SV 001-A

PRENTICE-HALL
ACCOUNTING

G. E. SYME, B. Com., C.A.

T. W. IRELAND, B.P.E.
Eric Hamber Secondary School

Prentice-Hall Canada Inc.,
Scarborough   Ontario

Canadian Cataloguing in Publication Data

Syme, G. E.
 Prentice-Hall accounting

Includes bibliographical references.
ISBN 0-13-715939-0

1. Accounting. I. Ireland, T. W. II. Title.

HF5635.S95 1990   657'.042   C89-095398-8

Also available:
Teacher's Guide 0-13-715756-8 (includes *Prentice-Hall Accounting* Computer Files)
Supplementary Material: Teacher's Key A (Chapters 1-12)   0-13-715715-0
                            Teacher's Key B (Chapters 13-18)   0-13-715723-1
                            Student Workbook A (Chapters 1-12)   0-13-715731-2
                            Student Workbook B (Chapters 13-18) 0-13-715749-5

PRENTICE-HALL INC., Englewood Cliffs, New Jersey
PRENTICE-HALL INTERNATIONAL, INC., London
PRENTICE-HALL OF AUSTRALIA, PTY., LTD., Sydney
PRENTICE-HALL OF INDIA, PVT., LTD., New Delhi
PRENTICE-HALL OF JAPAN INC., Tokyo
PRENTICE-HALL OF SOUTHEAST ASIA (PTE.) LTD., Singapore
EDITORA PRENTICE-HALL DO BRASIL, LTDA., Rio de Janeiro
PRENTICE-HALL HISPANOAMERICANA, S.A., Mexico

ISBN 0-13-715939-0

PROJECT EDITORS: John Metford, Denyse O'Leary
PRODUCTION EDITOR: Pam Young
MANUFACTURING: Lois Enns, Crystale Sheehan
DESIGN: Gail Ferreira Ng-A-Kien, Brant Cowie/ArtPlus Limited
TYPESETTING: Brant Cowie/ArtPlus Limited
PAGE MAKE-UP: Heather Brunton & Derek Meredith/ArtPlus Limited
TYPE OUTPUT: Tony Gordon Ltd.

Printed and bound in Canada by John Deyell Company

 2 3 4 5 6   JDC   95 94 93 92 91

To my son Steven, killed in a plane crash in Dryden, Ontario, on March 10, 1989. Your strength, talent, initiative, and contribution to the family are sorely missed.

G.S.

To Laura, Rebekah, and Kelsey, with love.

T.I.

Policy Statement

Prentice-Hall Canada Inc., School Division, and the authors of *Prentice-Hall Accounting* are committed to the publication of instructional materials that are as bias-free as possible. This text was evaluated for bias prior to publication.

The authors and publisher of this book also recognize the importance of appropriate reading levels and have therefore made every effort to ensure the highest degree of readability in the text. The content has been selected, organized, and written at a level suitable to the intended audience. Standard readability tests have been applied at several stages in the text's preparation to ensure an appropriate reading level.

Research indicates, however, that readability is affected by much more than word or sentence length; factors such as presentation, format and design, none of which are considered in the usual readability tests, also greatly influence the ease with which students read a book. These and many additional features have been carefully prepared to ensure maximum student comprehension. Further information is in the Introduction to the *Teacher's Guide*.

Contents

Acknowledgements

Developing an accounting textbook for today's market is a complex process. It takes a great deal of talent and experience to work from the authors' raw materials to a finished product. The authors know full well that the project would not be completed without expert assistance in many areas.

In particular, the authors wish to thank those at Prentice-Hall who have been involved in the production of this textbook. Steve Lane and Ian Lindsay were responsible for the planning and development from the outset. John Metford provided his skills of organization and language to structure the manuscript into its final form. Without the tireless efforts of Denyse O'Leary and Pam Young, the project would have withered on the vine. Their language skills and capacity for detail were invaluable.

We wish also to acknowledge the efforts of Susan Rance and Susan Howlett, project editors and Gail Ferreira Ng-a-Kien and Brant Cowie, art and design. In addition, we appreciate the advice of special reviewers Howard Lear of Kilarney Secondary School, Steve Edson of Nelson Boylan Secondary School, and Trevor Baker, former consultant to the Scarborough Board of Education. We would also like to thank Marlene Li and Sylvia Ma, students of Eric Hamber Secondary School, for their meticulous efforts.

Over the years Bill Riggs has made a prodigious contribution to the accounting package. His work is especially appreciated.

Preface

Prentice-Hall Accounting is an accounting program for one- and two-year courses in Canadian high schools. It provides a solid foundation in understanding the basic procedures of accounting. Our experience has proven the vital importance of the "basics." At the same time, the authors have responded fully to important developments in Canadian teaching practice and our economy. Our students will enter a computer workplace and must demonstrate skill and confidence with accounting software. Teachers know that the small businesses that create most new jobs want enterprising employees with transferable skills: communication, judgement, problem-solving, and sound business understanding. Consequently, *Prentice-Hall Accounting* supports classroom use of an industry-standard general ledger package; it teaches the use of the spreadsheet as a problem-solving tool and it offers a rich variety of problems and cases to develop understanding and transferable skills.

Sequence of topics The authors recognize that teachers will want to adjust the sequence of topics to fit their students' needs. The text follows the authors' preferred sequence. The service business is used to cover basic accounting theory and the complete accounting cycle in Chapters 2 through 10. Chapter 11 expands the theory and practice of accounting to the merchandising business. Students are then introduced to specialized journals, cash control, payroll, and end-of-period accounting. The last three chapters cover accounting for partnerships and corporations, and analyzing financial statements.

Chapter 1 introduces background topics such as the nature and types of business, the relationship between business and accounting, and accounting careers. Chapters 2 through 5 introduce accounting concepts in a simple, informal way. These chapters cover the balance sheet, the accounting equation, transaction analysis, the simple ledger, and accounting for revenue, expenses, and drawings. Chapters 6 through 9 build on students' understanding of basic concepts and procedures and take them through the accounting cycle. Chapters 6 and 7 cover source documents and the procedures of journalizing, posting, and balancing the ledger. Chapter 8 introduces the simple six-column work sheet and the balance sheet and income statement. Students complete the accounting cycle in Chapter 9, where they journalize and post simple adjusting and closing entries. Chapter 10 explains the role of subsidiary ledgers in a larger business.

As noted earlier, Chapter 11 treats the accounting procedures and transactions of a merchandising business. Chapter 12 covers specialized columnar journals which are still used in noncomputer accounting. Since Chapter 13, on cash control and banking, follows the merchandising business, students can grasp the need for cash and credit controls in business. Chapters 14 through 18 cover a variety of topics: payroll, end-of-period adjustments, partnership and corporation accounting, and analysis of financial statements.

Flexibility   Accounting is a cumulative subject, so the topics in the text are presented logically and systematically. Chapters 2 through 11 form the core of high school courses, and should probably be taught in order. Subsequent chapters can be selected and ordered as the teachers choose.

Classes of Different Ability   Accounting courses are usually unstreamed. *Prentice-Hall Accounting* provides a variety of high-quality assignment material. By adjusting the pace and selecting appropriate assignments, teachers can easily accommodate a wide range of student ability. With *Prentice-Hall Accounting*, a course emphasizing accounting theory is as easily developed as one emphasizing accounting procedures.

Questions, Exercises, Cases, Projects   Following each section of a chapter:
- Section Review Questions help students recall the content of the section.
- Section Exercises check comprehension and give immediate practice in new concepts.

At the end of each chapter:
- Using Your Knowledge questions give skill-oriented practice in various accounting routines, such as transaction analysis.
- Comprehensive Exercises put understanding of accounting principles into use — for example, in setting up the books for a business.
- For Further Thought questions ask students to combine their accounting knowledge with common sense and "real world" business practice.
- Cases are based on real business problems and require critical thinking.

After Chapters 12 and 13 two business simulations, Summary Exercise and Supplementary Exercise, integrate several chapters.

Accounting and the Computer   The spreadsheet and the Bedford Integrated Accounting System are presented extensively in *Prentice-Hall Accounting*. The generic spreadsheet and the Bedford package are covered in general terms first, followed by specific applications. Both types of computer accounting sections involve hands-on experience, but do not require specific hardware. Although these sections occur throughout the text, teachers who do not or cannot teach computer accounting can pass them by without difficulty.

Career and Entrepreneur Profiles   Each chapter includes a profile accompanied by discussion questions. Nine examine accounting as a career. The other nine feature Canadian entrepreneurs and describe the challenges of new business ventures.

Decision-Making, Problem-Solving, and Communication   *Prentice-Hall Accounting* provides ample opportunities for students to make judgements and solve business problems, using the cases, For Further Thought exercises, and the profiles. Teachers can assign these in a group setting to enhance problem-solving and communication skills. Asking for written reports will develop students' ability to write for business.

Student Workbooks and Teacher's Keys   Two student Workbooks supply working papers required to complete the exercises in the text. Two Teacher's Keys supply complete solutions for all text and Workbook exercises as well as suggested answers for review questions, case studies, and profile discussion questions.

Teacher's Guide   *Prentice-Hall Accounting* is supplemented by a comprehensive Teacher's Guide. For each chapter, the guide offers:

- Chapter Overviews
- Suggested Chapter Schedules
- Teaching Notes
- Comments on Exercises
- Teaching Masters
- Tests
- Computer Files disks for Computers in Accounting

It is impossible to overstate the value for today's students of a basic knowledge of accounting. Accounting skills can unlock the door to rewarding business careers. But an understanding of basic accounting concepts can help even those who do not enter business to manage personal finances or unravel an increasingly complex world economic picture.

To help students understand the value of accounting knowledge, we have tried to stress practical uses wherever possible. We have tried to capture students' interest with a stimulating assortment of concepts, problems, and issues. Students embarking on the study of accounting are taking the first steps toward promising futures. It is our hope that for these students, and for their teachers, *Prentice-Hall Accounting* will provide an invaluable resource and guide.

G.E.S.
T.W.I.

Accounting and Business

As a student just beginning the study of accounting, you would naturally like to know exactly what accounting is. There is no simple definition. Accounting is a system of dealing with financial information. Some aspects are simple, others are complex. It takes several years of serious study and practice to become a professional accountant.

1.1 WHAT IS ACCOUNTING ABOUT?

There are five main activities involved in accounting. These are:

1. gathering financial information about the activities of a business or other organization;
2. preparing and collecting permanent records. Records provide evidence of purchase, proof of payment, details of payroll, and so on. They also serve as the basis for dealings with other companies;
3. rearranging, summarizing, and classifying financial information into a more useable form;
4. preparing information reports and summaries:
   a. to help management reach decisions;
   b. to serve the needs of groups outside the business, such as bankers and investors;
   c. to measure the profitability of the business;
5. establishing controls to promote accuracy and honesty among employees. As businesses grow, owners can no longer look after everything alone. They have to hire others to help them. As soon as employees are hired, accounting controls become essential.

Accounting—An Information System

A good accounting system provides the answers to many questions. For example, owners and managers might seek answers to questions such as the following:

- Is the business earning enough profit?
- Are the selling prices of the products high enough?
- How much does ABC Company owe the business?
- How much does the business owe to XYZ Company?
- What is the value of all of the goods for sale?
- Do any of the goods for sale need to be restocked?
- To whom was cheque No. 502 issued?
- How much does it cost to produce product X?
- How much did John Smith earn last year?
- Are the customers paying their bills on time?
- Do we have enough money to meet our needs?
- How can we finance a business expansion?

Other persons, companies, or organizations might seek answers to the following questions:

- Should I lend money to this business? (a banker)
- Should I buy into this business? (a potential investor)
- Should I sell this business? (an owner)
- Is the business well run? (an absentee owner)
- Is the company growing satisfactorily? (an absentee owner)
- Can the business afford to pay more to its employees? (a labour union)
- Is the business paying the proper amount of income tax? (the government)

1.2 WHY STUDY ACCOUNTING?

A knowledge of accounting can be very useful in several ways.

Accounting as a Job

Those of you who decide to enter the business world will find employment more easily if you have a background in accounting. A large number of jobs require accounting and clerical skills. There are different levels of accounting occupations. The higher the level, the more training and experience is required, and the higher the salary offered.

Accounting in Daily Life

Having a working knowledge of accounting is an advantage in daily life. Whether or not you work in that field, an accounting background will help you with the language of business as well as accounting concepts. You will be better able to handle your personal business affairs, such as preparing a personal budget, keeping personal financial records, and preparing your income tax return. With an improved grasp of financial matters, you will be in a better position to take advantage of business opportunities, or to understand the operation of the organization where you work.

Owning Your Own Business

Many people want to own their own business. Those who achieve this goal soon find themselves faced with accounting tasks. They must do their banking. They must keep track of the amounts owed by their customers. They must keep accounting records for the government. They must produce an income statement for income tax purposes. They may have to prepare payrolls and make payroll deductions. Clearly, a knowledge of accounting is helpful in the small business sector—the fastest-growing segment of our economy. If a business is to be successful, the owner's ability to make sound management decisions based on good financial records is essential. Throughout this text, you will see profiles of persons who own their own businesses.

Professional Accountancy

Some of you may choose professional accounting as a career. By completing the requirements of one of the professional organizations of accountants, you can become a Chartered Accountant, a Certified General Accountant, or a Certified Management Accountant. Qualified professional accountants often hold senior management positions and have the right to practise as public accountants.

A **public accountant** is one who serves the general public for a fee in the same way as a doctor or a lawyer does. The main type of work done by public accountants is auditing. **Auditing** is the examination and testing of the books, records, and procedures of a business in order to be able to express an opinion about its financial statements. Public accountants also work as management consultants and tax advisors.

Professional accountants may choose industrial or institutional accounting rather than public accounting. *Industrial accountants* work for large companies such as IBM or Stelco. *Institutional accountants* work for the government, banks, large insurance companies, and similar organizations.

Complexity of Business

There are many laws laid down by the government concerning fair business practices, income taxes, and so on. Owners and managers of businesses must be fully aware of these laws in order to make good decisions. However, the laws have become so numerous and complex that only experts can thoroughly understand them. Fully qualified accountants know these laws. The increasing complexity of government regulations is the major reason why accounting is one of the fastest growing of all professions.

1.3   CHARACTERISTICS OF BUSINESS

The Nature of Business

There are businesses of all types throughout the country. Businesses are the economic framework upon which our society is built. But what is a business? Generally, a business involves the manufacture and/or sale of goods or services in order to earn a profit.

Most businesses fall within one of the following four main categories:

1. The Service Business

A **service business** sells a service to the public; it does not make or sell a product as its main activity. To picture a service business, think of a bowling alley, a transport company, or a medical clinic.

2. The Merchandising Business

A **merchandising business** buys goods and resells them at a higher price for a profit. To picture a merchandising business, think of a hardware store, a marina, a department store, a record store, or a fast-food restaurant.

3. The Manufacturing Business

A **manufacturing business** buys raw materials, converts them into a new product, and sells these products to earn a profit. To picture a manufacturing business, think of a construction company, a paper mill, or a steel plant. Other businesses, closely related to manufacturers, are called *producing businesses*. A farm, for example, produces milk, grain, and other foods. Other producing businesses include oil extraction, mining, forestry, hunting, and fishing.

4. The Non-Profit Organization

A **non-profit organization** may carry on activities to meet certain needs within society and not for profit. To picture these organizations, think of a church, a service club (such as the Rotary), a group working to help people (such as the Cancer Society), and a recreational club (such as a community hockey league).

Forms of Business Ownership

There are three main forms of business ownership. On a walk down any commercial street, you can see examples of each one.

1. You might notice a sign that reads "J. Wouk, Carpenter." This sign indicates that J. Wouk is in business for himself. He may work alone or others may work for him. This type of business is known as a **sole proprietorship**. The owner is a sole proprietor.
2. You might come across a sign that reads "Fogle, Silver, and Zimmerman, Accountants." This sign suggests that three persons share in the ownership and

operation of an accounting business. A business of this type, involving more than one owner, is known as a **partnership**.

3. You might find a sign that reads "Red River Homes Limited." This sign tells you that the business is a limited company or a corporation. A **limited company** or **corporation** is a special form of business that is owned by a number of persons called shareholders. Almost all large business operations are corporations, and some have several thousand shareholders.

1.4 THE NATURE OF ACCOUNTING

A typical accounting department has several employees. They can be seen operating computers and calculators, speaking on telephones, engaging in discussion, working with pen and paper, checking computer printouts, sorting out business papers, and so on. At first sight, it is difficult to see any differences among the types of work being done. But different activities are being performed.

The accounting department of a business includes a wide variety of functions. In a small business, one or two people may do all the necessary accounting work. In a large business, the accounting work may be divided into several departments, each of which may have many people working in it.

The following section examines some of these accounting tasks in a typical business and the people performing them.

Specific Accounting Tasks

The *credit manager* is Samuel Kwong. One of his responsibilities is to decide whether or not to let new customers buy the company's goods or services on credit. He is responsible for all aspects of accounts receivable (that is, money owing from customers). Sam makes sure that customers' accounts are recorded accurately and collected promptly. If an account becomes overdue, it is Sam who must encourage the customer to pay. Since the company has a large number of customers, Sam is a very busy person.

Sam has a secondary school diploma and has worked for his present employer for six years. Two years ago he enrolled in a program to become a qualified accountant. It will take three more years for him to complete the program. He is gaining valuable experience in his present position, but he realizes that he may have to change companies to improve his status.

The *cash receipts clerk* is Frank Liscombe. Among his duties, Frank opens, sorts, and distributes the mail. Any money received in the mail must be listed for record-keeping purposes. Then it is organized properly for deposit in the bank. Frank is responsible for making the bank deposit each day.

Frank recently graduated from high school, where he concentrated on business subjects. Although his marks were good, he has no desire to go to college at this time. He is quite happy at his present job. Working for a year or two will give him a chance to think about his future.

The *supervisor of payroll* is Janet Doucette. She and her staff prepare the company's weekly payroll. Janet has an important position. The company has a large number of employees, and they depend on Janet to have their cheques ready on time.

Janet has held several different accounting jobs since she left school 15 years ago. She has no formal training but over the years has acquired a great deal of expert knowledge concerning payroll accounting. She enjoys the challenge of being in charge of the payroll department.

The *accounts payable supervisor* is Susan Kusyk. Susan's position is also an important one. As bills are received from suppliers, they are sent to Susan's department. There, certain steps are taken to make sure that the bills are made out correctly and are proper charges against the business. Bills are not paid until Susan gives the final approval.

Although she is not a qualified accountant, Susan is a college graduate and has taken a number of accounting courses. Her goal is to complete one of the professional accounting courses. She knows that she will improve her career options if she becomes a qualified accountant.

The *chief accountant and office manager* is Dave Duncan. He is in charge of the accounting department. As the senior person, Dave must ensure that the accounting system and procedures are in place and that the system is running smoothly and efficiently.

Dave is a chartered accountant. He is the only one in the office who understands the entire system. If something goes wrong, Dave can be counted on to work it out. In addition to his many regular duties, Dave is part of the management team. He spends a lot of time preparing data and reports for management and participates actively in making management decisions.

Accounting Work in General

The accounting department of a business is expected to perform many activities. These belong in one of three categories:

1. Routine Daily Activities

These are activities that occur in the same way nearly every day of the year. They include processing bills, preparing cheques, daily banking, recording transactions, preparing business papers, and so on.

2. Periodic Accounting Activities

These are activities that occur at regular intervals. Paycheques are made ready every week or two. The bank accounts are checked every month. The financial reports are prepared each month and every year. Also, the income tax return is prepared every year as required by government regulation.

3. Miscellaneous Activities

Some accounting activities cannot be predicted. For example, if an accounting employee resigns, the position must be filled quickly. An advertisement is prepared, interviews conducted, and a selection made. Or a bank manager may call expressing concern over the size of the bank loan. A visit to the bank to discuss the matter may become necessary. Or a salesperson may call about a new machine that will reduce office costs. Time may be taken to see a demonstration of the equipment. In addition, professional accountants take part in meetings and activities put on by their association.

The Accounting Cycle

Accounting is thought of as occurring in cycles. Accounting activities are performed in relation to equal periods of time known as fiscal periods. The usual length for a fiscal period is one year. The **accounting cycle** can be thought of as the recurring set of accounting procedures carried out during each fiscal period. These accounting activities are carried out repeatedly, period after period. Figure 1.1 shows the recurring nature of accounting activity.

The accounting cycle really consists of two separate cycles. Figure 1.1 shows these with an inner and an outer ring. Some of the activities shown on the outer ring occur every day. Others occur only once a month. The activities on the inner ring normally occur once a year and are based on data provided by the activities of the outer ring.

It must be understood, however, that each cycle is built upon the cumulative results of previous cycles. The business does not have a fresh start each fiscal period.

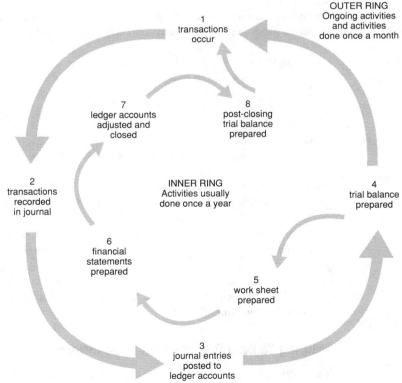

Figure 1.1   The accounting cycle.

1.5 BECOMING AN ACCOUNTANT

A great many accounting jobs exist in our society. Some are entry-level positions with small firms and require basic accounting skills only. Others are high-level positions requiring exceptional competence and training. Between these two extremes, there lies a vast range of accounting occupations in business. To fill these positions are many persons with different backgrounds and abilities, all calling themselves accountants. Some may have little or no formal training. Others may have studied at an advanced level for a number of years.

Accountants get their formal training either in high school, at college or university, or from a professional organization. In addition to formal studies in accounting, on-the-job experience is important. You are not really prepared to do professional accountancy until you have practical experience along with your formal training.

Most colleges and universities offer diplomas or degree courses in business. The study of accounting is included as part of the curriculum of these courses.

Professional Accounting Organizations

To be a fully qualified accountant you must complete the course prescribed by one of the three national professional accounting organizations.

Canadian Certified General Accountants' Association
Members' professional designation: CGA (Certified General Accountant)

The Society of Management Accountants of Canada
Members' professional designation: CMA (Certified Management Accountant)

Canadian Institute of Chartered Accountants
Members' professional designation: CA (Chartered Accountant)

Each of these national associations has provincial associations working within provincial requirements. The members of all three of these organizations are highly respected professional accountants.

At one time the accountancy profession was dominated by men. However, women have been entering the profession in increasing numbers. On four occasions in recent years women have won the Institute of Chartered Accountants' Gold Medal for obtaining the highest marks across Canada. Women now make up a significant proportion of all persons in accounting, and the percentage of women entering the profession is increasing annually.

Training To Be a Professional Accountant

To qualify as a professional accountant you will need further education after secondary school. You should examine the course requirements of each of the three accounting organizations carefully before you enroll. Each organization has its own requirements, which are not discussed here. It takes about five years after high school to become a qualified professional accountant. This includes a combination of part-time and full-time courses and work experience.

For admittance to the CGA course, a university degree is not required. This is an advantage for persons who do not choose to go on to university. You can enter the program and start to earn money right after high school. CGAs work in all areas of accounting.

The CMAs recently made it compulsory to have a university degree before qualifying. The CMAs place their emphasis on management accounting, and most of their graduates take management positions in business and industry. CMAs are regarded as being expert in cost accounting and industrial accounting.

The CAs represent the longest-standing body in the profession. The Canadian Institute of Chartered Accountants is generally regarded as the leading professional accounting organization. This is because its *Handbook* of accounting rules and standards is accepted by the other organizations. To enroll as a CA, you must be admitted to a university in a specific program laid down by the Institute.

All three organizations require practical experience to qualify. The Institute of Chartered Accountants, however, requires that this experience be obtained in the service of public accounting. This is obtained by working for a firm that offers accounting services to business, industry, and the general public, in the same way as a law firm does. The majority of public accountants are CAs.

To qualify as a CGA, CMA, or CA, you must pass a final examination. The final examinations for each organization are very demanding and are uniform across the country.

1.6 ACCOUNTING, BOOKKEEPING, AND COMPUTERS IN ACCOUNTING

Many people today still confuse "accounting" and "bookkeeping." But accounting and bookkeeping are different, although each is essential to the successful operation of a business. Computers are being used increasingly in both.

The Bookkeeper   The work of a bookkeeper is clerical in nature and for the most part concerned with routine matters. The term "bookkeeper" is gradually being replaced by the term "accounting clerk." Some of the jobs that a bookkeeper does are:

1. ensuring that transactions are properly recorded and that the necessary supporting documents are present and correct;
2. recording the accounting entries in the books of account and balancing the ledger as necessary;
3. making the payroll calculations and preparing the payroll cheques and other payroll records;
4. carrying out all necessary banking transactions.

The Accountant   The work of an accountant, on the other hand, is broader in scope and requires more education and experience. A professional accountant is usually responsible for maintaining the entire accounting system. Some of the things an accountant is concerned with are:

1. developing a system to ensure that correct data are entered into the accounting system;
2. ensuring that generally accepted accounting standards are met;
3. interpreting the data produced by the accounting system;
4. preparing reports based on the data output from the system;
5. participating in management meetings and assisting in making business decisions;
6. supervising the work of all accounting employees.

A qualified accountant has a high-level position. The top people in many large corporations are qualified accountants.

The Computer   The computer is ideal for use in an accounting environment. In accounting, there is a lot of recording, sorting, calculating, summarizing, storing, and working with numbers. The computer is good at all these activities. In addition, the computer can handle large quantities of data, and can produce data on video screen or by printout. Further, the computer is fast and can provide information for management quickly. Anyone intent on becoming an accountant will study computer courses as part of the curriculum.

Modern accounting offices use computers to run many different accounting packages (sets of programs that work together). Both accounting clerks and accountants regularly work with automated accounting programs and spreadsheets. As you progress through this text, you will have the opportunity to use real computer programs in accounting.

CHAPTER HIGHLIGHTS

Now that you have completed Chapter 1, you should:

1. have a broad understanding of the objectives of accounting;
2. know the four main kinds of businesses and the three forms of business ownership;
3. know the benefits to be gained by having a background in accounting;
4. know what is meant by *professional accountant* and *public accountant*;
5. know the type of work performed by an accounting department;
6. understand what is meant by the accounting cycle;
7. know the different ways that you can become an accountant;
8. know the three national professional accounting organizations.

ACCOUNTING TERMS

accountant
accounting
accounting clerk
accounting cycle
auditing
bookkeeper
corporation
limited company

manufacturing business
merchandising business
non-profit organization
partnership
public accountant
service business
sole proprietorship

CHAPTER QUESTIONS

1. How many main activities are involved in accounting?
2. Describe the fifth accounting activity discussed in the text.
3. Give three questions for which the accounting system can provide answers.
4. Name the two groups which benefit from the information provided by the accounting system.
5. Describe how a knowledge of accounting can help you in respect to employment.
6. Explain how a knowledge of accounting can help people who own their own business.
7. Describe the work of a public accountant.
8. Explain what "auditing" is.
9. Name three kinds of business besides the service business.
10. Name the four forms of business ownership.
11. Give one responsibility of the "credit manager."
12. Describe the work for which the accounts payable "supervisor" is responsible.
13. Give examples of a routine accounting activity and a periodic accounting activity.
14. Define the accounting cycle.
15. Name the three professional accounting organizations.
16. On the average, how long does it take, after enrolment, to become a qualified professional accountant?
17. Why are the Chartered Accountants regarded as being the leading body of professional accountants in Canada?
18. What special kind of work experience does the Chartered Accountants' organization require?
19. Describe briefly the nature of a bookkeeper's work.
20. What term is replacing the term "bookkeeper"?
21. Describe the scope of an accountant's work.
22. Explain why computer studies are now part of the curriculum of accounting courses.
23. Give two characteristics of the computer that make it ideal for use in accounting.

CHAPTER EXERCISES

Using Your Knowledge

1. A list of accounting terms is given below. **In your Workbook, in a numbered column, write down the term which matches the statement.**

   1. The professional accounting organization that does not require a university degree for admission.
   2. The professional accounting organization that emphasizes management accounting.
   3. The professional accounting organization that is considered the leader in the field.
   4. The department that is responsible for setting the terms of sale to customers and collecting the debts from customers.
   5. Formal accounting data, prepared at least once a year.
   6. The department that looks after the payment of bills for services and goods received.
   7. An organization whose main aim is to provide a service at little or no cost to the user.
   8. The recurring set of accounting procedures carried out during each fiscal period.
   9. A business that buys goods and resells them at a higher price for profit.
   10. The owner of a business who is in business alone.
   11. A special form of business that is owned by a number of persons called shareholders.
   12. Professional persons who offer their services as accountants to the general public.
   13. The examining and testing of the books, records, and procedures of a business in order to be able to express an opinion about the financial statements.
   14. A business that sells a service to the public and does not make or sell a product.
   15. A business that buys raw materials, converts them into a new product, and sells these products to earn a profit.

List of Accounting Terms

accounting cycle
accounts payable department
auditing
Certified General Accountants Association
corporation
credit department
financial statements
Institute of Chartered Accountants

manufacturing business
merchandising business
non-profit business
public accountants
service business
Society of Management Accountants
sole proprietor

---

2. Each of the statements below can be completed by filling in the blank(s) with one or more of the following: *bookkeeper, bookkeeping, accountant, accounting, accounting clerk.*

   In your Workbook, fill in the correct term in each of these statements.

   1. The work of a(n) _____ is clerical in nature.
   2. The work of a(n) _____ is concerned with routine matters.

3. The term _____ is gradually being replaced with the term _____ clerk.

4. A(n) _____ ensures that the supporting documents are present and correct for every transaction.

5. A(n) _____ ensures that generally acceptable accounting principles are followed.

6. A(n) _____ records the accounting entries in the books of account.

7. A(n) _____ makes the payroll calculations.

8. A(n) _____ prepares reports based on the data produced by the accounting system.

9. A(n) _____ carries out all the necessary banking transactions.

10. A(n) _____ participates in management meetings.

11. A qualified _____ has a high-level position.

12. For centuries, all _____ was handwritten.

13. Many small businesses still do their _____ by hand.

---

3. This exercise also appears in your Workbook.

1. Which of the following does not fit?
   a. An accounting clerk verifies source documents.
   b. An accounting clerk ensures that the ledger balances.
   c. An accounting clerk works neatly to guard against errors.
   d. An accounting clerk studies tax bulletins to keep up to date.

2. Which of the following does not fit?
   a. An accounting clerk works out accounting entries.
   b. An accounting clerk, together with the owner, compares this year's and last year's income statements.
   c. An accounting clerk records accounting entries in the books.
   d. An accounting clerk inquires about a suspected error made by the bank.

3. Which of the following does not fit?
   a. An accountant is a professional person.
   b. An accountant has a broad knowledge of "accounting."
   c. An accountant ensures the accuracy of the payroll deductions.
   d. An accountant discusses the business's "cash flow" with the owners.

4. Which of the following does not fit?
   a. An accountant talks about the final qualifying exams.
   b. An accountant investigates the credit rating of a new customer.
   c. An accountant is promoted to vice-president.
   d. An accountant is ill; a meeting with the bank manager has to be cancelled.

5. Which of the following does not fit?
   a. The computer is an ideal machine for use in an accounting environment.
   b. The computer can handle large quantities of data.
   c. The computer produces better profit figures.
   d. The computer can provide information for management very quickly.

CAREER
David Green / Student in Accounts

David Green says that as a kid growing up in Conception Bay, Newfoundland, he liked nothing better than a winter storm because it meant a day off school. To his surprise, when David studied accounting in high school, he found his courses interesting and enjoyable. He decided to continue his study of accounting and become a chartered accountant.

David is now a student in accounts, working toward a professional degree as a chartered accountant in the Co-operative Educational Program at Memorial University in St. John's. This program brings together the theory and practice of accounting. Students spend four months taking classes and then four months gaining practical experience by working for a chartered accountant.

During the four-year program, David will complete nine courses in accounting: two in taxation, one in auditing, two in economics, two in computer science, and four in business-related areas such as law and finance. At the end of the program, David will graduate with an Honours Bachelor of Commerce degree. He then must write the examination for chartered accountants, which actually involves four examinations, each four hours long.

To gain his practical experience, David works with McPherson, Scott and Co., a firm of chartered accoun-

tants in St. John's. The company has a wide range of clients, including car dealerships, charities, small manufacturers, and trust companies. Some of these companies have manual accounting systems, while others have computerized systems. As a result, David is exposed to a variety of accounting procedures.

This year, David is spending most of his time examining the accounting controls over cash to ensure accuracy and honesty. He advises clients when controls have to be strengthened.

David reviews and analyzes books of accounts to ensure that financial statements are presented fairly. He also helps one of the firm's chartered accountants to complete tax returns. Finally, David performs general bookkeeping for his clients; this includes journalizing, posting, banking, accounts receivable, and payroll. This on-the-job training provides David with the opportunity to experience and learn word processing, the use of electronic spreadsheets, data management, and communications.

According to the terms of David's program, the firm of chartered accountants is responsible for supervising him in all assignments. The accountants also submit a student evaluation to the university; this will be reviewed by David and the accountants together. David's student evaluation will be made available to employers who are considering hiring him.

If David succeeds in becoming a chartered accountant, he will have several career choices. He may decide to take a position in industry as an executive officer, or he may want to start his own accounting practice or join an accounting firm. At present, David intends to work for a corporation when he graduates.

David highly recommends the Co-operative Educational Program to all those who wish to advance their business careers. The combination of study and practical application means that graduates of the program are well equipped to meet the challenges of today's competitive business world.

DISCUSSION

1. Explain what is meant by the term "student in accounts."
2. List some of the duties David performs during the auditing process.
3. The phrase "the financial statements are presented fairly" sets out an important concept in accounting and auditing. In your opinion what do you think this expression means?
4. Discuss the career options open to David when he becomes a chartered accountant.
5. If you were in David's position and were to become a chartered accountant, what career option would you choose and why?
6. Write a report on the co-operative educational program in business offered at a university in your province. Include in your report the names of other Canadian universities that offer similar programs and the qualifications required to enrol. You can check the school guidance office and the library for this kind of information.

The Balance Sheet

2.1 **Financial Position**
2.2 **The Balance Sheet**
2.3 **Claims against the Assets**
2.4 **Generally Accepted Accounting Principles**
2.5 **Computers in Accounting The Accounting Spreadsheet**

Businesses need good accounting systems in order to produce records of day-to-day financial information, reports, and summaries. One of the most important uses of this information is to show the financial position of an individual or a business.

2.1 FINANCIAL POSITION

The concept of financial position is straightforward. It shows what a business owns, what it owes to others, and what its owner's investment is. The following steps outline how to determine the financial position of a business.

Step 1 **List the things the business owns that are worth money**; these are called **assets**. They do not have to be fully paid for. **Give a dollar value to each item and total the list.**

Step 2 **List and total the amounts owed by the business**; these are called **liabilities**.

Step 3 **Calculate the difference between the total assets and the total liabilities.** This difference is known as the **owner's equity** or **owner's capital**. A less common term is **net worth**.

The **financial position** of a business may be thought of as the status of the business, as represented by the assets, the liabilities, and the owner's equity.

Example:
Let us follow the three-step procedure given above to work out the financial position of Easy Rent-Alls on September 30, 19—. Easy Rent-Alls is owned by Jim Salas.

Step 1 **List what the business owns (assets); give a dollar value to each item and total the list.**

For Easy Rent-Alls the assets are as follows:

Cash on hand	$ 40.20
Bank balance	710.00
Amount owed by W. Boa	131.50
Amount owed by T. Burns	350.00
Land	48 000.00
Buildings	95 000.00
Rental equipment	75 364.70
Delivery truck	19 965.00
Total assets	$239 561.40

Step 2 List what the business owes (liabilities).

For Easy Rent-Alls, the liabilities are as follows:

Amount owed to Arrow Supply	$ 1 950.40
Amount owed to Best Repairs	1 250.00
Bank loan payable	15 000.00
Mortgage payable	65 200.00
Total liabilities	$83 400.40

Step 3 Calculate the difference between total assets and total liabilities.

The calculation is as follows:

Total assets	$239 561.40
Total liabilities	83 400.40
Difference	$156 161.00

The difference of $156 161.00 is Jim Salas's investment in the business. It is known as the owner's equity or capital.

The Fundamental Accounting Equation

Owner's equity is always worked out in the same way, by subtracting total liabilities from total assets. This relationship is always true and can be written in the form of an equation.

This **fundamental accounting equation** may be stated in this way:

$$A - L = OE \quad \text{(Assets – Liabilities = Owner's Equity)}$$

The equation may also be stated in another way:

$$A = L + OE \quad \text{(Assets = Liabilities + Owner's Equity)}$$

Now let us use the figures for Easy Rent-Alls to see the fundamental accounting equation at work.

$$A \quad - \quad L \quad = \quad OE$$

$$\$239\ 561.40 - \$83\ 400.40 = \$156\ 161.00$$

or

$$A \quad = \quad L \quad + \quad OE$$

$$\$239\ 561.40 = \$83\ 400.40 + \$156\ 161.00$$

The fundamental accounting equation is an extremely important concept in the study of accounting. As you will soon see, it is the basis for all accounting theory.

Accounts Receivable and Accounts Payable

Customers often buy goods or services from a business with the understanding that they will pay for them later. These customers then owe money to the business. They are in debt to the business. The debts owed represent a dollar value to the business. The business is right to include them as one of its assets.

These debts are known as **accounts receivable** (sometimes abbreviated A/R or A.R.). Each of the customers who owes money to the business is one of its debtors. A **debtor** is anyone who owes money to the business.

In turn, a business often purchases goods and services from its suppliers with the understanding that payment will be made later. The business is in debt to its suppliers. These debts represent a dollar obligation of the business. The business is right to include them as one of its liabilities.

Debts owed by the business are referred to as **accounts payable** (sometimes abbreviated A/P or A.P.). Each of the suppliers owed money by the business is one of its creditors. A **creditor** is anyone to whom the business owes money.

SECTION REVIEW QUESTIONS

1. Explain how to calculate a person's financial position.
2. Karen Lipka has assets of $150 000 and liabilities of $75 000. What is her equity?
3. If a business has an equity of $125 000 and liabilities of $75 000, how much are the assets worth?
4. Define asset.
5. Define liability.
6. Define owner's equity.
7. What is another term that means the same thing as equity?
8. What are accounts receivable?
9. What are accounts payable?
10. What is the term used to describe any supplier to whom the business owes money?
11. What is the term used to describe any company or person who owes money to a business?

SECTION EXERCISES

1. List eight assets that a small business might own.

2. List three liabilities that a small business might owe.

3. Classify each of the following as an asset or a liability:

Office Furniture	An amount owed by R. Jonas, a debtor
An amount owed to H. Krueger, a creditor	Mortgage Payable
Land	Trucks
Supplies	A Canada Savings Bond
Bank Loan	An account receivable
Buildings	An account payable
An unpaid heating bill	

4. If the total assets of a business are $37 486.49 and the total liabilities are $11 547.80, calculate the owner's equity.

5. On December 31, 19-1, A. Lower's accounting equation was as follows:

Assets ($150 000) – Liabilities ($70 000) = Equity ($80 000)
If during 19-2 the assets increased by $70 000 and the liabilities decreased by $20 000, calculate the owner's equity at December 31, 19-2.

6. If during 19-6 the equity increases by $52 000, and the assets increase by $26 000, what change has occurred to the liabilities?

7. If total assets increase by $10 000, and the equity increases by $5 000, what change has occurred in the liabilities?

8. If the liabilities increase by $15 000, and the equity decreases by $5 000, what change has occurred in the assets?

9. Paul Silva's assets and liabilities are listed below in alphabetical order.

Bank loan, $4 000; Building, $140 000; Cash, $1 435; City Service (a debtor), $960; Emerson Electric Ltd. (a creditor), $1 200; Equipment, $23 750; Francis and Company (a debtor), $350; Frank's Service Station (a creditor), $375; Mortgage on building, $76 000; Supplies, $370.

1. List the assets in one column and total them.
2. List the liabilities in another column and total them.
3. Calculate Paul Silva's equity.

10. Claude Pineau, a factory worker in Hull, Quebec, asks you to help him find out how much he is worth. From a discussion with him you find out the following facts:

   a. His bank balance is $754.

   b. He owns a home valued at $82 500 which has a mortgage on it of $12 500.

   c. He owns furniture and household equipment valued at $16 000.

   d. He owns a summer property valued at $65 000 which he bought entirely with money borrowed from the bank. Since the time of purchase he has paid back $20 000 of the loan.

   e. He has unpaid bills amounting to $1 560.

   f. He owes his father-in-law, M. Dupuis, the sum of $10 000 which he borrowed interest-free several years ago at the time he bought his home.

   List Claude Pineau's assets in one column, his liabilities in another, and calculate his net worth.

2.2   THE BALANCE SHEET

The formal way of presenting financial position is by means of a balance sheet. The balance sheet of Easy Rent-Alls is shown in Figure 2.1. A **balance sheet** is a statement showing the financial position of a business, person, or other organization on a certain date.

Easy Rent-Alls		Balance Sheet		September 30, 19—		
Assets			**Liabilities**			
Cash on Hand		40 20	Accounts Payable			
Bank Balance		710 —	– Arrow Supply		1950 40	
Accounts Receivable			– Best Repairs		1250 —	
– W. Boa		13 150	Bank Loan		15000 —	
– T. Burns		350 —	Mortgage Payable		65200 —	
Land		48000 —	Total Liabilities		83400 40	
Buildings		95000 —				
Rental Equipment		75364 70	Owner's Equity			
Delivery Truck		19965 —	J. Salas, Capital		156161 —	
Total Assets		239561 40	Total Liabilities and Equity		239561 40	

Figure 2.1   The balance sheet of a small business, Easy Rent-Alls.

The balance sheet is set up in the form of the fundamental accounting equation: $A = L + OE$. Assets appear on the left side, with the liabilities and owner's equity on the right side.

Preparing a Balance Sheet

The steps in preparing a simple balance sheet are shown in the following illustrations. The figures for Easy Rent-Alls are used in the example.

Step 1 Write in the statement heading on columnar paper as shown in Figure 2.2. The heading must indicate the name of the business, the name of the statement, and the date of the statement.

WHO:　The name of
　　　　the business

Easy Rent-Alls
Balance Sheet ◄──── WHAT:　The name of
　　　　　　　　　　　　　　　　the statement
September 30, 19—

WHEN:　The date of
　　　　　the statement

Figure 2.2　The heading on a balance sheet.

Step 2 Write in the sub-heading "Assets" at the top of the left side column. Underline the sub-heading. Then write in the assets on the left side as shown in Figure 2.3.

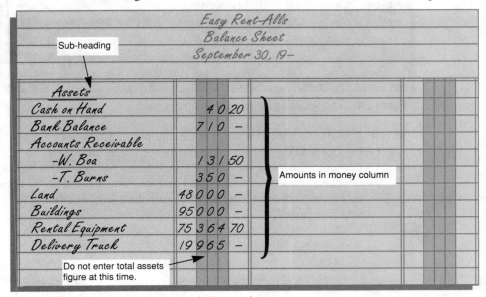

Easy Rent-Alls
Balance Sheet
September 30, 19—

Sub-heading

Assets		
Cash on Hand	4 0 20	
Bank Balance	7 1 0 –	
Accounts Receivable		
–W. Boa	1 3 1 50	
–T. Burns	3 5 0 –	Amounts in money column
Land	48 0 0 0 –	
Buildings	95 0 0 0 –	
Rental Equipment	75 3 6 4 70	
Delivery Truck	19 9 6 5 –	

Do not enter total assets figure at this time.

Figure 2.3　The assets listed on a balance sheet.

The assets are listed in the order of their liquidity. **Liquidity** means the ease with which the assets can be converted into cash. Cash and bank balance, being the most liquid, are listed first. Accounts receivable are listed next because they are usually collected within 30 days. The names of the customers are usually given in alphabetical order. Supplies and long-lasting assets are listed later because normally they are not converted into cash.

Step 3 Write in the sub-heading "Liabilities" at the top of the right side column. Underline the sub-heading. Then write in the liabilities on the right side as shown in Figure 2.4. The liabilities are listed in the order in which they will be paid. Suppliers' names are usually placed in alphabetical order.

Draw a line below the last liability to indicate addition. Then write in "Total Liabilities" and the total.

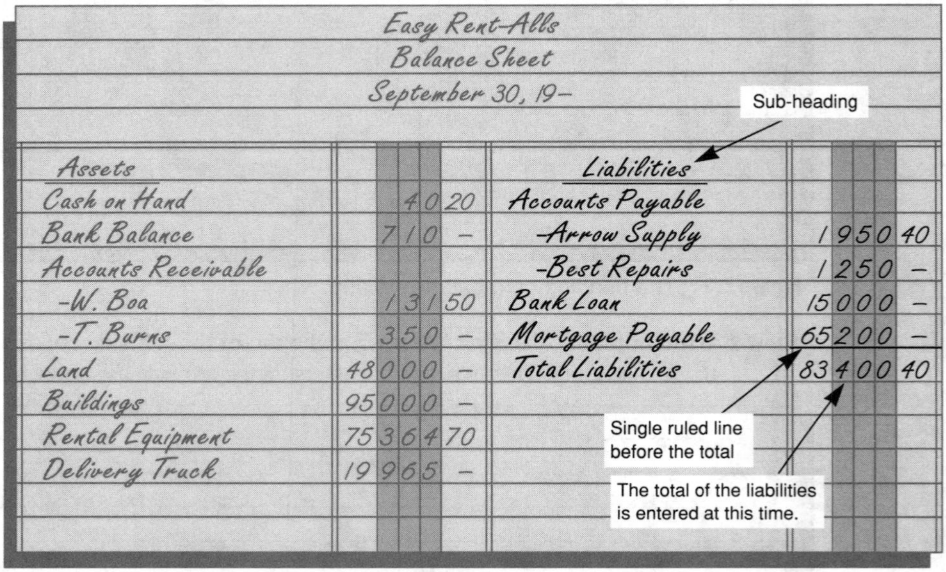

Figure 2.4 The liabilities listed on a balance sheet.

Step 4 Beneath the liabilities write in the sub-heading "Owner's Equity." Underline the sub-heading. Then write in the owner's name plus the word "Capital," and the equity figure as shown in Figure 2.5. As you know, this figure is the difference between the total assets and the total liabilities. You will have to obtain the total assets figure to calculate the equity, but do not write it in until step 5 on page 23.

Easy Rent-Alls						
Balance Sheet						
September 30, 19–						
Assets				Liabilities		
Cash on Hand		40 20		Accounts Payable		
Bank Balance		7 10 –		– Arrow Supply		1 95 0 40
Accounts Receivable				–Best Repairs		1 25 0 –
–W. Boa		1 3 1 50		Bank Loan		15 00 0 –
–T. Burns		3 50 –		Mortgage Payable		65 20 0 00
Land		48 00 0 –		Total Liabilities		83 40 0 40
Buildings		95 00 0 –				
Rental Equipment		75 36 4 70		Owner's Equity		
Delivery Truck		19 96 5 –		J. Salas, Capital		156 1 6 1 –

Sub-heading

The name of the owner and the word "Capital"

Figure 2.5   The owner's equity recorded on a balance sheet.

Step 5 Complete the balance sheet by writing in the final totals as shown in Figure 2.6. These totals are written on the first fully open line.

Easy Rentals						
Balance Sheet						
September 30, 19–						
Assets				Liabilities		
Cash on Hand		40 20		Accounts Payable		
Bank Balance		7 10 –		–Arrow Supply		1 95 0 40
Accounts Receivable				–Best Repairs		1 25 0 –
– W. Boa		1 3 1 50		Bank Loan		15 00 0 –
–T. Burns		3 50 –		Mortgage Payable		65 20 0 –
Land		48 00 0 –		Total Liabilities		83 40 0 40
Buildings		45 00 0 –				
Rental Equipment		75 36 4 70		Owner's Equity		
Delivery Truck		19 96 5 –		J. Salas, Capital		156 1 6 1 –
Total Assets		239 5 6 1 40		Total Liabilities and Equity		239 5 6 1 40

Figure 2.6   The completed balance sheet for a business.

On this line, write in "Total Assets" on the left side and "Total Liabilities and Equity" on the right side. Write in the totals. The two totals must be on the same line and agree. Place a single ruled line above and a double ruled line below each of the two totals.

Important Features of the Balance Sheet

1. A three-line heading is used. The heading tells:
   WHO?—the name of the organization or individual (if there is no business name);
   WHAT?—the name of the financial statement, in this case, the balance sheet;
   WHEN?— the date on which the financial position is determined.
2. The assets are listed on the left side of the balance sheet and the liabilities are listed on the right side.
3. The assets are listed in the order of their liquidity.
4. Under Accounts Receivable the customers' names are listed in alphabetical order.
5. The liabilities are listed in the order in which they normally would be paid.
6. Under Accounts Payable the suppliers' names are listed in alphabetical order.
7. The details of any item are fully disclosed on a balance sheet. For example, on the balance sheet of Easy Rent-Alls shown above, the used delivery truck is shown in the Assets section at its cost price of $19 965. The amount that is owed on the truck, $15 000 to the bank, is shown in the Liabilities section. This is more informative than to show the truck at $4 965, which is how much of it the business really owns.
8. The two final totals, one for each side of the balance sheet, are recorded on the same line and underlined with a double line.
9. The owner of a business will have assets and liabilities that are strictly personal and do not belong on the balance sheet of the business. Examples are: the family home, the family boat, and the amount owed on the family car. It is important to remember to keep business assets and liabilities separate from personal ones.

Basic Recordkeeping Practices

When To Abbreviate

Avoid using abbreviations on financial statements such as balance sheets except when listing a business name that includes an abbreviation. For example, General Bakeries Limited is the full name of a business; therefore, the word Limited should not be abbreviated. However, in the case of Canadian Electric Co., the abbreviation for "Company" is used because it is part of the formal name of the business.

Use of Columnar Paper

It is important for an accounting student to learn to use columnar paper. When columnar paper is used, notice how the figures are placed carefully in the columns. This is to help the accountant total the columns correctly. Observe also that dollar signs, periods, and commas are not used when recording amounts of money in columns.

When using columnar paper, even-dollar amounts may be shown by placing a dash in the cents column. Thus, in the following illustration, 12— is used instead of 12.00.

The two zeros are used on typed or printed reports, and are preferred by some on a financial statement such as the balance sheet.

Use of Ruled Lines

If a column of figures is to be totaled (added or subtracted), a single line is drawn beneath the column and the total is placed beneath this single line as shown below:

If a total happens to be a final total, such as the last amounts on the balance sheet, a double ruled line is drawn immediately beneath the total as shown below:

On most balance sheets, in order to place the two final totals on the same line, it is necessary to leave one or more blank lines between the figures in a column and the column total. When this is done, the single ruled line is placed close to the "total" figure and not immediately beneath the figures in the column. The following examples show this.

 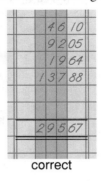

incorrect   correct

Neatness

It is most important that an accountant's work be neat and perfectly legible. This is necessary so that no one misinterprets the writing or the numbers. Although the work should never be untidy, it is not necessary for it to be beautiful—only neat and legible.

From the very beginning you should make it a habit to strive for neatness, accuracy, and clarity in all of your exercises. Be sure to use your ruler to make ruled lines beneath headings and in the columns.

SECTION REVIEW QUESTIONS

1. What is a balance sheet?
2. When does the name of the owner of a business appear in the heading of a balance sheet?
3. On which side of a balance sheet are the assets listed? The liabilities?
4. How is an automobile that is not fully paid for listed on a balance sheet?
5. What four items may be omitted when listing figures on columnar paper?
6. On which side of a balance sheet does a creditor appear?
7. What is meant by a single ruled line drawn beneath a column of figures?
8. Why is it important for an accountant's work to be neat?
9. When is a double ruled line drawn beneath a total?
10. When can short forms or abbreviations be used on financial statements?
11. Give two forms of the fundamental accounting equation.
12. Which is the most liquid asset?
13. In what order are liabilities listed on a balance sheet?
14. In what order are assets listed on a balance sheet?

SECTION EXERCISES

1. Kate Kramer is the owner and operator of The Kramer Company located in Revelstoke, B.C. On September 30, 19—, The Kramer Company had the following assets and liabilities. **Prepare the September 30 balance sheet for The Kramer Company.**

Assets

Cash on Hand	$ 106
Bank Balance	1 530
J. Crothers (debtor)	1 100
R. Zack (debtor)	370
Supplies	1 200
Furniture and Equipment	14 700
Delivery Equipment	20 100

Liabilities

Anglo Supply Co. (creditor)	740
C.P. Gregg (creditor)	3 000
Bank Loan	10 000

2. The New Western Company in Brandon, Manitoba, owned by Guy Albrecht, had the following assets and liabilities on March 31, 19—. **Prepare a balance sheet for the company, as of that date.**

Bank	$ 1 896
Tasty Beverages (debtor)	750
Food Haven (debtor)	400
Metro Mall (debtor)	1 235
Supplies	850
Furniture and Equipment	75 840
Land	50 000
Building	140 000
Trucks	35 000
Household Finance Company (creditor)	19 345
General Trading Company (creditor)	2 356
Lightning Electronics (creditor)	3 378
Bank Loan	10 000
Mortgage Payable	75 000

3. Michael Travis, the owner of Travis and Company located in Moncton, New Brunswick, gave the following list of assets and liabilities to a public accountant and asked him to prepare a balance sheet as of March 31, 19—. **Prepare the balance sheet as if you were the public accountant.**

Amounts owed to Travis and Company:

—G. Fordham	$ 1 042.16
—W. Gaines	743.86
—D. Samuelson	1 346.95

Amounts owed by Travis and Company to suppliers:

—Raymond and Company	125.00
—Gem Finance Co.	1 236.45
—Empire Insurance Co.	150.00
—Beacon Company	1 567.25
—General Supply Co.	15 540.00

Office Supplies	$ 326.40
Building	135 000.00
Bank Balance	4 946.03
Land	46 000.00
Office Equipment	11 960.00
Shop Equipment	3 535.00
Delivery Equipment	14 240.00
Bank Loan	25 000.00
Mortgage Payable	52 000.00

4. **Workbook Exercise: Finding errors on a balance sheet.**

2.3 CLAIMS AGAINST THE ASSETS

Who owns the assets of a business? The answer is: those persons who provided the funds used to acquire the assets. They have a claim against the assets of the business. If those persons who provided the funds are not the owners, they are called creditors.

A balance sheet shows who has a claim against the assets of a business. The balance sheet of Paramount Design, owned by Janet Korey, shows clearly who has a claim against the assets of her business.

Figure 2.7 The balance sheet of Paramount Design showing the claims against the assets.

As shown on the left side of the balance sheet, Janet's business assets are $43 763.10. The right side of the balance sheet shows that these assets, or the funds to obtain them, were provided by: the bank, $9 000; the other creditors, $1 905 and $750; and Janet herself, $32 108.10.

Expressed in another way, according to the fundamental accounting equation:

$43 763.10   = $9 000 + $1 905 + $750   + $32 108.10

Assets	Creditors' claims against the assets	Owner's claim against the assets

Creditors' Claims First

If a business is closed down, to whom do the assets belong? They still belong to the owners and creditors. But the claims of the creditors are settled first, and then the claim of the owner. This means that the owner has to accept any losses that might occur from selling off any assets. On the other hand, the owner benefits from any profits that might occur. The owner always gets what is left after the claims of the creditors have been paid.

Suppose that Janet Korey closed down the business, and in the process suffered a loss of $7 200 when selling off the assets. The equation shown above would not remain the same but would show the loss of $7 200 as follows:

$35 563.10   = $9 000 + $1 905 + $750   + $24 908.10

Assets (now all cash) down $7 200	Creditors' claims remain the same	Owner's claim down $7 200

SECTION REVIEW QUESTIONS

1. Who has a claim against the assets of a business?
2. How can you quickly find out who has a claim against the assets of a business?
3. Who has first claim against the assets of a business?
4. Who benefits from gains made in closing down a business?
5. Who suffers (primarily) from losses incurred in closing down a business?

SECTION EXERCISES

1. Joseph Litz is the owner of Bayliner Boat Charters, a business in Truro, Nova Scotia, that has six sailboats for hire. Mr. Litz has been able to make a comfortable living from renting out these boats during the sailing season.

The balance sheet of Bayliner Boat Charters is shown below.

BAYLINER BOAT CHARTERS
BALANCE SHEET
OCTOBER 31, 19—

Assets		Liabilities	
Bank	$ 900	Bank Loan	$ 18 000
Accounts Receivable	1 050	Accounts Payable	3 740
Supplies	1 250	Mortgage Payable	80 000
Property	175 000		$ 101 740
Equipment	4 390	Owner's Equity	
Boats	32 850	J. Litz, Capital	113 700
	$215 440		$ 215 440

Mr. Litz is past retirement age and is finding the business more than he can comfortably handle. He has attempted to sell it intact, but was unsuccessful. He has decided, therefore, to sell the assets for cash and pay off the claims of the creditors. In this way he can get his equity out of the business.

Mr. Litz hires a liquidator to help him. Through this person's services, the accounts receivable are collected in full. The supplies are sold for $500; the equipment is sold for $2 000; the boats are sold for $20 350; and the property is sold for $180 000. The liquidator charges $1 500.

Prepare a detailed calculation showing how much Mr. Litz will receive as a result of his claim against the assets.

2. Carla Mann is the owner of Carla's Interior Design in Yorkton, Saskatchewan. A new firm has come to town and Carla has accepted a position with them. Carla is closing down her own business and is in the process of selling the assets.

Just before she accepted her new position, the balance sheet of Carla's Interior Design was as follows:

CARLA'S INTERIOR DESIGN
BALANCE SHEET
JUNE 30, 19—

Assets		Liabilities	
Cash	$ 1 500	Bank Loan	$ 9 500
Accounts Receivable	7 870	Accounts Payable	1 250
Supplies	1 520		$10 750
Equipment	3 740	Owner's Equity	
Automobile	17 500	Carla Mann, Capital	21 380
	$32 130		$32 130

Carla was successful in selling the supplies for $1 200 cash and the equipment for $2 200 cash. She was also able to collect in cash all of the accounts receivable except for $870, which was considered to be uncollectable.

1. **Prepare a simple balance sheet on July 31, after disposing of the three assets mentioned above.**
2. **Suggest the simplest way to dispose of the remaining assets and thus complete the closing of the business.**

2.4　GENERALLY ACCEPTED ACCOUNTING PRINCIPLES

In performing their work, accountants follow a set of rules or standards known as *generally accepted accounting principles (GAAPs)*. GAAPs include a number of specific rules, practices, and procedures. Some are formal regulations and others set out what has become common practice over the years.

The Canadian Institute of Chartered Accountants (CICA) is the professional accounting organization that establishes the standards for accountants in Canada. The complete body of accounting knowledge and opinion is contained in the *CICA Handbook*. The handbook is prepared in looseleaf form so that it can be updated regularly. This is done by issuing revised pages in respect to new information or to replace information that has become incorrect.

Three GAAPs are introduced below. Others are introduced at appropriate times throughout the text. A list of GAAPs is given in the Appendix on page 841.

GAAP— The Business Entity Concept

The business entity concept provides that **the accounting for a business organization must be kept separate from the personal affairs of its owner, or from any other business or organization.** This means that the owner of the business should not place any personal assets, such as the family home, on the business balance sheet. The balance sheet of the business must reflect the financial position of the business alone. Also, when transactions of the business are recorded, any personal expenditures of the owner are charged to the owner. They are not allowed to affect the operating results of the business.

The balance sheet of Easy Rent-Alls in Figure 2.1 complies with the business entity concept. The balance sheet reflects the affairs of the business only. No personal assets or liabilities are included.

GAAP—The Continuing Concern Concept

The continuing concern concept assumes that **a business will continue to operate, unless it is known that it will not.** This is also known as the **going concern concept**.

The dollar values associated with a business that is alive and well are straightforward. For example, a supply of envelopes with the company's name printed on them would be valued at their cost price. This would not be the case if the company were going out of business. In that case, the envelopes would be difficult to sell because the company's name is on them. The values of such assets often cannot be determined until they are actually sold. When a company is going out of business, the values of the assets usually suffer because they have to be sold under unfavourable circumstances.

GAAP—The Principle of Conservatism

The principle of conservatism provides that **accounting for a business should be fair and reasonable.** In their work, accountants are required to make evaluations and estimates, to deliver opinions, and to select procedures. They should do this in such a way that assets or profits are neither overstated nor understated when uncertainty exists.

SECTION REVIEW QUESTIONS

1. Name the three leading accounting organizations in Canada.
2. Over the years what have the above organizations established?
3. In what publication are most of the rules of accounting found?
4. What does GAAP stand for?
5. Explain what is meant by the business entity concept.
6. Explain what is meant by the continuing concern concept.
7. Explain what is meant by the principle of conservatism.

SECTION EXERCISES

1. **This exercise also appears in your Workbook.**
   Kevin Kaghee is the owner of Central Paving Company in Charlottetown, P.E.I. His personal and business assets and liabilities are listed below.

   1. **Separate the list below into the two columns provided.**
   2. **Calculate the total assets and the total liabilities in each column.**
   3. **Calculate Kevin Kaghee's personal net worth and his equity in Central Paving Company.**

Assets	Amount	Business	Personal
Accounts Receivable	$ 27 460		
Boat and Motor	16 520		
Business Bank Balance	1 852		
Business Automobiles	48 054		
Furniture and Appliances	6 528		
Government Bonds of Owner	20 000		
House and Lot	99 600		
Office Furniture and Equipment	18 324		
Office Supplies	3 545		
Owner's Automobiles	18 657		
Paving Materials	55 326		
Personal Bank Balance	1 258		
Plant Property and Buildings	125 358		
Summer Cottage	65 874		
Trucks and Equipment	285 657		
Total Assets			
Liabilities			
Accounts Payable	3 500		
Business Bank Loan	56 000		
Mortgage on Plant Property	75 000		
Mortgage on House and Lot	60 000		
Mortgage on Summer Cottage	22 300		
Owed to Finance Co.—Business Equipment	136 522		
Total Liabilities			
Owner's equity			

2. **Answer the following questions in your Workbook.**

1. A customer who owes $500 to the business has recently died. The lawyers for the customer have told the business that there is only a one in four chance of the debt being paid.
   a. Should the amount be included on the balance sheet of the business?
   b. Which GAAP(s) affect this situation? Explain.

2. A contracting company is involved in a dispute over its bill to a customer. The bill for $500 000 was recently reduced to $400 000 by a decision of the courts. The company is now appealing the decision.
   a. Which amount should be taken into the accounts (recognized)?
   b. Which GAAP(s) affect this situation? Explain.

3. Six months ago you closed out your business. Now, a person has expressed an interest in acquiring the business. The potential buyer requests a current balance sheet, but you provide her with the one that was prepared just prior to closing.
   a. Will the balance sheet be accepted by the buyer and her accountant?
   b. Which GAAP(s) affect this situation? Explain.

4. Martha Higgins is currently trying to borrow some money from the bank. She has listed her personal automobile ($25 000) on the business balance sheet to make the statement look more attractive to the banker.
   a. Is this a reasonable thing to do?
   b. Which GAAP(s) affect this situation? Explain.

5. The manager of a business has heard that the business might be sold and that he might lose his job as a result. When preparing a balance sheet for the owner, the manager values everything as low as possible in order to discourage the prospective buyer. He claims that this practice is allowed by the principle of conservatism.
   a. Is the manager correct in his claim?
   b. Which GAAP(s) affect this situation? Explain.

6. A figure of $25 000 for computerized office equipment appears on a company balance sheet. Recently, better quality equipment has been developed and put on the market. However, the existing equipment still does an adequate job for the company, and the company has no intention of replacing it.
   a. Should the equipment figure be eliminated because it represents obsolete equipment?
   b. Which GAAP(s) affect this situation? Explain.

2.5 COMPUTERS IN ACCOUNTING: THE ACCOUNTING SPREADSHEET

You probably know about computer software that is purchased for use on a computer. A spreadsheet is software that can be programmed to do a number of tasks.

The first step in using a spreadsheet is to load the software into the computer's memory. On the computer's screen this will produce a grid like the one shown below in Figure 2.8.

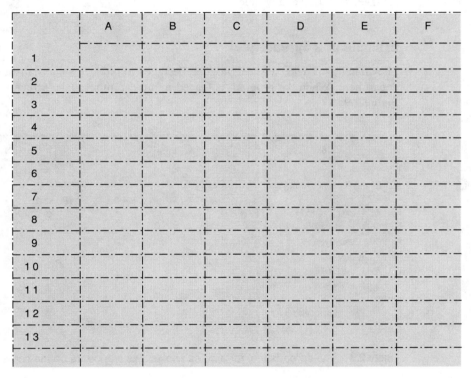

Figure 2.8   A spreadsheet as it might appear on the screen.

Each rectangle in the grid is known as a "cell." The cells are identified as A1, A2, B5, C8, and so on. Spreadsheets vary in size but are always larger than the screen. You cannot see all of the grid at one time. But you can see any part of the grid by moving it back and forth, or up and down, on the screen. This is done with the cursor keys or another device.

Information can be entered on the screen through the keyboard. The cursor is moved to the desired cell and the information is keyed in. This information is visible on the screen. For any screen cell the programmer can:

1. Leave the cell blank.
2. Enter a label, which is a string of letters or characters, such as a column heading.

3. Enter a numerical value.

4. Enter a formula.

The programmer can enter "hidden" formulas which do not appear on the screen but which are linked to the cells by the computer. Formulas are used to make the calculations for the final output of the spreadsheet program. There can be one formula for each cell. Any formula can be seen by looking at the "status" line which usually appears above the grid on the screen.

When a program is prepared and tested, it can be stored on a disk. It can be retrieved and used at any time.

Example of a Spreadsheet

Shown below is a spreadsheet program designed to produce some statistics for a sales department. When the program is loaded into the computer, the screen appears as in Figure 2.9.

	A	B	C	D	E	F
1						
2	XYZ SALES ANALYSIS					
3			PRODUCT	PRODUCT	PRODUCT	TOTALS BY
4	SALES PERSON		A	B	C	SALES PERSON
5	ANDERSON A.					
6	BROWN C.					
7	DAVIS C.					
8	GREEN B.					
9	HARRISON F.					
10						
11	TOTALS BY PRODUCT					

Figure 2.9   The spreadsheet for a sales analysis as it appears on the screen.

But what you see on the screen is not the complete program. There are hidden formulas that you cannot see on the grid. Figure 2.10 on p. 37 shows the complete program with the hidden formulas in faint print.

To use this program, it is merely necessary to key in the individual sales figures while the "calculator key" is turned off. When all of the figures are entered, the calculator key is turned on. Then, all of the vertical and horizontal totals are calculated automatically. The final output appears on the screen as shown in Figure 2.11 on p. 37. A copy of the final output can be obtained using the printer. The column and row identifiers will not be shown on the printout.

	A	B	C	D	E	F
1						
2	XYZ SALES ANALYSIS					
3			PRODUCT	PRODUCT	PRODUCT	TOTALS BY
4	SALES PERSON		A	B	C	SALES PERSON
5	ANDERSON A.					SUM(C5:E5)
6	BROWN C.					SUM(C6:E6)
7	DAVIS G.					SUM(C7:E7)
8	GREEN B.					SUM(C8:E8)
9	HARRISON F.					SUM(C9:E9)
10						
11	TOTALS BY PRODUCT		SUM(C5:C9)	SUM(D5:D9)	SUM(E5:E9)	SUM(F5:F9)

Means the sum of the figures entered in cells C5 to C9.

Figure 2.10   The spreadsheet for a sales analysis showing the hidden formulas associated with certain screen cells.

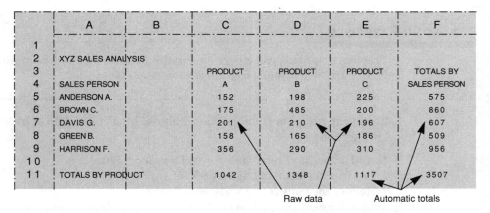

	A	B	C	D	E	F
1						
2	XYZ SALES ANALYSIS					
3			PRODUCT	PRODUCT	PRODUCT	TOTALS BY
4	SALES PERSON		A	B	C	SALES PERSON
5	ANDERSON A.		152	198	225	575
6	BROWN C.		175	485	200	860
7	DAVIS G.		201	210	196	607
8	GREEN B.		158	165	186	509
9	HARRISON F.		356	290	310	956
10						
11	TOTALS BY PRODUCT		1042	1348	1117	3507

Raw data   Automatic totals

Figure 2.11   The spreadsheet for a sales analysis in its final form. The raw data have been entered via the keyboard. The totals were calculated automatically.

A major advantage of the spreadsheet is how it handles error corrections or changes in data. For example, suppose that one of the sales figures had been entered incorrectly. By merely correcting the figure on the screen all of the calculations will be redone in seconds if the "calculator key" is on.

A simple balance sheet can be prepared using a spreadsheet program. Formulas are necessary to calculate: 1) the total assets; 2) the total liabilities; and 3) the owner's equity. All other information is in the form of labels or numerical values. If a name happens to be larger than one cell, two cells are used or the name can be abbreviated.

COMPUTER REVIEW QUESTIONS

1. What is a spreadsheet in data processing?
2. What is the first step in using a spreadsheet?

3. What is the name given to any position on the grid?
4. You cannot see all of the grid at one time. What do you do to see a part of the grid that is not presently on the screen?
5. How is a "label" entered into the spreadsheet?
6. How is a "value" entered into the spreadsheet?
7. In additon to labels and numeric values, what else is associated with a spreadsheet?
8. What can be done with a spreadsheet program once it is completed and tested?
9. When a spreadsheet program is loaded into the computer, what action must the user take to make use of it?
10. The text refers to hidden formulas. What does the text mean by a hidden formula?
11. What is shown in cell D7 of the spreadsheet in Figure 2.11?
12. For what purpose would formulas be used to prepare a balance sheet?
13. In Figure 2.11, if you were to change one of the sales figures, what would happen on the screen?

COMPUTER EXERCISES

1. **Prepare a spreadsheet program for the balance sheet of Easy Rent-Alls in Figure 2.1. When your program is completed, save it.**

2. **Load your program from question 1 above. Modify the data to include the following changes.**

   1. Add an account receivable for C. Orr for $1 500.
   2. Increase the cash on hand by $500.
   3. Reduce the bank loan by $10 000.
   4. Give the new totals for a) total assets, b) total liabilities, and c) owner's equity.

CHAPTER HIGHLIGHTS

Now that you have completed Chapter 2, you should:

1. understand what is meant by the financial position of a person or a business;
2. know the meaning of accounts receivable and accounts payable;
3. be able to prepare a simple balance sheet in proper form for a business or an individual;
4. understand the fundamental accounting equation;
5. understand the meaning of claims against the assets;
6. be able to use basic recordkeeping practices;
7. understand the concept of liquidity;
8. know three generally accepted accounting principles: the business entity concept, the continuing concern concept, and the principle of conservatism.

ACCOUNTING TERMS

accounts payable	fundamental accounting equation
accounts receivable	GAAP
asset	generally accepted accounting principles
balance sheet	going concern concept
business entity concept	liability
capital	liquidity
continuing concern concept	net worth
creditor	owner's equity
debtor	principle of conservatism
financial position	

CHAPTER EXERCISES

Using Your Knowledge

1. **For each of the following questions, write in your Workbook the letter that represents the best possible answer.**

   1. The financial position of a business is
   a. the difference between total assets and total liabilities.
   b. represented by the assets, the liabilities, and the capital.
   c. the same as the net worth of the business.

   2. If the total assets increase by $10 000 and the total liabilities decrease by $10 000, the capital will
   a. increase by $20 000.
   b. be unchanged.
   c. decrease by $20 000.

   3. Which one of the following is not true?
   a. $A - C = L$
   b. $A - L = C$
   c. $A + L = C$
   d. $A = L + C$

   4. A balance sheet shows
   a. all of the owner's assets and liabilities.
   b. a financial picture of the business on a certain date.
   c. the progress of the business over a period of time.

   5. Which one of the following is not true?
   a. The heading of a balance sheet shows the date as of which it was prepared.
   b. Assets are listed in the order of their liquidity.
   c. Accounts receivable are considered to be a liquid asset.
   d. Personal assets have no place on the business balance sheet.
   e. A truck which cost $10 000 and for which $6 000 is owed is listed on the balance sheet at $4 000.

6. Abbreviations may be used on financial statements
   a. when it is necessary to crowd things to conserve space.
   b. to save time in preparing the statements.
   c. in a company name if the abbreviation is a formal part of the name.
7. Which one of the following is least true? Columnar paper helps the accountant
   a. to add columns more accurately.
   b. to make records easier to read.
   c. to make the records more attractive.
   d. to make recordkeeping go more quickly.
8. Which one of the following is not true?
   a. Ruled lines are used to underline headings.
   b. Ruled lines are used to indicate that columns of numbers are to be totaled.
   c. Ruled lines are necessary to separate sections of the balance sheet.
   d. Ruled lines are doubled to indicate a final total.
9. Before a business is closed down, the equation for it is:
   Assets ($125 000) = Liabilities ($37 000) + Equity ($88 000)
   If assets of $70 000 are sold for $20 000, assets of $50 000 are sold for $90 000, and the remaining assets stay the same, the equation will become
   a. $55 000 = $37 000 + $18 000.
   b. $115 000 = $37 000 + $78 000.
   c. $75 000 = $37 000 + $38 000.
   d. $135 000 = $47 000 + $88 000.
   e. $115 000 = $27 000 + $88 000.
10. Which of the following is not true?
   a. In the liability section on a balance sheet, accounts payable may be listed first.
   b. On a balance sheet there are three main totals.
   c. On a balance sheet the owner's name only appears in the heading.
   d. On a balance sheet the final totals are always on the same line.

2. Shown below is the balance sheet of S. Magbool.

   Based on the limited information given, would you say that Magbool has any kind of a financial problem? Explain.

S. MAGBOOL
BALANCE SHEET
JANUARY 31, 19—

Assets		Liabilities	
Cash	$ 6 000	Accounts Payable	$ 35 000
Accounts Receivable	14 000	Mortgage Payable	60 000
Land	40 000		$ 95 000
Buildings	95 000	Owner's Equity	
Equipment	25 000	S. Magbool, Capital	85 000
	$180 000		$180 000

3. On December 31, 19—, you present your balance sheet, shown below, to the manager of the local bank, with the hope of obtaining a small bank loan. During your conversation with the manager, certain facts are brought out.
   a. About $8 000 owing from customers is considerably overdue.
   b. A yearly mortgage payment of $4 000 is due next March 1.
   c. All creditors' accounts are due within 30 days.
   d. The average earnings of the business for the past five years have been very good.

BALANCE SHEET
DECEMBER 31, 19—

Assets		Liabilities	
Cash	$ 5 000	Accounts Payable	$17 000
Accounts Receivable	25 000	Mortgage Payable	35 000
Land	10 000		$52 000
Equipment	20 000		
Building	30 000	Capital	38 000
	$90 000		$90 000

1. Would the bank manager grant the loan?
2. What concerns might the manager have?

For Further Thought

4. **Briefly answer the following questions.**

   1. The balance sheet is thought of as being a "snapshot" of the business. Explain this statement.
   2. Assets and liabilities can be thought of as things that can be touched or seen. For example, you can go into the parking lot and touch the automobile, or you can see the signed bank loan at the bank. The equity is not like this. Explain.
   3. Give reasons why businesspersons sell on credit when there is a chance that they will not be able to collect the debt.
   4. Work out another acceptable definition of a balance sheet besides the one given in the textbook.
   5. In three words, tell what information is contained in the heading of a balance sheet.
   6. Supplies are considered to be a more liquid asset than land. In a going concern, neither asset is expected to be sold for cash. Give an explanation for this.
   7. If a bank were to lend funds to a business, the bank would become a "secured" creditor. What does this mean? How does the bank accomplish it? Why do other creditors not do the same?
   8. The *CICA Handbook* is published in loose-leaf form so that it can be easily updated. Why do they use the loose-leaf system?

9. Given what you have learned so far, explain how the earnings of a business can be determined from its balance sheets if you know that the owner neither contributed nor withdrew any funds or other assets.

10. There is a saying in accounting: "Anticipate no profits and account for all possible losses." Which GAAP is this saying related to?

CASE STUDIES

CASE 1   *Considering the Purchase of a Business*

Your friends Joseph and Janice Dubois have recently inherited some money and want to use it to purchase a business of their own. They have come to you for advice regarding the possible purchase of a sand and gravel business. They learned about the sale of the sand and gravel business through an advertisement in the newspaper.

The business is being sold by K. Vako who has owned it for 20 years and wants a change because of failing health. The business has been profitable over the years, earning an average of $50 000 per year over the last 10 years.

The following balance sheet has been prepared by Mr. Vako personally.

VAKO SAND AND GRAVEL
BALANCE SHEET
DECEMBER 31, 19-6

Assets		*Liabilities*	
Bank	$ 500	Bank Loan	$ 30 000
Accounts Receivable	17 400	Accounts Payable	22 740
Supplies	1 100	Mortgage Payable	50 000
Land	40 700		$102 740
Buildings	38 000		
Equipment	67 600	*Owner's Equity*	
Gravel Deposits	200 000	K. Vako, Capital	262 560
	$365 300		$365 300

Mr. Vako is asking $250 000 for the business. This seems to be a very good price. It is less than his capital figure as shown on the balance sheet.

Work in a small group to help Joseph and Janice decide if they should buy the sand and gravel business. Prepare a list of questions that need to be answered and be ready to present your list to the class. To help you, a first question is already given below.

1. What condition is the equipment in and is it really worth $67 600?

Case 2   *Placing a Value on Assets*

Hilda Lahti is the owner of Custom-Made Products in Prince George, B.C. Originally, Custom-Made Products was a machine shop that produced custom work of many kinds. In the last few years the company has developed and patented a line of scaffolding equipment for contractors and builders. The scaffolding equipment produced by the company is better than that of its competitors. As a result, the company has had great success with the new product. At the same time, the custom machine shop division of the business has been doing poorly. There is a lot of competition from other machine shops in the community. In the last year the company earned $135 000. $110 000 of this was from the sale of scaffolding equipment and only $25 000 from the machine shop.

Recently, Hilda has decided to make a major change in the company operations. In particular, she has decided to get out of machine shop work. She intends to concentrate the entire energies of the company on expanding the markets for scaffolding, and developing new products of this type. The change in policy has been made official and the customers of the company have been notified.

The most recent balance sheet of the company, prepared at the request of the company's bank, provides the following information:

Assets	
Cash	$ 1 500
Accounts Receivable	20 540
Supplies	1 821
Land and Building	102 500
Machinery and Equipment	205 365
Automotive Equipment	65 385
Total Assets	$397 111
Liabilities	
Bank Loan	$105 000
Accounts Payable	11 850
Mortgage Payable	85 000
Total Liabilities	$201 850
Owner's Equity	$195 261

The bank manager who receives the above balance sheet notices that no adjustment has been made to show the company's decision to quit custom machine shop work. Inquiries reveal that the company has $155 000 of specialized machine shop equipment. This figure is included in the Machinery and Equipment figure of $205 365 on the balance sheet. It is generally agreed that the market for this type of equipment is quite poor. The company's equipment is outdated, and most other machine shops have already acquired modern computerized equipment.

Questions

1. Based on the preceding statement, why would the bank manager be concerned about the repayment of the bank loan?
2. What additional information would help the bank manager to evaluate the company's loan?
3. What needs to be done regarding the above balance sheet?
4. Assuming that a buyer for the machine shop equipment is found at a price of $35 000, what changes should be made on the balance sheet?
5. Prepare a simple balance sheet to show the changes.
6. What GAAP influenced you in your thinking?

ENTREPRENEUR
Samuel Essex / Sole Proprietor

In high school, Samuel Essex of Vernon, British Columbia, took a number of business courses, including accounting. After graduation, he was hired as a bookkeeper for a branch office of the Trane Service Agency, an international corporation. Samuel worked with cash receipts, accounts receivable, and accounts payable.

After two years, Samuel decided to leave and start his own business. Following months of preparation, he opened Sam's Fabric Shoppe in a rented store on Vernon's main street. The business has been extremely successful. Samuel sells a high-quality selection of fabrics, wool, and needlepoint supplies. He enjoys the independence, variety, and contact with people that owning one's own store provides.

As the sole proprietor of a small business, Samuel does all his own accounting; his training and experience in this area have proven invaluable. Although he is very busy, Samuel enrolled in a correspondence introductory accounting course at the university. This course acquainted him with some very important accounting principles: the business entity concept, and the principle of conservatism.

Today in his own business, Samuel's accounting duties include keeping track of accounts receivable and accounts payable and reconciling his monthly bank statement. He also has to make sure that the cor-

rect amount of sales tax is sent to the provincial government. Further, he must be certain to have enough stock on hand to meet the demands of his customers.

Samuel has recently approached his local bank for a loan of $10 000. He wants to purchase a microcomputer with a double disk drive, a printer and a software package for his general ledger and his merchandise inventory. This will enable him to manage a larger stock. By buying in larger quantities, Samuel hopes to take advantage of suppliers' discounts and increase his inventory. The loan manager, following standard procedure, has asked Samuel to produce a balance sheet for his business. Samuel's balance sheet contains the following assets, liabilities, and owner's equity:

SAM'S FABRIC SHOPPE
BALANCE SHEET
JUNE 30, 19--

Assets		Liabilities	
Cash on Hand	$ 50.00	Accounts Payable	
Bank Balance	3 000.00	Northcab Silk Co.	$ 1 800.00
Accounts Receivable		H.A. Kidd Co.	2 200.00
Bodley & Son	350.00		$ 4 000.00
Lukes	200.00		
Merchandise Inventory	17 000.00		
Supplies	1 400.00	Owner's Equity	
Furniture & Fixtures	13 000.00	Samuel Essex, Capital	42 000.00
Office Equipment	11 000.00		
	$46 000.00		$46 000.00

Having prepared the balance sheet, Samuel now sees that not all the assets belong to him. If the loan is granted, then the claims against the assets of Sam's Fabric Shoppe will total $14 000. Nonetheless, Samuel is determined to expand his business. He feels that the risk is justified by the prospect of increased success for his business, made possible through the use of new microcomputer equipment.

DISCUSSION

1. List some advantages and disadvantages of being a sole proprietor.
2. Discuss the types of merchandise inventory and supplies Samuel would have in his store.
3. How have Samuel's accounting courses helped him operate his business successfully?
4. Discuss how Samuel would use the microcomputer equipment in his business.
5. Examine Samuel's balance sheet. Can you see any reason why the bank manager might not grant the loan of $10 000?
6. What additional information might the bank manager want in order to grant this loan?
7. If Samuel were denied the loan from the bank, discuss other approaches he could take in order to obtain the $10 000 for the purchase of the computer equipment he is interested in.

Analyzing Changes in Financial Position

3.1 Business Transactions
3.2 Equation Analysis Sheet
3.3 Summary of Steps in Analyzing a Transaction
3.4 Introduction to Source Documents
3.5 Computers in Accounting   The Electronic Spreadsheet: A Modern Tool for Accountants

3.1 *BUSINESS TRANSACTIONS*

On any given day in a business many events occur that cause the financial position of the business to change. Each of these events is called a business transaction. A **business transaction** may be defined as a financial event that causes a change in financial position.

For example, suppose the business buys a new truck for which it pays $20 000 cash. This event is a transaction because it causes the financial position of the business to change. There would be an increase in the item Trucks of $20 000. There would be a decrease in the item Cash of $20 000.

Or suppose that the business owes $7 000 to City Finance and makes a payment of $1 000 against the debt. This event is also a transaction causing the financial position to change. The amount owed to City Finance would be reduced by $1 000. The cash on hand would be reduced by $1 000.

On the other hand, suppose that the city plumbing inspector inspects the building and leaves a letter suggesting some improvements. This is not a business transaction because no assets or liabilities have changed as a result of the activity.

SECTION REVIEW QUESTIONS

1. What is a business transaction?
2. Explain the following sentence: "Transactions are the raw materials of accounting."
3. Give an example of a transaction.
4. Give an example of an event in a business that is not a transaction.

SECTION EXERCISES

1. **Given that a transaction is a financial event that requires changing the statement of financial position, decide whether or not each of the following is a transaction.** The business is Best Consultants of Calgary, Alberta.

   1. $800 is paid by the business to Mercury Finance to reduce the amount owed to them.
   2. The owner, P. Dufour, withdraws $500 from the business for her own personal use.
   3. A new employee is needed in the payroll department. P. Dufour interviews Stan Martin for the job.
   4. A $700 consulting service is provided for Rita Bertoli on credit.
   5. The business pays the rent for the month, $500.
   6. The employee in question 3 above is hired to start work next Monday at $300 per week.
   7. The business purchases a new computer for cash at the price of $3 000.
   8. The computer in question 7 above is defective and is replaced at no cost to the business.

2. **This exercise also appears in your Workbook.**
   Given that a transaction is a financial event that requires changing the statement of financial position, decide whether or not each of the following is a transaction. You are working for Ace Collection Agency of Regina, Saskatchewan, owned by Ingrid Lencz.

   1. $40 cash was paid for gasoline for the company automobile.
   2. Ingrid Lencz paid $15 out of her own pocket for lunch.
   3. Ingrid's personal car was damaged and needed a $500 repair job.
   4. A $250 service was performed for a customer who paid cash.
   5. A leased typewriter broke down and needed to be replaced at no cost to the business. The man who came with the replacement said that the new machine was a $1 500 model.
   6. A customer who owed the business $1 200 makes a partial payment of $300.
   7. The business bank loan was reduced by a direct payment to the bank of $1 000.
   8. A burglar broke into the office and stole the leased typewriter. The business has 100 per cent replacement insurance to cover breaking and entering and theft.

3.2   EQUATION ANALYSIS SHEET

Your next step in the study of accounting is to learn how the various business transactions affect and change the financial position. To begin with, look at the balance sheet of Metropolitan Movers of Burnaby, B.C. on page 49.

METROPOLITAN MOVERS
BALANCE SHEET
—DATE—

Assets		Liabilities	
Cash	$13 500	Accounts Payable	
Accounts Receivable		Central Supply	$ 1 750
B. Cava	1 300	Loan Payable	
K. Lincoln	2 500	Mercury Finance	18 370
Equipment	11 500	Total Liabilities	$20 120
Trucks	24 500		
		Owner's Equity	
		J. Hofner, Capital	33 180
	_____		
Total Assets	$53 300	Total Liabilities and Equity	$53 300

Figure 3.1 The balance sheet of Metropolitan Movers.

The balance sheet of Metropolitan Movers shows the values of the assets, liabilities, and capital on a particular date. As business transactions occur, the values of assets, liabilities, and capital change. The balance sheet is not a suitable type of record on which to record these changes. Therefore, let us arrange the balance sheet items in a different manner. We will transfer the assets, liabilities, and capital from the balance sheet onto what we will call an equation analysis sheet. This sheet is ideal for studying and recording changes in financial position. In Figure 3.2 you can see the balance sheet items for Metropolitan Movers entered on an equation analysis sheet. Note that this arrangement is in the form of the fundamental accounting equation.

		ASSETS				LIABILITIES		OWNER'S EQUITY
	Cash	A/R		Equipment	Trucks	A/P	LoanPay'l	J.Hofner
		B. Cava	K. Lincoln			Central Supply	Mercury Finance	Capital
Beginning balances	13 500	1 300	2 500	11 500	24 500	1 750	18 370	33 180
			53 300		=	20 120	+	33 180

Figure 3.2 Equation analysis sheet for Metropolitan Movers.

Updating the Equation Analysis Sheet

Let us now examine how transactions affect financial position.

TRANSACTION 1 $1 200 cash is paid to Mercury Finance.

After this payment is made, the financial position shown in Figure 3.2 will no longer be correct. Two changes are necessary: Cash must be reduced by $1 200, and the amount owed to Mercury Finance must also be reduced by $1 200. These changes are recorded on the equation analysis sheet shown in Figure 3.3.

	ASSETS					LIABILITIES		OWNER'S EQUITY
	Cash	A/R		Equipment	Trucks	A/P	LoanPay'l	J.Hofner
		B. Cava	K. Lincoln			Central Supply	Mercury Finance	Capital
Beginning balances	13 500	1 300	2 500	11 500	24 500	1 750	18 370	33 180
Transaction 1	−1 200						−1 200	
New balances	12 300	1 300	2 500	11 500	24 500	1 750	17 170	33 180
			52 100		=		18 920	+ 33 180

Figure 3.3 Equation analysis sheet after transaction 1.

In analyzing transaction 1, observe that:

1. The amounts for Cash and Mercury Finance are updated: Cash is decreased by $1 200 and the debt owed to Mercury Finance is decreased by $1 200.
2. The amounts for the other items remain unchanged.
3. After the changes are recorded and the new totals determined, the equation is still in balance.

TRANSACTION 2   K. Lincoln, who owes Metropolitan Movers $2 500, pays $1 100 in part payment of the debt.

Can you figure out the changes to be made on the equation analysis sheet? Try to do this mentally before looking ahead at Figure 3.4.

	ASSETS					LIABILITIES		OWNER'S EQUITY
	Cash	A/R		Equipment	Trucks	A/P	LoanPay'l	J.Hofner
		B. Cava	K. Lincoln			Central Supply	Mercury Finance	Capital
Beginning balances	13 500	1 300	2 500	11 500	24 500	1 750	18 370	33 180
Transaction 1	−1 200						−1 200	
New balances	12 300	1 300	2 500	11 500	24 500	1 750	17 170	33 180
Transaction 2	+1 100		−1 100					
New balances	13 400	1 300	1 400	11 500	24 500	1 750	17 170	33 180
			52 100		=		18 920	+ 33 180

Figure 3.4 Equation analysis sheet after transaction 2.

In analyzing transaction 2, observe that:

1. The figure for Cash is increased by the amount received, $1 100.
2. The figure for K. Lincoln is decreased by $1 100. $1 400 is still owing on the debt.
3. After the changes are recorded, the equation is still in balance.

TRANSACTION 3   **Equipment costing $1 950 is purchased for cash.**

Again, try to make the changes mentally before looking at the entries recorded in Figure 3.5.

		ASSETS				LIABILITIES		OWNER'S EQUITY
	Cash	A/R		Equipment	Trucks	A/P	Loan Pay'l	J. Hofner
		B. Cava	K. Lincoln			Central Supply	Mercury Finance	Capital
Beginning balances	13 500	1 300	2 500	11 500	24 500	1 750	18 370	33 180
Transaction 1	−1 200						−1 200	
New balances	12 300	1 300	2 500	11 500	24 500	1 750	17 170	33 180
Transaction 2	+1 100		−1 100					
New balances	13 400	1 300	1 400	11 500	24 500	1 750	17 170	33 180
Transaction 3	−1 950			+1 950				
New balances	11 450	1 300	1 400	13 450	24 500	1 750	17 170	33 180
			52 100		=		18 920 +	33 180

Figure 3.5 Equation analysis sheet after transaction 3.

In analyzing transaction 3 observe that:

1. Cash is decreased by the amount paid, $1 950.
2. Equipment is increased by the cost of the equipment acquired, $1 950.
3. After the changes are recorded, the equation is still in balance.

TRANSACTION 4   **A new pick-up truck is purchased at a cost of $18 000. Metropolitan Movers pays $10 000 cash and arranges a loan from Mercury Finance to cover the balance of the purchase price. (Note:** This is considered to be a single transaction. Mercury Finance will pay $8 000 directly to the truck dealer, who will be paid in full.)

Again, try to work out the changes mentally before looking at the equation analysis sheet in Figure 3.6.

		ASSETS				LIABILITIES		OWNER'S EQUITY
	Cash	*A/R*		*Equipment*	*Trucks*	*A/P*	*Loan Pay'l*	*J. Hofner*
		B. Cava	*K. Lincoln*			*Central Supply*	*Mercury Finance*	*Capital*
Beginning balances	13 500	1 300	2 500	11 500	24 500	1 750	18 370	33 180
Transaction 1	−1 200						−1 200	
New balances	12 300	1 300	2 500	11 500	24 500	1 750	17 170	33 180
Transaction 2	+1 100		−1 100					
New balances	13 400	1 300	1 400	11 500	24 500	1 750	17 170	33 180
Transaction 3	−1 950			+1 950				
New balances	11 450	1 300	1 400	13 450	24 500	1 750	17 170	33 180
Transaction 4	−10 000				+18 000		+8 000	
New balances	1 450	1 300	1 400	13 450	42 500	1 750	25 170	33 180
		60 100				=	26 920	+	33 180

Figure 3.6 Equation analysis sheet after transaction 4.

In analyzing transaction 4 observe that:

1. Cash is decreased by the amount paid out, $10 000.
2. Trucks is increased by the cost of the new truck, $18 000.
3. The liability to Mercury Finance is increased by the additional amount borrowed, $8 000.
4. After the changes are recorded, the equation is still in balance.

TRANSACTION 5   **Metropolitan Movers completes a storage service for B. Cava at a price of $1 500. A bill is sent to Cava to indicate the additional amount that Cava owes.**

Work out the changes necessary and compare them with the equation analysis sheet in Figure 3.7.

| | ASSETS | | | | | LIABILITIES | | OWNER'S EQUITY |
| | Cash | A/R | | Equipment | Trucks | A/P | LoanPay'l | J.Hofner |
		B. Cava	K. Lincoln			Central Supply	Mercury Finance	Capital
Beginning balances	13 500	1 300	2 500	11 500	24 500	1 750	18 370	33 180
Transaction 1	-1 200						-1 200	
New balances	12 300	1 300	2 500	11 500	24 500	1 750	17 170	33 180
Transaction 2	+1 100		-1 100					
New balances	13 400	1 300	1 400	11 500	24 500	1 750	17 170	33 180
Transaction 3	-1 950			+1 950				
New balances	11 450	1 300	1 400	13 450	24 500	1 750	17 170	33 180
Transaction 4	-10 000				+18 000		+8 000	
New balances	1 450	1 300	1 400	13 450	42 500	1 750	25 170	33 180
Transaction 5		+1 500						+1 500
New balances	1 450	2 800	1 400	13 450	42 500	1 750	25 170	34 680
		61 600				=	26 920	+ 34 680

Figure 3.7 Equation analysis sheet after transaction 5.

Transaction 5 is not as simple to understand as the previous four. But "understanding" is vital to becoming a good accountant. Transaction 5 may be explained as follows:

1. Cava owes $1 500 more to Metropolitan Movers and therefore the figure for Cava is increased by $1 500.
2. No other asset or liability is affected.
3. J. Hofner's Capital is increased by $1 500.

There are two ways to explain this increase in capital. First, remember that Metropolitan Movers is in the business of providing a service to earn profit. When the service to Cava is completed, and Cava legally owes the $1 500, a gain has been made. Metropolitan Movers is then better off by the amount of this gain. This is recorded by increasing the capital of the owner, J. Hofner.

Second, the increase in capital can be shown by arithmetic. Remember that capital is the difference between the total assets and the total liabilities, and the adding of $1 500 to Equity is necessary to keep the equation in balance.

	ASSETS		LIABILITIES		CAPITAL
After transaction 5 (Figure 3.7)	$61 600	–	$26 920	=	$34 680
Before transaction 5 (Figure 3.6)	$60 100	–	$26 920	=	$33 180
			Increase in capital	=	$ 1 500

Clearly, there is an increase in capital of $1 500, which must be recorded on the equation analysis sheet.

TRANSACTION 6   J. Hofner, the owner, withdraws $500 for personal use.

Work out the necessary changes and then check your work against the equation analysis sheet in Figure 3.8.

| | ASSETS | | | | | LIABILITIES | | OWNER'S EQUITY |
| | Cash | A/R | | Equipment | Trucks | A/P | LoanPay'l | J.Hofner |
		B. Cava	K. Lincoln			Central Supply	Mercury Finance	Capital
Beginning balances	13 500	1 300	2 500	11 500	24 500	1 750	18 370	33 180
Transaction 1	−1 200						−1 200	
New balances	12 300	1 300	2 500	11 500	24 500	1 750	17 170	33 180
Transaction 2	+1 100		−1 100					
New balances	13 400	1 300	1 400	11 500	24 500	1 750	17 170	33 180
Transaction 3	−1 950			+1 950				
New balances	11 450	1 300	1 400	13 450	24 500	1 750	17 170	33 180
Transaction 4	−10 000				+18 000		+8 000	
New balances	1 450	1 300	1 400	13 450	42 500	1 750	25 170	33 180
Transaction 5		+1 500						+1 500
New balances	1 450	2 800	1 400	13 450	42 500	1 750	25 170	34 680
Transaction 6	− 500							− 500
New balances	950	2 800	1 400	13 450	42 500	1 750	25 170	34 180
			61 100				26 920 +	34 180

Figure 3.8 Equation analysis sheet after transaction 6.

In analyzing transaction 6 observe that:

1. Cash is decreased by $500, the amount withdrawn.
2. No other asset or liability is affected.
3. Capital is decreased by $500. After changing the cash figure, the difference between total assets and total liabilities is $34 180. This is $500 less than it was immediately before the transaction.
4. After the changes are recorded, the equation is still in balance.

TRANSACTION 7   One of the trucks requires an engine adjustment costing $75. The repair is paid for in cash when the truck is picked up.

Work out the necessary changes and then check your work against the equation analysis sheet in Figure 3.9.

	Cash	A/R B. Cava	A/R K. Lincoln	Equipment	Trucks	A/P Central Supply	LoanPay'l Mercury Finance	J. Hofner Capital
		ASSETS				**LIABILITIES**		**OWNER'S EQUITY**
Beginning balances	13 500	1 300	2 500	11 500	24 500	1 750	18 370	33 180
Transaction 1	−1 200						−1 200	
New balances	12 300	1 300	2 500	11 500	24 500	1 750	17 170	33 180
Transaction 2	+1 100		−1 100					
New balances	13 400	1 300	1 400	11 500	24 500	1 750	17 170	33 180
Transaction 3	−1 950			+1 950				
New balances	11 450	1 300	1 400	13 450	24 500	1 750	17 170	33 180
Transaction 4	−10 000				+18 000		+8 000	
New balances	1 450	1 300	1 400	13 450	42 500	1 750	25 170	33 180
Transaction 5		+1 500						+1 500
New balances	1 450	2 800	1 400	13 450	42 500	1 750	25 170	34 680
Transaction 6	− 500							− 500
New balances	950	2 800	1 400	13 450	42 500	1 750	25 170	34 180
Transaction 7	−75							−75
New balances	875	2 800	1 400	13 450	42 500	1 750	25 170	34 105
			61 025			=	26 920 +	34 105

Figure 3.9 Equation analysis sheet after transaction 7.

In analyzing transaction 7 observe that:

1. Cash is decreased by $75, the amount paid for the repair.
2. No other asset or liability is affected. The value of the truck on the equation analysis sheet is not increased because the engine was tuned up.
3. Capital is decreased by $75. After changing the cash figure, the difference between total assets and total liabilities is $34 105. This is $75 less than it was immediately before the transaction.
4. After the changes are recorded, the equation is still in balance.

Updating the Balance Sheet

The figures for an updated balance sheet for Metropolitan Movers are taken from the last line of the equation analysis sheet. Figure 3.10 shows the new balance sheet.

```
                    METROPOLITAN MOVERS
                       BALANCE SHEET
                         —DATE—

   Assets                        Liabilities
   Cash                $   875   Accounts Payable
   Accounts Receivable             Central Supply      $  1 750
      B. Cava            2 800      Mercury Finance       25 170
      K. Lincoln         1 400   Total Liabilities     $26 920
   Equipment            13 450
                                 Owner's Equity
   Trucks               42 500   J. Hofner, Capital      34 105
   Total Assets        $61 025   Total Liabilities and Equity  $61 025
```

Figure 3.10 The updated balance sheet of Metropolitan Movers.

SECTION REVIEW QUESTIONS

1. Name the form used in this chapter for analyzing transactions.
2. Explain how this form is related to the balance sheet.
3. Explain the mathematical way of telling if capital has increased after a business transaction.
4. How do you know if the changes for a transaction recorded on an equation analysis sheet were balanced?
5. Are there any transactions for which only one balance sheet item changes? How do you know?

SECTION EXERCISES

1. The opening financial position is shown here for Sheila's Interior Decorating, owned by Sheila Kostiuk. **In your Workbook, or on columnar paper, record in the correct columns the changes required for the transactions below. After each transaction, calculate the new totals and make sure that the equation balances.**

	ASSETS					LIABILITIES		OWNER'S EQUITY
	Cash	Accounts Receivable D. Murray	Supplies	Office Furniture	Truck	Accounts Payable Ace Supply	Pine Motors	S. Kostiuk Capital
Opening Balances	1 000	50						1 050

TRANSACTIONS

1. Stationery and supplies are purchased from Ace Supply, $75 on credit. They will be paid for within 30 days.
2. A new desk for the office costing $450 is purchased for cash.
3. D. Murray, a debtor, pays her debt in full.
4. A $100 service is performed for a customer who pays immediately in cash.
5. A used truck costing $6 500 is purchased from Pine Motors. A down payment of $500 is made. It is agreed that the remainder of the purchase price will be paid within three months.
6. $75 is paid to Ace Supply, a creditor.
7. The owner, Sheila Kostiuk, withdraws $100 from the business for her own use.

---

2. The balance sheet of Triangle Real Estate, at the close of business on September 30, 19—, is as follows:

TRIANGLE REAL ESTATE
BALANCE SHEET
SEPTEMBER 30, 19 ——

Assets		Liabilities	
Cash	$ 216	Account Payable	
Accounts Receivable		Acme Supply	$ 1 562
P. Adams	375		
J. Hahn	150	Owner's Equity	
N. Swartz	200	J. Morse, Capital	25 521
Supplies	4 175		
Equipment	21 967		
	$27 083		$27 083

1. **Record the above balance sheet figures on the equation analysis sheet provided in your Workbook.**
2. **Analyze the transactions of October 1, listed below, and record the necessary changes on the equation analysis sheet. After each transaction, ensure that the equation is still in balance.**
3. **After completing transaction 5, prepare a new balance sheet.**

TRANSACTIONS OF OCTOBER 1

1. $100 cash is received from N. Swartz in part payment of the amount owed by him.
2. $200 cash is paid to Acme Supply in part payment of the debt owed to them.
3. Supplies costing $95 are purchased for cash from the Standish Company.
4. Triangle Real Estate sells a home for A.J. Buhler. For this service, Triangle Real Estate receives a commission of $4 700 cash.
5. A new desk (Equipment) is purchased from Ideal Furniture for $950 cash.

3. Alliance Appliance Service, in Renforth, Ontario, owned by Wayne Dalli, has the
following assets and liabilities at the close of business on October 20, 19—.

Assets		Liabilities	
Cash	$ 1 395	Bank Loan	$ 5 000
Accounts Receivable		Mortgage Payable	52 700
N. Chang	100		
P. O'Neil	527		
Land	40 000		
Building	80 000		
Equipment	8 316		
Delivery Truck	19 750		

1. **Record the above items on an equation analysis sheet. Do not forget to calculate and include the capital figure.**
2. **Analyze the transactions of October 21, listed below, and record the necessary changes on the equation analysis sheet.**
3. **After completing transaction 5, calculate the new totals and ensure that the equation is still in balance. Then prepare a new balance sheet.**

TRANSACTIONS OF OCTOBER 21

1. The owner, in need of money for his personal use, draws $500 cash out of the business.
2. P. O'Neil pays her debt of $527.
3. A repair service is performed for a customer. The customer pays the full amount of the bill in cash, $90.
4. A new electrical tester is purchased and paid for in cash, $410.
5. The regular monthly mortgage payment is made, $900 in cash.

4. Workbook Exercise: Additional practice in using an equation analysis sheet.

3.3 SUMMARY OF STEPS IN ANALYZING A TRANSACTION

The following objectives will help you to analyze any transaction.

Step 1 **Identify all items (assets and liabilities) which must be changed and make all necessary changes.**

When thinking about the transaction, try to be logical and to use common sense.
• Carefully analyze the information given for any transaction.
• Classify each item affected as an asset or a liability.
• Decide whether each item affected is to be increased or decreased.

Step 2   **See if owner's equity has changed.**

Remember the accounting equation. For example, if assets decrease and there is a corresponding liability decrease, the owner's equity will not change. But if assets decrease and liabilities are unchanged, the equation must be balanced by a decrease in owner's equity. Eventually, you will be able to estimate whether or not owner's equity has changed. Generally, if a business is better off after a transaction, owner's equity has increased. If a business is worse off after a transaction, owner's equity has decreased.

Step 3   **Make certain that at least two of the individual items have changed.**

It is possible for several items—assets, liabilities, or owner's equity—to change but never only one.

Step 4   **Make sure that the equation is still in balance.**

The fundamental accounting equation must be respected: assets must equal liabilities plus owner's equity.

Developing Good Work Habits

The first step in the accounting process is to analyze a transaction to determine the financial changes that result from it. You must recognize the importance of performing this step correctly. Accounting must be accurate. Therefore you must be accurate.

You must also realize that the possible number of different transactions is very large. Do not think of trying to memorize all of the changes for all of the transactions. If you tried to rely on memory alone, you could not become a truly good accountant. Good accountants use their memory, of course, but they also rely on common sense, clear thinking, and a thorough understanding of accounting theory.

SECTION REVIEW QUESTIONS

1. In working out the changes caused by a transaction, what is the first objective? What is the second objective?
2. What do good accountants rely on besides their memory?
3. Why must accounting be done accurately?
4. What is a good clue as to whether capital has increased or decreased?
5. Assets increase by $10 000 with no corresponding change in liabilities. What change is there in capital?

3.4   INTRODUCTION TO SOURCE DOCUMENTS

Most of the activity within a business creates business papers or documents. These are necessary for a variety of reasons such as proof of purchase, proof of payment, and reference. The papers move from person to person and from department to department and are eventually filed.

Much of the activity mentioned above requires the making of accounting entries. Some of the transactions begin within the accounting department: the writing of a cheque, for example. Other transactions begin in other departments in the organization; for example, the purchasing of goods may be started by the Purchasing Department.

The accounting department must be informed of transactions regardless of where they originate. The accounting department must learn of any business activity that requires the making of an accounting entry. This is done by means of business papers, called source documents. They are called source documents because they are the source of the data that the accounting department uses to make the accounting entries. A *source document* is a business paper, such as a bill. It is the original record of a transaction and it provides the information needed when accounting for the transaction.

Examples of source documents include hydro bills, telephone bills, cheque copies, receipts, cash register summaries, and credit card statements. In Chapter 6, a full discussion is devoted to source documents, with illustrations. For now, remember:

1. accounting entries are made from business papers known as source documents, and
2. source documents are kept on file for reference purposes and as proof of transactions.

GAAP—The Objectivity Principle

This is a generally accepted accounting principle related to source documents.

The objectivity principle states that **accounting will be recorded on the basis of objective evidence**. Objective evidence means that different people looking at the evidence will arrive at the same values for the transaction. Simply put, this means that accounting entries will be based on fact, and not on personal opinion or feelings.

The source document for a transaction is almost always the best objective evidence available.

For example, the best objective evidence for the purchase of a new desk used in the business is the bill received from the retailer. The source document shows the amount agreed to by the buyer and the seller, who are usually independent of each other.

Auditors and others may want to ask questions about a business. Source documents are kept on file so that such questions can be easily answered.

SECTION REVIEW QUESTIONS

1. Give reasons why business papers are created within a business.
2. Where in the business do business papers originate?
3. What must happen to any business paper for which an accounting entry is necessary?
4. For accounting purposes what are these business papers called?
5. State and explain the objectivity principle.
6. Give some examples of source documents.
7. What happens to source documents after the accounting entries have been completed?

SECTION EXERCISES

1. **Examine the source document below and answer the questions that follow, using what you know so far.**

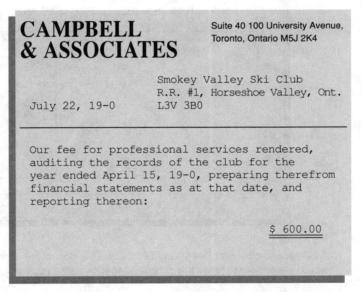

CAMPBELL
& ASSOCIATES

Suite 40 100 University Avenue,
Toronto, Ontario M5J 2K4

Smokey Valley Ski Club
R.R. #1, Horseshoe Valley, Ont.
July 22, 19-0   L3V 3B0

Our fee for professional services rendered,
auditing the records of the club for the
year ended April 15, 19-0, preparing therefrom
financial statements as at that date, and
reporting thereon:

$ 600.00

A professional bill received by Smokey Valley Ski Club. This bill came from a firm of chartered accountants and shows the charge for auditing the club's records and preparing its financial statements.

1. Who issued the bill?
2. Who received the bill?
3. When was the bill issued?
4. Does the bill say when payment is due?
5. In your opinion, what accounting changes will be made by the receiver?
6. For what service was the bill issued?
7. Does the bill represent good objective evidence? Why?

2. **Examine the source document below and answer the questions that follow, using what you know so far.**

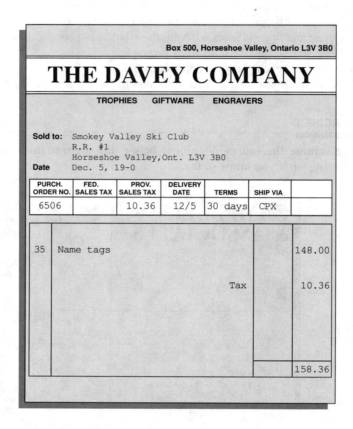

Box 500, Horseshoe Valley, Ontario L3V 3B0

THE DAVEY COMPANY

TROPHIES   GIFTWARE   ENGRAVERS

Sold to: Smokey Valley Ski Club
R.R. #1
Horseshoe Valley, Ont. L3V 3B0
Date Dec. 5, 19-0

PURCH. ORDER NO.	FED. SALES TAX	PROV. SALES TAX	DELIVERY DATE	TERMS	SHIP VIA	
6506		10.36	12/5	30 days	CPX	

35	Name tags		148.00
		Tax	10.36
			158.36

A bill received by Smokey Valley Ski Club. This document came from a small service business and shows the charge made for name tags worn by the members.

1. Who issued the bill?
2. Who received the bill?
3. When was the bill issued?
4. When were the goods delivered?
5. When is this bill due for payment?
6. Why was this bill issued?
7. In your opinion, what accounting changes will be made by the purchaser?
8. Was this a cash sale transaction?
9. Why does the bill represent good objective evidence?

3. **Examine the source document below and answer the questions that follow.**

SMOKEY VALLEY SKI CLUB	**015**
R.R. #1, Horseshoe Valley, Ont. L3V 3B0	

Nov. 12 19--

PAY TO THE
ORDER OF   Mid-West Ski Lifts and Equipment | $ 10 000.00

Ten Thousand ----------------------- xx DOLLARS

THE COMMERCIAL BANK

Smokey Valley Ski Club

per *A. Hart*
      R. Schwartz

⑈015⑈ ⑆11962⑈509⑆   7427⑈0⑈

1. What kind of source document is it?
2. Who issued the source document?
3. Who received the source document?
4. What do you think this source document is paying for?
5. As a result of this source document, two of the following are possible. Indicate which two are possible, and indicate which one of the two is more likely.
   a. An asset and a liability will both increase.
   b. An asset and a liability will both decrease.
   c. An asset will increase and another asset will decrease.
   d. An asset and equity will both decrease.

4. The accountant for a business received a memorandum from the owner. The memorandum stated that a new office desk recently installed in the owner's office was acquired at a cost of $2 500 and that it was paid for in cash by the owner personally.

1. **Why is the memorandum not objective evidence?**
2. **What is the best objective evidence in this case?**

3.5 COMPUTERS IN ACCOUNTING: THE ELECTRONIC SPREADSHEET: A MODERN TOOL FOR ACCOUNTANTS

An equation analysis sheet has been used in Chapter 3 of the text to record the effects of transactions and to calculate new balances. It is a type of work sheet that is an ideal application for an electronic spreadsheet as can be seen in Figure 3.11.

Cell References

A cell is identified by naming the column and the row where the cell intersects. In the example in Figure 3.11, the number 540 is found in cell B5. Each cell is given such an address so that it can be located and used mathematically.

	A	B	C	D	E	F	G
1		ASSETS		LIABILITIES		OWNER'S EQUITY	
2							
3		Cash	Equipment	Bank Loan	Note Payable	Capital	
4	Beg. Balances	$10 000	$5 000	$7 000	$1 000	$7 000	
5	Transaction 1	540				540	
6							
7							
8							
9							
10							
11							
12							
13							
14							
15	Totals	$10 540	$5 000	$7 000	$1 000	$7 540	
16	Equality Check:						
17		Assets:	$15 540		Assets:	$15 540	
18		Liabilities:	$8 000				
19		Equity:	$7 540	Liabilities and Equity:		$15 540	
20							

Figure 3.11 Typical design of an electronic spreadsheet.

Formulas and Functions

The electronic spreadsheet is ideal for analyzing changes in financial position. Unlike an ordinary equation analysis sheet, the electronic spreadsheet can show the column totals automatically each time that values are keyed in. It can also be used to show that the total assets are equal to the total liabilities plus the owner's equity.

Formulas

The user/programmer can create formulas and enter them into cells. A formula is a mathematical relationship involving the value to be displayed in a cell. The formula is evaluated by the computer and the value is directed into the cell. Cell C17 contains the formula =B15+C15 (which is hidden but can be seen on the status line). This is simply a directive to add the contents of cell B15 and cell C15 and place the resulting value in C17. The spreadsheet obeys by displaying $15 540 on the screen in cell C17.

Functions

A function is a more complex formula stored in the computer's memory, which can be called upon by the programmer/user. In Figure 3.11 the total of $10 540 at cell B15 was produced by the spreadsheet function: =SUM(B4··B14). This function instructs the computer to add all the cells from B4 to B14 inclusive and to place the resulting value in cell B15. In this case, the = sign is a prefix indicating that a function is to be performed; SUM is the name of the function, and the range of cells within the brackets is what the function will add.

Reproducing Cell Data

Spreadsheets can also reproduce the data from one cell to another. The total assets amount has been calculated at C17. To get this amount to appear again at F17, a cell reference is used. Simply move the cell pointer (the bright rectangle that highlights an entire cell) to cell F17 and enter =C17 (a prefix followed by the cell being referenced.) Cell references can also be used in this spreadsheet model to prepare a balance sheet that is instantly updated with each transaction. Simply move the cell pointer to another area of the spreadsheet. Type the appropriate titles and use cell references to duplicate the necessary figures from the equation analysis sheet.

Spreadsheet Advantages

Spreadsheets are now considered essential tools of business. There are a number of advantages of the spreadsheet for the accountant.

Speed   Speed is gained through automatic calculations. Formulas and functions compute new balances instantly. All you have to do is enter numbers (values). The calculation is completed as soon as you press the return key.

Accuracy   Formulas and functions normally display answers based on the contents of other cells. As long as the formula or function includes the correct cell addresses and is properly designed, there will be no mathematical errors.

Power   A vast number of cells can be designed to contain formulas, functions, and cell references that are based on the contents of another cell: A1, for example. If the contents of A1 are changed, then all of the cells that refer to A1 are immediately updated. This type of numerical power (often referred to as the "what if" capability) allows users to see immediately the effect of making changes in any of the variables. It is a tremendous analytical tool for accountants.

SPREADSHEET EXERCISES

Merrymen Window Washing: Question 7, p. 68

1. **1. Load the spreadsheet model named CH3 from your data disk into your computer.** You should now be viewing a portion of an equation analysis sheet.

2. **Notice that the opening balances have been entered on Row 5 and that they appear again on Row 17.** The cell contents of Row 5, however, are values entered through the keyboard. The contents of Row 17 are produced by functions built into the spreadsheet program. Moving the cell pointer to each of these cells and observing the status line will help you understand the difference.

3. **Examine cells B21 and C21 and see that the accounting equation is in balance.**

4. **Key in values for each transaction of Merrymen Window Washing. Begin with –800 at B6 (use the hyphen to indicate negative values). Notice what other cells change when the transaction is entered.**

5. **After all the transactions are entered, check the zero-proof column — column P — for any column that does not have a zero balance.** If you find one, then you have made an error which must be found and corrected.

6. **Check the accounting equation totals at the bottom of the spreadsheet model.** If the zero-proof column showed no errors, the accounting equation will balance — guaranteed.

Challenge Exercise

2. 1. **Move the cell pointer to a blank area of the spreadsheet and develop a model to produce the balance sheet for Merrymen Window Washing. Type in the titles and leave space for the amounts.**

2. **Use cell references to duplicate totals shown on the equation analysis sheet.** For example, to reproduce the Cash total, =B17 must be entered.

3. Once the balance sheet is completed, a change can be made to illustrate the power of the spreadsheet. **Assume that an error was made in the first transaction: only $80 was paid to Simplex Finance, not $800. Move the cell pointer to Row 6 and update the two cells affected. Move back to the balance sheet and note the new totals.** A new version was created instantly.

COMPUTER REVIEW QUESTIONS

1. What is a cell?

2. What are cell addresses and why are they necessary?

3. The contents of a cell may not be the same as seen on the spreadsheet screen. Explain.

4. Cell contents can be values, labels, formulas, functions, and cell references. Give an example of each.

5. Explain the difference between a formula and a function.

Communicate It

You and your sister are partners in a part-time landscaping business. She wants to use an equation analysis sheet identical to the one on page 49. You prefer to use a spreadsheet. **Prepare a written explanation to outline your position.**

CHAPTER HIGHLIGHTS

Now that you have completed Chapter 3, you should:

1. understand the factors that create changes in financial position;
2. be able to define "business transaction";
3. be able to work out the changes created in any of the assets, liabilities, or capital for any simple transaction;
4. be able to record a series of transactions on an equation analysis sheet;
5. be able to prepare a balance sheet from an equation analysis sheet;
6. be able to state the four steps in analyzing a business transaction;
7. know the purpose of source documents;
8. understand the objectivity principle.

ACCOUNTING TERMS

business transaction   objectivity principle

CHAPTER EXERCISES

Using Your Knowledge

1. Shown below is an equation analysis sheet for the business of Brad Provost, a painter and decorator in Sydney, Nova Scotia.

   Examine the entries made on this sheet. Then prepare a list of five transactions that would have caused the changes in the financial position indicated by the entries.

		ASSETS					LIABILITIES		OWNER'S EQUITY
	Cash	Accounts Receivable C. Sully	Receivable F. Vanweers	Supplies	Equipment	Bank Loan	Accounts Payable P. M. Co.	Payable Norpaints	B. Provost Capital
	400	135	250	1 500	8 500	500	300		9 985
1.	+250		−250						
2.				+150				+150	
3.	+300								+300
4.		+115							+115
5.	−300						−300		
	650	250	Ø	1 650	8 500	500	Ø	150	10 400

2. Shown below is an equation analysis sheet for the business of Brian Lee, an architect. **After studying this sheet, prepare a list of five transactions that would have caused the changes in financial position as shown.**

	ASSETS					LIABILITIES		OWNER'S EQUITY
	Cash	A/R L. Swan	Supplies	Equipment	Auto	Bank Loan	A/P High Finance	B. Lee, Capital
	500		1 300	7 000	17 000	4 000	5 000	16 800
1.	+500	+1 300						+1 800
2.	+1 500				−7 000		−5 000	−500
3.	−1 000				+20 000	+19 000		
4.	−150							−150
5.			−50					−50
	1 350	1 300	1 250	7 000	30 000	23 000	Ø	17 900

3. At December 31, 19-1, Dowse Company had assets totaling $85 000. At December 31, 19-2, the assets totaled $115 000. During the same period, liabilities increased by $35 000. **If the equity at the end of the first year amounted to $60 000, what was the amount of the owner's equity December 31 of the second year? Show how you arrive at your answer.**

4. Describe four transactions that would cause the owner's equity to decrease.

5. Describe two transactions that would cause the owner's equity to increase.

6. Workbook Exercise: Completing a schedule showing changes in total assets, total liabilities, and owner's equity for a series of transactions.

Challenge Exercise
7. Merrymen Window Washing is a business owned and operated by Carl Savich in Timmins, Ontario. On November 30, 19—, at the end of the day, the financial position of the business is as shown on the following balance sheet.

```
                    MERRYMEN WINDOW WASHING
                         BALANCE SHEET
                       NOVEMBER 30, 19—
```

Assets		Liabilities	
Cash	$ 2 750	Accounts Payable	
Accounts Receivable		Cleanall Co.	$ 124
T. Brock	420	Hipp Co.	475
D. Pederson	75	Loan Payable	
Supplies	880	Simplex Finance	8 560
Truck	15 050		$ 9 159
		Owner's Equity	
Equipment	12 947	C. Savich, Capital	22 963
	$32 122		$32 122

1. **Set up the balance sheet items on an equation analysis sheet. Leave a blank column for a new account payable.**
2. **Analyze the transactions of December 1, listed below, and record the necessary changes on the equation analysis sheet.**
3. **After completing the transactions, calculate the new totals, ensure that the equation is still in balance, and prepare a new balance sheet.**

TRANSACTIONS OF DECEMBER 1

1. The regular monthly instalment payment of $800 is paid to Simplex Finance.
2. $400 of supplies is purchased from Hipp Co. but not paid for.
3. $200 cash is received from T. Brock in part payment of his debt.
4. A new hoist is purchased from N.R.C. Co. for $2 125. A cash down payment of $300 is made. The balance of the purchase price is to be paid at a later date.
5. The old hoist, included in the Equipment figure at $550, is sold for $100 cash.
6. A $500 window-washing service is performed for D. Pederson. Pederson pays $575, both for this service and the balance to pay off the amount owed.
7. The truck was in a serious collision and is a write-off. The insurance company pays Merryman Window Washing $14 500 cash.
8. The loan payable to Simplex Finance is paid off.
9. A new truck costing $23 000 is purchased. An $8 000 down payment is made. The balance is financed through Simplex Finance.
10. The amount owed to Hipp Co. is paid in full.
11. Supplies valued at $50 are taken on a job and used up.

For Further Thought

8. Briefly answer the following questions.

1. Assume that your assets include a truck worth $7 000. Assume further that the truck represented by the $7 000 has recently been wrecked in an accident and

that you are negotiating with your insurance company for a settlement. What financial changes (if any) will be recorded at this time?

2. One of your customers slips on your icy walkway and is injured. You receive a letter from the customer's lawyer to the effect that the customer wants $10 000 in damages. What financial changes (if any) will be recorded as a result of this letter?

3. In your opinion, what is the difference between an account payable and a loan payable?

4. Explain why it is impossible for a balance sheet to be out of balance and to be correct.

5. Explain why it is possible for a balance sheet to be in balance and still be incorrect.

6. Explain why it is impossible for only a single item to change as a result of a business transaction.

7. Examine the simple chart below on which the scale is: one unit = $100.

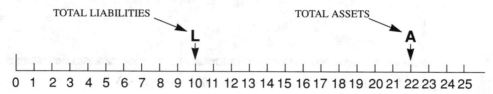

CAPITAL: **C = ?**

   a. What is the figure for total assets?
   b. What is the figure for total liabilities?
   c. Calculate the capital. How is it represented on the chart?

Now assume that a new desk is purchased for $200 cash.
   d. Mentally calculate the new figure for total assets.
   e. Mentally calculate the new figure for total liabilities.
   f. Mentally place these new figures on the chart. Will the capital figure change and, if yes, by how much? How does the chart show this?

8. Examine the chart below on which the scale is: one unit = $100.

C = ?

   a. What is the figure for total assets?
   b. What is the figure for total liabilities?
   c. Calculate the capital. How is it represented on the chart?

Now assume that there is a loss by water damage of supplies worth $300 and that there is no insurance coverage on the supplies.
   d. Mentally calculate the new figure for total assets.
   e. Mentally calculate the new figure for total liabilities.

f. Mentally place these new figures on the chart. Will the capital figure change and, if yes, by how much? How does the chart show this?

9. Explain why an equation analysis sheet is better than a balance sheet for recording accounting changes.

10. Name a source document that would not originate in the accounting office.

11. You are given 50 shares of a company by an aunt who has died. The share certificates show a face value of $10 each. Explain how you would arrive at a true value for the shares.

12. Describe what is meant by the term "at arm's length" in respect to "objectivity."

CASE STUDIES

CASE 1   *Is Money Better?*

Hannah and Tina are school friends of yours at Vanier High School in Clark's Harbour, Nova Scotia. The two girls happen to be discussing their personal fortunes at the moment. Hannah is feeling rich because she has $2 000 in a personal bank account. A distant aunt who died recently left her the money.

Tina feels pretty well off, too. She has less money but she also has some valuable possessions that were left to her by her grandmother. For reasons that she cannot explain, she feels that she is just as well off as Hannah.

You get into the conversation at lunch break. You suggest to the two girls that they each prepare a personal balance sheet. You explain how to go about it and how to estimate the value of non-cash items. The balance sheets, you say, will show who is better off financially.

The girls prepare their balance sheets according to your directions and come up with the following:

HANNAH'S BALANCE SHEET SEPTEMBER 30	
Assets	
Bank balance	$ 2 000
Clothes	1 500
Total	$ 3 500
Liabilities and Equity	
Debts owing	nil
Hannah's Capital	3 500
Total	$ 3 500

TINA'S BALANCE SHEET SEPTEMBER 30	
Assets	
Bank balance	$ 10
Stereo set	500
Jewellery	1 000
IBM shares	1 100
Clothes	1 200
Total	$ 3 810
Liabilities and Equity	
Debts owing	$200
Tina's Capital	3 610
Total	$ 3 810

When the two girls get together to compare balance sheets, they still cannot agree. Hannah thinks that she is better off because she has more cash and clothes. Tina disagrees because she has greater capital.

Discuss these balance sheets with Hannah and Tina. Explain to them how to measure a person's equity.

CASE 2   Can You Spend the Equity?

Raj Singh is a young man who has just inherited a business from his father who was killed in an accident. Raj has little business experience but is anxious to learn and willing to work hard.

The business has not been operating very profitably lately because it badly needs to replace outdated equipment. This will cost $35 000.

The latest balance sheet of the business shows the following:

Assets		Liabilities	
Cash	$ 3 000	Accounts Payable	$ 5 000
Accounts Receivable	17 000	Bank Loan	30 000
Land	30 000	Mortgage Payable	50 000
Building	50 000		$ 85 000
Equipment	20 000	Owner's Equity	35 000
	$120 000		$120 000

After examining the balance sheet, Raj believes that he sees the solution to the problem. He wants to use the equity to purchase the new equipment. The accountant hastens to point out to Raj that this is not possible. Raj demands an explanation.

Question
1. What explanation will the accountant give?

CASE 3   Checking Out a New Customer

Arthur Field, the owner of New Age Manufacturing, comes to you to arrange for the buying on credit of materials for his business. He advises you that the orders will amount to approximately one-half million dollars a year. This amount of new business could have a very beneficial effect on your company. You would even have to expand your own facilities to take advantage of it. You tell Mr. Field that you need time to consider the proposal.

Your banker advises you to find out as much as you can about New Age Manufacturing. You go to a credit investigation bureau. They provide you with the following balance sheet totals for New Age Manufacturing.

Assets	$450 000
Liabilities	445 000
Equity	5 000

Questions
1. What conclusion would you draw from the balance sheet totals?
2. What dangers are there in dealing with New Age Manufacturing?
3. Would you do business with Mr. Field? Explain.

CAREER
Melissa Porchuk / Student

Melissa Porchuk is now in her final year at Swift Current Comprehensive High School in Swift Current, Saskatchewan. Her future plans are to obtain a Bachelor of Commerce degree at the University of Regina and then to enroll in the Institute of Chartered Accountants program.

During her last two years in high school, Melissa has been studying accounting and computer concepts to prepare herself for a responsible position in the business world. She has enjoyed her accounting courses and her grades have been very good in this area.

Because she had taken accounting courses, Melissa was able to get a summer job in the accounting department of Agri-Co Freight Company, which specializes in the shipping of wheat and other locally produced grains.

During her first summer months at Agri-Co Freight, Melissa was responsible for checking the calculations on all sales invoices and preparing daily sheets of these invoices. She received payments from customers and recorded them in the customers' accounts. In addition, Melissa was responsible for checking the accuracy of various source documents for payment, such as telephone bills, purchase invoices, hydro bills, and tax bills.

During her second summer with Agri-Co Freight, the company changed from a manual system to a computer system for accounts receivable. Melissa studied computer systems in high school, and was very excited about the change. She continued to handle all customers' accounts, coded all sales invoices for computer entry, prepared cheque remittance forms to enter these payments in the computer, and completed all weekly and monthly accounts receivable balances for the computer.

Each month, Melissa received a computer printout of the accounts receivable and presented the total to the company controller for verification. She also issued monthly computer-produced customer statements.

Because she has controlled the paper flow of a wide variety of tasks within an accounting office, Melissa realizes that being organized, neat and accurate are extremely important.

Her accounting courses and work experience provide Melissa with a good base for further study. She finds it easier to concentrate on the concepts of accounting because she has already mastered the practical aspects.

Melissa is very pleased with the work she has done for Agri-Co Freight during the summer months. Her employers are so impressed with her work they would like her to return during the summer while she studies at university. They want her to accept a highly responsible position with the company once she has completed her education.

DISCUSSION

1. List five business transactions Melissa handles in her daily accounting routine.
2. Melissa is responsible for many source documents in her job. Name the source documents in Melissa's profile that would cause the Capital account to increase.
3. Explain how Melissa would code the sales invoices for entry in the computer.
4. Do you think "legible record-keeping" is necessary today, since most records are produced by computer?
5. One of Melissa's responsibilities is to check the accuracy of various source documents before payment. Explain how you would check the accuracy of telephone bills, purchase invoices, hydro bills and tax bills before these bills are paid.
6. Give examples of objective evidence that are illustrated in Melissa's career profile.

The Simple Ledger

4.1 Ledger Accounts
4.2 Debit and Credit Theory
4.3 Account Balances
4.4 Trial Balance

The purpose of Chapter 3 was to show you the effect that transactions have on financial position. In Chapter 3, you practised analyzing transactions and keeping a financial position up to date. The method used, the equation analysis sheet, was a very simple one. However, that method is not satisfactory when working with a complete business operation.

In an active business, many transactions occur each day. To be able to handle them all, accountants use a more complete system, based on the concepts of the previous chapter. While the system is more complex, it is also more efficient and orderly, and it is universally accepted.

4.1 LEDGER ACCOUNTS

In this chapter you will be learning the system used to maintain an up-to-date financial position. For this purpose, accountants long ago developed the account and the ledger.

An **account** is a page specially designed to record the changes in any of the individual items affecting the financial position. There is one account for each different item affecting the financial position. All the accounts together are called the ledger. A ledger is a group or file of accounts.

A **ledger** can be prepared in different ways (see Figure 4.1). The accounts can be prepared on cards to form a card ledger. They can be prepared on loose-leaf paper to form a loose-leaf ledger. Or the accounts can be recorded on a magnetic tape or magnetic disk to be used in a computerized system. All the methods are still in use, but computerized systems are becoming more and more common as computers and computer software improve.

Let us begin our study of ledger accounts by referring to the records of Pacific Trucking owned by Byron Rissien of Prince Rupert, B.C. The balance sheet of this business is shown in Figure 4.2.

a.

b.

Loose-leaf ledger (courtesy of Luckett
Loose Leaf, Ltd.).

Card ledger (courtesy of Luckett
Loose Leaf, Ltd.).

c.

d.

Magnetic tape (courtesy of
IBM Canada Ltd.).

Diskette.

Figure 4.1   Four forms of the ledger. Observe how the cartridge of magnetic tape has
replaced the much larger reels formerly used (lower left).

PACIFIC TRUCKING
BALANCE SHEET
JUNE 30, 19—

Assets		*Liabilities*	
Cash	$ 3 265	Bank Loan	$18 000
Accounts Receivable		Accounts Payable	
W. Caruso	150	Dini Bros.	1 516
R. Van Loon	620	Packham Products	3 946
Supplies	2 465		$23 462
Trucks	55 075	*Owner's Equity*	
Equipment	22 174	B. Rissien, Capital	60 287
	$83 749		$83 749

Figure 4.2   The balance sheet of Pacific Trucking.

The data from this balance sheet are used to set up the separate pages, called accounts. The dollar value for each item on the balance sheet gives the beginning value for that item's account.

Pacific Trucking will have 10 accounts, one account for each item on the balance sheet. These accounts are Cash, Account Receivable—R. Van Loon, Account Receivable—W. Caruso, Supplies, Trucks, Equipment, Bank Loan, Account Payable—Packham Products, Account Payable—Dini Bros., and B. Rissien, Capital. All these accounts together form the ledger for Pacific Trucking.

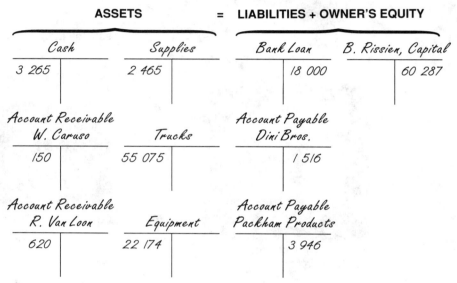

Figure 4.3   The simple ledger accounts of Pacific Trucking.

Figure 4.3 shows the information from the balance sheet of Pacific Trucking presented as accounts in a ledger. These accounts are called T-accounts because, as you can see, each one looks like a T. The T-account is a simple kind of account, used mainly to explain accounting theory. The formal account, the one actually used in business, will be introduced in a later chapter.

Important Features of Ledger Accounts

Using the above ledger as a guide, let us look at four important features of all ledger accounts.

1. Each individual balance sheet item is given its own specially divided page with the name of the item at the top. Each of these pages is called an account. In Figure 4.3, there are 10 accounts. You must learn to call them the Cash account, the R. Van Loon account, the Packham Products account, the Bank Loan account, and so on.
2. The dollar figure for each item is recorded in the account on the first line. This is the beginning value for the account.

3. It is especially important to record the dollar figure on the correct side of the account. For any item, the correct side is the side on which the item itself would appear on a simple balance sheet. Observe that for each of the *asset* accounts, the dollar amount is placed on the *left* side of the account page. For each of the *liability* accounts and the *owner's equity* account, the dollar amount is placed on the *right* side of the account page.

4. The ledger and the balance sheet both show financial position, although in different ways. If you have a ledger, a balance sheet can be prepared from it. If you have a balance sheet, a ledger can be prepared from it.

SECTION REVIEW QUESTIONS

1. Explain what an account is.
2. Define a ledger.
3. How many accounts are there in a ledger?
4. Name the different forms a ledger can take.
5. How have ledgers been prepared in the last 50 years?
6. The accounting records are commonly referred to as the "books." Why would this name be used?
7. Why are computerized accounting systems becoming very common?
8. Why are the beginning amounts for a ledger usually taken from a balance sheet?
9. What is the principal use of T-accounts?
10. Explain where the dollar amounts are placed in the accounts when setting up the beginning amounts in a ledger.

SECTION EXERCISES

1. The balance sheet for Stevens Woodworking is shown below.

STEVENS WOODWORKING
BALANCE SHEET
-DATE-

Assets		Liabilities	
Cash	$ 2 000	Bank Loan	$ 20 000
Accounts Receivable		Account Payable	
A. Marks	375	Gem Lumber	2 500
C. Prentice	1 150	Mortgage Payable	55 000
Land	30 000		$ 77 500
Building	45 000		
Equipment	27 800	*Owner's Equity*	
Truck	14 500	T. Stevens, Capital	43 325
	$120 825		$120 825

Set up the ledger for Stevens Woodworking in the T-accounts provided in your Workbook.

2. The balance sheet of Dr. Pauline Inaba is shown below.

DR. PAULINE INABA
BALANCE SHEET
-DATE-

Assets		*Liabilities*	
Cash	$ 500	Accounts Payable	
Accounts Receivable		A.B. Associates	$ 1 200
P. Auul	350	Medico Supply	2 300
S. Wouke	1 250		$ 3 500
Supplies	3 900		
Furniture and Equipment	18 320	*Owner's Equity*	
Automobile	21 040	Pauline Inaba, Capital	41 860
	$45 360		$45 360

Set up the ledger of Dr. Inaba in the T-accounts provided in your Workbook.

3. Shown below is the ledger of Lilly Wall, who operates an interior design business. The asset and liability account balances are given.

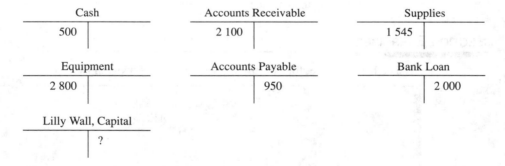

Show the fundamental accounting equation for Lilly Wall.

4.2 DEBIT AND CREDIT THEORY

In your work so far you have learned that the idea of "left side" and "right side" is important in accounting. This is especially true when using ledger accounts. The theory of accounting using ledger accounts is based entirely on the understanding that there are two distinct sides to every account page.

The two sides of an account page are described in the same way by accountants everywhere. **Debit** is the word associated with the left side of an account. **Credit** is the word associated with the right side of an account. There is no deeper meaning: debit means "left," credit means "right."

Remember that the two new terms apply to every account, as shown below.

Any Account	
left side	right side
DEBIT	CREDIT
(short form DR or Dr)	(short form CR or Cr)

These two new words—debit and credit—are probably the two most often used words in the accountant's vocabulary. Let us now begin to use these two new accounting terms ourselves. Looking back at the simple ledger in Figure 4.3, you will notice that the values of the assets were placed on the left side—the debit side—of their accounts. The values of the liabilities and of the capital were placed on the right side—the credit side—of their accounts. You may correctly conclude from this that asset accounts have debit values and that liability and capital accounts have credit values.

The Rules of Debit and Credit

Now you are familiar with the simple ledger and the terms debit and credit. You have discovered which side of the account to use to record the beginning value for each type of account. You are ready to learn how changes are recorded in the accounts. There is a simple set of rules for recording changes in accounts. For each type of account, record increases on its beginning value side and decreases on the other side. These rules are summarized, using the terms debit and credit, in the chart below:

Types of Accounts	INCREASES	DECREASES
ASSET accounts	DEBIT	CREDIT
LIABILITY and OWNER'S EQUITY accounts	CREDIT	DEBIT

Applying the Rules of Debit and Credit

To give you practice in using the new rules of debit and credit, a number of transactions of Pacific Trucking are analyzed on the following pages. In applying these rules to the transactions, you should try to do the analyses before reading the explanations. You must master the technique of analyzing transactions if you want to be a skilled accountant.

TRANSACTION 1   **$200 of supplies is purchased from Packham Products, to be paid for later.**

Analysis   To correctly analyze a transaction it is helpful in the initial stages to use a "transaction analysis sheet." This sheet, shown below, provides a place to organize your thoughts about the transaction. Proceed according to the following steps:

1 In column (1), write down the names of the accounts that are affected by the transaction. In this example:

(1) Account Names	(2) Asset, Liability, or Owner's Equity	(3) Increase (+) or Decrease (−)	(4) Debit or Credit	(5) Amount
Supplies				
Packham Products				

2 In column (2), write down whether each of these accounts is an asset, a liability, or the capital. In this example:

(1) Account Names	(2) Asset, Liability, or Owner's Equity	(3) Increase (+) or Decrease (−)	(4) Debit or Credit	(5) Amount
Supplies	Asset			
Packham Products	Liability			

3 In column (3), write down whether the accounts are to be increased or decreased. In this example:

(1) Account Names	(2) Asset, Liability, or Owner's Equity	(3) Increase (+) or Decrease (−)	(4) Debit or Credit	(5) Amount
Supplies	Asset	+		
Packham Products	Liability	+		

4 In column (4), write down whether the accounts are to be debited or credited. Apply the rules given in the previous section. In this example: to increase an asset you debit the account; to increase a liability you credit the account.

(1) Account Names	(2) Asset, Liability, or Owner's Equity	(3) Increase (+) or Decrease (−)	(4) Debit or Credit	(5) Amount
Supplies	Asset	+	DR	
Packham Products	Liability	+	CR	

5 In column (5), write in the amounts by which the accounts are increased or decreased. In this example:

(1) Account Names	(2) Asset, Liability, or Owner's Equity	(3) Increase (+) or Decrease (–)	(4) Debit or Credit	(5) Amount
Supplies	Asset	+	DR	200–
Packham Products	Liability	+	CR	200–

This final step completes what is known as the accounting entry for the transaction. An **accounting entry** may be defined as all of the changes in the accounts caused by one business transaction, expressed in terms of debits and credits.

An accountant would express the accounting entry for transaction 1 in the following way: debit Supplies and credit Packham Products, $200. Notice that the debited account and amount are stated first. The credited account and amount are stated second. After the changes are recorded in the appropriate account, the accounts appear as shown below:

Supplies	Account Payable Packham Products
2 465	3 946
200	200

Notice that the transaction includes both a debit and a credit, and that the total of debit and credit amounts is equal. This is the case with every transaction.

TRANSACTION 2 **$500 is paid to Dini Bros., in part payment of the amount owed to them.**

Analysis   This transaction is recorded on a transaction analysis sheet as follows:

(1) Account Names	(2) Asset, Liability, or Owner's Equity	(3) Increase (+) or Decrease (–)	(4) Debit or Credit	(5) Amount
Dini Bros.	Liability	–	DR	500–
Cash	Asset	–	CR	500–

An accountant would express the accounting entry as follows: debit Dini Bros. and credit Cash, $500.

After the changes are recorded, the accounts appear as shown below:

Cash	Account Payable Dini Bros.
3 265	500	500	1 516

TRANSACTION 3   **$200 cash is received from R. Van Loon in part payment of her debt.**

Analysis   The accounting entry for this transaction is worked out on the transaction analysis sheet as follows:

(1) Account Names	(2) Asset, Liability, or Owner's Equity	(3) Increase (+) or Decrease (−)	(4) Debit or Credit	(5) Amount
Cash	Asset	+	DR	200–
R. Van Loon	Asset	−	CR	200–

Read the changes as follows: debit Cash and credit R. Van Loon, $200.
   After the changes are recorded, the accounts appear as follows:

Cash		*Account Receivable* *R. Van Loon*	
3 265	500	620	200
200			

TRANSACTION 4   **A delivery service is provided for a customer at a price of $400. The customer pays cash at the time the service is completed.**

Analysis   The accounting entry for this transaction is worked out on the transaction analysis sheet as follows:

(1) Account Names	(2) Asset, Liability, or Owner's Equity	(3) Increase (+) or Decrease (−)	(4) Debit or Credit	(5) Amount
Cash	Asset	+	DR	400–
B. Rissien, Capital	Owner's Equity	+	CR	400–

Express these changes as follows: debit Cash and credit B. Rissien, Capital, $400.
   After the changes are recorded in the accounts, they will appear as shown below:

Cash		*B. Rissien, Capital*	
3 265	500		60 287
200			400
400			

TRANSACTION 5   **A used truck costing $8 000 is purchased from Dini Bros. A cash down payment of $2 500 is made at the time of the purchase and the balance is to be paid at a later date.**

Analysis   This transaction affects three accounts. The accounting entry for the transactions is worked out as follows:

(1) Account Names	(2) Asset, Liability, or Owner's Equity	(3) Increase (+) or Decrease (−)	(4) Debit or Credit	(5) Amount
Trucks	Asset	+	DR	8 000—
Cash	Asset	−	CR	2 500—
Dini Bros.	Liability	+	CR	5 500—

Read these changes: debit Trucks, $8 000; credit Cash, $2 500; credit Dini Bros., $5 500.

After the changes are recorded in the accounts, the accounts will appear as follows:

Cash		Trucks	Account Payable Dini Bros.	
3 265	500	55 075	500	1 516
200	2 500	8 000		5 500
400				

Notice that this transaction includes one debit but two credits. The total of the debit and the total of the credits are equal for the transaction.

TRANSACTION 6   **A delivery is completed for R. Van Loon at a price of $350. Van Loon does not pay for the service at the time it is provided but agrees to pay within 60 days.**

Analysis   The accounting entry for this transaction is worked out on the transaction sheet as follows:

(1) Account Names	(2) Asset, Liability, or Owner's Equity	(3) Increase (+ or Decrease (−)	(4) Debit or Credit	(5) Amount
R. Van Loon	Asset	+	DR	350—
B. Rissien, Capital	Owner's Equity	+	CR	350—

Read these changes: debit R. Van Loon and credit B. Rissien, Capital, $350.

After the changes are recorded in the accounts, they will appear as shown below:

Account Receivable R. Van Loon		B. Rissien, Capital
620	200	60 287
350		400
		350

TRANSACTION 7   **One of the lifting machines (part of Equipment) breaks down. $650 cash is spent on repairing the machine.**

(A common mistake made by students with this type of transaction is to increase the Equipment account. To help you to avoid this mistake, here is a clue: the owner is worse off financially because the machine had to be repaired.)

Analysis   This transaction is worked out on the transaction analysis sheet as follows:

(1) Account Names	(2) Asset, Liability, or Owner's Equity	(3) Increase (+) or Decrease (−)	(4) Debit or Credit	(5) Amount
Cash	Asset	−	CR	650−
B. Rissien, Capital	Owner's Equity	−	DR	650−

Read the changes: debit B. Rissien, Capital and credit Cash, $650.
After the changes are recorded, the accounts will appear as follows:

Cash		B. Rissien, Capital	
3 265	500	650	60 287
200	2 500		400
400	650		350

Double-Entry System of Accounting

Whenever a transaction occurs, changes must be made in the accounts. For each transaction, all of the account changes together must balance. They are known as the accounting entry for the transaction.

In this chapter so far, there have been seven transactions which are summarized in Figure 4.4.

Transaction	Account Names	Account Classifications A, L, OE	Debit or Credit	Amount
1	Supplies	A	DR	$ 200
	Packham Products	L	CR	$ 200
2	Dini Bros.	L	DR	$ 500
	Cash	A	CR	$ 500
3	Cash	A	DR	$ 200
	R. Van Loon	A	CR	$ 200
4	Cash	A	DR	$ 400
	B. Rissien, Capital	OE	CR	$ 400
5	Trucks	A	DR	$8 000
	Cash	A	CR	$2 500
	Dini Bros.	L	CR	$5 500
6	R. Van Loon	A	DR	$ 350
	B. Rissien, Capital	OE	CR	$ 350
7	B. Rissien, Capital	OE	DR	$ 650
	Cash	A	CR	$ 650

Figure 4.4 Seven accounting entries for Pacific Trucking.

As you have noticed, each of the above seven transactions balances within itself. The total of the debit amounts equals the total of the credit amounts. This is basic to the whole accounting process and is true for every possible transaction. If you ever find an accounting entry that does not balance within itself, you can be certain that it is not correct. On the other hand, a balanced entry is not necessarily a correct entry. If it is balanced, it means that it is probably correct. If it does not balance, there is no chance that it is correct.

Now you can understand why the system you have been working with is known as the double-entry system of accounting. In the **double-entry system of accounting** every transaction is recorded in the accounts in two steps. First it is recorded as a debit (or debits) and second as a credit (or credits) so that the total of the debit entries equals the total of the credit entries. The double-entry system of accounting is in general use throughout the business world.

SECTION REVIEW QUESTIONS

1. Explain the meaning of the words "debit" and "credit."
2. Explain the system that is used when setting up the beginning financial position in a ledger.
3. For what accounts does an increase mean "debit"?
4. For what accounts does a decrease mean "debit"?
5. For what accounts does an increase mean "credit"?
6. For what accounts does a decrease mean "credit"?
7. What is a transaction analysis sheet used for?
8. What is an accounting entry?
9. What special condition should be true of every accounting entry?
10. What condition is true for an accounting entry that does not balance?
11. What condition is true for an accounting entry that does balance?
12. Explain the meaning of the double-entry system of accounting.

SECTION EXERCISES

1. **Complete the following in your Workbook by writing in the words "increase" or "decrease" in the rectangles provided.**

ASSETS		=	LIABILITIES		+	OWNER'S EQUITY	
Debit	Credit		Debit	Credit		Debit	Credit

2. Flora Monday is the owner-operator of a fitness clinic. The ledger used in her business contains the following accounts:

> Cash
> Accounts Receivable (several)
> Supplies
> Furniture
> Equipment
> Automobile
> Accounts Payable (several)
> Flora Monday, Capital

Listed below are transactions of Flora's business. **Examine these transactions and record your analysis on the transaction analysis sheet provided in your Workbook and shown below.** To help you get a correct start, the first transaction has been done for you. **Be sure that each entry balances within itself.**

TRANSACTIONS

1. $300 cash is received from J. Parker, one of the accounts receivable. –
2. $200 of supplies is purchased for cash.
3. Little Bros., one of the accounts payable, is paid $100.
4. The owner withdraws $250 for her personal use.
5. A piece of new equipment costing $500 is purchased from Champion Sports. $125 cash is paid at the time of purchase with the balance of $375 to be paid within 30 days.
6. A new customer signs up for a fitness course. The $300 fee is paid in cash.

Transaction Analysis Sheet

Trans-action No.	Account Names	Asset, Liability, or Owner's Equity	Increase (+) or Decrease (−)	Debit or Credit	Amount
1.	Cash	Asset	+	DR	300–
	Acct. Receivable J. Parker	Asset	−	CR	300–

3. **Workbook Exercise: Additional practice in using a transaction analysis sheet.**

4. **Workbook Exercise: Completing a chart showing the accounts debited and the accounts credited for a series of transactions.**

4.3 ACCOUNT BALANCES

In the ledger of Pacific Trucking there are 10 accounts (see Figure 4.3). The following information is stored in each account:

1. the name of the account, which is written at the top;
2. the dollar value of the account and the indication of whether the value of the account is a debit or a credit.

Calculating the Balance of an Account

To calculate the balance of a T-account, two steps are performed. These two steps are shown in Figure 4.5, using accounts from the ledger of Pacific Trucking.

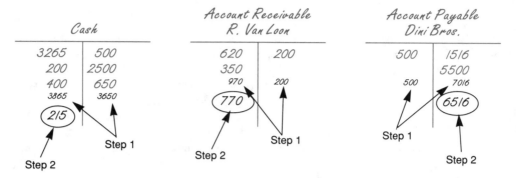

Figure 4.5 Calculating the balance of a T-account.

1 Add separately the two sides of the account. Use tiny pencil figures to write down these two subtotals, one beneath the last item on each side. These tiny totals are called **pin totals** or **pencil footings**.

2 a. Subtract the smaller total from the larger total.
   b. Write the result beside or beneath the larger of the two pin totals from Step 1. Circle this final amount.

The circled amount is the dollar value of the account. The side on which it is recorded indicates which type of balance it is, debit or credit. Together the two pieces of information represent the account balance. The **account balance** gives the dollar value of an account and shows whether it is a debit or credit value.

Interpreting the Balance of an Account

It is not enough simply to find the account balances. You must now learn to interpret the information stored in the accounts. They must mean something to you. Look at the accounts in Figure 4.5 and see what you can learn from them.

It should be clear what the account balances are. The Cash account has a balance of $215 and it is a debit balance because it is entered on the left side. Similarly, the R. Van Loon account has a balance of $770, debit, and the Dini Bros. account has a balance of $6 516, credit.

So far you are familiar with three types of accounts: assets, liabilities, and the capital. At this stage, all accounts fall into one of these categories. You already know that assets have debit balances and that liabilities and capital have credit balances.

It follows therefore that:

a. the Cash account is an asset because it has a debit balance.
b. the R. Van Loon account is an asset (an account receivable) because it has a debit balance.
c. the Dini Bros. account is a liability (an account payable) because it has a credit balance and is not the Capital account.

The Bank Account

Business people rely heavily on the banking system. The least expensive and most convenient way to make payments is by cheque (or electronic funds transfer). It should be clear that the handling of large quantities of cash on the premises should be avoided, where possible. There is always the danger of theft or loss of the cash. Also, the business has a responsibility to its employees to avoid putting temptation in front of them.

The most important reason that businesses use banking services is the convenience of making payments. It is much easier to send a cheque to someone than it is to deliver cash in person. This is especially true if the buyer and the seller are dealing with each other over a long distance. It is common practice to make all but very small payments by cheque. The charges for bank services are quite reasonable.

As a result, you can expect to see an account called Bank in the ledger rather than one called Cash. When money is received or paid out, it is the Bank account, not Cash, that is increased or decreased.

The words "bank" and "cash" are often used interchangeably. When an item is bought for cash, it is paid for at the time it is purchased. However, the payment is often made by cheque, and not by actual cash.

Cash and banking are discussed fully in Chapter 13.

Exceptional Account Balances

Occasionally, an account that would normally have a debit balance ends up with a credit balance and vice versa. Opposite balances like this are not necessarily the result of mistakes, although that possibility should certainly be checked out. There may be a good reason for an account to end up with a balance opposite to its normal one.

For example, suppose that Jack Evans, a customer, owes us $50. Suppose also that he sends a cheque for $55 in payment. His account will end up with a credit balance of $5, even though he is a customer and normally has a debit balance. The account balance is correct. It shows that the business owes Jack Evans $5. The account is temporarily a liability account.

A similar situation can affect the Bank account. For instance, we might spend more out of the bank account than we have in it (the bank would have to agree to this). Then we would end up with a credit balance in the Bank account. What does this credit balance mean? It means that the Bank account is temporarily in a liability position and that we are in debt to the bank.

Other transactions can bring about exceptional balances as well. Consider the following:

. you overpay an account payable;
. a customer with no account balance returns unsatisfactory merchandise for credit;
. you return goods for credit to a supplier with whom you have no account balance.
    Exceptional balances do not last long. Ordinary business activity usually causes them to return quickly to normal.

Expressing Money Amounts

Business people need to be able to verbally express amounts of money quickly and clearly. Over the years, a common way of verbally expressing amounts of money has evolved. Some examples are shown in the table below.

Amount	Expression
$ 0.17	seventeen cents
$ 1.75	one / seventy-five
$ 17.50	seventeen / fifty
$ 175.00	one seventy-five / dollars
$ 1 750.00	seventeen / fifty / dollars
$ 1 751.63	seventeen / fifty-one / sixty-three
$17 516.30	seventeen / five sixteen / thirty

SECTION REVIEW QUESTIONS

1. What three pieces of information does an account contain?
2. Explain the two steps in calculating the balance of a T-account.
3. How do you know which type of balance (debit or credit) an account has?
4. What kind of account has a debit balance?
5. What kind of account has a credit balance?
6. What does it mean if an account has an exceptional balance?
7. Give two examples of situations that result in an exceptional balance.
8. How would an accountant verbally express each of the following amounts: **(a)** $2 461.12 **(b)** $13 756.92 **(c)** $7. 42 **(d)** $756.00? Write it out as the accountant would say it.

SECTION EXERCISES

1. **The selected accounts below appear in your Workbook. Calculate their balances. Remember to make your pencil footings in tiny figures, and to circle the balance on the correct side of the account.**

Cash		Account Receivable H. Devrie		Account Payable P. Helka		R. Smart, Capital	
250	190	25	175	30	75	150	3 140
1 210	48	150		45	40		
360	512	70			175		
29		35					

1. **What does the debit balance in the H. Devrie account mean?**
2. **What does the credit balance in the P. Helka account mean?**

2. **The following three accounts have exceptional balances. Examine them and answer the questions that follow.**

Bank	Account Receivable P. Chu	Account Payable J. Reicher
500	100	300

   1. For each account explain what is unusual about the balance.
   2. For each account give a possible cause of the exceptional balance.

3. **A number of phrases appear below. To the right there are two columns, one headed "Debit" and the other headed "Credit." In your Workbook, indicate whether each phrase is best represented by the word "debit" or by the word "credit" by placing a check mark in the appropriate column.**

	Debit	Credit
1. The left side of an account.		
2. The balance of an account receivable.		
3. The balance of a supplier's account.		
4. A decrease in a liability.		
5. An exceptional balance in the Bank account.		
6. The balance in the Equipment account.		
7. The right side of an account.		
8. The balance in the Bank Loan account.		
9. An exceptional balance in an accounts payable account.		
10. The larger side of a liability account.		
11. A creditor's account.		
12. A customer's account.		
13. An increase in an asset.		
14. A debtor's account.		

4.4   TRIAL BALANCE

When setting up a ledger, as in Figure 4.3, the information for the accounts is usually obtained from a balance sheet. This way, the ledger begins in a balanced position. The total of the accounts with debit balances equals the total of the accounts with credit balances.

The changes caused by business transactions are recorded in the ledger. These changes are all in the form of balanced accounting entries, that is, entries where debits equal credits. As a result, the ledger should be balanced after each full accounting entry. Just as a balance sheet must balance, a ledger must also balance.

Periodically, it is necessary to check the accuracy of the ledger. This is done by means of a "trial balance." The taking off of a trial balance is a simple procedure to find out if the ledger is in balance. A **trial balance** is a listing of the account balances in a ledger. It is used to see if the dollar value of the accounts with debit balances is equal to the dollar value of the accounts with credit balances. To do this you simply add up all the debit balances, add up all the credit balances, and see if the two totals are the same. If they agree, the ledger is said to be **in balance**. If they do not agree, the ledger is said to be **out of balance**. The whole process, called **taking off a trial balance**, is usually done at the end of each week or month according to preference.

The completed ledger for Pacific Trucking is shown in Figure 4.6. Let us now see if it is in balance.

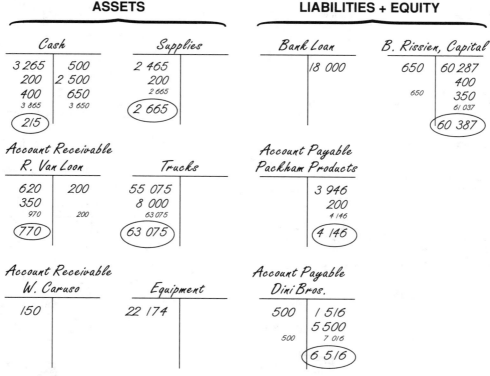

Figure 4.6   The completed ledger of Pacific Trucking.

Methods of Taking Off a Trial Balance

To take off a trial balance proceed as follows:

1 List all the accounts and their balances.
2 Place the debit balances in a debit column and the credit balances in a credit column.
3 Add up the two columns.
4 See if the two column totals are the same. Only if the two column totals are the same can you consider your ledger work to be correct.
5 Write a heading at the top. A heading is necessary on the trial balance. It must show the name of the individual or business, the title "Trial Balance," and, very importantly, the date.

The completed trial balance for the ledger on page 94 is shown in Figure 4.7.

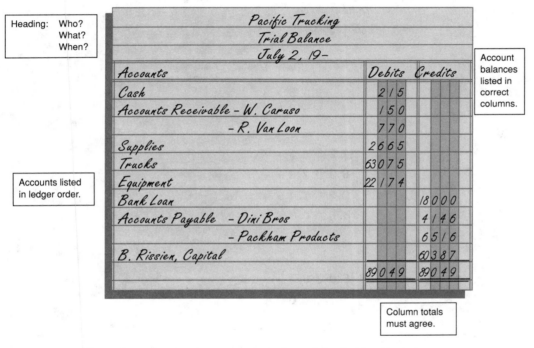

Heading: Who? What? When?

Account balances listed in correct columns.

Accounts listed in ledger order.

Pacific Trucking		
Trial Balance		
July 2, 19–		
Accounts	Debits	Credits
Cash	2 1 5	
Accounts Receivable – W. Caruso	1 5 0	
– R. Van Loon	7 7 0	
Supplies	2 6 6 5	
Trucks	630 7 5	
Equipment	22 1 7 4	
Bank Loan		18 0 0 0
Accounts Payable – Dini Bros		4 1 4 6
– Packham Products		6 5 1 6
B. Rissien, Capital		603 8 7
	890 4 9	890 4 9

Column totals must agree.

Figure 4.7 The trial balance for the ledger of Pacific Trucking.

Another way of taking off a trial balance is by using a printing calculator. This is a more convenient method and so is used very commonly.

The procedure is as follows:

1 Clear the machine by pressing the "total" button.
2 Enter the balances in the machine in ledger order.
Make sure to enter the: **debits** as +
                              credits as –

3 Take off a total by depressing the "total" button. If your ledger work is correct, the sum of the + entries will be equal to the sum of the – entries. Therefore, the total should be 0.00.

The adding machine method of taking off a trial balance is illustrated in Figure 4.8. Be certain that you understand the principle involved. Your work is arithmetically correct if you get zero for your tape total. Your work is incorrect if you do not get zero for your tape total. If this happens, you must begin a search for the error or errors.

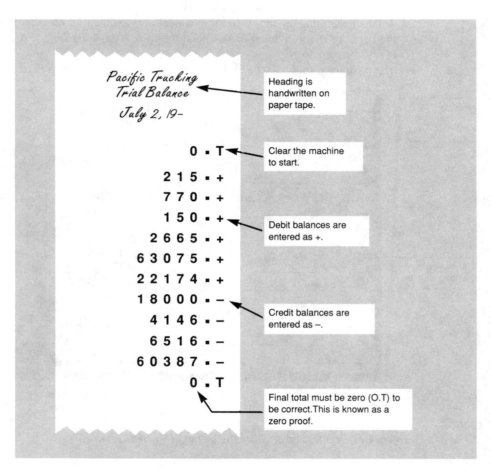

Figure 4.8 Trial balance done on a printing calculator.

Importance of the Trial Balance

It is important to an accountant to have the ledger in balance. The work is not accurate if the ledger is not in balance. A ledger out of balance is a certain sign that at least one error has been made in the accounts.

A good accountant does not rest until all errors are found and corrected. Moreover, the accountant must test the ledger fairly often. It is standard practice to take off a trial balance every month. Regardless of the method used, a trial balance should be kept on file for a year, or at the least until after the visit of the official auditors.

Trial Balance out of Balance

Trial balances do not work out on the first attempt most of the time. When the trial balance is out of balance, it means that at least one error has been made in the accounting process. It is the accountant's job to find and correct these errors. The errors may have been caused by faulty addition, by entering an item on the wrong side, and so on. Even if the ledger is in balance, it might still have errors in it. A ledger that is in balance proves only that it is mechanically or mathematically correct. The accountant may have made incorrect entries, but they were balanced ones. Errors such as these are often the most difficult to find.

It takes a methodical approach to locate accounting errors because they are often quite difficult to detect. Skill in finding errors is a great advantage to an accountant.

For now, there is a four-step procedure to follow if you find a ledger that does not balance. This method is expanded in Chapter 7 (see page 196). The four steps are:

1 re-add the trial balance columns;
2 check the figures from the ledger against those of the trial balance. Make sure that none are missing, none are on the wrong side, and none are for the wrong amount;
3 recalculate the account balances;
4 check that there is a balanced accounting entry in the accounts for each transaction.

You may be lucky enough to balance the ledger without having to go through all these steps. In this event, your task is finished and you can file your trial balance.

On the other hand, you may have completed all the steps and still not have balanced the ledger. When this happens, it means that you have made an error in one of the steps. You will have to go through the steps again, this time working more carefully. If all the steps are done correctly, the errors will be found, and the ledger will be balanced.

SECTION REVIEW QUESTIONS

1. Give a mathematical explanation of why a ledger should always balance.
2. Describe the procedure for balancing a ledger.
3. Describe how one takes off a trial balance when using a printing calculator.
4. Why is it important to balance the ledger?
5. How often should the ledger be tested by balancing it?
6. What happens to a completed trial balance?
7. For how long is a trial balance kept on file?
8. What does it mean if you complete the procedure for balancing a ledger and the ledger is still not in balance?

SECTION EXERCISES

1. Mr. J. Strom is the owner of a hardware store in Lethbridge, Alberta. At the end of the year he attempted to prepare a trial balance of the accounts in the general ledger as shown below. The balances themselves are correct. But Mr. Strom has no knowledge of double-entry bookkeeping and so he has made many errors in listing the balances.

Find the errors and prepare a corrected trial balance.

J. STROM
TRIAL BALANCE
DECEMBER 31, 19--

	Debit	Credit
Cash	$ 3 000	
Land	50 000	
Accounts Receivable–Jones		$ 10 940
Supplies	3 400	
Office Equipment	15 350	
Automobile		21 200
Building	140 000	
Accounts Payable–Smith	5 160	
Bank Loan		52 000
J. Strom, Capital		108 230
Mortgage Payable		78 500
	$216 910	$270 870

2. The ledger for C. Hernandez as of June 30, 19-6 is given below.

Cash		Account Receivable P. Onno		Account Receivable G. Slaught		Account Receivable R. Tamo	
5 000		850		1 124		3 500	

Supplies		Equipment		Automobiles		Account Payable J. Batt	
1 585		25 350		22 800			785

Account Payable W. Parker		Account Payable H. White		Bank Loan		C. Hernandez Capital	
	1 000		1 200		25 000		32 224

Prepare a trial balance for C. Hernandez as of June 30. Remember to write in the three-part heading.

3. The accounts and balances of Ceco Co. are arranged below in alphabetical order. **Prepare a trial balance of Ceco Co. with the accounts arranged in normal ledger order. Remember to write in the three-part heading. Date the trial balance June 30 of this year.**

Accounts and Balances	
Automobile	$22 500
Account Payable—Jondahl Co.	1 350
Account Payable—P. Swartz	4 250
Account Receivable—M. Legris	3 500
Account Receivable—W. Nishi	850
Bank Loan	10 000
C. Oke., Capital	27 471
Cash	7 000
Equipment	7 296
Supplies	1 925

4. **Workbook Exercise: Finding out why a simplified ledger does not balance.**

5. **Workbook Exercise: Finding out why a simplified ledger does not balance.**

CHAPTER HIGHLIGHTS

Now that you have completed Chapter 4, you should:

1. know what an account is and what a ledger is;
2. know the rules of debit and credit as they apply to assets, liabilities, and capital;
3. be able to record transactions in T-accounts and calculate an account balance;
4. know what the balance in a T-account means;
5. understand the concept of double-entry accounting;
6. be able to take off a trial balance using both the handwritten method and the machine method;
7. understand the importance of the trial balance;
8. be able to locate and correct errors in T-accounts.

ACCOUNTING TERMS

account	double-entry system of accounting	pin totals
account balance	in balance	taking off a trial balance
accounting entry	ledger	trial balance
credit	out of balance	
debit	pencil footings	

CHAPTER EXERCISES

Using Your Knowledge

1. Indicate whether each of the following statements is true or false by entering a "T" or an "F" in the space indicated in your Workbook. Explain the reason for each "F" response in the space provided.

   1. A number of individual balance sheet items may appear on one account page, as long as they are shown separately.
   2. Many accountants use the equation analysis sheet instead of the ledger.
   3. There is a page in the ledger for the total assets figure.
   4. T-accounts are ideal for small businesses.
   5. The first dollar amount recorded in an account is placed on the same side as it appears on a simple balance sheet.
   6. There is no account for capital because it can always be found by subtracting the total assets from the total liabilities.
   7. A transaction analysis sheet is a permanent accounting record.
   8. For every transaction, there is always one debit amount and one credit amount which are equal.
   9. A balanced accounting entry is a correct accounting entry.
   10. The balance of an account that is not zero must be either a debit or credit.
   11. The J.R. Dahl account in the ledger of C. Jacob is either an account payable or an account receivable.
   12. Eric Lai's account has a credit balance. This means that he purchased our services on credit.
   13. An exceptional balance merely means that it is opposite to what it would be normally.
   14. A customer is given a refund because of unsatisfactory service. The account of this customer would then have an exceptional balance.
   15. A ledger contains an exceptional balance. A trial balance cannot be taken until the exceptional item is transferred to another part of the ledger.
   16. A trial balance that is in balance proves that there are no errors in the accounts.
   17. A trial balance is taken using a printing calculator. When the "total" key is pressed, the figure 89.00 comes up. This is the amount of the error.
   18. The business buys supplies and pays cash. The accounting entry made in the accounts is Dr Cash and Cr Supplies. This causes the ledger to be out of balance.
   19. A correct trial balance needs to be kept only until the next one is taken.

2. **Workbook Exercise: Determining transactions from entries made in a T-account ledger.**

3. **Workbook Exercise: Determining transactions from entries made in a T-account ledger.**

4. The trial balance prepared by your company at the end of the month did not balance as a result of one error. In reviewing the entries for the month, the accountant noticed that one of the transactions, for the purchase of furniture and fixtures, was recorded as a debit to Furniture and Fixtures, $500, and a debit to Cash, $500. **Answer the following questions about this transaction:**

   1. Was the Cash account overstated, understated, or correctly stated on the trial balance? If overstated or understated, show by how much.
   2. Was the total of the debit column of the trial balance overstated, understated, or correctly stated? If overstated or understated, show by how much.
   3. Was the total of the credit column of the trial balance overstated, understated, or correctly stated? If overstated or understated, show by how much.

5. The accountant for M. Finney, owner of a janitorial service business, prepared a trial balance at the end of December. When Ms. Finney examined the trial balance, she noticed that the S. Pearson Co. had a debit balance of $375. Ms. Finney remembered depositing a cheque received from Pearson for that amount. She wants to know why a debit balance still exists on the records.

   Give three different explanations of how this could happen.

6. **State whether the following errors would cause a trial balance to be out of balance and by how much. Explain why or why not.**

   1. The entry to record the purchase of delivery equipment was omitted from the Delivery Equipment account, $150.
   2. A new desk was purchased for cash. Cash was credited but Office Supplies was debited instead of Office Equipment. The cost of the desk was $400.
   3. Cash of $100 was received from a client for services performed. Cash was debited for $100 and Capital was credited for $10.
   4. Cash of $500 was borrowed from the bank. Cash was credited for $500 and Bank Loan was debited $500.

7. **Examine the source document on p. 102 and answer the questions below.**

   1. Who issued the fees form?
   2. Who received the fees form?
   3. Why was the form issued?
   4. Who filled in the details on the form?
   5. In your opinion, when is the deadline for paying this bill?
   6. It states that a cheque is enclosed. Is it necessary that the amount of the cheque agree with the summary?
   7. In your opinion, what accounting entry will be made by Louis Tusek?
   8. Based on what you know so far, what accounting entry will be made by the Smokey Valley Ski Club?
   9. Was this a cash transaction?

ANNUAL FEES FORM

SMOKEY VALLEY SKI CLUB

Name _Louis Tusek_   Phone Home _325-6410_

Address _15 Cam Street_   Phone Bus. _325-4987_
                Street
Orillia
                City

List all family members who will be skiing:

Name	Age Dec. 1	Annual fee
Louis	35	250.00
Teresa	32	200.00
Ginger	12	125.00
Dene	8	125.00
Roger	6	125.00
	TOTAL FEE	825.00

I (the undersigned) hereby agree to comply with and be governed by the By-Laws, Rules and Regulations of the Club now or hereafter in force or as amended from time to time and I agree to be responsible for any debts incurred by members of my family.

Dated this _15th_ day of _November_ 19- _-_

Signature _Louis Tusek_

I enclose my cheque for _$ 825.00_

SMOKEY VALLEY SKI CLUB   R.R. #1, Horseshoe Valley, Ont. L3V 3B0

A fees form for a member of the Smokey Valley Ski Club. This form, together with a cheque, shows the annual payment for this member's family. The cheque is made out to the ski club and is deposited in the bank.

Comprehensive Exercises

8. A. Hoysted is a sign painter and truck letterer. Her business has the following assets and liabilities:

Assets		Liabilities	
Cash	$ 2 216	Bank Loan	$ 6 500
Accounts Receivable		Accounts Payable	
G. Anderson	357	Consumers' Supply	1 375
N. Ostrowski	402	Nu-Style Furniture	2 951
Office Supplies	2 980	Loan Payable, M. Hoysted	11 980
Painting Supplies	4 120		
Office Furniture	5 090		
Automobile	20 000		

1. **Set up A. Hoysted's financial position in the T-accounts provided in the Workbook. Include the equity account.**
2. **For the transactions listed below, record the accounting entries in T-accounts. If it is helpful for you, use a transaction analysis sheet.**

TRANSACTIONS

1. Received $200 cash from a customer for painting a sign.
2. Paid $500 to Consumers' Supply.
3. Received $402 cash from N. Ostrowski.
4. Sold an extra office desk (which is included in the Office Furniture figure at $450) to G. Brand at a price of $250. Brand paid $100 cash and owed the balance.
5. Reduced the bank loan by $1 000.
6. Paid the regular monthly bank loan payment, $500.
7. Paid the balance owing to Consumers' Supply.

3. **Calculate the account balances and balance the ledger by taking off a trial balance.**

---

9. Rainbow Real Estate is a business owned by Cathy Rogers. The assets and liabilities of the business are as follows:

Assets		Liabilities	
Cash	$ 1 056	Bank Loan	$ 19 000
Accounts Receivable		Account Payable	
D. Murray	1 351	Tuck Corporation	1 520
A. Niemi	2 516		
Office Supplies	1 115		
Furniture and Equipment	11 916		
Properties Owned	18 042		
Automobile	27 965		

The financial position of Rainbow Real Estate is set up in T-accounts in the Workbook. **For the transactions listed below, record the accounting entries in the T-accounts. Use a transaction analysis sheet if necessary. Calculate and record the balances in the accounts and take off a trial balance.**

TRANSACTIONS

1. Received $516 cash from A. Niemi.
2. Sold a home for V. Morris. For this service, Morris owes $4 150 to Rainbow Real Estate.
3. Paid $95 cash for office supplies.
4. Received $20 000 cash for sale of a property. (The property is included in the Properties Owned figure at $5 000.)
5. Paid $15 000 cash to the bank to reduce the amount of the bank loan.
6. Paid $520 cash to Tuck Corporation.
7. Paid $40 cash for a new headlight for the automobile.
8. Received $800 cash from D. Murray.
9. The owner withdrew $500 cash for her personal use.
10. Received $2 000 cash from V. Morris.
11. Paid the balance of the debt to Tuck Corporation in cash.
12. Purchased a new office desk at a cost of $600 from Pioneer Furniture but did not pay cash for it.
13. Sold a home for A. McIntosh. McIntosh paid Rainbow Real Estate $5 100 cash for the service.

For Further Thought

10. Briefly answer the following questions.

1. What size of business is likely to have a loose-leaf ledger?
2. In a handwritten ledger one can see the figures. How do you think the amounts are stored in a computerized system?
3. A ledger account does not have the word "asset," "liability," or "equity" recorded on it. How can you tell if the account is an asset, a liability, or equity?
4. Assets, liabilities, and equity can each be thought of as having a natural side. What is the natural side for an asset? a liability? equity?
5. The formal account, designed for handwritten records, has two distinct sides —the debit side and the credit side. Do you think that account data take this form when stored in the computer? Explain.
6. Try to express the following by writing it out as an accountant would say it.
   a. $51 326.26
   b. $7.50
   c. $750.00
   d. $3 145.00
   e. $31.45

7. Explain why the rules of debit and credit are identical for liabilities and equity.
8. Explain why you do not debit Automobiles when you pay to get a fender straightened out on your automobile.
9. Is the statement "For every debit there is a credit" perfectly true? Explain.
10. What is the purpose of pin totals? Why are they written in pencil? Is it all right to erase them at any time?
11. What assumption would you make if an account balance were given to you without your having been told if it is a debit or credit balance?
12. Suppose that you, an outsider to the business, were told that Sarah Jones had an account balance of $350. Can you tell if Sarah Jones is a debtor or a creditor?
13. What is an exceptional account balance? Would a better word be "unusual"? "opposite"? "abnormal"?
14. The method of taking off a trial balance using a printing calculator is referred to as the "zero proof method." Explain why this is so.
15. Why are trial balances taken at least once per month rather than once or twice a year?

CASE STUDIES

CASE 1   *Property Value on a Balance Sheet*

You are a loan officer with the Reliable Trust Company in Dryden, Ontario. On March 30, 19—, a young businessman, Gary Inch, comes to you in the hope of borrowing $75 000 for a business venture. When you inquire about his personal financial status, he presents you with the balance sheet shown below.

GARY INCH
BALANCE SHEET
MARCH 20, 19—

Assets		*Liabilities*	
Cash	$ 2 000	Accounts Payable	$ 5 300
Accounts Receivable	1 500	Mortgage Payable	30 000
Furniture	9 000		
Supplies	1 300		$ 35 300
Truck	17 000	*Owner's Equity*	
Building Lot	75 000	Gary Inch, Capital	70 500
	$105 800		$105 800

When examining this statement, you become concerned about the item Building Lot for $75 000. You have lived in Dryden for several years and you know that there are not many properties in town that are worth that much money.

Gary informs you that he bought the property one month ago for $30 000 and that he borrowed the entire sum from his father. This is shown properly on the statement as Mortgage Payable.

Your conversation with Gary indicates that he truly believes that the property will increase in value in the near future and that he has listed it at the amount he expects to sell it for. When you find out the location of the property, you realize that it is a piece of land that took over two years to sell.

Questions
1. What is your opinion about listing the property at $75 000? What GAAP is affected?
2. What would you say to Gary about this particular item?
3. Would you lend Gary the money based only on the financial data given to you? Explain.

CASE 2 *Choosing between Two Companies*

	Company A	Company B
Assets		
Cash	$21 500	$700
Accounts Receivable	3 000	59 500
Supplies	1 300	2 500
Equipment	15 600	42 400
Land and Building	54 000	150 000
Total	$95 400	$255 100
Liabilities and Equity		
Accounts Payable	$22 800	$45 900
Mortgage Payable	22 000	128 000
Owner's Equity	50 600	81 200
Total	$95 400	$255 100

Assume that each of the two companies has been forced out of business and must sell its assets for cash in order to pay its debts.

Questions
1. Are the values shown necessarily the values you could get? Explain.
2. Are there any problems associated with selling the assets? Explain any problems you see and why they occur.
3. Which company would you prefer to own? Explain.

ENTREPRENEUR
Paul Murphy / Fab-Tech Industries Ltd.

All his life, Paul Murphy has never taken "no" for an answer. In fact, overcoming obstacles that would shatter most of us has propelled Paul into a thriving career as a budding entrepreneur, the driving force behind Fab-Tech Industries Ltd. of Winnipeg.

Paul has always had restricted physical mobility, because Thalidomide was prescribed for his mother during her pregnancy. Opening doors, getting dressed, moving chairs to new locations have been difficult for Paul over the years. However, the insight he gained while overcoming these problems was invaluable when, as a young adult, he launched a successful business career.

Paul thrives on confrontation and challenge. "Just tell me no, say something can't be done, and I'm ready for the fight." His career began through a conversation with a family friend. She was looking for a mini van that would help her disabled daughter get around. Paul took the project on, seeking advice from Dennis Pohl, the technician who designed his specially built wheelchair.

In his direct style, Murphy tackled the problem by sliding under a mini van in the middle of a Chrysler showroom, much to the astonishment of the floor sales staff. With Pohl, he studied the possibilities and made the necessary changes to one of the vans.

Murphy and Pohl devised a wide-entry back area that did not alter the shape of the van. "When the van is closed, it looks no different from a standard vehicle that anybody might own," explains Murphy.

Paul's company, Fab-Tech Industries, started operations in 1988, financed with his own money and some financing and grants from the federal and provincial governments. His product, a modification kit that improves accessibility to mini vans for people confined to wheelchairs, sells for between $2 000 and $4 500. The design is being marketed continent-wide, and Paul is looking for distributors.

At present, however, Paul is building units to order only. This strategy prevents him from having too much product on hand at any one time. He has no employees and so contracts work out. As the company grows and the cash flow stabilizes, this strategy may no longer be appropriate.

Paul hopes to market his product to taxi companies, courier services, and equipment movers, where increased access and space are important. However, in the meantime, he consults with architects, engineers, property owners, and developers on barrier-free access for handicapped people. He hopes to present seminars on this topic. In

addition, he is researching and developing an exercise bed.

As with most new businesses, all has not been smooth sailing. Convincing people that the "disabled community" would buy his product has been difficult. Obtaining government certifications to use the modified vans as taxicabs has been another hurdle. "Once that is done, I think we should be able to sell as many as 100 to 150 units in a year. When the taxi companies start operating the van, people in wheelchairs can call a taxi and travel to their destination without the driver having to help the passenger into the cab and store the wheelchair," claims Murphy.

As a boy Paul had a keen interest in cars, in which he was encouraged by his father, a doctor. Together they tinkered in their home workshop. What began as a hobby Paul developed into a career adapted to his life with its physical restrictions.

By his own admission, Paul was not an outstanding student. However, Paul attributes the self-discipline in his business approach to his private school. High school courses such as accounting and business law provided him with the basic knowledge for operating a business. He gained his business expertise while experimenting with various career options once he was out of high school.

DISCUSSION

1. How has Paul's handicap affected his attitude towards new situations?
2. What characteristic is a positive force in Paul's life?
3. How is Paul a good example for young business hopefuls?
4. Explain briefly why Paul is a successful business person.

The Expanded Ledger: Revenue, Expense, and Drawings

5.1 Expanding the Ledger
5.2 Completing Ledger Theory
5.3 Computers in Accounting   Using Spreadsheets Efficiently

In Chapter 4, you were introduced to a number of ledger accounts and to the basic system of debit and credit.

In Chapter 5, new ledger accounts are introduced and the rules of debit and credit are expanded. The rules regarding the asset and liability accounts will not change. But the rules regarding the owner's equity account will be modified.

5.1 EXPANDING THE LEDGER

To date, you have been accustomed to having a single account for owner's equity. Any change in the equity of the business was recorded in that one account, no matter what caused the change. Now you must become familiar with a system in which the ledger has a number of accounts in an equity section. Each of the new accounts reflects a particular kind of transaction that affects owner's equity. In the expanded equity section you will see new accounts for:

revenues, which are related to the sales of goods or services;
expenses, which are the costs related to the revenues;
drawings, which represent the owner's personal withdrawals.

These three new accounts are defined and explained fully in the next section. An illustration of an expanded ledger is shown in Figure 5.1.

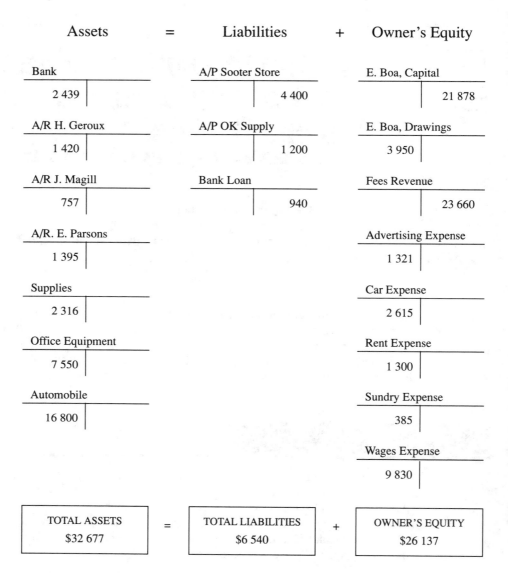

Figure 5.1   The expanded ledger of Eve Boa, a lawyer.

Purpose of Expanding the System

The new accounts in the equity section of the ledger have one main purpose: to provide essential information about the progress of the business. This information is needed by managers and owners to see if the business is being run profitably, and to help them make sound decisions.

Some of the information in the new accounts is used to prepare an income statement, such as the simple one illustrated in Figure 5.2. As you can see from the illustration, the income statement shows in a detailed way whether the business is profitable or not. The revenue and expense accounts are organized to show the net income (or net loss) of the business for a given period. This is discussed more fully later in this chapter and again in Chapter 8.

<table>
<tr><td colspan="3" align="center">HARRIS REAL ESTATE
INCOME STATEMENT
MONTH ENDED JANUARY 31, 19-4</td></tr>
<tr><td>*Revenue*</td><td></td><td></td></tr>
<tr><td>Commissions</td><td></td><td>$25 726.50</td></tr>
<tr><td>*Expenses*</td><td></td><td></td></tr>
<tr><td>Advertising</td><td>$1 236.25</td><td></td></tr>
<tr><td>Car Expenses</td><td>3 256.10</td><td></td></tr>
<tr><td>Miscellaneous Expense</td><td>952.30</td><td></td></tr>
<tr><td>Rent</td><td>1 250.00</td><td></td></tr>
<tr><td>Wages</td><td>1 860.00</td><td></td></tr>
<tr><td>Total Expenses</td><td></td><td>8 554.65</td></tr>
<tr><td>Net Income</td><td></td><td>$17 171.85</td></tr>
</table>

Figure 5.2   A simple income statement.

The ledgers that you have worked with so far have had a single equity account—the Capital account. Any changes in the equity of a business were recorded in that one account. However, this does not provide sufficient information about changes in owner's equity. Now you must become familiar with a ledger that has a number of accounts in an equity section. These new accounts are used to gather the figures that cause each type of change in equity.

Revenue

Selling goods or services produces revenue. **Revenue** is an increase in equity resulting from the sale of goods or services in the usual course of business. Consider the following transaction:

> Eve Boa, a lawyer, draws up a legal agreement for J. Basso, a client, and for her services is paid a fee of $250 in cash.

Analysis   This transaction increases both Bank and equity by the amount of $250. Before, you would have debited Bank and credited E. Boa, Capital. Now, you will debit Bank as before. But an increase in equity from business operations is revenue and must be credited to the Fees Revenue account. The transaction is recorded as follows:

If the service performed for J. Basso was sold on credit, the transaction would be recorded as:

Think along the following lines:

1. revenue represents an increase in equity;
2. an increase in equity requires a credit entry;
3. therefore, the Fees Revenue account is credited.

All similar transactions affecting fees revenue will be credited to the Fees Revenue account. The account will have a credit balance. The account balance will be the total fees earned for the fiscal period to date.

Usually, a business has only one revenue account and it is given an appropriate name. For example, a loan company earns its revenue in the form of interest. Its revenue account would likely be called Interest Revenue. A real estate company would have a revenue account called Commissions Earned. Suitable names for the revenue accounts of other types of businesses might be Rental Revenue, Fees Earned, Royalties, and so on.

GAAP—The Revenue Recognition Convention

The revenue recognition convention states that **revenue must be recorded in the accounts (recognized) at the time the transaction is completed.** Usually, this just means recording revenue when the bill for it is sent to the customer. If it is a cash transaction, the revenue is recorded when the sale is completed and the cash received.

It is not always quite so simple. Think of the building of a large project such as a dam. It takes a construction company a number of years to complete such a project. The company does not wait until the project is entirely completed before it sends its bill. Periodically, it bills for the amount of work completed and receives payments as the work progresses. Revenue is taken into the accounts on this periodic basis.

It is important to take revenue into the accounts properly. If this is not done, the income statements of the company will be incorrect and the readers of the financial statements will be misinformed.

Expense

There are certain costs associated with producing revenue—rent, wages, fuel, advertising, and so on. Each of these costs is known as an expense. An **expense** represents a decrease in equity. Consider the following transaction:

> Eve Boa pays her secretary the regular weekly wage of $400 in cash.

Analysis   This transaction requires that both Bank and equity be decreased by $400. The decrease to Bank is handled as before, by a credit to the account. But a decrease in equity from business operations is an *expense*. It must be debited to an expense account. In this example, the Wages Expense account is debited. The transaction is recorded as follows:

Think along the following lines:

1. expense represents a decrease in equity;
2. a decrease in equity requires a debit entry;
3. therefore, the Wages Expense account is debited.

The Wages Expense account, or any expense account for that matter, will normally receive debit entries. All wages will be accumulated in the one account. It will have a debit balance that is the total of the wages for the period to date.

There are many transactions that involve expenses. For example:

> Eve Boa receives the monthly furnace oil bill for $195 from Municipal Oil. The bill is not paid immediately.

The transaction is recorded as follows:

In any business, there are a number of expense accounts, each one representing a specific sort of decrease in equity. The name of the account tells the nature of the decrease. Typical expense accounts are: Rent Expense, Delivery Expense, Insurance Expense, Bank Charges, and Postage. Observe that the word "expense" is not always included in the account title where there is no doubt that it is an expense.

All expenditures are not for expenses. The purchase of a new building, for example, would be debited to an *asset* account called Buildings.

Net Income or Net Loss

It is from the revenue and expense accounts that a business can tell whether or not it has earned a net income (profit). **Net income** is the difference between the total revenues and the total expenses where the revenues are greater than the expenses. If the expenses are greater than the revenues, the business has suffered a **net loss**. Drawings are not a factor in calculating net income or net loss.

GAAP—The Matching Principle

The matching principle is an extension of the revenue recognition convention, which we looked at earlier. The **matching principle** states that **each expense item related to revenue earned must be recorded in the same time period as the revenue it helped to earn**. If this is not done, the financial statements will not measure the results of operations fairly.

For example, consider Karen Lepsoe who borrowed $20 000 to buy property. She intended to resell it at a profit. Six months later she sold the property for $28 000. On the surface it appears that a profit of $8 000 was made. But this fails to take into account the expenses associated with the transaction. The real profit from the transaction is calculated as follows:

Selling price of property		$28 000	
Deduct: Cost of property	$20 000		Costs and
Legal fees	400		expenses
Property taxes	350		matched
Bank interest	1 200		against
Realtor's commission	1 120		revenue
Total costs and expenses		23 070	
Net Profit		$ 4 930	

The matching principle will be considered more fully when we discuss "adjustments" in a later chapter. Adjustments are necessary to arrive at the proper figures for the financial statements.

Drawings

The owner of a business usually looks to the profits of the business to provide a livelihood. In a healthy business, the owner will be able to take funds (generated by profits) out of the business on a regular basis, much like a salary. These withdrawals of funds by the owner are known as **drawings** and represent a decrease in equity. Drawings are *not* expenses. They have nothing to do with determining the net income or net loss.

Cash is the most common item withdrawn by an owner for personal use. For example,

Eve Boa, the owner of the business, withdraws $300 to pay for personal expenses.

Analysis   This transaction requires that equity and Bank both be decreased by $300. The decrease to Bank is handled in the usual way, as a credit to that account. But this particular decrease in equity is not an expense and must be charged to the owner. The transaction is recorded as follows:

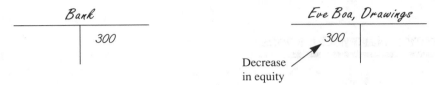

The Drawings account is also affected when the owner buys something for personal use but has the business pay for it. The owner may wish to take advantage of a special price that is offered to businesses but not to individuals. Or it may simply be that this form of payment is more convenient. In any event, when recording the transaction, the debit must be to Drawings.

For example, assume that Eve Boa purchases a new coffee-maker through the business for personal use. A bill for $85 for the coffee-maker arrives in the office from Baystore. The $85 is not an expense of the business. It must be charged to Eve Boa. The transaction is recorded as follows:

All entries affecting Drawings follow the rules of debit and credit. Drawings represents a decrease in equity, and decreases in equity require debit entries. Therefore, the Drawings account normally receives debit entries. All drawings will be gathered in this one account and it will have a debit balance.

Some other transactions that affect the Drawings account are:

• the owner takes assets other than cash out of the business for personal use. These could be something like a typewriter, a table, or merchandise.
• the owner collects a debt from a customer and keeps the money for personal use. The accounting clerks would have to be told of this.

Equity Section Summary

There are four types of accounts in the equity section.

1. Capital: This account will now contain the equity figure at the beginning of the fiscal period, plus new capital from the owner, if any.
The following three types of accounts are used to show changes in owner's equity from one period to the next.
2. Revenues: Increases in equity resulting from the sale of goods or services. A revenue account normally has a credit balance.

3. Expenses: Decreases in equity resulting from the costs of the materials or services used to produce the revenue. An expense account normally has a debit balance.
4. Drawings: Decreases in equity resulting from the owner's personal withdrawals. The Drawings account normally has a debit balance. Drawings is not a factor when calculating net income or loss.

SECTION REVIEW QUESTIONS

1. What new accounts are there in the equity section of the ledger?
2. What is the purpose of the Capital account in the expanded ledger?
3. What is the source of data for the income statement?
4. Define revenue.
5. Define expense.
6. Define drawings.
7. Which accounts in the equity section affect the calculation of net income?
8. Give three examples of transactions that affect drawings.
9. Explain the revenue recognition convention.
10. Explain the matching principle.

SECTION EXERCISES

1. **This exercise also appears in your Workbook.**

   A business has the beginning financial position recorded in the schedule on page 117. Ten simple transactions are listed in the left-hand column. **Work out the revised totals for assets, liabilities, and owner's equity after each transaction. Enter these totals in your Workbook. Complete the last two columns of the chart on p. 117 by recording: a) the amount of change in equity (if any), and b) whether the change in equity represents revenue, expense, or drawings.**

2. Eric Inahaba is in business for himself as a groundskeeper and gardener in Hamilton, Ontario. He cuts grass, weeds gardens, and trims trees and shrubs for a number of customers on a regular basis. The following accounts are in Eric Inahaba's ledger:

Bank	Account Payable—Pesticide Products
Account Receivable—G. Hung	Account Payable—Pro Hardware
Account Receivable—F. Sawchuck	E. Inahaba, Capital
Account Receivable—W. Scott	E. Inahaba, Drawings
Chemical Supplies	Revenue
Equipment	Advertising Expense
Truck	Miscellaneous Expense
Bank Loan	Telephone Expense
Account Payable—Banner News	Truck Expense

   In your Workbook record the following transactions, using the schedule provided in your Workbook.

Ex. 1 continued

	Total Assets	Total Liabilities	Owner's Equity	Change in Equity	Revenue? Expense? Drawings?
Starting position	10 000	6 000	4 000		
Transactions					
1. Purchased $400 of supplies for future use and paid cash.					
2. Reduced bank loan by $1 000.					
3. Received $800 cash from a debtor.					
4. Sold services for $900 cash.					
5. Sold services on credit, $1 500.					
6. Paid hydro for month just ended, $125.					
7. Owner withdrew $750 cash for personal use.					
8. Paid employee's wages, $600.					
9. Purchased truck on credit, $20 000.					
10. Owner took supplies for personal use, $250.					

Ex. 2 continued

TRANSACTIONS

July
2 Received a bill from Pesticide Products regarding the purchase of $125 worth of insecticide on account.
5 Received a bill from Pro Hardware for $150 for the purchase of a new ladder on account.
6 Issued a cheque for $100 to W. Decorte for part-time wages.
10 Received $50 from a customer for services performed for cash.
13 Issued a bill to G. Hung for $100 for services sold on account.
13 Received a bill from the *Banner News* regarding a $50 advertisement placed in the newspaper on account.
16 Issued a cheque for $175 to E. Inahaba, the owner, for his personal use.

19 Received a notice from the bank stating that $90 had been taken by them from the business's bank account to pay for interest charges on the bank loan.

20 Received a memo from E. Inahaba, the owner, stating that he had received $100 from a cash customer. The money was not put in the bank as usual but was kept by Mr. Inahaba.

3. **In your Workbook, complete each of the following statements with either the word "debit" or the word "credit."**

1. The Bank account normally has a _____ balance.
2. A Revenue account normally has a _____ balance.
3. An Expense account normally has a _____ balance.
4. Paying a creditor involves a _____ entry to the creditor's account.
5. The Drawings account receives a _____ entry when the owner withdraws money for personal use.
6. A lawyer gives a refund to a customer. The Bank account will receive a _____ entry and the Revenue account will receive a _____ entry.
7. Supplies are bought on credit. The Supplies account will receive a _____ entry and the supplier's account payable will receive a _____ entry.
8. The Drawings account will not normally receive _____ entries.
9. An increase in equity can be thought of as a _____ to the Capital account.
10. Net profit can be thought of as a _____ to the Capital account.
11. Net loss can be thought of as a _____ to the Capital account.
12. The owner takes a computer from the business for his personal (permanent) use. The Drawings account will receive a _____ entry.

4. **Workbook Exercise: Additional practice in recording accounting entries.**

5. A series of transactions for Ace Repair is given below. **A chart for the solution is given in the Workbook. Show the effect of each of the transactions on assets, liabilities, and owner's equity by placing checkmarks in the appropriate columns of the chart.** The first transaction is done for you.

TRANSACTIONS

1. Performed a service for a customer for cash.
2. Performed a service for a customer on credit.
3. Sold a typewriter for cash for its value as shown in the accounts.
4. Sold a typewriter for cash at less than its value as shown in the accounts.
5. Purchased an automobile on credit.
6. Paid cash to have the automobile repaired.
7. The owner took out cash for his personal use.
8. Paid an employee a weekly salary in cash.
9. The owner took an automobile out of the business for his permanent personal use.
10. Paid cash to the bank to reduce the bank loan.

Solutions Chart

No.	Asset		Liability		Revenue (Equity) (Increase)	Expense (Equity) (Decrease)	Drawings (Equity) (Decrease)
	Increase	Decrease	Decrease	Increase			
1	√				√		

5.2 COMPLETING LEDGER THEORY

Understanding Equity Relationships

It is important to understand the equity section of the ledger fully. In Figure 5.3, the expanded ledger of Eve Boa is presented in a way that will help you to gain this understanding.

Study Figure 5.3 and observe the following:

1. There are four types of accounts in the equity section of the ledger—capital, revenue, expense, and drawings.
2. The Capital account represents the beginning equity figure.
3. Changes in equity are recorded in the revenue, expense, and drawings accounts.
   * *Revenues* represent an increase in equity from normal business activity. Because they represent an increase in equity, they are recorded as credits in the equity section.
   * *Expenses* represent a decrease in equity from normal business activity. Because they represent a decrease in equity, they are recorded as debits in the equity section.
   * *Drawings* represent a decrease in equity as a result of the owner's personal withdrawals. Because they represent a decrease in equity, they are recorded as debits in the equity section.
4. The fundamental accounting equation is given at the bottom of the figure and shows that Eve Boa's ledger is in balance.
5. The difference between the total revenues and the total expenses is the net income or the net loss. *Net income* is the result if the revenues are greater than the expenses. *Net loss* is the result if the expenses are greater than the revenues. For Eve Boa, the net income is $8 209 (revenues of $23 660 less expenses of $15 451). The drawings have nothing to do with the calculation of net income or net loss.
6. The net income (or net loss) figure, together with the drawings figure, shows the increase or decrease in equity. For Eve Boa, there has been an increase in equity of $4 259 (increase from net income of $8 209 less a decrease from drawings of $3 950). If drawings are greater than net income, there will be an overall decrease in equity.
7. The following is the equity equation for Eve Boa.

Beginning Capital	+	Net Income	−	Net Loss	−	Drawings	=	Ending Capital
$21 878	+	$8 209	−	n/a	−	$3 950	=	$26 137

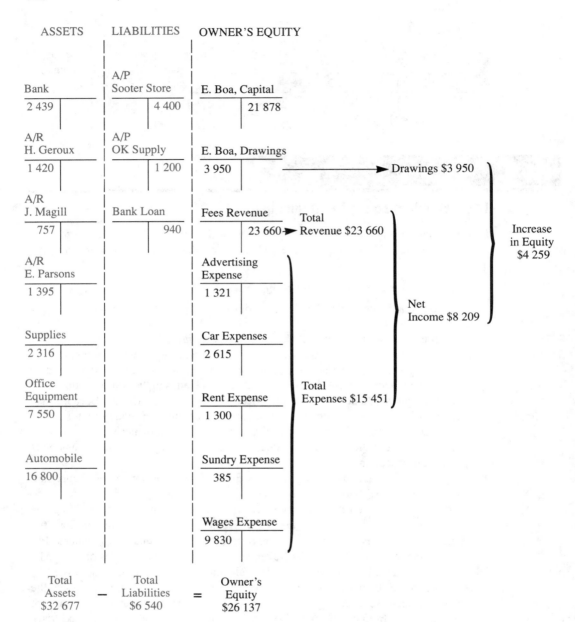

Figure 5.3   The expanded ledger of Eve Boa showing some important equity relationships.

The Fiscal Period

Now that you have learned about net income, it is time to introduce another new concept in accounting. Net income is measured over a specific length of time, called the fiscal period, or the accounting period. The **fiscal period** (also called the **accounting period**) is the period of time over which earnings are measured. All fiscal periods for a business are of the same length.

The earnings figure of a business does not mean anything if you do not know how long it took to produce those earnings. You would not be very informed about a business if all you knew about its net income was that it amounted to $4 000. You would not be very favourably impressed if it took one year to earn that amount. On the other hand, if the $4 000 was earned in only one week, you would probably be quite impressed.

In business today, the formal fiscal period is usually one year. The fiscal year does not have to be the same as the calendar year. It just has to run for 12 consecutive months. For example, a fiscal year could begin on July 1 and end on June 30 of the following year.

Half-yearly, quarterly, or monthly fiscal periods are used by some businesses. Managers can keep a close watch over their business by using short fiscal periods. Even when fiscal periods shorter than one year are used, it is still necessary to produce an annual income statement for income tax purposes.

GAAP—The Time Period Concept

The **time period concept** provides that **accounting will take place over specific time periods known as fiscal periods**. These fiscal periods are of equal length, and are used when measuring the financial progress of a business.

The Simple Income Statement

At regular intervals, the owner of a business will have an income statement prepared. The total of the expenses is deducted from the total of the revenue to arrive at the net income or net loss.

An income statement must be prepared annually to comply with income tax law. However, most business people will want to see income statements prepared more often so that they are kept informed about the progress of the business.

The income statement for Eve Boa, taken from the ledger as it appears in Figure 5.3, is shown in Figure 5.4. This statement is for a fiscal period of one month ended January 31.

EVE BOA
INCOME STATEMENT
MONTH ENDED JANUARY 31, 19—

Revenue		
Fees Revenue		$23 660
Expenses		
Advertising	$ 1 321	
Car Expenses	2 615	
Rent	1 300	
Sundry Expenses	385	
Wages	9 830	
Total Expenses		15 451
Net Income		$ 8 209

Figure 5.4   The simple income statement for Eve Boa.

Chart of Accounts

It is customary to number the accounts in the ledger. These numbers are used for identification and reference, particularly in computerized systems. The numbering system used in this text is the common three-digit one shown below. You will use these numbers in later chapters.

Assets		100-199
Liabilities		200-299
Owner's	Capital	300-399
	Drawings	
Equity	Revenues	400-499
	Expenses	500-599

A **chart of accounts** is a list of the ledger accounts and their numbers arranged in ledger order. Most businesses have copies of their chart of accounts available for their employees, and for outsiders such as auditors. Eve Boa's chart of accounts is shown in Figure 5.5. It is taken from the ledger in Figure 5.3. Notice the gaps left in case new accounts need to be inserted.

E. BOA
CHART OF ACCOUNTS

Assets		*Equity*	
Bank	No.105	E. Boa, Capital	No. 305
Accounts Receivable		E. Boa, Drawings	310
H. Geroux	110	Fees Revenue	405
J. Magill	115	Advertising Expense	505
E. Parsons	120	Car Expense	510
Supplies	125	Rent Expense	515
Office Equipment	130	Sundry Expense	520
Automobile	135	Wages Expense	525
Liabilities			
Accounts Payable			
Sooter Store	205		
OK Supply	210		
Bank Loan	215		

Figure 5.5   E. Boa, chart of accounts.

Debit and Credit in the Expanded Ledger

The ledger is now expanded to include revenues, expenses, and drawings. Thus, the rules of debit and credit must now include these new items. The complete rules of debit and credit are as follows:

TYPE OF ACCOUNT		TO INCREASE	TO DECREASE
Assets		Debit	Credit
Liabilities		Credit	Debit
Equity	Capital	Credit	Debit
	Revenue	Credit	Debit
	Expense	Debit	Credit
	Drawings	Debit	Credit

Debit and Credit Balances

An accountant needs to understand thoroughly the account balances in a ledger. At this stage it is not very difficult to tell whether an account is an asset or an expense, a liability or revenue. But it will not always be simple. Remember these rules:

1. Accounts with debit balances are normally either assets, expenses, or drawings.
2. Accounts with credit balances are normally either liabilities, capital, or revenue.

Trial Balance Procedure Unchanged

The new types of account do not change the trial balance procedure. Simply total the accounts with debit balances, total the accounts with credit balances, and see that the two totals agree. This is illustrated in Figure 5.6 with the trial balance of Eve Boa's ledger (Figure 5.1).

No.	Account	Debit	Credit
	E. Boa Trial Balance — date —		
105	Bank	2439 –	
	Accounts Receivable		
110	H. Geroux	1420 –	
115	J. Magill	757 –	
120	E. Parsons	1395 –	
125	Supplies	2316 –	
130	Office Equipment	7550 –	
135	Automobile	16800 –	
	Accounts Payable		
205	Sooter Store		4400 –
210	OK. Supply		1200 –
215	Bank Loan		940 –
305	E. Boa, Capital		21878 –
310	E. Boa, Drawings	3950 –	
405	Fees Revenue		23660 –
505	Advertising Expense	1321 –	
510	Car Expense	2615 –	
515	Rent Expense	1300 –	
520	Sundry Expense	385 –	
525	Wages Expense	9830 –	
		52078 –	52078 –

Figure 5.6   Trial balance of E. Boa's ledger.

Buying and Selling on Credit

Businesses with good reputations are able to buy goods on short-term credit. This is a convenient way to do business and is an accepted practice in general use. The purchaser is able to delay payment for a short period of time, usually 30 days. The buyer thus has time to inspect or test the goods thoroughly before paying for them, and can refuse to pay for the goods if they are not satisfactory.

The buying and selling of goods on short-term credit is quite common in our society. Therefore expect to see this type of transaction frequently in your exercises.

On Account

The term "on account" is used extensively in modern business. It is an essential part of business vocabulary. The term is used in four specific ways:

1. Suppose an item is purchased on credit. This means that it is not paid for at the time of purchase. This is a purchase on account. A **purchase on account** is a purchase that is not paid for at the time it is made.
2. Suppose an item is sold on credit; that is, it is not paid for at the time it is sold. This is a sale on account. A **sale on account** is a sale for which the money is not received at the time it is made.
3. Suppose money is paid out to a creditor to decrease the amount owed to the creditor. This is a payment on account. A **payment on account** is money paid to a creditor to reduce the amount owed to that creditor.
4. Suppose money is received from a debtor company to reduce the amount owed to us. This is a receipt on account. A **receipt on account** is money received from a debtor to reduce the amount owed by that debtor.

SECTION REVIEW QUESTIONS

1. What is a chart of accounts?
2. Who uses a chart of accounts?
3. Describe the account numbering system used in this text.
4. Prepare a chart of rules of debit and credit in their final form.
5. What types of account balances are normally found in an asset account? a liability account? a revenue account? an expense account? the Drawings account? the Capital account?
6. State the equity equation.
7. Why do businesses prefer to make purchases on credit?
8. The term "on account" is used in four ways. What are these four ways?
9. What must have happened previously, before you can receive money on account from a customer?

SECTION EXERCISES

1. **Using the table below, complete the exercise that follows in your Workbook.**

1.	Asset debit
2.	Asset credit
3.	Liability debit
4.	Liability credit
5.	Capital debit
6.	Capital credit
7.	Drawings debit
8.	Drawings credit
9.	Revenue debit
10.	Revenue credit
11.	Expense debit
12.	Expense credit

A series of transactions is given below. **Show the effect of the accounting entry for each transaction.** The first transaction is done for you.

1. Purchase a new car on account.

2. Receive payment on account from a customer.

3. Owner withdraws cash for personal use.

4. Owner starts a new business by investing cash.

5. The car is repaired and paid for in cash immediately.

6. Perform a service for a customer for cash.

7. Perform a service for a customer on account.

8. Purchase supplies for cash.

9. Receive a bill for gas and oil for the car.

10. Pay a creditor on account.

11. Throw out some ruined supplies.

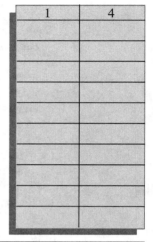

1	4

2. The ledger of Emily Stokaluk is given below as at March 31, 19—.

Bank	Accounts Receivable	Supplies
10 100	8 300	950

Land	Building	Equipment
35 000	110 000	22 000

Automobiles	Accounts Payable	Bank Loan
24 000	2 800	10 000

Mortgage Payable	E. Stokaluk, Capital	E. Stokaluk, Drawings
75 000	52 088	15 000

Fees Earned	Interest Earned	Advertising
132 500	1 000	1 200

Bank Charges	Building Maintenance	Gas and Oil
350	420	1 800

Light and Heat	Miscellaneous Expense	Repairs to Car
1 640	128	850

Wages
41 650

1. Prepare a trial balance in your Workbook.
2. Prepare a chart of accounts based on the numbering system used in the text.
3. Prepare a simple income statement (one month).

---

3. The ledger accounts of Karen's Air Service are shown below in alphabetical order.

Accounts Payable	Kathy Koy, Capital
Accounts Receivable	Kathy Koy, Drawings
Advertising Expense	Land
Airplanes	Legal Expense
Automobiles	Mortgage Payable
Bank	Revenue—Freight
Bank Charges	Revenue—Passengers
Building	Salaries
Building Repairs	Supplies
Equipment	Supplies Used
General Expense	Telephone
Insurance Expense	Wages

1. Rearrange these accounts into the usual ledger order.
2. Prepare a chart of accounts using the textbook numbering system as a guide.

---

4. Shown below and in your Workbook is a chart for the rules of debit and credit. Complete the chart in your Workbook by writing the words "increase" or "decrease" in the appropriate spaces.

Assets = Liabilities + Owner's Equity

Assets		Liabilities		Capital		Revenue	
DEBIT	CREDIT	DEBIT	CREDIT	DEBIT	CREDIT	DEBIT	CREDIT

Drawings		Expense	
DEBIT	CREDIT	DEBIT	CREDIT

5. **From the following information for the month ended November 30, 19—, prepare an income statement for Atlas Associates.**

Fees Earned, $31 700; Salaries Expense, $13 400; Rent Expense, $6 000; General Expense, $1 200; Advertising Expense, $600; Car Expense, $3 700; Light and Heat Expense, $3 500.

6. **In your Workbook complete the following schedule by filling in the blanks for each of the five separate equity section relationships.**

	1.	*2.*	*3.*	*4.*	*5.*
Beginning capital	6	6	15		62
Total revenues	10		29		
Total expenses	8	11		30	35
Net income or loss (–)		14	11	20	–5
Drawings	3	12		15	
Increase or decrease (–) in equity			–6		–10
Ending capital				10	

5.3 COMPUTERS IN ACCOUNTING: USING SPREADSHEETS EFFICIENTLY

One of the advantages of spreadsheets mentioned in Chapter 3 was speed. This specifically referred to how fast calculations can be performed. This advantage would be lost by accountants, however, if they had to spend a lot of time typing the large number of formulas and functions that a typical spreadsheet model contains.

To help accountants work efficiently, all spreadsheet programs have the time-saving ability to copy the contents of cells. Consider Figure 5.7.

	A	B	C	D	E
1			SALES REPORT		
2	BRANCH	1ST 6 MOS.	2ND 6 MOS.	TOTAL	COMMISSIONS
3					
4	KAMLOOPS	$45 000	$41 000	$86 000	$4 300
5	MEDICINE HAT	$32 000	$37 000	$69 000	$3 450
6	SASKATOON	$41 000	$38 000	$79 000	$3 950
7	WINNIPEG	$52 000	$47 000	$99 000	$4 950
8					
9	COMMISSIONS	5%			

Figure 5.7   Spreadsheeting a sales report.

The total for the Kamloops branch at D4 is produced by the formula =B4+C4. For the Medicine Hat branch the formula is identical except that the cells are on line 5. Similarly, the cells for the Saskatoon branch are on line 6 and for the Winnipeg branch on line 7. Instead of typing in the formulas one at a time, they can easily be inserted all at one time by using the COPY command. This is done by calling up the *command* menu, selecting the *copy* option, and following the computer's requests for information (prompts). The formula from D4 (the source cell) will be copied automatically into D5, D6, and D7 (the destination cells). The row references will adjust automatically so that the correct branch totals are produced.

Relative Cell References

The formula at D4 (=B4+C4) contains relative cell references. Simply put, these are row and column references that will change when the copy command is used.

The adaptability of relative cell references is one of the most useful features of spreadsheets. Hundreds of formulas can be created in seconds.

Absolute Cell References

There are times when an accountant does not want a cell reference to change when formulas are copied. Consider cell E4 in Figure 5.7. The formula to produce $4 300 is =D4*B9 (the * is the multiplication symbol used by spreadsheets). If this formula is copied downward, errors will result because the reference to B9 will change and the other totals in column D will not be multiplied by B9 which contains the commission rate of 5%.

To correct this problem, the B9 reference must be made absolute before the formula is copied. Most spreadsheets do this when $ signs are entered before the row and column references. For example, the formula at E4 should be =D4*B9. When this formula is copied down to E7, the formula will be =D7*B9. The reference to cell B9 has not changed, so that the totals for each of the branches get multiplied by 5%.

Relative cell references, then, change when they are copied; absolute cell references do not. An understanding of both is necessary if an accountant is to make speedy and accurate use of spreadsheets.

Choosing Commands

To load files, save files, print files, copy formulas, and perform many other tasks, spreadsheet users must have access to a number of commands. Some spreadsheets require a keyboard character (it is the "/" for Lotus 1,2,3) to be struck to show a list of commands. A letter will then be typed to select a command, and further options will appear. These spreadsheets are said to be character-based (See Figure 5.8).

Some spreadsheets have recently become more visual by allowing users to "pull down" menus in order to select commands. The cursor keys or a mouse may then be used to select further options (See Figure 5.9).

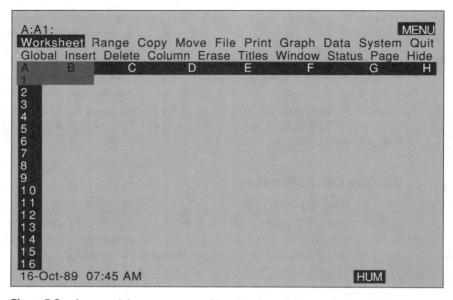

Figure 5.8   A spreadsheet program with a command menu.

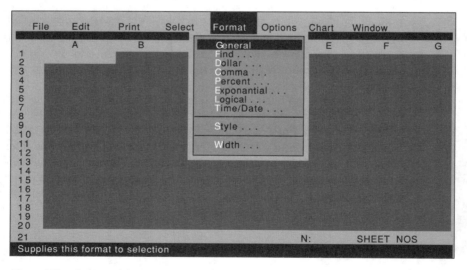

Figure 5.9   A spreadsheet program with a pull-down menu.

Regardless of the type of system your spreadsheet uses, to properly use the copy command you will be asked to identify the source cell or cells; these are the cells you are copying from. Then you will select the destination cell or cells which represent the location you are copying to. After completing the command and observing all the correct figures that were instantly produced, you will gain a new sense of number-crunching power.

SPREADSHEET EXERCISES

Professional Engineering and Consulting, Case 1, page 137

1. 1. **Load the spreadsheet model named CH5 from your data disk into your computer.** The income statements for Professional Engineering and Consulting should now be seen.
   2. **Note that the text does not ask for the change in every income statement item.** Such information is useful and with a spreadsheet, you will be able to produce the figures very quickly.
   3. The first calculation is the Consulting Revenue. **At F10, enter =D10–E10. If this formula produces the correct result, use the copy command to reproduce it.** The source cell is F10 and the destination cells are F11 to F31.
   4. Although your work is basically finished, you may want to improve the appearance of your model. **Where necessary, learn how to use your spreadsheet commands to format numbers with dollar signs, and to "blank" cells that show zero.**

Challenge Exercise

2. 1. Column G will be used to express the 19-7 expenses, total expenses, and net income as percentages of total revenue. Only one formula is again required: **at G17, divide the 19-7 Advertising by 19-7 Total Revenue. Learn the commands to format this cell to a percentage correct to two decimal places.**
   2. **Copy this formula down to G31.** Errors should result. **Examine the contents of some of the destination cells to understand why.**
   3. You should have determined that the destination cells were not divided by the Total Revenue cell. When the Total Revenue reference is copied downward, it must not change. It must be made absolute. **Edit the formula at G17 to =D17/D14 and repeat the copy command.**

COMPUTER REVIEW QUESTIONS

1. What is a relative cell reference?
2. What must be done to make sure that a cell reference is relative?
3. Why is the copy command necessary?
4. Explain the difference between a source cell and a destination cell.
5. Explain how to gain access to the copy command of your spreadsheet program.

Communicate It

Use the completed CH5 spreadsheet model to help prepare the report required by Part B of Case 1 on page 138. If you are using an integrated software package, copy the model to the word processing section. Also, spreadsheet programs can make charts and graphs. You can increase the effectiveness of your report by graphing key figures from the income statements.

CHAPTER HIGHLIGHTS

Now that you have completed Chapter 5, you should:

1. understand net income and net loss and be able to calculate both;
2. be able to prepare a basic income statement from supplied figures;
3. understand the importance of the income statement to owners, managers, and other interested parties;
4. understand that the data for the income statement are accumulated in special accounts in the equity section of the ledger;
5. be able to define revenue, expense, and drawings;
6. be able to make simple analyses and comparisons from given financial data;
7. be able to use the term "on account" in the four customary ways;
8. know the reason why businesses prefer to buy on credit;
9. know three new generally accepted accounting principles: the time period concept, the revenue recognition convention, and the matching principle.

ACCOUNTING TERMS

accounting period	net loss
chart of accounts	payment on account
drawings	purchase on account
expense	receipt on account
fiscal period	revenue
income statement	revenue recognition convention
matching principle	sale on account
net income	time period concept

CHAPTER EXERCISES

Using Your Knowledge

1. **For each of the accounts listed, indicate whether it would normally have a debit or credit balance.**

   Supplies; Advertising Expense; A. Bryce, Drawings; G. Wright, a creditor; Rent Expense; Fees Earned; Bank Loan; W. Magill, a debtor; A. Bryce, Capital; Mortgage Payable; Automobile.

2. Mrs. E. Foreman owns and operates a small florist shop in Gander, Newfoundland. She deposits all cash received in the bank and makes all payments by cheque. At the end of the last fiscal period, the Bank account showed a credit balance of $1 350 after all balances were found to be correct.

1. **Assuming no errors, how is it possible for the Bank, an asset account, to have a credit balance?**
2. **If, during the fiscal period, the revenues exceeded the expenses by $2 000 and the drawings amounted to $2 600, what is the net income figure for the period?**

3. The income statement of Bianco Company is shown below.

BIANCO COMPANY
INCOME STATEMENT
YEAR ENDED DECEMBER 31, 19—

Revenue		$47 416
Expenses		
Car Expense	$ 1 732	
Rent	3 500	
Utilities	1 075	
Wages	23 072	29 379
Net income		$18 037

Two errors were found in the books after the above statement was prepared:

a. A bill for $750 for automobile repairs had been incorrectly debited to Automobiles.
b. $5 000 of owner's drawings had been incorrectly debited to Wages.
Prepare a corrected income statement.

4. The account balances in the ledger of Pamela Garside, a sculptor, are shown on p. 134 in the T-accounts.

Pamela's auditor discovered the following errors when checking the records:
a. $150 of cash revenue was credited incorrectly to the Capital account.
b. $500 of the owner's drawings was debited incorrectly to the Wages account.
c. $400 of automobile expense was debited incorrectly to the Automobiles account.
d. $110 of equipment was incorrectly debited to Car Expense.

1. **In your Workbook, write out the changes in the accounts necessary to correct the above errors.**
2. The net income figure prior to the auditor's discoveries was determined to be $4 340. **What will the corrected income figure be?**

Bank	A.R. – P. Adler	A.R. – A. Jackson	Equipment
1 745	50	70	5 000

Supplies	Automobiles	A.P. – Century Finance	A.P. – B & B Stone
610	7 900	5 500	110

P. Garside, Capital	P. Garside, Drawings	Revenue	Car Expense
5 625	200	11 920	500

Light, Heat, Water	Rent	Wages
280	300	6 500

---

5. With the expanded ledger, the accounting equation now appears as shown below. **In your Workbook, complete the schedule by filling in the rectangles with the correct figures for Penny Company over a four-year period.**

	Assets	=	Liabilities	+	Beginning Capital	+	Revenues	–	Expenses	–	Drawings
End of											
Year 1	100	=	20	+	70	+	60	–	45	–	5
Year 2	120	=	30	+		+	90	–	60	–	
Year 3	130	=		+		+	105	–	80	–	20
Year 4		=	30	+		+	110	–	95	–	10

---

6. A partially completed summary of financial data is given below. The data pertain to the fundamental accounting equation for Hugh Miller over a period of two years.

	Assets	*Liabilities*	*Equity*
End of 19–1		$27 400	
End of 19–2			$19 300

In your Workbook fill in the missing figures, given that:

1. revenues for 19-2 are $42 000;
2. expenses for 19-2 are $22 000;
3. drawings for 19-2 are $18 000;
4. the assets decreased by $5 000 from the end of 19-1 to the end of 19-2.

Comprehensive Exercise

7. N.A. James, a public accountant, decided to begin a business of his own on October 1, 19—. At that time he invested in the business a bank balance of $5 000 and an automobile of $18 000.

Note on the Handling of Supplies in Exercises

It is common practice in accounting to allow the Supplies account to become incorrect during the accounting period, and to make it correct at the end of the accounting period. This is a technique used by accountants for convenience.

In your accounting entries:

- When supplies are purchased, make the following accounting entry for their cost.
   Dr Supplies and Cr Accounts Payable or Bank
- When supplies are used up in the business, make no accounting entry.

The technique for updating the Supplies account is treated in Chapter 9.

N.A. James
Chart of Accounts

101 Bank
110 Account Receivable—Jenkins and Co.
120 Office Supplies
125 Office Equipment
130 Automobile
210 Account Payable—Office Supply Company
301 N.A. James, Capital
302 N.A. James, Drawings
401 Fees Earned
505 Advertising Expense
510 Car Expense
515 Donations Expense
520 Miscellaneous Expense
525 Rent Expense

The accounts required are provided for you in the Workbook. Also, there is a ruled chart for you to write down the changes caused by the transactions.

1. Work out the changes for the above transaction. Record these changes on the chart provided and in the T-accounts.

2. For each of the transactions listed below, work out the changes for the transaction and record these changes on the chart provided and in the T-accounts.

TRANSACTIONS

1. Purchased $300 of office supplies for cash. Issued a cheque in payment.
2. Issued a cheque for $50 for an advertisement in a local newspaper.
3. Received a bill from Office Supply Company in regard to the purchase of a desk, a chair, and a filing cabinet at a total cost of $1 100 on account.
4. Mr. James was hired by a client, Jenkins and Co. At the conclusion of the work, Mr. James charged Jenkins and Co. $900 and issued a bill for this service performed on account.
5. B. Masters, a client, paid $100 in cash for a bookkeeping service. W. Shields, another client, paid $75 in cash for having her tax return prepared. The total of $175 was deposited in the bank.
6. A cheque for $100 was sent as a donation to the Salvation Army.
7. A cheque for $300 was received from Jenkins and Co. on account.
8. A cheque was issued to Office Supply Company in full payment of the balance of its account.
9. Paid Louis's Service Station $120 for gasoline and repairs to the business automobile. A cheque was issued right away.
10. Performed an accounting service for T. Wu and received $200 cash in full payment. The owner, N.A. James, did not deposit this money in the bank, but kept it for his personal use.
11. Issued a cheque for $750 in payment of the rent for the month of October.
12. Purchased $120 of office supplies from Grand and Toy. The purchase was paid for by cheque.
13. Issued a cheque for $50 for an advertisement in a local newspaper.
14. Issued a bill for $600 to Jenkins and Co. for accounting services performed on account.
15. Issued a cheque for $70 for postage stamps. (**Note:** Stamps are not considered to be supplies.)
16. Issued a cheque for $500 to the owner for his personal use.

3. Balance the ledger by means of a trial balance.
4. Prepare an income statement for the period, which is the month of October, 19—.

For Further Thought

8. Briefly answer the following questions.

1. In earlier chapters there was no income statement to show the net income of a business. How can the owner calculate net income without producing an income statement?

2. John earns a salary of $8 000 and Gary earns a salary of $10 000. Who has the better earnings? Explain.

3. The rules say that a credit entry is required to increase equity. Explain why an expense account, which is part of the equity, requires a debit entry to increase it.

4. Explain why there are usually only one or two revenue accounts but a number of expense accounts.

5. Which way would you organize the expense accounts in the ledger? Explain the reason for your choice.

6. What information from the financial statements would a banker for a business be particularly interested in?

7. A company may have fiscal periods of any length as long as it also produces a financial statement annually. Why does a company have to produce an annual statement?

8. Suppose that you were handed a ledger and asked to determine the equity. Describe two ways that this can be done.

9. Give appropriate names for the Revenue account for the following businesses:

   a. a doctor;   **d.** a dry cleaning company;
   b. a loan company;   **e.** a photographer;
   c. a real estate company;   **f.** a hairdresser.

10. You now know seven GAAPs. Name them.

11. A business could be quite profitable and yet have money problems. Give one reason why this might happen.

12. The text states that accounts with credit balances are either liabilities, equity, or revenue. Still, it is possible for the Bank account to have a credit balance. Explain this apparent inconsistency.

13. Give three reasons why businesses prefer to make their purchases on credit.

14. Why is it just as important to control the expenses of a business as it is to increase the revenue?

15. Bonanza Burger sells hamburgers for $.89. Burger Giant sells them for $1.09. And yet, Bonanza Burger makes a larger profit.
    Give two reasons why this is possible.

CASE STUDIES

CASE 1   *Analyzing an Income Statement Covering Two Years*

Shown on page 138 is an income statement for Professional Engineering and Consulting showing the figures for 19-7 and 19-6. Study these income statements and answer the questions that follow.

PROFESSIONAL ENGINEERING AND CONSULTING
INCOME STATEMENT
YEAR ENDED JUNE 30, 19-7 and 19-6

	19-7	19-6
Revenues		
Consulting	$ 62 250	$ 60 402
Construction	202 365	290 201
Designing	35 250	36 603
Total Revenue	$299 865	$387 206
Operating Expenses		
Advertising	$ 3 520	$ 3 400
Automobiles Expense	25 025	16 350
Bank Charges	15 850	1 200
Building Expenses	4 200	3 700
Equipment Maintenance	1 525	1 750
Insurance	5 014	2 000
Light, Heat, and Water	3 124	3 107
Miscellaneous Expense	312	250
Property Taxes	1 215	950
Telephone	1 507	704
Wages	102 301	78 201
Total Expenses	$163 593	$111 612
Net Income	$136 272	$275 594

Questions

Part A
1. Calculate the change in the total revenues.
2. Calculate the change in the total expenses.
3. Name the four expense accounts that show the greatest increase.
4. Calculate the change in the net income.

Part B
The owner, C. Haywood, is quite concerned about the dramatic decrease in net income from 19-6 to 19-7. Prepare a brief report explaining mathematically the drop in profit. A useful technique for you to attempt at this time is the making of percentage comparisons.

CASE 2   *Studying Results of Operation*

Shown on page 139 are the results of operation for Dr. Tanis Tamo for a five-year period.

DR. TANIS TAMO
OPERATING RESULTS (in thousands)

	19-1	19-2	19-3	19-4	19-5
Revenue					
Fees Earned	$143	$160	$184	$214	$239
Expenses					
Car Expense	$20	$22	$23	$25	$27
Insurance	8	8	9	12	13
Light & Heat	15	16	17	20	22
Office Expense	11	11	13	17	18
Rent	12	12	12	15	18
Telephone	5	5	6	7	8
Wages	20	22	28	30	33
Total Expenses	$91	$96	$108	$126	$139
Net Income	$52	$64	$76	$88	$100

Questions

1. On graph paper draw a five-year graph of a) the revenue, and b) the total expenses. This can be in the form of a bar graph or a line graph.
2. Are total expenses increasing as fast as revenue over the five years?
3. Which expense has the greatest percentage increase?
4. Which expense has the least percentage increase?
5. Revenues are expected to rise by only two per cent in 19-6. This is because the work-load is near its maximum. Dr. Tamo is anxious to increase her net income in 19-6 to $110 000. How can this possibly be done? Give a specific suggestion.

CASE 3   *Perspective on Financial Statements*

Neil Poje of Nolalu, Ontario, has an oil distribution business. The business has a $50 000 bank loan with a local bank. Following normal practice, the bank manager has requested a copy of the financial statements of the business for the latest year. Neil has provided her with audited financial statements. In simplified form, these statements are as follows:

POJE FUELS
INCOME STATEMENT
YEAR ENDED JUNE 30, 19—

Revenues		$250 000
Expenses		
Cost of Oil	150 000	
Other Expenses	65 000	
Total Expenses		215 000
Net Income		$ 35 000

POJE FUELS
BALANCE SHEET
JUNE 30, 19—

Assets

Cash	$ 5 000
Accounts Receivable	14 000
Inventory of Oil	100 000
Other Assets	70 000
Total Assets	$189 000

Liabilities and Equity

Bank Loan	$ 50 000
Accounts Payable	30 000
Total Liabilities	$ 80 000
Owner's Equity	109 000
Total Liabilities and Equity	$189 000

Questions

1. Why does a bank manager request financial statements?
2. In your opinion, should Neil Poje be satisfied with the net income figure?
3. Why might the bank manager be concerned about the bank loan?
4. Give an explanation for the business being short of cash.
5. The inventory of oil is shown at $100 000. What could happen to make this figure higher or lower?
6. What could the bank manager require (if it has not already been done) to make the bank's position more secure?
7. The bank manager will probably compare this set of financial statements with those of previous years. Of what use would this be?
8. If you were the bank manager, what action would you take regarding this loan?

CASE 4   *Analyzing the Records of a Business*

Shown on page 141 in comparative form are the account balances of Metro Haulage Company for the years 19-3, 19-4, 19-5, and 19-6. The net income figures for 19-4 and 19-5 are also shown.

	19-3	19-4	19-5	19-6
Assets				
Cash	$ 500	$ 500	$ 500	$ 500
Accounts Receivable	10 000	11 000	12 000	12 000
Supplies	1 000	1 000	1 100	1 100
Land and Building		100 000	100 000	100 000
Equipment	4 000	5 000	5 000	10 000
Trucks	25 000	25 000	50 000	50 000
Total Assets	$40 500	$142 500	$168 600	$173 600
Liabilities and Equity				
Accounts Payable	$ 5 500	$ 6 000	$ 6 000	$ 10 000
Bank Loan	10 000	10 000	25 000	
Mortgage Payable		80 000	75 000	70 000
Owner's Equity	25 000	46 500	62 600	93 600
Total Liabilities and Equity	$40 500	$142 500	$168 600	$173 600
Net Income (Profit)		$35 000	$40 000	

Questions

1. In 19-4:
  a. In detail, explain the increase in the total assets.
  b. What were the sources of the funds that were used to acquire the above assets?
  c. How much money did the owner take out of the business?
2. In 19-5:
  a. In detail, explain the increase in the total assets.
  b. In addition to the assets in a), what else were funds needed for?
  c. What were the sources of funds used to pay for a) and b) above?
  d. How much money did the owner take out of the business?
3. In 19-6:
  a. By how much did the total assets increase?
  b. For what else was money needed in 19-6?
  c. Where did the money come from to pay for a) and b) above?
  d. Calculate the profit of the company if the owner took $19 000 out of the business.

CAREER
Robert Hunt, CMA / Intermediate Accountant

Robert Hunt was born in Lennoxville, Québec, where his family lived until just after he finished high school. Robert enjoyed his accounting courses in high school to such a degree he decided to pursue an accounting career. His family moved to Sherbrooke, Québec, and thereafter, Robert went to work as a payroll clerk with C.P. Clare Ltd., a firm that manufactures computer parts and printers. As a payroll clerk, he calculated the hours worked by employees, calculated employee bonuses, and prepared various reports for the cost accountant. Since most of the company's business is done in French, it is fortunate for Robert that he is fully bilingual.

Robert soon decided to obtain a professional degree in accounting. He enrolled in the Certified Management Accountants (CMA) program and began taking courses at night, while working full time during the day. After a few years of study, Robert earned the right to use the letters CMA after his name.

Robert was quickly promoted to junior accountant. In this position, he controlled accounts receivable and accounts payable, prepared bank reconciliation statements, and kept track of the company's cash payments.

He presently works as an intermediate accountant for two of the companies controlled by Vitesse Transport Limitée, a firm that transports freight. He reports directly to the management accountant. His major duty is preparing two monthly financial statements: the income statement and the balance sheet. To prepare these statements, Robert must reconcile four different bank accounts each month. He must also maintain control of all fixed assets of the business and prepare the monthly trial balance of the general ledger. In addition to these duties, Robert makes sure that the company's taxes are paid. Finally, he prepares Statistics Canada reports for government use, providing a list of the company's major expenditures and other statistical information.

Robert's career in accounting is progressing well. If he continues his hard work and keeps himself informed through further study of generally accepted accounting principles, he should rise quickly to a key accounting position.

DISCUSSION

1. What are some of the accounting duties Robert performs?
2. Write a report on the Certified Management Accountants program. Include the following information in your report:
   • educational requirements;
   • business communications requirements;
   • fees;
   • number of courses to earn the CMA designation;
   • courses that are studied.
3. What generally accepted accounting principles are important to Robert when he prepares his financial statements?
4. Outline some of the duties of a cost accountant. What are some of the reports Robert would prepare for the cost accountant?
5. What do you think would be some of the advantages of being bilingual if you were to enter the business world in the future?
6. How does Robert maintain control over all the fixed assets of Vitesse Transport Limitée?
7. Why does a business such as Vitesse Transport Limitée have four different bank accounts?

The Journal and Source Documents

6.1 The Journal
6.2 Source Documents
6.3 Sales Tax

6.1 THE JOURNAL

In the last two chapters, you have practised analyzing transactions to determine what accounts were affected and whether the accounts should be debited or credited. You recorded the changes caused by transactions—referred to by accountants as *entries* —in ledger accounts called T-accounts.

However, ledger accounts alone do not satisfy all the needs of accounting. As we have seen, each transaction requires two or more entries which must balance. In a ledger, each entry is recorded in a separate account. The accounts are on different pages. Therefore as transactions mount up, the bits and pieces of the accounting entries become scattered throughout the ledger. The details for any one transaction become difficult to put back together. Yet this is often necessary to do. It is for this reason that accountants use another book, called a *journal*, to keep all the entries together, transaction by transaction. The entries are actually recorded in the journal *before* they are recorded in the ledger accounts.

A **journal** is a book in which the accounting entries for all transactions are *first recorded*, before they are recorded in the ledger accounts. Each transaction is recorded separately. The transactions are recorded in the order of their occurrence. In this way, the journal provides an important continuous record of all transactions.

The Two-Column General Journal

There are several different types of journals used in accounting. The simplest one, and the one you will study in this chapter, is the two-column general journal. A two-column general journal page is shown in Figure 6.1. You will see readily that it has two money columns, one for the debit amounts and one for the credit amounts. There are also columns for Date, Particulars (account names and explanations), and PR (Posting Reference, explained on page 186).

General Journal Facts

GENERAL JOURNAL   PAGE _16_

DATE		PARTICULARS	P.R.	DEBIT	CREDIT
Nov.	9	Supplies		135—	
		Bank			135—
		Letterhead and envelopes;			
		Cheque #40			
	12	Equipment		900—	
		Supplies		400—	
		Accs. Payl-Olivetti			1100—
		Bank			200—
		IBM typewriter, ribbons and			
		stationery; cheque #41			
	28	Accs. Payl-Woodwards		750—	
		Bank			750—
		Partial Payment; cheque #42			
Dec.	3	Accs. Recl- W. Hill		300—	
		Revenue			300—
		Service on account			
	17	Bank		5000—	
		Bank Loan			5000—
		Increase in bank loan			

Figure 6.1   A page from a two-column general journal.

Pages numbered consecutively

Each journal entry balances.

Blank line between transactions

A "compound entry" affects more than two accounts.

Abbreviations permitted

Simple brief explanations

There are five transactions recorded in the journal in Figure 6.1. The transactions are separated by blank lines, making it easy to recognize them individually. The accounting entries for the transactions are referred to as journal entries.

A **journal entry** is made up of all the accounting changes for one transaction, in the form in which it is written in the general journal. The transactions are recorded in the journal in a specific way. Notice that the debited account and amount are recorded first. The credited account and amount are recorded second and are indented. Notice that for each transaction there is at least one debit amount and one credit amount, and the total of the debit amounts is equal to the total of the credit amounts. This is the case with every complete journal entry.

Journalizing is the process of recording accounting entries in the journal. The journal is known as a **book of original entry** because each balanced accounting entry is recorded there first. The basic process of recording transactions first in the journal and then in the ledger is shown by the chart in Figure 6.2.

Transactions occur.	→	Transactions are recorded in a journal in order by date.	→	The accounting entries are transferred to the ledger accounts.

Figure 6.2   The first three steps in the accounting cycle.

Journalizing in the Two-Column General Journal

Recording the Date

The following is the customary procedure for recording the date in the date column of a journal.

1. **The year**   Enter the year in small figures on the first line of each page. Do not repeat it for each entry. Enter a new year at the point on the page where it occurs.
2. **The month**   Enter the month on the first line of each page. Do not repeat it for each entry. Enter a new month at the point where it occurs.
3. **The day**   Enter the day on the first line of each journal entry. The day is repeated no matter how many transactions occur on any given day.

Steps in Recording a Journal Entry

There are four steps in recording a general journal entry. These are as follows:

1 Enter the day in the date column.

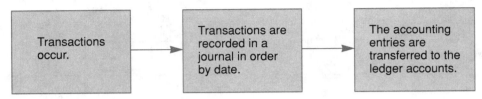

2 Enter the names of the accounts to be debited at the left margin of the Particulars column. Enter the debit amounts in the Debit money column.

DATE	PARTICULARS	P.R.	DEBIT	CREDIT
12	*Equipment*		9 0 0 —	
	Supplies		4 0 0 —	

3 Enter the names of the accounts to be credited. They are indented about 2.5 cm in the Particulars column. Enter the credit amounts in the Credit column.

12	Equipment		9 0 0 —			
	Supplies		4 0 0 —			
	Accs Payl – IBM				1 1 0 0 —	
	Bank				2 0 0 —	

4 Write a brief explanation for the entry beginning at the left margin of the Particulars column on the line beneath the last credit item.

12	Equipment		9 0 0 —			
	Supplies		4 0 0 —			
	Accs Payl – IBM				1 1 0 0 —	
	Bank				2 0 0 —	
	I.B.M. typewriter, ribbons and					
	stationery; cheque #41					

Usefulness of the General Journal

The chief purpose of the general journal is to provide a continuous record of the accounting entries in the order in which they occur. But this is not its only use.

The accounting clerk works out the accounting entries from the source documents and records them in the journal. The clerk can then see the work in an organized way. This is the time to check that each entry balances, and generally that everything is in order. A job done well at this stage reduces errors and prevents problems from occurring later.

The journal is also useful for reference purposes. It is often necessary to refer back to the journal to verify a transaction. This is particularly the case when balancing the ledger.

The Opening Entry

Every accounting entry is recorded first in the journal. This is done even for the very first accounting entry, the one that sets up the financial position from a balance sheet. The journal entry that starts the books off, or "opens" them, is known as the **opening entry**.

The opening entry for Shirley Cassar's photography business can be seen in Figure 6.3. The figures for this accounting entry came from a balance sheet prepared at the time.

Oct. 30	Bank	1 4 0 0 —			
	Supplies	2 4 2 5 —			
	Equipment	8 7 1 5 —			
	Automobile	19 5 5 0 —			
	Shirley Cassar, Capital			32 0 9 0 —	
	Opening financial position				
	of Shirley Cassar				

Figure 6.3   The opening entry for a small business.

SECTION REVIEW QUESTIONS

1. Explain what is meant by "the accounting entries become scattered throughout the ledger."
2. Why is a second book, the journal, necessary in accounting?
3. Define "journal."
4. What is a journal entry?
5. What is meant by "journalizing"?
6. Why is a journal known as a "book of original entry"?
7. Describe the appearance of a two-column general journal.
8. In the two-column general journal, how do you tell where one journal entry ends and another one begins?
9. Are abbreviations permitted in the journal?
10. Answer the following questions about the two-column general journal:
    a. Where is the year always entered?
    b. When do you re-enter the year?
    c. Where is the month always entered?
    d. When do you re-enter the month?
    e. What is the rule for recording the day of a transaction?
11. Which accounts are recorded first when recording a journal entry?
12. Which accounts are indented when recording a journal entry?
13. Describe how explanations are recorded in the journal.
14. Describe what is meant by the "opening entry".
15. What else does the journal provide besides a daily list of accounting entries?

SECTION EXERCISES

1. Tony's Repair Shop is owned and operated by Tony Castillo. The chart of accounts for his business is given below.

TONY'S REPAIR SHOP
CHART OF ACCOUNTS

Assets
105   Bank
110   A/R   C. Jacobs
115   A/R   D. Steiger
120   Supplies
125   Equipment

Liabilities
205   A/P   Western Electric
210   A/P   Ace Cartage

Owner's Equity
305   T. Castillo, Capital
310   T. Castillo, Drawings
405   Repair Revenue
505   Bank Charges
510   Light and Heat
515   Miscellaneous Expense
520   Rent
525   Truck Expense
530   Wages Expense

Journalize the following transactions for Tony's Repair Shop on page 17 of the two-column general journal provided in the Workbook.

TRANSACTIONS

19-5
Feb.

3   Paid the rent for February, $500 cash.
5   Paid $400 to Western Electric on account.
7   Performed a repair service for A. Abel for cash, $375.00.
10 The owner withdrew $200 cash for personal use.
11 Received $350 from C. Jacobs on account.
14 Paid $85 cash for repairs to the truck.
17 Paid $40 cash for gasoline for the truck.
24 Performed a repair service for D. Steiger on account, $275.
28 Paid $300 cash for wages for the month.

---

2. Paula Perna, a lawyer, has decided to open her own law office on June 1, 19-6. On that date she commenced business with the following assets and liabilities.

Assets		*Liabilities*	
Bank balance	$ 2 500	Acme Finance Company	$8 750
Law library	3 500	The Stationery Store	3 250
Office equipment	8 250		
Automobile	16 500		

1. Prepare a balance sheet for Paula Perna as of June 1, 19—.
2. Record the beginning financial position of Paula Perna on page 1 of a two-column general journal.
3. Journalize the following transactions for Paula Perna. Use the following chart of accounts.

Chart of Accounts

Assets	*Owner's Equity*
Bank	P. Perna, Capital
A/R R. Spooner	P. Perna, Drawings
A/R T. & R. Builders	Fees Earned
Office Supplies	Car Expense
Law Library	General Expense
Automobile	Rent Expense
Office Equipment	Wages Expense
Liabilities	
A/P Acme Finance	
A/P The Stationery Store	

TRANSACTIONS

June

1   Paid the rent for June, $500 cash.
2   Purchased typing and stationery supplies on account from The Stationery Store, $375.

3   Performed a legal service for cash, $200.
5   Performed a legal service on account for R. Spooner, $350.
8   Paid $1 000 cash to The Stationery Store on account.
10 Performed a legal service on account for T. & R. Builders, $1 100.
11 Received $350 on account from R. Spooner.
15 Paid $40 cash for gasoline for the business automobile.
20 Paid wages for part-time secretarial help, $250.
24 Paid $65 cash for postage.
24 Paid the regular monthly instalment to Acme Finance, $320.
30 Paula withdrew $450. Of this, $400 was for personal use and $50 was for gasoline for the business automobile.

3. The general journal shown below contains a number of errors. **Study the given journal and prepare a list describing these errors.**

GENERAL JOURNAL				PAGE	
DATE	PARTICULARS	P.R.	DEBIT	CREDIT	
Feb 3	Bank		200 —		
	Account Receivable – P. Simms			200 —	
	Partial payment from customer.				
Feb 7	Bank			50 —	
	Supplies		50 —		
	Pencils, pens, and papers				
	purchased from Reingolds.				
Feb 10	Bank		90 —		
	M. Farris, Capital		60 —		
	Equipment			250 —	
	Sold equipment ($250) for $90 cash.				
Feb 22	Account Payable – General Finance		315 —		
Feb 22	Bank			315 —	
	Account Receivable – N. Proulx		125 —		
	M. Farris, Capital			125 —	
	Service performed for cash.				
Mar 3	Supplies			20 —	
	Accounts Payable – Reingolds		20 —		
	Purchased folders on credit.				

4. A number of journal entries are shown below without dates or explanations. These entries are for a beauty shop operated by Kelly Marshall in Kapuskasing, Ontario.

   Examine these entries and prepare a list of transactions that could have caused them.

Bank	25	
Kelly Marshall, Capital		25
Supplies	30	
Bank		30
Kelly Marshall, Drawings	200	
Bank		200
Account Receivable—Jan Vasko	20	
Revenue		20
Supplies	70	
Account Payable—Fain Bros.		70

5. Rob Czank begins business with the following assets and liabilities: Cash, $1 200; Land, $42 500; Building, $85 900; Office Equipment, $3 900; Account Payable to Diamond Equipment, $350; Mortgage on Building, $32 560.

   After calculating the equity figure, record the opening entry for Rob Czank on August 1, 19— in a two-column general journal.

6. Described below are number of transactions of Clare Lehto Window Cleaning, located in Fredericton, New Brunswick. **On page 14 of a two-column general journal, record the journal entries for these transactions. Use the following accounts:**

   Bank
   Accounts Receivable—Various debtors
   Cleaning Supplies
   Accounts Payable—Various creditors
   C. Lehto, Capital
   C. Lehto, Drawings
   Revenue
   Miscellaneous Expense
   Telephone Expense
   Wages Expense

   ## TRANSACTIONS

   19-5

   April

   3   Received a cheque for $110 from P. Remus on account.
   6   Paid $300 to Walberg Bros. on account.
   9   Purchased $500 of cleaning supplies from Merrick Products on account.

10   Performed a cleaning service for a customer and received $157 cash in payment.
15   Paid the telephone bill in cash, $24.50.
19   The owner withdrew $400 for her personal use.
20   Paid $450 for wages.
25   Corrected an error in the accounts. The Supplies account had been debited $25 in error. The Miscellaneous Expense Account should have been debited.

6.2   SOURCE DOCUMENTS

As we have seen, transactions are first recorded by accounting personnel as journal entries. Where do these people obtain the information about the transactions? They obtain it from source documents. This topic was briefly introduced in Chapter 3. In this chapter, source documents will be studied in detail.

A number of business transactions are started outside the accounting department. These are transactions initiated not by accounting personnel, but by the owner, salespeople, department heads, managers, and other authorized people.

The accounting department is informed of the transactions by means of business papers which are sent to it. These business papers are called source documents. A **source document** is a business paper which shows the nature of a transaction and provides all the information needed to account for it properly. The accounting department uses the source documents as the basis for recording the accounting entries. Almost every accounting entry is based on a source document.

For some transactions there are no conventional source documents. The owner withdrawing money for personal use is an example. In such a case, the accounting entry must be supported by some other business paper or record. In this instance, a memorandum from the owner would be sufficient. In other cases, the supporting documents might be:

• detailed calculations prepared by the accounting department;
• a previous source document, such as a long-term rental agreement, which covers a series of transactions.

A company is required to keep source documents on file. They will be used within the office for reference purposes, locating errors, and so on. As well, source documents provide the factual evidence to verify transactions of the business. They provide the proof that the accounting records have been prepared accurately and honestly.

Several basic source documents will be explained and illustrated in the next few pages. For each, the journal entries are given and explained. They are considered to be basic source documents because they are used in the most common business transactions. A company called Masthead Marine, owned by David Scott of Vancouver, B.C., is used to illustrate these source documents and their journal entries. Masthead Marine is in the business of selling boats, marine equipment, and boat parts and supplies. The revenue account for Masthead Marine is called Sales.

Cash Sales Slip

A **cash sales slip** is a business form showing the details of a transaction in which goods or services are sold to a customer for cash. Usually, there is an original and two copies. The features of a cash sales slip and the uses for the copies are shown in Figure 6.4.

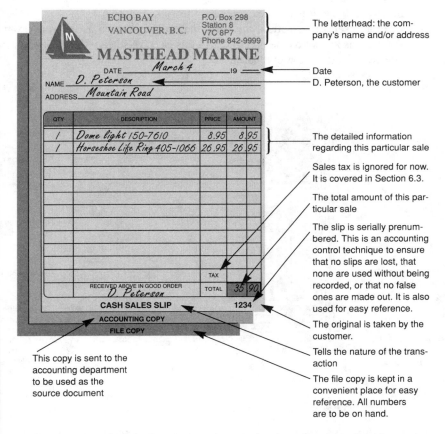

Figure 6.4　Cash sales slip representing a sale of goods or services for cash.

Journal Entry for a Cash Sales Slip

The accounting copy goes to the accounting department as the source document for the journal entry. For the above sales slip, the journal entry is:

	DR	CR
Bank	$35.90	
Sales		$35.90

A similar journal entry will be made for all cash sales slips.

Sales Invoice

Many businesses do not deal with the general public and therefore normally do not have cash sales. Businesses of this type make nearly all their sales on account. For each sale on account, a sales invoice is issued to the customer. A **sales invoice** is a business form showing the details of a transaction in which goods or services are sold on account. Usually there is an original and several copies. The features of a sales invoice and the uses for the copies are shown in Figure 6.5.

In any sales transaction, the party that sells is known as the vendor and the party that buys is known as the purchaser. In this case Masthead Marine is the vendor and S. & S. Boatworks is the purchaser.

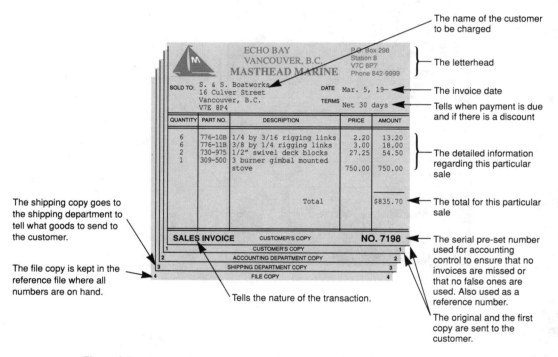

Figure 6.5 A sales invoice representing a sale of goods or services on account.

Journal Entry for a Sales Invoice

The accounting copy goes to the accounting department as the source document for the journal entry to record the sale. For this sales invoice the journal entry is:

	DR	CR
Account Receivable—S. & S. Boatworks	$835.70	
Sales		$835.70

A similar journal entry will be made for all sales invoices.

Dual Purpose Sales Slip

Some businesses dealing with the general public do business both for cash and on account. There is a business form that will handle both types of transaction. This is the dual purpose sales slip. A **dual purpose sales slip** is a business form showing the details of a transaction in which goods or services are sold either for cash or on account. There is a place on the form where the sales person checks off the type of transaction—cash, or charge. An example of a dual purpose sales slip is shown in Figure 6.6.

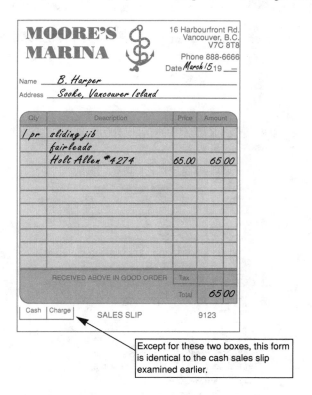

Figure 6.6   Dual purpose sales slip.

Journal Entry for a Dual Purpose Sales Slip

The journal entry for the source document shown above is:

	DR	CR
Account Receivable—B. Harper	$65.00	
Sales (Revenue)		$65.00

If the cash box had been checkmarked, the journal entry would have been

	DR	CR
Bank	$65.00	
Sales		$65.00

Purchase Invoice

Masthead Marine is not always the vendor company. Often, it makes purchases from other companies. Then it is the purchaser company. When Masthead Marine makes a purchase on account from a supplier, the company supplying the goods issues a sales invoice to Masthead Marine. When the vendor's invoice arrives at the office of Masthead Marine, it becomes a purchase invoice. A **purchase invoice** is a business form representing a purchase of goods or services on account. It is the name used in the office of the purchaser to differentiate between its own sales invoices and those of its suppliers.

Two examples of purchase invoices are shown in Figures 6.7 and 6.8.

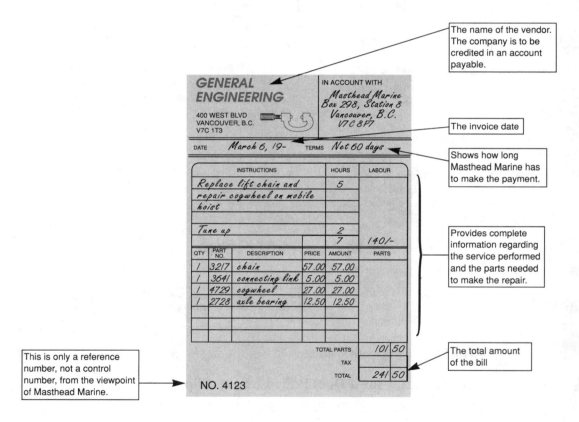

Figure 6.7   A purchase invoice for repairs to a lift truck.

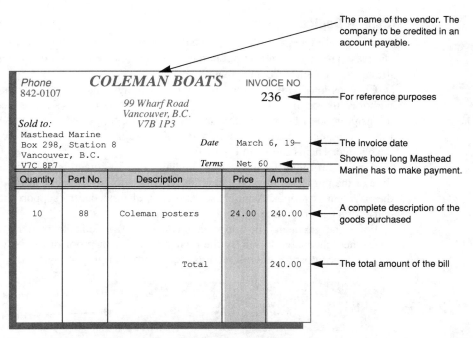

The name of the vendor. The company to be credited in an account payable.

For reference purposes

The invoice date

Shows how long Masthead Marine has to make payment.

A complete description of the goods purchased

The total amount of the bill

Figure 6.8   A purchase invoice for advertising posters.

Journal Entries for Purchase Invoices

Masthead Marine buys a variety of goods and services from numerous suppliers. No single journal entry will do for all the different items purchased. The account debited will depend on what particular goods or services are purchased. The account credited will always be the same—accounts payable.

The journal entry for the purchase invoice in Figure 6.7 is:

	DR	CR
Equipment Repairs	$241.50	
Account Payable—General Engineering		$241.50

The journal entry for the purchase invoice in Figure 6.8 is:

	DR	CR
Advertising Expense	$240.00	
Account Payable—Coleman Posters		$240.00

The above two entries show clearly:
• the account debited depends on the nature of the goods or services purchased;
• the account credited is always an account payable.

Cheque Copies

It has already been established that all payments are normally paid by cheque. The cheques themselves are sent out in the mail. A cheque copy is a document supporting the accounting entry for a payment by cheque.

Cheques may be issued for any number of things: cash purchases, wages, owner's withdrawals, payments on account, and so on. Most cheques are issued to pay for things previously bought on account and which are supported by purchase invoices on file. The purchase invoices being paid for are summarized on the tear-off portion of the cheque. This is shown in Figure 6.9.

A payment might be for a cash purchase, that is, something being paid for at the time of the purchase. In such a case, the cheque copy itself is not sufficient proof that the payment is proper. A purchase invoice is also needed to support the accounting entry for a cash purchase.

For some payments, no supporting voucher is needed. For owner's withdrawals, the cashed cheque endorsed by the owner is sufficient proof of proper payment. For wages, the company's payroll records are the proof of proper payment.

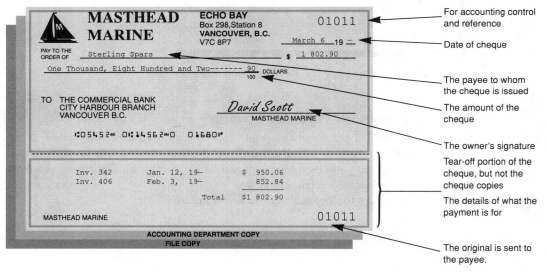

Figure 6.9   A cheque representing a payment made by the company. The accounting department copy of this cheque is the source document for the payment.

Journal Entry for a Cheque Copy

The accounting department copy is sent to the accounting department where it is used as the source document for the transaction. The debit part of the journal entry depends on the nature of the transaction. The credit part of the journal entry is always to Bank. For this particular cheque copy the journal entry is:

	DR	CR
Account Payable—Sterling Spars	$1 802.90	
Bank		$1 802.90

Cash Receipts Daily Summary

Each day, in business, some cheques or cash are usually received from customers. These are referred to as the "cash receipts." The cheques themselves cannot be kept to support the accounting entries. The cheques must be deposited in the bank. Therefore, before making the deposit a listing of the cash receipts is prepared by the mail clerk or another employee.

The **cash receipts daily summary** is a business paper which lists the money coming in from customers. The cash receipts list is the source document for the cash receipts accounting entries. This listing shows the names of the customers, the dollar amounts, and what the amounts are for in each case. To help prepare this form the clerk uses the information on the tear-off portions of cheques received, or remittance advices sent along with the cheques. A **remittance advice** is a form accompanying the cheque explaining the payment. Sometimes it is no more than a copy of the invoice.

A cash receipts daily summary is shown in Figure 6.10.

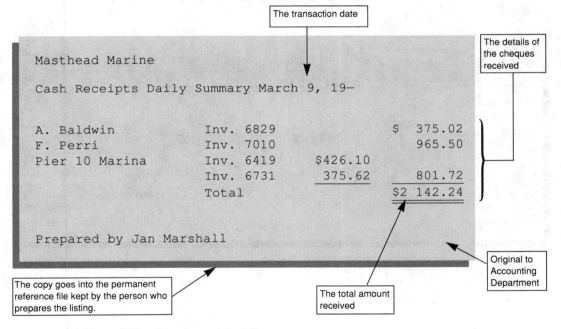

Figure 6.10   A cash receipts daily summary.

Journal Entry for a Cash Receipts Daily Summary

The original list goes to the accounting department as the source document for the accounting entry. For the cash receipts list above, the journal entry is:

	DR	CR
Bank	$2 142.24	
Account Receivable—A. Baldwin		$375.02
Account Receivable—F. Perri		$965.50
Account Receivable—Pier 10 Marina		$801.72

Bank Advices

There are times when the bank initiates a change in the bank account of a business. The bank informs the business of such a transaction by means of a bank advice or bank memo. A **bank debit advice** is a bank document informing the business of a decrease made in the business's bank account. A **bank credit advice** is a bank document informing the business of an increase made in the business's bank account.

In Figure 6.11, the Commercial Bank has sent a bank debit advice to Masthead Marine telling them that their account was charged interest on a bank loan.

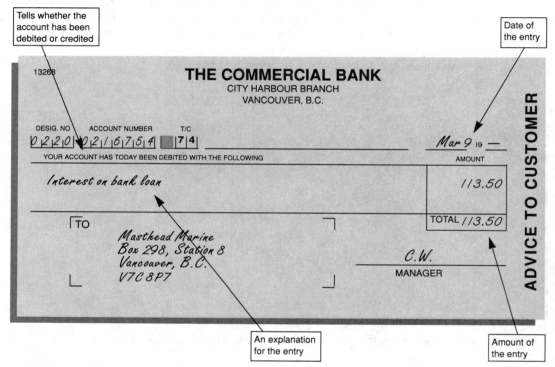

Figure 6.11   A bank advice.

Journal Entry for a Bank Advice

The bank advice goes to the accounting department as the source document for the journal entry. In this case the journal entry is:

	DR	CR
Bank Charges and Interest	$113.50	
Bank		$113.50

If the form had been a credit advice, the Bank account would have been debited and an appropriate account credited.

Summary of Source Documents and Related Journal Entries

Source Document	Transaction Description	Journal Entries	
		Account Debited	*Account Credited*
Cash sales slip	A sale of goods or services for cash	Bank	Sales
Sales invoice Charge sales slip	A sale of goods or services on account	Accounts Receivable	Sales
Purchase invoice	A purchase of goods or services on account	1. An expense account such as Advertising 2. An asset account such as Supplies or Equipment	Accounts Payable
Cheque copy	1. Paying an account payable 2. Cash purchase of an asset * 3. Cash payment for an expense * 4. Owner draws out money for personal use	1. A liability account such as Accounts Payable 2. An asset account such as Automobiles 3. An expense account such as Car Expense 4. The Drawings account	Bank
Cash receipts daily summary	The cheques received from customers on account	Bank	Accounts Receivable
Bank debit advice	Bank account decrease	Interest Expense	Bank
Bank credit advice	Bank account increase	Bank	Interest Earned

* Must be accompanied by a purchase invoice.

Additional Supporting Documents and Vouchers

In addition to the source documents listed above you may encounter the following:
• cash register slips;
• receipts, such as those for donations, or for postage;
• hydro bills, telephone bills;
• credit card or charge account statements;
• insurance endorsement certificates;
• written memos from the owner;
• bank statements;
• cash register internal tapes.

Number of Copies of Source Documents

There is no fixed number of required copies of business documents. Each business develops its own system to suit its own needs and preferences. Some owners and managers prefer a simple system, others a more elaborate one. The number of copies of any particular business document depends primarily on how elaborate the system is. Generally, the more elaborate the system, the greater the number of copies required to satisfy it.

GAAP—The Cost Principle

The cost principle states that **the accounting for purchases must be at the cost price to the purchaser**. In almost all cases, this is the figure that appears on the source document for the transaction. There is no place for guesswork or wishful thinking when accounting for purchases.

The value recorded in the accounts for an asset is not changed later if the market value for the asset changes. It would take an entirely new transaction based on new objective evidence to change the original value of an asset.

There are times when the above type of objective evidence is not available. In those instances, the transaction is recorded at fair market value, which must be determined by some independent means.

SECTION REVIEW QUESTIONS

1. Not all transactions requiring journal entries are initiated by the accounting staff. Explain.
2. How does the accounting department find out about all transactions?
3. What is a source document?
4. What is the principal use of source documents in the accounting department?
5. Give an example of a transaction for which there is no conventional source document.
6. Who else, besides the accounting department, may have reason to use the source documents on file?
7. What is the purpose of a cash sales slip?
8. Why is the cash sales slip regarded as less formal than the sales invoice?
9. Explain the essential difference between a sales invoice and a cash sales slip.
10. Explain who the "vendor" is.
11. Explain how to use the dual purpose sales slip.
12. What is a purchase invoice?
13. Explain why all journal entries for purchase invoices are not the same.
14. Why is a cheque not used as a source document?
15. What is the most common type of transaction for which a cheque is issued?
16. What supporting documents are needed for a cash purchase?
17. What is the supporting evidence for a payroll cheque?
18. Explain what cash receipts are.
19. Why is it necessary to prepare a cash receipts listing?

20. From what two sources does the clerk obtain the data to prepare the cash receipts listing?

21. Why do banks issue bank advices?

22. A bank debit memo requires a credit entry in the bank account of the business. Explain.

23. State the cost principle.

24. Why is an invoice regarded as an ideal source document?

SECTION EXERCISES

1. Answer the following questions related to the source document below.

1. What business document is it?

2. What is the purpose of the document?

3. Where does the information come from to prepare the list?

4. Why is a list prepared?

5. In the listing what does "on account" mean compared to "Invoice 4502"?

6. Give the journal entry that would be made as a result of the listing.

7. Who is G. Smalley?

SAYERS AND ASSOCIATES
CASH RECEIPTS DAILY SUMMARY
MARCH 14, 19—

Degagne Machine Shop	on account	$ 500.00
Kivella Bake Shop	Inv. 4502	315.43
Molner Paints	Inv. 3909	214.60
Robitaille Taxi	on account	200.00
G. Smalley	Total	$1 230.03

2. Answer the following questions related to the source document on p. 164.

1. What business document is it?

2. What is the purpose of the document?

3. Who is the issuer of the document?

4. Explain the purposes of the document number.

5. Give the journal entry that would be made by the issuer of the document.

```
┌──────────────────────────────────────────────────────────┐
│                                          Horseshoe Valley  │
│  DAVIDSON          ▲ ▲                    Ontario, L4M 4Y8  │
│  TREE             ▲ ▲ ▲                   Phone 321-8765    │
│  EXPERTS          ▲ ▲ ▲                                     │
│                                                            │
│                    Date    March 10   19 ———               │
│        NAME      F. Vailliant                              │
│        ADDRESS     Craighurst                              │
└──────────────────────────────────────────────────────────┘
```

QUANTITY	DESCRIPTION	PRICE	AMOUNT	
6	pruning of			
	mature trees,			
	removing dead			
	wood	30	180	–
2	cut down and			
	remove mature			
	trees	75	150	–
		TAX		
RECEIVED ABOVE IN GOOD ORDER		TOTAL	330	—

F. Vailliant

CASH SALES SLIP   2651

---

3. Answer the following questions related to the source document on p. 165.

1. What business document is it?

2. Who is the sender of the document? Who is the receiver?

3. To which business is this document the equivalent of a sales invoice? To which business is it a purchase invoice?

4. Give the journal entry that would be made by the sender of the document.

5. Give the journal entry that would be made by the receiver of the document.

Our file No. 3862

KNUTSEN AND TREBLEY
BARRISTERS, SOLICITORS

5200 Dufferin Street
Fredericton, New Brunswick
E3B 4A7

TO   Hansen and Company,
     Fredericton, New Brunswick,
     E3B 5B7

Re: Hansen and Company v. Lorimer Bros.
    Motor Vehicle Accident

   To our fee for all services herein, including office consultations, receiving instructions
and advising, obtaining police accident report
and interviewing witnesses, attending to issuing
Writ of Summons and arranging service thereof,
correspondence and negotiations with solicitors
for defendant and completion of settlement,
obtaining payment of settlement proceeds and
reporting to you, in all $450.00

Paid to issue Writ of Summons $17.00
Paid bailiff to serve Writ   21.50
Paid police for accident report 10.00   48.50

     Total fees and disbursements $498.50

This is our account set and subscribed
this 17th day of March, 19—. Per

P. Knutsen

---

4. The document on page 166 arrives at your place of business by mail. **Answer the following questions concerning it.**

   1. What business document is it?
   2. Who do you work for?
   3. Why was this document sent to your company?
   4. What does the broken line on the document represent?
   5. Explain the information beneath the broken line.
   6. Give the journal entry that would be made in the books of your company to record the source document.
   7. What happens to the upper part of this document?

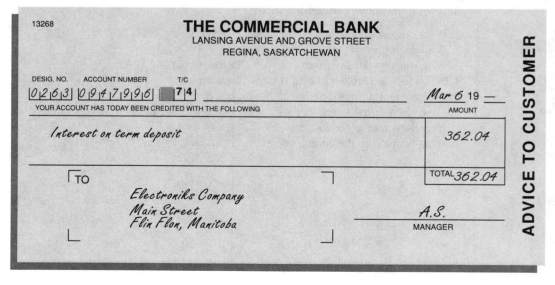

| CARBIDE TOOLS LIMITED | 4000 Essex Drive Vancouver, B.C. V7R 8S8 | No. 1101 |

May 10 ___ 19 —

PAY TO THE ORDER OF Presto-Can Company _____ $ 1 368.30

One Thousand, Three Hundred and Sixty-Eight---------- 30/100 **DOLLARS**

THE COMMERCIAL BANK
CITY HARBOUR BRANCH
VANCOUVER, B.C.

Marianne Mayo
CARBIDE TOOLS LIMITED

⑆030800301⑆⑈ 004⑆⑈030800301⑈

IN PAYMENT OF THE FOLLOWING

Invoice	Date	Amount
#6149	April 16	$ 217.02
#7002	April 30	400.12
#7109	May 7	751.16
	Total	$1 368.30

CARBIDE TOOLS LIMITED   1101

5. Answer the following questions related to the source document below.

1. What business document is it?
2. In whose books of account is a journal entry now necessary as a result of this source document?
3. Give the journal entry that would be made as a result of the source document.

| 13268 | **THE COMMERCIAL BANK** LANSING AVENUE AND GROVE STREET REGINA, SASKATCHEWAN | |

| DESIG. NO. | ACCOUNT NUMBER | T/C | | |
| 0 2 6 3 | 0 9 4 7 9 9 6 | 7 4 | *Mar 6* 19 — | AMOUNT |

YOUR ACCOUNT HAS TODAY BEEN CREDITED WITH THE FOLLOWING

Interest on term deposit 362.04

TO   *Electroniks Company Main Street Flin Flon, Manitoba*   TOTAL 362.04

A.S.
MANAGER

ADVICE TO CUSTOMER

6.3 SALES TAX

Sales tax is one way the federal and provincial governments raise funds. There is a lot of detailed regulation associated with sales tax: which items are taxed, which items are not, what forms are necessary, and so on. A business involved in the selling of goods or services needs someone in the office to be familiar with sales tax regulations. Government offices are set up in many communities to provide the necessary forms, regulations, and assistance.

This text will not deal with sales tax in a detailed way. Sales tax will be explained in simple terms only, to provide a view of the basic concepts and procedures.

Retail Sales Tax

A retail sales tax is charged by most provincial governments. A **retail sales tax** is a percentage tax based on the price of goods sold to a customer. The tax is added to the price and paid by the customer. The rates of tax vary from province to province and are established by the provincial governments. It is currently usual in Canada to tax the final consumer only. A sale from a wholesaler to a retailer would not be taxed.

Accounting for Sales Tax

The Purchaser

The purchaser of goods or services does no accounting for sales tax. The purchaser simply accounts for the transaction at the final figure on the sales slip, or invoice. This final figure includes the sales tax.

The Seller

The seller is charged with the responsibility of administering the sales tax. The seller is obliged to do the following:

1. calculate the tax and add it on to the normal price of the goods;
2. collect the tax from the customer;
3. accumulate the sales tax charged to the customers in a special liability account, called Sales Tax Payable;
4. pay the accumulated sales tax over to the government periodically. In some cases sales tax will be paid to the government before it is collected from the customer.

Sales Tax on a Cash Sale   The simplest transaction involving sales tax is the "cash sale." The seller determines the amount of the tax, adds it to the price, and collects the total from the customer. The cash sales slips used so far have not included sales tax. Now that we know about sales tax, this item will be included on the cash sales slips. Examine the cash sales slip in Figure 6.12.

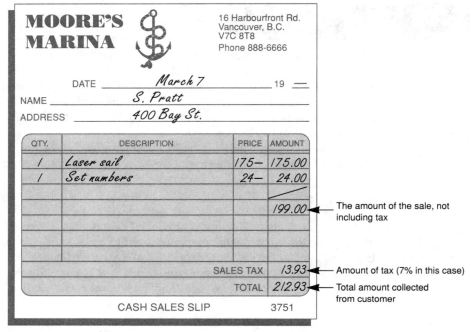

Figure 6.12   A cash sales slip on which a sales tax has been added.

Keep in mind that businesses do not forward immediately the tax they collect from customers every day. Sales tax must be paid to the government periodically, and therefore represents a liability payable to the government. Businesses accumulate the tax they collect in the Sales Tax Payable account. For the above sales slip, the journal entry is:

	DR	CR
Bank	$212.93	
Sales		$199.00
Sales Tax Payable		$13.93

Sales Tax on a Charge Sale   Sales tax is also added to a sale on account represented by a sales invoice. In Figure 6.13, a sales invoice is shown that includes a five per cent sales tax. With a charge sale the seller does not collect the tax at the time of the sale, but must wait until the customer pays his or her account. This is usually within 30 days.

The journal entry for the sales invoice on p. 169 is:

	DR	CR
Account Receivable—Marathon Recreation	$337.84	
Sales		$321.75
Sales Tax Payable		$16.09

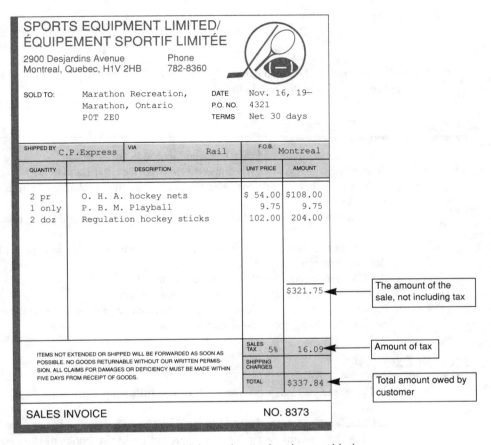

Figure 6.13 Sales invoice on which a sales tax has been added.

Remitting Sales Tax

Sales tax is collected for a month and then is paid over to the government. In most regions, the sales tax collected in any one month is to be paid to the government by the 15th of the following month. Taxes collected in January are to be paid by the 15th of February, and so on. From time to time, government auditors pay visits to businesses to check the accuracy of records, collections, and payments.

Assume that a total of $415.23 was recorded in the Sales Tax Payable account in the month of January. The T-account would appear as follows:

Sales Tax Payable
| | Jan   415.23 |

The account represents a liability owed by the business to the government. When the balance is paid, the journal entry to record the payment is:

	DR	CR
Sales Tax Payable	$415.23	
Bank		$415.23

The payment will clear the January balance. In the meantime, the sales tax items for February will be gathering in the account.

SECTION REVIEW QUESTIONS

1. Why do governments apply a sales tax on goods and services?
2. Where does one go to find out about sales tax rules and regulations?
3. What special accounting for sales tax is done by the purchaser of goods that have a tax added?
4. What four things is the seller of goods and services required to do regarding sales tax?
5. A cash sale of $100 is made. A sales tax of seven per cent is applied. How much does the customer pay?
6. What kind of account is the Sales Tax Payable?
7. Explain when to remit sales tax to the government.
8. Explain how a business person may be required to pay sales tax to the government before it has been collected from the customer.

SECTION EXERCISES

1. 1. Calculate the sales tax for each of the following if the rate of tax is five per cent.
   2. Calculate the total amount to be paid by the customer for each of the following.
   3. Give the journal entry for each transaction in the books of the vendor.

TRANSACTIONS

1. A cash sale of goods at a price of $75.
2. A cash sale of goods at a price of $120.
3. A charge sale of goods at a price of $58.60.
4. A charge sale of goods at a price of $98.00
5. A sale of goods at a price of $130 with a down payment of $50.

2. The invoice on page 171 was issued to Island Marina by Masthead Marine.

   1. Give the journal entry to be made in the books of the vendor.
   2. Give the journal entry to be made in the books of the purchaser, if the account to be debited is Merchandise Inventory.

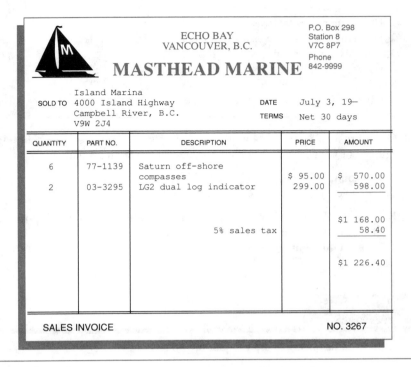

ECHO BAY
VANCOUVER, B.C.

MASTHEAD MARINE

P.O. Box 298
Station 8
V7C 8P7
Phone
842-9999

SOLD TO Island Marina
4000 Island Highway
Campbell River, B.C.
V9W 2J4

DATE July 3, 19—
TERMS Net 30 days

QUANTITY	PART NO.	DESCRIPTION	PRICE	AMOUNT
6	77-1139	Saturn off-shore compasses	$ 95.00	$ 570.00
2	03-3295	LG2 dual log indicator	299.00	598.00
				$1 168.00
		5% sales tax		58.40
				$1 226.40

SALES INVOICE   NO. 3267

3. Jack Pritchard paid $330.96, including five per cent sales tax, for some furniture.

1. **Calculate the price of the goods before the sales tax is added.**
   Use the following equation to solve for "price" (P):

$$P + \frac{5P}{100} = 330.96$$

2. **Calculate the sales tax on the goods.**
3. **Prove your work.**

4. **Examine the account below and answer the questions that follow.**

ACCOUNT *Sales Tax Payable*   No. *22*

DATE	PARTICULARS	PR	DEBIT	CREDIT	DR CR	BALANCE
Feb. 19- / 1	Forwarded				Cr	476 30
15			476 30			
28				242 95		
28				316 20	Cr	559 15
Mar. 15			559 15			
31				251 86		
31				302 19	Cr	554 05

1. How much sales tax was accumulated in January?
2. How much sales tax was accumulated in February?
3. What does the account balance represent?
4. How much sales tax was accumulated in March?
5. When will the sales tax accumulated in March be paid?
6. Give the journal entry that will be made for the transaction of April 15.

5. On February 28, 19—, Moore's Marina sold the goods shown below to Valerie Miniaci of Bear Island, Alberta. The sale was made on account.

| 2 | Grumman canoes | @ | $1 950.00 each |
| 4 | Paddles | @ | $215.00 a pair |

1. **In your Workbook write up the above sale on a dual-purpose sales slip. Sales tax at five per cent is to be added.**
2. **Give the journal entry in the vendor's books.**

CHAPTER HIGHLIGHTS

Now that you have completed Chapter 6, you should:

1. understand why a journal and a ledger are both used in the accounting process;
2. be able to record transactions in a two-column general journal;
3. be able to work out an opening entry from a balance sheet;
4. know the first three steps in the accounting cycle;
5. be able to recognize a number of basic source documents and understand the uses for the various copies;
6. know the journal entries for a number of source documents;
7. understand that source documents are part of an overall accounting system for controlling and recording accounting transactions;
8. understand the cost principle in recording transactions;
9. know the purpose of retail sales tax imposed by governments;
10. be able to calculate sales tax and to include sales tax in sales transactions;
11. know the journal entries for source documents containing sales tax;
12. know the journal entry for remitting sales tax to the government.

ACCOUNTING TERMS

bank credit advice
bank debit advice
book of original entry

cash receipts daily summary
cash sales slip
cost principle

dual purpose sales slip   purchase invoice
journal   remittance advice
journal entry   retail sales tax
journalizing   sales invoice
opening entry   source document

CHAPTER EXERCISES

Using Your Knowledge

1. **Identify the source document or documents that would support the following transactions:**

   a. debt paid on account
   b. supplies purchased for cash
   c. service performed on account
   d. money withdrawn by owner
   e. bank loan reduced
   f. donation paid by cash

   g. receipt from customer on account
   h. supplies purchased on account
   i. sale made on account
   j. service performed for cash
   k. bank interest charged
   l. hydro bill paid by cash

2. **The following exercise also appears in your Workbook.**

   Complete the following summary.

Nature of Transaction	Source Document or Documents	The Required Journal Entry	
		Account Debited	Account Credited
Payment on Account			
Sale on Account			
Bank Service Charge			
Cash Payment of Phone Bill			
Cash Received on Account			
Purchase of Equipment on Account			
Cash sale			

3. **The following exercise also appears in your Workbook.**

In the chart below, there is a list of numbered source documents to the left. To the right is a list of transactions. **You are to match the transactions with the source documents by writing the document number beside the transaction to which it relates.** Some transactions affect more than one source document. **In these cases, write in more than one document number.**

Source Document	Document Number	Document Transactions	Number
Bank Credit Memo	1	1. Owner withdraws money.	
Bank Debit Memo	2	2. Purchase of equipment on account.	
Cheque Copy	3	3. Payment on account.	
Cash Sales Slip	4	4. Cash sale.	
Sales Invoice	5	5. Cash payment for donation.	
Purchase Invoice	6	6. Purchase of office supplies by cash.	
Receipt Invoice	7	7. Sale on account.	
Cash Receipts List	8	8. Cheques received from customers on account.	
Owner's Written Memo	9	9. Increase bank loan.	
Sales Slip Received	10	10. Owner invests additional money in the business.	
Bank Statement	11	11. Bank service charge.	

4. **This exercise also appears in your Workbook.**

Indicate whether each of the following statements is true or false by placing a "T" or "F" in the space indicated. Explain the reason for each "F" response in the space provided.

1. Anyone in the business can initiate a business transaction.
2. Every journal entry is based on a source document.
3. The only purpose of source documents is to provide the basis for a journal entry.
4. A business that sells to its customers on a cash basis would not normally use a sales invoice.
5. The journal entry for all cash sales slips is essentially the same.

6. Sales invoices are used by businesses that make most of their sales on account.
7. For every sales invoice there is a debit to an account receivable.
8. Dual purpose sales slips are the choice of businesses that sell for cash and also on account.
9. Every sales invoice is also a purchase invoice.
10. The debit entry for every purchase invoice is always the same.
11. The supporting document for a payment on account is the tear-off portion of a cheque.
12. The credit entry for every cheque copy payment is always the same.
13. Cheques received are considered to be cash received.
14. The bank has no right to make deductions from the accounts of its customers.
15. We debit Bank when we receive a bank debit memo.
16. The cost principle states that every acquisition of assets is to be recorded at their cost price.
17. The best objective evidence of a purchase is a purchase invoice received at "arm's length."
18. Only provincial governments are allowed to levy retail sales taxes.
19. The purchaser of goods or services is required to make accounting entries for sales tax.
20. The Sales Tax account is an expense account.

Comprehensive Exercises

5. Described below are source documents for Wayne Siebert, a professional photographer in Kelowna, B.C. **Journalize these transactions in a two-column general journal, using the following accounts:**

Accounts—Bank
          Accounts Receivable—various debtors
          Photo Supplies
          Automobile Equipment
          Accounts Payable—various creditors
          Sales Tax Payable
          W. Seibert, Capital
          W. Seibert, Drawings
          Fees Earned
          Automobile Expense
          Bank Charges Expense

TRANSACTIONS

November
4   *Sales Invoice*
        No. 571 for $275 plus sales tax of $13.75 to R. Chevrier for photo services completed on account.
6   *Purchase Invoice*
        Received from Black's Photo in the amount of $265 for photo supplies received in good condition.

9 *Purchase Invoice*

Received from Texaco Oil in the amount of $165 for gasoline used in the company car.

10 *Cheque Copy*

No. 652 for $325 issued to the owner for his personal use.

12 *Cash Sales Slip*

No. 214 for $145 plus sales tax of $7.25 for photography work performed for cash.

15 *Bank Debit Memo*

From Commercial Bank in the amount of $35.50 for bank service charges.

20 *Memorandum*

From the owner stating that he had taken $75 of photo supplies for his personal work at home.

22 *Cash Receipt*

Received $412 from H. Walker on account.

25 *Cheque Copy*

No. 653 paying for the supplies purchased above on November 6.

28 *Purchase Invoice*

Received from Oakley Motors in the amount of $750 for body repairs done on the business automobile.

---

6. Champion Rent-All, a business in Parry Sound, Ontario, rents out tools and equipment. The accounts for the business are as follows:

Bank	Rental Revenue
Accounts Receivable—various	Bank Charges Expense
Supplies	Delivery Expense
Rental Tools and Equipment	Light, Heat, and Water Expense
Truck	Miscellaneous Expense
Accounts Payable—various	Rent Expense
Sales Tax Payable	Telephone Expense
Frank N. Mazur, Capital	Wages Expense
Frank N. Mazur, Drawings	

Journalize the transactions below in the two-column general journal provided in the Workbook.

TRANSACTIONS

October

2 *Cash Sales Slip*

No. 409, to W. Franklin, $52.50 plus 5% sales tax of $2.63; total $55.13.

4 *Charge Sales Slip*

No. 410, to G. Fairbridge, $87.50 plus 5% sales tax of $4.38; total $91.88.

5 *Purchase Invoice*

From Vulcan Machinery, No. 3062 for one hydraulic jack, a rental tool, $315.

8 *Cheque Copy*

No. 1475, to Fair Supply Company, $215.90 on account.

9 *Cash Sales Slip*
No. 411, to R. Gullett, $115.10 plus 5% sales tax of $5.76; total $120.86.
11 *Cash Receipt*
From P. Mathers, $402.20 on account.
15 *Cheque Copy*
No. 1476, to Municipal Hydro, for cash payment of hydro bill, $172.
17 *Cheque Copy*
No. 1477, to R. Klein, $512 for wages.
17 *Cash Sales Slip*
No. 412, to A. Heisse, $90 plus 5% sales tax of $4.50; total $94.50.
18 *Cheque Copy*
No. 1478, to the owner, Frank Mazur, for his personal use, $350.
22 *Credit Card Statement*
From Husky Oil Company, $209 for gas and oil used in the delivery truck.
24 *Bank Debit Memo*
For bank service charge, $42.50.
25 *Cheque Copy*
No. 1479, to R. Klein, $512 for wages.

---

7. Janet Nuttall is in business as a commercial artist in Winnipeg, Manitoba. The accounts for her business are shown below:

Bank
Accounts Receivable—various
Art Supplies
Equipment
Automobile
Accounts Payable—various
Sales Tax Payable
Janet Nuttall, Capital

Janet Nuttall, Drawings
Fees Revenue
Car Expenses
Electricity Expense
Miscellaneous Expense
Rent Expense
Telephone Expense

Journalize the transactions below in a two-column general journal. Add seven per cent on all sales transactions.

TRANSACTIONS

March
3 *Sales Invoice*
No. 192, to Mountain Distributors, $175.
4 *Sales Invoice*
No. 193, to Old Fort Trading Co., $300.
4 *Cheque Copy*
No. 316, to Central Garage for the cash payment for repairs to the business automobile, $115.
6 *Cheque Copy*
No. 317, to Twin City Hydro for the cash payment of the monthly hydro bill, $65.

10 *Purchase Invoice*
From C. & C. Equipment, No. 1401, for one large metal drawing table, $475.

10 *Cheque Copy*
No. 318, to Dejavu Art Supply for the cash payment for artist's supplies, $85.

13 *Cheque Copy*
No. 319, to the owner for her personal use, $350.

14 *Sales Invoice*
No. 194, to Display Design Company, $255.

14 *Cash Receipt*
From Victor Schilling, $150 on account

17 *Cheque Copy*
No. 320, to C. & C. Equipment, $475 on account.

19 *Sales Invoice*
No. 195, to Scoville Sales, $235.

20 *Cheque Copy*
No. 321, to Fleming Properties, for the monthly rent, $375.

23 *Purchase Invoice*
From Lougherys Limited, No. 634, for drafting and artist's equipment, $215.

25 *Cheque Copy*
No. 322, to Twin City Telephone, for cash payment of the monthly telephone bill, $28.50.

27 *Credit Card Statement*
From Imperial Oil, for the gas and oil used in the automobile, $71.40.

31 *Cash Receipt*
From Old Fort Trading Co., $300 on account.

---

8. **Comment briefly on each of the following. Be prepared to present your comments to the class.**

1. In a period of rising prices, the assets on the balance sheet will be understated. Therefore the balance sheet is misleading.

2. Joan Nordquist purchased the property next to her business at a price of $55 000. She wanted the property for a much-needed expansion to the business premises. One week later, Joan received an independent offer to purchase the property for $75 000 but turned it down. However, she instructed her accountant to increase the value of the property in the accounts to $75 000. In her opinion, a new value for the property was established by the offer to purchase.

3. Fred Hebert purchased a new piece of equipment for his business. The normal selling price of this equipment was $22 000. Fred was given a special price of $18 000 because he was a close friend of the dealer. Fred wondered which value should be used to record the equipment in the accounts.

4. A company ran out of cash even though it was a consistently good money-maker. How could this happen?

5. The Colossimo Company ordered a new van at a cost of $23 000 on March 19. It was agreed that Colossimo Company would not take delivery of the van until July 31. Colossimo Company does not know if it should record the transaction now.

6. Sarah Tolp inherited a used automobile upon the death of a relative. She brought it into her business. She instructed the accountant to record the car at a value of $25 000 but provided no business papers to support that figure.

For Further Thought

9. Briefly answer the following questions.

1. Name three jobs in a secondary school that carry the right to make purchases.
2. Explain the term "source document."
3. Give an example other than owner's drawings of a transaction for which there would be no normal source document.
4. In the Truck account there is a debit entry for a new truck in the amount of $25 000. You suspect that this figure is wrong. You find that the source document for the transaction is missing from the files when you look for it. How could you verify the amount?
5. Cash sales slips are pre-numbered as a control feature. What would you tell your employees to do about cash sales slips that were spoiled and had to be redone?
6. Explain how an invoice can be both a "sales invoice" and a "purchase invoice."
7. Cash sales slips are usually loaded into a metal container for ease in preparation. What happens to the copies immediately after they are prepared?
8. Why can the invoice numbers on purchase invoices not be used for control purposes by the buyer?
9. The person who receives the mail, makes out the cash receipts list, and deposits the receipts in the bank is not normally an employee in the accounting department. Explain why.
10. The rule states that assets are debited when they are increased. However, the bank issues a "debit" memo when it decreases the bank account. Explain.
11. Once the cost of an asset is recorded in the accounts, it is not normally changed regardless of its market value. Give some reasons for this rule.
12. Sales tax added on to an invoice in March has to be paid by April 15. However, the invoice in question may not be collected until May. Express an opinion on this.

CASE STUDIES

CASE 1   *Acquiring Assets in a Package Deal*

Ted Cyr is the owner of a large contracting company in Thomson, Manitoba. A competitor of Cyr's had gone bankrupt and his equipment was liquidated at a public auction. One particular lot of equipment attracted Cyr's attention. The lot included: one bulldozer, two dump trucks, one crane, one pavement roller, and a property on which there was a good-sized construction building and a sand pit. Before the auction, Cyr obtained the services of a professional appraiser to help him evaluate the lot for sale. The appraiser estimated the values as follows:

Appraised Values

Bulldozer	$ 60 000
Dump truck 1	12 000
Dump truck 2	6 000
Crane	120 000
Pavement roller	72 000
Land parcel	36 000
Construction building	30 000
Sand pit	24 000
Total	$360 000

Cyr decided in advance of the auction that he would bid as high as $300 000 for the lot. However, much to his satisfaction, he won the lot with a bid of only $234 000.

Cyr is a businessman who keeps proper books and records and complies with all accounting standards and conventions. He intends to set up the newly acquired assets properly in the accounts. He is not sure how to do this because they were acquired as a package. He is certain that the equipment and the land at least should be set up in separate accounts.

Cyr hires you, a public accountant, to prepare the accounting entries to record the new assets.

Questions
1. To set up the newly acquired assets, four asset accounts are used. What are these?
2. At what overall value should the newly acquired assets be set up in the accounts? What GAAP makes this necessary?
3. How can the appraised values be used to calculate cost values for the new assets?
4. Work out the cost values for the newly acquired assets, making sure that the total is equal to the auction price.
5. Give the journal entry to set up the assets and to record their payment.
6. Write a brief report outlining the steps in setting up the package of assets in the accounts.

CASE 2   Is a Profit Always a Profit?

In 19-2 Marjorie Maepea, a dealer in small sailboats in Summerside, Prince Edward Island, had a profitable year. She ended the 19-2 fiscal year by having an extra $50 000 in cash and was looking for a good business opportunity. For some time she had considered using the money to purchase a larger sailboat—to test the market in Summerside for larger boats. In particular, she looked at a 10-metre Tarzan selling for $50 000. However, she eventually abandoned the idea. Instead, she purchased a nearby piece of commercial property for which she paid $50 000.

At the end of 19-5, Marjorie sold the land that she had purchased in 19-2 for $80 000. She felt good about the deal. The profit of $30 000 looked good on the books and Marjorie again had cash available to pursue other interests. She again considered the move into larger sailboats and again looked at the new Tarzan 10, which was virtually unchanged from the 19-2 model. She was shocked to learn that the price for a 19-5 Tarzan 10 had risen to $74 000.

Questions

1. How much was the profit on the sale of the industrial property purchased in 19-2?
2. Assuming that there is a special income tax (capital gains tax) of 20 per cent on this type of profit, calculate the amount of the tax and the amount of the profit after deducting the tax.
3. How much free cash does Marjorie have available as a result of the land transaction?
4. Is Marjorie in any better position now than she was in 19-2 in respect to the purchasing of the Tarzan 10? Explain by means of a chart.
5. Based solely on the evidence presented in this case, did Marjorie really make a profit on the sale of the commercial property? Explain in terms of straight dollars and in terms of purchasing power.
6. What word is used to explain the increase in the value of the property and the boat?
7. Could Marjorie's book profit be called a *paper* profit?
8. Write a brief letter to the income tax authorities expressing your views on the 20 per cent capital gains tax as a source of revenue for the government.

CASE 3 *Profit before Sentiment?*

John Pemberton had worked for T.W. Jones as chief accountant for six months. He was proud of the efficiency and enthusiasm shown by his staff.

One day, John was visibly upset after returning from a meeting with Mr. Jones. At the meeting, Mr. Jones had suggested that John dismiss the two senior employees in his department and bring in two young employees at the bottom of the salary scale. This would save the company several thousand dollars a year. "There is no room for sentiment in the business world," Mr. Jones had said.

John knew that his department would survive without the senior employees. There were intermediate-level employees in the department who were waiting for an opportunity to move up to bigger responsibilities. There would be a slight inconvenience but not much more.

John considered the proposal for some time and could not feel comfortable with it. Both of the senior employees were older men, aged 55 and 60 respectively. John knew that it would not be easy for these men to find employment at the salary level they now enjoyed. Unfortunately, there was no union in the company to protect the rights of these men. John was also concerned about his own future. If he did not go along with the scheme, his employer would consider him "soft" and his job might be endangered.

Questions

1. Is Mr. Jones's scheme a good one from a strictly business point of view?
2. Is Mr. Jones's scheme legal?
3. Does John have the right to consider his own future ahead of the future of others?
4. What do you think John should do?

CAREER
Barbara Blaney, CA / Public Accountant

Barbara Blaney was born in Sydney, Australia. Her parents moved to Halifax when she was only three years old, so Barbara feels like a true Nova Scotian.

After high school, Barbara immediately enrolled at Dalhousie University to work towards a Bachelor of Commerce degree. When she graduated, Barbara had intended to go straight into the job market. Unfortunately, unemployment was high at the time. Barbara applied for a student loan and went back to Dalhousie to study for a Master of Business Administration degree with a concentration in accounting and information systems.

Upon graduation, Barbara articled for her C.A. designation with Clarkson, Gordon & Co., in their Halifax office. Because she held an M.B.A. degree, the Institute of Chartered Accountants granted Barbara advanced standing in many of the courses a C.A. student must take. With this advantage, she was able to complete all the requirements and pass the examinations for her C.A. designation in less than two years.

Barbara now had to make a decision. Based on her academic qualifications, she had many offers of employment, from chartered accountants, private industry and government. Her other choice was to set up her own accounting practice.

Barbara decided she would prefer to be her own boss. She set up her practice in a small town outside of Halifax. She hired a clerk-typist to handle the clerical work and two accounting clerks to help her handle the routine accounting functions. With a small business loan, she purchased a computerized accounting system. It consisted of two micro-computers, two disk drives, a printer, and software which could handle ledgers, payroll, inventory, and accounts receivable and payable.

Barbara visited the various small businesses in the community and convinced them to let her handle all their bookkeeping on the computer. For some of her clients, Barbara found it necessary to design sales invoices similar to those illustrated in this chapter. To have each business keep track of cheques received from customers, she set up a List of Cash Receipts form. She insisted that all businesses have numbered cheques and that the copies of purchase invoices be attached to each cheque copy as proof of payment.

Now Barbara visits her clients each week and collects all their source documents to take them back to the office. Using these source documents as input, her accounting clerks key the information into the computer using the permanent file for each business. The computer gives her a printout of the trial balances, income statements, and balance sheets.

Because the computer handles so much of the routine work, Barbara is able to spend more time in developing appropriate planning and forecasting activities. She is called upon to prepare income tax returns for her clients and also to make suggestions about how to save the businesses money. She is also requested to provide management services. She advises businesses about all aspects of sales, purchasing, accounting systems, and data processing.

Barbara is extremely pleased with her decision to set up her own accounting practice. She enjoys being her own boss and derives a great deal of satisfaction from making her own decisions. After a few difficult years in the beginning, Barbara's practice is now financially successful. This allows her to spend more time enjoying her favourite leisure activities, travelling and fishing.

DISCUSSION

1. What source documents did Barbara have her clients set up to control cash?
2. Discuss the advantages and disadvantages of setting up your own accounting practice.
3. Write a report on the Chartered Accountancy program. In your report, include the following information:
   • educational requirements;
   • experience requirements;
   • advanced standing;
   • number of courses to earn the CA designation;
   • courses that are studied.
4. Identify and explain the use of the source documents you recognize in Barbara's profile.
5. Write a report on the Master of Business Administration degree at a university of your choice. Find out the qualifications needed to enrol, the number of courses required for graduation, length of time the program takes to complete, and the average needed for graduation.
6. If you were in Barbara's position as a CA, how would you convince businesses to let you handle their bookkeeping systems?
7. Why does Barbara have the businesses attach copies of all purchase invoices to the cheque copies?
8. What are the various duties Barbara performs for her clients as a public accountant?
9. What are the advantages for Barbara of setting up her accounting practice in a small town rather than in Halifax?

Posting

7.1 Posting
7.2 Trial Balance Out of Balance
7.3 Computers in Accounting   Bedford Accounting

7.1 POSTING

You have now been introduced to the journal and the ledger, the two important books in the accounting process. You are now ready to learn to use these books "formally," just as accountants do.

The Balance Column Account

So far we have only considered the simple two-sided ledger account, showing debits on one side and credits on the other. However, a second style of ledger account, known as the balance column account, is actually more useful and convenient. The **balance column account** has three money columns, one for the debit amounts, one for the credit amounts, and a separate one for the balance. This allows the balances to stand out more clearly. It is the most commonly used account. The T-account and the balance column account are compared in Figure 7.1.

Opening an Account

An accounting entry often affects an item for which there is no account in the ledger. When this happens, it is necessary to open an account. **Opening an account** means preparing an account page and placing it in its proper place in the ledger. To open an account, proceed as follows:

1 Obtain an unused account page.
2 Write the name for the new account at the top of the page. The account name is known as the **account title** and will be written on the back of the page as well.
3 Write in the account number.
4 Insert the new account in its proper place in the ledger.

Both the front and the back of any account page are used for the same item.

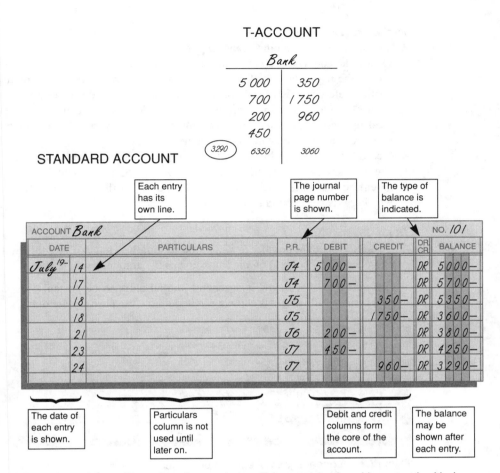

Figure 7.1 Comparison of entries made in a T-account (top) and in a standard balance column account.

Formal Posting

In the previous section you learned that each accounting entry is first recorded in the journal. It is then transferred, or "posted," to the ledger. **Posting** is the process of transferring information from the journal to the ledger. Every individual amount recorded in the journal must be posted separately. The six-step procedure for posting is described in the next section. Illustrations for posting debit and credit amounts are given in Figures 7.2—7.6.

Six Steps in Posting

For each individual amount entered in the journal, you must perform the following six steps. Five of these steps are performed in the ledger; one of the steps is performed in the journal.

In the Ledger

1 Turn to the proper account in the ledger.

2 Record the date. Use the next unused line in the account.

3 Record the page number of the journal (where the transaction is journalized) in the posting reference (P.R.) column of the account. Write the letter J (for Journal) in front of this number; for example, J14. As you will see later, several journals are used in accounting. Therefore, you must use a code to tell you which journal is being referred to. You can look ahead to see this on page 432.

4 Record the amount. Debit amounts are entered in the debit columns of the accounts. Credit amounts are entered in the credit columns of the accounts.

5 Calculate and enter the new account balance in the balance column. Indicate whether it is a debit or a credit balance.

In the Journal

6 Record the account number to which the posting was made. Enter this in the posting reference (P.R.) column on the same line as the amount being posted.

Example Shown below is a general journal entry to be posted. This is followed by a series of illustrations showing in detail how the postings are done.

GENERAL JOURNAL				PAGE	14
DATE	PARTICULARS	P.R.	DEBIT	CREDIT	
Aug 19- 14	Office Furniture		425 —		
	Bank			150 —	
	Accs Pay'l – Office Supply Company			275 —	
	Purchase of new desk				

Figure 7.2 A general journal entry to be posted.

1 Posting the debit amount

GENERAL JOURNAL				PAGE	14
DATE	PARTICULARS	P.R.	DEBIT	CREDIT	
Aug 19- 14	Office Furniture	110	425 —		
	Bank			150 —	
	Accs Pay'l – Office Supply Company			275 —	
	Purchase of new desk				

6 Go back and enter the account number.

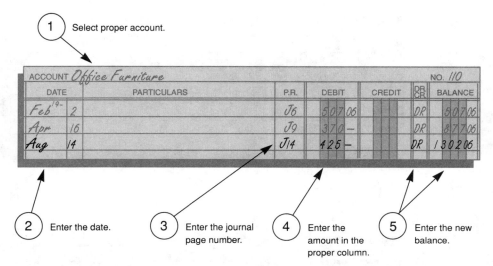

Figure 7.3   The debit item in the journal entry posted to the Office Furniture account.

2 POSTING THE FIRST CREDIT AMOUNT

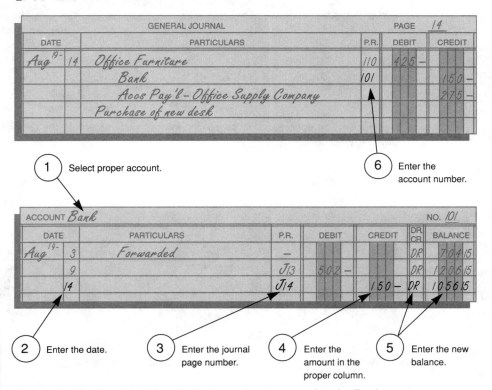

Figure 7.4   The first credit item in the journal entry posted to the Bank account.

3 POSTING THE SECOND CREDIT AMOUNT

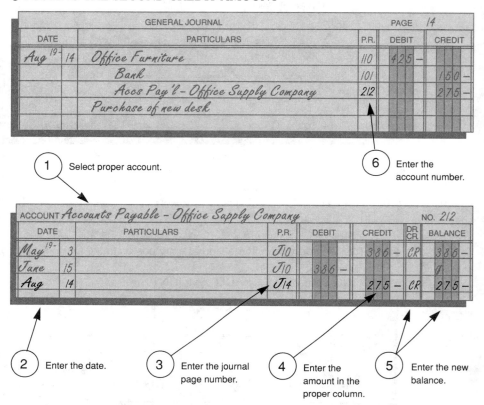

Figure 7.5   The second credit item in the journal entry posted to the Office Supply Company account.

After the journal entry is completely posted, the general journal and the three accounts involved appear as below.

The journal entry being posted

DATE	PARTICULARS	P.R.	DEBIT	CREDIT
Aug ¹⁹⁻ 14	Office Furniture	110	425 —	
	Bank	101		150 —
	Accs Pay'l – Office Supply Company	212		275 —

LEDGER ACCOUNTS

The ledger
accounts
affected

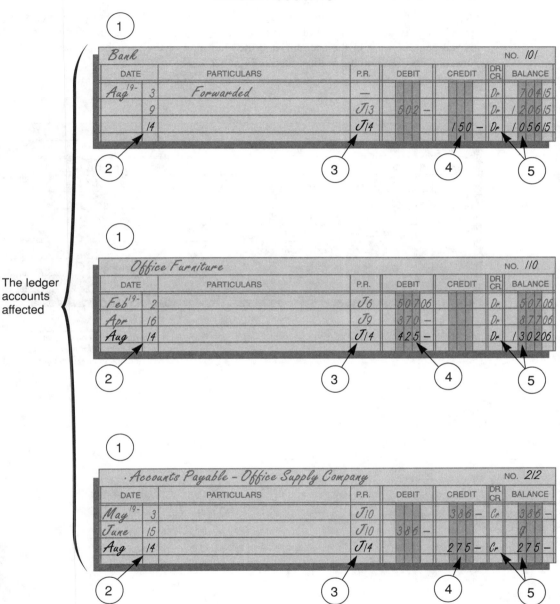

Figure 7.6   Six steps in the formal posting of a journal entry.

Cross-Referencing

Steps 3 and 6 of the foregoing posting sequence perform what is known as cross-referencing. Expressed in simple terms, **cross-referencing** is the recording of the journal page number in the account, and the recording of the account number in the journal. Cross-referencing is illustrated in Figure 7.7.

GENERAL JOURNAL				PAGE	37	
DATE		PARTICULARS	P.R.	DEBIT	CREDIT	
Nov. 19-	18	*Buildings*	120	2 4 7 5 —		
		P. Sloan, Capital	301	3 0 0 —		
		Bank			2 7 7 5 —	
		Purchase of materials to				
		add to buildings; some				
		materials taken by owner				

Figure 7.7   Cross-referencing.

The fact that no number has been recorded here means that the entry has not yet been posted.

LEDGER ACCOUNTS

Bank   NO. *101*

DATE		PARTICULARS	P.R.	DEBIT	CREDIT	DR CR	BALANCE
Nov.¹⁹⁻	15	Forwarded	—			Dr	3 0 2 7 50
	17		J36	4 1 2 90		Dr	3 4 4 0 40

Buildings   NO. *120*

DATE		PARTICULARS	P.R.	DEBIT	CREDIT	DR CR	BALANCE
Jan.¹⁹⁻	3		J30	18 4 3 2 —		Dr	18 4 3 2 —
Mar.	10		J32	2 1 7 0 —		Dr	20 6 0 2 —
Nov.	18		J37	2 4 7 5 —		Dr	23 0 7 7 —

P. Sloan, Capital   NO. *301*

DATE		PARTICULARS	P.R.	DEBIT	CREDIT	DR CR	BALANCE
Nov.¹⁹⁻	10	Forwarded	—			Cr	20 2 5 0 —
	15		J34	2 5 0 —		Cr	20 0 0 0 —
	18		J37	3 0 0 —		Cr	19 7 0 0 —

There are three reasons for cross-referencing.

1. Entries in accounts can be readily traced to their source in the general journal.
2. Entries in the journal can be traced to the accounts where they have been posted.
3. If the posting process is interrupted, it is easy to tell where to begin again. Journal amounts that have been posted will have the account number entered.

Correcting Errors in the Books

Over the years professional accountants have made it a rule not to erase. Erasures in the books might arouse the suspicions of the auditors, the official examiners of the books and records. Therefore, other methods are used for making corrections.

Errors Found Immediately

It is simple to correct an error that is found right away. Simply stroke neatly through the incorrect figures or letters and write in the correct ones immediately above. Figures 7.8 and 7.9 show this type of correction. An accounting clerk should learn to write small so that errors can be corrected easily.

GENERAL JOURNAL				P. *8*	
Date	Particulars	P.R.	Debit		Credit
Jun 16	*Cash*		*50 —*		
	A. ~~Abbot~~ Martin				*50 —*
	Payment of account balance				

Figure 7.8   Correcting a name in the journal.

ACCOUNT					DR. CR.	No. *5*
Date	Particulars	P.R.	Debit	Credit		Balance
Feb 19 *5*		*J3*	*64 10*		*DR*	*64 10*
8		*J6*	*131 75* ~~141 35~~		*DR*	*195 85* ~~205 95~~

Figure 7.9   Correcting an amount in an account.

Errors Found Later

The accounting department may not learn of an error until after quite some time has passed. In many cases, the error can be corrected by means of an accounting entry. For example, consider the following situation:

On July 5, an accounting clerk noticed that an invoice for $752 was debited to the wrong account. The invoice was clearly for supplies but had been debited to the Equipment account. The error was made on January 17, almost six months earlier.

The two accounts involved appear as shown in Figure 7.10:

Supplies

Date	Partcs	Dr	Cr	Balance
Jan 1	Forwarded			150 – Dr
Feb 12		370 –		520 – Dr
20		110 –		630 – Dr
Mar 30		50 –		680 – Dr
Apr 19		225 –		905 – Dr
May 12		70 –		975 – Dr
28		125 –		1100 – Dr
Jun 25		45 –		1145 – Dr

Equipment

Date	Partcs	Dr	Cr	Balance
Jan 1	Forwarded			7350 – Dr
Jan 17		752 –		8102 – Dr
Jun 5		1100 –		9202 – Dr

Figure 7.10   The two accounts affected by an incorrect posting.

The best way to correct an error of this type is with a correcting journal entry. A **correcting journal entry** is an accounting entry that cancels the effect of an error. In the above case, the entry is needed to cancel the $752 in the Equipment account and set it up in the Supplies account. This journal entry is:

	DR	CR
Supplies	$752.00	
Equipment		$752.00
To correct posting error made on		
January 17th.		

This method makes it unnecessary to squeeze $752 into the Supplies account, to stroke through and change several dollar amounts, and to change several trial balances.

After correction, the two accounts appear as shown in Figure 7.11.

Supplies

Date	Partcs	Dr	Cr	Balance
Jan 1	Forwarded			150 – Dr
Feb 12		370 –		520 – Dr
20		110 –		630 – Dr
Mar 30		50 –		680 – Dr
Apr 19		225 –		905 – Dr
May 12		70 –		975 – Dr
28		125 –		1100 – Dr
Jun 25		45 –		1145 – Dr
Jul 5		752 –		1897 – Dr

Equipment

Date	Partcs	Dr	Cr	Balance
Jan 1	Forwarded			7350 – Dr
Jan 17		752 –		8102 – Dr
Jun 5		1100 –		9202 – Dr
Jul 5			752 –	8450 – Dr

Figure 7.11   The two accounts after correction.

Forwarding Procedure

When an account page is full, the account must be continued on a new page. **Forwarding** is the process of continuing an account or journal on a new page by carrying forward the date and the balance from the completed page. The process of forwarding is illustrated in Figure 7.12.

a.

ACCOUNT T.J.Barker							NO. 4
DATE	PARTICULARS	P.R.	DEBIT	CREDIT	DR CR	BALANCE	
Feb¹⁹⁻ 7		J1	150 62		Dr	150 62	
9		J3	374 50		Dr	525 12	
11		J5		150 62	Dr	374 50	
12		J5	216 51		Dr	591 01	
16		J8	75 62		Dr	666 63	
18		J9		374 50	Dr	292 13	
19		J9	583 62		Dr	875 75	
21	Forwarded	J10		292 13	Dr	583 62	

b.

ACCOUNT T.J.Barker							NO. 4
DATE	PARTICULARS	P.R.	DEBIT	CREDIT	DR CR	BALANCE	
Feb¹⁹⁻ 21	Forwarded				Dr	583 62	

Forwarding is not posting.

Figure 7.12 The finished account page after being forwarded (a.) and the new account page with the balance brought forward (b.).

The Accounting Cycle

The total set of accounting procedures that must be carried out during each fiscal period is known as the "accounting cycle." The steps in the accounting cycle are introduced gradually throughout the text. Figure 7.13 shows the four steps in the accounting cycle that have been studied so far.

Transactions occur. Source documents. → Accounting entries recorded in journal. → Journal entries posted to the ledger accounts. → Ledger balanced by means of trial balance. → More to come

Figure 7.13 The first four steps in the accounting cycle.

SECTION REVIEW QUESTIONS

1. Name the two important books in the accounting process.
2. Name the simple account that shows debit amounts on one side and credit amounts on the other.
3. Name the style of account used most commonly.
4. Why is this style of account most useful?
5. Describe the steps in opening an account.
6. Where are accounting entries first recorded?
7. What is "posting"?
8. Give the five steps in posting that are performed in the ledger.
9. Give the one step in posting that is performed in the journal.
10. Describe "cross-referencing."
11. Give the three reasons for cross-referencing.
12. Describe the procedure for making a simple correction in the accounts or journal.
13. Describe the procedure for making a correction of an error found after some time has passed.
14. What is "forwarding"?
15. Name the first four steps in the accounting cycle.

SECTION EXERCISES

1. Two partially completed accounts are given below and also in your Workbook. **For each of these, complete the balance column by calculating and entering the balance after each entry. Be sure to indicate each time whether the balance is debit or credit.**

A.

Asset

Debit		Credit		Balance	
				DR/CR	Amount
1 000	00				
250	00				
310	00				
		1 250	00		
200	00				
350	00				
		860	00		
850	00				
		1 000	00		
1 500	00				
200	00				

B.

Liability

Debit		Credit		Balance	
				DR/CR	Amount
		3 500	00		
		1 600	00		
3 500	00				
1 000	00				
		2 000	00		
600	00				
2 000	00				
		450	00		
500	00				
		50	00		
		375	00		

2. Workbook Exercise: Posting transactions.

---

3. Workbook Exercise: Posting transactions.

---

4. Workbook Exercise: Forwarding an account balance.

7.2   TRIAL BALANCE OUT OF BALANCE

As you have already learned, sometimes the trial balance does not balance. It is your job as bookkeeper or accountant to find and correct the errors. Skill in finding errors is important to an accountant.

Figure 7.14 shows the five steps to be followed when a trial balance does not balance. Often, the error or errors will be detected before all the steps are carried out. However, if you finish the five steps and the account still does not balance, then you did not do them correctly. You will have to go through the sequence again, this time working with more care.

Short Cuts in Detecting a Single Error

It may take a lot of time to go through the routine described in Figure 7.14. Experienced accountants try to avoid this whenever they can. They usually try one of four quick tests first.

The initial step in any of the quick tests is to calculate the trial balance difference — the amount by which the trial balance is out. Then any of the following tests may be applied:

1. If **the trial balance difference is a multiple of 10**, such as 10 cents, one dollar, and so on, an error in addition has likely been made. Therefore, start with steps 1 and 3 of Sequence of Balancing Steps (involving addition) given in Figure 7.14.
2. Check both the ledger and the journal to see if **the trial balance difference is equal to an amount entered in the ledger or the journal.** Whenever you find such an amount, verify it to make sure that it has been handled correctly.
3. **If the trial balance difference is an even amount, divide it by two.** Then search (1) the trial balance, and (2) the ledger accounts for this amount. If an equivalent amount is found, check it carefully. In particular, look to see if a debit amount has been posted or transferred as a credit, or vice versa.

   An error of this type always produces a trial balance difference equal to twice the amount of the error. For example, consider the simplified trial balance shown on p. 198. It contains a single error. The $30 item listed as a credit should have been listed as a debit.

   Notice that the difference between the totals is $60, twice the amount of the error.

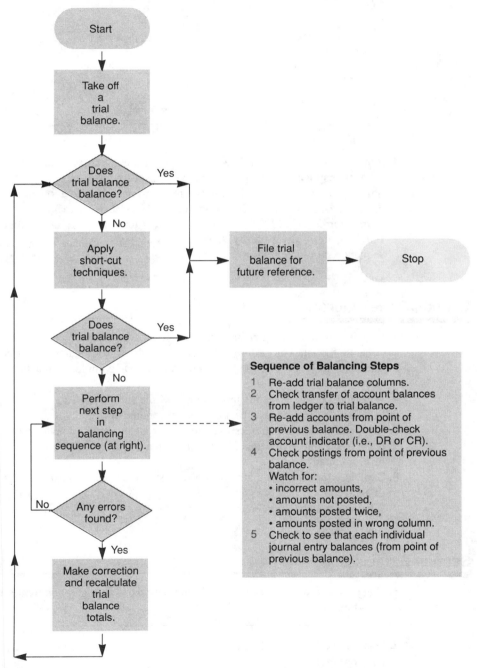

Figure 7.14   Flowchart of the procedure for balancing the general ledger.

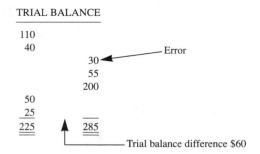

TRIAL BALANCE

```
110
 40
         30 ◄——————— Error
         55
        200
 50
 25
225    ▲   285
       |————————— Trial balance difference $60
```

4. If the trial balance is a multiple of 9, it is likely that a transposition error has occurred.

A **transposition error** is a mistake caused by changing the order of digits or omitting digits when transferring figures from one place to another. A transposition error has occurred when, for example, $35.60 is posted as $36.50, or when $1 200 is transferred as $120. **Such errors always produce a trial balance difference that is exactly divisible by 9.** When this happens, steps 2 and 4 of the checking sequence should be performed first.

SECTION REVIEW QUESTIONS

1. Why is skill in locating errors important to an accountant?
2. Give the five-step procedure to be followed when a trial balance does not balance.
3. What has to be done if the five-step procedure is completed, but the ledger is still not balanced?
4. What must be done before applying any of the short-cut tests?
5. What kind of error does a trial balance difference of $10 suggest?
6. In regard to the error in question 5 above, what steps would be followed first?
7. If the trial balance difference is not an even amount, which of the short-cut tests can be eliminated?
8. Explain what happens mathematically when an amount is posted to the wrong side of an account.
9. What is a transposition error?

SECTION EXERCISES

1. **Workbook Exercise: Locate and correct errors in a given journal, ledger, and trial balance.**

2. **Workbook Exercise: Locate and correct errors in a given journal, ledger, and trial balance.**

3. The four mini-exercises on pages 200 through 203 will give you practice at using the short-cut techniques for locating errors when a trial balance does not balance. **Each exercise has one error in it which you are to find. For each mini-exercise, go through the sequence of steps outlined below. Once you locate the error you need not continue with the subsequent steps.**

Short-Cut Steps to Locating an Error
1 Write down the trial balance difference.
2 Is it a multiple of 10 like $1, or $10, or $100? If *no*, go to step 3. If *yes*, then re-add the trial balance and re-add the accounts in the ledger.
3 Search the journal, ledger, and trial balance for an entry equal to the trial balance difference. Check any such entries to ensure that a posting was not missed or posted twice, or an account balance was not missed or listed twice.
4 Does the trial balance difference figure divide evenly by 9? If *no*, go to step 5. If *yes*, check for a transposition error in transferring account balances onto the trial balance or in posting from the journal to the ledger.
5 Is the trial balance difference an even amount? If *yes*, divide the amount by two and write down the result. Then search the records for this amount. Check any entry for this amount to ensure that the entry was not posted to the wrong side of an account, or an account balance was not listed on the wrong side of the trial balance.

1. Why does it not balance?

JOURNAL

PARTICULARS	DR	CR
Bank	4 500	
Equipment	3 600	
Capital		8 00
Supplies	73	
Accounts Payable		73
Expense	47	
Bank		47
Bank	195	
Revenue		195
Drawings	100	
Bank		100
Accounts Receivable	63	
Revenue		63
Supplies	38	
Bank		38

LEDGER

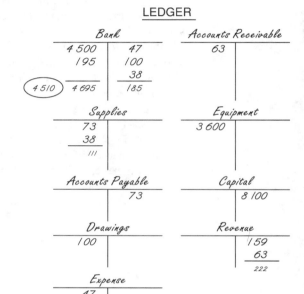

Bank

	4 500	47	
	195	100	
		38	
4 510	4 695	185	

Accounts Receivable

63

Supplies

73
38
111

Equipment

3 600

Accounts Payable

	73

Capital

	8 100

Drawings

100

Revenue

	159
	63
	222

Expense

47

TRIAL BALANCE

DR	CR
4 510	73
63	8 100
111	222
3 600	
100	
47	
8 431	8 395

2. Why does it not balance?

JOURNAL

PARTICULARS	DR	CR
Bank	3 000	
Equipment	2 000	
Capital		5 000
Supplies	490	
Bank		490
Accounts Receivable	155	
Revenue		155
Expense	56	
Bank		56
Expense	72	
Accounts Payable		72
Bank	312	
Revenue		312
Drawings	97	
Bank		97

LEDGER

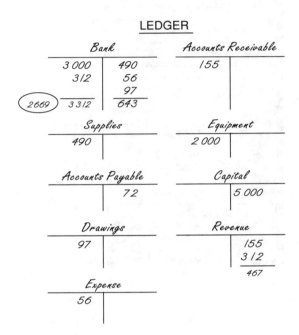

Bank

3 000	490
312	56
	97
(2669) 3 312	643

Accounts Receivable

155	

Supplies

490	

Equipment

2 000	

Accounts Payable

	72

Capital

	5 000

Drawings

97	

Revenue

	155
	312
	467

Expense

56	

TRIAL BALANCE

DR	CR
2 269	72
155	5 000
490	467
2 000	
97	
56	
5 467	5 539

3. Why does it not balance?

JOURNAL

PARTICULARS	DR	CR
Bank	2 500	
Equipment	7 000	
Capital		9 500
Accounts Receivable	371	
Revenue		371
Bank	269	
Revenue		269
Supplies	53	
Accounts Payable		53
Drawings	127	
Bank		127
Expense	86	
Bank		86
Expense	49	
Accounts Payable		49

LEDGER

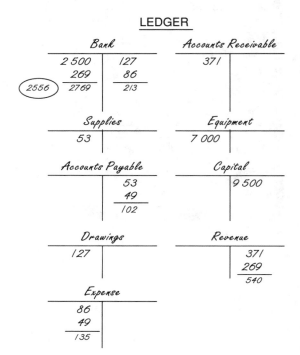

TRIAL BALANCE

DR	CR
2 556	102
371	9 500
53	540
7 000	
127	
135	
10 242	10 142

4. Why does it not balance?

JOURNAL

PARTICULARS	DR	CR
Bank	4 000	
Equipment	3 000	
Capital		7 000
Supplies	216	
Accounts Payable		216
Accounts Receivable	321	
Revenue		321
Expense	73	
Bank		73
Expense	34	
Accounts Payable		34
Drawings	41	
Bank		41
Bank	150	
Accounts Receivable		150

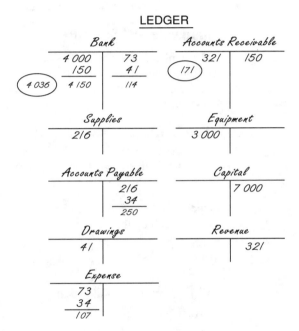

LEDGER

Bank

4 000	73
150	41
4 036 4 150	114

Accounts Receivable

321	150
171	

Supplies

216	

Equipment

3 000	

Accounts Payable

	216
	34
	250

Capital

	7 000

Drawings

41	

Revenue

	321

Expense

73	
34	
107	

TRIAL BALANCE

DR	CR
4 036	250
171	7 000
216	41
3 000	321
107	
7 530	7 612

7.3 COMPUTERS IN ACCOUNTING: BEDFORD ACCOUNTING

Once you have your Bedford accounting package set up and underway, it is easy to work with and gives impressive results. However, getting started is quite involved. Be prepared for some frustrations, and have your Bedford manual nearby for ready reference. The instructions that follow are for the IBM and IBM-compatible version of Bedford. There is also a version of Bedford for Macintosh computers called Simply Accounting.

Hardware and Software

The explanations given in this text are for a system that has a hard disk drive (**C**) and a floppy disk drive (**A**). If you have a different setup, a few of the commands and keystrokes will be different. This should present no real problem. Refer to your DOS systems manual or seek assistance from an experienced person.

The Bedford Diskette

The first thing to be done is to load your Bedford program onto the hard disk. Place the diskette into drive A and key in the following command:

```
C >  copy a:\bedford.exe c:\
```

Once this is done, put your program diskette away in a safe place. Now, whenever you want to call up the Bedford program, enter the following:

```
C >  cd\
C >  bedford
```

The Company Diskette

Save your company files on diskettes. You should use a separate diskette for each company. Place a diskette in drive A and enter:

```
C >  format a:
```

This ensures that you are using a formatted diskette. Second, make a directory on the diskette using a company code name. You are limited to eight characters when deciding on code names. Since the company that we will be working with is General Engineering, use the code name *geneng*. With the company diskette in drive A, key in the following:

```
C >  mkdir a:\geneng
```

You will now have a diskette ready for a company known as *geneng* as well as having the Bedford program set up on your hard disk. Mark the diskette "geneng."

Starting To Use Bedford

When you first call up the Bedford program from your hard disk, the screen display will be as shown in Figure 7.15 on p. 205.

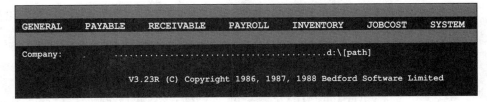

Figure 7.15   Screen display when Bedford is started.

At the top is the module menu. Beneath that the display is asking for: 1) the company name, and 2) the location of the company files. The information must be keyed in accurately. With the company diskette in drive A respond with the following:

Because no bookkeeping has been done yet, the diskette is empty except for its code name. The computer responds with the screen display shown in Figure 7.16.

```
 GENERAL    PAYABLE    RECEIVABLE    PAYROLL    INVENTORY    JOBCOST    SYSTEM

 Company:       A:\geneng

 There are no Company files at the end of the indicated path. Press RETURN if you wish to
 create a new set of Company Files or press ESCAPE if you wish to enter a different path.
```

Figure 7.16   Screen display where a new company is being started.

Respond by pressing the enter key. The screen display shown in Figure 7.17 appears.

```
 GENERAL    PAYABLE    RECEIVABLE    PAYROLL    INVENTORY    JOBCOST    SYSTEM

 Company:       A:\geneng                                   > 01-01-00
 Start:         ...... mmddyy                               <
 Conversion:                                                > 01-01-00
 Finish
```

Figure 7.17   Screen display asking for the initial dates.

The display is asking for three dates associated with the business known as *geneng*. When you enter these dates, they will replace the sample dates that appear to the right and will act as a reminder. The "mmddyy" shows the form in which the dates are to be entered. The three dates are:

Start   The date of the beginning of the fiscal period.
Conversion   The date as of which the account balances are entered in the company files.
Finish   The date of the end of the fiscal period.

Enter the dates that apply for Exercise 7 on page 212 of the text. These are as follows: Start, August 31, 19-9; Conversion, August 31, 19-9, and Finish, September 30, 19-9.

This is the only time you will be asked for these three dates — when the company file is first being set up. However, they can be changed if it becomes necessary. Refer to your manual if this need arises.

When these dates have been entered, all text disappears from the screen and you are left only with the module menu in which the first item, GENERAL, is highlighted with the rectangular pointer.

Menus and Keys

The main menu, called the module menu, runs across the page at the top. You can move the highlighted pointer to one of seven options with the cursor-left and the cursor-right keys. Move to GENERAL. Make your selection by pressing the cursor-down key. A pull-down menu appears beneath the heading GENERAL. The display on your screen becomes that shown below in Figure 7.18.

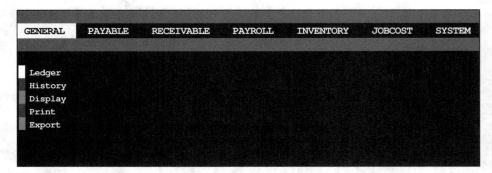

Figure 7.18   Screen display showing five options for the GENERAL module.

You now have a vertical menu with five choices. Use the cursor-up and cursor-down keys to move to the option you want. Move to Ledger and select it by pressing the cursor-right key. You are presented with another menu. Move down to and select the option Insert. You are presented with another menu. This is the way the Bedford menus work. The easiest way to back up through the series of menus to the module menu is with the ESC key.

Chart of Accounts

Now that you know how to use the menus, look at the built-in chart of accounts. You can display this by selecting GENERAL, Ledger, and either of the three choices in the next menu. Part of the built-in chart of accounts appears to the right. The rest of the chart can be accessed by using the cursor-down key.

You are not going to use this particular chart of accounts because it is not suitable for General Engineering. There is a way to change the chart of accounts. But it is a lengthy process and you are not asked to do it at this time. Instead, you will be given a set of company records with a suitable chart of accounts already set up. Load in model GENENG and look at the chart of accounts for General Engineering.

You can either display or print this chart of accounts at this stage. To display it, select GENERAL, Display, Chart. To print it, select GENERAL, Print, Chart. You can see immediately that the numbering system is the one used in the text with only a few minor differences. You can also display or print a trial balance by selecting GENERAL, Display, Trial, or GENERAL, Print, Trial. The trial balance shows that the accounts are set up but there has been no activity in them.

Getting the System READY

Your next task is to set up the beginning account balances for General Engineering. You will obtain the data for this from the balance sheet on page 213 of your textbook. There are six account balances to be set up.

For each account proceed as follows. Select GENERAL and History. You will be presented with a menu such as that shown in Figure 7.19.

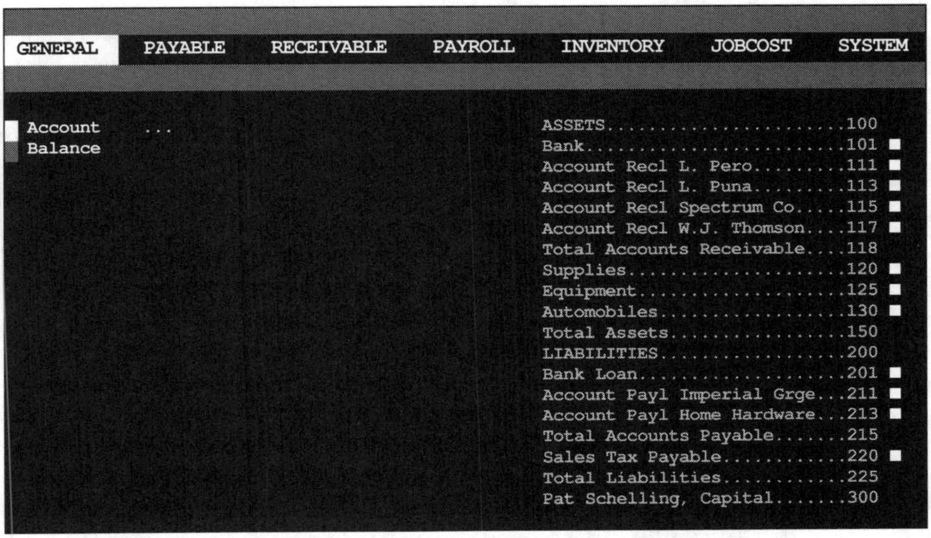

Figure 7.19   Screen display for entering account balances.

Enter 101, the account number for Bank. The word Bank will appear beside the word Account and the pointer will move to Balance. Enter 2000, with no dollar signs or commas. (A decimal point is needed if it is not an even dollar amount.) 2 000.00 will appear beside Balance and the pointer will move back to Account. At this point, the computer has not taken the data into its memory. The account and the balance remain on display for your approval. If you are satisfied that the information displayed is correct, press the Control and Enter keys at the same time. The computer accepts the data and moves back to the previous menu. Repeat the process for each of the remaining accounts. After the six account balances are entered, there is one more step before the system is "ready."

You cannot process transactions in this module until the system acknowledges that it is ready. You must now test the system to see if it will accept your accounts. Select SYSTEM, Default, Module, and General. The display shown in Figure 7.20 appears on the screen.

GENERAL	PAYABLE	RECEIVABLE	PAYROLL	INVENTORY	JOBCOST	SYSTEM

```
Start        08-31-89
Conversion   08-31-89
Finish       09-30-89
Ready        No
```

Figure 7.20   Screen display to test if the company files are ready.

The screen display shows No for Ready. Select Ready and the NO will be changed to YES. Now press the Control and Enter keys at the same time. If your accounts are in logical order and if your ledger is in balance the system will accept the module as being Ready. This should be the case for *geneng*. This opens the door to the next stage of Bedford accounting.

Escape back through the menus to the Module menu. Select GENERAL and you will see that the pull-down menu has changed. Now that the system is "ready" there is no further need for the History option. The History option is replaced by the Journal option which allows you to make general journal entries based on business transactions. Journalizing business transactions in Bedford is the topic of the computer section in Chapter 12.

The proper company name, not the code name, should be printed on the company reports. You must tell the computer what the company name is. Select SYSTEM, Default, Module, and System. A menu is presented in which the first item requested is the company name. Type in the company name, press Enter, and then press Control-Enter. The computer will now call your company by its proper name.

To exit the system, move to the module menu, select SYSTEM, and then finish. Your work will be saved automatically.

COMPUTER REVIEW QUESTIONS

1. What letter is associated with the hard disk drive? The floppy disk drive?
2. Give the command to be entered after the C prompt to place the Bedford program onto the hard disk.
3. Once the Bedford program is on the hard disk, what are the commands to call it up?
4. What does the text say about using diskettes for company files?
5. How many modules are there in Bedford accounting?
6. When the screen display asks for the company files, what is the keyboard response for a company called Romax?
7. Describe the three dates that the computer will ask for.
8. Describe the system Bedford uses for selecting options from menus.
9. What is the easiest way to back up through a series of menus?
10. Give the path of options that gives access to the chart of accounts.
11. Give the path of options that prints out the chart of accounts.
12. Give the path of options that displays the trial balance.
13. Explain what is meant by getting the system ready.
14. Explain how to test if a set of company files are ready.
15. Explain the consequences of the module not being ready.
16. What option change in one of the menus is made when the module becomes ready?
17. Give the path of options that allows you to enter the proper company name.
18. Explain how to exit the system and save your work.

COMPUTER EXERCISES

1. 1. **Load the model named "golflinx."** This model is designed for Exercise 8 on page 214 of your text.
   2. **Enter the account balances.** These will be found on the trial balance on page 215.

> **Note:** Enter the balance of the Drawings account as a minus number (–). This is because the Drawings account is in a credit section of the ledger. The computer will record any balances entered in this section as credit balances unless there is some indication to the contrary.

   3. **Make the system ready.**
   4. **Enter the company's formal name.**
   5. **Print out a chart of accounts and a trial balance. Check that the company name is correct.**

CHAPTER HIGHLIGHTS

Now that you have completed Chapter 7, you should:

1. be able to post journal entries and balance them correctly;
2. be able to work out an "opening entry" from a balance sheet and to "open" an account;
3. understand why both a journal and a ledger are used in the accounting process;
4. be able to use a balance column account correctly and with ease;
5. understand the purpose of cross-referencing;
6. know how to forward the balance of an account to a new page;
7. know the first four steps in the accounting cycle;
8. know how to make corrections in the journal and in the accounts, and how to make correcting journal entries;
9. be able to use correctly the short cuts in locating trial balance errors.

ACCOUNTING TERMS

account title	cross-referencing	posting
balance column account	forwarding	transposition error
correcting journal entry	opening an account	

CHAPTER EXERCISES

Using Your Knowledge

This exercise also appears in the Workbook.

1. **Indicate whether each of the following statements is true or false by placing a "T" or an "F" in the space indicated. Explain the reason for each "F" response in the space provided.**

   1. The chief advantage of the three-column account is that there is room for the account balance.
   2. Both sides of an account page (front and back) are used for the same item, for example, Bank.
   3. Entering the journal page number in the account is the sixth step in the posting process.
   4. The step described in 3. above is performed in the journal.
   5. The process of setting up an account is known as "forwarding."
   6. The fourth step in the accounting cycle, as we know it, is the taking off of a trial balance.
   7. It is not possible for the ledger to be out of balance and also to be correct.

8. If the trial balance difference is an even amount, the error could not be a transposition error.

9. If the trial balance difference is zero, the ledger is in balance.

10. Posting a debit item incorrectly as a credit produces a trial balance credit total that is smaller than the debit total by twice the amount of the error.

11. Only very rarely does a transaction affect only one account.

12. Ledger accounts are arranged alphabetically to make them easier to find.

13. The presence of the account number in the journal indicates that the posting of an item has been completed.

2. **Complete the chart in the Workbook about the effect of errors on a trial balance.**

Error Situations	*Trial Balance Will Not Balance*		*Trial Balance will balance but will not be correct*
	Debits greater than Credits by ($$)	*Credits greater than Debits by ($$)*	
1. An entire journal entry is posted as $400 instead of $100.			
2. A debit of $200 is posted twice.			
3. A debit of $150 is posted as a credit.			
4. The Bank account is over-added by $80.			
5. The Drawings account balance of $5 500 is missed when preparing the trial balance.			
6. The Revenue account balance of $72 000 is listed on the trial balance as a debit.			
7. An entire general journal entry for $325 is not posted.			
8. An entire general journal entry for $50 is posted in reverse.			
9. A $40 debit is not posted.			
10. A $500 credit is posted as $50.			
11. A debit of $60 to Bank was also posted to a customer's account.			
12. A $40 debit is posted as $400.			

3. An accounting clerk has prepared his trial balance as of June 30, 19—, and determines that total debits equal total credits. He breathes a sigh of relief and informs his boss that his ledger is in balance and that therefore the accounts are correct. His boss, a chartered accountant, tells him that this is not necessarily the case. She asks him to prepare a list of four possible errors that could occur and yet not cause the trial balance to be out of balance. **Prepare this list as if you were the accounting clerk.**

4. An employee working on his first trial balance discovers that the Furniture and Equipment account has a credit balance of $5 000 and a customer's account has a credit balance of $200. **Has the accountant made a mistake in his records or is this situation possible? Explain.**

5. You have been employed by Wilson Building Supplies as an accounting clerk. Your main duty is to record journal entries daily and post to the general ledger. Your procedure in posting is to post the entries by account order. For example, you first go through all your journal entries and post all Bank entries. You then proceed to the second account, and so on. **Explain the advantage of this method.**

6. Dean Perry posts from the journal to the ledger at the end of each week. Because he prepares a balance sheet once a year, he believes it is necessary to prepare a trial balance only once a year. **What are the disadvantages of taking a trial balance only once a year?**

Comprehensive Exercise

7. The accounts required for this exercise are shown in the chart of accounts below. If you are not using the Workbook for this exercise, allow 18 lines for the Bank account.

GENERAL ENGINEERING
CHART OF ACCOUNTS

101	Bank	301	Pat Schelling, Capital
111	A/R L. Pero	302	Pat Schelling, Drawings
113	A/R K. Puna	401	Service Revenue
115	A/R Spectrum Co.	505	Automobiles Expense
117	A/R W.J. Thomson	510	Bank Charges Expense
120	Supplies	515	General Expense
125	Equipment	520	Rent Expense
130	Automobiles	525	Telephone Expense
201	Bank Loan	530	Wages Expense
211	A/P Imperial Garage	535	Loss on Sale of Equipment
213	A/P Home Hardware		
220	Sales Tax Payable		

Pat Schelling, a millwright, began a business called General Engineering. His beginning financial position is shown in the following balance sheet:

GENERAL ENGINEERING
BALANCE SHEET
AUGUST 31, 19—

Assets		*Liabilities*	
Bank	$2 000	Bank Loan	$20 000
Supplies	1 450		
Equipment	14 732	*Owner's Equity*	
Automobiles	28 957	P. Schelling, Capital	27 139
	$47 139		$47 139

1. Journalize the opening entry and post it in the accounts.
2. Journalize and post the transactions for September shown below.

TRANSACTIONS

September

1 *Cheque Copy*
   To Rosewell Investments in the amount of $900 for the rent for the month.

3 *Purchase Invoice*
   From Home Hardware for $235 regarding supplies purchased on account.

5 *Sales Invoice*
   To W. J. Thomson, $3 500 plus $245 sales tax, for services rendered on account.
   To L. Pero, $2 000 plus $140 sales tax, for services rendered on account.

9 *Cash Sales Slip*
   Sold a piece of equipment for $500 cash (assume no sales tax). This piece of equipment had originally cost $1 200 and was included in the Equipment account at that figure. (**Note:** Although a sale has been made, this transaction does not affect the revenue account which is used only for the normal revenue of the business.)

10 *Sales Invoice*
   To Spectrum Co., $800 plus $56 sales tax, for services rendered on account.

11 *Cheque Copy*
   To the owner, for personal use, $500.

12 *Cheque Copy*
   To Home Hardware on account, $235.

15 *Purchase Invoice*
   Received from Imperial Garage charging for gasoline and oil used in the company automobiles, $342.

16 *Cheque Copy*
   Issued to the Marketplace for the cash purchase of supplies, $165. A bill for the supplies was attached to the cheque copy.

18 *Cash Receipt*
Received a cheque from W. J. Thomson in full payment of the account balance.

18 *Cheque Copy*
To the owner, repaying him for out-of-pocket expenses: Postage, $32; Parking, $40; and Gas and Oil for business purposes, $78; total $150.

19 *Bank Debit Memo*
Received a memorandum from the bank stating that $250 had been deducted from the business bank account for bank interest and bank service charges.

19 *Cheque Copy*
To an employee for wages, $575.

19 *Sales Invoice*
To K. Puna, $600 plus $42 sales tax, for services rendered on account.

22 *Memorandum*
From the owner, stating that the bank had acted on his instructions to reduce the bank loan by $2 000.

24 *Cheque Copy*
To Bell Telephone for $58 in payment of the telephone bill which was attached.

25 *Cash Receipt*
Received a cheque from L. Pero for $1 000 on account.

26 *Sales Invoice*
To W. J. Thomson, $400 plus $28 sales tax, for services rendered on account.

26 *Cheque Copy*
To the owner, for personal use, $450.

29 *Memorandum*
From the owner, stating that: 1) he had paid $190 out of his own pocket for supplies used for business purposes, and, 2) his Drawings account is to be credited for the above amount.

30 *Cheque Copies*
To an employee for wages, $570.
To Imperial Garage paying $342 on account.

30 *Purchase Invoice*
From Imperial Garage charging for gasoline and oil used in the company automobiles, $312.

3. **Balance the ledger by means of a trial balance.**
4. **Prepare an income statement for the month of September.**
5. **Prepare a simple balance sheet as at September 30. Remember that Equity = Assets – Liabilities.**

---

8. **The accounts required for this exercise are provided in the Workbook.**
The Harbour Golf Links, owned by Shirley Iris, operates a par-three golf course and a driving range. On September 30, 19-7, the trial balance of the business is as shown on page 215.

HARBOUR GOLF LINKS
TRIAL BALANCE
SEPTEMBER 30, 19-7

No.	Accounts	DR	CR
100	Bank	$ 3 750.20	
105	Supplies — Golf Course	10 236.00	
110	Supplies — Office	3 265.25	
115	Property	95 000.00	
120	Buildings	85 360.00	
125	Automotive Equipment	40 956.00	
130	Maintenance Equipment	22 650.60	
201	Bank Loan		$120 000.00
205	Account Payable — Main Supply		1 890.65
210	Account Payable — Blair's Automotive		
215	Account Payable — Pro Equipment		3 582.10
220	Mortgage Payable		100 000.00
301	Shirley Iris, Capital		37 802.96
305	Shirley Iris, Drawings	18 000.00	
401	Revenue — Golf		52 655.00
405	Revenue — Food		9 250.50
500	Automotive Expenses	5 963.01	
505	Bank Charges	6 842.25	
510	Light, Heat, and Water	2 850.45	
515	Maintenance Expense	7 230.85	
520	Miscellaneous Expense	1 525.75	
525	Mortgage Interest Expense	4 500.00	
530	Telephone Expense	685.55	
535	Wages Expense	16 365.30	
		$325 181.21	$325 181.21

1. **Journalize and post the transactions below and on page 216 for the month of October. Use page 28 of the journal.**

October

2   *Cheque Copy*
     No. 652, cash purchase of miscellaneous expense item, $155.

4   *Purchase Invoice*
     From Main Supply, for fertilizer, $950.20.

5   *Bank Debit Memo*
     Bank charges and loan interest for September, $1 250.

7   *Cheque Copy*
     No. 653, for wages for the week, $650.

8   *Cash Receipts*
     Cash receipts for previous week, golf $2 005, food $490, total $2 495.

9   *Cheque Copy*
    No. 654, to Main Supply, payment of debt owing, $1 890.65.
10 *Purchase Invoice*
    From Blair's Automotive, truck repairs, $220.
11 *Purchase Invoice*
    From Pro Equipment, golf course supplies, $176.40.
13 *Cheque Copy*
    No. 655, to the owner, for personal use, $1 500.
14 *Cheque Copy*
    No. 656, for wages for the week, $700.
15 *Cash Receipts*
    Cash receipts for previous week, golf $1 920, food $470, total $2 390.
17 *Purchase Invoice*
    From Pro Equipment, repairs to lawnmowers, $400.
18 *Cheque Copy*
    No. 657, to Axoil, cash purchases of gas and oil, $42.25.
20 *Cheque Copy*
    No. 658, to Greco Investments, mortgage payment, interest $750, principal
    $1 000, total $1 750.
21 *Cheque Copy*
    No. 659, for wages for the week, $680.
22 *Cash Receipts*
    Cash receipts for previous week, golf $2 200, food $500, total $2 700.
23 *Cheque Copy*
    No. 660, to Pro Equipment, partial payment of debt owing, $2 000.
24 *Purchase Invoice*
    From Main Supply, for office supplies, $95.
25 *Purchase Invoice*
    From Blair's Automotive, for auto equipment repairs, $290.
26 *Cheque Copy*
    No. 661, for the cash purchase of miscellaneous expense item, $85.
28 *Cheque Copy*
    No. 662, for the wages for the week, $620.
29 *Cash Receipts*
    Cash receipts for the previous week, golf $2 010, food $580, total $2 590.
30 *Cheque Copy*
    No. 663, cash payment for hydro for the month, $165.
31 *Cheque Copy*
    No. 664, cash payment for telephone for the month, $75.
31 *Cheque Copy*
    No. 665, to the owner, for personal use, $1 500.

2. **Balance the ledger by means of a trial balance.**
3. **Prepare a simple income statement for the 10 months ended October 31.**
4. **Prepare a simple balance sheet as of October 31. Remember that**
   Assets – Liabilities = Owner's Equity.

For Further Thought

9. Briefly answer the following questions.

1. People who work in accounting departments usually describe themselves as "accountants" regardless of how well qualified they are. Give your opinion of this practice, with reasons.
2. Is the person in charge of the payroll of a large business an important employee? Explain.
3. Not long ago, you earned your accountant's qualification while employed by Superior Tire Manufacturing Company. You have recently taken a new position with the General Life Insurance Company. Your new position presents you with many new challenges directly related to the accounting function. Explain what differences you might encounter and why they would be there.
4. Your teacher asks you to give the accounting entry for the purchase of supplies for cash. You begin your response, "Credit Bank and————." Your teacher stops you, believing that you are incorrect. Why would the teacher think so?
5. The accounts shown in your Workbook are usually only a few lines long. In actual practice they are a full page long. When setting up your ledger, would you put one account on the front side of the page, and a different account on the back? Support your answer with good reasons.
6. When cross-referencing, some accountants just use check marks. What are the advantages and disadvantages of this technique?
7. An accounting error that is found after quite some time would be corrected by a journal entry. Why would this method be used instead of stroking out incorrect figures and writing in the correct ones?
8. A posting intended for Smith's account in the accounts receivable ledger was incorrectly made to Smythe's account. How would this error be detected?
9. Many students prefer to look at the *Teacher's Keys* when they have an exercise that does not balance. Why is this a bad habit?
10. If your ledger does not balance by $5 and you have been unable to find the error after a four-day search, is it all right simply to change one of the accounts to force it into balance? Justify your opinion.

CASE STUDIES

CASE 1 *To Fire or Not To Fire?*

Sylvia Lomax is a recently qualified chartered accountant. Her first position after graduation has been chief accountant with Mayflower Movers of Saskatoon, Saskatchewan. Shortly after taking this position, she placed an advertisement in local newspapers for an experienced bookkeeper. She hired Steve Sheba, one of several applicants for the job.

Steve's first task in his new position was to take off a trial balance. This task usually took about half a day to complete. Steve began work on the trial balance in the afternoon of his first day on the job. At the end of the day the ledger was not yet balanced. Again at the end of the second day the ledger was not yet balanced.

Sylvia waited patiently for two more days for the task to be completed. When it was still not done at the day's end, she became concerned about Steve Sheba.

Questions

1. Should a bookkeeper be able to balance any ledger?
2. Has Sylvia allowed enough time for Steve to have balanced the ledger?
3. Is Sylvia right to be concerned about Steve?
4. Who is at fault here: Steve, or Sylvia? Give reasons for your choice.
5. What should Sylvia do to correct this situation?

CASE 2   *Frustration for the Auditor*

Pera Painting, of Montréal, Québec, has applied to the bank for a loan. The bank manager has some doubts about this customer. The owner of Pera Painting is Warren Dean, an aggressive young man with a reputation in the community for fast living. The records that Dean has submitted to the bank indicate that the business is quite profitable. However, Dean's recordkeeping techniques are unusual, and the bank manager is unsure about their accuracy. The bank manager asks Noel Des Roches, a public accountant, to audit the books.

Noel soon learns about Dean's methods. While at high school, Dean took an accounting course. Now he does his own bookkeeping. In order to save time, Dean does not use a journal but records all accounting entries directly in the accounts. In addition, he keeps a file of all business papers. He claims that he has never had a problem in backchecking on a transaction.

Noel finds it a slow process trying to figure out which debits correspond to which credits in the ledger. He always seems to need Dean to explain things to him and Dean is usually out on a job. On the third day, Noel finds that he cannot proceed further until Dean explains some puzzling entries. Unfortunately, Dean in not available, having left for a week's skiing in Europe.

Shown below are the unverified entries in the accounts. (These are not all of the accounts and entries of the business, but only the ones that Noel has not yet figured out.)

Bank		Acc Rec'l—P Watt	Materials	Property
5 000	5 000	5 000	5 000	10 000
	10 000			

Automobile	Acc Pay'l—C.P. Paints	City Loan Co.
10 000	5 000	5 000

Questions
1. From an office clerk, Noel learns the following:
   a. Dean bought either a car or an investment property from a customer. There was some talk of offsetting the customer's account balance against the cost price.
   b. Dean has a habit of taking some of the files home with him. Since there are no files or banking records in the office pertaining to the car or the property, Noel assumes that Dean has taken them home. Because Dean lives alone, these records are unavailable.

   Prepare a list of transactions that would explain the entries in the accounts.
2. Eventually, Noel realizes that he can't finish the audit until Dean returns from Europe, and reports this to the bank manager. The bank manager asks Noel to write up a report for Dean. Noel is to explain the difficulties he has encountered with Dean's records and how these difficulties can be avoided by using conventional accounting procedures.

   Write this report as if you were Noel Des Roches.

Case 3 *Is Bank Accounting Different?*

Accounting is one of Susan Lott's favourite subjects at school. She often talks at the dinner table about what she has learned in class that day. Susan's brother Ed has no formal accounting training, but is a junior clerk at a bank and is involved in bank accounting. One evening, Ed questions Susan's explanation of debit and credit theory. Ed claims that a customer's bank account is increased by means of a credit and decreased by means of a debit, and he produces a bank statement to prove it. Susan admits that her brother is right, and the next day Susan brings the issue up in her accounting class. As she suspected, her accounting teacher has a logical explanation.

Question
1. Write out a brief explanation of this issue as if you were the teacher.

Case 4 *Does Automated Accounting Use Standard Theory?*

Andy, another relative of Susan Lott, works as a clerk in the data processing and computer centre of a large corporation in Montréal. He claims that accounting is no longer done as Susan is learning it. Susan has now spent several months studying accounting. She is upset at Andy's suggestion that she is learning outmoded techniques.

Questions
1. Is there a different theory of accounting when it is computerized?
2. Even though accounting systems may use different journals and ledgers, do they use different theories of accounting? Explain.

ENTREPRENEUR
Lesley Hayes / Electraslide Corporation

Most people have two choices in life: they can work for someone else, or they can go into business for themselves. Lesley Hayes learned as a young person the trials and rewards of the second option, starting your own business.

In 1977, as a 15-year-old high school student in Calgary, Alberta, she joined Junior Achievement of Canada (JA). Through this organization, high school students "learn by doing" how business works in a free enterprise system.

One of JA's programs enables groups of 12 to 15 teenage achievers to form their own companies. They manufacture and sell a product or service of their choice. Looking for experience that would help her plan her future, Lesley joined her first JA company, Barntiques, as vice-president of marketing and production. The students, with the help of adult volunteer advisors from the Petrofina Corporation, decided to produce Memory Boxes. Made originally by pioneers out of barn boards, these boxes commemorated a first harvest, with compartments of seeds, dried flowers, etc. Barntiques raised the money needed to start the business by selling $2.00 shares to family and friends.

As part of her job, Lesley spent countless hours after school finding better ways to manufacture the boxes. A very streamlined process was developed to overcome the production problems. Then, when orders started pouring in, she and her fellow entrepreneurs worked overtime making extra boxes.

Thrilled by the excitement and fun of her first business success working with her friends, Lesley was elected president of another JA business the following year. Called the Rack Shack, the company made spice racks that sold for $9.99. This simple product, which required only 10 production steps, turned out to be a sales winner. Two-dollar shareholders received 130 per cent back on their investment when the company was liquidated a year later. Rack Shack also won JA's Alberta Company of the

Year award, Lesley was named President of the Year, Achiever of the Year, Salesperson of the Year, and received the Executive Award.

From her hands-on JA experience, Lesley learned production controls to make good quality products on time. She also developed the skill of getting the most out of co-workers as well as herself. Dealing fairly and ethically with the competition was easy because they were all her friends in JA. But it was the luxury of being able to learn and make mistakes on a relatively small scale in JA that gave her the confidence and desire she needed to eventually launch her own business.

After graduating from high school, Lesley attended the Alberta College of Art and earned a four-year diploma in Visual Communications. Seeing the trend towards computer graphics, she then spent a year at Sheridan College studying computer art and design. To obtain experience before starting her own business, Lesley worked for computer art firms

in Calgary and Vancouver, where she quickly moved up from night artist to full partner. Along the way, she learned how to write a business plan, raise funds, produce budgets, and deal with clients.

In 1987, she struck out on her own, creating the Electraslide Corporation, which produces slides for audiovisual presentations, mainly for large oil firms. The company has grown at an annual rate of 35% a year, with expected sales of $250,000 for 1989.

Lesley credits JA and her work experience with teaching her how important efficient systems are. They keep track of everything from production and sales to payroll, financing, and other expenses. Without knowing what is going on, she says, you won't be able to control costs or create profits.

Lesley's advice to young people considering a business career is that success is 10 per cent inspiration, 90 per cent perspiration, and 100 per cent commitment.

DISCUSSION

1. Why did Lesley want to join Junior Achievement?
2. How do you think the adult volunteer advisors might help students taking part in Junior Achievement programs?
3. How do you think Lesley's experience with Junior Achievement helped her in her career plans?
4. Why did Lesley not go into business for herself immediately after graduation from college?
5. What, according to Lesley, are the most important factors for a business career?

The Work Sheet and Formal Financial Statements

8.1 The Six-Column Work Sheet
8.2 Formal Financial Statements: Income Statement
8.3 Formal Financial Statements: Balance Sheet

In the preceding chapters, you learned about the system for recording transactions in the books of account. Next you will learn the technique used to prepare the income statement and the balance sheet.

Financial statements are prepared from the information provided by the ledger accounts. They are prepared at the end of the fiscal period and whenever else they may be required. The preparation of formal financial statements is normally the work of senior accounting staff or professional accountants.

8.1 THE SIX-COLUMN WORK SHEET

Purpose of the Work Sheet

Accountants use a business form called a work sheet to help prepare the financial statements. A **work sheet** is an informal business paper used to organize and plan the information for the financial statements. The work sheet is prepared on columnar accounting paper, usually in pencil so that changes may be made easily. Accountants normally use an eight-column work sheet in order to include further information. You will study the eight-column work sheet in Chapter 9. The six-column work sheet is used at this time to present the new concepts as simply as possible.

Control Accounts for Accounts Receivable and Accounts Payable

When you look at your first work sheet you will see a difference in the way accounts receivable and accounts payable are handled. You will see that there are no debtors' names associated with the Accounts Receivable account or creditors' names associated with the Accounts Payable account. What you see on the work sheet are the Accounts Receivable *control* account and the Accounts Payable *control* account. The **Accounts Receivable control account** represents the sum of the balances of all the individual Accounts Receivable accounts. The **Accounts Payable control account** represents the sum of the balances of all the individual Accounts Payable accounts.

Having two control accounts instead of dozens or hundreds of individual debtors' and creditors' accounts streamlines the work sheet. It produces a single figure for accounts receivable and a single figure for accounts payable. This is more efficient for preparing work sheets and provides a more effective presentation on the balance sheet.

The details about the accounts of individual debtors and creditors are kept in separate records. The formal procedure for maintaining control accounts and the separate records for debtors and creditors is the topic of Chapter 10.

Steps in Preparing a Work Sheet

1 Write in the heading on the work sheet paper. Examine the heading in Figure 8.1 carefully. Observe the precise way that the fiscal period is described.

Vulcan Rentalls	Work Sheet			Year Ended December 31, 19--		
ACCOUNTS	TRIAL BALANCE		INCOME STATEMENT		BALANCE SHEET	
	DR	CR	DR	CR	DR	CR

Figure 8.1   Recording the heading on the work sheet.

2 Enter all accounts with their balances in the first two columns, as shown in Figure 8.2. It is essential that the trial balance columns be correct before you continue. There is no hope of producing a correct work sheet if the trial balance does not balance.

3 Extend each of the amounts from the trial balance columns into one of the four columns to the right as in Figure 8.3. The process is simple and logical. Revenue and expense items are extended into the Income Statement columns. These are the items that make up the net income or net loss. All other items—assets, liabilities, capital, and drawings—are extended into the Balance Sheet columns. Observe that the drawings are not a net income item and are not transferred to the Income Statement section.

Be careful to transfer amounts accurately, and to record debit amounts in debit columns and credit amounts in credit columns. Be sure, too, that no single amount is transferred to two places and that no item is missed.

4 Balance the work sheet, as shown in Figure 8.4. There are four steps in balancing the work sheet.

a. Total each of the four right-hand money columns and write in the totals.

b. Calculate the difference between the two Income Statement columns (in our example, $35 579.01), then the difference between the two Balance Sheet columns (again, $35 579.01), and see that the two differences are equal.

Valcan Rentalls	Work Sheet						Year Ended December 31, 19--	
		TRIAL BALANCE		INCOME STATEMENT		BALANCE SHEET		
ACCOUNTS		DR	CR	DR	CR	DR	CR	
Bank		3 4 5 7 15						
Accounts Receivable		19 4 0 2 50						
Supplies		1 2 4 0 -						
Equipment		20 4 0 0 -						
Automobiles		32 9 3 6 57						
Accounts Payable			5 2 9 6 10					
Sales Tax Payable			5 6 1 11					
Bank Loan			10 0 0 0 -					
R. Tessier, Capital			50 0 0 0 -					
R. Tessier, Drawings		24 0 0 0 -						
Sales			95 9 0 7 -					
Advertising Expense		7 5 6 -						
Bank Charges Expense		1 7 4 2 -						
Car Expense		6 5 7 5 80						
Miscellaneous Expense		1 7 5 -						
Rent Expense		12 0 0 0 -						
Telephone Expense		1 2 0 0 -						
Utilities Expense		1 3 7 0 -						
Wages Expense		36 5 0 9 19						
		161 7 6 4 21	161 7 6 4 21					

Figure 8.2   Recording the trial balance on a work sheet.

If they are not the same, the work sheet does not balance. It is mathematically impossible for the work sheet to be correct if it does not balance. Therefore, you should not proceed to the preparation of the financial statements until all errors have been found and corrected.

c. Record the balancing figure on the work sheet in two places, as shown in Figure 8.4. Since the revenues are greater than the expenses, the balancing figure represents a net income. Record the balancing figure on the debit side of the income statement columns and on the credit side of the balance sheet columns. The balancing figure appears on the credit side of the balance sheet section, since the net income represents an increase in the capital.

Notice that the balancing figure ($35 579.01) is placed in two locations on the work sheet: in the outer two of the last four columns. This is normal when there is a profit.

d. Rule and show the final column totals as shown in Figure 8.4.

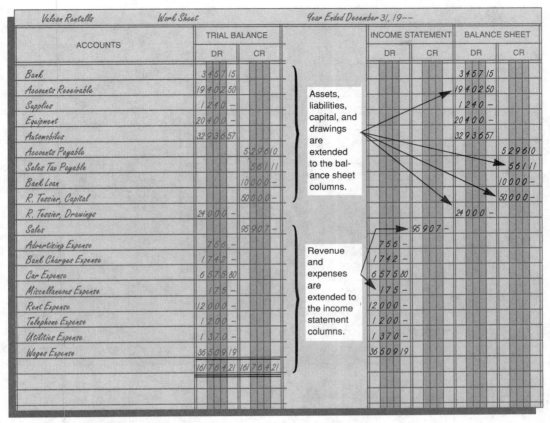

Figure 8.3   Extending the amounts on a work sheet.

Vulcan Rentalls — Work Sheet — Year Ended December 31, 19--

ACCOUNTS	TRIAL BALANCE DR	CR	INCOME STATEMENT DR	CR	BALANCE SHEET DR	CR
Bank	3457 15				3457 15	
Accounts Receivable	19402 50				19402 50	
Supplies	1240 -				1240 -	
Equipment	20400 -				20400 -	
Automobiles	32936 57				32936 57	
Accounts Payable		5296 10				5296 10
Sales Tax Payable		561 11				561 11
Bank Loan		10000 -				10000 -
R. Tessier, Capital		50000 -				50000 -
R. Tessier, Drawings	24000 -				24000 -	
Sales		95907 -		95907 -		
Advertising Expense	756 -		756 -			
Bank Charges Expense	1742 -		1742 -			
Car Expense	6575 80		6575 80			
Miscellaneous Expense	175 -		175 -			
Rent Expense	12000 -		12000 -			
Telephone Expense	1200 -		1200 -			
Utilities Expense	1370 -		1370 -			
Wages Expense	36509 19		36509 19			
	161764 21	161764 21	60327 99	95907 -	101436 22	65857 21
Net Income			35579 01			35579 01
			95907 -	95907 -	101436 22	101436 22

Balancing figure

Figure 8.4 Balancing the work sheet (net income situation).

Net Income or Net Loss

The balancing figure on the work sheet tells the amount of the net income or net loss for the fiscal period. A look at the Income Statement columns tells which of the two it is. A net income has been earned if the total revenues (credit column) are greater than the total expenses (debit column). A net loss has been incurred if the total expenses (debit column) are greater than the total revenues (credit column).

Finalizing the work sheet for a loss situation is done slightly differently than for a profit situation. The balancing figure is placed in the **inner two of the last four columns** when there is a loss. A balancing figure of $356.07 is shown in Figure 8.5.

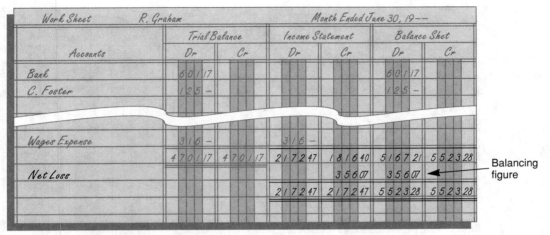

Balancing
figure

Figure 8.5 Balancing the work sheet (net loss situation).

The Work Sheet and the Financial Statements

Owners and business executives rarely look at the raw data of actual financial records. They rely on the accounting department to maintain the records properly and to process the data into a more meaningful form. The owners and executives want to see finished accounting reports and financial statements. It is up to the accounting department to produce first-class reports and statements.

A completed work sheet contains all of the information needed to prepare the income statement and the balance sheet. Develop the habit of looking only to the work sheet for this information. It is the best, and sometimes the only, source of the information. Figures 8.6, 8.7, and 8.8 show how the income statement and the balance sheet of Vulcan Rentalls are prepared directly from the work sheet.

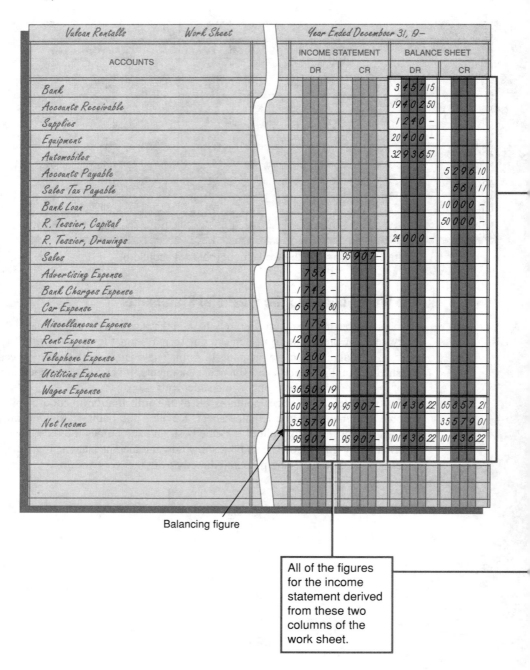

Vulcan Rentalls	Work Sheet		Year Ended December 31, 19—		
ACCOUNTS		INCOME STATEMENT		BALANCE SHEET	
		DR	CR	DR	CR
Bank				3457 15	
Accounts Receivable				19402 50	
Supplies				1240 —	
Equipment				20400 —	
Automobiles				32936 57	
Accounts Payable					5296 10
Sales Tax Payable					561 11
Bank Loan					10000 —
R. Tessier, Capital					50000 —
R. Tessier, Drawings				24000 —	
Sales			95907 —		
Advertising Expense		756 —			
Bank Charges Expense		1742 —			
Car Expense		6575 80			
Miscellaneous Expense		175 —			
Rent Expense		12000 —			
Telephone Expense		1200 —			
Utilities Expense		1370 —			
Wages Expense		36509 19			
		60327 99	95907 —	101436 22	65857 21
Net Income		35579 01			35579 01
		95907 —	95907 —	101436 22	101436 22

Balancing figure

All of the figures for the income statement derived from these two columns of the work sheet.

Figure 8.6 A partial work sheet for Vulcan Rentalls, giving the information for the financial statements shown in Figure 8.7 and Figure 8.8.

Vulcan Rentalls				
Balance Sheet				
December 31, 19–				
Assets				
Current Assets				
Bank			3 457 15	
Accounts Receivable			19 402 50	
Supplies			1 240 –	24 099 65
Plant and Equipment				
Equipment			20 400 –	
Automobiles			32 936 57	53 336 57
				77 436 22
Liabilities and Owner's Equity				
Current Liabilities				
Accounts Payable			5 296 10	
Sales Tax Payable			561 11	
Bank Loan			10 000 –	15 857 21
R. Tessier, Capital				
Balance, January 1			50 000 –	
Net Income	35 579 01			
Drawings	24 000 –			
Increase in Capital			11 579 01	
Balance, December 31				61 579 01
				77 436 22

Figure 8.7   The balance sheet, prepared from the amounts in the "balance sheet" columns of the work sheet.

Vulcan Rentalls		
Income Statement		
Year Ended December 31, 19–		
Revenue		
Sales		95 907 –
Operating Expenses		
Advertising Expense	756 –	
Bank Charges Expense	1 742 –	
Car Expenses	6 575 80	
Miscellaneous Expense	175 –	
Rent Expense	12 000 –	
Telephone Expense	1 200 –	
Utilities Expense	1 370 –	
Wages Expense	36 509 19	
Total Operating Expenses		60 327 99
Net Income		35 579 01

Figure 8.8   The income statement, prepared from the amounts in the "income statement" columns of the work sheet.

(Left margin note, pointing to balance sheet:) of the figures the balance ⋯eet derived ⋯m these two ⋯lumns of the ⋯rk sheet.

More on the Accounting Cycle

You have already learned that there is a certain set of procedures to be followed during a fiscal period. Journalizing, posting, and balancing of the ledger are carried out by junior employees. The next two steps involve the preparation of the work sheet and the financial statements. They are carried out by senior people. All the steps together constitute the accounting cycle.

The six steps of the accounting cycle studied so far are shown in Figure 8.9 below.

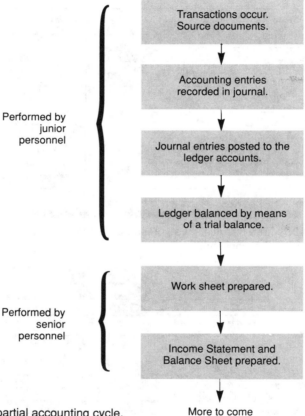

Performed by junior personnel

Transactions occur. Source documents.

Accounting entries recorded in journal.

Journal entries posted to the ledger accounts.

Ledger balanced by means of a trial balance.

Performed by senior personnel

Work sheet prepared.

Income Statement and Balance Sheet prepared.

More to come

Figure 8.9 Steps in the partial accounting cycle.

SECTION REVIEW QUESTIONS

1. When are financial statements prepared?
2. In the accounting department, who usually prepares the financial statements?
3. Name and describe the form used by accountants to help them prepare the financial statements.
4. Explain an important aspect of step 2 in completing a work sheet.
5. Which kinds of accounts are extended to the balance sheet columns?

6. How do you know if the work sheet balances?
7. Why is it important to balance the work sheet?
8. Why is the Drawings account not extended to the Income Statement section?
9. How do you tell if the business has made a profit or suffered a loss?
10. Why do managers and owners usually not look at the actual accounting records?
11. What records do the managers and owners look at?
12. Why should an accounting department be concerned about producing first-rate reports and statements?
13. Where is the best place for an accountant to obtain all of the necessary information for the balance sheet and the income statement?
14. Give the six steps in the accounting cycle so far.

SECTION EXERCISES

1. **For each account listed below, indicate whether it would be extended to Income Statement Debit, Income Statement Credit, Balance Sheet Debit, or Balance Sheet Credit.** (A chart for this exercise is provided in the Workbook.)

Accounts Payable	Bank Loan
Miscellaneous Expense	Accounts Receivable
Revenue	Automobile
Advertising Expense	Bank
Wages Expense	G. Rojek, Drawings
Mortgage Payable	Sales
Light and Heat Expense	Bank Charges Expense
Equipment	Rent Expense
G. Rojek, Capital	Supplies
Delivery Expense	Trucks

2. **From the simplified data shown below, complete a work sheet for N. Foreman and Company for the month ended April 30, 19—.** (Profit situation)

TRIAL BALANCE APRIL 30, 19—

Bank	$ 750.20	
Accounts Receivable	15 375.10	
Supplies	1 250.00	
Equipment	18 500.00	
Automobiles	29 375.00	
Bank Loan		$30 000.00
Accounts Payable		5 331.00
N. Foreman, Capital		25 000.00
N. Foreman, Drawings	3 000.00	
Fees Revenue		18 200.00
Bank Charges Expense	250.00	
Car Expense	1 750.00	
Miscellaneous Expense	512.20	
Light and Heat Expense	746.00	
Rent Expense	1 100.00	
Telephone Expense	276.50	
Wages Expense	5 646.00	
	$78 531.00	$78 531.00

3. **Workbook Exercise: Additional practice in completing a work sheet. (Loss situation)**

4. The trial balance for Boa Bodyworks and Repairs for the year ended December 31, 19-8, is given below.

BOA BODYWORKS AND REPAIRS
TRIAL BALANCE
DECEMBER 31, 19-8

	DR	CR
Bank	$ 723.50	
Accounts Receivable	23 356.05	
Supplies	1 420.00	
Land	54 000.00	
Building	102 500.00	
Automobiles	35 256.20	
Equipment	25 750.00	
Bank Loan		$ 30 000.00
Accounts Payable		5 365.25
Sales Tax Payable		568.35
B. Boa, Capital		188 975.87
B. Boa, Drawings	48 000.00	
Revenue — Bodywork		135 315.02
Revenue — Repairs		66 214.98
Advertising Expense	850.00	
Automobile Expense	4 569.33	
Bank Charges Expense	3 485.00	
General Expense	1 258.90	
Light and Heat Expense	2 585.00	
Materials Expense	36 750.25	
Telephone Expense	1 585.00	
Wages Expense	84 350.24	
	$426 439.47	$426 439.47

Prepare a six-column work sheet for the above. (Profit situation)

5. The work sheet on page 233 contains a number of errors.

1. **Locate the errors, make the necessary corrections, and balance the work sheet.** A work sheet for you to use has been provided in the Workbook.
2. **State what the control account balances would be for accounts receivable and accounts payable.**

6. **Workbook Exercise: Steps in the Accounting Cycle**

Work Sheet	The Arthur Company				Month Ended Oct. 31, 19—	
Accounts	Trial Balance		Income Statement		Balance Sheet	
	Dr	Cr	Dr	Cr	Dr	Cr
Bank	1722 16				1722 16	
Acc. Rec'l - J. Young	323 –				323 –	
Acc. Rec'l - M. Watson	72 –				72 –	
Acc. Rec'l - H. Chan	116 –				116 –	
Supplies	1255 –				1255 –	
Office Equipment	5863 –				5863 –	
Automobiles	13200 –				13200 –	
Acc. Pay'l - O.K. Supply		421 72				421 72
Acc. Pay'l - City Hydro		116 42				116 42
Acc. Pay'l - Slick Oil Co.		331 19				331 19
Bank Loan		10000 –				10000 –
P. Arthur, Capital		10504 82				10504 82
P. Arthur, Drawings	1000 –		1000 –			
Revenue		4903 17		4903 17		
Advertising	465 12		465 12			
Automobile Expense	270 –				270 –	
Bank Charges	56 40		56 40			
Miscellaneous Exp.	113 74		113 74			
Rent	400 –		400 –			
Salaries	1280 –		1280 –		1280 –	
Telephone	25 60		25 60			
Utilities	115 30					
	26277 32	26277 32	2340 86	5903 17	12230 16	21074 15
Net Income			3562 31			8843 99
			5903 17	5903 17	12230 16	29918 14

8.2 FORMAL FINANCIAL STATEMENTS: INCOME STATEMENT

The Formal Income Statement

You learned previously that revenues and expenses together produce a net income or a net loss. You also learned that this information is summarized on the income statement, and that it is very important information. The income statement tells the owners and managers how the business is doing, that is, whether or not it is profitable. These people will be keenly interested in this information because their livelihoods and the continuation of the business depend on profitability.

By definition, an **income statement** is a financial statement that summarizes the items of revenue and expense, and shows the net income or net loss of a business for a given period of time. The formal income statement of Cherub Air Service is shown in Figure 8.10.

You should note carefully the main components of the formal income statement as shown in Figure 8.10.

1. The **Heading** gives: • name of business;
   • name of statement;
   • accounting period for which the figures have been accumulated.
2. The **Revenue** section shows an increase in equity resulting from the proceeds of the sale of goods or services in the ordinary course of business.
3. Two types of revenue are shown in the statement for Cherub Air Service.
4. The **Expense** section shows decreases in equity resulting from the cost of the goods or services used to produce the revenue.
5. Expenses are shown in detail.
6. The **Net Income** or **Net Loss** figure. Net Income is the difference between total revenues and total expenses, if the revenues are greater than the expenses. In this case:

Revenues	$252 931
Expenses	−166 970
Net Income	$ 85 961

Net income is also known as net profit. Net income is not cash. Net Loss occurs if the expenses are greater than the revenues.

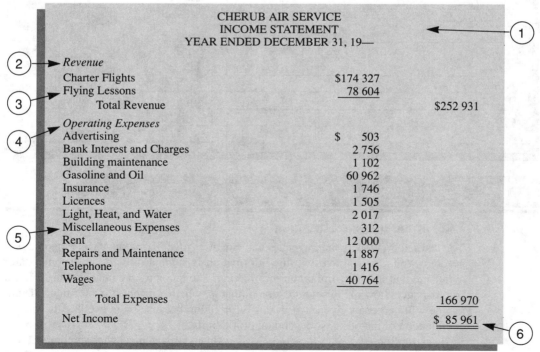

Figure 8.10   The income statement for Cherub Air Service showing a two-column presentation.

The Income Statement Put to Use

By Owners and Managers

The income statement is a very useful tool. It tells the owners or managers if their business is earning a profit and how much the profit is. The income statement is helpful to them in forming company goals and policies, and in making business decisions.

A business will not survive long if it does not earn a profit. All of the figures making up the profit or loss may be seen on the income statement. The figures for the current year may be compared with those for the prior year or years. Unfavourable trends or problems may be seen quickly and can then be corrected. Successful businesspeople make good use of the information on the income statement.

By Bankers

Bankers will want to see the financial statements of any business to which they lend money. Bankers need to know if the borrower will be able to repay the loan. Financial statements help inform bankers about the condition of a business.

By Income Tax Authorities

Every business is required by law to prepare an income statement once each year. The net income figure of a proprietorship must be included on the owner's income tax return. The income statement must be sent to the government along with the owner's income tax return.

SECTION REVIEW QUESTIONS

1. What are the two classifications on the simple income statement?
2. How do you calculate net income? Net loss?
3. Name the three persons or groups who use the income statement.
4. Why are owners keenly interested in the income statement?
5. Why are bankers interested in seeing the income statement of a business to which the bank has loaned money?
6. Name one type of business which must produce an income statement for the government.
7. Explain why the income statement in question 6 above is needed.

SECTION EXERCISES

1. Shown below is the simple income statement for Jott Consultants.

JOTT CONSULTANTS		
INCOME STATEMENT		
MONTH ENDED OCTOBER 31, 19-8		
Revenue		
Consulting Fees		$42 657.00
Operating Expenses		
Advertising Expense	$ 1 200.50	
Bank Charges Expense	252.65	
Car Repairs Expense	1 852.60	
Gasoline and Oil Expense	2 528.10	
Rent Expense	1 200.00	
Salaries Expense	12 400.00	
Telephone Expense	356.50	
Utilities Expense	256.90	
Total Expenses		20 047.25
Net Income		$22 609.75

Study the above statement and answer the questions that follow.

1. What three things are included in the heading?
2. Explain how the date for the income statement will differ from the date used on the balance sheet for this business.
3. On what day did the previous fiscal period end?
4. How is the net income calculated?
5. Explain why the individual expenses are entered in the first of the two columns.

2. Given on page 237 is a completed partial work sheet.
From this work sheet prepare a simple income statement.

Provident Services	Work Sheet	Year Ended June 30, 19-5		
		Income Statement		
Accounts		Debit	Credit	
Bank				
Accounts Receivable				
Supplies				
Land				
Building				
Equipment				
Automobiles				
Accounts Payable				
Sales Tax Payable				
J. Hori, Capital				
J. Hori, Drawings				
Commissions Earned			$135 269.25	
Advertising Expense		$ 2 400.00		
Automobile Expense		8 352.10		
General Expense		1 252.14		
Light and Heat Expense		3 525.40		
Telephone Expense		1 741.20		
Wages Expense		55 365.01		
		72 635.85	135 269.25	
Net Income		62 633.40		
		$135 269.25	$135 269.25	

3. There are a number of errors in the income statement below for Mayfare Plumbing, owned by James Fare.

INCOME STATEMENT
JAMES FARE
DECEMBER 31, 19-5

Revenue		
Sales and Service		$127 416.00
Operating Expenses		
Advertising	$ 1 150.50	
Bank Charges	1 750.00	
Depreciation of Automobile	4 296.—	
Gas and Oil	4 935.—	
Light, Heat, and Power	3 975.12	
Materials Used	15 906.—	
Miscellaneous	257.00	
Telephone	250.00	
Wages	$18 076.09	
Total Expenses		55 095.71
Net Profit		$ 72 320.29

1. **Identify the errors and list them in the space provided in your Workbook.**
2. **Calculate the correct net income.**

8.3 *FORMAL FINANCIAL STATEMENTS: BALANCE SHEET*

Balance Sheet—Account Form and Report Form

The balance sheets that you are going to work with in this chapter are different from those you learned about earlier. The previous balance sheets were shown in account form. The **account form of balance sheet** is one on which the information is presented in a side-by-side, or horizontal, format.

In this chapter you will study a style of balance sheet known as the report form. The **report form of balance sheet** is one on which the information is presented in a one-above-the-other, or vertical, format. The two styles are contrasted in Figure 8.11. The report form of balance sheet is common because it uses standard-sized paper.

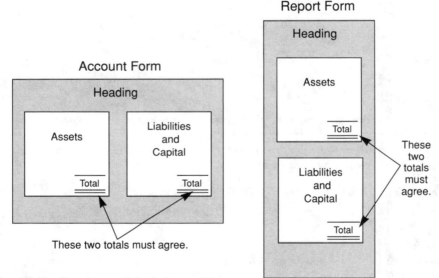

Figure 8.11   Two forms of the balance sheet.

Formal Balance Sheet

The balance sheet introduced in this chapter is a classified one. A **classified balance sheet** is one in which the data is grouped according to major categories. A sample classified balance sheet is shown in Figure 8.12. Observe the overall appearance of this balance sheet carefully. Be sure to relate the marginal notes to the sample statement. In particular, note the meanings of the terms "current assets," "plant and equipment," "current liabilities," and "long-term liabilities" and the way that the "equity" is presented. You will learn more about classified statements as you progress through the text.

You should note carefully the main components of the classified balance sheet as shown in Figure 8.12.

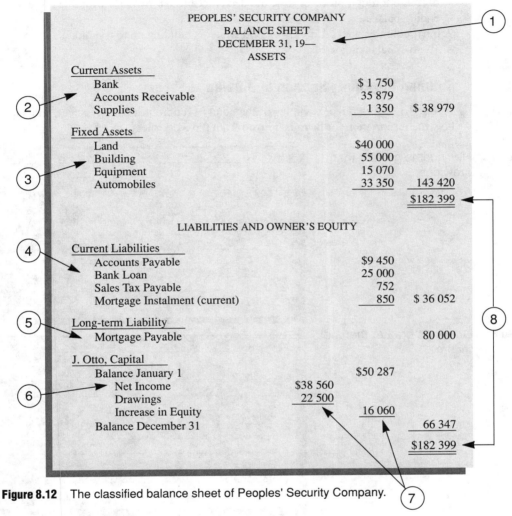

PEOPLES' SECURITY COMPANY
BALANCE SHEET
DECEMBER 31, 19—
ASSETS

Current Assets		
Bank	$ 1 750	
Accounts Receivable	35 879	
Supplies	1 350	$ 38 979
Fixed Assets		
Land	$40 000	
Building	55 000	
Equipment	15 070	
Automobiles	33 350	143 420
		$182 399

LIABILITIES AND OWNER'S EQUITY

Current Liabilities		
Accounts Payable	$9 450	
Bank Loan	25 000	
Sales Tax Payable	752	
Mortgage Instalment (current)	850	$ 36 052
Long-term Liability		
Mortgage Payable		80 000
J. Otto, Capital		
Balance January 1		$50 287
Net Income	$38 560	
Drawings	22 500	
Increase in Equity		16 060
Balance December 31		66 347
		$182 399

Figure 8.12   The classified balance sheet of Peoples' Security Company.

1. The **Heading** gives: • name of business
   • name of statement
   • date on which the balance is taken.
2. **Current Assets**: assets that will be converted into cash within one year and assets that will be used up within one year.
3. **Plant and Equipment or Fixed Assets**: long-term assets held for their usefulness in producing goods or services.
4. **Current Liabilities**: short-term debts, payment of which is expected to occur within one year.
5. **Long-term Liabilities**: debts of the business that are not due within one year.

6. Capital: total assets minus total liabilities.

This section is organized to show clearly the beginning balance, the increase or decrease through profit or loss, the decrease through owner's withdrawals, and the ending balance.

7. Inner columns are used to list individual items building up to a subtotal.

8. The two balancing totals.

Building the Equity Section of a Balance Sheet

Figure 8.13 gives three examples of the equity section of a balance sheet, and shows how the information for them is derived from the work sheet.

Case 1. Net income greater than drawings.

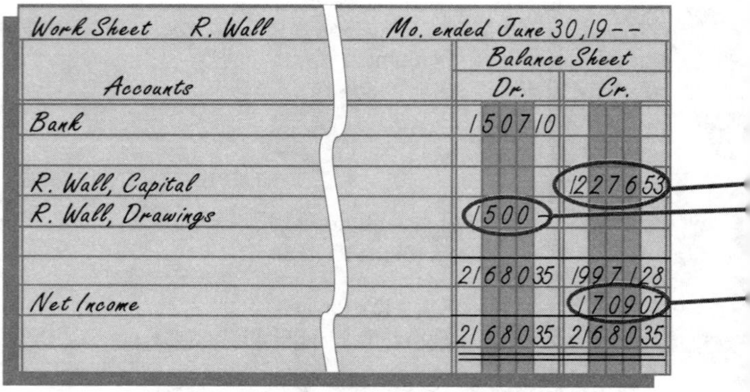

Case 2. Drawings greater than net income.

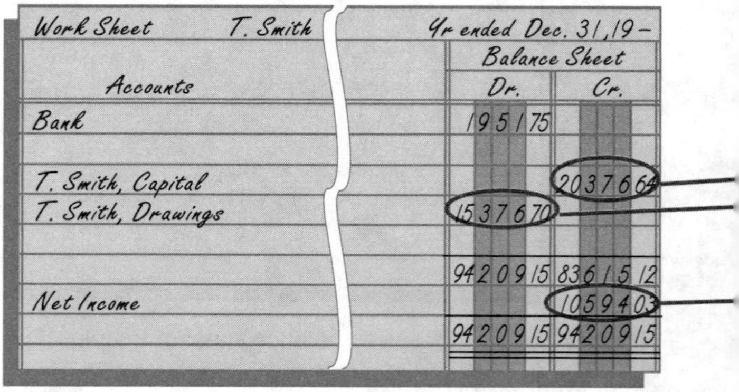

Case 3. A loss.

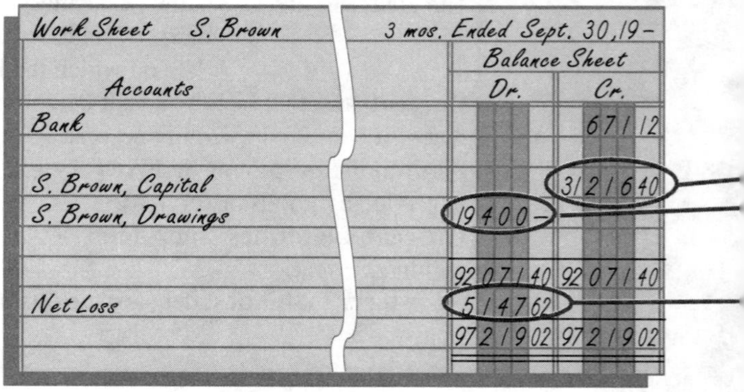

Figure 8.13 Equity items are transferred from the work sheet (left) to the balance sheet (right) for three different situations.

R. Wall, Capital					
Balance June 1			12 27 6 53		
Net Income	1 7 09 07				
Drawings	1 5 00				
Increase in Capital			2 09 07		
Balance June 30				12 4 8 5 60	

T. Smith, Capital					
Balance January 1			20 3 7 6 64		
Net Income	10 5 9 4 03				
Drawings	15 3 7 6 70				
Decrease in Capital			4 7 8 2 67		
Balance December 31				15 5 9 3 97	

S Brown, Capital					
Balance, July 1			31 2 1 6 40		
Net Loss	5 1 4 7 62				
Drawings	1 9 4 00				
Decrease in Capital			24 5 4 7 62		
Balance September 30				6 6 6 8 78	

Understanding the Equity Section of the Balance Sheet

The three equity sections from the previous page are examined again below from a different viewpoint. Figure 8.14 tells us that in each case, the equity section starts with the capital figure at the beginning of the fiscal period, shows the changes in capital during the period, and finishes with the capital at the end of the period.

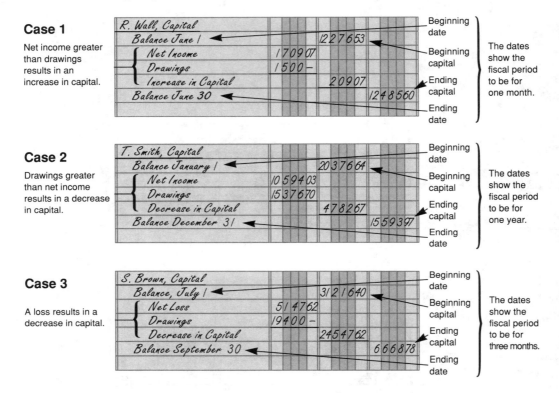

Case 1

Net income greater than drawings results in an increase in capital.

Case 2

Drawings greater than net income results in a decrease in capital.

Case 3

A loss results in a decrease in capital.

Figure 8.14   Three equity sections showing how equity changes in a fiscal period.

Typed or Printed Financial Statements

In the business world, financial reports are usually typewritten or printed. However, as a student you will find it more convenient to prepare your statements in handwritten form.

Shown on page 243 in Figure 8.15 is a typical typewritten balance sheet. Observe in particular the way in which dollar signs are used.

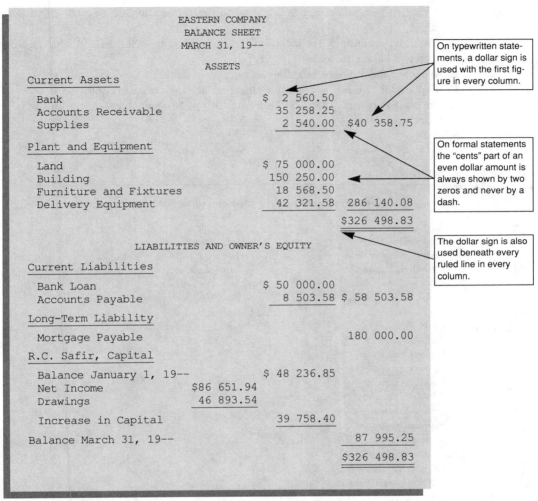

EASTERN COMPANY
BALANCE SHEET
MARCH 31, 19--

ASSETS

Current Assets

Bank	$ 2 560.50	
Accounts Receivable	35 258.25	
Supplies	2 540.00	$40 358.75

Plant and Equipment

Land	$ 75 000.00	
Building	150 250.00	
Furniture and Fixtures	18 568.50	
Delivery Equipment	42 321.58	286 140.08
		$326 498.83

LIABILITIES AND OWNER'S EQUITY

Current Liabilities

| Bank Loan | $ 50 000.00 | |
| Accounts Payable | 8 503.58 | $ 58 503.58 |

Long-Term Liability

| Mortgage Payable | | 180 000.00 |

R.C. Safir, Capital

Balance January 1, 19--		$ 48 236.85	
Net Income	$86 651.94		
Drawings	46 893.54		
Increase in Capital		39 758.40	
Balance March 31, 19--			87 995.25
			$326 498.83

> On typewritten statements, a dollar sign is used with the first figure in every column.

> On formal statements the "cents" part of an even dollar amount is always shown by two zeros and never by a dash.

> The dollar sign is also used beneath every ruled line in every column.

Figure 8.15   An example of a typed financial statement.

SECTION REVIEW QUESTIONS

1. In what style were the balance sheets of the early chapters prepared?
2. Describe the account form of the balance sheet.
3. Describe the report form of the balance sheet.
4. Give the accountancy meaning of the word "classified."
5. Name the two asset classifications on the simple balance sheet in Figure 8.12.
6. Give another accepted name for "Plant and Equipment."
7. Name the two liability classifications on the simple balance sheet.
8. Describe how the capital is presented on the new form of balance sheet.

9. Describe how the columns are used in the preparation of a classified balance sheet.
10. The equity section of the balance sheet is made up from three figures on the work sheet. What are these three figures?
11. What set of conditions produces an increase in equity?
12. Explain the two sets of conditions that produce a decrease in equity.
13. In what two ways, besides the print, do typed financial statements differ from handwritten ones?

SECTION EXERCISES

1. **Classify the accounts given below into one of the categories named at the right.**

Accounts	*Categories*
Accounts Payable	Current Assets
Accounts Receivable	Plant and Equipment
Advertising Expense	Current Liabilities
Automobiles	Long-term Liabilities
Bank Charges Expense	Owner's Equity
Bank Loan	Revenue
Bank	Operating Expense
Buildings	
Commissions Earned	
Delivery Expense	
F. Ryback, Capital	
F. Ryback, Drawings	
General Expense	
Insurance Expense	
Mortgage Payable (Current Instalment)	
Mortgage Payable (Non-current portion)	
Postage Expense	
Rent Expense	
Supplies	
Telephone Expense	
Wages Expense	

2. Shown on p. 245 is the unclassified balance sheet for The Boat Repair Centre, owned by Anna Rodriguez of Kenora, Ontario.

   1. Give the total of the current assets.
   2. Give the total of the fixed assets.
   3. Give the total of the current liabilities.
   4. Give the total of the long-term liabilities.

5. Explain why there is an increase in capital.
6. Explain why the equity section begins on October 1 and ends on September 30.
7. What is the amount of the total mortgage payable?

THE BOAT REPAIR CENTRE
BALANCE SHEET
SEPTEMBER 30, 19-4

Assets

Bank	$ 2 125.00
Accounts Receivable	15 256.36
Office Supplies	1 500.00
Repair Supplies and Materials	15 236.00
Land	36 000.00
Building	48 000.00
Equipment	16 250.00
Truck	22 356.90
	$156 724.26

Liabilities

Accounts Payable	$ 5 216.35
Bank Loan	10 000.00
Mortgage Instalment due within one year	2 000.00
Mortgage Payable	48 000.00
	$ 65 216.35

Owner's Equity

A. Rodriguez, Capital

Balance October 1, 19-3		$80 356.00
Net Income	$35 615.20	
Drawings	24 463.29	
Increase in Capital		11 151.91
Balance September 30, 19-4		91 507.91
		$156 724.26

3. In your Workbook complete the following schedule by filling in the blanks.

Items	Opening Capital	Net Income or Net Loss (−)	Drawings	Ending Capital
a.	$30 000	$15 000	$10 000	$
b.	50 000	−2 000	7 000	
c.	70 000	32 000		75 500
d.		16 000	19 500	33 200
e	56 000		30 000	40 000
f.	45 000		25 000	15 000
g.	22 000		10 000	28 000
h.		25 000	18 000	42 000
i.	120 000	42 000		112 000

4. **Prepare the equity section of the balance sheet from the data given for each case below.**

Owner's name	T. Hunter	S. Robb	W. Head
Fiscal period	Year ended December 31, 19—	Three months ended March 31, 19—	Month ended May 31, 19—
Opening capital	$27 042.62	$19 641.25	$20 196.74
Net income	39 171.04	22 462.67	(Loss) 3 750.20
Drawings	35 000.00	25 575.00	10 047.17

5. **From the following data prepare the classified balance sheet in report form for Fraser River Enterprises for the year ended December 31, 19-5.**

	DR	CR
Bank	$ 1 500.85	
Accounts Receivable	33 654.87	
Supplies	2 698.31	
Automobiles	42 546.49	
Equipment	33 258.00	
Bank Loan		$34 000.00
Accounts Payable		3 692.43
Sales Tax Payable		841.10
T. Patterson, Capital		63 555.67
T. Patterson, Drawings	42 800.00	
Net Income		54 369.32

6. Given below is a completed partial work sheet.
   From this work sheet prepare a classified balance sheet in report form.

Stanley Park Enterprises	Work Sheet	6 Months Ended June 30, 19-5	
		Balance Sheet	
Accounts		Debit	Credit
Bank		3 050.15	
Accounts Receivable		26 750.85	
Supplies		3 500.00	
Land		100 000.00	
Building		124 364.00	
Equipment		75 352.00	
Automobiles		42 500.00	
Accounts Payable			4 125.55
Sales Tax Payable			650.00
J. Hori, Capital			366 485.95
J. Hori, Drawings		56 000.00	
Commissions Earned			
Advertising Expense			
Car Expense			
Light and Heat Expense			
Telephone Expense			
Wages Expense			
		431 517.00	371 261.50
Net Income			60 255.50
		431 517.00	431 517.00

CHAPTER HIGHLIGHTS

Now that you have completed Chapter 8, you should:

1. understand the purpose of a work sheet;
2. be able to complete a six-column work sheet;
3. know the two forms of the balance sheet, the account form and the report form;
4. know the meaning of "formal" and "classified" with respect to financial statements;
5. be able to prepare a formal income statement and a classified balance sheet;
6. understand that the data for the financial statements comes directly from the work sheet;
7. understand the three variations of the equity section of a balance sheet;
8. know the first six steps in the accounting cycle;
9. know the three groups that use financial statements.

ACCOUNTING TERMS

accounts payable control account
accounts receivable control account
balance sheet—account form
balance sheet—report form
classified balance sheet
control account
current liability

current asset
fixed asset
long-term liability
plant and equipment
work sheet
income statement

CHAPTER EXERCISES

Using Your Knowledge

1. Stacey Worrell, an accounting student, has discovered a slight variation in the procedure for balancing a work sheet. Her method is shown below.

Work Sheet — Morton Enterprises	Mo. Ended Dec. 31, 19—					
Accounts	Tr. Bal.		Inc. St.		Bal. Sht.	
	Dr	Cr	Dr	Cr	Dr	Cr
Bank	12—				12—	
Acc Rec'l – G. Flavelle	8—				8—	
Supplies	15—				15—	
Equipment	40—				40—	
Truck	120—				120—	
Acc. Pay'l – Tops Hardware		17—				17—
V. Maswich, Capital		141—				141—
V. Maswich, Drawings	75—				75—	
Revenue		300—		300—		
General Expense	10—		10—			
Light and Heat	50—		50—			
Rent	90—		90—			
Telephone	8—		8—			
Wages	30—		30—			
	458—	458—	188—	300—		
Net Income			112—			112—
			300—	300—	270—	270—

1. Give your opinion of this method.

2. Explain why the balance sheet columns balance with the $112 net income figure included, but would not if the figure were excluded.

2. Given below is the trial balance for Chen and Associates at November 30, 19-7

CHEN AND ASSOCIATES
TRIAL BALANCE
NOVEMBER 30, 19-7

	DR	CR
Bank	$ 950.25	
Accounts Receivable	8 525.45	
Supplies	350.00	
Automobile	19 500.00	
Equipment	22 300.00	
Accounts Payable		$ 3 569.28
Sales Tax Payable		753.52
T.C. Chen, Capital		43 298.91
T.C. Chen, Drawings	5 400.00	
Fees Earned		21 366.00
Advertising Expense	655.30	
Bank Charges Expense	29.55	
Car Expense	1 388.74	
Miscellaneous Expense	55.35	
Rent Expense	1 000.00	
Salaries Expense	8 400.00	
Telephone Expense	144.75	
Utilities Expense	288.32	
	$68 987.71	$68 987.71

1. Complete a six-column work sheet (one-month fiscal period).
2. Prepare a simple income statement.
3. Prepare a classified balance sheet in report form.

3. The trial balance of Ying Lo, a lawyer, on June 30, 19-5, after a fiscal period of six months, is as follows:

Bank	$ 516.20	
Accounts Receivable	9 255.50	
Office Supplies	1 525.00	
Office Equipment	10 356.00	
Automobile	19 255.65	
Professional Library	5 363.25	
Accounts Payable		$ 2 858.25
Ying Lo, Capital		34 024.81
Ying Lo, Drawings	20 000.00	
Fees Earned		55 285.00
Car Expense	4 592.36	
Light and Heat Expense	589.25	
Miscellaneous Expense	1 254.85	
Rent Expense	7 200.00	
Salaries Expense	9 235.00	
Telephone Expense	3 025.00	
	$92 168.06	$92 168.06

Complete a six-column work sheet and prepare the formal financial statements.

4. The trial balance of Star Delivery, owned by Danielle Nowak, on December 31, 19-4, after a fiscal period of one year, is as follows:

Bank	$ 1 852.25	
Accounts Receivable	15 325.00	
Office Supplies	1 863.00	
Furniture and Equipment	7 258.36	
Land	45 500.00	
Buildings	52 365.50	
Automobile	9 255.65	
Trucks	36 252.95	
Accounts Payable		$ 3 859.25
Bank Loan		25 000.00
Mortgage Payable		75 000.00
Danielle Nowak, Capital		58 099.98
Danielle Nowak, Drawings	32 000.00	
Revenue		125 254.00
Gas and Oil Expense	26 215.24	
Insurance Expense	2 657.25	
Miscellaneous Expense	1 526.85	
Telephone Expense	965.32	
Truck Repairs	4 240.65	
Utilities Expense	1 575.65	
Wages Expense	48 359.56	
	$287 213.23	$287 213.23

Complete a six-column work sheet and prepare the financial statements.

5. **This exercise also appears in the Workbook.**
For each of the following, check off the most appropriate response in the space provided.

1. Financial statements are prepared:
   a. once a year.
   b. at the end of the fiscal period.
   c. whenever management requires it.
   d. all of the above.
   e. none of the above.
2. A work sheet is:
   a. one of the books of account.
   b. one of the financial statements.
   c. used instead of the financial statements.
   d. all of the above.
   e. none of the above.
3. Extending amounts on a work sheet means:
   a. adding to the amounts because of additional transactions.
   b. placing debit amounts in debit columns and credit amounts in credit columns.
   c. transferring amounts into the Balance Sheet section or the Income Statement section

  d. all of the above.

  e. none of the above.

4. The process of balancing the work sheet involves:

  a. totaling the four right-hand money columns.

  b. calculating the difference between the two money columns in each of the last two sections.

  c. ensuring that the differences in b) above are equal to each other.

  d. all of the above

  e. none of the above

5. A work sheet will not balance if:

  a. the Telephone Expense amount is extended to the Balance Sheet section Debit column.

  b. the Drawings amount is extended to the Income Statement section Debit column.

  c. the Capital amount is extended to the Balance Sheet section Debit column.

  d. all of the above.

  e. none of the above.

6. You can tell what the net income or net loss figure is by:

  a. looking at the balancing figure in the Balance Sheet section of the work sheet.

  b. looking at the balancing figure in the Income Statement section of the work sheet.

  c. looking at the equity section of the completed balance sheet.

  d. all of the above.

  e. none of the above.

7. All of the following statements, except one, are false. Indicate which statement is true.

  a. The report form of balance sheet is the only style used in the real business world.

  b. The report form of balance sheet is common because it uses standard-sized paper.

  c. The report form of balance sheet is horizontal in form.

  d. The style of the report form of balance sheet eliminates the need for "balancing" totals.

  e. The report form of balance sheet is more difficult to understand.

8. All of the following statements, except one, are false. Indicate which statement is true. On a classified balance sheet:

  a. Automobiles are not included in the Fixed Assets section because their value decreases over time.

  b. A mortgage payable is deducted from the asset, Building.

  c. Supplies are not included as a current asset because they are normally converted into cash.

  d. A bank loan is included in long-term liabilities.

  e. The values shown for the fixed assets are not necessarily their true market value.

9. All of the following statements, except one, are true. Indicate which statement is false.

  a. The data in the books of account are considered to be "raw" data.

  b. Accountants are judged on the basis of the accounting statements and reports that they prepare. Therefore their work should be first-class in form and content.

c. All of the data necessary for the financial statements can be found on the work sheet.

d. An overall decrease in capital can occur in two ways. An overall increase in capital can occur in only one way. Therefore, decreases in capital are more common.

e. The beginning balance in the equity section of the balance sheet is not always that of January 1.

10. During a fiscal period a business suffered a loss of $12 000, began the period with a capital balance of $20 000, and ended the period with a debit balance of $2 000. The drawings for the fiscal period were:

  a. $ 6 000
  b. $10 000
  c. $30 000
  d. $18 000
  e. $14 000.

For Further Thought

6. Briefly answer each of the following questions.

1. The subtotals of the Balance Sheet columns do not agree by exactly the amount of the net income. Explain why this is so.

2. If the Equipment account balance in the Trial Balance section of the work sheet is extended incorrectly to the Income Statement debit column, the work sheet will still balance. Why is this so?

3. List three errors that would cause a work sheet to be out of balance.

4. Which form of the balance sheet—report form or account form—gives the better presentation of the financial statement? Give reasons for your answer. Obtain a copy of a financial report of a public corporation and see what form is used.

5. Describe how columns are used efficiently in the preparation of financial statements.

6. What is probably the most significant observation that can be made from a classified balance sheet?

7. What can a public accountant do for the owner of a business to ensure that the accounting department does its work properly?

8. Your friend in the accounting class has difficulty preparing the equity section of the balance sheet. Explain how to do this for all three situations.

9. Is the owner's equity the amount that the owner would get from the sale of the business, or is it merely the amount of the owner's capital as shown by the books?

10. Explain why it is better to use a work sheet for the preparation of the financial statements, rather than work directly from the ledger.

CASE STUDIES

CASE 1 *Interpreting Balance Sheets*

Firewood Supply is a small business operated on a seasonal basis by Gerry Riel in St. Boniface, Manitoba. Comparative condensed balance sheets for the business for the 19-1 and 19-2 seasons are shown below.

FIREWOOD SUPPLY
BALANCE SHEET
DECEMBER 31, 19–2
(With comparative figures for 19–1)

	19-1	*19-2*
Assets		
Bank	$ 2 000	$ 3 000
Accounts Receivable	14 000	20 000
Equipment	15 000	15 000
Truck	15 000	29 000
	$46 000	$67 000
Liabilities and Equity		
Accounts Payable	$10 000	$20 000
Bank Loan	14 000	14 000
Owner's Equity	22 000	33 000
	$46 000	$67 000

Questions
1. Calculate the net income for 19-2 if the owner's drawings amounted to $15 000.
2. Explain how the accounts receivable would increase by $6 000.
3. Describe the business's ability to pay its debts.
4. The assets increased from $46 000 to $67 000. Explain in detail where the funds came from to acquire the assets.

CASE 2 *Financing Student Council Activities*

At the beginning of the school year, the Riverview High School student council has inherited a bank balance that was overdrawn by $935. The council has no assets.

The members of the council executive are extremely concerned and have asked you, the treasurer, to examine the records of the council to find out the reasons for the poor financial position. They have also asked you to make recommendations for providing good management in the coming year.

As a result of your investigation you find out that the previous council began its year with a positive bank balance of $200 and an inventory of 500 fully paid-for T-shirts which had cost $1 each.

The bank book shows that the following transactions took place during the previous year.

	Cheques	Deposits	Balance
Beginning balance			$ 200
Sale of student cards (940 × $2.50)		$2 350	2 550
Cost of printing student cards	$ 350		2 200
Grant to drama club	1 000		1 200
Proceeds from dance (Nightmare)		2 000	3 200
Profit on refreshments (Nightmare)		70	3 270
Charge for musicians (Nightmare)	1 500		1 770
Grant to choir	1 000		770
Proceeds from sale of 500 T-shirts		375	1 145
Proceeds from variety show		140	1 285
Grant to athletic department	1 000		285
Proceeds from dance (Brainstorm)		300	585
Charge for musicians (Brainstorm)	1 600		−1 015
Profit on refreshments (Brainstorm)		80	−935

The previous student council had decided to have only top-notch entertainment at dances. Although this meant that the musical groups were expensive, a large profit was expected to be made on every dance. However, the "Brainstorm" dance fizzled because of bad weather and poor scheduling.

The T-shirts were sold at a bargain rate in order to promote school spirit. The three $1 000 grants were normal annual commitments made to the three school organizations.

Questions
1. Rearrange the above data to show more clearly how the bank balance dropped from $200 to negative $935.
2. Describe the factors which, in your opinion, contributed directly to the poor financial position.
3. Give recommendations for better managing the financial affairs of the student council in the future.
4. Suggest ways to remedy the negative bank balance.

CASE 3   *Responsibility for Loss?*

Sue Zabjek, a history teacher, had 90 students who needed textbooks. The local bookstore had not provided good service in previous years. Therefore, to save money for her students and to avoid delay, Sue decided to buy the textbooks directly from the publisher. Sue clearly stated to her classes that she intended to sell the books at cost with no profit to her. The books arrived with an invoice for $1 350.

Sue's system for selling the books was very informal. As students crowded around her desk, Sue would take money from each one, give out a text, put the money in her drawer, and then repeat the process.

At the end of a week, Sue decided to take stock of her sales. She found that she had $1 050 in her desk. She also had 14 unsold books. By simple arithmetic, Sue calculated that she was missing either $90 or six books.

Before deciding on a course of action, Sue surveyed her classes to learn the status of the texts. Her survey showed that 76 students had their texts and 14 did not.

Questions
1. a. Did the publisher send the correct number of books?
   b. How could the shortage have been caused? Give three possibilities.
   c. Describe measures that Sue could have taken to prevent such an occurrence.

Sue did not believe that she should bear the $90 loss. Therefore, she decided to increase the charge per book by $1 for all 90 students. The increased price of the text was still lower than the bookstore price of $18.50. However, when she announced her decision to her students she met considerable resistance.

A few students refused to pay as a matter of principle, and others began to follow suit. They claimed that the teacher had agreed to sell the texts at cost price and should keep her word. These students did not believe they should be penalized for the teacher's failure to take adequate precautions.

Another student, whose father owned the bookstore, was furious at the price increase. From the beginning she had felt that Sue's plan brought unfair competition against her father. Now she could no longer restrain herself; she registered a formal complaint to the school principal against the teacher. The principal did not like to get involved, but finally agreed to discuss the matter with the teacher.

Questions
2. a. Should a teacher be allowed to bypass local competition in the purchase of textbooks? Give reasons for your answer.
   b. Should Sue Zabjek have to suffer the $90 loss, or is her course of action a reasonable one? Give reasons to support your response.
   c. What should the principal say to Ms. Zabjek?

CASE 4   *Solving a Money Problem*

The Harper Valley Ski Club is a small private ski club in Creston, B.C. When the club was first established it was expected to be strictly private. There are 100 family memberships. The original members paid about $4 000 for their shares. However, the current market value for shares is only about $2 000.

Over the years the club has never had an easy time financially, but has managed to avoid serious difficulties. However, in 19-2 the club experienced a hardship brought on by two factors. First, the club installed snowmaking equipment at a cost of $200 000 for which the funds were borrowed from the bank. Second, bank interest rates rose to 20 per cent.

For the 19-2—19-3 ski season the financial statements of the club showed the following.

Harper Valley Ski Club Balance Sheet		Harper Valley Ski Club Income Statement	
ASSETS		REVENUE	
Bank	$ 1	Ski Fees	$300 000
Accounts Receivable	4 000	EXPENSES	
Land and Building	150 000	Bank Interest	$ 40 000
Equipment	500 000	Other Expenses	265 000
Total	$654 001	Total Expenses	$305 000
LIABILITIES AND EQUITY		Net Loss	$ 5 000
Bank Loan	$200 000		
Accounts Payable	5 000		
Capital	449 001		
Total	$654 001		

The financial situation has made many members dissatisfied for the following reasons:
1. There has been an extra assessment on the members to cover the losses.
2. The club has no funds with which to make any improvements. To manage these would take an annual net income of at least $25 000.
3. The situation is making it difficult for members who wish to leave the club (moving away, etc.) to sell their shares.
4. There is no apparent end to the problem.

Questions
1. Which expense is there a possibility of eliminating?
2. What are the average ski fees per member?
3. At the current market price, how many new shares would have to be sold to raise enough cash to pay off the bank loan?
4. Assume that this number of shares were sold.
   a. How much money would be brought in?
   b. What is the most logical way to spend this money?
   c. The income statement would be affected in two ways. Give the two ways and the amounts involved.
   d. What would the new net income figure be?
5. **Assume that you were asked to advise the members how to solve their financial problem. Prepare a brief report outlining your suggestions.**

CAREER
Carol Smalley / Accounts Payable Supervisor

While Carol Smalley was attending R. H. King Collegiate in Scarborough, Ontario, she particularly enjoyed the accounting courses she took as part of a business and commerce program. This background helped her to get a job as a cashier with State Farm Insurance upon graduation. After less than a year in this position, she was promoted to commissions clerk.

Since then, Carol's accounting career has been wide and varied. From State Farm Insurance, Carol moved into International Business Machines as an accounts payable clerk. Her responsibilities there included organizing the invoices for payment, insuring that discounts for early payment were made, and matching invoices to packing slips and purchase orders so that payment could be approved by the general manager.

After a year and a half with IBM, Carol left her job to start a family. Then after a four-year absence from the work force, she joined Prentice-Hall Canada Inc., a publishing company. She began by working in the customer service department and later moved to the accounts receivable department as a collection clerk. Eventually, after three years as

an accounts payable processor, Carol was promoted to accounting operations administrator.

In this position, Carol gained invaluable experience in setting up accounting systems on a personal computer. Her main responsibility during this time was to set up a fixed asset system in which all furniture and equipment, corporate computers, microcomputers, and distribution and production equipment were listed by serial number and cost value. In this way, they could much more easily be reconciled with the general ledger. She also learned a great deal about Prentice-Hall's procedure for handling royalties (payments paid to authors) and travel and entertainment expenses. With her knowledge in this area, Carol wrote the company's Procedures Manual on the handling of royalty expenses.

Recently, Carol was promoted once again. She is now accounts payable supervisor, responsible for overseeing five other employees. The accounts payable department looks after payment of all expenses, including inventory and royalties. Carol oversees the input and processing of all payable expenses.

Although a great many of Carol's present skills were learned on the job, she feels that her high school accounting courses gave her a firm foundation. They taught her not only basic accounting concepts and procedures, but also the importance of organization, accuracy, and thoroughness.

DISCUSSION

1. What are the accounting jobs Carol has held since graduating from high school?
2. How have Carol's accounting courses helped her in her career?
3. List the information that is placed on a computer data form.
4. What were Carol's duties as an accounts payable clerk while employed at IBM?
5. List all the source documents Carol has handled in her various accounting positions.

Completing the Accounting Cycle

9.1 Simple Adjustments and Expanded Work Sheets
9.2 Closing Entries Concepts
9.3 Journalizing and Posting the Closing Entries
9.4 Computers in Accounting   Increasing Spreadsheet Power

In Chapter 8 you learned about the six-column work sheet and its use in preparing formal financial statements. In this chapter you will learn how to make adjusting entries on an eight- or ten-column work sheet, and how to close the books at the end of a fiscal period.

9.1 SIMPLE ADJUSTMENTS AND EXPANDED WORK SHEETS

The Adjustment Process

Financial statements are used extensively to assist in making business decisions. Therefore it is important for financial statements to be accurate, up to date, and consistent from year to year. The responsibility for these documents rests entirely with the company's accountants. When preparing financial statements, the accountants must ensure that

1. all accounts are brought up to date;
2. all late transactions are taken into account;
3. all calculations have been made correctly;
4. all GAAPs have been complied with.

Bringing the account data up to date at statement time is known as "making the adjustments." The accounting entries produced by this process are known as the adjusting entries. An **adjusting entry** is one made to assign amounts of revenue or expense to the proper accounting period before finalizing the books for the fiscal period.

Adjusting entries are necessary because the books of account are allowed to become inexact between statement dates. This does not mean inaccurate. Rather, it means that certain things have been left undone. The accounts do not need to be perfectly accurate between statement dates. Time, effort, and money can be saved by leaving some things undone. However, at statement time, the omissions must be put right. If the accounts were not adjusted then, a correct net income or net loss would not be determined.

There are numerous situations where it is convenient to allow the accounting records to become inexact during the accounting period. The following is a good example.

> On July 1, Markell Company lends $18 250 to its president John Fumo. He is given a favourable interest rate of six per cent. No date is specified for repayment. Interest on the loan is to be paid annually each July 1. The company has a December 31 year-end.

Technically, Fumo owes the company $3 a day for interest on the loan. This is calculated as follows: $18 250 × 6/100 × 1/365 = $3. Precise accounting would require making the following accounting entry once each day.

	DR	CR
Interest Receivable—John Fumo	$3	
Interest Earned		$3

If it were done this way, 193 such entries would be recorded before the year-end. Clearly, there is little purpose in this. The total interest owed is neither large nor important. It can be computed in a matter of seconds when necessary.

The full amount of the interest due—$549 in this case—will be recorded with one adjusting entry at the year-end.

Adjusting Entries and the Work Sheet

The first place that adjusting entries are recorded is on the work sheet. As the work sheet is prepared, the adjusting entries are worked out and recorded in a section headed Adjustments. This requires two additional columns on the work sheet after the trial balance columns. The work sheet is balanced and finalized before any adjusting entries are recorded in the accounts. To show how this is done, a work sheet for Cassidy Cartage is started in Figure 9.1. You will be shown how the adjusting entries are recorded on the work sheet as we proceed.

Adjusting for Supplies Used

Supplies is an account that is allowed to become inexact during the accounting period. When supplies are purchased their cost is debited to the Supplies account. But as supplies are used, no attempt is made to record the usage. It is simply too much of a nuisance to make an accounting entry each time supplies are used, or even once a day. Therefore, no such entries are made. As a result, the Supplies account is not correct at the end of the fiscal period. However, the matching principle requires that the account be made correct when financial statements are prepared. This is done by means of an adjusting entry.

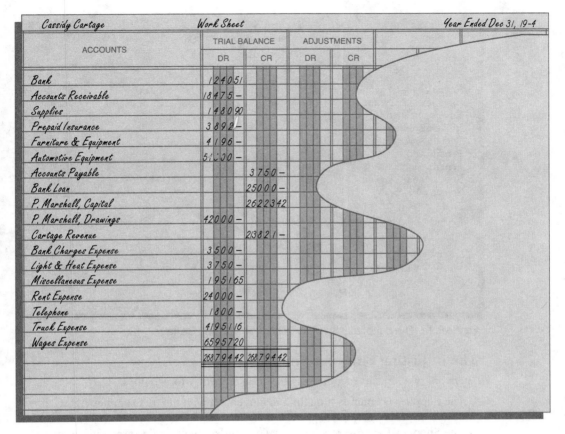

Figure 9.1   The trial balance of Cassidy Cartage recorded on the work sheet.

Calculating the Amount of the Adjustment for Supplies

The balance in the Supplies account should be equal to the cost of the supplies that are actually on hand, the ones that were not used. Therefore, the first task in working out the supplies adjustment is to take a "physical inventory" of supplies. This involves the preparation of a listing like the one shown in Figure 9.2.

The Supplies figure on the trial balance for Cassidy Cartage is $1 480.90. The inventory listing shows $526.00. The difference between the two figures, $954.90, is the dollar amount of the supplies used (or spoiled, or stolen). It is the figure used in the adjusting entry.

CASSIDY CARTAGE
SUPPLIES INVENTORY
DECEMBER 31, 19–4

Description	Quantity		Cost	Value
Envelopes, #10, white	2	boxes	$ 29.00	$ 58.00
Envelopes, #8, white	3	boxes	23.50	70.50
Envelopes, manila	37		.25	9.25
Ball pens, blue	15		.22	3.30
Pencils, black, HB	75		.95	71.25
Pencils, red	32		.89	28.48
Pencils, auto .5	3		7.85	23.55
Scotch tape, 1 cm	12		4.50	54.00
Scotch tape, 2 cm	8		6.50	52.00
Paper clips, regular	16	boxes	1.89	30.24
Paper clips, jumbo	5	boxes	3.50	17.50
Gummed labels, #505	3	pkgs	6.50	19.50
Elastic bands	5	boxes	3.59	17.95
			Total	$526.00

Figure 9.2 The supplies inventory listing for Cassidy Cartage.

The Adjusting Entry for Supplies

There are two objectives in making the adjusting entry for supplies.

1. The Supplies account is brought into agreement with the true supplies figure shown on the inventory listing.
2. The Supplies Expense account is made to reflect the supplies used during the fiscal period, as required by the matching principle.

The adjusting entry shown below achieves these two objectives.

	DR	CR
Supplies Expense	$954.90	
Supplies		$954.90

The adjusting entry for supplies is not journalized at this time. It is only recorded in the adjustments section of the work sheet as shown in Figure 9.3.

Observe that the adjusting entry is referenced on Figure 9.3 with a circled numeral "1."

Adjusting for Insurance Used

There are times in business when expense items are paid for in advance. This presents no special problem if the period covered by the expense item (rent, for example) falls entirely within the fiscal period. However, some items (insurance, for example) are for a period that does not correspond to the fiscal period and may affect the following fiscal period as well. Items of this nature are called prepaid expenses and require special accounting treatment at statement time.

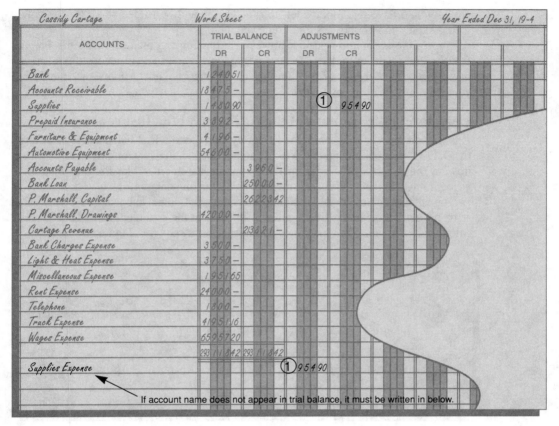

Figure 9.3   The supplies adjustment recorded on the work sheet.

A **prepaid expense** is one that is paid for in advance but whose benefits extend into the future. The most common prepaid expense is insurance. A business can purchase insurance to cover possible losses in respect to automobiles, buildings, contents, crops, and so on. When you purchase insurance, you usually pay for one year's coverage in advance. Occasionally, an insurance company will give businesses insurance for a period longer than one year.

When prepaid expenses are purchased they are usually debited to a prepaid expense account. For insurance, the account is called Prepaid Insurance. The accounting entry to purchase insurance is

	DR	CR
Prepaid Insurance	$$$$	
Bank, or Accounts Payable		$$$$

As time passes, prepaid insurance gradually decreases in value until it runs out. Let us say that you purchased car insurance for one year on March 1 at a cost of $600. On September 1 the insurance coverage would be half-used. It would only have a refund value of $300 (less a service charge). On December 31, the company's year-end, the policy would have two months left to run. This would be valued at $100. The policy would expire on February 28 if not renewed.

During the accounting period, however, no attempt is made to keep the Prepaid Insurance account up to date. No accounting entries are made to record the insurance that is used up. Because of this, the balance in the Prepaid Insurance account is not generally correct from day to day.

Calculating the Amount of the Adjustment for Insurance

Again, working with the example of Cassidy Cartage, the trial balance shows a figure of $3 892 for prepaid insurance. We know that this balance is wrong. However, we are now in the process of preparing the financial statements. The Prepaid Insurance account must be made correct by means of an adjusting entry.

The balance in the Prepaid Insurance account must be made equal to the total value remaining in all of the insurance policies in force at the statement date. This figure is calculated by means of an insurance listing such as is shown in Figure 9.4.

Company	Policy Date	Term	Expiry Date	Premium	Unused Fraction	Value Remaining
Acme	Aug 1, 19–4	1 yr	Jul 31, 19–5	$ 816	7/12	$ 476
Fidelity	Aug 1, 19–4	1 yr	Jul 31, 19–5	1 248	7/12	728
Guarantee	Mar 1, 19–4	1 yr	Feb 28, 19–5	948	2/12	158
Fireman's	Nov 1, 19–4	1 yr	Oct 31, 19–5	1 152	10/12	960
						$ 2 322

PREPAID INSURANCE LISTING
DECEMBER 31, 19–4

Figure 9.4   A prepaid insurance listing.

The prepaid insurance schedule shows $2 322. This is the value of the insurance that belongs to a future period. The prepaid insurance figure on the trial balance shows $3 892. The difference between the two figures, $1 570, is the dollar amount of the insurance used up. It is the figure used in the adjusting entry.

The Adjusting Entry for Insurance Used

The adjusting entry for prepaid insurance accomplishes two things.

1. The Prepaid Insurance account is brought into agreement with the insurance schedule.
2. The Insurance Expense account is made to reflect the insurance used during the fiscal period, as required by the matching principle.

The following journal entry achieves these objectives:

	DR	CR
Insurance Expense	$1 570	
Prepaid Insurance		$1 570

The adjusting entry is not journalized at this time. It is entered in the adjustments section of the work sheet as shown in Figure 9.5.

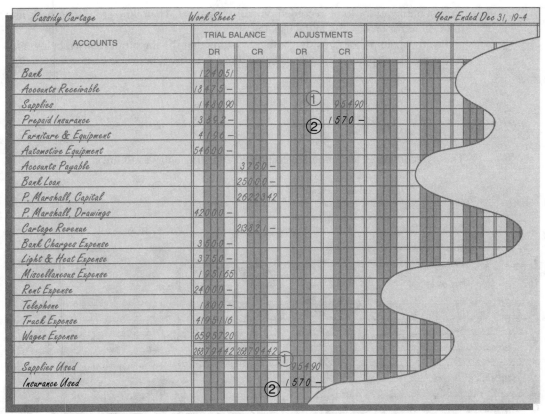

Figure 9.5 The insurance adjustment recorded on the work sheet.

Adjusting for Late Purchase Invoices

You have already seen a number of "laws" (or GAAPs) used by accountants. You can now appreciate that an accountant must be on the watch for items that require special handling when the time comes to prepare financial statements. Among the items to which an accountant gives special attention are late-arriving purchase invoices.

Goods and services are often bought and received toward the end of an accounting period. The bills for these items may not arrive until the subsequent fiscal period. Of course, that is the wrong fiscal period for them. The matching principle states that expenses are to be recognized in the same period as the revenue that they helped to earn. This means that the accounting department must see to it that all items are recorded in their proper accounting period in order to arrive at a proper determination of net income.

The financial statements cannot be completed until two to three weeks after the end of the accounting period. This period of waiting is necessary and sufficient for the late arrival of purchase invoices from suppliers. During this waiting period, the accounting department examines all purchase invoices in order to separate out those that affect the fiscal period just ended. The ones that are set aside are summarized into an accounting entry to be recorded on the work sheet. Then they are placed back into the system for processing in the usual manner.

For the example of Cassidy Cartage, assume that the three bills shown below represent the "late" purchase invoices belonging to the fiscal period just ended.

Late Purchase Invoices	
Telephone	$ 45
Truck repair	496
Typewriter repair	85
Total	$626

These late invoices are summarized into an adjusting entry as follows:

	DR	CR
Telephone Expense	$ 45	
Truck Expense	496	
Miscellaneous Expense	85	
Accounts Payable		$626

Figure 9.6 The adjustment for late invoices recorded on the work sheet, and the adjustments column balanced.

This adjusting entry is shown on the work sheet for Cassidy Cartage in Figure 9.6. The purchase invoices are then absorbed into the regular accounting system to be checked, recorded, and eventually paid in the new fiscal period.

The 10-Column Work Sheet

Before extending the work sheet, some accountants prefer to work out an adjusted trial balance right on the work sheet. To do this, they add two additional columns, headed Adjusted Trial Balance, after the two adjustments columns on the work sheet as shown in Figure 9.7. This makes 10 columns in all.

The amounts to be entered in the adjusted trial balance columns are determined as follows.

1 Calculate the value of the first four columns for each item. This may involve adding or subtracting, depending on what is contained in the four columns.
2 Transfer the value—one debit amount or one credit amount—to the corresponding column of the adjusted trial balance section.

You can see this by looking at the supplies line of the work sheet for Cassidy Cartage which is worked out below in Figure 9.7.

For supplies, the debit of $1 480.90 and the credit adjustment of $954.90 taken together are worth $526.00, debit. The $526.00 debit is the amount that is carried over to the adjusted trial balance section.

Cassidy Cartage	Work Sheet								Year Ended December 31, 19-4	
Accounts	Trial Balance		Adjustments		Adjusted T. B.		Income Statement		Balance sheet	
	Debit	Credit	Debit	Credit	Debit	Credit	Debit	Credit	Debit	Credit
Supplies	1480 90			954 90	526 -					
Accounts Payable		3750 -		626 -		4376 -				

Figure 9.7 A partial work sheet with adjusted trial balance columns.

Look also at the Accounts Payable line in Figure 9.7. For Accounts Payable, the credit of $3 750.00 and the credit adjustment of $626.00 taken together are worth $4 376.00, credit. The $4 376.00 credit is the figure that is carried over to the adjusted trial balance section.

The 10-column work sheet for Cassidy Cartage, completed to the point of the adjusted trial balance, is shown in Figure 9.8.

Cassidy Cartage	Work Sheet						Year Ended Dec 31, 19-4
ACCOUNTS	TRIAL BALANCE		ADJUSTMENTS		ADJ. TRIAL BALANCE		
	DR	CR	DR	CR	DR	CR	
Bank	1240 51				1240 51		
Accounts Receivable	18475 –				18475 –		
Supplies	1480 90			① 954 90	526 –		
Prepaid Insurance	3892 –			② 1570 –	2322 –		
Furniture & Equipment	4196 –				4196 –		
Automotive Equipment	54600 –				54600 –		
Accounts Payable		3750 –		③ 626 –		4376 –	
Bank Loan		25000 –				25000 –	
P. Marshall, Capital		26223 42				26223 42	
P. Marshall, Drawings	42000 –				42000 –		
Cartage Revenue		21382 1 –				21382 1 –	
Bank Charges Expense	3500 –				3500 –		
Light & Heat Expense	3750 –				3750 –		
Miscellaneous Expense	1951 65		③ 85 –		2036 65		
Rent Expense	24000 –				24000 –		
Telephone	1800 –		③ 45 –		1845 –		
Truck Expense	4195 16		③ 496 –		4244 16		
Wages Expense	65957 20				65957 20		
	268794 42	268794 42					
Supplies Expense			① 954 90		954 90		
Insurance Expense			② 1570 –		1570 –		
			3150 90	3150 90	269420 42	269420 42	

Figure 9.8   A partial work sheet showing the adjusted trial balance section.

Once the adjusted trial balance columns are balanced, the amounts in this section are extended to the income statement and balance sheet sections. Each item belongs in one of the income statement columns or one of the balance sheet columns. Debit values are transferred to debit columns and credit values are transferred to credit columns.

Those who favour the 10-column work sheet feel that its use reduces mechanical errors, which results in a saving of time, with fewer frustrations.

The Eight-Column Work Sheet

The adjusted trial balance section is included on the 10-column work sheet to make the preparation of the work sheet more straightforward. It is suitable for inexperienced accountants and for students. However, most accountants reach a level of performance where they do not need to use these two columns. They use an eight-column work sheet which does not include a section for an adjusted trial balance.

Completing the Work Sheets

You have now completed the first two sections of the work sheet, the trial balance section and the adjustments section. You already know that the work sheet must be extended to the last four columns for the income statement and balance sheet.

The steps involved in extending the eight-column work sheet are as follows:

1 Determine the value of the first four columns for each item.
2 Transfer the value found in step 1 above directly to one of the last four columns of the work sheet—the income statement and balance sheet sections. Debit values are transferred to debit columns and credit values are transferred to credit columns.

Most accountants wait until all of the adjusting entries are recorded and balanced on the work sheet before doing the extensions. Then they perform all of the extensions at one time.

Balancing the Work Sheet for Cassidy Cartage

The process of balancing the work sheet is identical to that learned in the previous chapter. This involves:

1 totaling each of the last four columns;
2 determining the difference between the two income statement columns, ($ 67 760.09), and the difference between the two balance sheet columns ($67 760.09);
3 ensuring that the two differences in 2 above are the same. If they are not, then the work sheet does not balance, and contains one or more errors. These must be found and corrected before the financial statements are prepared.
Figure 9.9 shows the balanced work sheet for Cassidy Cartage.

The difference between the two income statement columns is $67 760.09, and the difference between the two balance sheet columns is also $67 760.09. The work sheet is balanced.

Journalizing and Posting the Adjusting Entries

So far the adjusting entries have been recorded only on the work sheet. Once the work sheet is completed, the adjusting entries must be recorded in the accounts.

Journalize and post *all and only* those adjusting entries that appear in the adjustments section of the work sheet. This is no time for discovering new adjustments. The adjustment decision process took place when the work sheet was prepared. Now it is simply a matter of putting these adjustments into the accounts.

This can be done by individual entries as shown in Figure 9.10, or in one grand entry as is done by many accountants. The entries are usually dated on the last day of the fiscal period. They are headed "adjusting entries" so there is no need for explanations.

Cassidy Cartage — Work Sheet — Year Ended Dec 31, 19-4								
ACCOUNTS	TRIAL BALANCE		ADJUSTMENTS		INCOME STATEMENT		BALANCE SHEET	
	DR	CR	DR	CR	DR	CR	DR	CR
Bank	124051						124051	
Accounts Receivable	18475-						18475-	
Supplies	148090			(1) 95490			526-	
Prepaid Insurance	3892-			(2) 1570-			2322-	
Furniture & Equipment	4196-						4196-	
Automotive Equipment	54600-						78000-	
Accounts Payable		3750-		(3) 626-				4376-
Bank Loan		25000-						25000-
P. Marshall, Capital		2622342						2622342
P. Marshall, Drawings	42000-						42000-	
Cartage Revenue		213821-				213821-		
Bank Charges Expense	3500-				3500-			
Light & Heat Expense	3750-				3750-			
Miscellaneous Expense	195165		(3) 85-		203665			
Rent Expense	24000-				24000-			
Telephone	1800-		(3) 45-		1845-			
Truck Expense	4195116		(3) 496-		4244716			
Wages Expense	6595720				6595720			
	26879442	26879442						
Supplies Expense			(1) 95490		95490			
Insurance Expense			(2) 1570-		1570-			
			315090	315090	14606091	213821-	12335951	5559942
Net Income					6776009			6776009
					213821-	213821-	12335951	12335951

Figure 9.9 The extended and balanced eight-column work sheet for Cassidy Cartage.

Adjusting Entries

Dec. 31	Supplies Expense		95490	
	Supplies			95490
31	Insurance Expense		1570-	
	Prepaid Insurance			1570-
31	Miscellaneous Expense		85-	
	Telephone Expense		45-	
	Truck Expense		496-	
	Accounts Payable			626-

Figure 9.10 The adjusting entries for Cassidy Cartage.

After these adjusting entries have been journalized and posted, the ledger accounts will be updated. The updated ledger for Cassidy Cartage is shown in Figure 9.11.

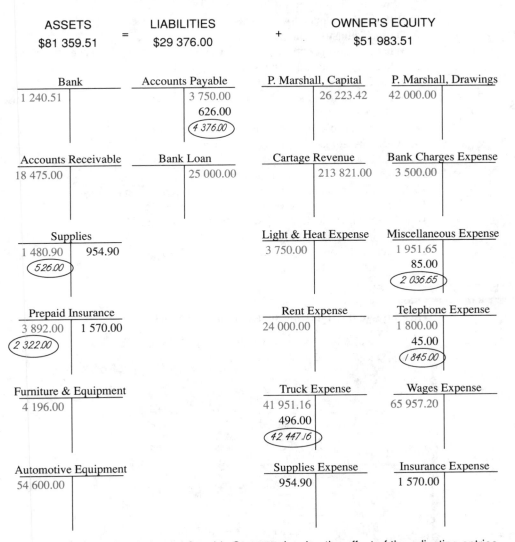

ASSETS	=	LIABILITIES	+	OWNER'S EQUITY
$81 359.51		$29 376.00		$51 983.51

Figure 9.11 The ledger of Cassidy Cartage showing the effect of the adjusting entries.

The person who records the adjusting entries does not have to be the one who prepares the work sheet. There is a particular set of procedures to follow and it works in all cases. It is often necessary for an accountant to make use of the work of others.

SECTION REVIEW QUESTIONS

1. Why are adjusting entries necessary?
2. Why are accounts allowed to become inexact between statement dates?
3. Define "adjusting entry."
4. What accounting entry in regard to supplies is ignored between statement dates?
5. What accounting entry in regard to supplies is not ignored?
6. What GAAP is involved in regard to the adjustment for supplies?
7. What has to be done at the end of the fiscal period before the "supplies used" can be calculated?
8. Give the basic adjusting entry for "supplies used."
9. Where are adjusting entries first recorded?
10. What is a prepaid expense?
11. What is the most common prepaid expense?
12. Name the account that is debited when insurance is paid for in advance.
13. What must be done before the "insurance used" can be calculated?
14. What is the basic adjusting entry for insurance used?
15. Explain what a late purchase invoice is.
16. Describe the process of extending the work sheet.

SECTION EXERCISES

1. Complete the following schedule in your Workbook.

Supplies	Trial Balance Figure	Supplies Closing Inventory Figure	Supplies Expense Figure
1.	$300.00	$100.00	200
2.		$175.00	$250.00
3.	$950.00		$740.00

Prepaid Insurance	Trial Balance Figure	Prepaid Insurance Final Calculation	Insurance Expense Figure
1.	$875.00	$325.00	
2.	$925.00		$315.00
3.		$410.00	$375.00

2. If the Supplies account has a debit balance of $2 018, use the following information to complete the inventory sheet and make the adjusting entry in the T-accounts in your Workbook.

Inventory Item	Quantity	Unit Price	Value	
Rubber bands	3 boxes	$ 1.50 per box		
Envelopes #8	10 boxes	32.00 per box		
Envelopes #10	4 1/2 boxes	36.00 per box		
Envelopes, manila	2 boxes	28.00 per box		
Typing paper	4M sheets	15.60 per M		
Letterhead	10M sheets	22.50 per M		
Copy paper	4M sheets	10.00 per M		
Carbon paper	2 boxes	6.00 per box		
Paper clips	12 boxes	1.50 per box		
Staples	15 boxes	4.10 per box		
Pencils, regular	4 doz.	5.50 per doz.		
Pencils, red	2 doz.	6.10 per doz.		
		Total		

3. A one-year insurance policy was purchased on September 1, 19-1 for $216.

 1. **Calculate the portion of the cost of this insurance policy to be charged to each of the years ended December 31, 19-1 and 19-2.**
 2. **Calculate the value of the prepaid insurance for this policy as of December 31, 19-1.**

4. **For each of the following insurance policies calculate the value of the prepaid insurance at the year-end date shown.**

Policy	a.	b.	c.
Purchase date	Oct. 1, 19–4	Oct. 1, 19–4	Oct. 1, 19–4
Year-end date	Dec. 31, 19–4	Dec. 31, 19–5	Oct. 31, 19–4
Term of policy	1 year	2 years	1 year
Premium	$360	$360	$456

Policy	d.	e.	f.
Purchase date	Mar. 1, 19–1	June 1, 19–6	July 1, 19–4
Year-end date	Dec. 31, 19–1	June 30, 19–6	Dec. 31, 19–5
Term of policy	1 year	1 year	2 years
Premium	$120	$276	$192

5. **Use T-accounts to help you do this exercise in your Workbook.**

The Guilford Glass Shop began business on October 1, 19-0. Its first fiscal year ended on September 30, 19-1. On January 1, 19-1, $720 was paid for a truck licence for the 19-1 calendar year.

1. **Give the accounting entry to record the above transaction.**
2. **Calculate the value for prepaid licences of September 30, 19-1.**
3. **Calculate the truck licence expense for the fiscal period ended September 30, 19-1.**
4. **Give the adjusting entry necessary at September 30, 19-1.**

On January 1, 19-2, $720 was paid for the truck licence for the 19-2 calendar year.

5. **Give the balance in the Prepaid Licences account after recording the above payment.**
6. **Calculate the value for prepaid licences of September 30, 19-2.**
7. **Calculate the truck licence expense for the fiscal period ended September 30, 19-2.**

6. The work sheet for P. Pahl and Company is shown below with the trial balance figures already entered.

Work Sheet		P. Pahl and Company							Year Ended December 31, 19-8	
Accounts	Trial Balance		Adjustments		Adjusted T. B.		Income Statement		Balance sheet	
	Debit	Credit	Debit	Credit	Debit	Credit	Debit	Credit	Debit	Credit
Bank	1800 –									
Accounts Receivable	19500 –									
Supplies	1000 –									
Ppd. Insurance	1750 –									
Equipment	22000 –									
Automobile	21000 –									
Accounts Payable		4360 –								
P. Pahl, Capital		54040 –								
P. Pahl, Drawings	15000 –									
Fees Earned		60300 –								
Car Expense	3800 –									
General Expense	2950 –									
Miscellaneous Exp.	700 –									
Rent Expense	7200 –									
Wages Expense	22000 –									
	118700 –	118700 –								

1. **Using the additional information given below, complete a 10-column work sheet in the Workbook.**
2. **Journalize the adjusting entries in a two-column general journal.**
3. **Post the adjusting entries to the T-account ledger provided in the Workbook, and take off an adjusted trial balance.**

Optional

4. Prepare an income statement and a balance sheet.

Additional Information

1. The value of the supplies on hand at the year-end amounted to $700.
2. The prepaid insurance at the year-end was calculated at $800.
3. Late-arriving invoices pertaining to the 19-8 fiscal period were for:

Car Expense	$ 75
General Expense	100
Total	$175

---

7. The work sheet for Mission Marketing is shown below with the trial balance figures already entered.

Work Sheet	Mission Marketing								Year Ended December 31, 19-5		
Accounts	Trial Balance		Adjustments		Adjusted T. B.		Income Statement		Balance sheet	
	Debit	Credit	Debit	Credit	Debit	Credit	Debit	Credit	Debit	Credit
Bank	3000 —									
Accounts Receivable	21600 —									
Supplies	4250 —									
Ppd. Insurance	1254 —									
Equipment	19200 —									
Automobile	44200 —									
Accounts Payable		7345 —								
C. Ans, Capital		71275 —								
C. Ans, Drawings	40000 —									
Fees Earned		135700 —								
Car Expense	13214 —									
Light and Power Exp.	2800 —									
Miscellaneous Exp.	1563 —									
Rent Expense	18000 —									
Wages Expense	45239 —									
	214320 —	214320 —								

1. **Using the additional information given below, complete a 10-column work sheet in your Workbook.**
2. **Journalize the adjusting entries in a two-column general journal.**
3. **Post the adjusting entries to the T-account ledger provided in the Workbook and take off an adjusted trial balance.**

Optional

4. Prepare an income statement and a balance sheet.

Additional Information

1. The value of the supplies on hand at the year-end was $950.

2. The prepaid insurance at the year-end was calculated to be $680.

3. Late-arriving invoices pertaining to the 19-5 fiscal period were for:

Car expense	$150
Miscellaneous expense	50
Light and power expense	$115
Total	$315

8. The work sheet for J. Soo and Associates is shown below with the trial balance figures already entered.

Work Sheet				J. Soo and Associates			Year Ended December 31, 19-5			
Accounts	Trial Balance		Adjustments		Income Statement		Balance sheet			
	Debit	Credit	Debit	Credit	Debit	Credit	Debit	Credit		
Bank	2500 –									
Accounts Receivable	11500 –									
Supplies	1950 –									
Ppd. Insurance	624 –									
Equipment	9200 –									
Automobile	18350 –									
Accounts Payable		6230 –								
J. Soo, Capital		36662 –								
J. Soo, Drawiangs	7500 –									
Commissions		35650 –								
Car Expense	3214 –									
Light and Power Exp.	1563 –									
Miscellaneous Exp.	902 –									
Rent Expense	6000 –									
Wages Expense	15239 –									
	78542 –	78542 –								

1. **Using the additional information given below, complete an eight-column work sheet in your Workbook.**
2. **Journalize the adjusting entries in a two-column general journal.**
3. **Post the adjusting entries to the T-account ledger provided in the Workbook and take off an adjusted trial balance.**

Optional
4. **Prepare an income statement and a balance sheet.**

Additional Information
1. The value of the supplies on hand at the year-end was $640.
2. The prepaid insurance at the year-end was calculated to be $260.
3. Late-arriving invoices pertaining to the 19-5 fiscal period were for:

Car Expense	$ 50
Miscellaneous Expense	65
Total	$115

9.2 CLOSING ENTRIES CONCEPTS

In the last section you saw how adjusting entries are calculated and recorded on the work sheet for use in preparing the financial statements. This achieved one of the most important purposes of the accounting process. However, accounting is cyclical in nature. Remember the "time period concept." It states that financial reporting, on net income in particular, is done in equal periods of time. The accounts must now be made ready for the next cycle.

The final stage of the accounting cycle is to prepare the accounts for the next fiscal period. To do this, you must understand which accounts have balances that do not continue from one period to the next.

Real Accounts and Nominal Accounts

Asset and liability accounts, as well as the owner's capital account, are considered to be *real* accounts. **Real accounts** are ones whose balances continue into the next fiscal period. Examples of real accounts include Bank, Trucks, and Accounts Payable.

On the other hand, Revenue, Expense, and Drawings accounts are considered to be temporary equity accounting and are known as *nominal* accounts. **Nominal accounts** are ones whose balances do not continue into the next fiscal period. Nominal accounts, with the exception of the Drawings account, are related to the income statement, and the income statement deals only with a single fiscal period. All nominal accounts begin each fiscal period with a nil balance.

A special nominal account, called the *Income Summary* account, is used only during the closing entry process. The **Income Summary account** summarizes the revenues and expenses of the period. The temporary balance in this account represents either the amount of net income or the amount of net loss.

Closing Out the Nominal Accounts

Once the income statement for a period has been completed, the balances in the nominal accounts are no longer useful. These "old" balances in the nominal accounts must be removed to make the accounts "fresh" for the next accounting period. There must be no balance left in any nominal account to start off a new fiscal period. This process is known as closing the accounts, closing out the accounts, or clearing the accounts. **Closing an account** means to cause it to have no balance. The nominal accounts are closed out at the end of every fiscal period, as explained in detail in the next section.

As you know, during any fiscal period the total equity of a business is not contained in a single account. It is contained in a number of accounts in the equity section of the ledger. The Capital account shows the equity balance at the beginning of the period. Any changes in equity during the period are contained in Revenue, Expense, and Drawings accounts, which are the nominal accounts. Closing the *nominal* equity accounts involves moving the values collected in those accounts into the one *real* equity account, the Capital account. This is the way the Capital account is updated to show the final equity figure at the end of each fiscal period.

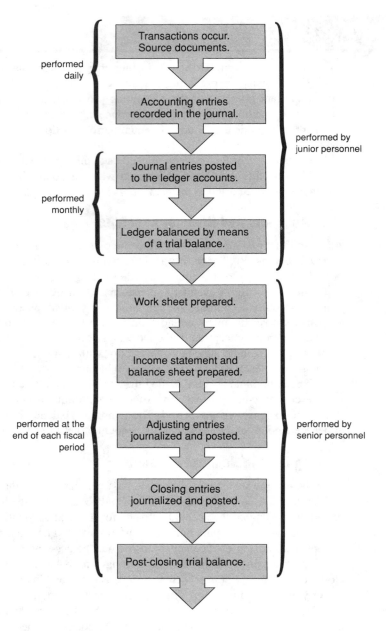

Figure 9.12   The complete accounting cycle.

End-of-Period Procedure

There are a number of things to be done at the end of each fiscal period. These are:

1 Bring accounts up to date by journalizing and posting the adjusting entries. You will recall that some accounts were allowed to become inexact during the fiscal period. These were updated on the work sheet and on the financial statements, and later journalized and posted to the accounts.

2 Close the nominal accounts to prepare them for the next fiscal period. This involves journalizing and posting the closing entries. This is done in two phases.

   1. Transfer the balances of the revenue and expense accounts to the new Income Summary account.
   2. Transfer the balances of the Income Summary and Drawings accounts to the Capital account.
   Now all the nominal accounts have zero balances. But the Capital account, which continues to the next fiscal period, has an updated balance. You will be shown how to do this in the next section.

3 Take off a post-closing trial balance. There is a lot of room for making errors in the process of journalizing and posting the adjusting and closing entries. A trial balance is taken off to ensure that the ledger is still in balance. A **post-closing trial balance** is one that is taken as soon as the closing entries have been posted.

Complete Accounting Cycle

The post-closing trial balance is the final step in the accounting cycle. Figure 9.12 on page 278 shows the steps in the accounting cycle in its final form.

SECTION REVIEW QUESTIONS

1. Explain the time period concept.
2. What does the final stage of the accounting cycle involve?
3. What is a real account?
4. What is a nominal account?
5. What are nominal accounts also called?
6. Which accounts in the ledger are the nominal accounts?
7. Why are "old" balances cleared out of the nominal accounts?
8. Explain what is meant by "closing an account."
9. What three things must be done at the end of the accounting period?
10. What steps have been added to the accounting cycle in this chapter?

SECTION EXERCISES

1. A list of accounts appears below. **Indicate which of these are nominal accounts.**

Accounts

Accounts Payable
Accounts Receivable
Advertising Expense
Automobiles
Bank
Bank Charges Expense
Bank Loan
Building
Capital—Sylvia Magill
Car Expenses
Delivery Expense
Drawings—Sylvia Magill
Equipment

Insurance Expense
Land
Legal Expense
Mortgage Payable
Postage Expense
Rent Expense
Revenue from Commissions
Salaries Expense
Sales
Supplies
Supplies Expense
Telephone Expense
Wages Expense

2. A simplified ledger appears on page 281 and in your Workbook.

   1. **Calculate the total assets, total liabilities, and the owner's equity. Prove the accuracy of your figures.**
   2. **By stroking out and/or changing balances, show what the account balances would be after the closing entries were completed.**

3. **Workbook Exercise: Completing a chart showing the steps in the accounting cycle.**

4. **Complete each of the following statements by writing in your Workbook the appropriate word or phrase from the list on page 281.**

   1. Accounting is _____ in nature.
   2. The _____ states that financial reporting is done in equal periods of time.
   3. Asset and liability accounts are considered to be _____ accounts.
   4. _____ are ones that have their balances continue on into the succeeding fiscal period.
   5. Revenue, expense, and drawings accounts are considered to be _____ accounts.
   6. The balances in _____ do not continue into the _____ fiscal period.
   7. Another name for a nominal account is a _____.
   8. Nominal accounts begin each fiscal period with _____.
   9. The process of removing the "old" balances from the nominal accounts is known as _____.
   10. _____ means to cause it to have no balance.
   11. During a fiscal period the Capital account shows _____.
   12. Changes in equity during a fiscal period (except for additional investments by the owner) are contained in _____ accounts.

13. At the end of the fiscal period the ledger is brought up to date by _____.

14. One of the final steps in the accounting cycle is to bring the Capital account _____ and to _____ the nominal accounts.

15. The final step in the accounting cycle is _____.

List of Words and Phrases

a nil balance	nominal accounts
close out	real
closing an account	real accounts
closing the accounts	revenue, expense, and drawings
cyclical	temporary equity account
next	the balance at the beginning of the period
journalizing and posting the	the post-closing trial balance
adjusting entries	time period concept
nominal	up to date

Bank		Bank Loan		S. Mosar, Capital		S. Mosar, Drawings	
100			300		740	750	

Accounts Receivable		Accounts Payable		Advertising Revenue		Sales Revenue	
200			150		1750		450

Supplies				Bank Charges		Light and Heat	
50				20		40	

Equipment				Miscellaneous Exp.		Printing Expense	
1050				5		500	

Rent		Telephone	
250		25	

Wages	
400	

9.3 JOURNALIZING AND POSTING THE CLOSING ENTRIES

You have just studied the objectives of the closing entries. Now you will learn how to achieve those objectives.

The source of the data for the closing entries is the work sheet. All of the necessary figures for the closing entries exist in one convenient place on the work sheet. To explain the closing entry process, let us continue with the work sheet and the ledger for Cassidy Cartage which you worked with in section 9.1.

There is no single way that closing entries must be recorded. This text uses a four-step approach to the closing entries. Shown below, in Figure 9.13, is the work sheet for Cassidy Cartage with the figures for the four steps clearly outlined.

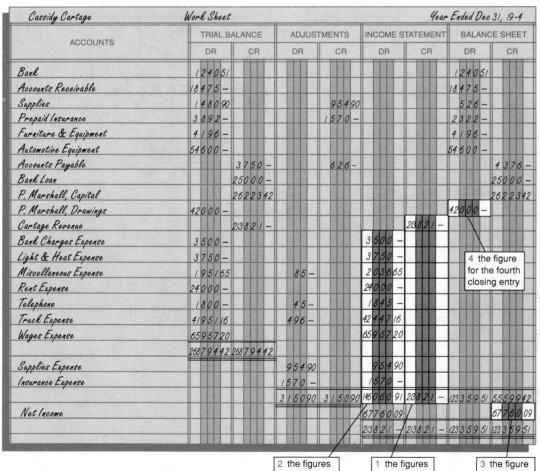

Cassidy Cartage	Work Sheet						Year Ended Dec 31, 19-4	
ACCOUNTS	TRIAL BALANCE		ADJUSTMENTS		INCOME STATEMENT		BALANCE SHEET	
	DR	CR	DR	CR	DR	CR	DR	CR
Bank	1240 51						1240 51	
Accounts Receivable	18475 -						18475 -	
Supplies	1480 90			954 90			526 -	
Prepaid Insurance	3892 -			1570 -			2322 -	
Furniture & Equipment	4196 -						4196 -	
Automotive Equipment	54600 -						54600 -	
Accounts Payable		3750 -		626 -				4376 -
Bank Loan		25000 -						25000 -
P. Marshall, Capital		26223 42						26223 42
P. Marshall, Drawings	42000 -						42000 -	
Cartage Revenue		213821 -				213821 -		
Bank Charges Expense	3500 -				3500 -			
Light & Heat Expense	3750 -				3750 -			
Miscellaneous Expense	1951 65		85 -		2036 65			
Rent Expense	24000 -				24000 -			
Telephone	1800 -		45 -		1845 -			
Truck Expense	41951 16		496 -		42447 16			
Wages Expense	65957 20				65957 20			
	268794 42	268794 42						
Supplies Expense			954 90		954 90			
Insurance Expense			1570 -		1570 -			
			3150 90	3150 90	146060 91	213821 -	123359 51	55599 42
Net Income					67760 09			67760 09
					213821 -	213821 -	123359 51	123359 51

4 the figure for the fourth closing entry

2 the figures for the second closing entry

1 the figures for the first closing entry

3 the figure for the third closing entry

Figure 9.13 Completed work sheet for Cassidy Cartage.

Closing Entry No. 1

The first closing entry transfers the balances in the revenue account(s) to a new nominal account called Income Summary. *Use all of the figures—including the subtotal —to formulate your entry.* The figures for this closing entry are found in the Income Statement section credit column of the work sheet, as outlined in Figure 9.13.

Since revenues have credit balances, debit entries are needed to close them out. Knowing this will help you work out the first closing entry for Cassidy Cartage, which appears below in Figure 9.14.

	Closing Entries			
Dec	31	*Cartage Revenue*	2 13 82 1 –	
		Income Summary		2 13 82 1 –

Figure 9.14 The first closing entry for Cassidy Cartage.

Closing Entry No. 2

The second closing entry transfers the balances in the expense accounts to the Income Summary account. The figures for this closing entry are found in the Income Statement section debit column of the work sheet as outlined in Figure 9.13. *Use all of the figures down to and including the subtotals, and no others.*

Since expenses have debit balances, credit entries are needed to close them out. Understanding this will help you work out the second closing entry for Cassidy Cartage, which appears below in Figure 9.15.

	31	*Income Summary*	1 46 06 0 91	
		Bank Charges Expense		3 5 00 –
		Light & Heat Expense		3 7 50 –
		Miscellaneous Expense		2 03 6 65
		Rent Expense		24 0 0 –
		Telephone Expense		1 8 45 –
		Truck Expense		42 4 47 16
		Wages Expense		65 9 57 20
		Supplies Expense		9 5 4 90
		Insurance Expense		1 5 70 –

Figure 9.15 The second closing entry for Cassidy Cartage.

The ledger of Cassidy Cartage after the second closing entry is shown below in Figure 9.16.

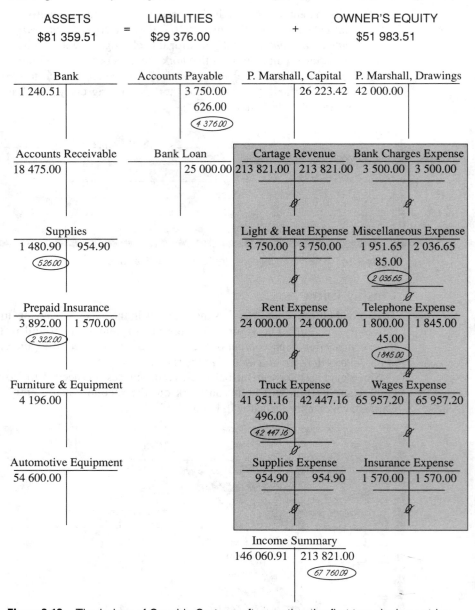

| ASSETS | | LIABILITIES | | OWNER'S EQUITY |
| $81 359.51 | = | $29 376.00 | + | $51 983.51 |

Bank
1 240.51

Accounts Payable
3 750.00
626.00
4 376.00

P. Marshall, Capital
26 223.42

P. Marshall, Drawings
42 000.00

Accounts Receivable
18 475.00

Bank Loan
25 000.00

Cartage Revenue
213 821.00 | 213 821.00
0

Bank Charges Expense
3 500.00 | 3 500.00
0

Supplies
1 480.90 | 954.90
526.00

Light & Heat Expense
3 750.00 | 3 750.00
0

Miscellaneous Expense
1 951.65 | 2 036.65
85.00
2 036.65
0

Prepaid Insurance
3 892.00 | 1 570.00
2 322.00

Rent Expense
24 000.00 | 24 000.00
0

Telephone Expense
1 800.00 | 1 845.00
45.00
1845.00
0

Furniture & Equipment
4 196.00

Truck Expense
41 951.16 | 42 447.16
496.00
42 447.16
0

Wages Expense
65 957.20 | 65 957.20
0

Automotive Equipment
54 600.00

Supplies Expense
954.90 | 954.90
0

Insurance Expense
1 570.00 | 1 570.00
0

Income Summary
146 060.91 | 213 821.00
67 760.09

Figure 9.16 The ledger of Cassidy Cartage after posting the first two closing entries.

The equity section of the ledger is considerably changed at this point. All of the revenue and expense accounts now have nil balances. They have been closed out. Only three accounts in the equity section have a balance. Observe that the total of the equity section remains at $51 983.51. Ignoring the accounts with nil balances, the equity section appears as follows.

P. Marshall, Capital	P. Marshall, Drawings	Income Summary	
26 223.42	42 000.00	146 060.91	213 821.00
			_(67 760.09)_

The balance in the Income Summary account represents either the amount of net income or the amount of net loss. It will be closed out to the owner's Capital account.

The Income Summary account for Cassidy Cartage now contains the following:

- the total revenues of $213 821.00 on the credit side;
- the total expenses of $146 060.91 on the debit side;
- the account balance of $67 763.09 credit which is the net income figure.

If a loss had been suffered, the debit side of the account would have been greater than the credit side, and the account would have a debit balance.

Closing Entry No. 3

The third closing entry transfers the balance in the Income Summary account to the owner's Capital account. The amount is easily picked up from the work sheet. If the Income Summary account has a credit balance, it will take a debit entry to close it. If the account has a debit balance, it will take a credit entry to close it. The third closing entry for Cassidy Cartage appears below in Figure 9.17.

	31	Income Summary	6776009	
		P. Marshall, Capital		6776009

Figure 9.17   The third closing entry for Cassidy Cartage.

Closing Entry No. 4

The fourth closing entry transfers the balance of the Drawings account to the Capital account. Again, the figure for this entry is easily picked up from the work sheet. Since the Drawings account always has a debit balance, a credit entry is needed to close it. The fourth closing entry for Cassidy Cartage appears below in Figure 9.18.

	31	P. Marshall, Capital	42000—	
		P. Marshall, Drawings		42000—

Figure 9.18   The fourth closing entry for Cassidy Cartage.

The ledger for Cassidy Cartage, with all four closing entries posted, appears in Figure 9.19 below. The objectives of the closing entries have been achieved. The Capital account shows the true balance, and the nominal accounts are cleared and ready for the next fiscal period.

ASSETS		LIABILITIES	+	OWNER'S EQUITY
$81 359.51	=	$29 376.00		$51 983.51

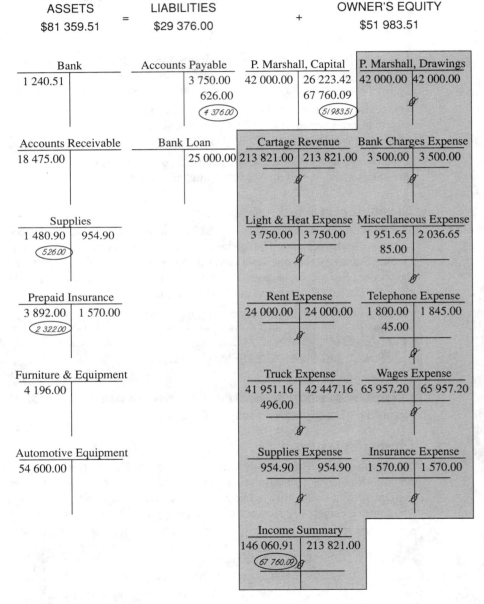

Figure 9.19   The ledger of Cassidy Cartage after all four closing entries have been posted.

Closing Entries—Summary

The four closing entries do the following:

1. close out the revenue account(s) to the Income Summary account;
2. close out the expense accounts to the Income Summary account;
3. close out the Income Summary account to the Capital account;
4. close out the Drawings account to the Capital account.

Post-Closing Trial Balance

The accuracy of the ledger must be checked after you have finished journalizing and posting the adjusting and closing entries. This is done by taking off the post-closing trial balance.

The post-closing trial balance for Cassidy Cartage is shown below in Figure 9.20.

CASSIDY CARTAGE
POST-CLOSING TRIAL BALANCE
DECEMBER 31, 19-4

	DR	CR
Bank	$ 1 240.51	
Accounts Receivable	18 475.00	
Supplies	526.00	
Prepaid Insurance	2 322.00	
Furniture & Equipment	4 196.00	
Automotive Equipment	54 600.00	
Accounts Payable		$ 4 376.00
Bank Loan		25 000.00
P. Marshall, Capital		51 983.51
	$81 359.51	$81 359.51

Figure 9.20   The post-closing trial balance for the ledger of Cassidy Cartage.

Uses of the Work Sheet

You have already used a work sheet and are aware of its usefulness in preparing the financial statements. However, there are other uses for a work sheet.

A work sheet is beneficial in the following ways:

1. A work sheet provides a method of organizing the figures for the financial statements. It contains all of the up-to-date figures for the statements in one convenient place.
2. A work sheet lets the accountant see the effect of adjusting entries before they are recorded in the accounts. Accountants sometimes have a choice in how to handle an adjustment.
3. A work sheet proves the arithmetic accuracy of the figures before they are used in the financial statements.
4. A work sheet is the source for obtaining all of the information for recording the adjusting and the closing entries.

SECTION REVIEW QUESTIONS

1. What is the normal source of the information for the closing entries?
2. Explain exactly how to obtain the information for the first closing entry.
3. Explain exactly how to obtain the information for the second closing entry.
4. In what new account are the revenues and expenses summarized?
5. What does the balance in the Income Summary account represent (before it is closed out)?
6. What is the purpose of a post-closing trial balance?
7. Why is a post-closing trial balance briefer than a regular trial balance?
8. Give the four uses of a work sheet.

SECTION EXERCISES

1. Shown below is the completed work sheet for Dr. E. Santala of Porcupine, Ontario. **In your Workbook, journalize the adjusting and closing entries for Dr. Santala.**

Dr. E Santala, Dentist	Work Sheet				Year Ended Dec. 31, 19-4			
ACCOUNTS	TRIAL BALANCE		ADJUSTMENTS		INCOME STATEMENT		BALANCE SHEET	
	DR	CR	DR	CR	DR	CR	DR	CR
Bank	13750 10						13750 10	
Accounts Receivable	3749 0 —						3749 0 —	
Supplies	1035 0 —			7250 —			310 0	
Prepaid Insurance	590 6 —			4050 —			1856 —	
Equipment	6443 4 17						6443 4 17	
Investment - Govt. Bonds	10000 0 —						10000 0 —	
Accounts Payable		4365 —						4365 —
E. Santala, Capital		20431 5 77						20431 5 77
E. Santals, Drawings	8000 0 —						8000 0 —	
Fees Earned		18037 4 —				18037 4 —		
Interest Earned		7500		2500 —		10000 —		
Bank Charges Expense	170 —				170 —			
Light & Heat Expense	2957 —				2957 —			
Miscellaneous Expense	1436 50				1436 50			
Rent Expense	3000 0 —				3000 0 —			
Telephone Expense	2759 —				2759 —			
Wages & Salaries Expense	4730 2 —				4730 2 —			
	39655 4 77	39655 4 77						
Supplies Expense			7250 —		7250 —			
Insurance Expense			4050 —		4050 —			
Bond Interest Receivable			2500 —				2500 —	
			13800 —	13800 —	9592 4 50	19037 4 —	30313 0 27	20868 0 77
Net Income					9444 950			9444 950
					19037 4 —	19037 4 —	30313 0 27	30313 0 27

2. Shown below is the completed work sheet for R. Tompko who operates a barber shop in Revelstoke, British Columbia.

In your Workbook:

1. journalize the adjusting and closing entries in the general journal provided.
2. post the adjusting and closing entries in the general ledger provided.
3. take off a post-closing trial balance.

Golden Tresses Hair Stylists	Work Sheet						Year Ended Dec. 31, 19—	
	TRIAL BALANCE		ADJUSTMENTS		INCOME STATEMENT		BALANCE SHEET	
ACCOUNTS	DR	CR	DR	CR	DR	CR	DR	CR
Bank	790 —						790 —	
Supplies & Materials	2755 —		800 —	1055 —			2500 —	
Prepaid Insurance	2450 —			1625 —			825 —	
Equipment	17370 —						17370 —	
Accounts Payable		1075 —		800 —				1875 —
R. Tompko, Capital		9922 —						9922 —
R. Tompko, Drawings	42000 —						42000 —	
Revenue		98370 —				98370 —		
Advertising Expense	1200 —				1200 —			
Bank Charges Expense	96 —				96 —			
Light & Heat Expense	2104 —				2104 —			
Materials Used Expense	6950 —		1055 —		8005 —			
Miscellaneous Expense	1902 —				1902 —			
Rent Expense	6000 —				6000 —			
Wages Expense	25750 —				25750 —			
	109367 —	109367 —						
Insurance Expense			1625 —		1625 —			
			3480 —	3480 —	46682 —	98370 —	63485 —	11797 —
Net Income					51688 —			51688 —
					98370 —	98370 —	63485 —	63485 —

3. Workbook Exercise: Journalizing and posting adjusting and closing entries from a completed work sheet and taking off a post-closing trial balance.

4. Indicate whether each of the following statements is true or false by placing a "T" or an "F" in the space indicated in your Workbook. Explain the reason for each "F" response in the space provided.

1. Journalizing and posting the adjusting and closing entries is a routine task that can be done by any knowledgeable accounting clerk.

2. All of the data required to journalize the adjusting and closing entries can be found on the work sheet.

3. It can be assumed that all adjustments have been thought of once the work sheet is completed.

4. The adjusting entries must be journalized and posted to bring the ledger into agreement with the figures on the financial statements.

5. An explanation is needed for each individual adjusting entry being journalized.

6. The adjusting and closing entries in the journal are dated as of the end of the fiscal period.

7. The closing entries can only be processed using the four-step method.

8. The figures for the first closing entry (as described in the textbook) are taken from the income statement section, debit column, of the work sheet.

9. Since revenue accounts have debit balances, credit entries are needed to close them out.

10. The second closing entry (as described in the textbook) transfers the balances in the expense accounts to the Income Summary account.

11. When the adjusting entries and the first two closing entries are journalized and posted, all of the accounts in the equity section of the ledger except three will have nil balances.

12. A loss has been suffered if the Income Summary account has a credit balance before it is closed out.

13. The first two entries in the Income Summary account are the same as the subtotals of the income statement section of the work sheet.

14. The Income Summary account is not closed out if a loss occurs.

15. A work sheet is not necessary in a computerized system because the mathematical accuracy of the figures is assured.

9.4 COMPUTERS IN ACCOUNTING: INCREASING SPREADSHEET POWER

Speed, accuracy, and power are three advantages that spreadsheets give to accountants. In Chapters 3 and 5, speed was emphasized — speed in calculations and speed in entering cell contents by using the copy command. In this chapter the subject of spreadsheet power is further examined.

Spreadsheet power means the speedy display of useful information even when complex computations are involved. To produce spreadsheet power, many mathematical functions must be built in to perform the special calculations.

Choosing Functions

A function is a built-in mathematical computation (usually complex). Some spreadsheet programs have in excess of 100 functions. Instead of attempting to master every function, you should examine the spreadsheet manual to see what functions are available. Then, when you have a specific task to perform, choose the one to satisfy your needs.

For example, Figure 9.21 shows a listing of contract numbers and their dollar amounts.

	A	B	C	D	E
1	LIST OF CONTRACTS				
2	CONTRACT #	AMOUNT			
3	1	35 356.78			
4	2	37 457.20			
5	3	42 987.10			
6	4	35 702.56			
7	5	30 607.25			
8	6	45 096.24			
9	7	47 098.23			
10	8	41 678.88			
11	9	43 786.34			
12	10	35 261.98			
13	11	30 567.45			
14	12	47 657.34			
15	13	44 987.45			
16	14	30 588.75			
17	15	47 888.30			
18	16	41 876.45			
19	17	30 588.25			
20	18	47 099.12			
21	19	39 045.28			
22	20	32 456.78			
23					
24					
25	MAXIMUM				
26	MINIMUM				

Figure 9.21   A list of contracts and amounts.

If you want the spreadsheet to show the amount of the largest contract, there is a spreadsheet function to help you. When you enter =MAX(B3..B22) at cell B25, the figure 47 888.30 will appear at B25 instantly. Notice that the structure of this function is the same as the SUM function with which you are already familiar. First, a prefix is entered. In this case it is the "=" sign, but some software uses a different symbol. This is followed by the name, followed by the range of cells to be examined.

To display the smallest number in the list, use =MIN(C14..C18) at cell B26. The figure 30 567.45 will appear there instantly. The name of the function often reveals its purpose. MAX stands for maximum; MIN for minimum. It does not take much guesswork to see the purpose of other commonly used functions, such as AVG, or COUNT.

Logical Functions

Accountants make decisions as a matter of daily routine. Can spreadsheets help accountants by making logical decisions? The answer is yes — to a limited extent. To illustrate the logical power of a spreadsheet, consider the relatively simple bookkeeping task of placing the net income or net loss on the work sheet. Let us examine this task by looking at the spreadsheet in Figure 9.22. You can work along at your computer by loading spreadsheet model CH9-1. This spreadsheet has been completed except for the last two lines.

	A	B	C	D	E	F	G	H	I	J
1	Worksheet			Mission Marketing				Year Ended December 31, 19-5		
2			Trial Balance		Adjustments		Income Statement		Balance Sheet	
3	Accounts		DR	CR	DR	CR	DR	CR	DR	CR
4	BANK	3 000							3 000	
5	ACCOUNTS RECEIVABLE	21 600							21 600	
6	SUPPLIES	4 250				3 300			950	
7	PREPAID INSURANCE	1 254				574			680	
8	EQUIPMENT	19 200							19 200	
9	AUTOMOBILE	44 200							44 200	
10	ACCOUNTS PAYABLE		7 345			315				7 660
11	C. ANS, CAPITAL		71 275							71 275
12	C. ANS, DRAWINGS	40 000							40 000	
13	FEES EARNED		135 700					135 700		
14	CAR EXPENSE	13 214			150		13 364			
15	LIGHT AND POWER EX	2 800			115		2 915			
16	MISCELLANEOUS EX	1 563			50		1 613			
17	RENT EXPENSE	18 000					18 000			
18	WAGES EXPENSE	45 239					45 239			
19		214 320	214 320							
20	SUPPLIES EXPENSE				3 300		3 300			
21	INSURANCE EXPENSE				574		574			
22					4 189	4 189	85 005	135 700	129 630	78 935
23	Net Income or Net Loss									

Figure 9.22   The spreadsheet model showing the almost completed work sheet for Mission Marketing.

Chapter 8 of your text referred to the net income or net loss on the work sheet as the balancing figure. Recall that if there is a net income, the balancing figure is placed in the outer two of the last four columns (columns G and J). If there is a net loss, the balancing figure is placed in the inner two of the last four columns (columns H and I).

For this model to be useful time after time, four cells — G23, H23, I23, and J23 — have to be programmed to make a logical decision. The decision is straightforward: show the balancing figure or show zero. By searching the manual, you will find a function to make this happen. In this case, the IF function does the job.

The structure of the IF function is as follows: =IF (conditional statement, true response, false response). The prefix, the function name, and the brackets are familiar to you. But the three items separated by commas which are contained within the brackets are new. Let us examine how to use this function for cell G23.

The correct reasoning for cell G23 goes like this: if revenues are greater than expenses, calculate and show the net income. If revenues are not greater than expenses, show zero. A correct IF function entered at G23 can say this. Examine the correct IF function below.

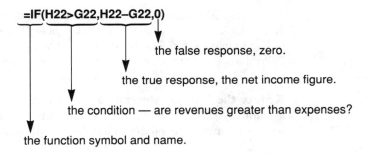

the false response, zero.

the true response, the net income figure.

the condition — are revenues greater than expenses?

the function symbol and name.

In the example that we are using, there is a profit. Therefore the condition is true. H22 is greater than G22 and as a result the cell at G23 will display the net income figure of 50 695. If the condition had been untrue, a zero (0) would have been displayed.

Enter the above function at cell G23 of your model and you will see the display instantly. Now, try to enter the similar functions for H23, I23, and J23 plus those to complete the work sheet totals. The functions for G23, H23, I23, and J23 are given below in case you have difficulty.

Functions for model CH9-1	
Cell	Function
G23	= IF (H22>G22, H22–G22, 0)
H23	= IF (G22>H22, G22–H22, 0)
I23	= IF (I22<J22, I22–J22, 0)
J23	= IF (J22<I22, I22–J22, 0)

You should now have some idea of how useful the IF function can be. With it, accountants can be immediately alerted to costs that are too high, sales projections that are too low, and all kinds of other management information.

SPREADSHEET EXERCISES

1. **Perform the following:**

   1. Load the spreadsheet model named CH9-2 for Cassidy Cartage.
   2. Enter the adjustments for supplies ($954.90) and prepaid insurance ($2 076.00) in columns E and F. After the adjustments have been entered, use the SUM function to total these two columns.
   3. Use formulas involving + and − to extend the work sheet. For example, the formula to extend the Supplies line, +C6+E6–F6, would be entered in cell I6. A similar formula will have to be entered for each balance sheet item and each income statement item. To some extent, you can save time by using the COPY command.
   4. Use the SUM function to subtotal the last four columns.
   5. Use the IF function to complete the balancing line of the work sheet.
   6. Use simple +,− formulas or SUM functions to complete the work sheet.
   7. Print a copy of the work sheet. Save the spreadsheet for possible future use.

2. **Reduce the Cartage Revenue account and increase the Accounts Payable account by $200 000 to produce a loss. Check to see that your spreadsheet has been programmed properly to handle a profit and a loss.**

Challenge Exercise

3. The IF function can be used at cell A26 to have the spreadsheet display the words Net Income and the words Net Loss as the true or false responses. **Simply enter the text or label, enclosed in quotation marks, "Net Income," for example. Be sure to test your work.**

COMPUTER REVIEW QUESTIONS

1. What is meant by spreadsheet power and why is it important to accountants?
2. "Upon buying a spreadsheet program, the first thing an accountant should do is master all of the mathematical functions available." Comment on this statement.
3. An example of a conditional statement is "IF A1=100". Write three other conditional statements. Each one must contain a mathematical symbol.
4. What is the purpose of commas in the structure of the IF function?
5. Many spreadsheets allow users to enter text as the true or false response of an IF function. The words must be enclosed in quotation marks. Write an IF function that displays a written warning to an accountant that total expenses are too high.

Communicate It

Your friend is having trouble understanding the IF function. **Using your own words, write a brief explanation that will improve his comprehension. Include an example that he can relate to.**

CHAPTER HIGHLIGHTS

After you have completed Chapter 9, you should:

1. understand why adjusting entries are necessary;
2. be able to make the adjusting entries for supplies, prepaid insurance, and late-arriving invoices;
3. be able to use ten-column and eight-column work sheets;
4. know which accounts are nominal ones and which accounts are real ones;
5. understand the purpose of nominal accounts and why they must be cleared;
6. understand the purpose of the Income Summary account;
7. know the complete accounting cycle;
8. know the four benefits of the work sheet;
9. be able to journalize and post the adjusting and closing entries;
10. know the purpose of the post-closing trial balance.

ACCOUNTING TERMS

adjusting entry
closing an account
Income Summary account
nominal account
post-closing trial balance
prepaid expense
real account

CHAPTER EXERCISES

Using Your Knowledge

1. Luciano Massaro owns a beauty parlor in Yorkton, Saskatchewan. Shown below is the trial balance for his business after the first two months of business in 19-8.

LUCIANO MASSARO
TRIAL BALANCE
FEBRUARY 28, 19-8

	DR	CR
Bank	$ 1 802.50	
Accounts Receivable	13 550.00	
Supplies	2 017.00	
Prepaid Insurance	2 150.00	
Equipment	7 200.00	
Automobile	18 000.00	
Accounts Payable		$ 4 316.00
Luciano Massaro, Capital		33 690.92
Luciano Massaro, Drawings	11 000.00	
Revenue from Sales		47 976.00
Automobile Expense	1 940.20	
Bank Charges Expense	96.00	
Light and Heat Expense	2 402.00	
Miscellaneous Expense	200.22	
Rent Expense	1 000.00	
Telephone Expense	310.00	
Wages Expense	24 315.00	
	$85 982.92	$85 982.92

1. **Using the additional information provided below, complete an eight-column work sheet.**

Additional Information
1. Supplies on hand at February 28th—$1 512.
2. Prepaid insurance as of February 28th—$1 550.
3. Late-arriving invoice—Car repair bill—$75.

2. **Prepare an income statement and a classified balance sheet.**
3. **Journalize the adjusting and closing entries.**
4. **Post the adjusting and closing entries to the ledger provided in the Workbook.**
5. **Take off a post-closing trial balance.**

Comprehensive Exercise

2. The general ledger trial balance of the *Oakville Journal*, after a fiscal period of one year, is given on page 297. Additional information is also provided.

OAKVILLE JOURNAL

TRIAL BALANCE

DECEMBER 31, 19-8

	DR	CR
Bank	$ 2 750.00	
Accounts Receivable	15 317.20	
Supplies and Materials	23 795.16	
Prepaid Insurance	4 200.00	
Land	75 000.00	
Buildings	105 000.00	
Equipment	95 700.00	
Automotive Equipment	75 325.00	
Accounts Payable		$ 9 216.42
Bank Loan		100 000.00
Mortgage Payable		110 000.00
R. Lucht, Capital		122 638.91
R. Lucht, Drawings	50 000.00	
Revenue—Advertising		218 946.00
Revenue—Circulation		91 315.00
Bank Interest and Charges Expense	12 150.00	
Building Maintenance Expense	3 220.00	
Car Expense	4 960.50	
Light and Heat Expense	11 350.00	
Miscellaneous Expense	5 940.13	
Mortgage Interest Expense	5 500.00	
Postage Expense	1 240.00	
Office Salaries Expense	34 319.15	
Sales Promotions Expense	2 750.00	
Truck Expense	26 334.19	
Telephone Expense	2 946.00	
Wages Expense	94 319.00	
	$652 116.33	$652 116.33

From the above trial balance, with the additional information below, do the following in your Workbook:
1. **Complete the work sheet.**
2. **Prepare the income statement and the balance sheet for 19-8.**
3. **Journalize the adjusting and closing entries.**
4. **Post the adjusting and closing entries in the T-accounts provided.**
5. **Take off a post-closing trial balance.**

Additional Information
1. The value of materials and supplies at the year-end amounted to $8 013.56.
2. The value of unexpired insurance at the year-end amounted to $1 325.00.
3. Late bills arriving in January, 19-9 which pertain to the 19-8 fiscal period are as follows:

Supplies and Materials	$ 509.60
Car Expense	200.00
Truck Expense	746.20
Miscellaneous Expense	35.00
Total	$1 490.80

3. **1.** During 19-1, its first year of operation, Magna Company purchased $2 852.12 of office supplies.

2. At the end of 19-1 the office supplies on hand were valued at $1 325.60.

3. During 19-2 Magna Company purchased $2 956.75 of office supplies.

4. At the end of 19-2 the office supplies on hand were valued at $1 500.50.

In the Supplies account and the Supplies Expense account provided in your Workbook, show in logical order the effect of:

a. the office supplies purchased;

b. the supplies expense adjusting entries;

c. the supplies expense closing entries.

4. **Use T-accounts and prepaid insurance listings to help you with this exercise.**
During its first year of operation, Force Company purchased the following insurance policy.

	Company	Policy Date	Term	Premium
19-1	Genuine	March 1	1 year	$240

1. Calculate the prepaid insurance at the end of 19-1.

2. Calculate the insurance expense for 19-1.

3. Give the adjusting entry for insurance used in 19-1.

During its second year of operation, Force Company purchased the following additional insurance policies.

	Company	Policy Date	Term	Premium
19-2	Genuine	Mar 1	1 year	$240
	Regal	Sept. 1	1 year	144
	Standard	Nov. 1	1 year	120

4. What is the balance in the Prepaid Insurance account at the end of 19-2 before any adjusting entry?

5. Calculate the value of prepaid insurance at the end of 19-2.

6. What is the insurance expense for 19-2?

7. Give the adjusting entry for insurance used in 19-2.

8. Prove the insurance expense figure for 19-2 by calculating it in another way.

5. **Use T-accounts and prepaid insurance listings to help you with this exercise.**
   During its first two years of operation, Quest Company purchased the following insurance policies.

	Company	Policy Date	Term	Premium
19-1	Surety	March 1	2 years	$240
	Royal	July 1	1 year	120
	State	October 1	1 year	240
19-2	Crown	August 1	1 year	240

   1. **How much was spent on insurance in 19-1?**
   2. **What is the value of the prepaid insurance at the end of 19-1?**
   3. **What is the insurance expense for 19-1?**
   4. **Give the adjusting entry for insurance used in 19-1.**
   5. **What is the balance in the Prepaid Insurance account at the end of 19-2 before any adjusting entry?**
   6. **Calculate the value of prepaid insurance at the end of 19-2.**
   7. **What is the insurance expense for 19-2?**
   8. **Give the adjusting entry for insurance used in 19-2.**

Using Your Knowledge

6. Pest Exterminators of Halifax, Nova Scotia, suffered a fire in which many important accounting records were destroyed. You have been hired to assist them in reconstructing their records. Shown below are three items that were not destroyed because the firm's bookkeeper had been preparing them at home. **From the data below, reconstruct the work sheet for Pest Exterminators.**

   Item 1: To help you with the Balance Sheet columns on the work sheet.

PEST EXTERMINATORS
POST-CLOSING TRIAL BALANCE
DECEMBER 31, 19—

	DR	CR
Bank	$ 1 200	
Accounts Receivable	15 350	
Supplies	1 850	
Prepaid Insurance	900	
Land	40 000	
Buildings	72 400	
Equipment	15 350	
Truck	42 284	
Accounts Payable		$ 6 743
Bank Loan		40 000
Joan Budd, Capital		142 591
	$189 334	$189 334

Item 2: To help you with the Adjustment columns of the work sheet.

PEST EXTERMINATORS
ADJUSTING ENTRIES
DECEMBER 31, 19—

	DR	CR
Supplies	$ 176	
Miscellaneous Expense	102	
Truck Expense	250	
Accounts Payable		$ 528
Supplies Used	2 276	
Supplies		2 276
Insurance Used	1 900	
Prepaid Insurance		1 900

Item 3: To help you with the Income Statement columns of the work sheet and with the drawings and net income.

PEST EXTERMINATORS
CLOSING ENTRIES
DECEMBER 31, 19—

	DR	CR
Revenue	$126 375	
Income Summary		$126 375
Income Summary	78 133	
Bank Interest and Charges		5 162
Light and Heat		2 700
Miscellaneous Expense		1 048
Telephone		1 050
Truck Expense		13 291
Wages		50 706
Supplies Used		2 276
Insurance Used		1 900
Income Summary		
Joan Budd, Capital		48 242
Joan Budd, Capital	40 000	
Joan Budd, Drawings		40 000

7. Given the following limited information, prepare the closing entries for O. Como.

O. COMO		
BALANCE SHEET		
NOVEMBER 30, 19—		
Assets		
Bank		$100
Accounts Receivable		300
Supplies		70
		$470
Liabilities		
Accounts Payable		$150
Owner's Equity		
Balance November 1		$170
Net Income	$650	
Drawings	500	
Increase in Equity		150
Balance November 30		320
		$470

O. COMO	
INCOME STATEMENT	
MONTH ENDED NOVEMBER 30, 19—	
Revenue	$1 800
Expenses	
General Expense	$ 50
Utilities	100
Wages	1 000
	$1 150
Net Income	$ 650

8. John, a student in accounting, comes to you, his teacher, with the following difficulty. After a great deal of time and effort, John has failed to balance the post-closing trial balance, and has become quite frustrated. "Everything was going fine," he states. "My balance sheet balanced. My income statement agreed. I just can't figure it out." John's balance sheet, income statement, and post-closing trial balance are given on page 302.

1. **How can you tell quickly which figure(s) on the post-closing trial balance are probably the incorrect ones?**
2. **Which figure(s) are wrong in this trial balance?**
3. **Explain what error or errors John has made.**

BALANCE SHEET		
Assets		
Bank	$1 301	
Accounts Receivable	7 406	
Supplies	385	
Land	21 900	
Buildings	75 382	
Equipment	19 462	
		$125 836
Liabilities		
Bank Loan	$12 000	
Accounts Payable	5 726	
Mortgage Payable	51 672	$ 70 398
Owner's Equity		
Beginning balance	$71 314	
Net Loss	$ 876	
Drawings	15 000	
Decrease in equity	15 876	
Ending balance		55 438
		$125 836

INCOME STATEMENT		
Revenue		$19 462
Expenses		
Advertising	$ 3 902	
Delivery	3 764	
Wages	12 000	
Utilities	672	20 338
Net Loss		$ 876

POST-CLOSING TRIAL BALANCE		
Bank	$ 1 301	
Account Receivable	7 406	
Supplies	385	
Land	21 900	
Buildings	75 382	
Equipment	19 462	
Bank Loan		$ 12 000
Accounts Payable		5 726
Mortgage Payable		52 672
Owner's Equity		57 190
	$125 836	$127 588

For Further Thought

9. **Briefly answer the following questions.**

1. Explain why the time period concept pertains more to the income statement than to the balance sheet.

2. The Bank account is ongoing or continuous in nature. Explain.

3. Is the owner's Capital account a nominal account? Explain.

4. Assume that the nominal accounts are not closed out at the end of a fiscal period. Explain how this affects account data for the next fiscal period.

5. Assume that the accounts are updated and closed out at the end of an accounting period. For how long will the account balances remain accurate?

6. Usually, the owner's Capital account is up to date only on the last day of the fiscal period. Why does this not create a problem for the users of the financial data?

7. What would be the best first step toward balancing a post-closing trial balance that did not balance?

8. You are given a completed work sheet prepared by another employee. You are asked to process the adjusting and closing entries. Explain why this will be no problem for you.

9. Suppose that, when you are performing the task in question 8 above, you detect that an adjusting entry was overlooked or forgotten in error. What, if anything, would be done about this?

10. Assume that the first two closing entries have been processed. What does it mean if the Income Summary account has a credit balance? Is the amount of the credit balance significant?

CASE STUDIES

CASE 1   *A Mix-Up in Year-End Accounting*

Brenda James is a self-employed public accountant in Wallenstein, Ontario. She performs a variety of accounting services for a number of clients within a 300 kilometre radius of her office. At the present time she happens to be working in a small town about 120 kilometres from home.

While there, Brenda receives a telephone call from her office regarding a problem with the work of another client in the town where she is located. Before returning home, Brenda pays a visit to this other client, Academy of Music, to provide assistance.

Academy of Music does its own accounting up to the trial balance stage. Brenda does the year-end accounting. She has recently provided Academy of Music with a set of financial statements and a list of adjusting and closing entries for the client to journalize and post. The client takes off the post-closing trial balance.

The accounting clerk for Academy of Music sensed that something was wrong with the list of adjusting and closing entries. He decided not to process them until he talked to Brenda. Brenda has to work with data available in the client's office because all of her working papers are at her office. To prepare to study the situation, she gathers together the following:

A.

ACADEMY OF MUSIC
BALANCE SHEET
DECEMBER 31, 19-2

Assets

Current Assets

Bank	$ 3750	
Accounts Receivable	18 184	
Supplies	300	
Prepaid Insurance	630	$22 864

Plant and Equipment

Equipment	$27 375	
Automobile	18 012	45 387
Total Assets		$68 251

Liabilities and Owner's Equity

Current Liability

Accounts Payable		$5 085

F. Oke, Capital

Balance January 1		$52 330
Net Income	$37 836	
Drawings	27 000	
Increase in Capital	10 836	
Balance December 31		63 166
Total Liabilities and Equity		$68 251

B.

ACADEMY OF MUSIC
INCOME STATEMENT
YEAR ENDED DECEMBER 31, 19–2

Revenue

Fees Earned	$95 300

Operating Expenses

Bank Charges	$ 102
Car Expense	16 222
Light and Heat	3 825
Miscellaneous Expense	370
Rent	6 000
Telephone	500
Wages	28 375
Supplies Used	650
Insurance Used	1 420
	57 464
Net Income	$37 836

C.

ACADEMY OF MUSIC
ADJUSTING AND CLOSING ENTRIES
DECEMBER 31, 19–2
(provided by Brenda James)

	DR	CR
Adjusting Entries		
Supplies Used	810	
Supplies		810
Insurance Used	1 080	
Prepaid Insurance		1 080
Car Expense	210	
Miscellaneous Expense	160	
Accounts Payable		370
Closing Entries		
Fees Earned	81 316	
Income Summary		81 316
Income Summary	51 672	
Bank Charges		1 120
Car Expense		13 280
Light and Heat		3 307
Miscellaneous Expense		215
Rent		5 400
Telephone		400
Wages		25 060
Supplies Used		810
Insurance Used		1 080
Income Summary	25 388	
F. Oke, Capital		25 388
F. Oke Capital	20 000	
F. Oke, Drawings		20 000

Questions

1. How can Brenda tell if something is wrong?
2. Is the list of adjusting and closing entries the correct one? Explain.
3. Does the list supplied have anything to do with Academy of Music? Explain.
4. Give the most likely explanation for the error.
5. Work out the adjusting entries from the information that you have available. Start to prepare a new list of the correct adjusting and closing entries.*
6. Work out the closing entries and complete the list of adjusting and closing entries.

* You can do this by restructuring the work sheet, starting with the Balance Sheet and Income Statement columns and working backwards.

continued

ACADEMY OF MUSIC
UNADJUSTED GENERAL LEDGER
December 31, 19–2

Bank	Accounts Receivable	Supplies	Prepaid Insurance
3 750	18 184	950	2 050

Equipment	Automobile	Accounts Payable	F. Oke, Capital
24 375	19 780	4 370	39 586

F. Oke, Drawings	Fees Earned	Bank Charges	Car Expenses
27 000	95 300	102	15 707

Light and Heat	Miscellaneous Expense	Rent	Telephone
3 675	370	6 000	450

Wages	Supplies Used	Insurance Used	Income Summary
28 375			

CASE 2 *Once a Liability, Always a Liability?*

Birch Contracting Company in Nanaimo, B.C., was obliged by law to provide vacation pay to every employee equal in amount to two per cent of the gross pay of the employee. This liability for vacation pay became due and payable on June 1 of each year.

Most of the company's work was seasonal in nature and required a lot of manual labour. Therefore, Birch Contracting employed many migrant workers who stayed for only one season. These workers were often new Canadians who did not know Canadian laws and regulations.

Birch Contracting provided for the necessary vacation pay and the accounting entries were properly recorded in the books. However, the company made no effort to contact former employees when the payment came due. Locating former employees was difficult, time-consuming, and often impossible. Therefore, the company chose to wait until the employees made the contact. Consequently, all former employees who did not contact the company were never paid their vacation pay.

Over a period of years, the liability for vacation pay as shown by the ledger grew to a sizable amount. The company accountant felt that something should be done about the liability, but the owner directed her to leave things as they were.

Questions
1. Is the company policy a reasonable one?
2. Should an unpaid liability be left on the books indefinitely?
3. What two advantages are gained by leaving the unpaid liability on the books indefinitely?
4. How would correct accounting practice deal with the above situation?

ENTREPRENEUR
Mai Mackenzie / West Vancouver Finishing School

The adage "experience is the best teacher" aptly applies to Scots-born Mai Mackenzie, founder and director of the West Vancouver Finishing School, located across Burrard Inlet from Vancouver, B.C.

Ms. Mackenzie has managed to turn her first-hand experience of the cultures, customs, and business practices of Asian peoples into a finishing school. Her school is both for young people aged 18 to 25 who plan to enter the business world and for business people wanting to learn how to conduct themselves in the Far East.

During 10 years spent with British Airways, Ms. Mackenzie learned a great deal about the cultures, customs, and languages of Southeast Asian countries. But her most intensive practical experience came afterward, when she and her first husband, a journalist, lived and worked for 12 years in Malaysia, Singapore, and Hong Kong. Together they drove through the jungles interviewing men and women in far-flung villages.

After her husband's death, Mai and her two young sons returned to London, England. There she married school master David Mackenzie and the family moved to British Columbia. In 1986 she opened West Vancouver Finishing School. Since then support has grown from both the business community and young people, some of whom come from as far away as Mexico and Japan to enroll. The school now has a teaching staff of five, and the 1989-90 enrolment is expected to double that for 1988-89. Among Mai Mackenzie's larger business clients have been B.C. Telephone, Royal LePage Real Estate, and Wardair.

Mai's goal is to help business people avoid spending thousands of dollars on hotel bills, promotion, wining and dining prospective clients, and then at the end of the trip returning home empty-handed. Mai has seen this happen to those who are unprepared for business in the Orient. "They get back on the airplane and say it was a nice trip but nothing happened."

"A lot of people want to know about the whole Pacific Rim because they are expanding into it," says Mai. "I tell them that what applies in Thailand, for example, won't work in Japan."

In Mai's view, a business person must carefully prepare for the trip to Asia. Her courses help by providing an overview of a country's culture, geography, and history. They also focus on travel, currency, the media, dietary needs, hotels, advertising, public relations, and seminar and meeting facilities. She invites representatives from airlines, banks, and Asian governments to address her classes on what to expect in Pacific Rim countries. Some of her courses touch on the wines and cuisines of various Asian nations.

She suggests that Occidentals try to look at Asia through Asian eyes, not their own Western eyes, if they wish to be accepted in Asian society and do business there. Says Mai, "I have lived in Asia so long that I can see how Westerners make mistakes. With Asians, you never know if you've made a social blunder. They won't tell you. They will be pleasant because they have been trained to be polite. They don't want you to lose face. They smile and shake your hand and you go off thinking you have done very well. But you'll never hear from them again."

Mai believes that, for young people, finishing school bridges the gap between high school and career or college. "That gap is a scary time," she says. "Many young people who graduate from high school are afraid of what lies ahead for them. We need to give students a backup system after leaving high school in order to keep their talents alive and to help them find their rightful place in society. That's what we attempt to do in our school."

DISCUSSION

1. What programs does West Vancouver Finishing School offer to students?
2. What special skills does Mai Mackenzie have for teaching business-related courses?
3. How is the world "shrinking" in terms of business?
4. Explain the disappointment experienced by Westerners attempting to do business in Asia.
5. Why should Western business people learn about the culture of the country in which they plan to do business?
6. How might courses offered by West Vancouver Finishing School prepare students just out of high school for the future?

Subsidiary Ledger Accounting

As a business grows, its ledger grows too, but in a special way. The increase in the ledger comes mostly from having more accounts for customers and creditors. The other ledger accounts seldom increase in number; they only increase in the size of their balances.

Figure 10.1 illustrates the growth of a ledger. The number of accounts for customers and creditors increases. But the number of other accounts remains about the same.

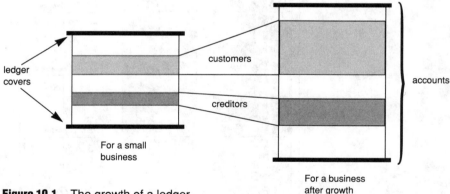

Figure 10.1 The growth of a ledger.

Some large businesses—Bell Canada, for example—have ledgers that contain many thousands of customers' accounts.

In Chapters 8 and 9, the individual accounts of customers and creditors were not included on the work sheet or on the balance sheet. It was the total of the customers' accounts and the total of the creditors' accounts that were used. These were called *control* accounts. What you were not told at that time was that the individual customers' accounts and the individual creditors' accounts are not even kept in the main ledger, now to be called the *general ledger*. In fact, they are kept in separate ledgers known as *subsidiary ledgers*. This is all part of a more efficient accounting system.

A growing business reaches a point where additional office help is needed to handle the increase in accounting and other duties. At the same time, the owner of the business will be trying to keep costs down by hiring the least expensive employees. They are persons whose skills, training, and experience are at an early stage of development. The system of subsidiary ledgers and control accounts makes it possible to have the work related to subsidiary ledgers done by junior employees under the supervision of a few senior persons. This is usually the case in a mature business.

10.1 SUBSIDIARY LEDGER THEORY

The bookkeeping for customers' and creditors' accounts is ideally suited to a division of work. It makes good business sense to separate these accounts from the rest of the ledger. Then they can be looked after independently by accounting clerks.

To begin the study of subsidiary ledgers, examine the T-accounts ledger in Figure 10.2. This is a typical ledger except that the number of customers' and creditors' accounts is very small.

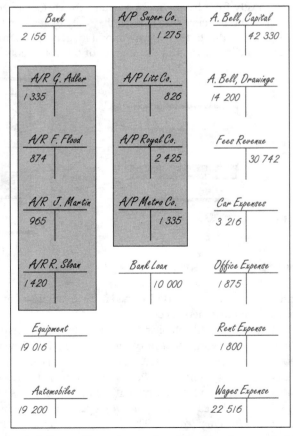

Figure 10.2   A simple ledger with customers' and creditors' accounts highlighted.

From this ledger extract all of the accounts of customers (Accounts Receivable) and all those of creditors (Accounts Payable). Set them aside in two separate groups. This is shown in Figure 10.3. In each new group, arrange the accounts in alphabetical order.

By definition, a group of accounts is a ledger. Therefore, each of the two new groups of accounts is a ledger. The accounting system now contains three ledgers.

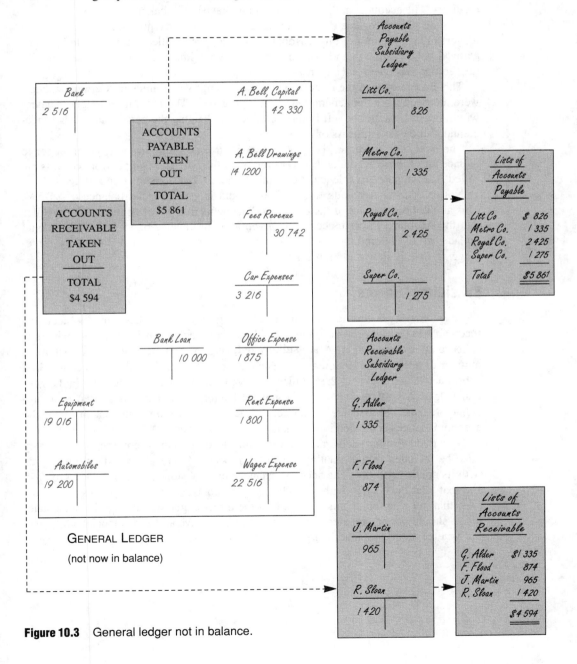

Figure 10.3   General ledger not in balance.

The ledger of customers' accounts is known as the accounts receivable ledger. The **accounts receivable ledger** is a book or file containing all of the accounts of customers. The accounts in this ledger normally have debit balances.

The ledger of creditors' accounts is known as the accounts payable ledger. The **accounts payable ledger** is a book or file containing all of the accounts of ordinary creditors. The accounts in this ledger normally have credit balances.

It is necessary for each ledger to have its own identity now that there are three ledgers in the system. For this reason, the main ledger is called the general ledger. The **general ledger** is the main ledger of a business containing accounts for assets, liabilities, equity, revenues, and expenses.

The change-over to the three-ledger system is not yet completed. Certain accounts were removed from the general ledger in Figure 10.3. Therefore it no longer balances within itself. It cannot be left in this condition. Balancing the general ledger is fundamental to the whole process of accounting.

The next step, therefore, is to open two control accounts in the general ledger to replace all of those accounts that were removed from it. The two control accounts are called Accounts Receivable and Accounts Payable. They are shown in Figure 10.4.

Notice that the Accounts Receivable account is given a debit balance of $4 594. This amount replaces all of the customers' accounts that were removed. Observe also that the Accounts Payable account is given a credit balance of $5 861. This amount replaces all of the creditors' accounts that were removed. The final state of the three-ledger system is shown in Figure 10.4.

Subsidiary Ledgers

We now have two new ledgers in our accounting system. These are the accounts receivable ledger and the accounts payable ledger. Each of these two new ledgers is called a subsidiary ledger. A **subsidiary ledger** is a separate ledger that contains a number of accounts of a similar type such as accounts receivable. The accounts in a subsidiary ledger make up the detailed data for one related control account in the general ledger. A **control account** is a general ledger account that is related to a subsidiary ledger. The balance in the control account represents the sum of all of the account balances contained in the related subsidiary ledger.

Now that subsidiary ledgers have been introduced into the accounting system, they must be included in the monthly balancing process. A subsidiary ledger must agree with its control account. The account balances in a subsidiary ledger must be totaled, and that total must agree with the balance of the control account. If it does not, errors exist that must be found and corrected. In the three-ledger system, the financial statements should not be prepared until the three ledgers have all been balanced. Only then can you feel confident that the figures are correct.

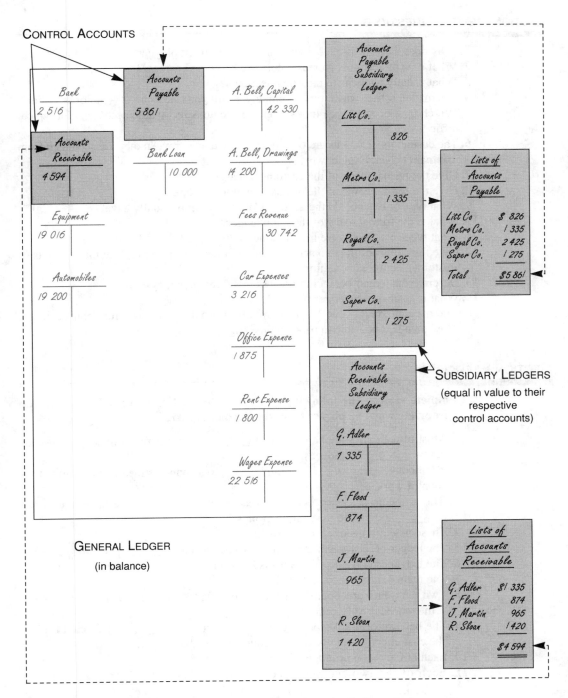

Figure 10.4   General ledger in balance in a simple three-ledger system.

SECTION REVIEW QUESTIONS

1. Why does a business have both junior and senior employees?
2. What type of accounts increase most in a growing business?
3. What usually happens to the other accounts?
4. In a mature office, which type of employee will you find more of—junior or senior?
5. Which type of employee looks after the accounts receivable accounts in a typical office?
6. The customers' accounts are considered to be a ledger when they are separated from the main ledger. Explain why.
7. Give the formal name of the customers' ledger.
8. Give the formal name of the ordinary creditors' ledger.
9. What type of balance do the accounts of the creditors usually have?
10. What is the formal name of the main ledger?
11. What type of accounts are found in the main ledger?
12. Give the names of the two accounts in the main ledger that replace the accounts of customers and trade creditors.
13. Describe the ledger-balancing process in a three-ledger system.
14. What is a subsidiary ledger?
15. The accounts receivable ledger normally has only accounts with debit balances. How then is it possible to balance this ledger?

SECTION EXERCISES

1. **Complete each of the following statements by writing in your Workbook the appropriate word or phrase from the list on page 315.**

   1. Most office duties are handled by _____ employees under the supervision of a few _____ employees.
   2. The bookkeeping for _____ and _____ accounts is ideally suited to a division of work.
   3. The accounts of customers and the accounts of creditors are taken out of the _____ and placed in separate groups.
   4. These new groups of accounts are arranged _____.
   5. The ledger of customers' accounts is known as the _____.
   6. The ledger of creditors' accounts is known as the _____.
   7. The main ledger is now called the _____.
   8. Two accounts are opened in the general ledger to replace those that were removed. These are called _____ and _____.
   9. The balance of the Accounts Receivable account is _____ the total of all of the customers' accounts in the accounts receivable ledger.
   10. Each of the two new ledgers is known as a _____.
   11. Each of the two summary accounts in the general ledger is known as a _____.

12. At the end of every month the subsidiary ledgers must be _____ with their respective control accounts.

List of Words and Phrases

Accounts Payable Control	creditor
Accounts Receivable Control	customer
Accounts Payable ledger	equal to
Accounts Receivable ledger	general ledger
Accounts Payable	junior
Accounts Receivable	ledger
alphabetically	senior
balanced	subsidiary ledger
control account	

---

2. The trial balance of Proctor's Pet Store in Weyburn, Saskatchewan, is shown below.

PROCTOR'S PET STORE
TRIAL BALANCE
JUNE 30, 19—

Bank	$ 1 150	
Accounts Receivable		
P. Shewchuk	350	
J. Britt	920	
C. Powell	1 500	
D. Zecca	500	
W. Pritz	2 900	
Supplies	1 550	
Equipment	15 037	
Accounts Payable		
Cleaners' Supply House		$ 900
Wendall's Store		250
Arnwell Animal Hospital		1 500
Tracy Proctor, Capital		18 122
Tracy Proctor, Drawings	11 000	
Revenue		29 435
Light and Heat Expense	2 475	
Miscellaneous Expense	316	
Rent Expense	12 000	
Telephone Expense	509	
	$ 50 207	$ 50 207

1. **Calculate the total value of the accounts receivable accounts.**
2. **Calculate the total value of the accounts payable accounts.**
3. T. Proctor changes over to a three-ledger system of accounting, with subsidiary ledgers and control accounts. **Perform the following:**
   a. **Show the general ledger trial balance.**
   b. **Show the accounts receivable subsidiary ledger listing in alphabetical order and make sure it agrees in total with the general ledger control account.**
   c. **Show the accounts payable subsidiary ledger listing in alphabetical order and make sure it agrees in total with the general ledger control account.**

3. Hans Schmidt operates a repair shop in Thessalon, Ontario. On December 31, 19— the trial balance for the business included the following accounts of customers and suppliers.

Customers		Trade Suppliers	
Aho, Armas	$ 95.20 Dr	Biltmore Plumbing	$ 215.00 Cr
Bilous, Stan	526.00 Dr	Fleming Door Frames	85.00 Cr
Cobb, John	1 552.00 Dr	Goodrich Rubber	352.00 Cr
Dealice, Guido	956.30 Cr	Hlady Aluminum	1 565.00 Cr
Franzmann, Sheila	1 230.00 Dr	Host Rent-a-Car	295.10 Cr
Hickey, George	29.60 Dr	Ideal Woodcraft	75.00 Dr
James, Leslie	3 750.00 Dr	Imperial Trailers	335.60 Cr
Mutz, J.	642.00 Dr	KBM Supply	1 525.00 Cr
Robbenhaur, M.	1 200.80 Dr	Urbanski Tile	743.25 Cr
Torma, Mike	175.10 Cr		
Wen, William	478.30 Dr		

Answer the following questions.

1. What should the balance be in the Accounts Receivable control account?
2. What should the balance be in the Accounts Payable control account?
3. Give the most likely explanation for the credit balances in the list of customers' accounts.
4. Give the most likely explanation for the debit balance in the list of suppliers' accounts.
5. What figure should appear on the balance sheet for accounts receivable? Explain your answer.
6. Would it be proper to transfer the two credit balances from the receivables to the payables, and the one debit balance from the payables to the receivables? Give some points for and against such an action.
7. Suppose that the transfer suggested above was made. What would the balances be in the control accounts?

10.2 SUBSIDIARY LEDGER SYSTEMS

Bookkeeping for Accounts Receivable

The flowcharts in Figures 10.5 and 10.6 show the clerical procedures needed to look after accounts receivable. A thorough examination of these flowcharts will show you how to maintain the accounts receivable ledger. The work of the accounts receivable clerk is shown in the first figure, and the work of the general ledger clerk is shown in the second. Be sure to read the Notes to Flowcharts that follow on page 319.

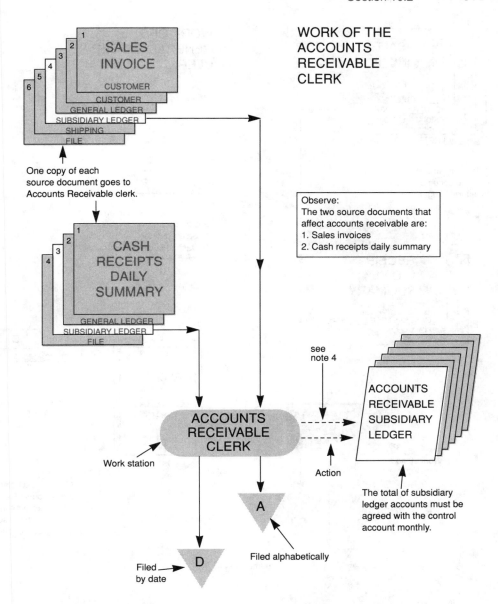

WORK OF THE
ACCOUNTS
RECEIVABLE
CLERK

Figure 10.5   Accounts receivable system. Work of the accounts receivable clerk.

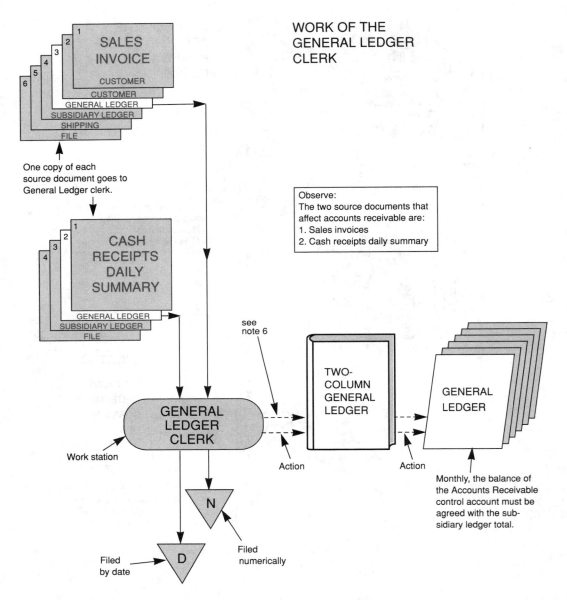

Figure 10.6   Accounts receivable system. Work of the general ledger clerk.

Notes to flowcharts

1. There are two source documents that affect accounts receivable.
   These are: a. *sales invoices*, and
   b. *cash receipts daily summaries.*
2. There are a number of copies of each of the source documents.
3. One copy of each source document is forwarded to the *accounts receivable clerk* (Figure 10.5).
4. The work of the accounts receivable clerk requires:
   a. *for each sales invoice*—a debit entry to a customer's account;
   b. *for each receipt on account*—a credit entry to a customer's account;
5. A different copy of each source document is forwarded to the *general ledger clerk* (Figure 10.6).
6. The work of the general ledger clerk requires an accounting entry for **every** source document.
   a. *For each sales invoice*, the accounting entry is:

	DR	CR
Accounts Receivable	$$$$	
Sales (Revenue)		$$$$
Sales Tax Payable		$$$$

   b. *For each receipt on account*, the accounting entry is:

	DR	CR
Bank	$$$$	
Accounts Receivable		$$$$

7. The subsidiary ledger is updated daily and balanced with its control account monthly.

Balancing the Ledgers

There are three ledgers to balance in a three-ledger system. The procedure for balancing the general ledger remains the same. However, the subsidiary ledgers must also be balanced. This is usually done by the subsidiary ledger clerk as follows.

A subsidiary ledger must be balanced with its control account as shown in Figure 10.7.

The procedure is simple.

1 Make sure that the subsidiary ledger and the control account are posted to the same point in time. Then:
2 Total all of the account balances in the subsidiary ledger.
3 Match the total against the balance of the control account in the general ledger.

If the two totals agree, then the subsidiary ledger is in balance. If the two do not agree, then the subsidiary ledger is not in balance. This means that there are errors to be found and corrected somewhere in the ledgers.

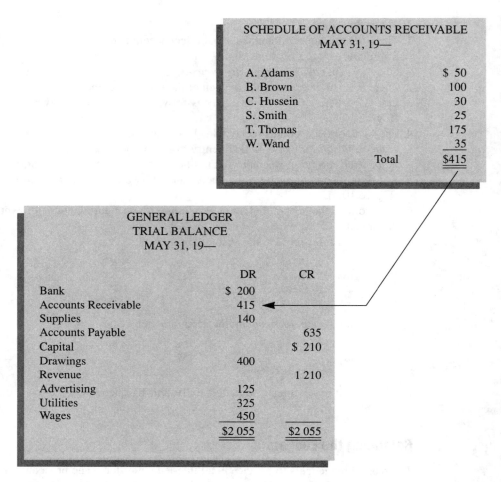

Figure 10.7   Balancing a subsidiary ledger with its control account.

Accounting Controls

The three-ledger system forms part of the overall theory of "internal control."

The accounting clerk who maintains the subsidiary ledger does so independently. This person has no access to cash and no involvement with any other accounting records that affect accounts receivable.

The general ledger clerk who prepares the accounting entries from the source documents works independently. This person does not initiate any source documents.

The general ledger and the two subsidiary ledgers are all maintained independently of each other. When they are brought into balance with each other at the end of each month, they prove that the work of the employees involved is both accurate and honest.

Bookkeeping for Accounts Payable

The previous section explained the procedures for maintaining the accounts receivable. The accounts payable can be handled by a very similar set of procedures.

The highlights of a system for accounts payable are:

1. There are two source documents that affect accounts payable.
   These are: a. *purchase invoices* (see **Note 1** below), and
   b. *cheque copies—on account only* (see **Note 2** below).
2. The accounts payable subsidiary ledger is maintained by the accounts payable clerk.
3. The work of the accounts payable clerk requires:
   a. *for each purchase invoice*—a credit entry to a creditor's account;
   b. *for each cheque copy (on account)*—a debit entry to a creditor's account.
4. The general ledger is maintained by the general ledger clerk.
5. The work of the general ledger clerk requires the making of accounting entries for every source document.
   a. *For each purchase invoice*, the accounting entry is:

	DR	CR
An asset or an expense*	$$$$	
Accounts Payable		$$$$

   *The account affected depends on what was purchased.

   b. *For each cheque copy on account*, the accounting entry is:

	DR	CR
Accounts Payable	$$$$	
Bank		$$$$

6. The subsidiary ledger is balanced with the control account monthly.

Note 1. Each purchase invoice goes through a rigorous series of verifying checks before being recorded in the accounts. It is important to ensure that: a) the goods or services were actually ordered, b) the goods or services are the right ones and were received in good condition, c) the price on the invoice is the agreed price, and d) there are no errors or omissions on the invoice.

Note 2. Not all cheques issued affect accounts payable. For example, a cheque issued to the owner for personal use, or a cheque for a cash purchase of supplies, does not affect accounts payable.

Non-Routine Entries to Subsidiary Ledgers

You have seen that accounting systems are designed so that the information flows to the office clerks by means of business source documents. Such transactions do not fit into the regular accounting routine.

For example, suppose that Naomi Kuper, the owner of a business, collects a $200 account in full from a customer, B. Marr. Ms. Kuper happens to be short of cash at the time. She keeps the money for her personal use instead of turning it in to the business.

First, Ms. Kuper would inform the accounting department of the transaction. She has no wish to deceive anyone. The accountant would make the following accounting entry in the journal:

	DR	CR
N. Kuper, Drawings	$200	
Accounts Receivable		$200
To record the collection by N. Kuper of the account of B. Marr. Funds were kept by N. Kuper for her personal use.		

There is no regular source document for this type of transaction. Without the source document, the accounts receivable clerk will not learn about the transaction in the usual way. The accountant understands this, and will make the entry in the subsidiary ledger personally, or will inform the clerk by means of a written memo. The accountant must attend to this promptly because the subsidiary ledger must be kept up to date.

Keeping Subsidiary Ledgers Up to Date

Customers' and creditors' accounts should be entered promptly. Customers' accounts are usually posted daily so that any communication with the customer is up to date. However, there is normally a slight delay in posting creditors' accounts because it takes time to complete the verification of the purchase invoices.

It is no longer necessary to keep the general ledger right up to date. The posting of the general ledger can be left until the end of the month now that the customers' and creditors' accounts are kept separately. At that time, the posting is done more efficiently, in one concentrated effort.

Standard practice is to balance all three ledgers once a month, after all postings have been completed.

It is possible to keep track of the daily bank balance in various ways without having to keep the general ledger Bank account up to date.

Locating Errors When a Subsidiary Ledger Does Not Balance

When a subsidiary ledger does not balance, a search for the errors must be made. In looking for errors, remember that for every amount entered in a subsidiary ledger there must be an equivalent amount entered in the control account, and vice versa.

In your search for errors, there is no need to go back in the accounts beyond the current month. The ledgers are balanced at the end of every month and the trial balances are kept on file as proof. If errors exist in the accounts, they must have been made after the last balancing was done.

SECTION REVIEW QUESTIONS

1. What are the two source documents that affect accounts receivable?
2. How do the clerks who look after the different ledgers learn about the transactions?
3. Describe the work done by the accounts receivable clerk.
4. Describe the work done by the general ledger clerk.
5. Why is the accounts receivable ledger updated daily?
6. Normally, a subsidiary ledger will not balance with its control account if both ledgers are not posted up to the same point in time. Explain.
7. What has to be done if a subsidiary ledger does not balance with its control? Whose responsibility is it?
8. Describe how to take off a subsidiary ledger trial balance.
9. There is a "control" aspect to the system of subsidiary ledgers and control accounts. Describe this.
10. What are the two source documents that affect accounts payable?
11. Why is the accounts payable ledger not perfectly up to date?
12. Why is it necessary to keep the accounts receivable accounts up to date but not the general ledger accounts?
13. What is the advantage of posting once a month in the general ledger?
14. If an error exists in the accounts it will have occurred since the last balancing. Explain.

SECTION EXERCISES

1. **Study the flowcharts in Figures 10.5 and 10.6 and answer the following questions.**

    1. How many copies of sales invoices are shown?
    2. How many copies of cash receipts daily summaries are shown?
    3. How many copies of each of the above are forwarded to accounting personnel?
    4. What eventually happens to all of the copies of the source documents that are received in the accounting department?
    5. What happens to the original of sales invoices?
    6. What do the solid lines with arrows indicate?
    7. Describe the work done by the subsidiary ledger clerk.
    8. Describe the work done by the general ledger clerk.
    9. What do broken lines with arrows indicate?
    10. How often are the subsidiary ledgers balanced?

2. **Develop two flowcharts that represent the accounts payable system. These two charts should be similar to the two charts in the textbook representing the accounts receivable system.**

3. **Workbook Exercise: Complete a chart showing which source documents affect which subsidiary ledgers and how they affect the general ledger.**

4. Your office duties with the Quick Distributing Co. include those of the accounts receivable clerk. You are to post daily to the customers' accounts from the business documents that you receive.

On the morning of each working day, the following business documents arrive on your desk:

a. Copies of all sales invoices issued on the previous working day by the Sales Department.

b. A listing of the day's cash receipts, prepared first thing each morning by the clerk who opens the mail.

1. Set up the accounts receivable ledger as of June 30, 19—, from the following detailed trial balance. If you are using the Workbook, the ledger is set up for you.

QUICK DISTRIBUTING CO.

ACCOUNTS RECEIVABLE TRIAL BALANCE

JUNE 30, 19—

Adams Bros., 12 Mountain Avenue	Inv. No. 480	$ 67.20	
	507	94.20	$ 161.40
Cozo & Son, 620 Main Street	512		75.65
A.G. Farmer, 120A Blackwell Ave.	514		315.62
S.P. Handy, Ltd., 75 Porter Ave.	484	216.25	
	511	200.22	416.47
R. Mortimer, 60 Hawley Crescent	470	516.25	
	496	621.90	
	505	608.36	1 746.51
Renforth Sales, 192 Dale Place	510		137.62
Vista Limited, 2001 Central Ave.	515		50.00
			$2 903.27

2. Make the entries to the customers' accounts from the following business papers. In the particulars columns, enter invoice numbers.

Transactions

July

2 *Invoices*
   No. 516, Adams Bros., $59.24.
   No. 517, Renforth Sales, $145.50.
   Cash Receipts
   A.G. Farmer, No. 514, $315.62.
   S.P. Handy, Ltd., No. 484, $216.25.

3 *Invoice*
   No. 518, Cozo & Son, $75.85.
   Cash Receipts
   Nil

4 *Invoices*

   No. 519, A.G. Farmer, $217.90.

   No. 520, The Williams Company, 417 Lake Street $150.00.

   Cash Receipts

   Adams Bros., No. 480, $67.20.

   R. Mortimer, No. 470 & No. 496, $1 138.15.

5 *Invoices*

   No. 521, Vista Limited, $94.95.

   No. 522, S.P. Handy, Ltd., $104.16.

   No. 523, R. Mortimer, $56.00.

   Cash Receipt

   Renforth Sales, No. 510, $137.62.

6 *Invoices*

   No. 524, Adams Bros. $167.07.

   No. 525, The Williams Company, $75.00.

   Cash Receipts

   Cozo & Son, No. 512, $75.65.

   Vista Limited, No. 515, $50.00

3. Take off a trial balance of the subsidiary ledger as of July 6 and balance the subsidiary ledger with the control account. The senior accountant has arrived at a control figure of $2 048.45.

---

5. On September 30, 19—, the detailed accounts payable trial balance of Magnetic Controls Company was as follows:

MAGNETIC CONTROLS COMPANY
ACCOUNTS PAYABLE TRIAL BALANCE
SEPTEMBER 30, 19—

		Inv. No.		
Daiton Enterprises	106 Fleet Street, Barbary	516		$ 430.74
Gordon & Associates	7400 King Street, Oak City	B7407		216.92
Henderson Associates	Box 65, Welton	16421	$ 507.00	
		16907	615.00	1 122.00
Kohler, R.M.	141 Nixon Avenue, Barbary	615		104.70
North State Packaging	1500 Middle Road, Lennox	901		74.87
Orenson & Company	560 The Eastway, Dayson	1604	$1 046.26	
		1809	516.15	1 562.41
Riggs, J.B.	75 Baxter Road, Estwing	74621		502.00
Smithers, P.R.	106 Farr Street, Wibbling	74		57.05
Union Advertising	7900 Primeau Avenue, Marks County	16352	$ 436.21	
		17201	702.16	
		17306	518.90	1 657.27
				$5 727.96

1. Set up the accounts payable ledger of Magnetic Controls Company. If you are using the Workbook the ledger is already set up for you.

2. From the selected business documents listed below, perform the duties of the accounts payable clerk by making the entries to the accounts payable ledger. Record the source document numbers in the subsidiary ledger accounts.

TRANSACTIONS

October

1   *Purchase Invoices*
    Smithers, P.R., No. 104, $151.89.
    North State Packaging, No. 1046, $57.25.
    Cheque Copies
    No. 65720, Union Advertising, on account, $800.
    No. 65721, Henderson Associates, Inv. 16421, $507.

2   *Purchase Invoices*
    Wrouse & Reid, 14 Kay Street, Saxton, No. 597G, $316.29.
    Union Advertising, No. 18002, $505.
    Orenson & Company, No. 1856, $216.
    Cheque Copies
    No. 65772, Daiton Enterprises, Inv. 516, $430.74.
    No. 65723, Orenson & Company, on account, $500.

5   *Purchase Invoices*
    Gordon & Associates, No. B7502, $315.20.
    Kohler, R.M., No. 719, $174.90.
    Riggs, J.B., No. 74998, $472.47.
    Cheque Copies
    No. 65734, North State Packaging, Inv. 901, $74.87.
    No. 65735, Union Advertising, balance of Inv. 17201, $338.37.

6   *Purchase Invoices*
    Daiton Enterprises, No. 702, $375.62.
    Henderson Associates, No. 17436, $1 746.21.
    Cheque Copy
    No. 65739, Gordon & Associates, Inv. B7407, $216.92.

7   *Purchase Invoices*
    Henderson Associates, No. 17807, $65.25.
    Kohler, R.M., No. 792, $107.64.
    Wrouse & Reid, No. 602B, $392.61.
    Cheque Copies
    No. 65744, Henderson Associates, Inv. 16907, $615.
    No. 65745, Orenson & Company, balance of Inv. 1604., $546.26.
    No. 65746, Wrouse & Reid, Inv. 597G, $316.29.
    No. 65747, Smithers, P.R., Inv. 74, $57.05.

3. Take off an accounts payable ledger trial balance and see that it agrees with the balance of the control account. The correct account figure is $6 221.79.

6. The simplified general ledger and subsidiary ledgers of Blue Bell Company are given below in T-accounts. These accounts are set up for you in the Workbook. If you are not using the Workbook, you will have to set up the ledger on blank paper, making room for the accounting entries to come.

General Ledger

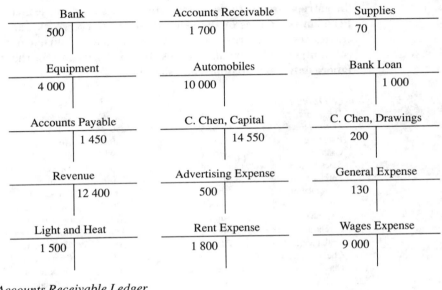

Bank	Accounts Receivable	Supplies
500	1 700	70

Equipment	Automobiles	Bank Loan
4 000	10 000	1 000

Accounts Payable	C. Chen, Capital	C. Chen, Drawings
1 450	14 550	200

Revenue	Advertising Expense	General Expense
12 400	500	130

Light and Heat	Rent Expense	Wages Expense
1 500	1 800	9 000

Accounts Receivable Ledger

Aube	Crozier	Elyk
300	200	150

Isola	Perrier	Tams
500	300	250

Accounts Payable Ledger

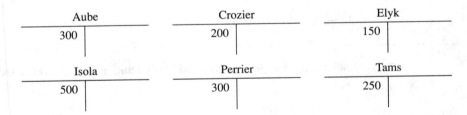

Ace Co.	Delta Co.	Galaxy Co.
225	150	75

Meteor Co.	Sun Co.	Venus Co.
300	400	300

Required:

1. **Ensure that the subsidiary ledgers are in balance with their respective control accounts to start with.**
2. **Perform the duties of the accounts receivable clerk. Select from the source documents shown below those that affect the accounts receivable and make the entries directly to the T-accounts in the subsidiary ledger.**
3. **Perform the duties of the accounts payable clerk. Select from the source documents shown below those that affect the accounts payable and make the entries directly to the T-accounts in the subsidiary ledger.**
4. **Perform the duties of the general ledger clerk. Work out the accounting entries for the source documents shown below, journalize them in a two-column general journal, and post to the T-accounts in the general ledger. Ignore dates, explanations, and sales tax.**

Source Documents

No.	*Document*	*Name*	*Amount*	*Explanation*
1.	Sales invoice	Crozier	$220	Sale on account
2.	Purchase invoice	Ace Co.	150	Advertising
3.	Cash receipt	Elyk	150	On account
4.	Sales invoice	Perrier	175	Sale on account
5.	Purchase invoice	Sun Co.	130	Supplies
6.	Cash receipt	Isola	300	On account
7.	Sales invoice	Tams	40	Sale on account
8.	Cheque copy	Sun Co.	400	On account
9.	Purchase invoice	Meteor Co.	350	Light and heat
10.	Cash receipt	Perrier	300	On account
11.	Cheque copy	Ace Co.	225	On account
12.	Cheque copy	Venus Co.	300	On account
13.	Cash sales slip	Winters	175	Cash sale
14.	Cheque copy	Chen	320	Drawings

5. **Balance the three ledgers.**

7. **Workbook Exercise: Journalizing and balancing in a simple three-ledger system.**

10.3 CUSTOMER'S STATEMENT OF ACCOUNT

You have seen that a business keeps detailed records of the accounts of its customers. A business needs to notify its customers about the status of their accounts if it expects to be paid promptly. Businesses do this by sending statements of account regularly to their customers. A **statement of account** is a record of a customer's account for a period of time, usually one month. It gives the customer a history of the account for the month, and the balance owing at the end of the month. The statement of account is used as a gentle request for payment.

The method of preparing statements of account depends on how much automation there is in the accounting system.

Manual Accounting System

The following method is used in a manual system of accounting.

1. The customers' accounts are kept in a subsidiary ledger in the way that you have seen. Each customer is given an account page on which all transactions of the customer are recorded. The entries continue on the account page until it is filled. Then the account balance is forwarded to a new page and the process continues.

2. A statement of account is prepared on a separate form and sent to each customer at the end of each month. The statement of account starts with the last balance shown on the previous statement. It then shows the transactions for the ensuing month and ends with the balance at the end of that month. Figure 10.8 shows a manual statement of account. Companies which have a great many customers may use a cycle billing procedure. Rather than process all customer statements at the end of the month, customers can be billed for periods within the month on the basis of account numbers, alphabetical listings, or other combinations. This permits the work to be done throughout the month, reducing the work load at the end of the month.

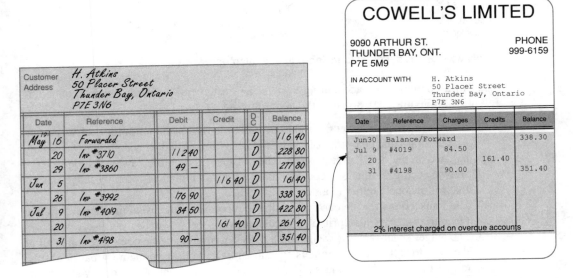

Figure 10.8   The ledger account and the statement of account for the month of July for H. Atkins.

Automated Accounting System

The manual system for producing customers' statements is too slow and time-consuming for a business with a large number of customers. A business with many credit customers requires a system that uses electronic equipment.

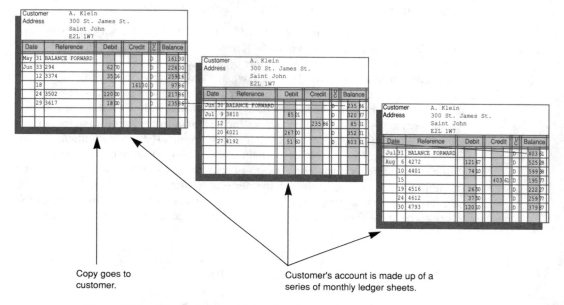

Copy goes to customer.

Customer's account is made up of a series of monthly ledger sheets.

Figure 10.9   A series of machine-printed statements for A. Klein.

In a computerized accounting system the customers' accounts are maintained as shown in Figure 10.9. Some of the highlights are:

1. A new ledger sheet is set up in the subsidiary ledger each month for each customer. The ending balance on the old ledger sheet is forwarded to become the beginning balance on the new (current) sheet. The old sheet is then filed away. As Figure 10.9 shows, each customer's account is made up of a number of monthly ledger sheets that follow one another in a series.

2. The transactions for the current month are recorded in the usual manner except that the entries are machine printed and calculated.

3. The ledger sheets are not created on a daily basis. Instead, the computer stores all of the data for all of the customers for the entire month in its memory banks. At the end of the month, it produces all of the customers' accounts and monthly statements in a single operation that may take only a few hours. An individual customer's account can be examined at any time simply by calling it up on the computer screen.

4. If the ledger sheets are prepared in duplicate, the copy is used as the customer's statement of account. The customer receives an exact copy of the account when this system is used. Banks use this method to produce bank statements for chequing accounts and business current accounts.

The computer can easily be programmed to produce two originals at little additional time or expense. This saves having to use messy carbon paper.

Figure 10.10 shows a computer-produced statement sent to a customer from a national department store. It is easy to show a great deal of information on computer-produced statements.

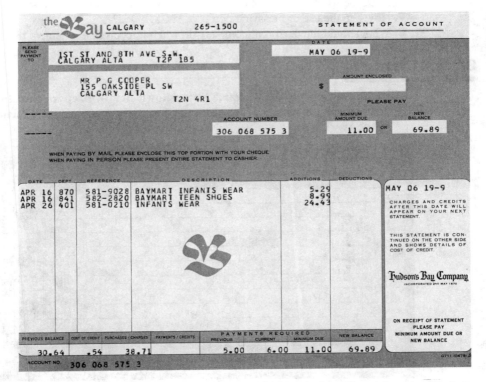

Figure 10.10 Computer-produced statement of account of a national department store.

Statements of Account and the Customer

You have seen that a business produces a statement of account for each customer each month. Let us now examine this important document from the customer's point of view.

A statement of account should always be checked by the customer for errors. Although the degree of accuracy in business recordkeeping is remarkably high, errors and oversights do occur. The customer should keep a file of statements of account and of the bills for purchases and returns made. Along with adequate banking records, these enable the customer to check each statement of account as it arrives. All errors should be reported to the suppliers.

SECTION REVIEW QUESTIONS

1. Why does a business notify its customers about the status of their accounts?
2. What is a statement of account?
3. Describe what a statement of account looks like if a manual system is used.
4. Explain how manual accounts differ physically from automated accounts.
5. In a computerized system, can customers' accounts be kept up to date if they are not printed out each day? Explain.
6. Describe what a statement of account looks like if a computerized system is used.
7. How can the use of messy carbon paper be avoided?
8. What should the person or company do when it receives a statement of account?

SECTION EXERCISES

1. **From the account of Richard Kott, shown below, prepare the statement of account for the month of April on the Biway Supply Company form provided in the Workbook.**

ACCOUNT	R. Kott, 30 Beechwood Crescent, Baton Place, Manitoba							No.	
DATE	PARTICULARS	PR	DEBIT	CREDIT	Dr Cr	BALANCE
Feb. 28	Balance Forwarded				Dr	431 20
Mar. 12	#3162		7570		Dr	50690
18	on account			300 —	Dr	20690
26	#3230		17460		Dr	38150
31	#3319		29650		Dr	67800
Apr. 5	on account			13120	Dr	54680
12	#3457		9640		Dr	64320
19	#3516		21950		Dr	86270
24	on account			500 —	Dr	36270
28	#3680		31520		Dr	67790
May 2	#3775		6130		Dr	73920
15	on account			4680	Dr	69240

2. Michele Penna received the statement of account shown on page 333.
   Michele keeps complete records of her dealings with other businesses. An examination of her files reveals the following:

   a. A check mark on Lakeside Supply's statement of account for March showed that the balance of $372.16 had been found to be correct.

   b. Four bills of sale from Lakeside Supply showed that the purchases during the month were as follows:

April 9	No. 3126	$115.70
14	No. 3296	131.50
23	No. 3410	164.53
27	No. 3592	15.16

Lake Street Thunder Bay Ont. P9Z 1R3			Phone **326 1900**	

Lakeside Supply

In Account With

Michele Penna
1402 Archibald Street
Thunder Bay, P9Z 4Y6

Date	Reference	Charges	Credits	Balance
Mar 31	Balance Forward			372.16
Apr 9	#3126	115.70		
14	Payment Received		200.00	
17	#3296	131.50		
20	#3384	274.35		
23	#3410	164.53		
27	#3592	15.16		873.40

2% Interest on Overdue Accounts

c. The cheque register entries showed that two payments had been made to Lakeside Supply during the month as follows:

April 10 No. 376 $200.00
      30 No. 390   172.16

1. What discrepancies are there between Michele's records and the company's?

2. Give probable reasons for these discrepancies.

3. Suggest what Michele should do regarding these discrepancies.

---

3. The Metropolitan Telephone Company follows the practice of sending monthly statements to its nearly one million customers. However, the accounting department has found it difficult to achieve the company's goal of sending out statements within one week of the month's end.

Suggest an alternative approach to statement preparation that might be acceptable to the company.

CHAPTER HIGHLIGHTS

Now that you have completed Chapter 10, you should:

1. know what a subsidiary ledger is and what a control account is;
2. understand the theory of the three-ledger system of accounting;
3. know how accounts receivable and accounts payable are presented on a balance sheet;
4. understand a simple accounting system for accounts receivable and for accounts payable;
5. know the source documents and the accounting entries that affect accounts receivable and accounts payable;
6. know how to handle non-routine transactions that affect subsidiary ledgers;
7. be able to locate errors in a subsidiary ledger that is out of balance;
8. understand the accounting control features of the three-ledger system;
9. know how a customer's statement of account is prepared manually and by computer.

ACCOUNTING TERMS

accounts payable ledger   general ledger
accounts receivable ledger   statement of account
control account   subsidiary ledger

CHAPTER EXERCISES

Using Your Knowledge

1. This exercise appears in your Workbook.
For each part of each statement below place a "T" (for true) or an "F" (for false) in the spaces provided.
Assume that the system described in the chapter is used.

1. An entire journal entry, for a $500 purchase invoice for supplies, is not recorded. As a result,
 a. The general ledger still balances.
 b. Two accounts in the general ledger have incorrect balances.
 c. The accounts payable ledger does not agree with its control account.
 d. The total in the accounts payable ledger is $500 more than the balance in the control account.
2. A cheque for $400 received from a customer is posted to the customer's account as a credit of $40. As a result,
 a. The general ledger does not balance.
 b. The accounts receivable ledger does not agree with its control account.

c. The total of the accounts receivable ledger is greater than the balance in the control account.

d. The accounts receivable ledger equals the control account but contains one or more errors.

3. $208 cash received from a customer is recorded correctly in the journal and general ledger but is credited to the customer's account as $280. To correct this error the accountant should:

a. Credit the customer's account $72.

b. Debit the customer's account $72.

c. Debit the control account $72.

d. Credit the control account $72.

4. A sales transaction for $800 is entered in the general journal as follows:

Revenue	$800	
Accounts Receivable		$800

As a result of this entry:

a. The general ledger trial balance does not balance.

b. The accounts receivable ledger disagrees with the control account by $800.

c. The balance in the Revenue account is incorrect by $800.

d. The balance in the Revenue account is incorrect by $1 600.

5. A purchase invoice for $250 is posted in the accounts payable ledger as a debit. As a result,

a. The accounts payable ledger does not equal the control account.

b. The difference between the accounts payable ledger and the control account is $250.

c. The difference between the accounts payable ledger and the control account is $500.

d. The general ledger balances.

6. A debit of $1 200 is not posted to a customer's account in the accounts receivable ledger. As a result,

a. The Revenue account and the Accounts Receivable account are both incorrect.

b. The general ledger remains in balance.

c. The balance of the control account is greater than the total of the accounts receivable ledger by $1 200.

d. The balance of the control account is smaller than the total of the accounts receivable ledger by $1 200.

---

2. **Analyzing the Effect of Errors**

At the end of June, the accountant for Marcus Company finds that the total in the accounts receivable subsidiary ledger does not agree with the balance in the control account. The subsidiary ledger total is $13 125 and the control figure is $13 500.

The accountant's investigation reveals five errors. **Complete a schedule to show the effect of correcting each of the following errors. Be sure to arrive at the correct accounts receivable figure.**

Errors

1. A sales invoice for $300, recorded correctly in the control account, was not posted to the subsidiary ledger.
2. A sales invoice for $325, recorded correctly in the control account, was posted twice in error to the customer's account in the subsidiary ledger.
3. A cash receipt for $100, recorded properly in the subsidiary ledger, was omitted from the control account.
4. A cash receipt for $75, recorded correctly in the control account, was posted to the wrong side of the customer's account in the subsidiary ledger.
5. An invoice for $500, posted correctly in the control account, was posted as $50 in the subsidiary ledger.

3. At the end of May, 19—, Ken Nakamoto found that the accounts receivable ledger and its control account were out of balance. His efforts to balance the ledger uncovered the errors set out below.

Errors

1. A sales invoice for $600 was posted in the subsidiary ledger as $660.
2. A cash receipt on account for $300 was not posted in the subsidiary ledger.
3. A sales invoice for $500 was missed entirely by the general ledger clerk.
4. The debit entry pertaining to a sales invoice for $800 was posted in the general ledger as a credit.
5. A sales invoice for $550 was not posted in the subsidiary ledger.
6. A sales invoice for $750 was missed entirely, by both the subsidiary ledger clerk and the general ledger clerk.
7. A cash receipt on account for $280 was not posted in the subsidiary ledger.

Required:
Given that the subsidiary ledger figure (before balancing) is $32 456,
a. determine the correct total for the subsidiary ledger and the control account;
b. calculate the control figure before any corrections were made.

4. **In your Workbook complete the chart shown on page 337 by placing check marks in the appropriate boxes.**

Source Document	In the Subsidiary Ledger						In the General Ledger											
	Which subsidiary ledger is affected?		Will the account be increased or decreased?		Will the account be debited or credited?		The accounting entry will be											
							Bank		Accounts Receivable		Accounts Payable		Asset or Expense		Revenue	
	A/R	A/P	In-crease	De-crease	Dr	Cr	Dr	Cr	Dr	Cr	Dr	Cr	Dr	Cr	Dr	Cr
purchase invoice																
cash receipt on account																
sales invoice																
cheque copy on account																

5. **Workbook Exercise: Challenge—completing a chart analyzing the effect of errors in a three-ledger system.**

Comprehensive Exercise

6. Rachel Bragg is a public accountant in Dartmouth, Nova Scotia. On March 31, 19—, her general ledger trial balance is as follows:

R. BRAGG
GENERAL LEDGER TRIAL BALANCE
MARCH 31, 19—

No.	Account	Debit	Credit
101	Bank	$ 1 850.00	
105	Accounts Receivable	7 220.00	
110	Supplies	2 750.00	
115	Office Equipment	18 400.00	
120	Automobile	24 700.00	
205	Accounts Payable		$ 6 449.70
301	R. Bragg, Capital		47 374.15
302	R. Bragg, Drawings	12 000.00	
401	Fees Income		31 650.00
505	Car Expense	3 295.60	
510	Light and Heat Expense	950.20	
515	Miscellaneous Expense	375.40	
520	Rent Expense	3 000.00	
525	Telephone Expense	516.15	
530	Wages Expense	10 416.50	
		$85 473.85	$85 473.85

1. **Set up the general ledger accounts as of March 31, 19—.**(Two Workbook ledger accounts are required for Bank.) If you are using the Workbook the ledger is already set up for you.

2. Set up the accounts receivable ledger as of March 31, 19—. Observe that the total of the four accounts is equal to the balance of the control account in the general ledger. If you are using the Workbook the ledger is already set up for you.

The accounts receivable ledger on March 31, 19—, contains the following accounts:

Blue Cab Company	16 Fox Street	Inv. No. 74	$1 920.00
Champion Store	175 Main Street	75	750.00
Oasis Restaurant	325 Second Street	76	1 550.00
Village Restaurant	400 Main Street	77	3 000.00
			$7 220.00

3. Set up the accounts payable ledger as of March 31, 19—. Observe that the total of the four accounts is equal to the balance of the control account in the general ledger. If you are using the Workbook the ledger is already set up for you.

The accounts payable ledger on March 31, 19—, contains the following accounts.

M. Ball, Consultant	430 Red Road, Bigtown	$1 700.00
R. & R. Supply	151 King Street	2 740.00
Stirling Company	46 River Road	759.50
Tom's Garage	705 Victoria Street	1 250.20
		$6 449.70

4. Each day you are to perform the duties of both the accounts receivable clerk and the accounts payable clerk. From the list of business transactions shown below, you are to make the entries daily to any customers' or creditors' accounts affected. Although it will be necessary for you to work directly from the list of transactions, try to imagine that you are working directly from the source documents themselves. Also, remember that not all business transactions affect the accounts of customers and creditors.

TRANSACTIONS

April
1 *Cheque Copy*
   No. 105, to P. Walters, $1 000, monthly rent.
3 *Sales Invoice*
   No. 78, to Blue Cab Company, $800.
5 *Cash Receipt*
   From Oasis Restaurant, $1 000, on account.
8 *Purchase Invoice*
   From Tom's Garage, $295, gasoline and oil.
9 *Cheque Copy*
   No. 106, R. & R. Supply, $740, on account.

12 *Sales Invoice*
    No. 79, to Champion Store, $500.
    No. 80, to Village Restaurant, $1 000.

15 *Cheque Copy*
    No. 107, to Municipal Telephone, $75.50, telephone for month.

    Cash Receipt
    From Blue Cab Company, $1 920, on account.

19 *Sales Invoice*
    No. 81, to Oasis Restaurant, $390.

22 *Purchase Invoice*
    From Stirling Company, $210, for supplies.

24 *Cheque Copies*
    No. 108, to M. Ball, $1 000, on account.
    No. 109, to Stirling Company, $759.50, on account.

30 *Cheque Copies*
    No. 110, to Municipal Hydro, $90, electricity for month.
    No. 111, to R. Carter, $300, part-time wages for month.

5. **Each day you are to perform the duties of the junior accountant. Journalize each of the above transactions in the two-column general journal. Do not post to the general ledger accounts until the end of April.**

6. **As the junior accountant, you are to post the general journal to the general ledger at the end of the month. Then you are to take off a general ledger trial balance. It is your responsibility to see that the ledger balances.**

7. **As the accounts receivable clerk, you are to take off a trial balance of the accounts receivable ledger as of April 30, 19——. It is your responsibility to see that the accounts receivable ledger balances with the control account.**

8. **As the accounts payable clerk, you are to take off a trial balance of the accounts payable ledger as of April 30, 19——. It is your responsibility to see that the accounts payable ledger balances with the control account.**

7. **Workbook Exercise: Practice in a three-ledger system.**

For Further Thought

8. **Briefly answer the following questions.**

1. What do the terms "division of labour" and "specialization" have to do with accounts receivable?

2. Subsidiary ledgers are looked after by junior persons. Explain why.

3. Why are subsidiary ledger accounts usually arranged alphabetically?

4. Do all creditors' accounts go in the accounts payable ledger? Explain.

5. Can there be other control accounts besides accounts receivable and accounts payable?

6. Is it enough to show just the total of accounts receivable on the balance sheet? Explain.

7. Assume that the accounting department receives only one copy of each sales invoice and cash receipts daily summary. How could all of the accounting be done using such a system?

8. Subsidiary ledger clerks do not make balanced accounting entries. Explain.

9. Where will the errors be found if the subsidiary ledger does not agree with its control account? In the general ledger? In the subsidiary ledger? In both?

10. What prevents the accounts receivable clerk from obtaining the money from a customer, pocketing it, and crediting the customer's account?

11. In a computerized system the general ledger is not one continuous record. Explain.

12. You are instructed by the owner that a certain customer has died and that her account will not be collectable. What should be done with the account? What accounting entry or entries should be made?

13. The general ledger clerk receives a copy of every source document. The subsidiary ledger clerks receive copies of some source documents only. Explain why this is so.

14. Neither the general ledger nor the subsidiary ledgers contain any errors. Yet the subsidiary ledgers do not balance with their respective control accounts. Explain how this is possible.

15. Explain why it is not necessary to keep the general ledger up to date on a daily basis.

CASE STUDIES

CASE 1   *Overcoming a Lack of Control over Accounts Receivable*

When Brian Barnes went to work as the chief accountant for Durante Paving Company, he quickly noticed that the system of handling accounts receivable was quite different from any system that he had encountered before. The system was theoretically simple and worked as follows:

a. The production department issued sales invoices and sent them to the accounting department. The accounting department, after making the appropriate accounting entries, filed these invoices in an "unpaid invoices" file, arranged alphabetically by customer.

b. As payments were received from customers, the appropriate invoices were withdrawn from the unpaid file, stamped PAID, and filed in a "paid invoices" file.

c. The file of unpaid invoices represented the accounts receivable subsidiary ledger of the company.

Each month, the accounting department prepared a detailed list of the unpaid invoices for the owner. When the owner, Mr. Durante, looked over this list, he always found errors in it, such as an item on the list that he knew had been paid, or an item listed twice and showing slightly different amounts. Mr. Durante was annoyed by these errors, and often accused the accounting department of incompetence. Barnes was also concerned because, since joining the company, he hadn't once been able to balance the subsidiary ledger with the general ledger control account. Barnes launched an investigation to find and overcome the weakness in the system. He found no fault with his own staff members, who performed their duties correctly. But he did find a serious problem with the "unpaid invoices" file. Other employees, particularly engineers and production foremen, were continually using the file, inserting and removing invoices without notifying the accounting department. These employees claimed that they needed the invoices for reference when discussing charges with customers, renegotiating a price, and so on. The engineering department did not keep its own file of invoices on special numbered forms. The invoices were typed up on ordinary letterhead paper.

Questions

1. The production engineers and foremen misused the "unpaid invoices" file. Give examples of specific occurrences that would create errors in the accounts receivable.

2. Suggest changes to the system that would allow the accounting department to gain control over the accounts receivable.

3. After fixing the accounting system, Barnes sees the owner, Mr. Durante, remove an invoice from the file without notifying the accounting department. How should Barnes handle this problem?

CASE 2   *Is the Policy Good or Bad?*

Joan Webster, the owner of a small business, decides that she should "look after Number One," as she puts it.

Webster has a thorough system of recordkeeping for accounts receivable. She makes certain that every debt is collected on time, and her collection record is extremely good. However, Webster has an entirely different attitude toward accounts payable. "Why," she asks, "should I keep records of how much I owe to others? Let them keep track of how much I owe them. And, if they don't do a thorough job of it, maybe I'll get away without paying for something." She believes that other businesses should control their accounts receivable as she controls hers.

As a result of this policy, Webster's procedure for handling incoming purchase invoices is very casual. After the purchase invoices are received and checked, they are placed in a pile on an office desk. The pile represents the accounts payable of the business, but no accounting entries are made to record them.

The purchase invoices stay in the pile on the desk until a request for payment is made. Then Webster removes the particular invoice in question and authorizes its payment. When the cheque in payment is issued, the purchase invoice is then accounted for as if it were a cash purchase of goods or services. The purchase invoice is filed with the cheque copy.

Questions

1. Is Webster's policy a reasonable one? Explain.

2. Would Webster's accounts be useful in providing information for management decisions?

3. When financial statements are prepared, how should the pile of unpaid bills be handled?

CASE 3   *Evaluating the Creditworthiness of Two Companies*

The simplified financial statements for two different companies appear below:

	Company A	Company B
Balance Sheet Data		
December 31, 19—		
Assets		
Bank	$ 1 000	$ 2 000
Accounts Receivable	30 000	8 000
Other Assets	80 000	74 000
Total	$111 000	$84 000
Liabilities and Equity		
Bank Loan	$ 25 000	—
Accounts Payable	5 000	$ 5 000
Owner's Equity	81 000	79 000
Total	$111 000	$84 000
Income Statement Data		
Year Ended December 31, 19—		
Revenue	$ 90 000	$80 000
Expenses		
Bank Interest	$ 5 000	—
Other Expenses	50 000	$43 000
Total Expenses	$ 55 000	$43 000
Net Income	$ 35 000	$37 000

Required:
You receive a loan application for $50 000 from each of the above companies to finance an expansion program. Analyze the above data and write a report on the creditworthiness of each of the two companies. In your report, address the following:
1. the percentage of accounts receivable compared to revenue;
2. how company A has financed its accounts receivable;
3. the effect issue 2 above has had on the net income;
4. the danger of the large accounts receivable figure being caused by overdue and uncollectable accounts;
5. whether or not you would grant the loans, and under what conditions.

ENTREPRENEUR
Sylvia Kish / Sylvia Kish Wardrobes

In 1979 Sylvia Kish and her husband were planning to move to Atlantic Canada to pursue their dream of getting into the hotel business. While they were in their home town of Preeceville, Saskatchewan, to bid their families farewell, a lucky twist led to the creation of one of Saskatchewan's most successful and innovative women's wear operations.

The owner of a Preeceville fabric store that carried a few items of clothing offered to sell the operation to Sylvia. The little business wasn't doing well — about $26 000 a year in sales.

But Sylvia decided to try it, even though she had no previous business experience.

She planned to learn the business as an employee at the minimum wage, then to review the situation after a year. That year saw the store's volume increase tenfold — and Sylvia was hooked on the business. She borrowed $28 000 from the bank to buy the business and additional funds to expand the inventory.

Kish believed that the whole province would shop at her store if she was imaginative enough.

Her idea was to help busy women build a complete wardrobe. But she had to attract clients from hundreds of miles away. After a new building was erected, extraordinary service that included catered lunches in a cozy lounge, tea, and loads of attention made women from Regina, Saskatoon, and Winnipeg flock to Preeceville for a day of pampering and professional advice.

Starting with an interview to determine the client's needs, Sylvia's of Preeceville created an individual look for each customer. The service included a computerized listing of all items purchased at the store. If a client needed a special article of clothing in a hurry, a phone call to Sylvia's would result in a hand-selected item being shipped by overnight express. Word of mouth coupled with aggressive advertising made Sylvia's of Preeceville the "in place" for women's clothing.

Kish wondered why her obvious natural talent for business had never surfaced before. Back at her high school, she found that her aptitude tests pointed to a career in business. But that option was not advanced by the school's counsellors.

After eight years in Preeceville, Kish relocated her business in Regina, Saskatchewan's capital (population, 175 000), a far cry from Preeceville (population 1 200). But the move was necessary to keep the business, renamed Sylvia Kish Wardrobes, growing.

Annual sales presently total about $1.25 million, and Kish's client base is still expanding. She believes that if she could get people to drive for several hours to Preeceville, she should be able to attract buyers from around the world to Regina. Working with airlines and local hotels, she has designed a package to entice clients from far and near who are looking for her style of full service.

Being unique is the key to Kish's success. "Do it your own way. Don't be a clone," she advises. Kish examined franchising her unique concept in retailing but decided against it. Instead, she is planning to expand in Regina, where she is involved with the community. She was recently elected as president of the Saskatchewan Chamber of Commerce, the first time a woman has held the post.

Success does not mean that all problems are over. Rapid growth of the business has meant that special attention has to be paid to securing enough money to finance the growing inventory. Kish stresses that "Being honest with financial advisors, such as bankers and accountants, is a must."

DISCUSSION

1. Why did Kish start out as an employee at minimum wage?
2. What was the basic premise on which she created the business?
3. How was Sylvia's of Preeceville different from other women's clothing stores?
4. Why did she decide to relocate the business?
5. What would you say is Kish's special talent?
6. Why is uniqueness a key to her success?

11 Accounting for a Merchandising Business

11.1 THE MERCHANDISING BUSINESS

So far we have studied only service businesses. These are the businesses that sell services rather than goods. Now, however, you are ready to study accounting for the merchandising or trading business. A **merchandising business** is a business that buys goods and sells them at a profit.

There are different categories of merchandising business. A **wholesaler** is a merchandising business that buys goods from manufacturers and sells to retailers. A **retailer** is a merchandising business that buys goods from wholesalers and manufacturers and sells to the public.

Merchandise Inventory

Businesses which buy goods for the purpose of selling them at a profit are dealing in merchandise. The quantity of merchandise on hand is known as **merchandise inventory** or **stock-in-trade**

The type of merchandise included in inventory varies from business to business. For instance, the merchandise inventory of a lumber company consists of various types and sizes of wood products. The merchandise inventory of a food retailer consists of a variety of food commodities. The merchandise inventory of an automobile dealer consists of new and used cars as well as replacement parts.

Two Aspects of Merchandise Inventory

Figure 11.1 shows the two aspects of merchandise inventory—goods sold and goods unsold. Assume that a business had $120 000 of goods available for sale during a fiscal period, and that $25 000 of these goods was still on hand (unsold) at the end of the period.

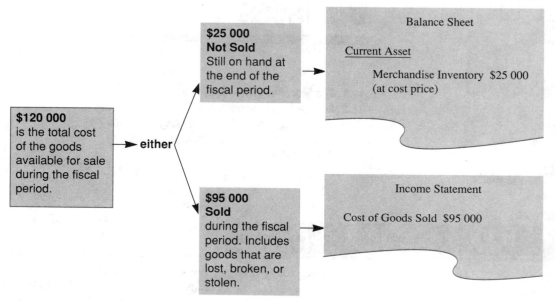

Figure 11.1   A diagram showing the two aspects of merchandise inventory.

Periodic Inventory Method

Over the years, accounting for inventory has been done most commonly by the periodic method. It has been the popular choice because it is inexpensive. The **periodic inventory method** is one in which the inventory is counted and valued only at the end of each fiscal period. This usually means once a year. Businesses that use this method do not keep up-to-date inventory records nor do they calculate the cost of the goods sold figure between statement dates.

Another method, the perpetual method which is described in section 5, is becoming more common in recent years because of the increased use of computers in business.

The Inventory Cycle

Merchandise is generally sold fairly quickly in a successful business. The business has to renew its stock regularly in order to have sufficient quantities on hand. Merchandise moves in and out of the business in a regular pattern as shown in the diagram above in Figure 11.1.

1. There is inventory at the beginning of the accounting period.
2. Merchandise is sold and moves out more or less continually during the accounting period.
3. Merchandise is replaced by the purchase of new stock from time to time.
4. The inventory at the end of the accounting period is more or less the same as at the beginning.

The simplified data below show that the typical pattern holds true whether we are speaking in terms of units or dollars.

	Units	Dollars
Beginning inventory	1 700	$ 42 500
Purchases	5 500	143 000
Total goods available for sale	7 200	$185 500
Merchandise sold	5 800	149 100
Ending inventory	1 400	$ 36 400

This data can be shown in the form of an equation as follows:

Cost of beginning inventory	+	Cost of merchandise purchased	−	Cost of merchandise sold	=	Cost of ending inventory
$42 500	+	$143 000	−	$149 100	=	$36 400

Merchandise Inventory and the Financial Statements

When the periodic inventory method is used, no effort is made during the fiscal period to find out either the figure for the cost of the goods sold or the figure for the goods on hand (unsold). This creates a problem at statement time because the statements cannot be prepared without these two figures.

Physical Inventory

When the periodic inventory method is used, it is necessary at statement time to take a physical inventory. A **physical inventory** is the procedure by which the unsold goods of a merchandising business are counted and valued (at cost price). This ending inventory figure is significant in three respects:

1. It is an important current asset on the balance sheet.
2. It is needed to calculate the cost of goods sold figure for the income statement.
3. It will be used as the beginning inventory figure for the next accounting period.

Merchandise Inventory on the Balance Sheet

A merchandising business buys goods to sell to its customers. Therefore, it keeps a stock of goods on hand. This inventory of goods usually has a large dollar value and must be included as an asset on the balance sheet. Merchandise inventory is listed as a current asset because it will normally be sold and converted into cash within one year. It is listed at its cost price, and not its selling price, in accordance with the cost principle. Merchandise inventory on a balance sheet is shown in Figure 11.2.

```
                        HARDY'S HARDWARE
                         BALANCE SHEET
                          JUNE 30, 19—

                             Assets

Current Assets
    Bank                                    $  1 205
    Accounts Receivable                       18 305
    Merchandise Inventory (at cost)           42 582         $ 62 092

Prepaid Expenses
    Supplies                                $  3 526
    Insurance                                  3 564            7 090

Plant and Equipment
    Store Equipment                         $25 658
    Delivery Equipment                        18 350          44 008

                                                            $113 190
```

Figure 11.2   A partial balance sheet showing merchandise inventory as a current asset.

Cost of Goods Sold on the Income Statement

You have seen that the inventory that *was not sold* belongs on the balance sheet. Similarly, the cost of the inventory that *was sold*, known as the **cost of goods sold**, belongs on the income statement.

An item that is sold for $100 may have cost around $75. This leaves a profit of $25 before deducting for other expenses. Clearly, the cost of any item sold is a very significant expense. The total cost of all of the items sold is usually the biggest expense figure for a merchandising business.

Since no attempt was made to determine the cost of goods sold figure during the period, it has to be obtained by a calculation. This calculation, based on the inventory equation shown to you previously, is as follows:

Cost of		Cost of		Cost of		Cost of
beginning inventory	+	merchandise purchased	–	merchandise sold	=	ending inventory

A simple mathematical rearrangement of this equation gives the cost of goods sold formula. It is this formula that is used to calculate the cost of goods sold figure when the periodic inventory system is used.

Cost of		Cost of		Cost of		Cost of
beginning inventory	+	merchandise purchased	–	ending inventory	=	merchandise sold

To calculate the cost of goods sold, three figures are needed to substitute for the terms in the formula. These are:

1. the beginning inventory figure, which is last year's ending inventory figure;

2. the merchandise purchased figure, which is accumulated during the period in an account called Purchases (you will read about this in the next section);
3. the ending inventory figure which is obtained by taking a physical inventory—by counting and valuing the entire inventory.

These data are presented on the income statement as shown in Figure 11.3.

MASTER TRADING COMPANY
INCOME STATEMENT
YEAR ENDED DECEMBER 31, 19–6

Revenue

Sales		$231 967

Cost of Goods Sold

Inventory, January 1	$55 325	
Purchases	120 402	
Cost of Goods Available for Sale	$175 727	
Less Inventory, December 31	57 350	
Cost of Goods Sold		118 377

Gross Profit	$113 590

Operating Expenses

Bank Charges	$375	
Building Maintenance	875	
Car Expense	3 582	
Light and Heat	1 850	
Miscellaneous	275	
Rent	12 000	
Telephone	957	
Wages	36 587	
Total Operating Expenses		$56 501
Net Income		$57 089

Figure 11.3 A simple income statement for a merchandising business.

Observe the following:

1. The cost of goods sold figure is considered so significant that the statement is prepared in two stages.
2. The first stage determines the gross profit. The **gross profit** is the difference between the selling price and the cost price of the goods sold. It can also be seen as the profit figure before deducting other expenses. The gross profit is a figure that the merchant will watch carefully. It is important to have enough gross profit to cover expenses and leave a sufficient net profit.
3. The cost of goods sold calculation is shown on the statement.
4. Expenses are now headed Operating Expenses.

Limitation of the Periodic Inventory Method

When the periodic inventory method is used, financial statements cannot be obtained unless a physical inventory is taken. This is a time-consuming procedure that often makes it necessary to close down business operations for a day or two. Why is the periodic method used so extensively despite this limitation? The answer is simple. The periodic method is much less expensive than the perpetual method. This is important for small businesses, such as drugstores and hardware stores, that have to keep track of inventories made up of large number of different items.

SECTION REVIEW QUESTIONS

1. Describe a service business.
2. Describe a merchandising business.
3. Define the terms "wholesaler" and "retailer."
4. Describe the merchandise inventory of a drugstore.
5. Give another name for merchandise inventory.
6. What has happened to the goods available for sale that are not on hand?
7. Where is merchandise inventory listed on the balance sheet?
8. Explain the importance of the cost of goods sold figure.
9. Explain the meaning of gross profit.
10. What types of businesses will use the periodic inventory method?
11. Explain why a small variety store would choose to use the periodic inventory method.
12. Give the four steps in the inventory cycle.
13. Give the cost of goods sold formula.
14. Why is it necessary to take a physical inventory when using the periodic inventory method?

SECTION EXERCISES

1. **Workbook Exercise: Completing a multiple-choice exercise regarding merchandise inventory.**

2. **For each of the following businesses, state five specific items that would normally be found in the merchandise inventory.**

   1. auto dealer;
   2. builder's supply dealer;
   3. furniture and appliance store;
   4. sports store;
   5. grocery store;
   6. hardware store;
   7. photography store;
   8. electronics store;
   9. department store.

3. **Workbook Exercise: Completing a chart regarding selling prices, cost prices, and gross profits.**

4. **The chart shown below also appears in the Workbook.**

   1. **Complete the chart by filling in the blank spaces.**

	Year 1	Year 2	Year 3
Beginning inventory	100 units	units	units
Merchandise purchased	units	900 units	units
Goods available for sale	800 units	units	units
Merchandise sold	units	1 000 units	800 units
Ending inventory	300 units	units	50 units

   2. **If the units cost $5 each throughout Year 3, work out the Cost of Goods Sold section of the income statement.**

5. **For each of the following calculate the cost of goods sold and the gross profit.**

	Sales	Beginning Inventory	Purchases	Ending Inventory
1.	$125 000	32 000	74 250	33 500
2.	$750 585	85 600	410 360	88 300
3.	$288 635	65 550	110 357	60 548
4.	$174 000	33 800	82 640	33 500
5.	$255 324	48 500	150 650	50 300

6. **Given below is a list of accounts and their balances for a merchandising business as well as the ending inventory figure. From these data calculate the cost of goods sold figure.**

   The ending inventory figure is $15 600.

Accounts	Balances	Accounts	Balances
Bank	$ 1 500	Car Expense	5 500
Accounts Receivable	22 450	Power Expense	2 150
Merchandise Inventory	14 500	Rent Expense	9 000
Supplies	1 300	Wages Expense	13 890
Automobile	18 000		
Equipment	22 000		
Accounts Payable	4 532		
T. Wilkes, Capital	77 558		
T. Wilkes, Drawings	12 000		
Sales	82 600		
Purchases	41 300		
Advertising	1 100		

7. Given below is a trial balance and the ending inventory figure for General Retail Company after a fiscal period of one month.

GENERAL RETAIL COMPANY
TRIAL BALANCE
JUNE 30, 19-3

Accounts	Debit	Credit
Bank	$ 3 000	
Accounts Receivable	29 350	
Merchandise Inventory	24 500	
Supplies	1 250	
Automobile	17 500	
Equipment	35 000	
Accounts Payable		7 222
T. Wilkes, Capital		79 528
T. Wilkes, Drawings	5 000	
Sales		55 325
Purchases	18 300	
Freight-in	275	
Advertising	500	
Car Expense	750	
Power Expense	900	
Rent Expense	1 000	
Wages Expense	4 750	
	$142 075	$142 075

Given that the ending inventory figure is $25 350, answer the following:

1. Give the beginning inventory figure.
2. Give the ending inventory figure.
3. Give the selling price of the goods sold.
4. Calculate the cost price of the goods sold.
5. Calculate the gross profit.
6. Calculate the total operating expenses.
7. Calculate the net profit.

11.2 ACCOUNTING PROCEDURES FOR A MERCHANDISING BUSINESS

So far you have learned the following facts about the periodic inventory system for a merchandising business.

• The final inventory figure must be included on the balance sheet as a current asset.
• The cost of goods sold figure must be included on the income statement.
• Neither the inventory figure nor the cost of goods sold figure is known during the accounting period.
• The cost of goods sold figure can be calculated by means of the formula developed in the previous section.

Now you will learn about the accounts that are needed for accounting for the cost of goods sold and merchandise inventory.

The Merchandise Inventory Account

Under the periodic inventory method, the merchandise inventory of a business is kept in two accounts. One of these is the Merchandise Inventory account. It shows the inventory figure as of the beginning of the accounting period.

At the fiscal year-end, the inventory is counted and valued at cost price to arrive at the merchandise inventory grand total for the financial statements. The inventory account is adjusted to equal the updated figure. This becomes the beginning inventory figure for the next fiscal period. This periodic inventory adjustment is the only accounting entry made to the Merchandise Inventory account.

You will now find a Merchandise Inventory account appearing in the assets section in most of your trial balances. Remember that the account represents the balance that was updated at the end of the preceding fiscal period. For your purposes, the balance of the Merchandise Inventory account represents the beginning inventory for the current period.

The Purchases Account

Purchases is the other account where the merchandise inventory of a business is kept. The merchandise purchased during the fiscal period is collected in the Purchases account. "Purchases" is a short version of "Purchases of Merchandise for Resale." The Purchases account is found in the expense section of the ledger. Some accountants place it as the first account in that section. If merchandise for resale is purchased for cash, the accounting entry (at the cost price) is:

	DR	CR
Purchases	$$$$	
Bank		$$$$

If merchandise for resale is purchased on account, the accounting entry (at the cost price) is:

	DR	CR
Purchases	$$$$	
Accounts Payable		$$$$

Be sure you understand that it is the purchase of merchandise inventory that is being discussed here. Other items purchased are handled in the usual way. For example, if a tire company buys office supplies, then Office Supplies is debited. However, if a tire company buys tires for sale to its customers, then Purchases is debited.

The Sales Account

The revenue account for a merchandising business is called "Sales." If goods are sold for cash, the accounting entry (at the selling price) is:

	DR	CR
Bank	$$$$	
Sales		$$$$

If goods are sold on account, the accounting entry (at the selling price) is:

	DR	CR
Accounts Receivable	$$$$	
Sales		$$$$

When a business sells goods, the physical inventory is reduced. However, no accounting entries are made to record this decrease in inventory when the periodic system is used. It is easier to allow the inventory to be inexact during the fiscal period and to correct it at the end. You will be shown how to do this later in the chapter.

The Freight-in Account

Freight on incoming merchandise is considered to be one of the costs of the goods. The **Freight-in account** is used to accumulate any transportation charges on incoming goods.

These charges are kept separate from transportation charges on outgoing goods which are recorded in Delivery Expense. Freight-in is accumulated separately because it is a cost related to the goods purchased and must be included in the calculation of the cost of goods sold. The Freight-in account is usually placed right after the Purchases account in the ledger.

The charges for freight-in or delivery expense are usually found on invoices from trucking companies, railways, or other transportation companies. If a business has its own trucks, these charges may be found on bills related to the running of the equipment such as bills for gasoline, oil, and repairs.

Duty refers to the special charges imposed by the government on certain goods imported from a foreign country. If any duty is being charged, it is handled in the same way as freight-in, and debited to a Duty account.

SECTION REVIEW QUESTIONS

1. Why is the final inventory figure included on the balance sheet?
2. How is the cost of goods sold figure determined for inclusion on the income statement?
3. In what two accounts in the general ledger is merchandise inventory recorded?
4. What does the balance in the Merchandise Inventory account represent during the fiscal period?
5. What prices are used to value the merchandise inventory?
6. What is the account title "Purchases" a short version of?
7. Give the accounting entry for the purchase of merchandise for resale on account.
8. Give the accounting entry for the purchase of a delivery truck for cash.
9. What is the revenue account usually called in the ledger of a merchandising company?
10. If the periodic inventory method is used, what accounting step is ignored when a sale is made? Try to give the accounting entry for this step.
11. What charges are recorded in the Freight-in account?
12. Are the following accounts real or nominal ones?
    a. Merchandise Inventory
    b. Purchases
    c. Freight-in
    d. Duty

SECTION EXERCISES

1. **Journalize the following transactions in two-column general journal form for Excel TV and Stereo:**

TRANSACTIONS

December
1 Received an invoice, No. 435, from Paramount Manufacturing for a shipment of television sets, $3 045.00.
2 Received an invoice, No. B616, from Murray Transport Company for transportation charges on the above shipment of television sets, $435.
3 Received an invoice, No. 7042, from Swiss Stationers for a shipment of office forms and supplies to be used in the business, $236.
4 Issued Sales Invoice, No. 789, to W. Parker for stereo speakers and electronic parts, $417.
5 Issued Cash Sales Slip, No. 143, for the cash sale of merchandise from the store, $92.
6 Received an invoice, No. 902, from Haniko Electric for a shipment of electronic parts, $2 678.

2. **Workbook Exercise: Additional practice in journalizing transactions.**

3. **In your Workbook, complete each of the following statements by inserting in the spaces provided the most appropriate word or phrase from the list given below.**

   1. The final inventory figure appears on the _____ and on the _____.
   2. Neither the _____ nor the _____ is known during the accounting period.
   3. The cost of goods sold figure is _____ using a _____.
   4. Merchandise inventory is kept in two accounts. These are _____ and _____.
   5. The _____ normally shows the merchandise inventory figure as of the _____.
   6. At the fiscal year-end, the inventory is counted and valued at _____.
   7. The Merchandise Inventory account is adjusted _____.
   8. The _____ is the only accounting entry made to the Merchandise Inventory account.
   9. Merchandise purchased during the fiscal period is debited to the _____.
   10. The "Purchases" account is a short form of _____.
   11. If merchandise is purchased on account, the account debited is _____.
   12. If a tire company purchases office supplies, the account debited is _____.
   13. For a merchandising business, the sales account is the _____.
   14. When a business using the periodic inventory method sells goods, there is no accounting entry to record the _____.
   15. The Freight-in account is used to accumulate _____.

   List of Words and Phrases

at the end of the fiscal period	inventory figure
balance sheet	merchandise inventory
beginning of the fiscal period	Merchandise inventory account
calculated	office supplies
cost of goods sold figure	purchases
cost prices	Purchases account
decrease in inventory	purchases of merchandise for resale
formula	Revenue account
income statement	transportation charges on incoming goods
inventory adjustment	

4. **Complete the following chart in your Workbook.**

Opening Inventory	Purchases	Freight-in	Closing Inventory	Cost of Goods Sold
$20 000	40 000	5 000	25 000	
$29 000	50 000	1 000	30 000	
$12 000		1 000	15 000	50 000
	$90 000	8 000	39 000	101 000
$50 000	100 000		60 000	100 000
$75 000	200 000	5 000		200 000

11.3 WORK SHEET FOR A MERCHANDISING BUSINESS

There are three new accounts for you to learn to handle on the work sheet and on the statements. These accounts are shown below in T-accounts.

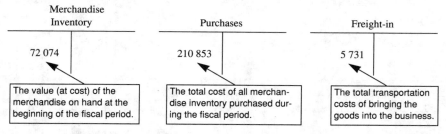

As you already know, the figures for the financial statements are obtained from a completed work sheet. Therefore, you must learn to handle these new accounts on the work sheet.

You will see these new accounts on the partial work sheet in Figure 11.4 and Figure 11.5. Study these two illustrations carefully to see how the accounts are dealt with, and why they are handled as they are.

Accountants use this technique because it is an easy and effective one. A simple three-step procedure on the work sheet produces the figures necessary for the financial statements.

HOW IT IS DONE

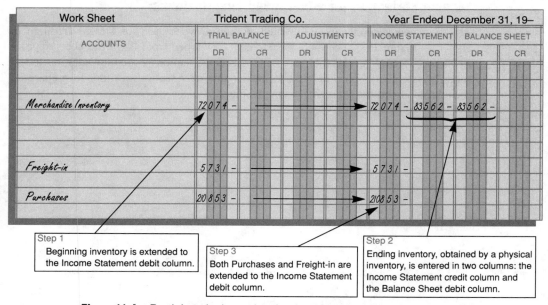

Figure 11.4 Partial work sheet showing how Merchandise Inventory, Purchases, and Freight-in are handled on a work sheet.

WHY IT IS DONE

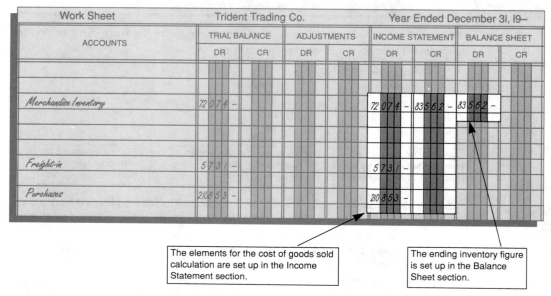

Work Sheet	Trident Trading Co.				Year Ended December 31, 19–			
ACCOUNTS	TRIAL BALANCE		ADJUSTMENTS		INCOME STATEMENT		BALANCE SHEET	
	DR	CR	DR	CR	DR	CR	DR	CR
Merchandise Inventory	72 074 –				72 074 –	83 562 –	83 562 –	
Freight-in	5 731 –				5 731 –			
Purchases	210 853 –				210 853 –			

The elements for the cost of goods sold calculation are set up in the Income Statement section.

The ending inventory figure is set up in the Balance Sheet section.

Figure 11.5 Partial work sheet explaining how the Merchandise Inventory, Freight-in, and Purchases are related to financial statements.

Income Statement for a Merchandising Business

The three new accounts are highlighted on the full work sheet for Trident Trading Co. shown in Figure 11.6. The income statement developed from this work sheet appears in Figure 11.7. Note that the Cost of Goods Sold section is a major addition to the income statement. You will have to master this new section in order to prepare an income statement for a merchandising business.

Work Sheet	Trident Trading Co.						Year Ended December 31, 19–	
ACCOUNTS	TRIAL BALANCE		ADJUSTMENTS		INCOME STATEMENT		BALANCE SHEET	
	DR	CR	DR	CR	DR	CR	DR	CR
Bank	4072 –						4072 –	
Accounts Receivable	27340 –						27340	
Merchandise Inventory	72074 –				72074 –	83562 –	83562 –	
Supplies	2840 –			2560 –			280 –	
Prepaid Insurance	4242 –			2915 –			1327 –	
Equipment	24316 –						24316 –	
Automobiles	37416 –						37416 –	
Accounts Payable		15270 –		565 –				15835 –
Bank Loan		10000 –						10000 –
Sales Tax Payable		2210 –						2210 –
R. Kehoe, Capital		125064 –						125064 –
R. Kehoe, Drawings	40000 –						40000 –	
Sales		377508 –				377508 –		
Advertising	1141 –				1141 –			
Bank Charges	2651 –				2651 –			
Car Expenses	4749 –		250 –		4999 –			
Delivery Expenses	1377 –				1377 –			
Freight-in	5731 –				5731 –			
Light & Heat	3673 –		315 –		3988 –			
Miscellaneous Expense	1507 –				1507 –			
Purchases	208853 –				208853 –			
Rent	12000 –				12000 –			
Salaries	24000 –				24000 –			
Telephone	1850 –				1850 –			
Wages	48220 –				48220 –			
	530052 –	530052 –						
Supplies Expense			2560 –		2560 –			
Insurance Expense			2915 –		2915 –			
			6040 –	6040 –	395866 –	461070 –	218313 –	153109 –
Net Income					65204 –			65204 –
					461070 –	461070 –	218313 –	218313 –

Figure 11.6 The full work sheet for Trident Trading Co.

TRIDENT TRADING CO.
INCOME STATEMENT
YEAR ENDED DECEMBER 31, 19—

Revenue

Sales		$337 508

Cost of Goods Sold

Merchandise Inventory, January 1	$ 72 074	
Purchases	210 853	
Freight-in	5 731	
Goods Available for Sale	$288 658	
Less: Merchandise Inventory, December 31	83 562	205 096
Gross Profit		$172 412

Operating Expenses

Advertising	$ 1 141	
Bank Charges	2 651	
Car Expenses	4 999	
Delivery Expense	1 377	
Insurance Used	2 915	
Light and Heat	3 988	
Miscellaneous Expense	1 507	
Rent	12 000	
Salaries	24 000	
Supplies Used	2 560	
Telephone	1 850	
Wages	48 220	107 208
Net Income		$ 65 204

Figure 11.7   The income statement for Trident Trading Co. showing the cost of goods sold section.

Closing Entries for a Merchandising Business

A very interesting result occurs when the closing entry process, described in Chapter 9, is applied to a merchandising business. The process very neatly cancels out the old inventory figure and sets up the new one. In other words, the closing entry process automatically updates the inventory account at the end of the fiscal period.

You can see how this is done by studying the simplified data in Figures 11.8 to 11.10.

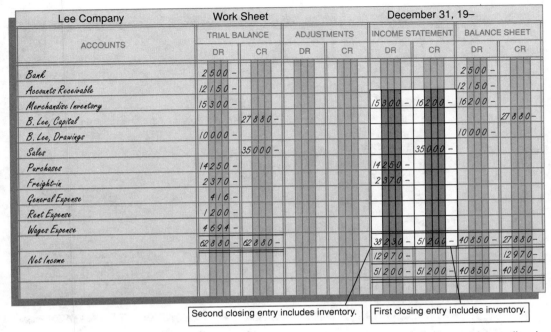

Lee Company	Work Sheet				December 31, 19–			
ACCOUNTS	TRIAL BALANCE		ADJUSTMENTS		INCOME STATEMENT		BALANCE SHEET	
	DR	CR	DR	CR	DR	CR	DR	CR
Bank	2500 –						2500 –	
Accounts Receivable	12150 –						12150 –	
Merchandise Inventory	15300 –				15300 –	16200 –	16200 –	
B. Lee, Capital		27880 –						27880 –
B. Lee, Drawings	10000 –						10000 –	
Sales		35000 –				35000 –		
Purchases	14250 –				14250 –			
Freight-in	2370 –				2370 –			
General Expense	416 –							
Rent Expense	1200 –							
Wages Expense	4694 –							
	62880 –	62880 –			38230 –	51200 –	40850 –	27880 –
Net Income					12970 –			12970 –
					51200 –	51200 –	40850 –	40850 –

Second closing entry includes inventory.   First closing entry includes inventory.

Figure 11.8   A simplified work sheet with the figures for the first and second closing entries outlined.

		GENERAL JOURNAL		
		Closing Entries		
Dec	31	Merchandise Inventory	16200 –	
		Sales	35000 –	
		Income Summary		51200 –
	31	Income Summary	38230 –	
		Merchandise Inventory		15300 –
		Purchases		14250 –
		Freight-in		2370 –
		General Expense		416 –
		Rent Expense		1200 –
		Wages Expense		4694 –
	31	Income Summary	12970 –	
		B. Lee, Capital		12970 –
	31	B. Lee, Capital	10000 –	
		B. Lee, Drawings		10000 –

Figure 11.9   The four closing entries, derived from the work sheet, Figure 11.8.

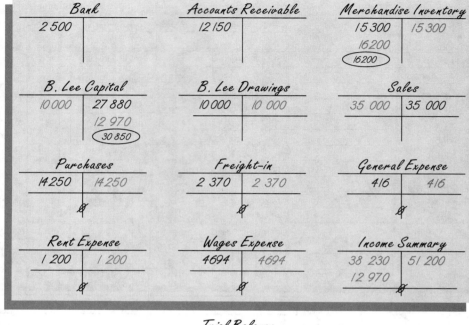

Trial Balance

DR	CR
2 500	30 850
12 150	
16 200	
30 850	30 850

Figure 11.10   The general ledger after completing the closing entries. The account balances before the closing entries are entered in black.

As you can see, the closing entry process has had the following effects:

• it has closed out all of the equity accounts except Capital;
• it has updated the Capital account. The new balance is $30 850;
• it has adjusted the Merchandise Inventory account. The new balance is $16 200.
  This balance will remain in the account until the next set of closing entries is recorded.

SECTION REVIEW QUESTIONS

1. Name the three new accounts that appear on the work sheet of a merchandising company.
2. What does the trial balance figure for Merchandise Inventory represent?
3. What does the trial balance figure for Purchases represent?
4. What important function must be carried out before the work sheet can be completed?

5. Explain in detail how to extend the Merchandise Inventory line.
6. Explain how to extend the Purchases line.
7. Explain how to extend the Freight-in line.
8. Where are the figures found for the Cost of Goods Sold section of the income statement?
9. Why is the Cost of Goods Sold section of the income statement so important?
10. Is the closing entry process basically the same as when first introduced?
11. What must one be careful of when recording the first two closing entries?
12. What new result occurs after processing the first two closing entries?
13. Where is the information for the closing entries found?
14. What is the total effect of all of the closing entries?

SECTION EXERCISES

1. **The partially completed work sheet shown below also appears in the Workbook.**

   1. Complete the work sheet. The ending inventory figure is $43 700.
   2. Prepare an income statement.
   3. Prepare a balance sheet.
   4. Journalize the closing entries.

Work Sheet	Bok Trading Company				Year Ended December 31, 19 –			
ACCOUNTS	TRIAL BALANCE		ADJUSTMENTS		INCOME STATEMENT		BALANCE SHEET	
	DR	CR	DR	CR	DR	CR	DR	CR
Bank	500–							
Accounts Receivable	18300–							
Merchandise Inventory	39600–							
Supplies	2500–			1200–				
Prepaid Insurance	1800–			1150–				
Equipment	27850–							
Accounts Payable		7400–		350–				
Sales Tax Payable		7200–						
R. Bok, Capital		62890–						
R. Bok, Drawings	10000–							
Sales		94310–						
Purchases	41500–		300–					
Freight-in	950–							
Light & Heat	2750–							
Miscellaneous Expense	350–		50–					
Rent	4800–							
Telephone	1500–							
Wages	19400–							
	171800–	171800–						
Supplies Expense			1200–					
Insurance Expense			1150–					

2. Shown below is the trial balance for Small Engine Sales and Service at December 31, 19—, the end of an annual fiscal period.

1. **Complete the work sheet in your Workbook, using the following additional information.**
   a. Closing inventory of merchandise—$35 651
   b. Closing inventory of supplies—$350
   c. Closing inventory of parts and materials—$4 560
   d. Unexpired insurance at December 31—$600
   e. Late bills—none.
2. **Prepare an income statement.**
3. **Prepare a balance sheet.**
4. **Journalize the adjusting and closing entries.**

SMALL ENGINE SALES AND SERVICE

TRIAL BALANCE

DECEMBER 31, 19—

	DR	CR
Bank	$ 520	
Accounts Receivable	12 680	
Merchandise Inventory	36 050	
Supplies	1 975	
Parts and Materials	10 350	
Prepaid Insurance	1 150	
Equipment	18 600	
Truck	18 000	
Accounts Payable		$ 5 360
Bank Loan		9 500
Sales Tax Payable		320
H. Rohr, Capital		48 500
H. Rohr, Drawings	25 000	
Revenue—Sales		80 362
Revenue—Service		66 215
Bank Charges	410	
Freight-in	862	
Light and Heat	2 240	
Miscellaneous Expense	650	
Purchases	52 795	
Rent	3 600	
Telephone	1 250	
Truck Expense	5 825	
Wages	18 300	
	$210 257	$210 257

5. **Post the adjusting and closing entries to the T-accounts provided in the Workbook.**
6. **Take off a post-closing trial balance.**

3. Shown below is the completed work sheet for Barbini Stone Products.

1. Journalize the adjusting and the closing entries in the general journal.
2. Post the adjusting and closing entries to the T-accounts provided in the Workbook.
3. Take off a post-closing trial balance.

Work Sheet	Barbini Stone Products				Year Ended December 31, 19 –			
ACCOUNTS	TRIAL BALANCE		ADJUSTMENTS		INCOME STATEMENT		BALANCE SHEET	
	DR	CR	DR	CR	DR	CR	DR	CR
Bank	3250 –						3250 –	
Accounts Receivable	34650 10						34650 10	
Merchandise Inventory	43700 –				43700 –	40500 –	40500 –	
Supplies	3400 50			2104 –			1296 50	
Prepaid Insurance	2090 –			950 –			1140 –	
Land	35000 –						35000 –	
Building	95000 –						95000 –	
Equipment	53400 –						53400 –	
Trucks	76000 –						76000 –	
Accounts Payable		42375 40		1135 –				43510 40
Sales Tax Payable		1354 80						1354 80
T. Barbini, Capital		266079 05						266079 05
T. Barbini, Drawings	36000 –						36000 –	
Sales		232250 –				232250 –		
Advertising	2570 –		100 –		2670 –			
Freight-in	3705 –		70 –		3775 –			
Light and Heat	12316 –				12316 –			
Miscellaneous Expense	1750 –		25 –		1775 –			
Purchases	80702 50		940 –		81642 50			
Telephone	1250 –				1250 –			
Wages	57275 15				57275 15			
	542059 25	542059 25						
Supplies Expense			2104 –		2104 –			
Insurance Expense			950 –		950 –			
			4189 –	4189 –	207457 65	272750 –	376236 60	309944 25
Net Income					65292 35			65292 35
					272750 –	272750 –	376236 60	376236 60

11.4 *MERCHANDISE RETURNS AND ALLOWANCES*

When a sale is made on account, the seller issues a sales invoice and makes the appropriate accounting entry. No further action is necessary for most sales transactions except to ensure that the customer pays the account.

In the Books of the Vendor

Occasionally, however, a correction or a cancellation of a sales invoice is necessary. Consider the sales invoice in Figure 11.11.

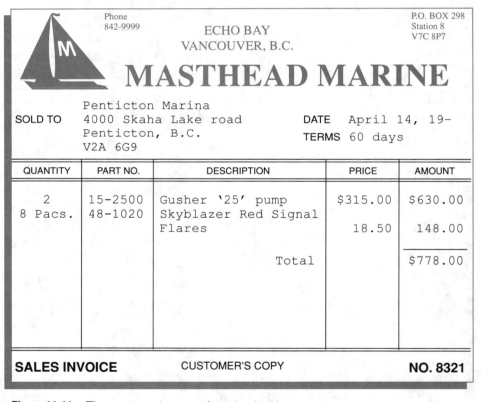

Phone 842-9999	ECHO BAY VANCOUVER, B.C.		P.O. BOX 298 Station 8 V7C 8P7

MASTHEAD MARINE

SOLD TO	Penticton Marina 4000 Skaha Lake road Penticton, B.C. V2A 6G9	DATE April 14, 19– TERMS 60 days	

QUANTITY	PART NO.	DESCRIPTION	PRICE	AMOUNT
2	15-2500	Gusher '25' pump	$315.00	$630.00
8 Pacs.	48-1020	Skyblazer Red Signal Flares	18.50	148.00
		Total		$778.00

SALES INVOICE   CUSTOMER'S COPY   **NO. 8321**

Figure 11.11   The customer's copy of a sales invoice.

Masthead Marine, the vendor, will make the following accounting entry for this invoice. In this example there is no sales tax.

	DR	CR
Accounts Receivable	$778.00	
Sales		$778.00

In T-accounts:

Accounts Receivable (Penticton Marina)		Sales	
778			778

The purchaser in this transaction is Penticton Marina. Assume that Penticton Marina learns that the Skyblazer flares are defective. Penticton Marina will notify the seller, Masthead Marine, that the flares are defective and are being returned. Penticton Marina will expect its account to be decreased by Masthead Marine.

Credit Invoice

The standard procedure in this situation is for the seller to issue a credit invoice. A **credit invoice**, or a **credit note**, is a "minus" invoice issued by the vendor to reverse a charge that was previously made on a regular sales invoice. Credit invoices are used to adjust, correct, or cancel a charge to a customer's account for any of the following reasons:

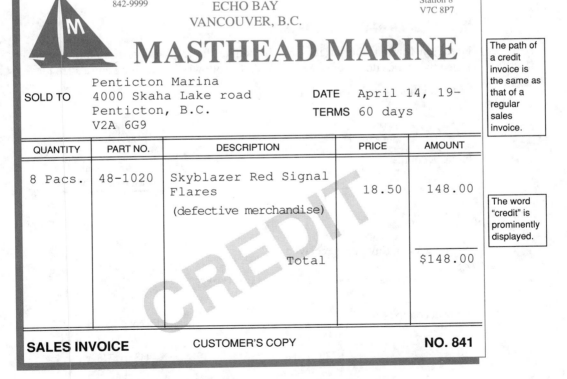

Figure 11.12 The customer's copy of a credit invoice.

- the goods prove to be defective and are returned;
- the goods prove to be less than satisfactory but are kept by the customer. In this case, the customer will be given an allowance (a reduction) off the invoice price;
- an error is made on the sales invoice. In this case, the error will be made right.

In our example, Masthead Marine issues the credit invoice shown in Figure 11.12.

A credit invoice has the opposite effect from a regular sales invoice. The customer's account and the sales account will be decreased. Masthead Marine will make the following accounting entry for the credit invoice.

	DR	CR
Sales	$148.00	
Accounts Receivable		$148.00

After the credit invoice is processed by Masthead Marine, the effect in the accounts is as follows:

Accounts Receivable (Penticton Marina)			Sales	
778	148		148	778
630				*630*

The balance in Penticton Marina's account has been correctly reduced to $630.

In the Books of the Purchaser

Penticton Marina, the purchaser, will handle the transaction in a similar manner. When the source documents are received, the following accounting entries are made.

When the (purchase) invoice is received:

	DR	CR
Purchases	$778.00	
Accounts Payable		$778.00

In the accounts:

Purchases	Accounts Payable (Masthead Marine)
778	778

When the credit invoice is received:

	DR	CR
Accounts Payable	$148.00	
Purchases		$148.00

In the accounts:

Purchases			Accounts Payable (Masthead Marine)	
778	148		148	778
630				*630*

Cash Refunds

The cash sale is a very common business transaction. But dissatisfaction can occur with cash sales as well as with charge sales. A customer who has paid cash for merchandise which has to be returned will usually receive a refund. A **cash refund** is the return of money to the buyer from the seller when merchandise is returned.

In principle, the accounting for refunds is similar to that for credit invoices. However, when a refund is given:

- no credit invoices are issued. Neither accounts receivable nor accounts payable is affected;
- instead, cash is handed over, or a cheque is issued. The accounting entry to record the transaction affects the Bank account. A refund cheque issued for goods returned requires the following accounting entry.

	DR	CR
Sales	$$$$	
Bank		$$$$

Returns and Allowances Accounts

Some businesses, such as large department stores, want detailed information about returns and allowances. They want to know what proportion of their sales was returned by their customers. They also want to know what proportion of their purchases (of merchandise) they returned to their suppliers. Businesses that require this specialized information get it by accumulating it in special "returns and allowances" accounts.

Sales Returns and Allowances Accounts

Figure 11.13 contrasts the two different methods of handling returns and allowances for sales.

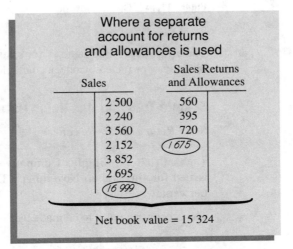

Figure 11.13   Chart showing the two methods of handling sales and returns and allowances.

Take note of the following observations.

- The single account at the left produces an account balance which represents the net sales figure. To obtain the returns and allowances figure, the account would have to be analyzed.
- The two accounts at the right produce two account balances. One represents the total sales figure. The other represents the total returns and allowances figure.

Purchases Returns and Allowances Accounts

The concept is exactly the same for purchases returns and allowances. Figure 11.14 contrasts the two different methods of handling returns and allowances for purchases.

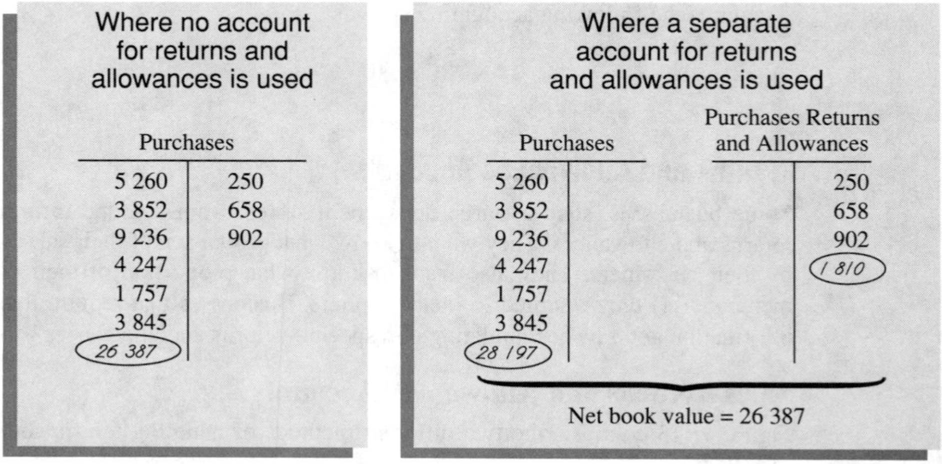

Figure 11.14   Chart showing the different methods of handling purchases returns and allowances.

The effect here is the same as for sales on page 369. The two accounts provide information not provided by one account alone.

Sample Transactions Using Returns and Allowances Accounts

Sales Returns and Allowances

TRANSACTION 1   **Simplex Company sells $500 of goods to A. Moss. An invoice is issued for the sale on November 12, 19—. Sales tax is added at the rate of five per cent.**

The accounting entry to be made by Simplex Company is as follows:

	DR	CR
Accounts Receivable—A. Moss	$525.00	
Sales		$500.00
Sales Tax Payable		$25.00

TRANSACTION 2 A portion of the goods sold to A. Moss is defective and is returned. Simplex Company issues a credit invoice for $180 plus sales tax of $9.

The accounting entry to be made by Simplex Company is as follows:

	DR	CR
Sales Returns and Allowances	$180.00	
Sales Tax Payable	9.00	
Accounts Receivable—A. Moss		$189.00

The effect of the above entries in the accounts is shown below:

Accounts Receivable (A. Moss)		Sales Tax Payable		Sales		Sales Returns and Allowances
525	189	9	25		500	180

Net sales = $320

Purchases Returns and Allowances

TRANSACTION 1 On June 12, 19—, Baytown Drug Market receives a shipment of drugs and the sales invoice for them from Drug Wholesale Company in the amount of $1 147.

The accounting entry to be made by Baytown Drug Market is as follows:

	DR	CR
Purchases	$1 147	
Accounts Payable (Drug Wholesale)		$1 147

TRANSACTION 2 On June 14, Baytown Drug Market notices that a number of packages in the shipment from Drug Wholesale are damaged. The damaged goods are returned for credit and a credit invoice for $438 is received from Drug Wholesale.

The accounting entry to be made by Baytown Drug Market is as follows:

	DR	CR
Accounts Payable—Drug Wholesale	$438	
Purchases Returns and Allowances		$438

The effect of the above entries in the accounts is shown below:

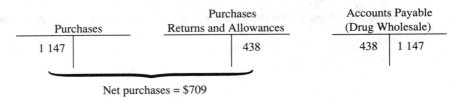

Purchases		Purchases Returns and Allowances		Accounts Payable (Drug Wholesale)	
1 147			438	438	1 147

Net purchases = $709

Returns and Allowances on the Income Statement

Both sales returns and allowances and purchases returns and allowances appear on the income statement of companies that use them. They are treated as deductions from sales and from purchases respectively. Their inclusion on the statement makes it a slightly more difficult statement to prepare. The income statement of Trident Trading Co. (page 360) is shown again in Figure 11.15 as it would appear if returns and allowances accounts were used.

TRIDENT TRADING CO.
INCOME STATEMENT
YEAR ENDED DECEMBER 31, 19—

Revenue			
Sales		$398 659	
Less Returns and Allowances		21 151	
Net Sales			$377 508
Cost of Goods Sold			
Merchandise Inventory, January 1		$72 074	
Purchases	$229 209		
Less Returns and Allowances	18 356		
Net Purchases		210 853	
Freight-in		5 731	
Goods Available for Sale		$288 658	
Less: Merchandise Inventory, December 31		83 562	205 096
Gross Profit			$172 412
Operating Expenses			
Advertising		$ 1 141	
Bank Charges		2 651	
Car Expense		4 999	
Delivery Expense		7 717	
Insurance Used		2 915	
Light and Heat		3 988	
Miscellaneous		1 507	
Rent		12 000	
Salaries		24 000	
Supplies Used		2 560	
Telephone		1 850	
Wages		48 220	113 548
Net Income			$ 58 864

Figure 11.15   The income statement of Trident Trading Co. including returns and allowances.

Revised Cost of Goods Sold Formula

To handle all types of business situations, the cost of goods formula is changed slightly. The revised formula shows "Net Cost of Merchandise Purchased." This takes into account the likelihood that there will be some returns and allowances during the period. The formula, in its final form, is as follows:

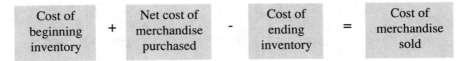

Cost of beginning inventory + Net cost of merchandise purchased − Cost of ending inventory = Cost of merchandise sold

SECTION REVIEW QUESTIONS

1. What form is issued when a sale is made on account?
2. When a sale is made on account and the customer is satisfied, what does the company expect the customer to do?
3. What happens when a customer is dissatisfied with the merchandise?
4. What business form is issued when a customer's account is adjusted downward?
5. Describe how a credit invoice is different from a regular invoice.
6. What is another name for a credit invoice?
7. For what three reasons are credit invoices issued?
8. Using the simplest system studied so far, give the accounting entry for the issuing of a credit invoice.
9. What is a cash refund?
10. Using the simplest system studied so far, give the accounting entry for a cash refund for merchandise returned by a customer.
11. Why do some businesses keep "returns and allowances" accounts?
12. Briefly explain the difference between accounting for a business that keeps returns and allowances accounts and one that does not.
13. Using the simplest system studied so far, give the accounting entry for a credit note for $100 for goods returned to a supplier.
14. Using returns and allowances accounts, give the accounting entry for a credit note for $100 for goods returned to a supplier.
15. Explain how to handle returns and allowances accounts on the income statement.

SECTION EXERCISES

1. **Examine the two source documents on pages 374 and 375 and answer the questions that follow.**

   1. From the point of view of Acadia Equipment and Supply, what source document is document A?
   2. From the point of view of Cornwallis Construction, what source document is document A?
   3. What source document is document B?

A.

EQUIPMENT RENTAL INVOICE

BOX 100, HALIFAX, N.S., B3L 2Z4

PHONE 233 6767

ACADIA
EQUIPMENT AND SUPPLY

CONTRACT NO.	DATE SHIPPED	SHIPPED VIA	INVOICE NUMBER
402	Sept. 10	Acadia	D4023

BILLING NO.	DATE RETURNED	RETURNED VIA	INVOICE DATE
36	Sept. 13	Acadia	Sept.14, 19--

RENTED TO   Cornwallis Construction
20 Cornwallis Street
Halifax, Nova Scotia
B3K 1A1

TERMS
Net 30 days

SHIPPED TO

Same

OVERDUE ACCOUNTS
2% per month

STOCK NO.	DESCRIPTION	NO. DAYS WEEKS, MOS.	RATE	AMOUNT
146	Forklift truck	3 days	$100.00	$300.00

4. Which company is the sender of the documents?

5. Which company is the purchaser?

6. Give the accounting entries for these two documents as if you were the accountant for Acadia Equipment and Supply. Acadia Equipment and Supply does not use returns and allowances accounts.

7. Give the accounting entries for these two documents as if you were the accountant for Cornwallis Construction. Cornwallis Construction does not use returns and allowances accounts.

B.

```
                              CREDIT INVOICE
BOX 100, HALIFAX, N.S., B3L 2Z4                    PHONE 233 6767

ACADIA
EQUIPMENT AND SUPPLY
```

CONTRACT NO.	DATE SHIPPED	SHIPPED VIA	INVOICE NUMBER
402	Sept. 12		C1129

BILLING NO.	DATE RETURNED	RETURNED VIA	INVOICE DATE
36	Sept. 13		Sept.19, 19--

RENTED TO   Cornwallis Construction
             2016 Cornwallis Street
             Halifax, Nova Scotia
             B3K 1A1

TERMS
Net 30 days

SHIPPED TO

OVERDUE ACCOUNTS
2% per month

STOCK NO.	DESCRIPTION	NO. DAYS WEEKS, MOS.	RATE	AMOUNT
146	Credit allowed due to malfunction of forklift truck	1/2	$100.00	$50.00

2. **Journalize the following transactions of Copeland's Furniture Mart.** Copeland's Furniture Mart does not use returns and allowances accounts.

   1. May 31 Cash Sales slip #1060 to A. Rosen for sale of goods $155 plus sales tax of $10.85; total $165.85; payment received in full.
   2. June 4 Cash Refund slip #1075 to A. Rosen for return of goods $155 plus sales tax of $10.85; total $165.85; cash refunded in full.

3. **Workbook Exercise: Additional practice in journalizing accounting entries from source documents.**

4. Jasper Company does not keep separate accounts for returns and allowances. The Sales account and the Purchases account for Jasper Company for a one-year period are represented on page 376.

Sales							No. 405	
Date		Particulars	PR	Debit	Credit	D/C	Balance	
Dec	31	For the year	J40		376 462 09			
	31	For the year	J40	47 650 32		C	328 811 77	

Purchases							No. 505	
Date		Particulars	PR	Debit	Credit	D/C	Balance	
Dec	31	For the year	J40	186 235 32				
	31	For the year	J40		27 356 04	D	158 879 28	

1. Give the gross sales figure.
2. Give the sales returns and allowances figure.
3. Give the net sales figure.
4. Give the gross purchases figure.
5. Give the purchases returns and allowances figure.
6. Give the net purchases figure.
7. Explain briefly how having separate returns and allowances accounts would help the management of this company.

5. From the following partial work sheet prepare the income statement for Tonk Traders to the point of reaching the gross profit figure.

Work Sheet Tonk Traders	Year Ended December 31, 19—	
Accounts	Income Statement	
	DR	CR
Merchandise Inventory	43 250.40	48 901.25
Sales		102 356.00
Sales Returns and Allowances	4 698.23	
Freight-in	6 235.14	
Purchases	60 258.20	
Purchase Returns and Allowances		9 562.45

11.5   PERPETUAL INVENTORY

There are many businesses for which the periodic inventory system is not adequate. Perhaps the most prominent of these are large department stores and large general merchandise and auto parts stores. Competition forces these businesses to use the *perpetual inventory system* which provides up-to-the-minute information about the company's stock. This is information that would not be possible if the periodic system were used.

How It Works

The **perpetual inventory system** is one in which a detailed record of items in stock is kept up to date on an ongoing basis. Not many years ago, this was possible for only a few businesses. It took many employees at considerable cost to produce the information on a card file. Additions to the inventory were made from copies of *receiving reports* which represented goods coming into the plant. Deductions from the inventory were made from copies of *shipping orders* which represented goods going out of the plant. An example of a perpetual inventory card is shown in Figure 11.16.

INVENTORY CONTROL CARD

Stock Number *L591*   Maximum *500 DOZ.*

Description *200 Watt Light Bulbs*   Minimum *50 DOZ.*

Location: Row *17* Bin *35*

Date	Reference	Unit Cost	Quantity Received	Quantity Shipped	Balance on Hand
Nov. 19- 5	*Balance Forward*				*216*
11	*S.O. 436*			*100*	*116*
14	*S.O. 501*			*40*	*76*
19	*S.O. 530*			*35*	*41*
21	*S.O. 539*			*20*	*21*
22	*R.R. 1074*	*41¢*	*450*		*471*
25	*S.O. 561*			*75*	*396*

Figure 11.16   A card from a perpetual inventory file.

Today computers are able to do the work far more effectively at a reasonable cost. With a computerized system, the inventory records are kept on a computer disk. The system is organized numerically with each item being given a unique code. As goods are received from suppliers, receiving reports are made out. Copies of these reports are then sent to the data entry clerk who enters the items into the inventory. If purchased goods are returned, the appropriate deductions from inventory are made.

The more technically complex part of the system happens in the store. Here each cash register is a point-of-sale terminal connected to the store's main computer. As items are sold, the cashier's duties include entering the code numbers and the quantities sold via the cash register keyboard or by means of an electronic scanner. The information is transferred directly to the store's central computer which is programmed to make the appropriate deductions from the inventory. Sales returns are generally handled by a separate department, usually the customer service department.

As good as the system is, it doesn't automatically know when goods are lost, stolen, or broken. Therefore, a manual check of the inventory is required. This is usually carried out on a random basis throughout the year. The quantity of individual items on hand is counted and compared with the book inventory shown by the computer. Any differences are adjusted to agree with the quantity counted manually.

Benefits of the Computerized Inventory Control System

A company using a modern computerized inventory control system benefits because:

1. Up-to-the-minute inventory information is available in detail. Given the unique code for an item through a terminal device, the computer can give back any information about the item that is stored in its memory. This may include a complete description of the product and the quantity on hand. Employees working on the floor are able to view the information on the screen of the terminal device and use the information in dealing with the customers.

   Office employees can view selected output either on the screen or by means of a printout. An example of a computerized printout for inventory is shown in Figure 11.17.

   An inventory status report such as the one shown above is usually produced once a day. As you can see, the listing shows the number on hand for each item as well as a maximum and minimum figure. The system alerts management when the quantity of any item becomes low and should be reordered.

   The reason this is important to a merchandising business is that an inventory that is larger than it should be costs money both to purchase and to provide the storage space for. This is money that the business can put to better use in other ways, particularly, for example, in reducing the bank loan. However, an inventory that is smaller than it should be is also a problem, for it creates the danger of running out of individual items and thus of losing sales.

2. Using this system, the business can know the value of the total inventory on hand at any time. Having this figure available makes it possible to produce financial statements and reports at a moment's notice. This gives management a chance to find out what is happening with many items. Management is thus able to take swift action to correct or avoid problems.

INVENTORY STATUS REPORT							
STOCK NUMBER	DESCRIPTION	OLD BALANCE	QUANTITY RECEIVED	QUANTITY SHIPPED	NEW BALANCE	MAXIMUM	MINIMUM
EH-3703	BALL HAMMER 8 OZ	74	0	33	31	100	40
EH-3704	BALL HAMMER 16 OZ	52	50	26	76	100	25
EH-3705	BALL HAMMER 24 OZ	24	170	19	175	200	25
EH-3707	BALL HAMMER 32 OZ	36	150	170	16	200	25
EH-3709	BALL HAMMER 40 OZ	47	0	6	41	200	25
EG-4119	CLAW HAMMER 13 OZ	12	35	1	46	50	15
EG-4126	CLAW HAMMER 16 OZ	74	0	32	42	200	50
EG-4131	CLAW HAMMER 16 OZ (STANLEY)	156	0	53	103	300	100
EG-4132	CLAW HAMMER 16 OZ (NEOPHRENE HANDLE)	13	0	5	8	25	10
EG-4135	CLAW HAMMER 16 OZ (LEATHER HANDLE)	90	200	5	285	300	100
EG-4108	TACK HAMMER 8 OZ	54	95	3	146	150	50
EH-3725	BRICK HAMMER	12	60	2	70	75	25
BE-5263	RUBBER MALLET 14 OZ	32	0	12	20	100	25
BE-5266	RUBBER MALLET 28 OZ	27	70	13	84	100	25
EH-3753	SLEDGE HAMMER 6 LB	40	0	20	20	100	25
EH-3755	SLEDGE HAMMER 8 LB	11	90	3	98	100	25
EH-3757	SLEDGE HAMMER 10 LB	5	45	3	47	50	10
EG-3203	HAND DRILL 1/4 INCH	37	0	13	24	100	25
EG-3206	HAND DRILL 1/4 INCH HEAVY DUTY	46	0	15	31	100	25
EG-3224	AUTOMATIC PUSH DRILL (8 BITS)	56	0	27	29	100	25

Figure 11.17   A partial daily inventory status report produced by computer.

SECTION REVIEW QUESTIONS

1. Describe the perpetual inventory system.
2. Which type of business is most likely to use the perpetual inventory system?
3. Before the use of computers, what form did a perpetual inventory system take?
4. Name the source document for additions to inventory in a manual system.
5. Name the source document for deductions from inventory in a manual system.
6. In a department store environment how are the deductions made from the inventory after a sale?
7. Is it necessary to count the inventory when a perpetual system is used? Explain.
8. Explain how a clerk on the floor of a modern store can benefit from the use of a computerized inventory system.
9. Name a computer-produced inventory report that would be made daily.
10. Why is it desirable to keep the inventory as low as possible?
11. What danger is there from keeping too low an inventory?
12. Why is it undesirable to have too high an inventory?
13. What advantage is there to having daily financial reports?

SECTION EXERCISES

1. **Indicate whether each of the following statements is true or false by entering a "T" or an "F" in the space indicated in the Workbook. Explain the reason for each "F" response.**

   1. Competition forces department stores to use the perpetual inventory system.
   2. The periodic inventory system produces information not possible with the perpetual inventory system.
   3. The copies of receiving reports are the source documents for data entry to increase the perpetual inventory.
   4. Deductions from the perpetual inventory are made only through the cash register in a computerized perpetual inventory system.
   5. In a computerized inventory system each inventory item is given a special code number.
   6. There is no reason to take a physical inventory in a computerized perpetual inventory system.
   7. Any differences between the book figures and the manual count figures in a perpetual inventory system require a correction to the book figures.
   8. Given the unique code for an item, the computer can give back any information about the item that is stored in its memory.
   9. In a computer-produced inventory system, goods are ordered when the quantity on hand becomes less than the maximum required.
   10. A computerized inventory system provides management with immediate feedback, making it unnecessary to solve problems.

---

2. **Complete each of the following statements by writing in your Workbook the appropriate word or phrase from the list on page 381.**

   1. Additions to inventory are usually made from copies of _____ .
   2. _____ forces department stores to use the perpetual inventory system.
   3. In a computerized inventory system each inventory item is given a _____ .
   4. A computerized inventory system provides management with _____ feedback which it can use to _____ problems.
   5. Given the unique code for an item, the computer can give back any information about the item that is _____ in its _____ .
   6. A computer-produced inventory status report makes it possible to compare the inventory on hand with suggested _____ and _____ quantities.
   7. The _____ inventory system produces information not possible with the _____ inventory system.
   8. Deductions from inventory are usually made from copies of _____ or through _____ in a modern store.
   9. Any differences between the _____ figure and the actual figure require an _____ to the book figure.
   10. Even in a computerized inventory system a _____ of the stock is necessary.

List of Words and Phrases

adjustment	memory
avoid	periodic
book	perpetual
competition	point-of-sale terminal
count	receiving reports
immediate	shipping orders
maximum	stored
minimum	unique code

3. Two inventory cards from the perpetual inventory file of Outpost Marine are included in the Workbook. These cards are shown on page 382.

   1. **From the source documents listed below choose those that pertain to the two selected inventory items and record the increases or decreases on the cards as if you were the inventory clerk.**
   2. **Assume that the quantities on hand are the latest ones purchased. Calculate the cost value for these two inventory items for inclusion in a summary for the grand inventory total.**

Source Documents		Stock No.	Quantity	Unit Price
March 1	Shipping Order No. 921	730-0320	5	
1	Shipping Order No. 922	713-3011	6	
2	Receiving Report No. 630	736-0551	10	5.10
3	Shipping Order No. 923	714-1018	35	
	Receiving Report No. 631	375-1000	20	10.50
4	Receiving Report No. 632	931-4014	25	9.05
5	Shipping Order No. 924	730-0320	15	
8	Receiving Report No. 633	423-6757	5	25.60
	Shipping Order No. 925	713-3011	10	
10	Receiving Report No. 634	703-1912	25	.50
11	Receiving Report No. 635	602-4210	20	1.45
	Shipping Order No. 926	705-1912	15	
12	Shipping Order No. 927	707-1129	100	
15	Receiving Report No. 636	713-3011	35	9.40
18	Receiving Report No. 637	920-0012	24	2.55
19	Shipping Order No. 928	730-0320	2	
20	Receiving Report No. 638	640-3121	30	40.25
23	Shipping Order No. 929	713-3011	15	
25	Receiving Report No. 639	730-0320	25	16.00
30	Shipping Order No. 930	730-0320	12	
31	Shipping Order No. 931	713-3011	20	
	Receiving Report No. 640	715-6745	12	5.20

INVENTORY CONTROL CARD

Stock Number	730–0320	Maximum	30
Description	SCHAEFER CHEEK BLOCK	Minimum	10
Location: Row	16 Bin 3		

Date	Reference	Unit Cost	Quantity Received	Quantity Shipped	Balance on Hand
Feb. 20	Forward	15.50			28
26	S.O. 904			5	23

INVENTORY CONTROL CARD

Stock Number	713–3011	Maximum	50
Description	BARTON CAM CLEAT	Minimum	20
Location: Row	20 Bin 14		

Date	Reference	Unit Cost	Quantity Received	Quantity Shipped	Balance on Hand
Feb. 24	Forward	9.20			37
26	S.O. 910			10	27

4. The following statement shows the results of operation for two successive years.

1. In your Workbook, fill in the blanks to complete the statement.

2. Suppose that on December 31, 19-8, the merchandise inventory was miscounted. Instead of $25 000 as shown, it was counted as $21 000.

   a. What effect would this understatement have on the net income figure for 19-8?

   b. What effect would it have on the net income figure for 19-9?

3. What effect, if any, would the above noted error have on the balance sheet for 19-8?

THE WALTON COMPANY
INCOME STATEMENT
YEARS ENDED DECEMBER 31, 19–8 AND 19–9

	19-8	19-9
Sales	$100 000	$120 000
Costs of Goods Sold		
Opening Inventory	$ 20 000	$ 25 000
Purchases		
Goods Available for Sale	$	$ 63 000
Less Closing Inventory	25 000	
Cost of Goods Sold	$	$
Gross Income	$ 65 000	$
Expenses	$	$ 37 000
Net Income	$ 33 000	$ 42 000

5. **This exercise also appears in your Workbook.**

Shown below are some of the accounts (in T-account form) from the ledger of Master Trading Company. Master Trading Company has a computerized accounting system and is able to keep its inventory and cost of goods accounts up to the minute. There is no account for Purchases. Assume that the bank account has a balance of $40 000.

Bank	Sales
40 000	

Merchandise Inventory	Cost of Goods Sold
50 000	

Record the journal entries for the following transactions directly into the ledger accounts. Ignore freight-in and sales tax.

TRANSACTIONS

1. Purchased merchandise for cash at a cost of $10 000.
2. Sold goods for cash. The goods, recorded in the inventory at $6 000, are sold for $11 000. (There are two aspects of this transaction to record.)
3. Sold goods for cash. The goods, recorded in the inventory at $9 000 are sold for $15 000. (There are two aspects of this transaction to record.)
4. Purchased merchandise for cash at a cost of $3 000.

CHAPTER HIGHLIGHTS

Now that you have completed Chapter 11 you should:

1. know what is meant by the terms merchandising business, wholesaler, and retailer;
2. know what is meant by merchandise inventory or stock-in-trade;
3. understand that the total cost of goods available for sale during a fiscal period is either 1) on hand, or 2) sold, broken, lost, or stolen;
4. be able to include merchandise inventory correctly on the balance sheet and on the income statement;
5. understand what is meant by gross profit;
6. know the difference between the periodic and the perpetual inventory methods;
7. know the inventory cycle and the cost of goods calculation;
8. know the accounting entries for 1) the purchase and sale of merchandise inventory, 2) freight-in, and 3) duty;
9. understand the accounting entries that affect the Merchandise Inventory account;
10. understand the need to take an end-of-period inventory;
11. be able to prepare a work sheet for a merchandising business;
12. be able to record the closing entries for a merchandising business;
13. understand the concept of merchandise returns and allowances;
14. be able to identify a credit invoice and to make the accounting entries for a credit invoice issued and a credit invoice received;
15. know the accounting entries for a cash refund;
16. understand why some businesses use special accounts for returns and allowances;
17. know the accounting entries for transactions that affect returns and allowances accounts;
18. be able to prepare an income statement that includes returns and allowances accounts.

ACCOUNTING TERMS

cash refund	merchandising business
cost of goods sold	periodic inventory method
credit invoice	perpetual inventory system
credit note	physical inventory
duty	retailer
freight-in account	stock-in-trade
gross profit	wholesaler
merchandise inventory	

CHAPTER EXERCISES

Using Your Knowledge

1. **In a two-column general journal record the accounting entries for the following selected transactions of Industrial Supply owned by Otto Graf.** Industrial Supply uses the periodic inventory system and does not use returns and allowances accounts. **Choose your own account names.**

TRANSACTIONS

May

1 *Sales Invoice No. 501*
   To Hewitt Construction for sale of merchandise on account; $656.00 plus 7% sales tax, total $701.92.

2 *Bank Debit Advice*
   For interest and bank charges for April; $65.85.

4 *Cheque Copy No. 1002*
   Issued to the owner for his personal use; $500.

5 *Purchase Invoice*
   Received from Dofasco for merchandise for resale; $1 072.14.

8 *Credit Invoice*
   Received from Great Lakes Wood Products; allowance for defective goods; $585.00

9 *Sales Invoice No. 502*
   To Northern Contracting for sale of merchandise on account; $846.00 plus 7% sales tax, total $905.22.

10 *Cheque Copy No. 1003*
   Issued to the Provincial Treasurer in payment of the sales tax for April; $1 754.34.

11 *Cheque Copy No. 1004*
   Issued to the Post Office for the cash purchase of postage stamps; $160.

12 *Cash Receipt*
   Received from Arrow Electric on account; $625.95.

15 *Credit Invoice No. 503*
   Issued to Handy Made Products for unsatisfactory goods returned; $585.00 plus 7% sales tax, total $625.95.

16 *Cheque Copy No. 1005*
   Issued to Olympia Distributors on account; $755.65.

19 *Cash Sales Slip No. 12520*
   Issued to T. Maloney for the cash sale of merchandise; $102.50 plus 7% sales tax, total $109.68.

22 *Cheque Copy No. 1006*
   Issued to Speedy Muffler for the cash purchase of a new muffler system for the truck; $166.92.

24 *Cheque Copy No. 1007*
   Issued to Bell Canada for the cash payment of the telephone bill for one month; $65.35.

25 *Cash Receipt*
   Received from Easy Products on account; $1 000.

26 *Purchase Invoice*
   Received from Pacific Transport for Transportation charges on incoming merchandise; $896.50.

29 *Credit Note*
   Received from Kohler Generators for merchandise returned; $2 850.

31 *Cheque Copy No. 1008*
   Issued to P. Vanderkam for wages; $950.74.

---

2. Workbook Exercise: Journalizing transactions involving returns and allowances accounts.

---

3. **Indicate whether each of the following statements is true or false by placing a "T" or an "F" in the space indicated in your Workbook. Explain the reason for each "F" response in the space provided.**

   1. A "wholesaler" is a "merchandiser." Therefore, a "merchandiser" is a "wholesaler."
   2. Some of the goods found in the inventory of a hardware store are also goods found in the inventory of a building supply store.
   3. Merchandise inventory is on the balance sheet under Prepaid Expenses.
   4. The cost of goods sold figure normally includes the cost of goods that are lost, stolen, or broken.
   5. The merchandise inventory of a drug store is calculated by counting all of the goods on hand and multiplying by the selling prices marked on the goods.
   6. An item that cost $40 and sold for $80 produced a gross profit of 50 per cent of the selling price.
   7. The difference between the selling price and the cost price of the goods for a fiscal period is also the net income figure before any operating expenses are deducted.
   8. The goods not sold represent the ending inventory.
   9. The goods sold at selling prices represent the revenue figure.
   10. The perpetual inventory system has not been commonly used because of the amount of work required to keep track of the many individual items in the inventory.
   11. A used car business could easily use the perpetual inventory system because the number of items in its inventory is quite small.
   12. XYZ department store uses the periodic inventory method. It must take a physical inventory at least once a year.
   13. A perpetual inventory results in a "calculated" inventory figure. The inventory quantities shown on a perpetual inventory listing should be checked by actually inspecting the inventory from time to time. This would make clear whether or not any goods were stolen.

14. If the beginning inventory was 10 000 units and the ending inventory was 12 000 units, the business sold more units than it purchased.
15. The merchandise inventory figure can be found during the fiscal period from the Merchandise Inventory account.
16. The Purchases account is used to accumulate all purchases during the period.
17. When a business that uses the periodic method sells goods, no accounting entry is made to reduce the merchandise inventory. If it were made, the entry would be debit Cost of Goods Sold and credit Merchandise Inventory.
18. The Freight-in account is used to accumulate all transportation charges during the fiscal period.
19. Freight-in is considered to be a cost of the goods acquired.
20. On the work sheet the Purchases figure in the trial balance is extended to the Income Statement section, Debit column.
21. On the work sheet the Merchandise Inventory figure in the trial balance is extended to the Balance Sheet section, Debit column.
22. Both the beginning and the ending inventory figures are shown on the income statement of a merchandising company.
23. The Merchandise Inventory account is automatically adjusted by the closing entries.
24. A credit invoice is issued by the vendor and received by the buyer.
25. The accounting entry for a credit note issued is either:

	DR	CR
Accounts Receivable	$$$$	
Sales		$$$$
or		
Accounts Receivable	$$$$	
Sales Returns and Allowances		$$$$

4. **From the partial work sheet shown on page 388:**

1. **prepare an income statement and a balance sheet.**
2. **journalize the closing entries.**

| Work Sheet   Master Trading Company   Year Ended December 31. 19— | | | | |
| | Income Statement | | Balance Sheet | |
Accounts	Dr	Cr	Dr	Cr
Bank			950.85	
Accounts Receivable			37 372.50	
Merchandise Inventory	45 957.00	43 500.00	43 500.00	
Supplies			1 350.00	
Prepaid Insurance			1 865.00	
Equipment			28 040.00	
Automobiles			25 350.00	
Accounts Payable				26 210.70
Sales Tax Payable				1 027.52
Bank Loan				25 000.00
Grace Strom, Capital				62 855.29
Grace Strom, Drawings			30 000.00	
Sales		216 350.50		
Sales Returns & Allowances	4 092.00			
Purchases	75 316.20			
Purchases Returns & Allowances		7 621.90		
Freight-in	1 592.00			
Advertising	1 585.00			
Bank Charges	2 685.00			
Car Expense	8 356.00			
Delivery Expense	5 695.21			
General Expense	1 632.25			
Light and Heat	1 875.25			
Rent	12 000.00			
Telephone	1 115.33			
Wages	47 256.32			
Supplies Used	2 563.00			
Insurance Used	2 417.00			
	214 137.56	267 472.40	168 428.35	115 093.51
Net Income	53 334.84			53 334.84
	267 472.40	267 472.40	168 428.35	168 428.35

5. General Marine is a company that maintains a perpetual inventory that includes several hundred items. Two of the items listed on the February 28th inventory are:

Item	Code	Quantity on Hand
Harken Blocks	460	32
Proctor Tiller Extenders	911	25

1. Shown on page 389 are the source documents for inventory items received and inventory items shipped during the month of March. **From this list of source documents, select those that pertain to the two items above and calculate the number of each of the two items on hand at the end of March.**

Date	Source Document	Stock Number	Quantity
May	1 Shipping Order	460	8
	2 Shipping Order	911	5
	Receiving Report	551	10
	3 Shipping Order	1018	35
	4 Receiving Report	1000	20
	Receiving Report	4014	25
	Shipping Order	460	10
	8 Receiving Report	6757	5
	Shipping Order	911	8
	11 Receiving Report	1912	25
	Receiving Report	4210	20
	12 Shipping Order	1912	15
	Shipping Order	1129	100
	15 Receiving Report	911	40
	18 Receiving Report	112	24
	Shipping Order	460	2
	20 Receiving Report	3121	30
	23 Shipping Order	911	15
	25 Receiving Report	460	30
	Shipping Order	460	15
	30 Shipping Order	911	12
	31 Receiving Report	6745	12

2. If the price of the items purchased on March 25 was $46 each, calculate the value of item #460 for the inventory.

6. The Sutton Hardware Store takes inventory only at the end of the calendar year because of the inconvenience involved. The gross profit of the business is stable and averages 40 per cent. On January 31, at the end of the first month of business, the ledger included the following five account balances.

Merchandise Inventory	$ 51 920
Sales	103 850
Purchases	73 950
Freight-in	1 258
Operating Expenses	22 357

Use the above information to estimate the closing inventory. Then prepare a condensed income statement for the month of January.

7. The accountant for a small company prepared an income statement which showed a net income figure of $38 525. The company's bank requested an audit of this statement. The following errors were found by the auditor who checked the books and records:

1. The $4 200 cost of installing new equipment had been charged to Repair Expense instead of to Equipment.
2. A $100 credit to Purchase Returns and Allowances was incorrectly credited to Sales Returns and Allowances.
3. Repairs to Automobiles was incorrectly overstated by the amount of $1 500.
4. No adjusting entry for supplies was made. The ledger showed a balance for supplies of $2 850; the supplies counted at the year-end amounted to $840.
5. The ending inventory figure used by the company accountant was $32 650 but there were a number of errors in arriving at that figure. The auditor revised the ending inventory figure to be $29 350.

Calculate the net income figure that would appear on the audited income statement.

8. Hiram Retail is a family owned department store in Winnipeg, Manitoba. When the physical inventory was taken at the year-end, an entire department was overlooked. As a result the inventory was understated by $10 000.
Use some hypothetical figures to help you answer the following questions.

1. How will the inventory understatement affect the cost of goods sold?
2. How will the inventory understatement affect the gross profit?
3. How will the inventory understatement affect the net income?
4. How will the inventory understatement affect the balance sheet?
5. What would be your answers to questions 1 to 4 if the $10 000 error had been an inventory overstatement?
6. If you were the manager of a company and were looking for a way to make the profit appear higher, what might you consider doing?
7. If you were the owner of a company and were considering cheating to save on income tax, what might you consider doing?

For Further Thought
9. **Briefly answer the following questions.**

1. Paula Waukey is the owner of a paper products business. Her company makes available a large variety of papers and paper-related products such as disposable towels, coffee filters, table covers, disposable coffee cups, and so on. Paula's customers could buy more cheaply by dealing directly with the manufacturers of the products. However, they continue to do business with Paula. Explain why Paula's customers choose to do business with her.
2. A road building company might have several inventories on hand. These could include office supplies, sand, stone, asphalt, and gasoline. Explain the difference between these inventories and merchandise inventory.
3. The text indicates that merchandise that is lost, broken, or stolen, is lumped in with cost of goods sold. Explain the logic of this.
4. Merchandise inventory on hand at the end of the fiscal period is listed on the balance sheet at its cost price. Indirectly, some inventory is listed on the income statement at its selling price. Explain.

5. Give a logical reason for showing the gross profit separately on the income statement.
6. Having a computerized inventory system allows a business to carry a smaller total inventory. Explain why this is possible. What is the advantage of being able to carry a smaller inventory?
7. The text states that the selling prices of goods are marked on the merchandise, but not the cost price. Why is the cost price not marked on the goods?
8. The merchandise sold is listed in two places on the income statement. Explain why this is done.
9. Explain why the closing inventory is valued at its cost price.
10. Explain why freight-in is included in the cost of goods sold calculation.
11. Give a logical reason why a business would close down for a day or two in order to take inventory.
12. Many businesspeople who use the periodic inventory system would rather not bother with inventory taking. However, they do it anyway. Explain why.
13. Explain why inventory count tickets are pre-numbered.
14. Assume that a large department store wants to take a quick inventory with some sacrifice of accuracy, to give it a rough idea of its progress. Try to devise a method of shortening the inventory procedure to give a reasonably close result.
15. The method of handling the merchandise inventory on the work sheet may be thought of as a "manipulation" rather than as an "adjustment." Explain.
16. Which financial statement do you think is of the most interest to a banker? Explain your answer.
17. What do you think is the most common error made by students when doing the closing entries for a merchandising business?
18. Explain how the credit note got its name.
19. In purchase transactions where there are returns and allowances involved, it is normal to wait until all of the source documents are received before making payment. Why would this be done?
20. Some businesses refuse to give a refund for merchandise returned. Explain how they handle this type of transaction.

CASE STUDIES

CASE 1 *Analyzing Income Statements*

Shown on page 392 are the income statements for two different companies in the furniture business.

INCOME STATEMENTS
YEAR ENDED DECEMBER 31, 19—

	Company A	Company B
Revenue		
Sales	$121 206	$415 072
Cost of Goods Sold	70 704	211 686
Gross Profit	$ 50 502	$203 386
Operating Expenses		
Advertising Expense	—	$ 43 072
Bank Charges Expense	$ 990	5 765
Building Maintenance Expense	140	3 500
Delivery Expense	10 403	35 206
Insurance Expense	509	1 532
Licenses Expense	120	435
Light, Heat, and Water Expense	1 850	5 775
Miscellaneous Expense	119	717
Rent Expense	4 800	12 000
Telephone Expense	275	716
Wages Expense	10 402	40 307
Total Expenses	$ 29 608	$149 025
Net Income	$ 20 894	$ 54 361

Questions

1. Describe your mental picture of these two companies (large or small, high profile or low profile, etc.) giving specific reasons for your impression.
2. B's expenses are much larger than A's, and yet B is able to earn more than twice the net income of A. How is this possible?
3. The relationship between the cost price of the goods and the selling price of the goods is crucial in any business. Consider the following analysis for Company A:

Sales	$121 206—100%
Cost of Goods Sold	$ 70 704— 58%

Company A's goods cost 58% of their selling price.

    a. Calculate this same percentage figure for Company B.

    b. If the figure for Company B were 58 per cent, the same as for Company A, how much lower would Company B's net income be?

CASE 2   *Irregularity Disclosed by Income Statement*

Mark Trewin is the owner of Spyhill Ski Shop. His accountant has just handed him the financial statements for the year. The income statement is shown on p. 393 in condensed form.

SPYHILL SKI SHOP
INCOME STATEMENT
YEAR ENDED JUNE 30, 19—

Revenue			
Sales		$110 000	100%
Costs of Goods Sold			
Opening Inventory	$ 36 500		
Purchases	67 000		
	$103 500		
Deduct Closing Inventory	36 000	67 500	61%
Gross Profit		$ 42 500	39%
Operating Expenses		29 000	27%
Net Income		$ 13 500	12%

Mark is upset by this statement, and suggests to his accountant that an error has been made. His accountant assures him that everything was checked and double-checked because of the low net income figure. No error was found.

Mark is particularly troubled by the gross profit figure. The operating expenses appear to be normal. Mark explains that all of his merchandise is marked up 100 per cent and that there have been no special sales needed to move the goods. In other words, Mark feels that the gross profit should be at its normal figure of approximately 50 per cent.

Because he has to be away a great deal, Mark relies heavily on his store manager. In past years Jill Zaba was the manager and no problems were encountered. A year ago, Jill left for a better position. This year the store was managed by Jon Yeo. Jon came from out of town and not much is known about him.

Questions

1. Assuming that the sales figure is correct, what should the figure for cost of goods sold have been?
2. What is the most likely reason for the high figure for cost of goods sold?
3. Try to show the cost of goods sold section as it would appear if there had been no irregularity.
4. Suggest how the owner can correct any irregularities.

CHALLENGE

CASE 3   *A Scheme To Save Income Tax?*

Vince Lyons owns a large and profitable sporting goods business in Regina, Saskatchewan. He has recently had a run of bad luck on the stock market, which has left him very short of funds. Unfortunately, he is badly in need of money to pay his income tax, which is almost due.

Vince desperately needs a way to reduce the amount of income tax that he will have to pay. After much searching, he comes up with a scheme that he thinks may work. He describes this scheme to his wife, Louisa, to get her reaction.

Vince explains to Louisa that his income tax is based primarily on the net income of the business. He shows her condensed figures for the current year and the projected figures for next year. These are shown below.

	This year's actual figures	Next year's projected figures
Sales	250 000	300 000
Cost of Goods Sold		
Beginning inventory	50 000	60 000
Purchases	147 500	170 000
Goods available for sale	197 500	230 000
Deduct ending inventory	60 000	65 000
	137 500	165 000
Gross Profit	112 500	135 000
Expenses	65 000	75 000
Net Income	47 500	60 000

	This year's actual figures (modified)	Next year's projected figures (modified)
Sales	250 000	300 000
Cost of Goods Sold		
Beginning inventory	50 000	40 000
Purchases	147 500	170 000
Goods available for sale	197 500	210 000
Deduct ending inventory	40 000	65 000
	157 500	145 000
Gross Profit	92 500	155 000
Expenses	65 000	75 000
Net Income	27 500	80 000

Vince proposes to understate this year's ending inventory by $20 000, causing the net income to be understated by the same amount. This way, Vince expects to reduce his tax bill by $7 000.

Vince does not consider this action to be dishonest. He explains to Louisa that an understatement this year will cause an overstatement the next year. He shows her the figures as they would appear containing the suggested inventory change. As Vince points out, the net income for the two years is still $107 500 whichever way it is calculated. Although he will pay less tax this year, he will make it up by paying more next year. Rather than cheating, he is simply postponing tax payment for a while. According to Vince, he will have no problem paying his taxes next year.

Questions
1. Is Vince correct when he claims that the net income for two years remains the same no matter how it is arrived at?
2. Will Vince be breaking the law?
3. Does the scheme offer a hidden benefit to Vince apart from the $7 000 tax deferral?
4. What dangers do you see in this scheme?

CHALLENGE

CASE 4   *Understating Inventory on Tax Returns*

Carol Menzies is the owner of Classic Glass and Mirror. In the years 19-1 through 19-5, Carol submitted the following income statements to the income tax department.

SCHEDULE OF REPORTED NET INCOME FOR CLASSIC GLASS AND MIRROR (in thousands of dollars)					
Year	1	2	3	4	5
Sales	200	220	250	280	320
Costs of Goods Sold					
Opening Inventory	40	30	30	40	40
Purchases	90	115	140	160	190
Goods Available	130	145	170	200	230
Less Closing Inventory	30	30	40	40	50
Costs of Goods sold	100	115	130	160	180
Gross Profit	100	105	120	120	140
Operating Expenses	60	65	70	70	80
Net Income	40	40	50	50	60

The above statements are correct except in one respect. Carol has understated the closing inventory figures in each of the five years. The true ending inventory figures are respectively $40, $50, $70, $80, and $100 (thousands).

The government income tax rates during this period of time are given in the schedule below. Carol has paid her income taxes promptly.

GOVERNMENT INCOME TAX RATES (in thousands of dollars)	
Net Income	*Rate*
$ 1 — $20	20%
$21 — $30	24%
$31 — $40	28%
$41 — $50	32%
$51 — $60	36%
$61 — $70	40%
$71 — $80	44%
$81 — $90	48%
$91 — $100	52%
Over $100	56%

Questions
Part A
1. Recalculate the net incomes to reflect the correct inventory figures.
2. Record the answers to the following questions.
   a. Record the amount by which the inventory is understated for each of the five years.
   b. Record the amount by which the net income is understated for each of the five years.
   c. Calculate and record the income tax on the reported net income figures for each of the five years.
   d. Calculate and record the (correct) income tax on the revised net income figures for each of the five years.
   e. Calculate and record the saving in income tax for each of the five years.
   f. Assume that the owner used the tax money saved to reduce her bank loan on which interest at 12 per cent was charged. Calculate and record the interest saved in each year. To help you in this calculation, the income tax saved in the first year would accumulate for four years. The interest saved for that year is: ($4 800 × 1.12 × 1.12 × 1.12 × 1.12) – $4 800 = $2 752.89
   g. Calculate and record the accumulated total income tax and interest saved by the end of the fifth year.

Questions
Part B
The tax department was tipped off anonymously that Carol Menzies was cheating on her income tax. Carol was paid a surprise visit by the tax auditors who uncovered all of Carol's misrepresentations. The income tax authorities decided:

- to levy a fine of $10 000;
- to leave the tax returns for Years 1 to 4 untouched;
- to record the correct closing inventory of $100 000 on the 19-5 income statement and to calculate the tax on the revised 19-5 figure according to the tax table;
- to charge interest on the unpaid taxes at the rate of 12 per cent, the same rate Carol was charged by her bank.

1. Calculate the tax bill facing Carol as a result of the income tax audit.
2. Give possible reasons to explain why Carol misrepresented the inventory in 19-1.
3. Give possible reasons why Carol continued to misrepresent inventories in subsequent years.
4. If the auditors had decided to recalculate each of the net incomes for the five years, the extra expense to Carol would have been less. Explain why.

ENTREPRENEURS
Gyle Graham, Guy Louis, and Su Ann Lim / Pacific Edge Trade Group

Like the bumblebee, which isn't supposed to fly, three young Vancouver entrepreneurs shouldn't succeed in marketing Canadian products in Japan, the toughest consumer market in the world. But Gyle Graham, Guy Louis, and Su Ann Lim have been doing it anyway.

In 1986, while still in their twenties, this trio, who met in university, formed Pacific Edge Trade Group Canada Ltd. to sell Canadian products in Japan. They started the company with their own capital, less than $1 000. For the first two years they financed it themselves. By 1989 sales reached $2 million, a growth rate of 500 per cent, and they are still growing.

Pacific Edge acts as the marketing arm in Japan for small Canadian manufacturers. Sometimes it will suggest modifications to a client, to make a product more popular with Japanese consumers.

At the outset, Pacific Edge avoided the traditional Japanese way of getting products to consumers through a chain of expensive intermediaries — distributors, wholesalers, and trading houses. By selling directly to retailers, Pacific Edge competes successfully with Japanese producers.

By the time Pacific Edge was formed, all three partners had travelled extensively in the Far East and gained much experience in the business practices and customs of Asian peoples. In addition, Su Ann, who has her Master's degree in Business Administration, has found her education to be a good foundation for her work.

Gyle, who lives and works in Tokyo, is now an old hand at promoting Canadian products there. Like his Chinese-Canadian partners, Gyle speaks Japanese. In fact, he speaks it so fluently that the national

Japanese television network, NHK, has used him on its news programs. He even starred in a Japanese-language TV comedy show — quite a feat for someone who was born and raised in Vancouver by Scottish-Canadian parents.

Gyle's national exposure has transformed him into somewhat of a celebrity in Japan. Mike "The Interrogator" Wallace interviewed him on the prestigious CBS-TV program, *60 Minutes*, as a result. Being well known has also helped Gyle to promote Pacific Edge products at a minimum cost or free. Other Western business people must spend thousands of dollars on promotion in order to break into the Japanese market.

"Typically," says Su Ann, "small Canadian businesses do not have the expertise or management time to promote their own products in Japan. They don't speak Japanese and they aren't right there to see what's happening. We do it for them. For certain lines we are also the distributor."

Their first successful line was a plush toy teddy bear manufactured in Hamilton, Ontario, by Binkley Toys. Despite claims that the Far East monopolizes the toy market, the Binkley bear has been a consistent best seller.

At present Pacific Edge mostly handles top-quality Canadian sporting equipment and clothing. One of its greatest successes has been a folding kayak, designed and built by Feathercraft Kayaks on Granville Island in Vancouver. The Feathercraft kayak has outsold every other imported make in Japan, including the popular models made by the giant Klepper Company of West Germany.

The partners are proud of their Canadian products, describing them as the best in the world. But "the Japanese," says Guy, "are very good at researching and making a competitive product. Our role is to provide feedback to our Canadian suppliers and manufacturers, alerting them to the possibility of competition so that they can produce better products at a lower price."

DISCUSSION

1. What is the traditional Japanese way of channelling goods to consumers?
2. What marketing approach is used by Pacific Edge?
3. Why was post-university experience important to each of the three partners in their business?
4. How was Gyle's media experience important to the business?
5. What handicaps do Western business people face when doing business in Japan and other Pacific Rim clients?
6. Use the library to prepare a list of Pacific Rim countries and the languages spoken by those countries.

Specialized Journals

12.1 The Synoptic Journal
12.2 The Five-Journal System
12.3 Cash Discounts
12.4 Computers in Accounting   Using Bedford in the Accounting Ledger

By this point, you have gained a fairly complete understanding of the accounting process. You are now ready to study accounting techniques designed to make the accounting process more efficient.

12.1 *THE SYNOPTIC JOURNAL*

In the business world, the two-column general journal is used mainly for non-routine transactions. Routine, or ordinary, transactions are generally recorded in "specialized" journals. The synoptic journal is a specialized journal designed for small businesses with only a few accounting employees. It would not be used in a computerized system.

The synoptic journal is a journal with a number of columns to accumulate accounting entries. Most special journals have a number of columns and are known as multi-columnar journals.

Journalizing in the Synoptic Journal

An illustration of a synoptic journal is shown in Figure 12.1. Observe the special money column headings for Bank debit, Bank credit, Accounts Receivable debit, Accounts Receivable credit, Accounts Payable debit, Accounts Payable credit, Sales credit, Purchases debit, and Sales Tax Payable credit.

SYNOPTIC JOURNAL												MONTH OF _____ 19 __				PAGE __
DATE	CUSTOMER SUPPLIER	REF NO	BANK		ACCOUNTS RECEIVABLE		ACCOUNTS PAYABLE		SALES OR INCOME	PURCHASES	SALES TAX PAYABLE	OTHER ACCOUNTS			
			DR	CR	DR	CR	DR	CR	CR	DR	CR	ACCOUNT	P.R.	DR	CR

Figure 12.1   A page from a synoptic journal.

A synoptic journal need not be identical to the one in the illustration. The headings depend to some extent on the nature of the business. For example, a service business would not need a column for purchases. Also, a synoptic journal may be designed with more columns than shown in the illustration.

The idea of the synoptic journal is to have special columns in which to sort items during the journalizing process. This saves time later when entries are posted. The individual items in the special columns are not posted singly. It is the totals of the special columns that are posted. Only one posting is needed for each special column.

For example, assume that 50 individual amounts have been entered in the Bank debit column of a synoptic journal. It is the total of these 50 amounts, not each separate amount, that is posted. The accounting department saves a good deal of time and effort by posting totals rather than individual amounts.

In theory, one could have a special column for every general ledger account. However, this would make the journal too cumbersome to be practicable. In practice, special columns are set up only for items that occur frequently. A general section is provided for other items. Accounts in this section are posted individually.

Journalizing in the synoptic journal is easy. Obtain a sheet of "synoptic" paper and try the following sample entries for Consumers' Trading Company.

TRANSACTION 1   May 4: Cash Sales Ticket No. 57: Sale of $256.00 of merchandise for cash; tax of $17.92; total, $273.92.

You should have no trouble working out the accounting entry for this transaction as follows:

	DR	CR
Bank	$273.92	
Sales		$256.00
Sales Tax Payable		17.92

In the synoptic journal this accounting entry would be recorded as follows:

DATE	CUSTOMER SUPPLIER	REF NO	BANK DR	BANK CR	ACCOUNTS RECEIVABLE DR	ACCOUNTS RECEIVABLE CR	ACCOUNTS PAYABLE DR	ACCOUNTS PAYABLE CR	SALES OR INCOME CR	PURCHASES DR	SALES TAX PAYABLE CR	OTHER ACCOUNTS ACCOUNT	P.R.	DR	CR
May 4	Cash Sale	57	273 92						256 -		17 92				

SYNOPTIC JOURNAL   MONTH OF May   19 —   PAGE 41

TRANSACTION 2   May 5: Sales Invoice No. 165: Issued to Paul Rogan; sale of $412.00 of merchandise on account; sales tax of $28.84; total, $440.84.

The accounting entry for this transaction is:

	DR	CR
Accounts Receivable (P. Rogan)	$440.84	
Sales		$412.00
Sales Tax Payable		28.84

In the synoptic journal this entry follows the previous entry in the manner shown below. Observe that no explanations are necessary for routine transactions. Also, remember that the postings to the subsidiary ledgers are made directly from source documents.

SYNOPTIC JOURNAL			BANK		ACCOUNTS RECEIVABLE		ACCOUNTS PAYABLE		SALES OR INCOME	PURCHASES	SALES TAX PAYABLE	OTHER ACCOUNTS				MONTH OF May 19 — PAGE 41
DATE	CUSTOMER SUPPLIER	REF NO	DR	CR	DR	CR	DR	CR	CR	DR	CR	ACCOUNT	P.R.	DR	CR	
May 4	Cash Sale	57	273 92						256 -		17 92					
5	P. Rogan	155			440 84				412 -		28 84					

TRANSACTION 3   May 6: Purchase Invoice: Received from Empire Wholesale for merchandise purchased on account; $816.00.

The accounting entry for this transaction is:

	DR	CR
Purchases	$816.00	
Accounts Payable (Empire Wholesale)		$816.00

In the synoptic journal the entry is recorded as shown below.

SYNOPTIC JOURNAL			BANK		ACCOUNTS RECEIVABLE		ACCOUNTS PAYABLE		SALES OR INCOME	PURCHASES	SALES TAX PAYABLE	OTHER ACCOUNTS				MONTH OF May 19 — PAGE 41
DATE	CUSTOMER SUPPLIER	REF NO	DR	CR	DR	CR	DR	CR	CR	DR	CR	ACCOUNT	P.R.	DR	CR	
May 4	Cash Sale	57	273 92						256 -		17 92					
5	P. Rogan	155			440 84				412 -		28 84					
6	Empire Wholesale							816 -		816 -						

TRANSACTION 4   May 7: Purchase Invoice and Cheque Copy No. 74: For the cash purchase of supplies from Deluxe Stationers; $235.40.

The accounting entry for this transaction is:

	DR	CR
Supplies	$235.40	
Bank		$235.40

In the synoptic journal the entry is recorded as shown below.

SYNOPTIC JOURNAL			BANK		ACCOUNTS RECEIVABLE		ACCOUNTS PAYABLE		SALES OR INCOME	PURCHASES	SALES TAX PAYABLE	OTHER ACCOUNTS				MONTH OF May 19 — PAGE 41
DATE	CUSTOMER SUPPLIER	REF NO	DR	CR	DR	CR	DR	CR	CR	DR	CR	ACCOUNT	P.R.	DR	CR	
May 4	Cash Sale	57	273 92						256 -		17 92					
5	P. Rogan	155			440 84				412 -		28 84					
6	Empire Wholesale							816 -		816 -						
7	Deluxe Stationers	74		235 40								Supplies		235 40		

The purchase of supplies does not happen frequently. Therefore, there is no special column for Supplies and the item is entered in the Other Accounts section.

TRANSACTION 5   May 7: Cheque Copy No. 75: Paid the rent for the month to Arrow Realty, $800.

The accounting entry for the transaction is:

	DR	CR
Rent Expense	$800.00	
Bank		$800.00

In the synoptic journal, the accounting entry is recorded as shown below.

SYNOPTIC JOURNAL				MONTH OF May	19 —						PAGE 41		
DATE	CUSTOMER SUPPLIER	REF NO	BANK DR	BANK CR	ACCOUNTS RECEIVABLE DR	ACCOUNTS RECEIVABLE CR	ACCOUNTS PAYABLE DR	ACCOUNTS PAYABLE CR	SALES OR INCOME CR	PURCHASES DR	SALES TAX PAYABLE CR	OTHER ACCOUNTS ACCOUNT · P.R. · DR	OTHER ACCOUNTS CR
May 4	Cash Sale	57	273 92						256 -		17 92		
5	P. Regan	155				440 4			412 -		28 4		
6	Empire Wholesale							8 16		8 16			
7	Deluxe Stationers	74					235 40					Supplies 235 40	
7	Arrow Realty	75		800 -								Rent Expense 800 -	

Rent Expense is recorded in the Other Accounts section because it is an infrequently occurring item.

Additional Transactions

A number of additional transactions of a routine nature are listed below. Try to journalize them on your own before comparing your work with the synoptic journal entries in Figure 12.2.

May

10   *Cheque Copy No. 76*
        Issued to A. Baldwin on account; $173.50.
      Cheque Copy No. 77
        Issued to G. English & Co. on account; $500.00.

11   *Cash Receipt*
        Received from R. Mayotte on account; $352.00.
      Cash Receipt
        Received from P. Fuhr on account; $620.00.

13   *Cheque Copy No. 78*
        Issued to M. Cham in payment of wages; $585.00.
      Cheque Copy No. 79
        Issued to D. Adams in payment of wages; $650.00.

14   *Sales Invoice No. 166*
        Issued to M. Delgaty for merchandise sold on account; $196.00 plus $13.72 sales tax; total $209.72

Sales Invoice No. 167

Issued to Carl Holm for merchandise sold on account; $240.00 plus $16.80 sales tax; total $256.80.

17 *Purchase Invoice*

Received from Continental Railway for freight charges on incoming merchandise $436.50.

18 *Purchase Invoice*

Received from Budget Oil for gasoline and oil used in the delivery truck; $262.54.

19 *Cheque Copy No. 80*

Issued to P. Kerr, the owner, for personal use; $800.00.

20 *Cheque Copy No. 81 together with Purchase Invoice*

Issued to Ideal Supply in payment of merchandise purchased for cash; $475.00.

21 *Purchase Invoice*

Received from Circle Supply for supplies purchased on account; $267.50.

Purchase Invoice

Received from Deluxe Stationers for the purchase on account of a new office desk at a cost of $1 053.95 and merchandise at a cost of $224.70; total $1 278.65.

24 *Memorandum from Owner*

To the effect that the company has borrowed $5 000 from the bank effective immediately.

26 *Cheque Copy No. 82*

Issued to Empire Wholesale on account; $400.00.

Purchase Invoice

Received from Prairie Manufacturing for the purchase of merchandise on account; $750.00.

26 *Cash Receipt*

Received from R. Stoddard on account; $300.00.

27 *Cheque Copy No. 83*

Issued to M. Cham for wages; $585.00.

Cheque Copy No. 84

Issued to D. Adams for wages; $650.00.

31 *Sales Invoice No. 168*

Issued to Purity Company for the sale of merchandise on account; $540.00 plus $37.80 sales tax; total $577.80.

Balancing the Columnar Journal

At the bottom of every journal page, and at the end of every month, a procedure called *cross balancing* is performed on the synoptic journal, or on any columnar journal. **Cross balancing** is the process of checking the grand total of all the debit columns against the grand total of all of the credit columns to make sure that the two grand totals agree. The steps in cross balancing a columnar journal are described below. Refer to Figure 12.2 as you study these steps.

1. Immediately beneath the last entry on the page, and in ink, draw a single ruled line across all money columns of the journal.
2. Separately, total (foot) each money column and write in the total in small pencil figures just beneath the single ruled line. You will recall that these tiny pencil figures are known as pencil footings or pin totals.
3. Using a printing calculator, separately add all the pin totals of the debit columns and all the pin totals of the credit columns. Include all columns of the journal. These two sums should yield the same grand total. The journal is in balance if the two sums are the same. The journal is out of balance if the two sums are not the same. A journal out of balance indicates that at least one error has been made in its preparation. You may not proceed to the posting of the journal until all errors have been located and corrected.
4. When the journal is balanced, write in the column totals in ink immediately beneath the pin totals.
5. In ink, draw a double ruled line across all money columns immediately beneath the inked-in column totals.

Forwarding in the Columnar Journal

A new journal page is started at the beginning of each month. Also, during the month a new page must be started whenever a page is filled up. When a new page is started during the month, it is customary to start it off with the balanced totals from the bottom of the previous page. The totals at the end of one page are ''forwarded'' to the next page. This procedure is illustrated in Figure 12.3.

SYNOPTIC JOURNAL   MONTH _May_

DATE	CUSTOMER SUPPLIER	REF NO	BANK		ACCOUNTS RECEIVABLE		ACCOUNTS
			DR	CR	DR	CR	DR
May 19- 4	Cash Sale	57	273 92				
5	P. Rogan	165			440 84		
6	Empire Wholesale						
7	Deluxe Stationers	74		235 40			
7	Arrow Realty	75		800 -			
10	A. Baldwin	76		173 50			173 50
10	English & Co.	77		500 -			500 -
11	R. Mayotte		352 -			352 -	
11	P. Fuhr		620 -			620 -	
13	M. Cham	78		585 -			
13	D. Adams	79		650 -			
14	M. Delgaty	166			209 72		
14	Carl Holm	167			256 80		
17	Continental Railway						
18	Budget Oil						
19	P. Kerr	80		800 -			
20	Ideal Supply	81		475 -			
21	Circle Supply						
21	Deluxe Stationers						
24	Continental Bank		5000 -				
26	Empire Wholesale	82		400 -			400 -
26	Prairie Manufacturing						
26	R. Stoddard		300 -			300 -	
27	M. Cham	83		585 -			
27	D. Adams	84		650 -			
31	Purity Company	168			577 80		
			6545 92	5853 90	1485 16	1272 00	1073 50 3

Figure 12.2 Synoptic journal with entries for one month.

PAGE _41_

SALES OR INCOME CR	PURCHASES DR	SALES TAX PAYABLE CR	OTHER ACCOUNTS			
			ACCOUNT	P.R.	DR	CR
256 –		17 92				
412 –		28 84				
	816 –					
			Supplies		235 40	
			Rent		800 –	
			Wages		585 –	
			Wages		650 –	
196 –		13 72				
240 –		16 80				
			Freight-in		436 50	
			Delivery Exp.		262 54	
			Drawings		800 –	
	475 –					
			Supplies		267 50	
	224 70		Office Equip.		1 053 95	
			Bank Loan			5 000 –
	750 –					
			Wages		585 –	
			Wages		650 –	
540 –		37 80				
1 644 00	2 265 70	115 08			6 325 89	5 000 00

Debits 0 ·	T	Credits 0 ·	T
6 545 · 92	+	5 853 · 90	+
1 485 · 16	+	1 272 · 00	+
1 073 · 50	+	3 811 · 19	+
2 265 · 70	+	1 644 · 00	+
6 325 · 89	+	115 · 08	+
		5 000 · 00	
17 696 · 17	T	17 696 · 17	T

Cross balancing the synoptic journal

A SYNOPTIC PAGE JUST COMPLETED

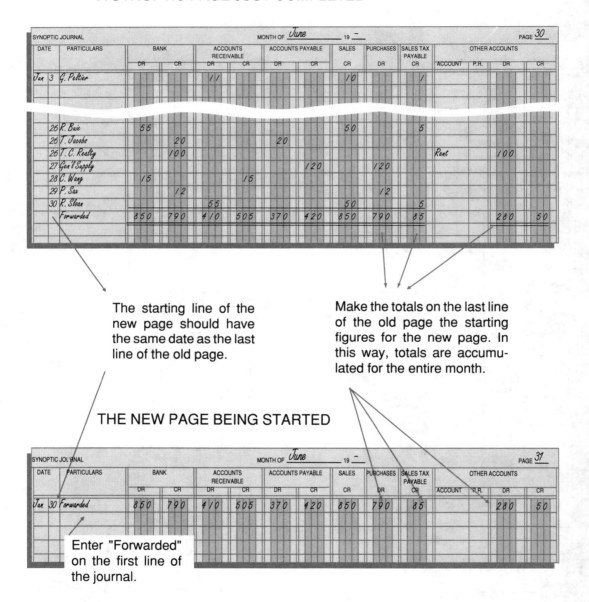

The starting line of the new page should have the same date as the last line of the old page.

Make the totals on the last line of the old page the starting figures for the new page. In this way, totals are accumulated for the entire month.

THE NEW PAGE BEING STARTED

Enter "Forwarded" on the first line of the journal.

Figure 12.3　Forwarding in the synoptic journal.

Posting the Synoptic Journal

Let us recall some facts about posting in general before discussing how to post the synoptic journal. First, posting to the general ledger is done once a month. Therefore the synoptic journal is posted once a month because it is posted to the general ledger. Second, posting to the subsidiary ledgers is done directly from source documents. The subsidiary ledger posting is done daily by an accounting clerk not involved with the general ledger.

Posting the synoptic journal requires a different procedure because it is a multi-columnar journal. The basic procedure is illustrated in Figure 12.4, using a simplified example. Study the example carefully, and observe that:

- the synoptic journal is balanced before posting is begun;
- for each of the "special" columns, the column totals are posted rather than the individual amounts within the columns. By posting only the totals, a great deal of time is saved;
- the Other Accounts section lists items that are generally unrelated. Therefore, the individual amounts contained within the columns in this section have to be posted separately. Posting the Other Accounts section of the synoptic journal is very similar to posting from a two-column general journal.

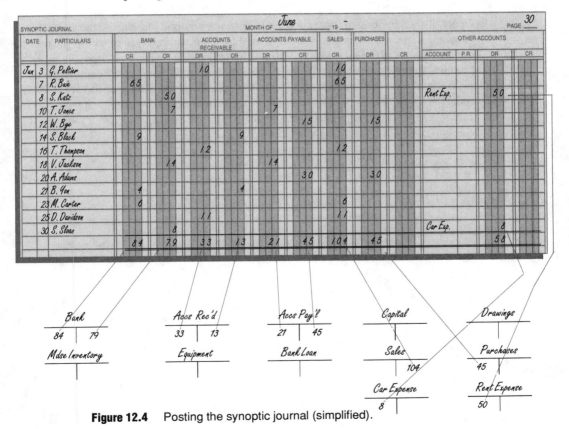

Figure 12.4   Posting the synoptic journal (simplified).

Formal Technique for Posting the Synoptic Journal

Figure 12.5 shows an example of formal posting from the synoptic journal. Observe the following details:

- the entries in the accounts are dated for the last day of the month;
- "Sn" or "SN" and the journal page number are used in the accounts when cross-referencing;
- the following rules apply when cross-referencing in the journal:
  1. the account number is entered in brackets immediately beneath the column total being posted;
  2. for items in the Other Accounts section, the account number is entered in the Posting Reference column beside the amount being posted;
- the account balances are not calculated until all the postings are completed.

The synoptic journal after being entirely posted appears as shown in Figure 12.6, with the posting reference numbers entered.

Two-Journal System

Generally, accounting offices make use of both the synoptic journal and the two-column general journal. The synoptic journal is used by a junior employee to record the routine transactions of the business. The two-column general journal is used by a senior accounting person to record entries of a non-routine, and usually more complex, nature.

In a two-journal system each journal is prepared independently of the other. At the end of every month, each of the journals is posted separately to the general ledger. If the general ledger does not balance, the search for errors must include both journals. The chart on page 411 illustrates the process.

TWO-JOURNAL SYSTEM

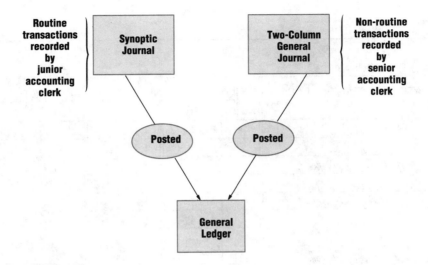

Variations in Journalizing in the Synoptic Journal

1. Debit entries may be entered in Credit columns and credit entries may be entered in Debit columns, but they must be circled, or written in red. This special treatment of an entry indicates that its effect in the column is the opposite to that specified in the column heading. When the column is totaled, the circled item must be subtracted to give the proper total. A refund or a credit invoice would be handled in this way (see Figure 12.7 on page 416).

2. Most accounting entries require only one line in the synoptic journal. However, there are times when two or more lines may be required. This occurs when at least two of the accounts affected by the transaction need to be entered in the Other Accounts section of the journal (see Figure 12.7 on page 416).

SYNOPTIC JOURNAL (Partial)

SYNOPTIC JOURNAL								
DATE	PARTICULARS	CHQ NO	BANK		ACCOUNTS RECEIVABLE		ACCC	
			DR.	CR.	DR.	CR.	DR	
May 19- 4	*Cash Sale*		56 -					
5	*Paul Boxer*				112 -			
6	*Empire Wholesale*							
7	*Deluxe Stationers*	74		37 20				
7	*Arrow Realty*	75		400 -				
31	*Purity Company*				96 -			
			1627 -	2550 90	628 -	571 -	37	
			(1)	(1)				

GENERAL LEDGER (Two accounts only)

ACCOUNT *Bank*						NO. *1*	
DATE	PARTICULARS	P.R.	DEBIT	CREDIT	DR CR	BALANCE	
Mar. 19- 31	*Balance brought forward*	-			DR	135 1 40	
Apr. 30		*Sₙ 41*	1630 20				
30		*Sₙ 41*		1264 19	DR	17 17 41	
May 31		*Sₙ 42*	1627 -				
31		*Sₙ 42*		2550 90			

Figure 12.5 Formal posting from the synoptic journal. The illustration shows only three posting

| | | SALES | PURCHASES | *Supplies* | OTHER ACCOUNTS | | | |
BLE	NO.	CR	DR.	*DR.*	ACCOUNT	P.R.	DR.	CR.
	57	5 6 -						
	165	1 1 2 -						
6 -			3 1 6 -					
				3 7 20				
					Rent Expense	58	4 0 0 -	

MONTH OF *May* 19 —   PAGE *42*

| | 168 | 9 6 - | | | | | | |
| 4 ²² | | 6 8 4 - | 7 7 6 - | 1 5 3 20 | | | 2 3 9 6 ²² | 1 0 0 0 - |

	OUNT *Rent Expense*						NO. *58*	
DATE	PARTICULARS	P.R.	DEBIT	CREDIT	DR/CR	BALANCE	
r. 30	*Balance brought forward*	—			DR	8 0 0 -	
ay 31		*Sr42*	4 0 0 -				

ledger accounts.

DATE		PARTICULARS	CHQ NO	BANK DR.	BANK CR.	ACCOUNTS RECEIVABLE DR.	ACCOUNTS RECEIVABLE CR.	ACCO DR
May	4	Cash Sale		56 -				
	5	Paul Boxer				112 -		
	6	Empire Wholesale						
	7	Deluxe Stationers	74		37 20			
	7	Arrow Realty	75		400 -			
	10	A. Baldwin	76		73 50			7
	10	G. English & Co.	77		46 20			4
	11	R. Smith		96 -			96 -	
	11	F. Jones		375 -			375 -	
	13	M. Field	78		312 -			
	13	R. French	79		285 -			
	14	M. Birch				250 -		
	14	Y. Ash				170 -		
	17	Continental Railway						
	18	Budget Oil						
	19	G. Ripley	80		300 -			
	20	Ideal Supply	81		300 -			
	21	Circle Supplies						
	21	Deluxe Stationers						
	24	Crescent Bank		1000 -				
	26	Empire Wholesale	82		200 -			20
	26	Prairie Mfg.						
	26	R. Stoddard		100 -			100 -	
	27	M. Field	83		312 -			
	27	R. French	84		285 -			
	31	Purity Company				96 -		
				1627 -	2550 90	628 -	571 -	3 7
				(1)	(1)	(2)	(2)	(21

Figure 12.6   Synoptic journal showing posting references.

May – 42

BLE		NO.	SALES CR.	PURCHASES DR.	*Supplies DR.*		ACCOUNT	P.R.	DR.	CR.
		57	5 6 –							
		165	1 1 2 –							
6 –				3 1 6 –						
					3 7 20					
						Rent Expense	56	4 0 0 –	
						Wages Expense	58	3 1 2 –	
						Wages Expense	58	2 8 5 –	
		166	2 5 0 –						
		167	1 7 0 –						
7 50						Freight-in	55	8 7 50	
4 72						Delivery Exp.	53	6 4 72	
						Ripley Drugs	32	3 0 0 –	
				3 0 0 –					
6 –					4 6 –				
0 –					7 0 –	Office Equip.	9	3 5 0 –	
						Bank Loan	22		1 0 0 0 –
0 –				1 6 0 –					
						Wages Expense	58	3 1 2 –	
						Wages Expense	58	2 8 5 –	
		168	9 6 –						
4 22			6 8 4 –	7 7 6 –	1 5 3 20			2 3 9 6 22	1 0 0 0 –
			(41)	(51)	(4)				

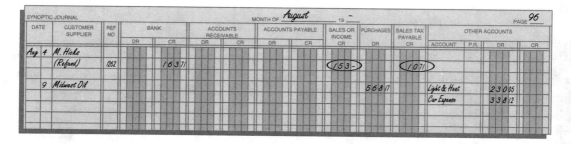

Figure 12.7 Variations in recording in the synoptic journal.

SECTION REVIEW QUESTIONS

1. The two-column general journal is mostly used for what type of transaction?
2. For what type of transaction are the specialized journals used?
3. Define "multi-columnar" journal.
4. Why does each line of the synoptic journal usually balance?
5. Explain how the synoptic journal saves time when entries are posted.
6. For which items are special columns set up in the synoptic journal?
7. Explain how to balance a synoptic journal.
8. Explain how to forward the synoptic journal.
9. Explain how to cross-reference in the synoptic journal.
10. Why is a general journal usually used along with a synoptic journal?
11. Describe how to record a debit entry in a credit column. How is the entry handled when the columns are being totaled?
12. Explain why some accounting entries require more than one line in the synoptic journal.

SECTION EXERCISES

1. **Indicate whether each of the following statements is true or false by entering a "T" or an "F" in the space indicated in your Workbook. Explain the reason for each "F" response in the space provided.**

   1. A non-routine transaction is one that is out of the ordinary.
   2. The synoptic journal is ideally suited to a large company.
   3. A synoptic journal is a multi-columnar journal.
   4. In the synoptic journal there would be a special column for Sales Tax Payable because it is a frequently occurring item.
   5. The headings in a synoptic journal are always the same as those shown in the textbook.

6. The main advantage of the synoptic journal is time saved in journalizing transactions.

7. An advantage of the synoptic journal is that it is not necessary to balance the accounting entry for every transaction.

8. The synoptic journal is balanced at the end of every month and at the end of every page.

9. The accuracy of the synoptic journal is checked by cross balancing.

10. The synoptic journal should be cross balanced before the final totals are inked in and the journal ruled off.

11. It is customary to forward the totals from one page of the synoptic journal to the next.

12. The total of the Other Accounts debit section is posted as a debit to the general ledger.

13. The postings from the synoptic journal are dated the last day of the month.

14. No cross-referencing is necessary when using a synoptic journal.

15. A two-journal system provides a different route for non-routine transactions.

16. A debit amount can be entered in a credit column if it is circled.

17. Every entry in the synoptic journal takes only one line.

---

2. **On page 19 of the synoptic journal of Donway Distributing, record the transactions listed below for the month of August, 19—. Add sales tax of seven per cent on all sales of merchandise. Use the following chart of accounts.**

DONWAY DISTRIBUTING
Chart of Accounts
101 Bank
105 Accounts Receivable
110 Merchandise Inventory
115 Supplies
118 Land
120 Building
125 Office Equipment
201 Accounts Payable
205 Bank Loan
210 Sales Tax Payable
215 Mortgage Payable
305 A. Orlando—Capital
310 A. Orlando—Drawings
405 Sales
505 Purchases
510 Freight-in
515 Advertising
520 Building Maintenance
525 Car Expense
530 Interest and Bank Charges

535 Light and Heat
540 Miscellaneous Expense
545 Telephone
550 Wages

TRANSACTIONS

August

2 *Cheque Copy No. 702*
   To D. Macdonald; for painting of the business premises; $856.00.

3 *Sales Invoice No. 210*
   To N. Rae; sale of goods on account; $184.00 plus sales tax.
   Cash Receipt
   From Viceroy Homes; on account; $150.00.

5 *Cheque Copy No. 703*
   To T. Vint; for wages; $290.00.
   Cash Sales Slip No. 91
   To M. Franci; cash sale of merchandise; $85.00 plus sales tax.

8 *Cheque Copy No. 704*
   To Cash; for cash purchase of postage stamps; $320.00. (Cashed by an
   employee who purchased the stamps.)
   Sales Invoice No. 211
   To Atlas Stores; sale of goods on account; $502 plus sales tax.

9 *Purchase Invoice*
   From Diamond Wholesalers; merchandise purchased on account; $925.00.

10 *Purchase Invoice*
   From Continental Railway; for freight charges on incoming goods; $315.00.

11 *Cash Sales Slip No. 92*
   To J. Vincent; cash sale of merchandise; $150.00 plus sales tax.

12 *Cheque Copy No. 705*
   To Vance Brothers; on account; $300.00.
   Cheque Copy No. 706
   To T. Vint; for wages; $290.00.

15 *Cheque Copy No. 707*
   To *Century News*; for newspaper advertisement; $42.00.
   Cheque Copy No. 708
   To A. Orlando; for owner's personal use; $300.00.

18 *Cash Sales Slip No. 93*
   To A. Anderson, cash sale of merchandise; $55.00 plus sales tax.

19 *Cheque Copy No. 709*
   To Merry Manufacturing; on account; $500.00.
   Cheque Copy No. 710
   To T. Vint; for wages; $290.00.
   Cash Receipt
   From J. Regnault; on account; $200.00.

22 *Cheque Copy No. 711*
        To Trade Group; mortgage instalment; $356.75 ($285.20 is debt reduction; $71.55 is interest expense).
    Sales Invoice No. 212
        To T. Schmidt; sale of goods on account; $170.00 plus sales tax.
23 *Purchase Invoice*
        From Deluxe Oil Company; $240.00 ($180.00 for business use; $60.00 for personal use by owner).
24 *Bank Debit Advice*
        From General Bank; for service charge; $42.00.
25 *Cheque Copy No. 712*
        To A. Orlando; for owner's personal use; $500.00.
26 *Cash Sales Slip No. 94*
        To K. Beka; cash sale of merchandise; $110.00 plus sales tax.
    Cheque Copy No. 713
        To T. Vint; for wages; $290.00.
29 *Purchase Invoice*
        From Federated Supply; for the purchase of merchandise; $1 240.00.
30 *Cheque Copy No. 714*
        To Public Utilities Commission; for hydro charges for month; $146.00.
31 *Sales Invoice No. 213*
        To Brian Keep; sale of goods on account; $190.00 plus sales tax.
    Cash Receipt
        From J. Klassen; on account; $400.00.

After recording the transactions do the following:
   1. Cross balance and rule the journal.
   2. Summarize the postings that would be made to the general ledger. List the information in three columns: Account; Debit Amount; Credit Amount. Show that the postings are balanced by totaling the two money columns.

3. **This exercise also appears in your Workbook.**
    Shown on p. 420, in condensed form, are the synoptic journal and the T-account general ledger of Plastic Products, owned by Jean Webb.
    1. Post the synoptic journal to the general ledger. Ignore dates and cross-references. Use check marks to indicate that postings are completed.
    2. Take off a general ledger trial balance.

Synoptic Journal

SYNOPTIC JOURNAL		BANK		ACCOUNTS RECEIVABLE		ACCOUNTS PAYABLE		SALES	PURCHASES	SALES TAX PAYABLE	OTHER ACCOUNTS			
DATE	PARTICULARS	DR	CR	DR	CR	DR	CR	CR	DR	CR	ACCOUNT	P.R.	DR	CR
Jun 20	Forwarded	1800	1450	2150	1970	1270	1350	1750	1460	160				
23	Laine	55						50		5				
23	Moore		60								Rent		60	
24	Park			110				100		10				
25	Reid	80			80									
25	Ruel		250			250								
25	Sacerty		20								Telephone		20	
26	Bass						150		150					
26	Clayton						300		300					
27	Delski		40								Wages		40	
27	Eady						90				Car Exp.		90	
27	Green		70								Freight		70	
27	Hook	400			400									
30	Klaus		230			230								
30	McCoy	88						80		8				
30	Nagy			77				70		7				
30	Perry			44				40		4				
		2423	2120	2381	2450	1750	1890	2090	1910	194			280	

General Ledger

Bank	Accounts Receivable	Mdse Inventory	Supplies
70	350	900	100

Equipment	Bank Loan	Accounts Payable	Sales Tax Payable
2 000	1 000	150	300

J. Webb, Capital	J. Webb, Drawings	Sales	Bank Charges
3020	500	4 500	40

Car Expenses	Freight-in	General Expenses	Purchases
500	100	90	1 700

Rent	Telephone	Utilities	Wages
300	50	1 220	750

4.   **Workbook Exercise: Posting the synoptic journal to a simple ledger.**

Comprehensive Exercise

5. F. Dunn is the sole proprietor of Crest Hardware in Iona, N.S. He operates the store with the assistance of his wife and some occasional part-time help. Mrs. Dunn works in the store and is also responsible for all direct aspects of accounting. The financial statements are prepared annually from her records by a professional accountant.

The books of account are very simple and consist of a general ledger, an accounts receivable ledger, an accounts payable ledger, and a synoptic journal. The last page used in the synoptic journal is page 72.

Most of the sales of the business are cash sales. The rate of sales tax is seven per cent. The cash receipts are deposited in the bank on a daily basis. All payments are made by cheque.

The number of accounts in both subsidiary ledgers is very small. Mr. Dunn grants credit to only a few customers and buys his stock from only a few suppliers. Because of the small number of debtors and creditors the subsidiary ledger routine is very simple. All transactions are recorded in the synoptic journal and the postings to the subsidiary ledgers are made directly from the source documents.

The three ledgers of Crest Hardware are set up in the Workbook from the following trial balances.

CREST HARDWARE
TRIAL BALANCE
JUNE 30, 19--

101 Bank	$ 12 400.00	
105 Accounts Receivable	13 365.25	
110 Merchandise Inventory	46 090.20	
115 Supplies	1 395.00	
120 Store Equipment	20 906.00	
130 Delivery Equipment	19 500.00	
201 Accounts Payable		$10 265.35
205 Sales Tax Payable		2 240.00
210 Loan Payable—Federal Finance		8 550.85
301 F. Dunn, Capital		89 952.08
302 F. Dunn, Drawings	6 000.00	
401 Sales		48 585.50
505 Delivery Expense	5 258.00	
510 Freight-in	956.23	
515 General Expense	2 953.10	
520 Purchases	14 120.00	
525 Rent Expense	2 400.00	
530 Wages Expense	14 250.00	
	$159 593.78	$159 593.78

CREST HARDWARE
ACCOUNTS RECEIVABLE TRIAL BALANCE
JUNE 30, 19--

R. Lai (Invoice 1407)	$ 4 072.15
G. Langford (Invoice 1431)	6 316.20
R. Potts (Invoice 1436)	2 976.90
	$13 365.25

CREST HARDWARE
ACCOUNTS PAYABLE TRIAL BALANCE
JUNE 30, 19--

City Hardware Supply (their Invoice No. 17421)	$ 6 742.10
Special Steel Products (their Invoice No. 147A)	3 523.25
	$10 265.35

1. Record the journal entries in the synoptic journal for the transactions listed below. Post to the subsidiary ledgers on a daily basis. No names are recorded in the synoptic journal for cash sales.

TRANSACTIONS

July

2 *Cash Sales Slip* No. 206
      $216.00 plus sales tax.
      Sales Invoice
      No. 1475, to R. Lai, $190.00 plus sales tax.
      Purchase Invoice
      No. 18021, from City Hardware Supply, $1 264.25, for purchase of merchandise.
3 *Cash Sales Slip* No. 207
      $102.00 plus sales tax.
      Cash Receipt
      From R. Lai, $4 072.15 on account.
5 *Cash Sales Slip* No. 208
      $55.00 plus sales tax.
6 *Cash Sales Slip* No. 209
      $350.00 plus sales tax.
      Cheque Copy
      No. 316, to R. Niosi, $98, wages for part-time help.
7 *Cash Sales Slip* No. 210
      $140.00 plus sales tax.
      Purchase Invoice
      No. 18340, from City Hardware Supply, $2 316.25, for purchase of merchandise.
      Cheque Copies
      No. 317, Special Steel Products, $500, on account.
      No. 318, City Hardware Supply, $6 742.10 paying No. 17421.
      No. 319, F. Dunn, $250, drawings.
9 *Cash Sales Slip* No. 211
      $260.00 plus sales tax.
10 *Cash Sales Slip* No. 212
      $75.00 plus sales tax.
      Sales Invoice
      No. 1476, to G. Langford, $590 plus sales tax.
12 *Cash Sales Slip* No. 213
      $40.00 plus sales tax.
      Purchase Invoice
      No. 192A, Special Steel Products, $375.00 for purchase of merchandise.
      Cheque Copy
      No. 320, to J. Sacco, $100 wages for part-time help.
13 *Cash Sales Slip* No. 214
      $250.00 plus sales tax.

Cheque Copy

    No. 321, to Special Steel Products, $3 023.25 balance of 147A.

14 *Cash Sales Slip* No. 215

    $185.00 plus sales tax.

Sales Invoice

    No. 1477, to R. Potts, $311.00 plus sales tax.

Purchase Invoice

    No. 1244, from Clix Oil Company, $275.00 for gasoline and oil used in the delivery truck.

Cheque Copies

    No. 322, F. Dunn, $150, drawings.

    No. 323, to Provincial Treasurer, $2 240.00, paying sales tax for previous month.

16 *Cash Sales Slip* No. 216

    $175.00 plus sales tax.

Cash Receipt

    From G. Langford, $6 316.20 in payment of invoice No. 1431.

17 *Cash Sales Slip* No. 217

    $225.00 plus sales tax.

Purchase Invoice

    No. 344, Joe Jay Transport, $375.15, charges for transportation on incoming merchandise.

19 *Cash Sales Slip* No. 218

    $240.00 plus sales tax.

Cheque Copy

    No. 324, to Oak Investments, $400, for the rent for the month.

20 *Cash Sales Slip* No. 219

    $142.00 plus sales tax.

21 *Cash Sales Slip* No. 220

    $264.00 plus sales tax

Cheque Copy

    No. 325, to F. Dunn, $250, drawings.

23 *Cash Sales Slip* No. 221

    $89.00 plus sales tax.

Sales Invoice

    No. 1478, to R. Lai, $311.00 plus sales tax.

Cheque Copies

    No. 326, to D. Phin, $75 part-time wages.

    No. 327, to Public Utilities Commission, $176.10 cash payment of electricity and water bills.

    No. 328, to City Telephone Company, $149.00 cash payment of telephone bill.

24 *Cash Sales Slip* No. 222

    $248.00 plus sales tax.

Cash Receipt

    From R. Lai, $203.30, invoice No. 1475.

---

26 *Cash Sales Slip* No. 223
    $55.00 plus sales tax.
    Cheque Copy
    No. 329, to City Hardware Supply, $1 264.25, for invoice No. 18021.
27 *Cash Sales Slip* No. 224
    $80.00 plus sales tax.
28 *Cash Sales Slip* No. 225
    $343.00 plus sales tax.
    Cheque Copy
    No. 330, to F. Dunn, $250, drawings.
    Purchase Invoice
    No. 18472, from City Hardware Supply, $350.00 for store supplies.

2. Balance the synoptic journal.
3. Post the synoptic journal to the general ledger.
4. Balance the general ledger.
5. Balance the subsidiary ledgers.

12.2 *THE FIVE-JOURNAL SYSTEM*

The synoptic journal described in the previous section is suitable only for a very small business or organization. The reason is that only one person at a time can work on it. Most businesses soon grow to a point where more than one person needs to be involved in the journalizing process. Systems using more than one journal have been developed

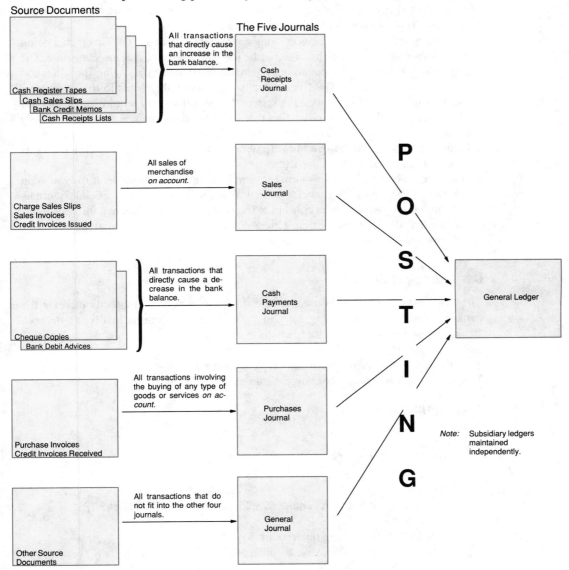

Figure 12.8 Basic structure of the five-journal system.

for this reason. The five-journal system is such a system. However, it should be kept in mind that these journals are not used in a computerized system.

The **five-journal system** is one in which five separate journals are operated at the same time, each journal restricted to a particular type of transaction. The basic structure of the five-journal system is illustrated in Figure 12.8. As you can see, the accounting entries are channelled from the various source documents into the five separate journals. Each journal is restricted to a particular type of transaction. Each of the journals is posted individually to the general ledger. As before, the subsidiary ledgers are posted independently from separate copies of the source documents.

There are two main advantages to using a number of journals. The first is that doing so allows several people to be involved in the journalizing process at the same time. The second is that it makes the accounting system more efficient by allowing specialization of duties among the staff. The five-journal system inevitably leads to the accounting clerks becoming specialists within the system. Large offices may require a specialist for each journal. Smaller offices often find that one person can handle two journals very well. A natural relationship exists between sales and cash receipts. There is also a natural relationship between purchases and cash payments. These pairs make very effective units of work within the accounting department.

Learning to operate the five-journal system is not going to be difficult for you. You will find no difference in the general journal. Also, each of the new ''special'' journals is a columnar journal similar in concept to the synoptic journal. The real difference lies in the fact that all of the routine transactions do not go into a single journal. Instead, they are channelled into one of four special journals.

Cash Receipts Journal

The **cash receipts journal** is used to record all transactions that directly increase the bank balance. Every accounting entry in the cash receipts journal involves a debit to Bank. The two most common transactions in the cash receipts journal are ''cash sales'' and ''receipts on account.''

A partially completed page from a typical cash receipts journal is shown in Figure 12.9. It was prepared from the source documents listed below.

TRANSACTIONS

February
  4 *Cash Sales Slip No. 64*
       Issued to R. Lentz; merchandise $118.00; sales tax $8.26; total $126.26.
     Cash Sales Slip No. 65
       Issued to M. Reid; merchandise $78.25; sales tax $5.48; total $83.73.
  5 *Cash Receipts*
       Received from T. Song on account; $500.00.
       Received from P. Yurick on account; $160.50.
  6 *Cash Sales Slip No. 66*
       Issued to G. Ostrum; merchandise $105.00; sales tax $7.35; total $112.35.

6   *Cash Receipt*
    Received from K. Pape on account; $106.47.
7   *Bank Credit Advice*
    Received from Centennial Bank; for interest earned; $725.00.
8   *Cash Sales Slip No. 67*
    Issued to C. Drew; merchandise $85.25; sales tax $5.97; total $91.22.

Special Considerations

- The cash receipts journal is a columnar journal and follows the rules for all columnar journals.
- Cash sales go in the cash receipts journal. Sales on account go in the sales journal. If a sale is partly for cash and partly on account, it goes into the cash receipts journal.

CASH RECEIPTS JOURNAL		MONTH OF *Feb*	19____				PAGE *16*
DATE	PARTICULARS	OTHER ACCOUNTS CR			SALES TAX PAYABLE CR	SALES CR	ACCOUNTS RECEIVABLE CR	REF. NO.	BANK DR
		ACCOUNT	P.R.	AMOUNT					
Feb 4	R. Lentz				8 26	1 1 8 -		64	1 2 6 26
4	M. Reid				5 48	7 8 25		65	8 3 73
5	F. Song						5 0 0 -		5 0 0 -
5	P. Yurich						1 6 0 50		1 6 0 50
6	C. Ostrum				7 35	1 0 5 -		66	1 1 2 35
6	K. Pape						1 0 6 47		1 0 6 47
7	Centennial Bank	Interest Inc.		7 2 5 -					7 2 5 -
8	C. Drew				5 97	8 5 25		67	9 1 22

Figure 12.9   A partially completed page of a cash receipts journal.

Sales Journal

The sales journal is used to record all transactions involving the sale of merchandise on account. Transactions related to sales on account are the only ones entered in the sales journal. The source documents for entries to the sales journal are sales invoices, credit invoices, and charge sales slips.

A partially completed page from a sales journal is shown in Figure 12.10. It was prepared from the following transactions.

TRANSACTIONS

February
5   *Sales Invoice No. 652*
    Issued to R. Rau; merchandise $59.00; sales tax $4.13; total $63.13.
    Charge Sales Slip No. 125
    Issued to L. Sauve; merchandise $84.50; sales tax $5.92; total $90.42.

6 *Credit Invoice No. 653*

    Issued to C. Myzk for unsatisfactory merchandise returned; merchandise $145.00; sales tax $10.15; total $155.15.

    Sales Invoice No. 654

        Issued to R. Halfmoon; merchandise $245.85; sales tax $17.21; total $263.06.

7 *Charge Sales Slip No. 126*

    Issued to H. Didyk; merchandise $110.25; sales tax $7.72; total $117.97.

8 *Sales Invoice No. 655*

    Issued to A. Han; merchandise $65.00; sales tax $4.55; total $69.55.

Special Considerations

- Only special columns are used in the sales journal.
- The rules for columnar journals apply to the sales journal.

SALES JOURNAL   MONTH OF _Feb._ 19 —   PAGE _22_

DATE		PARTICULARS	REF. NO.	SALES TAX PAYABLE CR			SALES CR	ACCOUNTS RECEIVABLE DR
Feb	5	R. Rau	652	4 13			59 -	63 13
	5	L. Sauve	125	5 92			84 50	90 42
	6	C. Myzk (credit)	653	10 15			45 -	55 15
	6	R. Halfmoon	654	17 21			245 85	263 06
	7	H. Didyk	126	7 72			110 25	117 97
	8	E. Han	655	4 55			65 -	69 55

Figure 12.10   A partially completed page of a sales journal.

Cash Payments Journal

The **cash payments journal** is used to record all transactions that directly decrease the bank balance. Every accounting entry in the cash payments journal results in a credit to Bank. The most common type of transaction recorded in the cash payments journal involves the issuing of a cheque. Cheques may be issued for a number of reasons.

Figure 12.11 shows a partially completed page of a cash payments journal. The journal was prepared from the following transactions.

TRANSACTIONS

February

3 *Cheque Copies*

    No. 72; issued to Collins Bros. on account; $250.00.

    No. 73; issued to Taylor Company on account; $550.00.

4   *Bank Debit Advice*

   Received from Centennial Bank; for bank service charges; $54.65.

   Cheque Copies

   No. 74; issued to B. Sims for wages; $650.21.

   No. 75; issued to C. Tett for wages; $702.35.

5   *Cheque Copies*

   No. 76; issued to D. Wedow, the owner, for personal use; $1 000.

   No. 77; issued to Harbour Trade Centre for the cash purchase of merchandise
   for resale; $905.65.

   No. 78; issued to Kyro's Supply; for the cash purchase of supplies; $323.73.

   No. 79; Issued to Superior Engineering; a down payment on the purchase of
   equipment costing $5 029.00; $1 000.

Special Considerations

- The cash payments journal is sometimes called the cash disbursements journal.
- The cash payments journal follows the rules for columnar journals.
- Purchases for cash go into the cash payments journal. Purchases on account go into
  the purchases journal. A purchase that is partly paid for by cash goes into the cash
  payments journal.

PAYMENTS JOURNAL   MONTH OF *Feb* 19 –   PAGE *19*

DATE		PARTICULARS	OTHER ACCOUNTS DR			WAGES DR	PURCHASES DR	ACCOUNTS PAYABLE DR	REF. NO.	BANK CR
			ACCOUNT	P.R.	AMOUNT					
Feb	3	Collins Bros.						250 -	72	250 -
	3	Taylor Company						550 -	73	550 -
	4	Centennial Bank	Bank Charges		54 65					54 65
	4	B. Sims				650 21			74	650 21
	4	C. Tett				702 35			75	702 35
	5	D. Wedow	Drawings		1000 -				76	1000 -
	5	Harbour Trading					905 65		77	905 65
	5	Kyro's Supply	Supplies		323 73				78	323 73
	5	Superior Eng'g	Equipment		5029 -			4029 -	79	1000 -

Figure 12.11   A partially completed page of a cash payments journal.

Purchases Journal

The **purchases journal** is used to record all transactions involving the buying of goods
or services on account. Every accounting entry in the purchases journal results in a credit
to Accounts Payable. The suppliers' invoices are the source documents for entries in the
purchases journal.

A partially completed page of a purchases journal is shown in Figure 12.12. The journal was prepared from the following transactions.

TRANSACTIONS

February

3 *Purchase Invoice*
   Received from Williams Equipment; for repairs to warehouse equipment; $562.50.

4 *Purchase Invoice*
   Received from Acklands; for warehouse and office supplies; $762.58.
   Purchase Invoice
   Received from Pascoe's; for items charged to miscellaneous expense; $145.36.

5 *Purchase Invoice*
   Received from Reliable Trading; for merchandise for resale; $2 500.00.
   Purchase Invoice
   Received from Mason and Mason; for merchandise for resale; $1 950.00.

6 *Purchase Invoice*
   Received from Grand Trunk Railway; for transportation charges on incoming merchandise; $256.00.
   Purchase Invoice
   Received from Hector Oil Company; for gas and oil used in the company automobiles; $315.62.

Special Considerations

. The purchases journal follows the rules for all columnar journals.

. The accountant for a business may file purchase invoices alphabetically or numerically. Where numerical order is used, a reference number must be placed on every purchase invoice received.

PURCHASES JOURNAL   MONTH OF _Feb_____ 19_____   PAGE _31_____

| DATE | PARTICULARS | OTHER ACCOUNTS DR | | | CAR EXPENSE DR | SUPPLIES DR | PURCHASES DR | REF. NO. | ACCOUNTS PAYABLE CR |
		ACCOUNT	P.R.	AMOUNT					
Feb 3	Williams Equip.	Bldg. Mntnce		5 6 2 50				120	5 6 2 50
4	Acklands					7 6 2 58		121	7 6 2 58
4	Pascoe's	Msc. Exp.		1 4 5 36				122	1 4 5 36
5	Reliable Trading						2 5 0 0 -	123	2 5 0 0 -
5	Mason & Mason						1 9 5 0 -	124	1 9 5 0 -
6	Grand Trunk Rwy.	Freight-in		2 5 6 -				125	2 5 6 -
6	Hector Oil				3 1 5 62			126	3 1 5 62

Figure 12.12   A partially completed page of a purchases journal.

Posting in the Five-Journal System

The four special journals must be cross balanced and ruled before they can be posted at the end of each month. The procedure for balancing a columnar journal was learned in the previous section. Basically, you must add the debit column totals, add the credit column totals, and see that the two sums are the same. If the sums are equal, the journal is ruled and ready for posting.

You have already learned how to post the general journal. You have just learned how to post a columnar journal. This is almost all that you need to know to post in the five-journal system.

Each journal is posted separately but in a handwritten system the order in which they are posted does not matter. No attempt to balance the ledger should be made until all five journals have been posted.

There is no change in the way subsidiary ledgers are handled. They are still posted directly from copies of source documents and are balanced against their control accounts monthly.

Cross-Referencing

When several journals are used it becomes necessary to identify them specifically by means of a code. For example, page 17 of the general journal is identified as GJ17. Each of the several journals is given its own simple code as follows.

Journal	Code
Cash Receipts	CR
Cash Payments	CP
Sales	S
Purchases	P
General	GJ or J
Synoptic	SN or Sn

The sample account shown below in Figure 12.13 uses the new coded posting references in an account.

Figure 12.13 A ledger account showing the journal codes.

SECTION REVIEW QUESTIONS

1. Why is the synoptic journal suitable only for a small business or organization?
2. Describe the five-journal system.
3. Give the two main advantages of using a number of journals.
4. Describe the types of transactions that go in each of the four special journals.
5. What are the two most common transactions that are entered in a cash receipts journal?
6. How do you handle a sale that is partly on account and partly for cash?
7. Why is a "general" section not needed in the sales journal?
8. Every accounting entry in the cash payments journal has one common element. What is it?
9. Give another name for the cash payments journal.
10. What is the source document for all entries in the purchases journal?
11. In what order are the journals posted in a five-journal system?
12. What codes are used for cross-referencing in the five-journal system?

SECTION EXERCISES

1. A list of transactions appears below. **From this list select and record those transactions that would be recorded in the cash payments journal.**

TRANSACTIONS

April
1 The owner, Patricia Sopinka, increased her equity in the business by depositing her personal cheque for $1 000 in the business bank account.
2 Issued cheque No. 40 to J. Chekov for the cash purchase of supplies, $155.15.
3 Issued sales invoice No. 70 to M. Kosir. This was for the sale of merchandise of $180 plus sales tax of seven per cent.
5 Received a purchase invoice from Sue Brown Manufacturing for the purchase of merchandise, $791.80.
8 Issued cheque No. 41 to Chong Supply Co. for the cash purchase of merchandise, $342.40.
9 Received a cheque from Carol Padovik on account, $350.
10 Issued cheque No. 42 to Municipal Hydro for the cash purchase of electricity for one month, $78.
12 Received a purchase invoice from District Supply for the purchase of supplies, $450.47.
15 Issued cheque No. 43 to Sharon Maki Wholesale on account, $750.
17 Issued sales invoice No. 71 to Carole's Catering. This was for the sale of merchandise of $250 plus sales tax of seven per cent.
19 Received a debit memo from the bank for service charges for one month, $54.00.
22 Received a memo from the owner stating that she had collected $200 on account from P. Walker but had kept the money for her personal use.
24 Cash sales slip No. 72 was issued for the cash sale of merchandise, $85 plus sales tax of $5.95.

25 Issued cheque No. 44 for the cash payment of the telephone bill for one month, $45.
30 Issued cheque No. 45 to Projects Inc. on account, $1 000.

Cross balance the journal.

---

2. **In which of the five journals would each transaction below be recorded?**

TRANSACTIONS

1. A cheque is issued to a supplier on account.
2. A purchase invoice is received from a supplier of merchandise.
3. A cheque is received on account from a customer.
4. A cash sale is made to a customer.
5. A sale on account is made to a customer.
6. A cheque is issued to the owner for his personal use.
7. A cheque is issued to pay the wages for the period.
8. A sales invoice is issued.
9. A correcting entry is made to transfer a debit amount from the Supplies account to the Miscellaneous Expense account.
10. A cheque is issued to pay for a cash purchase of merchandise.
11. A bank debit advice for a service charge is received.
12. A cheque is issued to a supplier on account.
13. A cheque is issued to pay for the monthly rent.
14. A bank debit advice is received with respect to a bad cheque.
15. A bank credit advice is received with respect to interest earned.
16. A new typewriter is purchased and a down payment is required. A cheque is issued.
17. The owner collects a debt from a customer but keeps the money for his personal use.
18. The owner spends a sum of money out of his own pocket for business purposes and is reimbursed by means of a cheque.

---

3. 1. **Journalize the transactions shown below in the five journals of Domino Wholesale Company.** The accounts for Domino Wholesale Company are as follows:

Bank	Purchases
Accounts Receivable	Freight-in
Merchandise Inventory	Bank Charges
Supplies	Delivery Expense
Equipment	General Expense
Accounts Payable	Light, Heat, and Water
Sales Tax Payable	Postage Expense
Anna Popov, Capital	Rent Expense
Anna Popov, Drawings	Telephone Expense
Sales	Wages Expense

TRANSACTIONS   (**Note:** Seven per cent sales tax to be added to all sales)

Date	Source Document	No.	Name	Explanation	Amount
May 1	Cheque copy	75	Morris and Hannah	Rent for May	$425.00
2	Purchase Invoice		Grinnelco	Merchandise	378.00
2	Cash receipt		R. Jones	On account	436.80
4	Cash sales slip	97	A. Racicot	Merchandise sold	70.00
4	Information memo			An error was discovered in the general ledger. An amount of $30 which had been debited to General Expense should have been debited to Supplies.	30.00
5	Cheque copy	76	P. Fobert	Wages	275.00
8	Sales invoice	317	C. Perry	Goods sold	215.00
9	Cash receipt		S. Storey	On account	95.00
9	Purchase invoice		Wonder Mfg.	Supplies	110.25
9	Cheque copy	77	A. Popov	Personal use	300.00
10	Purchase invoice		Pressed Fittings	Merchandise	435.75
10	Sales invoice	318	Mercer Company	Goods sold	190.00
11	Cash receipt		R. Russell	On account	200.00
12	Purchase invoice		Newday Supplies	Supplies	210.00
12	Cheque copy	78	General Supply	On account	$125.50
15	Purchase invoice		Baldwin's	Supplies	78.75
15	Sales invoice	319	T. Ward	Goods sold	216.00
16	Credit invoice issued	320	C. Perry	Merchandise returned $70 plus $4.90 tax	74.90
16	Cash receipt		R. Grant	On account	150.00
17	Cash sales slip	98	P. Fuhrman	Goods sold	65.00
17	Sales invoice	321	B. Adler	Goods sold	195.00
18	Cheque copy	79	Provincial Treasurer	Sales tax for prior month	497.07
19	Purchase invoice		Continental Railway	Freight-in	96.40
19	Sales invoice	322	G. Nolan	Goods sold	110.00
19	Information memo			An error was detected in the accounts receivable ledger. An amount of $62 which should have been credited to J. Walker's account was credited in error to M. Walker's account.	62.00
22	Cheque copy	80	Bell Telephone	Telephone	52.70

Date	Source Document	No.	Name	Explanation	Amount
May 22	Cheque copy	81	Baldwin's	Cash purchase of supplies	26.25
23	Sales invoice	323	W. Phillips	Goods sold	280.00
23	Cash sales slip	99	P. Leonard	Goods sold $190 Down payment $50	190.00 50.00
23	Cash sales slip	100	H. Fogh	Goods sold	370.00
24	Credit invoice received		Grinnelco	For goods returned $55 plus tax	58.85
25	Bank debit memo		Western Bank	Bank service charge	34.70
25	Cheque copy	82	A. Popov	Personal use	300.00
26	Cheque copy	83	O.K. Welding	On account	150.00
29	Cheque copy	84	A. Popov	Repaying owner for expenditures that she made for business purposes. Charge: General Expense 35.00 Supplies 110.00	145.00
29	Bank debit memo		Western Bank	NSF cheque of R. Russell	200.00
30	Cheque copy	85	S. Tybo	Wages	300.00
31	Purchase invoice		Jim's Garage	Gas and oil used in the delivery vehicle, $124.80; in the owner's car, $62.50	187.30

2. Balance and rule each of the five journals.

4. Workbook Exercise: Posting and balancing in a five-journal system (simplified).

5. Workbook Exercise: Journalizing, posting and balancing in a five-journal system (unsimplified).

12.3 *CASH DISCOUNTS*

You are probably already acquainted with cash discounts. They are usually offered on the bills for utilities in the home, such as the water, hydro, gas, or oil bills.

A **cash discount** is a reduction of the amount of a bill if payment is made on or before the discount date stated on the bill. The purpose of a cash discount is to encourage the customer to pay promptly. Many businesses, like utility companies, offer cash discounts to their customers.

Terms of Sale

Every business establishes certain terms of sale with its customers. The phrase **terms of sale** refers to the arrangements made with customers as to when the goods or services are to be paid for and whether a cash discount is offered.

There are various terms of sale. The most common ones are outlined below.

Standard Terms of Sale

1. **C.O.D.** Cash on delivery. The goods must be paid for at the time they are delivered.
2. **On Account** or **Charge**. The full amount of the invoice is due at the time the invoice is received but a brief time, usually 25 days, is given to make payment.
3. **30 Days** or **Net 30**. The full amount of the invoice is due 30 days after the date of the invoice.
   60 Days or **Net 60**. The full amount of the invoice is due 60 days after the date of the invoice.
4. **2/10,N/30**. This is read as "two per cent, ten, net thirty" or just "Two, ten, net thirty." If the bill is paid within 10 days of the invoice date, a cash discount of two per cent may be taken. Otherwise, the full amount of the invoice is due 30 days after the invoice date.
   1/15,N/60. If the bill is paid within 15 days of the invoice date, a cash discount of one per cent may be taken. Otherwise, the full amount of the invoice is due 60 days after the invoice date.

The terms of sale often depend on the customer's reputation for reliability in paying. A reliable customer of long standing will probably be granted very favourable terms. A new customer, about whom little is known, may be expected to pay cash on delivery, at least for a short time.

The terms of sale are recorded on the sales invoice as shown in Figure 12.14. Every time a sale is made and an invoice is sent out, the customer is reminded of the terms for payment. Also, the terms are usually recorded on the customer's account card, so that the credit manager, the sales manager, and other interested people may refer to them easily.

Accounting for Cash Discounts

Accounting for a cash discount begins at the time a credit sale is made to a customer and an invoice offering a cash discount is issued. Examine the invoice shown in Figure 12.14, for which Masthead Marine is the seller and Nanaimo Marina is the buyer.

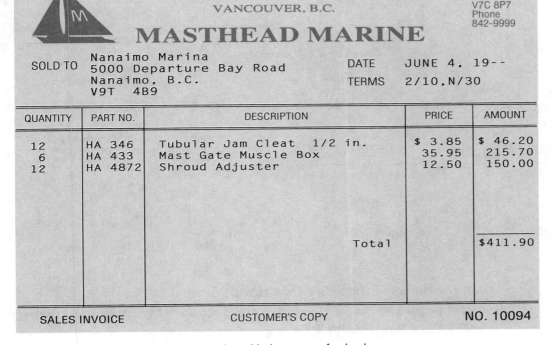

		ECHO BAY VANCOUVER, B.C.			P.O. Box 298 Station 8 V7C 8P7 Phone 842-9999
		MASTHEAD MARINE			

| SOLD TO | Nanaimo Marina
5000 Departure Bay Road
Nanaimo, B.C.
V9T 4B9 | | DATE | JUNE 4, 19-- | |
| | | | TERMS | 2/10,N/30 | |

QUANTITY	PART NO.	DESCRIPTION	PRICE	AMOUNT
12	HA 346	Tubular Jam Cleat 1/2 in.	$ 3.85	$ 46.20
6	HA 433	Mast Gate Muscle Box	35.95	215.70
12	HA 4872	Shroud Adjuster	12.50	150.00
			Total	$411.90

SALES INVOICE   CUSTOMER'S COPY   NO. 10094

Figure 12.14   A sales invoice with the terms of sale shown.

In the Books of the Buyer (Nanaimo Marina)

The invoice, when received by Nanaimo Marina, becomes a purchase invoice. For this purchase invoice, the following accounting entry is recorded in the purchases journal.

	DR	CR
Purchases	$411.90	
Accounts Payable (Masthead Marine)		$411.90

In the T-accounts the effect is:

Purchases		Accounts Payable (Masthead Marine)	
411.90			411.90

Someone in the accounting department of Nanaimo Marina will be responsible for checking the purchase invoices to see if any discounts are offered. Where discounts are offered, special treatment is necessary to ensure that payment is made within the discount period.

In this case the cheque is made out for $403.66. This amount is arrived at by deducting the two per cent discount ($8.24) from the amount of the invoice ($411.90). The tear-off portion of the cheque will show that the cheque is in payment of invoice No. 10094, and that a discount of $8.24 has been deducted.

From the cheque copy, the following accounting entry is made in the cash payments journal.

	DR	CR
Accounts Payable (Masthead Marine)	$411.90	
Discounts Earned		$ 8.24
Bank		403.66

The cumulative effect of the two transactions in the T-accounts is:

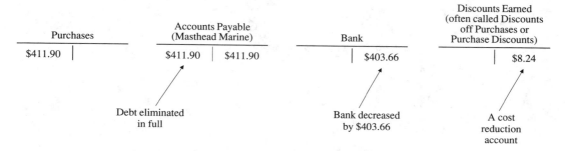

In the Books of the Seller (Masthead Marine)

From the data on the sales invoice copy, Masthead Marine makes the following accounting entry in the sales journal.

	DR	CR
Accounts Receivable (Nanaimo Marina)	$411.90	
Sales		$411.90

The effect in the T-accounts is:

Accounts Receivable (Nanaimo Marina)	Sales
$411.90	$411.90

Upon receiving Nanaimo Marina's cheque for $403.66, Masthead Marine includes the cheque on the Daily List of Cash Receipts. A copy of the listing is forwarded to the accounts receivable clerk for posting to the customer's account in the subsidiary ledger. This clerk checks any discounts taken to see that they are calculated correctly and are within the discount period. The customer's account is credited with the gross amount, in this case $411.90.

From the listing an accounting entry is also recorded in the cash receipts journal as follows:

	DR	CR
Bank	$403.66	
Discounts Allowed	8.24	
Accounts Receivable (Nanaimo Marina)		$411.90

After this accounting entry, the cumulative effect in the accounts is:

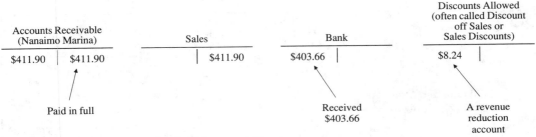

Additional Cash Discount Facts

1. Occasionally, a customer takes a late discount. In other words, the customer takes the discount after the discount period has passed.

    Business people try to be reasonable when faced with this situation. There may be postal delays to consider. No business wants a reputation for being cheap. At the same time, a business does not want to be taken advantage of by its customers.

    If a business decides to disallow a late discount, the usual practice is to cash the customer's deficient cheque and to credit the customer's account with the amount of the cheque only, not the gross amount. This will leave a small balance in the account. It is good business to write a polite letter requesting the customer to make up the deficiency.

2. The Discounts Earned account is often referred to as the Discount off Purchases or Purchase Discounts account. The Discounts Allowed account is often referred to as the Discount off Sales or Sales Discounts account.

3. Every business will try to take advantage of the cash discounts offered by its suppliers. Therefore, entries to the Discounts Earned account can be expected to occur frequently. These entries will normally require a special column when a columnar journal is used.

4. Not all businesses offer cash discounts to their customers. A business that does not offer cash discounts will not have a Discounts Allowed account.

5. Occasionally, an invoice is received on which there is a cash discount, and some time before the discount date a portion of the goods is returned or an allowance granted. In a case such as this, the usual procedure is to take the discount on the net cost of the goods, that is, the invoice figure less the credit note amount. Also, the discount date is adjusted to start from the date shown on the credit note.

Cash Discounts on the Income Statement

There is more than one way of handling cash discounts on the income statement. The method selected depends on the amount of the discounts and the preference of the accountant. If the amounts involved are small, they might be combined into another account such as Miscellaneous Expense. A more formal method is shown in Figure 12.15. When the formal method is used, Discounts Allowed and Discounts Earned are treated as deductions from Sales and from Purchases respectively.

TRIDENT TRADING CO. INCOME STATEMENT YEAR ENDED DECEMBER 31, 19--			
Revenue			
Sales		$403 955	
Less Returns and Allowances	$21 151		
Discounts Allowed	5 296	26 447	
Net Sales			$377 508
Cost of Merchandise Sold			
Inventory, January 1		$ 72 074	
Purchases	$233 567		
Less Returns and Allowances	$18 356		
Discounts Earned	4 358	22 714	
Net Purchases		210 853	
Freight-in		5 731	
Merchandise Available for Sale		$288 658	
Less: Inventory, December 31		83 562	205 096
Gross Profit			$172 412
Operating Expenses			
Advertising		$ 1 141	
Bank Charges		2 651	
Car Expenses		4 999	
Delivery Expenses		1 377	
Insurance Used		2 915	
Light and Heat		3 988	
Miscellaneous Expense		1 507	
Rent		12 000	
Salaries		30 340	
Supplies Used		2 560	
Telephone		1 850	
Wages		48 220	113 548
Net Income			$ 58 864

Figure 12.15 The income statement of Trident Trading Co., including discounts allowed and discounts earned.

SECTION REVIEW QUESTIONS

1. Define "cash discount."
2. Define "terms of sale."
3. Why would a business sell goods C.O.D.?
4. Why would the buying firm accept C.O.D. as the terms of sale?
5. What does the term "Net 30" mean?
6. What does the term "2/10,N/30" mean?
7. Where would the customer see the terms of sale for a transaction?
8. Where could the manager of a business see the terms of sale for any customer?
9. How does a business ensure that cash discounts are taken when available?
10. Which account—Discounts Allowed or Discounts Earned—is associated with a sales transaction?
11. What is another name for Discounts Allowed?
12. What is another name for Discounts Earned?
13. A business may not have an account for Discounts Allowed. Explain why.
14. Assume that there is a sales transaction followed by a sales return, and that there is a discount offered. On what figure is the discount calculated? On what date does the discount period begin?
15. Where does "Discounts Allowed" appear on the income statement?
16. Where does "Discounts Earned" appear on the income statement?

SECTION EXERCISES

1. **Complete the following schedule by calculating the amount of the payment that is necessary in each case. Where credit notes are involved, assume that the discount period is adjusted to start from the date on the credit note. This chart appears in your Workbook.**

Date of Invoice	Amount of Invoice	Terms of Sale	Amount of Credit Note	Date of Credit Note	Date Payment is Made	Amount of Payment Required
Mar 12	$ 52.50	2/10,n/30	-	-	Mar 20	
May 18	47.25	Net 30	-	-	May 27	
Sep 4	115.50	3/15,n/60	-	-	Oct 10	
Feb 6	1 050.00	1/20,n/60	$126.00	Feb 18	Mar 6	
Oct 19	588.00	2/10,n/30	42.00	Nov 5	Nov 27	
Aug 27	882.00	2/15,n/60	168.00	Sep 7	Sep 10	

2. Complete the following schedule by calculating the date that payment is required to pick up the discount, and the amount of the payment required. This chart appears in your Workbook.

Date of Invoice	Amount of Invoice	Terms of Sale	Amount of Credit Note	Date of Credit Note	Date Payment is Made	Amount of Payment Required
May 14	$ 147.00	2/10,n/30	-	-		
Apr 15	315.00	3/20,n/60	$42.00	May 1		
Jun 3	220.05	2/10,n/60	78.75	Jun 20		
Nov 20	59.25	2/15,n/60	36.75	Dec 2		

3. 1. a. In two-column general journal form, record the accounting entry for the invoice shown below in the books of Circle Supply.

```
900 Park Street          Circle Supply          Maple City

SOLD TO  Watson Construction
         1500 Randell Road
         Maple City   X3Y 7N5       INVOICE NUMBER  715
DATE August 3, 19--                 TERMS 2/10,n/30

Quantity   Description        Unit Price   Amount
10 boxes   #10 Woodscrews      $5.50       $55.00
2          Standard Crowbars    4.10         8.20
                                            63.20
           5% Sales Tax                      3.16
                                           $66.36
```

b. On August 12 a cheque in the amount of $65.03 is received from Watson Construction. In two-column general journal form, show the accounting entry to be recorded in the books of Circle Supply.

2. Watson Construction charges the merchandise shown on the above invoice to an account called Small Tools and Supplies. Show the journal entries for the above two transactions that will be made in the books of Watson Construction. Use appropriate dates.

4. 1. a. In the books of Circle Supply, in two-column general journal form, show the accounting entry to be recorded for the invoice below.

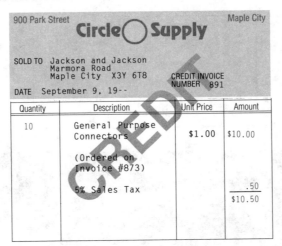

900 Park Street			Maple City
Circle ◯ Supply			

SOLD TO Jackson and Jackson
         Marmora Road
         Maple City   X3Y 6T8   INVOICE NUMBER 873

DATE September 3, 19--   TERMS   2/10,n/30

Quantity	Description	Unit Price	Amount
100	General Purpose Connectors	$1.00	$100.00
	5% Sales Tax		5.00
			$105.00

b. Some of the goods are found to be inadequate and are returned for credit. The following credit invoice is issued. **Show the accounting entry in general journal form to record this credit invoice in the books of Circle Supply.** Circle Supply does not use a Returns and Allowances account.

900 Park Street			Maple City
Circle ◯ Supply			

SOLD TO Jackson and Jackson
         Marmora Road
         Maple City   X3Y 6T8   CREDIT INVOICE
                                   NUMBER 891

DATE   September 9, 19--

Quantity	Description	Unit Price	Amount
10	General Purpose Connectors	$1.00	$10.00
	(Ordered on Invoice #873)		
	5% Sales Tax		.50
			$10.50

c. On September 19, a cheque is received in full payment of the sales invoice, less the credit invoice, less the cash discount. **Show the accounting entry in general journal form to record the receipt of this cheque.**

2. Record the accounting entries to be made for the above transactions in the books of Jackson and Jackson. Use appropriate dates. The goods affect the Supplies account.

12.4 *COMPUTERS IN ACCOUNTING: USING BEDFORD IN THE ACCOUNTING CYCLE*

Your knowledge of spreadsheets gives you an appreciation of the speed, accuracy, and power that they offer accountants. At this stage of your learning, you will unquestionably appreciate accounting software even more. Packages such as Bedford do the posting, take off a trial balance, and prepare the financial statements. Your bookkeeping tasks are essentially reduced to analyzing source documents and making journal entries.

Making Journal Entries

From the module menu, the GENERAL option must be chosen in order to gain access to the general ledger module. This is the section of Bedford that will allow general journal entries to be made. To get to the module (main) menu of Bedford, you will be asked to enter the "using" date. This is the date for this session's entries. The next step is to choose JOURNAL. Once this is done, menus similar to the ones in Figure 12.16 are displayed.

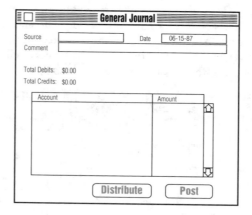

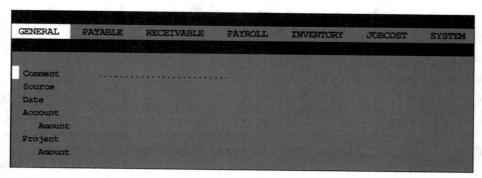

Figure 12.16 Bedford's general journal menus in both Macintosh and IBM-compatible versions.

Each of the general journal options has fields, which are spaces that allow you to enter data. COMMENT and SOURCE permit you to enter a comment and a source document number. Bedford presently requires an entry of some type in these fields. If you want the fields left blank, press the space bar before striking the return key.

The DATE option is for the date of the journal entry. Each time a journal entry is made, a date is shown beside this field. This is called the DEFAULT selection. (Defaults are selections that automatically appear in software because they are expected to be chosen often by users.) If the DEFAULT date is correct, selecting it will be faster than retyping the date. You make this selection by pressing both the shift key and the return key together.

In the ACCOUNT field enter the number of the account to be debited or credited. Bookkeepers usually start with a debit entry. A chart of accounts can be displayed on the screen, or the bookkeeper can refer to a printout, as a guide.

After the dollar amount of the debit has been entered in the AMOUNT field, the cursor returns to ACCOUNT so that the next account number may be identified. Very often, this account will be the credit entry of the transaction. The PROJECT and AMOUNT options are for the JOBCOSTING module; they will not be explored in this text.

To illustrate the journalizing process using the IBM and IBM-compatible version of Bedford, suppose Michael Pezim started a business on October 5, 19-4, by investing $20 000 of his personal funds. The following data would be entered into the journal fields:

COMMENT: Opening entry

SOURCE: *Space bar*
Mr. Pezim does not yet have remittance slips, so no source document number is available.

DATE: *Shift/Return*
This is the method of selecting the default date (October 5, 19-4) on IBM and IBM-compatible systems. The default date is the same as the USING date, which is identified in the process of loading Bedford.

ACCOUNT: 101
This is the number of the Cash account.

AMOUNT: 20 000
This is the amount of the Cash debit.

ACCOUNT: 301
This will display M. Pezim, Capital account.

AMOUNT: *Shift/Return*
Pressing Shift/Return accepts the default amount of $20 000. Bedford assumes that since the debit to Cash was $20 000, the credit to M. Pezim, Capital, will be $20 000 also. Accepting this default amount is faster than retyping and it reduces the chance of error.

In the event of compound entries (more than two accounts affected), the default amount may not then be appropriate. Each amount must be typed separately.

Posting

The above entry is finished, but it is not yet posted. To do this on IBM and IBM-compatible systems, the Return key is struck and the Left Arrow key is pressed. This takes you to the preceding menu. The entry is now posted, and the JOURNAL option can be selected once more if further entries are to be made.

Error Prevention

When a journal entry is posted, it cannot be erased. To correct the effects of an erroneous journal entry, further journal entries are required. The correction process is time-consuming.

To help reduce errors, Bedford permits you to see the journal entry in a familiar format. For example, to view the above journal entry on an IBM or IBM-compatible computer, press the F2 key after the credit amount is entered. The computer monitor will instantly look like Figure 12.17.

GENERAL	PAYABLE	RECEIVABLE	PAYROLL	INVENTORY	JOBCOST	SYSTEM

	DEBITS	CREDITS
101 Cash	20 000.00	
301 M. Pezim, Capital		20 000.00
	20 000.00	20 000.00

Figure 12.17   Journal entry displayed in a familiar format.

A display such as the one above provides visual confirmation that the journal entry is exactly what the bookkeeper wants. If an error is discovered, striking the F2 key again will bring back the journal entry fields. The contents of these fields can then be adjusted individually; or, if the bookkeeper wants to eliminate the entire entry and start again, the Esc key may be pressed. The Esc key will return the cursor to the previous menu, but it will not post the entry.

Error Correction

Viewing the journal entry before posting is recommended for every transaction. Nevertheless, errors will occur and will be posted. Since Bedford is a secure accounting system, posted data cannot be erased. One method to correct an erroneous entry is to reverse it and then correct it. In other words, undo it and redo it.

Suppose the opening journal entry for Michael Pezim's business is mistakenly posted as a debit to Cash of $2 000 and a credit to M. Pezim, Capital, of $2 000. The correct debit and credit figure is $20 000. Using the undo/redo method, the correcting journal entries are as shown in Figure 12.18.

GENERAL	PAYABLE	RECEIVABLE	PAYROLL	INVENTORY	JOBCOST	SYSTEM

			DEBITS	CREDITS
10-31-87	J1	To cancel the entry of Oct. 05,		
		301 M. Pezim, Capital	2 000.00	–
		101 Cash	–	2 000.00
10-31-87	J2	To record the investment of Oct. 05,		
		101 Cash	20 000.00	–
		301 M. Pezim, Capital	–	20 000.00

Figure 12.18   Correcting journal entries.

The first entry is the opposite of the erroneous journal entry, and thus cancels its effects. The second entry contains the proper figures. An alternative method of correction is to debit Cash $18 000 and credit M. Pezim, Capital, $18 000. This brings the balance of both accounts up to the intended figure of $20 000. Although this method requires only one journal entry, it may become confusing in some situations.

Using Negative Numbers

Some accounting software packages require all credit entries to be identified with negative numbers. Bedford does not. Instead, it requires negative numbers when a bookkeeper wants to decrease an account balance. Since asset accounts decrease differently from liability and equity accounts, care must be taken.

The balances of asset accounts decrease when credits are posted. The balances of liability and equity accounts decrease when debits are posted. For example, if a business pays $1 000 to a supplier on account, both Cash (an asset) and Accounts Payable (a liability) decrease. Bedford requires both amounts to be entered as – $1 000.

If a credit customer pays $3 000 on account, an asset increases (Cash) and an asset decreases (Accounts Receivable). Bedford requires the Cash figure to be entered as $3 000 and the Accounts Receivable figure as – $3 000.

The balances of expense accounts increase with debits. Therefore, to journalize the payment of monthly rent of $2 000, the Rent Expense amount is entered as $2 000 and the Cash amount is entered as – $2 000. (**Note:** Bedford allows the negative sign to be entered either before or after the number.)

The use of negative numbers emphasizes the point that a sound understanding of accounting is essential for the successful operation of accounting software. Bedford does help to some extent, however. For example, with the above rent transaction, Bedford will show the default amount of the Cash entry as – $2 000. The program is sophisticated enough that an increase to an expense account is assumed to cause a decrease to an asset account, so the negative sign is put in automatically. To improve your efficiency with negative numbers, always check the default amount. If it is correct, select it. Also, viewing the journal entry before posting (i.e., using the F2 key) is imperative.

Saving Your Work

Bedford posts a journal entry as soon the Left Arrow key is pressed and the cursor returns to the previous menu. It is important to remember, however, that the entry is only posted in the temporary memory of the computer. If electrical power is interrupted, the work will be lost. Minimize your losses by saving the posted entries to the disk at least every 15 minutes. On IBM and IBM-compatible computers, the SAVE option appears when the SYSTEM menu is pulled down. On Macintosh computers, the SAVE option is under the FILE menu.

Advantages of Accounting Software

Speed When you work with pen and paper, you know that completing the journal entries is only a fraction of your work. When you reach the same stage with accounting software, you can simply print the ledger, trial balance, income statement, and balance sheet within a matter of minutes.

Accuracy While you can always make incorrect journal entries, you cannot make balancing errors with accounting software. Bedford, for instance, will not allow you to post an entry where debits do not equal credits. This is why the trial balance is always in balance.

Power This is the quick return of useful information. Financial statements are used by management to make important decisions. Since accounting software allows financial statements to be produced so rapidly and easily, management will receive them more quickly and more often.

COMPUTER EXERCISE

1. Your teacher may ask you to complete a number of the text exercises that are ready to be used with Bedford. The first one is General Engineering, Chapter 7, Exercise 7, page 212. The procedures for this exercise, and all of the general ledger exercises, are outlined below.

   1. Load Bedford into the main memory of your computer.

   2. Identify the directory (IBM and IBM-compatibles) or folder (Macintosh) that contains the files of the company in the exercise. For example, the name of the directory for General Engineering is GENENG.

   (**Note:** Accounts and opening balances have been entered for each exercise. **Your teacher will require you, however, to make the general ledger READY for journal entries.** This is a short procedure that allows you to have your name printed on each statement, and it will let your teacher assign you a specific year for the journal entries so that your work will be further personalized. Your teacher will give you additional instructions.)

3. Complete the journal entries. Use comments and source document numbers when appropriate. Always view your journal entries in their familiar format before you post them. Save your journal entries to the disk every 15 minutes.
4. When you have completed the journal entries, ask your teacher about which statements to print and which exercises to do next.

COMPUTER REVIEW QUESTIONS

1. Why are fields included in some computer programs?
2. What are defaults? Why are they included in computer programs? Give two examples of defaults in Bedford.
3. After entering the amounts of a journal entry in Bedford, the Esc key will return the cursor to the previous menu and thus post the entry. Which part of the preceding statement is true and which is false?
4. What is the undo/redo method of journal error correction? Use an example in your answer.
5. A business pays $3 000 of its bank loan. What accounts require negative numbers when using Bedford to journalize this transaction?

Communicate It

You and Clara Pegotty are partners in a small catering business, which does not have an abundance of cash. Since the business already owns a computer and a spreadsheet program, Clara suggests that you design a spreadsheet model to handle the bookkeeping activities. **Write a memorandum that details your reactions to Clara's suggestion. If possible, use a word processing program.**

CHAPTER HIGHLIGHTS

Now that you have completed Chapter 12, you should:

1. understand the advantages of a multi-columnar journal;
2. be able to journalize, cross balance, post, and forward in a synoptic journal;
3. know the advantages of the synoptic journal;
4. understand the reason for a two-journal system;
5. know the variations in journalizing in the synoptic journal;
6. understand the advantages of the five-journal system;
7. be able to journalize and post in the five-journal system;
8. understand the purpose of offering a cash discount;
9. know the accounting entries for discounts earned and discounts allowed;
10. know how discounts earned and discounts allowed are presented on the income statement.

ACCOUNTING TERMS

C.O.D.
cash discount
cash payments journal
cash receipts journal
cross balancing
five-journal system

multi-columnar journals
purchases journal
sales journal
synoptic journal
terms of sale

CHAPTER EXERCISES

Using Your Knowledge

1. **Indicate whether each of the following statements is true or false by placing a "T" or an "F" in the space indicated in your Workbook. Explain the reason for each "F" response in the space provided.**

   1. The general journal is not normally used if the business has a synoptic journal.
   2. There is a special column for every general ledger account in the synoptic journal.
   3. The chief disadvantage of the synoptic journal is that you have to post column totals.
   4. An accounting entry that takes more than one line cannot be recorded in the synoptic journal.
   5. There would be a special column for Rent Expense in the synoptic journal.
   6. The synoptic journal is balanced at the end of every page.

7. The date used when formally posting the synoptic journal is the last day of the month.
8. A credit to Sales in the synoptic journal would normally be entered in the Other Accounts credit column.
9. All sales of merchandise are recorded in the sales journal.
10. The cash payments journal is also known as the cash disbursements journal.
11. Additional cash invested in the business by the owner would be recorded in the general journal.
12. A bank debit advice requires an entry in the cash receipts journal.
13. The five-journal system inevitably leads to the clerks becoming specialists within the system.
14. The general ledger would not balance if only four of the five journals were posted.
15. A purchase partly for cash and partly on account would be recorded in the purchases journal.

2. Two columns of a synoptic journal are totaled incorrectly, but the errors offset each other. The total of the Sales column is $2 000 more than it should be, and the total of the Accounts Receivable credit column is $2 000 less than it should be.
   1. **What will be the effect on the accounts? On the ledger? On income? On total assets?**
   2. **How might the errors be detected?**

3. Before posting to the general ledger, the equality of the debit and credit column totals in the journals should be proved. Suppose that this was not done, and that the total of a column in the cash receipts journal was incorrectly increased by $100.
   1. **How would this error first be discovered?**
   2. **What steps would normally be followed to find the cause of the error?**

4. M. Lunney Co. has two bank accounts, one with a balance on deposit of $100 000 and one for payroll, which is overdrawn by $5 000. The bank charges interest on the $5 000.
   Is the bank's practice fair? Explain.

5. N. Howard conducts a small retail business. At the time of a sale she collects the tax from the customer but makes no attempt to distinguish on her books between the amount of the sale and the amount of the sales tax. In her entries involving cash sales she debits Cash and credits Sales for the total amount.
   a. **If Howard's total sales for the month amount to $52 500, how much sales tax would she remit to the provincial treasurer if the rate of tax is five per cent? Assume that all sales are taxable.**
   b. **What entry would be made to record the sales tax?**

6. Bob Jarvis, the accountant for Wright Brothers, sets up an accounting system to eliminate the accounts receivable and accounts payable ledgers. All invoices owing to creditors and all invoices due from customers are kept in separate file folders until paid. When invoices are paid, they are removed from the customers' and creditors' files and placed in a file for paid invoices. At the end of the month the unpaid files are totaled and these totals agree with the balances in the control accounts in the general ledger.

What advantages and disadvantages are there to such a system?

7. Shoe store owner D. Mugami made approximately 300 credit sales and 100 credit purchases each month. Mr. Mugami recorded all these sales and purchases in a general journal. A friend asked him why he did not use a sales journal and a purchases journal. Mr. Mugami replied that he did not understand their use. He believed that they simply divided the work among several people. Since he did his own accounting, he had no need for these special journals.

Is division of labour the only reason for using special journals? Explain.

8. A review of the accounting records of Nixon Co. disclosed the following errors.
   1. Cash received from H. Latimer for $285.00 was entered correctly in the cash receipts journal, but posted to the accounts receivable ledger as $258.00.
   2. An invoice for 45 cartons at $1.75 each shipped to Best Drug Store was extended and entered in the sales journal as $87.75.
   3. Cash of $65.00 was entered correctly in the cash receipts journal as received from M. Smith, but was posted in the accounts receivable ledger to the account of M. Smythe.
   4. The footings of the "Purchases" column in the cash payments journal were overstated by $100.
   5. A cheque for $150 payable to G. Graham for legal fees was entered incorrectly in the cash payments journal as $160. The journal has not yet been posted.

   Discuss how these errors should be corrected.

9. 1. **Give the accounting entries in general journal form for each of the following source documents as they would be made in the books of Circle Supply.** Circle Supply uses Returns and Allowances accounts.
   2. **Give the accounting entries in general journal form for each source document as they would be made in the books of Kitchen Cabinetry. The Supplies account is to be charged for the goods.**

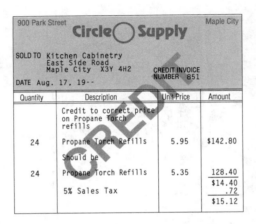

Quantity	Description	Unit Price	Amount
1 Ctn	#35 Copper Wire	$65.00	$ 65.00
24	Propane Torch Refills	5.95	142.80
			$207.80
	5% Sales Tax		10.39
			$218.19

900 Park Street   Circle Supply   Maple City

SOLD TO Kitchen Cabinetry
         East Side Road
         Maple City   X3Y 4H2
                               INVOICE NUMBER 802
DATE Aug. 9, 19--   TERMS 2/10,n/30

---

900 Park Street   Circle Supply   Maple City

SOLD TO Kitchen Cabinetry
        East Side Road
        Maple City   X3Y 4H2
                            CREDIT INVOICE
                            NUMBER 851
DATE Aug. 17, 19--

Quantity	Description	Unit Price	Amount
	Credit to correct price on Propane Torch refills		
24	Propane Torch Refills	5.95	$142.80
	Should be		
24	Propane Torch Refills	5.35	128.40
			$14.40
	5% Sales Tax		.72
			$15.12

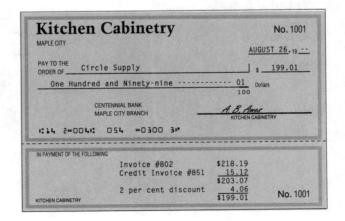

Kitchen Cabinetry   No. 1001

MAPLE CITY

                                    AUGUST 26, 19 --

PAY TO THE
ORDER OF ___ Circle Supply ___ $ 199.01

One Hundred and Ninety-nine ----------- 01 Dollars
                                      100

CENTENNIAL BANK
MAPLE CITY BRANCH   A. B. Ames
                                    KITCHEN CABINETRY

⑈14 2⑈004⑈ 054 ⑈0300 3⑈

IN PAYMENT OF THE FOLLOWING

                  Invoice #802 $218.19
                  Credit Invoice #851   15.12
                                      $203.07
                  2 per cent discount   4.06
KITCHEN CABINETRY $199.01   No. 1001

10. **Prepare an income statement from the following partial work sheet.**

Work Sheet   Superior Trading Company   Year ended December 31, 19--

Accounts	Income Statement		Balance Sheet	
	Dr	Cr	Dr	Cr
Bank				
Accounts Receivable				
Merchandise Inventory	44 323.40	43 750.00		
Supplies				
Prepaid Insurance				
Equipment				
Automobiles				
Accounts Payable				
Sales Tax Payable				
Bank Loan				
Grace Strom, Capital				
Grace Strom, Drawings				
Sales		201 245.50		
Sales Returns & Allowances	4 102.00			
Purchases	73 219.20			
Purchases Returns & Allowances		5 625.00		
Freight-in	1 501.00			
Advertising	1 426.00			
Bank Charges	2 247.00			
Car Expenses	8 135.00			
Delivery Expense	5 535.00			
Discounts Allowed	3 525.24			
Discounts Earned		1 023.65		
General Expense	1 505.15			
Light and Heat	1 785.25			
Rent	12 000.00			
Telephone	1 052.25			
Wages	46 056.35			
Supplies Used	2 203.00			
Insurance Used	2 075.00			
	210 690.84	251 644.15		
Net Income	40 953.31			
	251 644.15	251 644.15		

Comprehensive Exercises

11. **Workbook Exercise: Journalizing, posting, and balancing with five journals and three ledgers. Bristol Appliances.**

12. **Workbook Exercise: Locating and correcting errors in a five-journal system.**

Challenge Exercise

13. **Record the following selected transactions of Wholesale Food Distributors in general journal form. In working out your answers, bear in mind the following:**
    1. A few of the transactions are dependent on previous ones.
    2. Wholesale Food Distributors maintains separate accounts for Purchases Returns and Allowances and for Sales Returns and Allowances.
    3. The amounts of certain cheques (receipts and expenditures) have been left for you to decide.

TRANSACTIONS

November
3 *Sales Invoices*
    No. 962, Palmer's Grocery, $496.26; terms, 2/10,n/30; add five per cent sales tax.
    No. 963, Grey's Market, $376.14; terms, 2/10,n/30; add five per cent sales tax.
    No. 964, Alec's Groceteria, $197.26; terms, 2/10,n/30; add five per cent sales tax.
4 *Cheque Copy*
    No. 404, to D. K. Knight, $100, loan to an employee to help her overcome a personal hardship.
5 *Purchase Invoice*
    No. 213, from Gordon Canners, $1 260, dated No. 2; terms 3/20,n/60, for merchandise purchased.
6 *Bank Debit Note*
    From City Bank, $75.10, cheque returned NSF from Doyle's Grocery.
7 *Cheque Copy*
    No. 412, to Outboard Motor Sales, $425; instructions from J.D. Doan, the owner, to pay for a new outboard motor delivered to her cottage for personal use.
8 *Purchase Invoice*
    No. 5698, from Elmer Canners, $1 050; for merchandise purchased; terms, Net 60 days, dated Nov. 6.
10 *Credit Note Received*
    No. 445, from Gordon Canners, $147, dated No. 9; allowance granted on invoice No. 213 for incorrect goods.
11 *Cheque Copy*
    No. 447, to Jane Brown's, $475, to pay for C.O.D. delivery of a new office desk.
12 *Cash Receipt*
    Cheque from Grey's Market, paying sales invoice No. 963.

Credit Note Issued

No. 1007, to Palmer's Grocery, $56.70 including five per cent sales tax, for defective merchandise returned; discount period adjusted to begin on November 12.

14 *Credit Note Received*

No. 565, from Burlington Fruit Growers Association, $2 332.80, correcting their invoice No. 412, which was issued incorrectly in the amount of $2 592 instead of $259.20. (Note: This is neither a ''return'' nor an ''allowance.'')

18 *Cheque Copy*

No. 474, to G. Simcoe, $47.25; cash refund for defective merchandise that had been returned, $45, sales tax, $2.25.

22 *Cash Receipt*

Cheque from Palmer's Grocery, paying invoice No. 962 and credit note No. 1007 less discount.

25 *Cheque Copy*

No. 491, to Gordon Canners, paying sales invoice No. 213 and credit note No. 445 less discount.

26 *Cheque Copy*

No. 497, to Elmer Canners, paying invoice No. 5698.

30 *Cash Receipt*

Cheque from Alec's Groceteria, paying sales invoice No. 964.

For Further Thought

14. Briefly answer the following questions.

1. Northern Contracting is a small company with fewer than a dozen employees. The formal accounting of Northern Contracting is performed by a public accountant. The owner and his wife do the clerical routines. Why would the public accountant not be expected to perform the clerical routines? Specifically, name the tasks that the owners would probably have to do themselves.

2. Pet World and Salon uses a synoptic journal in which no columns for accounts receivable are provided. Give a reason for omitting these columns.

3. In the synoptic journal, there is no column for Sales debit. A debit entry to sales may be entered in the Sales credit column provided that it is circled. How else could the debit entry to Sales be recorded?

4. After cross balancing the synoptic journal, an accountant found (by good fortune) that one of the totals was incorrect. How then could the journal have cross balanced?

5. A very small business uses a synoptic journal. This business does not have independent clerks to maintain subsidiary ledgers, nor does it prepare copies of source documents for posting to subsidiary ledgers. Suggest a system of posting to subsidiary ledgers for this business.

6. A company which uses a synoptic journal sold goods to a customer for cash and issued a cash sales slip. When recorded in the synoptic journal, the sales slip was entered in the Accounts Receivable debit column. Would the synoptic journal cross balance? How might the error be detected?

7. You are taking over as the accountant for a small company which has been using only a two-column general journal. You have decided to change to a two-journal system including a synoptic journal. How would you go about selecting the headings for the columns?

8. The accountant for ABC Company was physically disabled and was not able to write small. Inked-in totals beneath pin totals were an impossibility for her. However, she knew only too well the need for testing to see that the journal was in balance before inking in the totals. Suggest an alternative procedure for this accountant.

9. The new bookkeeper for XYZ Company did not know about forwarding the synoptic journal during the month. At the end of May there were five independently balanced pages of the synoptic journal. How would you handle this situation?

10. The owner of a business at one time did the bookkeeping for the business and understood the system perfectly. On one occasion, she came to inform the present bookkeeper that she had collected money from a customer for a cash sale but had pocketed the money. The bookkeeper was temporarily absent and so the owner recorded the transaction herself. In what journal would she record the transaction? How much would the choice of journals matter?

11. An accounting clerk entered a sale on account in the general journal. What difficulties might this action create?

12. The text states that a natural relationship exists between sales and cash receipts. Explain this statement.

13. Assume that five different people look after the five different journals in a five-journal system. Would it be better for each of the five to be involved in the posting or to assign the task to one individual? Explain.

14. There could be more than five journals in an accounting system. Name one other journal that would be a sensible addition to the system.

15. The textbook and Workbook do not have many columns in their columnar journals. This is because the sizes of the pages are limited. In real situations more columns would be desirable. In what two ways could an accountant obtain journal pages with more columns?

16. You have just posted the cash payments journal but have not yet done the cash receipts journal. You notice that the Bank account has a credit balance. Is this a problem? Explain.

17. An accounting clerk posts the Discounts Allowed figure of $185 from the cash receipts journal to the debit side of the Discounts Earned account. Will this cause the ledger to be out of balance? Will this produce an incorrect net income figure, and if so, by how much?

18. Some accountants prefer to account for cash discounts on purchases in a way different from that described in the text. When a cash discount is allowed on a purchase, it is calculated immediately and deducted on the invoice in order to arrive at a net purchase figure. The accounting entry for the transaction is recorded at this net figure. Consequently:

a. For a $100 purchase of merchandise, with a two per cent discount, what will the accounting entry be?

b. If the discount period is 10 days and payment is made on time, what will the accounting entry be to record the payment?

c. If payment is not made within the discount period, how much must be paid?

d. Figure out the accounting entry for question c above.

e. The accounting entry in question d above reveals an important piece of information. What is it? Explain.

CASE STUDIES

CASE 1   *No Journal!*

Assume that you have just taken a job with Goodwood Construction as a senior accounting clerk. You are somewhat surprised by the accounting system Goodwood uses, described below. In your previous position you had become accustomed to the traditional five-journal system.

Goodwood does not use a traditional purchases journal or cash payments journal. In fact, Goodwood does not use a journal for these transactions. Here is the system used by Goodwood:

1. when a purchase invoice is received, it is verified in all respects;

2. no entry is made in a journal. Instead, the cheque to pay the purchase invoice is prepared. A simplified example of the type of cheque used is shown below;

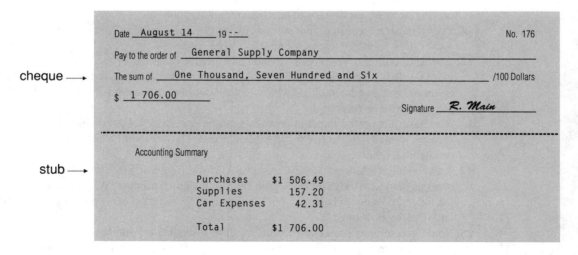

3. the original cheque and the cheque copy are forwarded to the accounting department;

4. the cheque itself is filed temporarily until time for payment arrives. Payment is looked after by another employee;

5. the cheque copies are accumulated by the month in a two-hole binder. This file of cheque copies is used for reference purposes during the month;
6. at the end of the month the file of cheque copies becomes the basis for one grand accounting entry for all the cheque copies. The procedure is to go through the file a number of times, each time making an addition of one particular item. For example, all of the purchases might be added the first time through, all of the supplies the second time through, and on the third pass, all of the car expenses. Eventually all the individual charges are subtotaled by account. The grand total of all the individual subtotals, of course, has to balance with the total of all the cheques. It is not an easy process because there is a lot of room for making errors. One grand accounting summary is eventually prepared. An example is shown below.

ACCOUNTING SUMMARY
CHEQUE COPIES
MONTH OF AUGUST, 19--

Purchases	$25 326.12
Supplies	2 568.21
Car Expenses	4 352.78
—	$$
—	$$
—	$$
—	$$
—	$$
Total	$42 158.63
Total Cheques	$42 158.63

The above summary is used as the source document for one accounting entry to record all the cheque copies for the month. The large, compound entry is recorded in the general journal. The entry is made as if all the cheques were paid even though many of them would still be on hand.

Questions
1. Why would a system like this be used?
2. What difficulties or inconveniences can you see in such a system?
3. How should the cheque copies be filed? Is there a need for more than one file?
4. How should the cheques not issued be dealt with at the month end? At statement time?
5. What is your general impression of the system? Would you adopt it? Give reasons.
6. Give a name to this system.

CASE 2   *Squeeze Play*

Highway Construction is a firm that builds major roads and highways. Its contracts frequently involve substantial sums of money. Consequently, its accounts receivable and accounts payable are quite sizeable.

Highway Construction obtains large quantities of raw materials, supplies, and services from numerous smaller companies. These are always purchased on credit, and the amounts of money involved are usually considerable. Individual bills of $100 000 or more are not uncommon. At the time of purchase, Highway Construction always agrees to the supplier's terms of sale. These terms usually request payment within 30 days with no discounts.

In road construction, cash inflows are often slow and irregular. As a result, Highway Construction makes no attempt to adhere to the terms laid down by the suppliers. It pays its debts when its own cash position is good. Often, the suppliers have to wait for as long as 90 to 100 days.

Small suppliers can seldom afford to wait 100 days for customers to pay large sums of money. Small suppliers have their own debts to pay, and payrolls to meet. Therefore, Lequita Adkins, the chief accountant for Highway Construction, receives many telephone calls urgently requesting immediate payment of overdue accounts.

Lequita is experienced at dealing with these suppliers. Over the years she has worked out a neat scheme for handling their requests for payment. First, she expresses surprise that the supplier did not know that Highway Construction always takes 90 days to pay its suppliers. Lequita then goes on to say that the only exception to this policy is if a supplier offers a two per cent cash discount. The supplier is usually desperate for the money and agrees to the two per cent discount, which at the time may seem trivial.

Lequita Adkins claims that she makes money for Highway Construction with this scheme, even if she has to borrow the money at 15 per cent to make the payment. She says that she can back up the claim with calculations.

Questions
1. Is Lequita Adkins a sharp businessperson? Explain.
2. Is Lequita's policy an ethical one?
3. On a bill for $200 000, how much is a two per cent discount?
4. Is Lequita correct when she states that she makes money for the company with this scheme? Prove your answer with a calculation.

CASE 3   *Crook or Saint?*

R. C. Bews was obsessed with building his business. He had started out by using an inheritance to establish a small paving company. Since then, R. C. had fashioned Bews Construction Limited into one of the major road construction companies in Ontario.

R. C. was a man of mixed temperament. He was often pleasant and kind, but he could be ruthless in business. R. C. could fire an employee without a twinge of conscience. His workers quickly learned not to waste a penny.

If performance is judged by profit alone, R. C. was a good businessperson. Between 19-1 and 19-9, Bews Construction Limited's net income was never lower than $500 000 (before income tax). In two of those years, it was over $1 000 000.

Bews Construction was located in Toronto, Ontario. Metropolitan Toronto is a major city; its population then was over two million. The surrounding area, consisting of a number of counties, had an equivalent population. Four million people drive a lot of cars, and require a great many well-maintained roads and highways. Road and highway construction and maintenance is a function of government. Therefore, the bulk of Bews Construction Limited's business was with city, county, and provincial government departments.

R. C. always tried to foster good relationships with each government employee that he dealt with, whether a major executive or simply a project inspector on the site. R. C. wined and dined these employees, and also made sure that he was in a position to grant them favours. He always made it a point to have extra tickets for the big hockey or baseball game. If a theatre attraction was sold out, R. C. could always find an extra pair of tickets for a grateful executive. He kept a long Christmas list of civic employees. The least important recipients were given bottles of liquor, while the most important received colour television sets. Rarely was a gift refused. During the hot summer months, a very comfortable lakefront cottage, complete with boat and car, was kept fully stocked and available for important officials.

R. C. claimed to be an honest man who expected nothing in return for his generosity. The gifts merely expressed his appreciation for the past friendship and cooperation of the recipient. The gifts also allowed him to share his prosperity with those people who had innocently contributed to the growth and development of his company.

Questions
1. Was R. C. a good businessperson?
2. What is your opinion of his policy of giving favours?
3. Is this policy consistent with his attitude toward his own employees?
4. Do you believe R. C.'s claim that there are no strings attached to his gifts? Discuss.
5. Suggest some advantages that R. C. might gain from his policy.
6. Are there any unfair income tax advantages to the company? To the recipients of the gifts?
7. If you had to express R. C.'s policy in one word, what would it be?

ENTREPRENEUR
Greig Clark / College Pro Painters

Some business persons are natural entrepreneurs. With no formal lessons or training, they know instinctively what to do. Greig Clark is one of these.

Even as a youngster growing up in his home town of Thunder Bay, the signs were there. On one occasion Greig picked his mother's rhubarb with the intention of peddling it from door to door. He saw the situation as a business opportunity. His mother took a different view, which caused Greig to have his first business setback. That venture failed but Greig's spirit remained intact.

Greig got into house painting in 1970 to finance his education at the University of Western Ontario. For most students this was simply a matter of finding summer employment with a local company.

But Greig didn't follow that path for two reasons. One, it wouldn't pay enough money. Two, he wouldn't be his own boss. He began to think about a small business of his own.

After considering a few alternatives, Greig decided that house painting was the answer to his needs. It did not require a lot of start-up capital. It wasn't highly technical. And local painting companies left some room for improvement. At the time, it didn't occur to him that knocking on doors and being turned down again and again would be difficult emotionally.

Greig clearly remembers meeting his first customer. He didn't know how much to charge because he had no idea of the quantity or type of paint to use, nor the number of hours it would take. He had to stall the customer while he went to the local library and the paint store for advice and information. Fortunately, the homeowners were not aware of his predicament. Perhaps they sensed his personal commitment to complete the job. This he did, and with it came his first (small) profit.

Greig's competence increased with each new job. A new-found confidence helped him win customers. As his small business succeeded, his principal objective, to fund his university education, was realized. In 1974 Greig graduated as an MBA from the University of Western Ontario.

Many business hopefuls are

stopped dead in their tracks by the inevitable snags. But not Greig. He knew instinctively that these obstructions were not barriers, but hurdles. The most serious obstacles in the early stages were government regulations for unemployment insurance, Canada Pension Plan, income tax, workers' compensation, and so on. Each detailed booklet of rules and regulations was intimidating even to the strongest person. But they simply could not be ignored. When Greig applied his energy to mastering the booklets, in each case, as he knew would happen, there was the inevitable breakthrough.

From the very beginning Greig had a keen sense of the value of records. He kept records and files about each job. These proved invaluable in determining such things as what to charge a new customer, the amount of paint required for a job, and the number of man-hours needed.

Eventually, these records were developed into a highly organized and streamlined system which served as the basis for the next stage of Greig's career — the College Pro Painters franchise.

Greig set up branch offices, staffed by university students using his proven methods for estimating, marketing, writing contracts, preparing payroll, accounting, and so on. Greig provided an operations manual and personally conducted workshops and training sessions. Thus, the student operators would start out using a proven formula, and the frustrations of starting a new business would be minimized. In turn, Greig would receive 10 per cent of the profits.

These were lean times for Greig but after six branches proved successful, he knew he had a winning formula. He decided to abandon other career plans and commit himself to the College Pro Painters concept. To say that it has been successful is an understatement. In 1988 there were 450 outlets in Canada and the United States, with gross annual sales of $35 million. Greig became a millionaire in 1981, after only four years.

Greig Clark's remarkable story tells how an inexperienced young man took an ordinary task — the painting of a house — and turned it into a large and profitable enterprise. It should inspire many young people to give of themselves for the sake of a simple, novel idea.

DISCUSSION

1. What is meant by a *natural* entrepreneur?
2. Why did Greig go into business for himself rather than take a job with a local company?
3. Why did Greig choose house painting for his business?
4. How is Greig's perception of obstacles different from that of most young people?
5. How did Greig's records eventually help him with the College Pro Painters concept?
6. How would the franchisees learn about Greig's methods?

Summary Exercise

Travel Trailers

Travel Trailers is a business owned and operated by Charles Fowler. The business earns its income from the selling and servicing of mobile homes and trailers. All sales and service transactions are subject to a five per cent sales tax.

Travel Trailers is able to treat the sale of every unit as a cash transaction. This is possible because of special arrangements made with an independent finance company. Travel Trailers receives payment in full for every unit sold. For units sold on credit, the finance company pays Travel Trailers and arranges to collect from the customer on the instalment plan.

1. **Set up the general ledger of Travel Trailers as of May 31, 19— from the following combined chart of accounts and general ledger trial balance.** If you are using the Workbook, the ledger is already set up for you.*

TRAVEL TRAILERS
GENERAL LEDGER TRIAL BALANCE
MAY 31, 19—

101	Bank	$ 11 751.75	
110	Accounts Receivable	2 483.25	
115	Merchandise Inventory	125 423.00	
120	Supplies	1 151.00	
125	Prepaid Insurance	2 650.00	
130	Equipment	28 472.00	
140	Delivery Truck	22 000.00	
201	Accounts Payable		$ 19 987.00
205	Bank Loan		120 000.00
210	Sales Tax Payable		1 694.24
305	C. Fowler, Capital		43 410.51
310	C. Fowler, Drawings	15 000.00	
405	Sales		189 423.51
410	Discounts Earned		1 034.20
505	Purchases	96 581.75	
510	Freight-in	1 174.72	
515	Bank Charges and Interest	4 516.50	
520	Delivery Expense	5 650.20	
525	Insurance Expense		
530	Light and Heat	4 350.40	
535	Miscellaneous Expense	994.58	
540	Rent	6 250.00	
545	Supplies Used		
550	Telephone	1 376.20	
555	Wages	45 724.11	
		$375 549.46	$375 549.46

* You can do the general ledger part of this exercise using Bedford. The trial balance is set up on the computer disk for your convenience.

2. Set up the accounts receivable ledger of Travel Trailers as of May 31, 19—from the information shown below. If you are using the Workbook, the ledger is already set up for you.

Customer	Address	Invoice	Amount
B. Fraser	15 Gay Street	634	$ 367.50
W. Hoyle	49 First Street	635	78.75
A. Newman	250 Fort Road	629	262.50
Schell Brothers	96 Garrison Avenue	633	1 060.50
N. Thompson	20 Wilson Avenue	630	624.75
L. Walker	4 Dennis Avenue	631	89.25
			$2 483.25

3. Set up the accounts payable ledger of Travel Trailers as of May 31, 19— from the following information. If you are using the Workbook, the ledger is already set up for you.

Supplier	Address	Reference	Amount
Double-G Industries	Manortown	420	$10 575.00
Maynard's Cartage	49 Larry Lane		nil
Modern Mobile Homes	West City	2213	2 100.00
National Hardware	64 Venture Street	2309	2 787.00
Parker Manufacturing	10 Bergen Street		nil
Windsor Manufacturing	Windsor	404	4 525.00
			$19 987.00

4. Travel Trailers uses five journals in its accounting system as shown below.

Sales Journal   *Page 19*

Date	Particulars	Ref. No.	Sales Tax Payable CR		Sales CR	Acc's Rec'l DR

Purchases Journal   *Page 74*

Date	Particulars	Other Accounts DR			Freight-in DR	Supplies DR	Pchs's DR	Ref. No.	Accs Pay'l CR
		Account	PR	Amount					

Cash Receipts Journal   *Page 37*

Date	Particulars	Other Accounts DR			Acc's Rec'l CR	Sales Tax Payable CR	Sales CR	Ref. No.	Bank DR
		Account	PR	Amount					

Cash Payments Journal   *Page 84*

Date	Particulars	Other Accounts DR			Wages DR	Drawing DR	Accs Pay'l DR	Ref. No.	Bank CR
		Account	PR	Amount					

General Journal   *Page 5*

Date	Particulars	PR	Debit	Credit

Journalize the following transactions for June. Use the journal page numbers shown. Post to the subsidiary ledgers daily directly from the source documents. Terms of sale are Net 30 unless noted otherwise.

TRANSACTIONS

June

1   *Sales Invoice*
    No. 636, to A. Newman, for repairs to trailer; $590 plus sales tax.
    Cheque Copy
    No. 755, to General Real Estate, for the rent for June; $1 250.

2   *Sales Invoice*
    No. 637, to L. Walker, for trailer parts; $900 plus sales tax.
    Cheque Copy
    No. 756, to Double-G Industries, on account; $5 000.

3   *Purchase Invoices*
    From Parker Manufacturing, No. 40, for supplies; $247.80; terms 2/10,N/30.
    From Double-G Industries, No. 472, for trailer parts; $1 551.20.

4   *Cash Receipts List*
    From W. Hoyle, on account; $78.75.
    From Federated Finance Company, No. 7042, for the sale of a trailer; selling price, $12 700; sales tax $635; total $13 335.
    Bank Debit Advice
    From Central Bank, for interest on bank loan for May; $1 200.

5   *Cheque Copies*
    No. 757, to C. Fowler, for personal use; $1 000.
    No. 758, made out to Cash, for the wages for the week; $2 178.50.
    Sales Invoice
    No. 638, to N. Thompson, for trailer repairs and parts; $1 370 plus sales tax.

8   *Cheque Copy*
    No. 759, to J.C. Pat Supply, for the cash purchase of supplies, $243.50, and miscellaneous expense, $135.25; total $378.75.
    Memorandum
    Correction required: $56.20 of Miscellaneous Expense had been debited to Freight-in in error.

9   *Cash Receipts List*
    From A. Newman, on account; $262.50.
    Purchase Invoices
    From Windsor Manufacturing, No. 452, for trailer parts; $1 452.00.
    From Maynard's Cartage, No. 64, for transportation charges on incoming merchandise; $217.50; terms 2/10,N/30.

10 *Bank Debit Advice*
    From Central Bank, to reduce the bank loan; $10 000.
    Sales Invoice
    No. 639, to B. Fraser, for trailer parts; $450 plus sales tax.

Cash Receipts List
From Federated Finance Company, No. 7043 for the sale of a trailer; selling price, $14 500; sales tax, $725; total $15 225.

Credit Note Issued
No. 27, to A. Newman, for unsatisfactory goods returned; $125 plus sales tax.

Cheque Copies
No. 760, to Modern Mobile Homes, payment in full of account; $2 100.
No. 761, to Double-G Industries, on account; $5 000.

Purchase Invoice
From Windsor Manufacturing, No. 481 for a new trailer; $14 500.

11   *Sales Invoice*
No. 640, to Schell Brothers, for trailer parts and service; $1 575 plus sales tax.

Cheque Copy
No. 762, to C. Fowler, the owner, for personal use; $500.

12   *Cash Receipts List*
From Schell Brothers, on account; $1 500.
From B. Fraser, on account; $367.50.
From N. Thompson, on account; $500.

Cheque Copy
No. 763, made out to Cash, for the wages for the week; $2 042.75.
No. 764, to Parker Manufacturing, paying invoice No. 40 less the two per cent discount; $242.84.
No. 765, to Craighurst Garage, cash payment for repairs to delivery truck, $420.

15   *Cash Receipts List*
From Federated Finance Company, No 7044, for the sale of a trailer; selling price, $10 200; sales tax $510; total $10 710.

Cheque Copies
No. 766, to Provincial Treasurer, paying sales tax for May; $1 694.24.
No. 767, to Windsor Manufacturing, on account; $15 000.

16   *Purchase Invoices*
From Maynard's Cartage, No. 82, for transportation charges on incoming goods; $182.50; terms 2/10,N/30.
From National Hardware, No. 2412, for trailer parts; $259.
From Double-G Industries, No. 515, for a new trailer; $17 680.
From Windsor Manufacturing, No. 499, for trailer parts; $283.50.

17   *Sales Invoice*
No. 641, to W. Hoyle, for trailer servicing; $110 plus sales tax.

Cheque Copy and Sales Slip
No. 768, to Emerald Store, for the cash purchase of miscellaneous expense items; $140.50.

18   *Cheque Copies*
No. 769, to C. Fowler, owner's personal use; $1 200.
No. 770, to National Hardware, on account; $2 787.
No. 771, to Maynard's Cartage, paying invoice No. 64 less the two per cent discount; $213.15.

19   *Credit Note Received*
     From Double-G Industries, price adjustment on invoice No. 515; $1 050.
     Purchase Invoice
     From National Hardware, No. 2480, for trailer parts; $409.50.
     Cheque Copy
     No. 772, made out to Cash, for the wages for the week; $2 040.
22   *Sales Invoice*
     No. 642, to L. Walker, for trailer parts and service; $290 plus sales tax.
     Purchase Invoice
     From Parker Manufacturing, for trailer parts; $358.80; terms 2/10,N/30.
     Memorandum
     The owner had collected $89.25 from L. Walker (for invoice No. 631) but had kept the money for personal use.
24   *Cash Receipts List*
     From Federated Finance Company, No. 7045, for the sale of a trailer; selling price, $11 500; sales tax, $575; total $12 075.
25   *Cheque Copy*
     No. 773, to C. Fowler, for personal use; $350.
     No. 774, to Maynard's Cartage, paying invoice No. 82 less the two per cent discount; $178.85.
     No. 775, to Humber Fuels, cash payment for fuel and oil for the delivery truck, $399.
     Bank Debit Advice
     From Central Bank, to reduce the bank loan; $5 000.
26   *Sales Invoice*
     No. 643, to A. Newman, for trailer repairs; $236 plus sales tax.
     Cheque Copies
     No. 776, to Windsor Manufacturing, on account; $1 760.50.
     No. 777, made out to Cash, for the wages for the week; $2 452.00.
     No. 778, to City Hydro, for hydro for the month; $495.80.
     No. 779, to Bell Telephone, for telephone for the month; $202.00.
29   *Cash Receipts List*
     From B. Fraser, on account; $472.50.
     From Schell Brothers, on account; $1 214.25.
     Purchase Invoice
     From National Hardware, No. 2561, for supplies; $930.
30   *Sales Invoice*
     No. 644, to W. Hoyle, for trailer servicing; $230 plus sales tax.

5. Balance the special journals.

6. Post the five journals to the general ledger.

7. Balance the general ledger as of June 30.

8. Balance the subsidiary ledgers as of June 30.

9. Prepare an eight-column work sheet using the additional information below:
   a) Supplies on hand at June 30th, $1 300.
   b) Prepaid Insurance as of June 30th, $1 599.
   c) Late purchase invoices: Purchases $740.
                             Miscellaneous Expense $102.
   d) Merchandise inventory at June 30th, $136 120.

10 Prepare an income statement (six-month fiscal period) and a balance sheet as of June 30th.

11. Journalize and post the closing entries.

12. Take off a post-closing trial balance.

13 Cash Control and Banking

The word "cash" can be used in both a narrow and a broad sense. In its narrow sense, cash means dollar bills and coins. In its broad sense, cash also includes cheques, bank balances, and other items such as credit card vouchers or money orders—anything that can be deposited in a bank account.

Cash in this broad sense is vital to a business. The principal objective of a business is to earn a profit. This profit must eventually be converted into cash. A business needs cash to pay its bills, to meet its expenses, to reward its owners, and so on.

A small quantity of cash is generally kept on hand in the office. However, a business keeps most of its cash in the safety of a bank account.

13.1 PERSONAL BANKING

Banks and other financial institutions, including trust companies, provide essential services for both businesses and individuals. Our modern economy would grind to a halt if the services of banks were suddenly withdrawn.

The principal services provided by banks are:

- the safekeeping of money;
- the processing of cheques and bank credit card vouchers, and facilitating the "electronic transfer of funds" between people and/or businesses;
- the lending of money to businesses and individuals;
- the processing of "bank" credit card transactions (discussed in detail in a later section);
- the handling of foreign currencies.

Basic Personal Bank Accounts

Banks provide pamphlets which explain the types of accounts, current interest rates, and service charges that they offer. These rates and charges will change from time to time.

There is a surprisingly large variety of types of bank accounts available to the public. The three most common bank account types are summarized below. Details were provided by the Bank of Nova Scotia. Other types of accounts provide combinations of the features described below.

PERSONAL BANK ACCOUNTS—SUMMARY

Pure Savings Account	*Daily Interest Savings Account*	*Personal Chequing Account*
Interest is added to the balance quarterly. This interest is calculated on the minimum monthly balances for the period. There is no interest if the minimum balance is less than $50 for the period.	Interest is added to the balance, calculated on the daily closing balance. The interest rate is slightly lower than for a pure savings account.	No interest is added.
No cheques are allowed.	No cheques are allowed.	$.43 is charged for each cheque.
One free withdrawal or transfer each quarter for each $200 minimum quarterly balance; thereafter $.43 each.	Two free withdrawals or transfers each month; thereafter, there is a $1 charge for each transaction.	$.43 is charged for each withdrawal.
A passbook record of the account is provided.	A passbook record of the account is provided.	A bank statement is provided each month. All cashed cheques are returned to the depositor.

A bank statement for a personal chequing account is shown in Figure 13.1.

Keeping Personal Bank Records

It is a good practice to keep a detailed record of your transactions and bank balance. There are three good reasons for this:

1. You will know your true bank balance at any time. This helps you avoid the embarrassment of writing cheques when there is no money in the account. Writing cheques that "bounce" is not good for your reputation, costs you money, and could damage your credit rating. It is difficult to borrow money if your credit rating is poor.
2. You can easily check back on any particular payment, or analyze your payments for income tax or other purposes.
3. You will have a means of checking the accuracy of the bank's record. This is useful if there is any discrepancy between the bank's record and your own.

The simplest form of personal record is the three-column booklet which banks usually hand out free of charge.

Scotia Bank
THE BANK OF NOVA SCOTIA

85092
Wascana Mall
726-3690

MR ALFRED JARRY
330 VICTORIA STREET
REGINA, SASKATCHEWAN
S4R 1J8

ACCOUNT NUMBER

0000-00

STATEMENT OF		FROM	TO	PAGE
SCOTIA CHEQUING ACCOUNT		FEB. 21, 19--	MAR. 21, 19--	1

DESCRIPTION	DEBITS	CREDITS	DATE M D	BALANCE
BALANCE FORWARD			02 21	361 18
DEPOSIT		2192 26	02 22	2553 44
CHEQUE 46	29 99			
CHEQUE 73	600 00			
CHEQUE 72	136 00		02 25	1787 45
CHEQUE 74	182 00		02 28	1605 45
CHEQUE 48	58 19			
CHEQUE 75	70 00			
CHEQUE 101	29 00		03 01	1448 26
TRANSFER FROM 0474320		2000 00		
CHEQUE 50	172 37			
CHEQUE 47	134 02		03 05	3141 87
CHEQUE 103	40 53			
CHEQUE 102	20 00		03 06	3081 34
CHEQUE 77	2000 00		03 07	1081 34
CHEQUE 76	158 51		03 08	922 83
CHEQUE 106	42 79			
CHEQUE 105	96 00		03 11	784 04
CHEQUE 49	15 97		03 14	768 07
CHEQUE	150 00		03 15	618 07
CHEQUE 107	22 00		03 19	596 07
SERVICE CHARGE	5 36		03 21	590 71

NO. OF DEBITS	TOTAL AMOUNT – DEBITS	NO. OF CREDITS	TOTAL AMOUNT – CREDITS	NO. OF ENCLOSURES	MORE ITEMS ON PAGE
19	3,962.73	2	4,192.26	18	

PLEASE EXAMINE THIS STATEMENT PROMPTLY – REPORT ERRORS OR OMISSIONS TO THE BANK WITHIN 30 DAYS OF RECEIPT OF THE STATEMENT

Figure 13.1   A bank statement for a personal chequing account.

NSF Cheque

A cheque is not cash. It is merely a slip of paper on which a formal promise to pay is written. When you accept a cheque you gamble that the cheque will be good. Most of the time cheques are good. But often enough they are not, so individuals and business people must be cautious.

   If you accept a cheque from someone, it will probably pass through these stages:

1 You will either cash the cheque or deposit it in your bank account. In either case the bank will require that you endorse the cheque by signing it on the reverse side. By endorsing the cheque you are legally contracting to guarantee the cheque should anything go wrong with it. Endorsement is discussed on page 491.
2 The bank gives you cash or credits your account with the amount of the cheque;
3 Your bank forwards the cheque through the bank clearinghouse to the bank of the person who issued the cheque;
4 The issuer's bank attempts to deduct the amount of the cheque from the issuer's bank account. The deduction will be made if the balance in the account is large enough to cover the cheque.

If the Funds Are Insufficient

5 If the balance is not large enough, the bank stamps the cheque "Not Sufficient Funds" (NSF) and sends it back to your bank. The cheque has now been "dishonoured"; in common speech, it has "bounced." An NSF cheque is one that was not cashed when presented to the issuer's bank because there were not sufficient funds in the issuer's bank account to cover the amount of the cheque;
6 The dishonoured cheque is then returned to your bank. Your bank will immediately deduct the amount of the worthless cheque from your account. Remember, you have already received the money or had your account increased, and you did agree to guarantee the cheque;
7 There is a service charge of $10 or more charged to the issuer of a dishonoured cheque. The innocent party also has to pay a charge of around $5.
8 Now you attempt to contact the person who gave you the worthless cheque, in order to recover your money. This may not be easy.
9 If the cheque above was one received by a business, an accounting entry would have been made through the cash receipts journal when the cheque was first received. For example, the entry might have been:

	DR	CR
Bank	$150.00	
Accounts Receivable (R. Walters)		$150.00

Once it is known that the cheque has been dishonoured (bounced), this entry will have to be reversed by an exactly opposite entry recorded in the cash payments journal. The entry will be:

	DR	CR
Accounts Receivable (R. Walters)	$150.00	
Bank		$150.00

Certified Cheque

To avoid the nuisance of a dishonoured cheque, as well as the possible loss of money, you can insist on any cheque offered to you being certified. A **certified cheque** is one for which the bank takes the funds out of the issuer's account in advance. It puts them in a special account to honour the cheque when it is presented.

The person who issues the cheque takes it to his or her bank to be certified. The funds are removed from the bank account at that time; the cheque is boldly marked CERTIFIED with a special stamp and returned to the issuer. There is a small bank charge for the service. The person to whom the cheque is issued can clearly see that it is certified and can be confident that it will not bounce.

You should ask for cash or a certified cheque when you are dealing with a stranger and when the amount of money involved is large. This might be the case if you were selling a used car by means of a newspaper advertisement.

Post-Dated Cheque

There are times when it is appropriate to write a post-dated cheque. A **post-dated cheque** is one that is dated for some time in the future. For example, a cheque written on January 15 but dated for March 1 is a post-dated cheque.

The usual reason for issuing post-dated cheques is to meet a series of payments such as for a mortgage. Usually, at the beginning of each year, 12 cheques, dated January 1, February 1, and so on, are given to the mortgage-holder. The mortgage-holder can then cash one of the cheques on the first day of each month.

You might also choose to write a post-dated cheque to pay off a personal loan. This gives the appearance of having made the payment, but in fact payment is delayed until a future date, payday, for example. You then have time to get money into your bank account.

SECTION REVIEW QUESTIONS

1. What are the five main services provided by banks?
2. Name the three most common types of personal bank accounts.
3. On which type of bank account is interest added?
4. Which type of bank account gives the highest rate of interest?
5. For which type of bank account is a bank statement provided?
6. Which type of bank account is best for writing cheques?
7. Name the three most common bank forms used with personal bank accounts.
8. Describe the simplest form of personal bank record.
9. What is an NSF cheque?
10. What is the simplest way to endorse a cheque?
11. What is meant by the word "bounced" in connection with banking?
12. Why does the bank have the right to take the amount of an NSF cheque out of the depositor's account?
13. What is a certified cheque?

14. Why would a person request a certified cheque?
15. What is a post-dated cheque?
16. Why would a person issue a post-dated cheque?

SECTION EXERCISES

1. **Complete each of the following statements by writing in your Workbook the appropriate word or phrase from the list below.**

    1. Banks provide _____ for both individuals and businesses.
    2. One of the essential services provided by banks is the _____ of money.
    3. Another of the essential services provided by banks is the _____ of money.
    4. Of the three most common types of personal bank accounts, the _____ gives the highest rate of interest.
    5. A bank statement is provided each month with the _____.
    6. A _____ record of a savings account is provided.
    7. It is advisable for the individual to keep a _____.
    8. The _____ is the simplest form of personal bank record.
    9. A cheque that the bank will not cash because of insufficient funds is known as an _____.
    10. A _____ is one for which the bank takes the funds out of the account in advance.
    11. A certified cheque will not _____.
    12. A _____ is one that is dated for some time in the future.
    13. The usual reason for writing post-dated cheques is in respect to a _____ such as for a mortgage.

    List of Words and Phrases

bounce	personal chequing account
certified cheque	post-dated cheque
essential services	pure savings account
lending	safekeeping
NSF cheque	series of payments
passbook	three-column booklet
personal bank record	

2. **Indicate whether each of the following statements is true or false by placing a "T" or an "F" in the space indicated in your Workbook. Explain the reason for each "F" response in the space provided.**

    1. A pure savings account is designed for the person who makes very few withdrawals.
    2. You are not allowed to write cheques on a pure savings account. Therefore, you can only get money out of a pure savings account by closing out the account.
    3. The interest rate on a daily interest savings account is always about one-half a point higher than it is on a pure savings account.

4. A passbook record of a savings account can only be updated at the bank.

5. The personal chequing account is not intended to be used for saving money.

6. There is no limit to the number of cheques that can be written on a personal chequing account.

7. A personal bank record is not really necessary because the bank keeps a record of your account.

8. If Joan Arnott's bank balance as shown by the bank is $352, she can write a cheque for that much money with no fear of its bouncing.

9. A cheque is considered to be cash, but it is not assured cash until it has been cleared by the banking system.

10. The purpose of endorsing a cheque is so the bank can compare the endorsement with the signature card.

11. When you deposit a cheque the bank gives you immediate credit for the amount even though the cheque might bounce.

12. You visit your sister-in-law's bank to cash a cheque for $100 that she has given to you. The bank informs you that there is only $90 in your sister-in-law's account and gives you the $90.

13. You should request cash or a certified cheque when you sell a used car to a stranger.

14. On March 15, 19-1, a bank would not cash a cheque dated March 20, 19-1.

---

3. Pugh & Co. made a cash sale to H. Vernon for $55 plus $2.75 sales tax for a total of $57.75. Vernon gave a cheque in payment. A few days after depositing the cheque in the bank, Pugh & Co. was notified by its bank that Vernon's cheque was NSF.

1. What entries would Pugh & Co. record at the time of making the sale?
2. What entries would record the fact that the cheque is NSF?

---

4. Pugh & Co. sold goods on account to H. Vetiri. The goods were priced at $107, the sales tax was $5.35, and the total was $112.35. The next month, Pugh & Co. received a cheque from Vetiri for $112.35 and deposited it in the bank. A few days later, the company was informed that the cheque had bounced. Discussion with Mrs. Vetiri disclosed that she was temporarily short of funds and would pay the bill in the near future.

1. What entries would be made by Pugh & Co. at the time of the sale?
2. What entries would be made by Pugh & Co. upon receipt of Vetiri's cheque?
3. What entries would record the fact that the cheque is NSF?

13.2 BANK CREDIT CARDS

Credit cards are used so much in our society that we can visualize a society without money—a cashless society. Credit cards are available for department stores such as Sears and Eaton's, oil companies such as Petro-Canada and Esso, and other large retail outlets such as Canadian Tire. We are so used to credit cards that many individuals and merchants would be badly affected if their use were ever discontinued.

Most smaller retail outlets do not offer their own company credit cards. For them the alternative is Visa or Mastercard. These are credit cards sponsored by the major chartered banks. With bank credit cards, consumers can make purchases on short-term credit at any retail outlet that accepts the bank's credit cards. The illustrations used in the text are supplied by the Bank of Nova Scotia, one of the sponsoring banks of the Visa card. The concepts are the same or similar for any bank credit card.

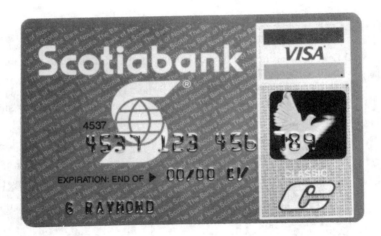

Figure 13.2 A Visa card.

Accounting for Bank Credit Card Transactions

1 The first step in a bank credit card transaction occurs when the customer makes a purchase, or returns goods, in a store that accepts the customer's credit card. After checking that the card is in good standing, the store clerk will:
   a. write up the sale on a credit card slip or "credit" voucher;
   b. run the sales slip through the imprinting device using the customer's credit card as shown in Figure 13.3. This prints the customer's name and identification number and the merchant's name and identification number on the sales slip.
   c. give one copy of the sales slip to the customer and keep two for the store. One of these will be forwarded to the bank along with the bank deposit.
2 The merchant will probably have a number of bank credit card transactions each day. The sales slips for these transactions must be kept in a safe place during the day.

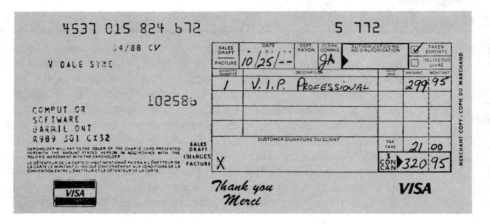

Figure 13.3   A completed Visa sales slip.

3 During or at the end of the day, the credit card slips are prepared for inclusion in the
  bank deposit. This involves:
  a. summarizing all of the slips for the day to obtain daily totals;
  b. writing in the totals onto a Merchant Deposit Summary as shown in Figure 13.4;

Figure 13.4   Visa merchant deposit summary slip.

  c. placing the credit card slips and the summary into a special envelope provided
    by the bank;
  d. recording the gross amount from the summary slip on the bank deposit slip. You
    will see how this is done on page 492.

4 When preparing the accounting entries for the day, the credit card slips must be included. In theory, the accounting entry is:

	DR	CR
Bank	$$$$	
Sales		$$$$
Sales Tax Payable		$$$$
Credit card slips for the day		

Credit Card Charges

When the merchant makes a bank deposit, the bank credits the account with the total value of the deposit, including full value for credit card slips. Thus the merchant receives quick payment for credit card sales and does not have to worry about collecting from the customer.

However, the bank does not provide the credit card service free of charge. The banks earn revenue from the service by applying three types of charges.

1. Transaction fees to the buyers, and interest on advances and overdue balances.
2. An annual fee charged to each merchant.
3. Discounts taken off the credit card slips deposited by the merchants. The merchant does not really get full value for the gross amount of the credit card slips. Each month, the merchant is charged a percentage of all of the slips for the month. The amount of the charge is deducted from the merchant's account. The merchant first sees the amount of the deduction on the bank statement. The journal entry necessary for the transaction is as follows:

	DR	CR
Credit Card Discount Expense*	$$$$	
Bank		$$$$
*(or, simply, Bank Charges)		

SECTION REVIEW QUESTIONS

1. Which types of companies were the first to offer credit cards?
2. Which types of stores use major bank credit cards?
3. The merchant who includes bank credit card slips in the bank deposit does not get full credit for them. Explain.
4. In what three ways do the banks earn revenue from bank credit cards?

SECTION EXERCISES

1. **Complete each of the following statements by writing in your Workbook the appropriate word or phrase from the list on page 480.**

   1. Today's society is often referred to as a _____ society.
   2. Credit cards sponsored by the chartered banks are _____ and _____.
   3. Bank credit cards can be used in most _____.

4. During or at the end of the day the credit card slips are prepared for inclusion in the _____.

5. The merchant does not get full value for the _____ of the credit card slips.

6. Each month the bank charges the merchant with a _____.

List of Words and Phrases

bank deposit	Mastercard
cashless	retail stores
discount fee	Visa
gross value	

---

2. **Indicate whether each of the following statements is true or false by placing a "T" or an "F" in the space indicated in your Workbook. Explain the reason for each "F" response in the space provided.**

1. Small retail outlets do not offer their own company credit cards because they prefer not to sell on credit.
2. Carrying a bank credit card is like having plastic money.
3. The use of credit cards slows things down at the cash register.
4. During or at the end of the day, the bank credit card slips are included in the bank deposit.
5. The two common bank credit cards are Visa and Mastercard.
6. Bank credit card services would probably not have become widely available without the development of the computer.
7. The merchant never has to worry about collecting his or her money if a customer offers a credit card in payment.
8. When accounting for the day's bank credit card sales, the debit is to Accounts Receivable (credit card centre).

---

3. Shown below and on page 481 are two Visa vouchers. **Study these two vouchers, then answer the questions that follow.**

A.

B.

```
4537 015 824 672                    6 706
    04/88 CV
   V DALE SYME

                  102585
  COMPUT OR
  SOFTWARE
  BAR IE ONT
  N989 501 CX32
```

Credit voucher / Note de crédit: 10/30/-- ... 10/27/-- ... 160.45
NOT SATISFACTORY
1 TEXT CRAFT ... 149 95
TAX TAXE 10 50
$ CDN CAN 160 45

PLEASE RETAIN THIS COPY AS A RECORD OF YOUR TRANSACTION
CONSERVEZ CETTE COPIE COMME PREUVE DE VOTRE TRANSACTION

VISA

1. What type of transaction does voucher A represent?
2. What type of transaction does voucher B represent?
3. Are these vouchers related? Explain your reasoning.
4. Give the name of the merchant.
5. Give the name of the customer.
6. When does the merchant get paid for voucher A?
7. How will voucher B be handled when making up the bank deposit of October 30?
8. What is the value of the net sales for the two vouchers including sales tax?
9. How much will the merchant be charged for these two vouchers if the discount rate is 2.75 per cent? How will the merchant pay the discount?
10. How much money will the merchant realize from these two vouchers?

---

4. A Visa statement for Robin Goodfellow appears on page 482. **Examine this statement, then answer the questions that follow.**

1. What is the statement date?
2. What is the due date shown on the statement?
3. What is Robin Goodfellow's account balance as of the statement date?
4. How many purchases were made during the statement period?
5. What is the value of the purchases made during the statement period?
6. How many payments were made during the statement period?
7. What is the amount of the payments made during the statement period?
8. What is the minimum amount that is due?
9. What percentage of the outstanding balance is the minimum amount?
10. What is this customer's credit limit?
11. How much interest was charged during the statement period?

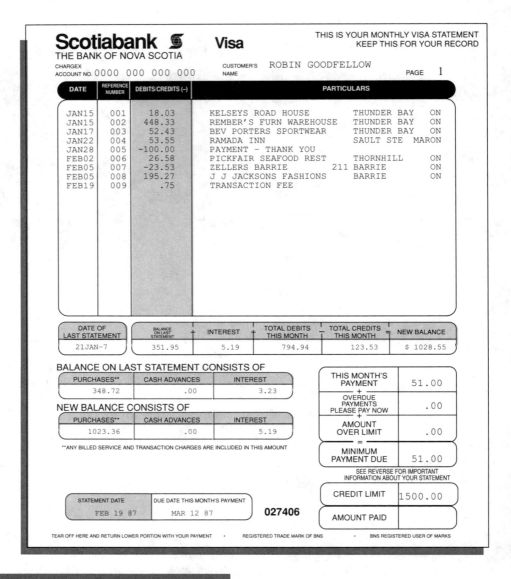

13.3 BANKING FOR A BUSINESS

A large part of business banking has to do with "cash receipts." The cash receipts of a business are the funds taken in from business operations. These funds must be carefully controlled and deposited in the bank promptly.

Daily Cash Receipts

The cash receipts of a business are usually received in one of the following three ways.

1. Mail Receipts

A business that sells on credit usually receives payment from its customers by way of cheques through the mail. Each business day the clerk in charge of the mail separates out any cheques received and prepares a listing of them. The clerk then gives the cheques up to the accounting department for deposit to the bank. You previously saw this cash receipts list in Chapter 6. The mail clerk is usually someone who does not work in the accounting department. Using an independent person in this way is a control technique that helps to ensure that the funds received will be handled and recorded properly. The usual accounting entry is:

	DR	CR
Bank	$$$$	
Accounts Receivable		$$$$

2. Over-the-Counter Sales

Some small businesses sell only a few goods over the counter, and place the money received in a drawer or cash box. It is customary for a business of this type to use dual-purpose sales slips. A sales slip, and a forms register in which to keep sales slips, are illustrated in Figure 13.5. The slips are prenumbered to ensure that all slips can be accounted for. This is a simple but effective accounting control technique. Cash sales, charge sales, refunds, returns for credit, and receipts on account can all be processed using the dual-purpose sales slips.

Courtesy of Moore Business
Forms and Systems Division

Figure 13.5   A dual-purpose sales slip and a forms register machine.

Proving the Cash   For each transaction a copy of the sales slip is kept in the lower section of the register. At the end of every business day a control procedure known as **proving the cash** or balancing the cash is carried out. The sales slips for the day are analyzed and a summary prepared such as the one shown below in Figure 13.6.

SALES SUMMARY	DATE *November 12* 19 –									
SIGNATURE *R.S.*	SALES		SALES TAX		TOTAL					
CHARGE SALES SLIPS	2	705	60		189	39	2	894	99
LESS CREDITS		316	20		22	13		338	33
NET CHARGE SALES SLIPS	2	389	40		167	26	2	556	66
CASH SALES SLIPS	3	716	21		260	13	3	976	34
LESS REFUNDS		296	30		20	74		317	04
NET CASH SALES SLIPS	3	419	91		239	39	3	659	30
RECEIPTS ON ACCOUNT								500	00
TOTAL CASH PER SLIPS							4	159	30
ACTUAL CASH ON HAND							4	149	30
CASH SHORT √ OR OVER ☐								10	–
TOTALS	5	809	31		406	65	6	215	96

Figure 13.6   A daily sales summary for a dual-purpose sales slip system.

The cash on hand by actual count at the end of every business day should be equal to the net cash sales figure on the summary. If it is not, there is a cash shortage or a cash overage as shown.

The summary, slips, and cash are forwarded to the accounting department for further processing. The accounting entry for the above summary is as follows:

	DR	CR
Accounts Receivable	$2 556.66	
Bank	4 149.30	
Cash Short or Over	10.00	
Accounts Receivable		$ 500.00
Sales		5 809.31
Sales Tax Payable		406.65

Cash short or over is explained fully on page 490.

3. Cash Register Receipts

Today, most retail businesses are equipped with one of two types of sophisticated cash register. One type is the point of sale terminal. A **point of sale terminal** is an electronic cash register that is connected to a central computer, which is the heart of a sophisticated information system. The other type is the stand-alone electronic cash register which is not connected to a computer. Cash registers today can continually interact with a computer to provide up-to-the minute information for use by both management and store personnel. For example:

- Jerry Henry purchases a new drill, using his charge card. The transaction is processed through a cash register. Immediately, Jerry's account and the inventory figure for drills are updated.
- Sylvia Murphy visits a department store to settle the balance of her overdue account. A clerk, using a computer terminal, calls up the details of Sylvia's account. Sylvia pays the balance of her account.
- Jim Star visits a department store to purchase a bicycle tire but cannot find the size he needs on the floor. He asks a store clerk if that size is available. The clerk, through a computer terminal, calls up the inventory status of the item and is able to tell Jim that the store does have the size in stock.

Even stand-alone cash registers have many valuable features. Today's operator may never have to make a mental or manual calculation. Price, sales tax, discount, and change computations can all be handled automatically, eliminating any possibility of error. As well, a number of accumulators are at work as transactions occur, building up totals to be printed out later. A typical stand-alone cash register is illustrated in Figure 13.7.

Change Fund (Float)   The change fund or float is a small quantity of money, usually between $50 and $100, in small bills and coins. This fund is used to make change for customers. It is placed in the cash drawer of the cash register at the beginning of each business day. At the close of the day, small bills and coins equalling the amount of the float are taken from the cash register drawer and put safely away. This is the float for the next business day.

The float is created in the first place by issuing and cashing a cheque made out to Cash. The accounting entry for the transaction is:

	DR	CR
Cash Float	$$$$	
Bank		$$$$

Detailed Audit Tape   Cash registers are used for transactions other than just cash sales. Charge sales, Visa sales, receipts on account, credit notes, and payments for small expenditures (known as "paid outs') can all be processed using a cash register. A duplicate sales slip, or similar document, is required for all transactions except cash sales. A copy of the sales slip is kept in the cash drawer.

As transactions occur during the day, the details are stored inside the cash register on a paper tape known as the detailed audit tape or the audit strip. The audit strip is a continuous record on tape of all transactions during the day. It is the equivalent of a series of customers' take-home receipts all joined together. Each transaction is given an individual reference number by the machine, in consecutive order. This makes it convenient for checking back on any particular transaction.

The daily totals are shown on the audit strip in Figure 13.8. Remember that a special key must be inserted in the control lock before the machine will release the totals. This key is kept under the control of a supervisor. The daily totals are needed to prove the cash and to work out the accounting entry for the day. A detailed audit tape, with explanations of the various codes, is illustrated in Figure 13.8.

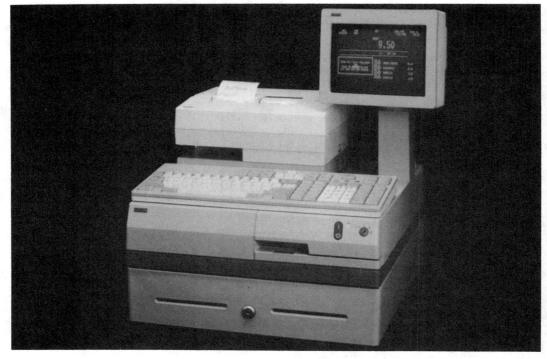

NCR 7052 Hardware

The NCR 7052 is a fully programmable retail workstation designed to control point-of-service functionality and peripheral support.

• Cabinet
– Integrated
– Modular

• Memory
– 640 KB
– 1.6 MB

• Keyboard
– 32-key
– 56-key
– 109-key (POS and alphanumeric)

• Display
– 2 x 20 Line Display
– 22.5 cm Video (Graphics interface)

• Communications
– StarLAN
– M-11

• Printer
– 46 Column Slip
– 42 Column Receipt
– 42 Column Journal

• Cash Drawer
– With or without Till, Lid and Tray

Optional features include:

• Integrated Stripe Reader with Pin Pad
• Customer Display
• Second Cash Drawer
• Hand Held, Flat Deck and Presentation Scanners
• Peripheral Communications

Figure 13.7   A typical stand-alone electronic cash register. Courtesy National Cash Register of Canada Limited. Note the features designed to give information on cash control.

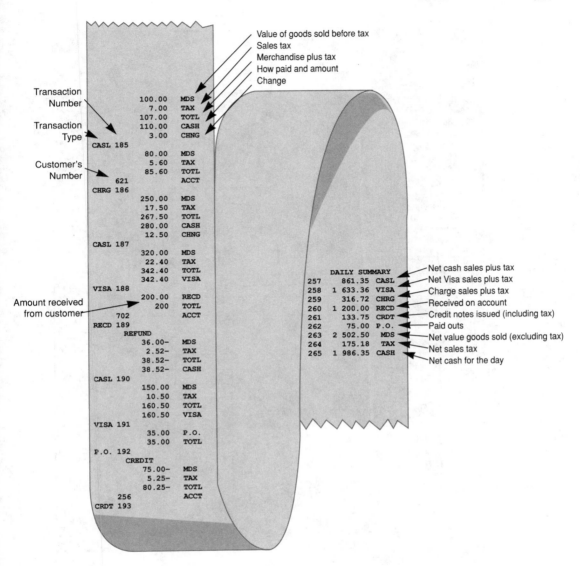

Figure 13.8   A cash register detailed audit tape (simplified).

Proving the Cash   Where a cash register is used, the cash is proved at the end of every business day. A modern cash register can produce most of the figures required on a daily balancing form (in this text called the Cash Proof and Accounting Summary). At the end of the day a blank form is inserted into the document printing device on the machine and the day's totals are machine-printed under the control of a supervisor. A completed form is shown in Figure 13.9.

CASH PROOF AND ACCOUNTING SUMMARY

DATE _March 18_____ ,19 ___ —

	TO LINE NO.	TOTALS
CASH REGISTER TOTALS		
Cash Sales less Refunds (Incl. Tax)	—	861.35
Visa Sales less Visa Returns (Incl. Tax)	2	1 633.36
Charge Sales (Incl. Tax)	3	316.72
Received on Account	8	1 200.00
Returns for Credit (Incl. Tax)	9	133.75
Paid Outs	—	75.00
Sales less Returns	10	2 502.50
Sales Tax (Net)	11	175.18
CASH PROOF		
Total Cash Received less Paid Outs	—	1 986.35
Cash by Actual Count	1	_1 975.35_
Cash Short	7	
Cash Over	12	_11.00_
PAID OUTS BREAKDOWN		
Account _Supplies_	4	_40.00_
Account _Miscellaneous Expense_	5	_35.00_
Account _____	6	
Total Paid Outs		75.00

ACCOUNTING ENTRY

LINE NO.	ACCOUNTS		DR	CR
1	Cash _1 975.35_			
2	Visa _1 633.36_ Total to Bank →		3 608 71	
3	Account Rec'l (Charge Sales)		316 72	
4	Asset or Expense _Supplies_		40 —	
5	Asset or Expense _Misc. Expense_		35 —	
6	Asset or Expense _____			
7	Cash Short or Over		11 —	
8	Accounts Rec'l (Rec'd on A/c)			1 200 —
9	Accounts Rec'l (Ret'd for Cr.)			133 75
10	Sales			2 502 50
11	Sales Tax Payable			175 18
12	Cash Short or Over			
	BALANCING TOTALS		4 011 43	4 011 43

CASHIER'S SIGNATURE   _Keith Hernandez_

Figure 13.9 The cash proof and accounting summary form.

A copy of the machine-produced cash proof and accounting summary form is retained by the cashier. The cashier should then follow the procedure outlined below and on page 489.

1 Remove the cash and the vouchers from the cash drawer and separate them from each other.

2 Prove the cash as follows:

 a. Remove the float and place it in safekeeping for the next business day.

b. Count the remaining cash carefully. Write the total in on the line for Cash by Actual Count on the balancing form. This amount should agree with the machine-produced figure immediately above it for Total Cash Received less Paid Outs. If these two figures do *not* agree, the difference represents either a cash shortage or a cash overage. It is recorded on the line that reads Cash Short or the line that reads Cash Over. In Figure 13.10 a shortage of $11.00 is recorded.

3 Total specific voucher groups and see that they agree with their corresponding summary figures. This is done in several categories:

    a. Bank credit card sales slips are agreed with the summary figure of $1 633.36.

    b. The charge sales slips of the business itself are agreed with the summary figure of $316.72.

    c. "Received on account" slips are agreed with the summary figure of $1 200.

    d. "Returns for credit" slips are agreed with the summary figure of $133.75.

    e. "Paid out" bills are agreed with the summary figure of $75.

4 Analyze the paid out bills and break them down by ledger account. Enter the details on the summary form. The example shows $40.00 for Supplies and $35.00 for Miscellaneous Expense.

5 Complete the Accounting Summary section of the form from the data above it. This section shows the accounting entry for the day's receipts. Transfer the figures with a line number to their left down to the appropriate line number in the Accounting Summary section. When all appropriate figures are transferred, the accounting summary section should balance. If it does not, the form has not been completed correctly and must be checked over until the error or errors are found.

6 Forward the cash, vouchers, and daily balance form to the accounting department. The accounting department will see that the money is deposited promptly in the bank, and make the appropriate accounting entries in the cash receipts journal as shown in Figure 13.10.

Cash Receipts Journal Month of March, 19 —									
Date	Particulars	Other Accounts Cr.			Sales Tax Payable Cr.	Sales Credit	Acc's Rec'l		Bank Dr
		Account	P.R.	Amount			Dr	Cr	
12	Cash Summary	Supplies		40 –	175 18	2 502 50	316 72	1 200 –	3 608 71
		Misc. Exp.		35 –				133 75	
		Cash Short		11 –					
		or Over							

Figure 13.10 The daily cash register accounting summary recorded in the cash receipts journal.

Cash Short or Over

Businesses that deal with the public in cash experience cash shortages and cash overages. Some businesses hold their clerks responsible for shortages and overages. That is, the clerks may keep any overages, but must make up any shortages out of their own pockets. No shortages or overages are recorded in the books when this policy is adopted.

Other firms accept the shortages and overages as part of doing business. Any shortages or overages must be recorded in a Cash Short or Over account. Any shortages are entered as debits to the account. Any overages are recorded as credits to the account.

At any particular time, the balance in the account represents either a shortage (expense, debit) or an overage (income, credit) depending on the type of balance in the account. It is usual for the account to end up with a debit balance. This is because customers who have been given too little change are more likely to complain than those who have been given too much change.

The Current Bank Account

With business bank accounts, there is usually more work involved for the bank's employees. For example, checking the coins and currency in a business's deposit can be quite time-consuming. People in business are expected to use a type of bank account known as the current account. A **current bank account** is one designed especially for the use of business people. The principal features of a current bank account are outlined below. There may be slight variations of these features from one bank chain to another.

* No interest is added.
* There is one free deposit, electronic funds transfer, or cheque per monthly statement period for each full $500 of minimum monthly credit balance.
* Thereafter, there is a small charge for each deposit, electronic funds transfer, or cheque processed per monthly statement period.
* There is a small minimum charge each monthly statement period.
* A bank statement is provided each month.
* The paid cheques are returned to the depositor each month along with the bank statement.
* Books of duplicate deposit slips are provided free of charge.

Preparing the Business Deposit

During the business day, the day's receipts are prepared for deposit. It is best to make the deposit as soon as possible to avoid having a large amount of money on the premises. However, the nature of some businesses makes them unable to complete this task until after banking hours. They must use the night depository service.

The person preparing the deposit must keep the following in mind:

1. Bills must be sorted by denomination for ease of counting;
2. Coins are to be wrapped when there are sufficient quantities;

3. Banks require that the depositor endorse (that is, guarantee) each cheque by signing it on the reverse side. Businesses endorse all cheques FOR DEPOSIT ONLY as shown in Figure 13.11. Usually, a business has an approved rubber stamp with which to make the endorsements. The endorsement shown in Figure 13.11 is a restrictive endorsement. A **restrictive endorsement** is one that places conditions on the cashing or depositing of the cheque. In the illustration nothing could happen to this cheque except that it be deposited in the account of Tech Industries Limited. If the cheque was lost or stolen, it could not be cashed. If, on the other hand, a cheque is endorsed in blank—that is, with just a signature, it could possibly be cashed by anyone who happened to get hold of it;

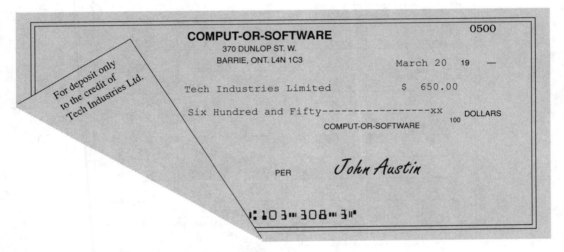

Figure 13.11   A restrictive endorsement on the back of a cheque.

4. The completed deposit slip must agree with the cash proofs and the accounting entries;
5. A duplicate deposit slip, stamped by the bank, must be obtained as the company's receipt for the deposit. The bank retains the original. If a night depository is used, the bank will mail out the receipted duplicate deposit slip. A completed deposit slip is shown in Figure 13.12 on p. 492.

SECTION REVIEW QUESTIONS

1. Name the three most common types of cash receipts of a business.
2. What is the usual reason a business would receive "mail" receipts?
3. What business form is commonly used by a business that sells goods over the counter?
4. Describe the basic process of proving the cash for a business that sells goods over the counter.
5. Cash registers today can be more than just cash registers. Explain.
6. What is meant by a stand-alone cash register?
7. Name several features of a typical stand-alone cash register.

cheques		Scotiabank **THE BANK OF NOVA SCOTIA**	

CREDIT ACOUNT NO. 000-00	DATE Oct 8 19—

NAME Pine Valley Golf	

PARTICULARS	AMOUNT
Jones	75 –
Archer	125 –
Lem	125 –
Singh	75 –
Yaremeo	75 –

TOTAL CHEQUES (CARRY FORWARD)	475 –

CURRENT ACCOUNT DEPOSIT

CREDIT ACCOUNT NO. 000-00	DATE Oct 8 19—

NAME Pine Valley Golf	

DEPOSITED BY S

16	x 1	16 –
41	x 2	82 –
17	x 5	85 –
8	x 10	80 –
12	x 20	240 –
	x 50	
	x 100	
	COIN	78 35
SUB-TOTAL	TELLER	581 35
VISA		378 50
U.S CHEQUES		
U.S. CASH		
* TOTAL CHEQUES (BROUGHT FORWARD)		475 –
SUB-TOTAL		1434 85
U.S. EXCHANGE (PLUS/MINUS)		
* GRAND TOTAL		1434 85

CURRENT ACCOUNT DEPOSIT

Figure 13.12   A completed deposit slip for a business.

8. Describe what the "float" is.
9. What types of transactions can be processed using a cash register?
10. Describe the two principal features of a detailed audit tape.
11. Give the name of the cash register balancing form used in this text.
12. The cash register summary totals are printed out on the detailed audit tape at the end of the day. Where else can they be printed?
13. Why are there cash overages or cash shortages?
14. Which is the more common—cash overage or cash shortage? Explain.

15. Who uses a current bank account?
16. Which personal bank account is similar to the current bank account?
17. When preparing a business deposit, what must be done with the coins?
18. How is a cheque endorsed for a business deposit?
19. What is meant by a "restrictive" endorsement?

SECTION EXERCISES

1. **Complete each of the following statements by writing in your Workbook the appropriate word or phrase from the list below.**

   1. The _____ of a business represent the money taken in from business operations.
   2. It is customary for a business that _____ to receive payment from its customers by way of cheques through the mail.
   3. Cheques received in the mail are _____ by the mail clerk before being deposited in the bank.
   4. Sales slips are _____ to ensure that all slips are accounted for.
   5. In a business where goods are sold for cash, the cash is _____ at the end of the day.
   6. An electronic cash register that is connected to a central computer is known as a _____.
   7. A small quantity of money used to start the cash register activity for the day is known as a _____.
   8. Cash registers can be used for transactions other than just _____.
   9. As transactions occur during the day, the details are stored inside the cash register on a paper tape known as the _____ or the _____.
   10. At the end of each day the daily balance form, the cash, and the vouchers are forwarded to the _____.
   11. Cash _____ are more common than cash _____.
   12. Businesses are required by the banks to use a _____.
   13. All cheques received by the business are endorsed _____ before being deposited.
   14. Business deposit slips are prepared in _____.
   15. When preparing the cash for deposit, bills are sorted by _____.

List of Words and Phrases

accounting department	duplicate
audit strip	for deposit only
balanced	listed
cash float	overages
cash receipts	point-of-sale terminal
cash sales	prenumbered
current bank account	sells on credit
denomination	shortages
detailed audit tape	

2. **Using the information given below, perform the following:**

   1. **Complete the sales summary and cash proof on the sheet provided in your Workbook.** The business does not accept Visa or Mastercard.

   2. **Write out the accounting entry for the day's transactions from the details on the summary sheet.**

Vouchers

Voucher	Transaction	Sale	Tax	Total
No. 57	Cash sale	$315.00	$22.05	$337.05
No. 58	Charge sale	206.00	14.42	220.42
No. 59	Cash sale	392.00	27.44	419.44
No. 60	Cash refund	102.00	7.14	109.14
No. 61	Cash sale	740.00	51.80	791.80
No. 62	Charge sale	315.00	22.05	337.05
No. 63	Charge sale	216.00	15.12	231.12
No. 64	Cash sale	375.00	26.25	401.25
No. 65	Cash refund	208.00	14.56	222.56
No. 66	Credit note	58.00	4.06	62.06
No. 67	Cash sale	374.00	26.18	400.18
No. 68	Credit note	216.00	15.12	231.12

Cash in Drawer, after Removing Change Fund

Bills $1 × 56   Coins 1¢ × 937
        $2 × 19   5¢ × 251
        $5 × 29   10¢ × 311
       $10 × 80   25¢ × 652
       $20 × 23
       $50 × 6

3. The cash register daily totals shown below for February 28, 19—, are machine-printed on the daily balance form given in your Workbook.

   1. **Complete the remainder of the form.**

   2. **Show that the vouchers agree with the appropriate summary figures.**

Additional Information

a. *Cash Register Daily Totals*

     $1 325.73 CASL
       843.16 VISA
       295.00 RECD
        40.00 P.O.
       525.37 CHRG
        87.74 CRDT
       170.52 TAX
    2 436.00 MDS
    1 580.73 CASH

b. *Cash on Hand, Including $50 Float*

   Bills $20 × 46   Coin 1¢ × 263
       $10 × 40   5¢ × 130
        $5 × 31   10¢ × 166
        $2 × 28   25¢ × 192
        $1 × 21

c. *Vouchers on Hand*

       Sales slip No. 75, credit note for $48.15
       Sales slip No. 76, charge sale for $124.12
       Sales slip No. 77, Visa sale for $273.92
       Sales slip No. 78, received on account, $75
       Sales slip No. 79, Visa sale for $181.90
       Sales slip No. 80, Visa sale for $218.28
       Sales slip No. 81, received on account, $125
       Sales slip No. 82, charge sale for $401.25
       Supplier's bill, for postage, $16.00
       Sales slip No. 83, Visa sale for $78.11
       Sales slip No. 84, credit note for $39.59
       Sales slip No. 85, received on account, $95
       Sales slip No. 86, Visa sale for $90.95
       Supplier's bill, for supplies, $24.00

4. **Workbook Exercise: End-of-day balancing procedure in a cash register environment.**

5. **Assume that the Cash Short or Over account is posted daily as in the account below. Examine the account and answer the following questions.**

Date	Particulars	P.R.	Debit	Credit	DR CR	Balance
Cash Short or Over						
July 19– 3			10 –			
4			2 –			
7				5 –		
10			20 –			
11				1 –		
12			5 –			
14				50		
17				1 50		
18			2 –			
20			1 –			
24			10 –			
25				75		
26			3 –			
27			10 –			
28			5 –			
31			1 –		Dr	60 25

1. **On how many days was there a cash shortage?**
2. **On how many days was there a cash overage?**

3. Is the net result for the month an overage or a shortage?
4. Does this account as it stands represent an expense or an income?

6. At the end of a business day, Joanne Adamson is responsible for preparing the night deposit for Marks and Associates. The deposit is to be made up from the currency and Visa slips shown below.

1. **Prepare the deposit on the form provided in the Workbook for June 10, 19—. Use account no. 756210.**
2. **Make the deposit agree with the accounting entry figure of $8 978.29.**

Currency

Bills	$1 ×	57
	$2 ×	85
	$5 ×	42
	$10 ×	78
	$20 ×	101
	$50 ×	22
	$100 ×	8
Coin	1¢ ×	151
	5¢ ×	86
	10¢ ×	158
	25¢ ×	141

Visa Slips

James	$109.14
Carter	83.46
Paracy	483.64
DeCorte	102.72
Hill	24.61
Melnyk	630.23
Thrower	85.60

Cheques

Thompson	$362.73
Meyer	55.64
Bogard	911.64
Geyer	155.50
Metsopoulis	228.98
Morris	189.95
Savela	334.91
Webb	25.68

13.4 ACCOUNTING CONTROLS FOR CASH

Every business establishes some kind of accounting system or set of procedures. The owner of a business should make the time and effort to establish a good system, one that has strong "internal control."

Internal Control

An accounting system that promotes employee honesty, accuracy, and efficiency is considered to have good internal control. **Internal control** is the set of accounting procedures established to protect the assets from theft and waste, ensure accurate accounting data, encourage efficiency, and adhere to company policies.

No internal control is necessary in a small business where the owner functions alone. But as the business grows and employees are hired, accounting controls become a factor in managing the business. Where there are a large number of employees, a good system of internal control is essential. A business should not take chances about its employees' honesty and dedication. It should take whatever steps it can to protect itself.

A good system of internal control can be quite involved and highly detailed. Some fundamental rules of good internal control are:

1. Where possible, two different people should be processing and preparing accounting documents independently of each other and their work must agree.
2. The person who records transactions or prepares accounting records should not also control or handle the physical assets.
3. All assets should be kept in a safe place. Two authorized persons should be present when negotiable assets are dealt with. (Negotiable assets are the ones that can easily be converted to cash.)
4. Only a few key employees should be allowed to approve and authorize transactions.
5. An independent public accountant should periodically carry out an audit to ensure that the accounting system is being followed correctly. If weaknesses are found, the system should be improved.
6. Responsibilities should be clearly established. It should be easy to tell who is responsible for errors or missing assets.

Procedures for the Control of Cash

Internal control affects all aspects of a business but is especially needed for cash. Cash is the single item most likely to be stolen outright by employees. Cash is the item most likely to be embezzled, that is, secretly stolen, with the help of falsified accounting records. Cash has no special marks to identify it, and is easily exchanged for other goods or services.

The following are internal control measures specially designed to protect the cash of a business.

1. Separate duties. In general, the same people should not handle the cash and keep the records for the cash. For example, the person who opens the mail and prepares the daily list of mail receipts should not be a member of the accounting department. If this procedure is followed, a theft can only take place if two or more employees decide to act together. (This is known as collusion.) A mail clerk who acted alone would be caught easily. Suppose, for instance, that the mail clerk managed to cash a customer's cheque for personal use. The customer's account would not be credited with the amount of the cheque and there would eventually be a complaint. An investigation would point to the mail clerk who had access to the cheque.

2. Deposit funds daily. The total cash receipts for the day should be deposited by the end of that day. This keeps the amount of cash in the office to a minimum. Theft is both prevented and discouraged. Banks provide a night depository system for the benefit of businesses who take in cash outside of banking hours.

3. Deposit funds intact. All of the cash receipts of each business day should be deposited intact. Cash received during the day should not be available for making payments or for borrowing by employees. The only exception to this rule is for cash register "pay outs" which are controlled by the cash register audit strip.

4. Make all payments by cheque. Except for petty cash expenditures, all payments should be supported by documents and follow a rigid set of approvals. Payment should never be by cash, only by cheque. When all payments are made by cheque and all cash receipts are deposited intact, the records prepared by the company correspond to the records prepared by the bank. It is then possible to compare the one against the other. This control technique, known as the bank reconciliation, is described in the next section.

5. Endorse cheques "For Deposit Only." Then each cheque can only be credited to the business's bank account and cannot be cashed in any other way.

6. Prepare deposit slips in duplicate. The deposit slip shows the details of the deposit. It is useful if any question arises regarding the deposit. The teller should stamp a duplicate of the deposit slip and the business should retain it as a receipt.

7. Use cash registers in retail stores. Cash registers or point-of-sale terminals should be used in retail outlets of any size and the cash receipts should be balanced every day. The audit strip and the balancing form become the source documents for the entries to the accounting system.

8. Reconcile bank accounts monthly. As was mentioned above, the company's and the bank's records can be compared, or "reconciled." If a company has more than one bank account, each one should be reconciled monthly.

Bank Reconciliation

Since both the bank and the business keep a record of the same funds, you might expect the month-end balance shown by the bank statement to agree with the month-end balance shown by the general ledger Bank account. This rarely happens.

Usually, the bank statement balance differs from the Bank account balance in the general ledger. How then can the accounting department be certain that either record is correct? The accuracy of both balances is proven by a process known as the bank reconciliation. A **bank reconciliation** is a routine procedure to determine why the balance on deposit in the bank does not agree with the balance on deposit as shown by the books of the company. The procedure involves a thorough investigation of the two sets of records and ends only after all the causes of the difference are uncovered. The process is completed by the preparation of a bank reconciliation statement. A **bank reconciliation statement** is a statement showing the causes for the difference between the bank balance as shown by the bank and the bank balance as shown in the general ledger of the depositor. An example of a bank reconciliation statement is shown in Figure 13.13.

	Boxwell and Company				
	Bank Reconciliation Statement				
	March 31, 19—				
Bank's Record			**Company's Record**		
Balance per statement	1204.90		Balance per ledger		1157.76
Add Late Deposit	300.51		Deduct: Error in		
	1505.41		recording cheque #697		
			for postage.		
Deduct Outstanding Cheques			Was recorded as $25.60		
#702 $60.00			Should have been 26.50		
#705 72.40			Difference .90		.90
#709 51.90					1156.86
#710 175.00					
#711 2.75	362.05		Deduct: Bank service		
			charge not recorded		
			in company books		13.50
True balance	1143.36		True balance		1143.36

Figure 13.13   A bank reconciliation statement.

Steps in Reconciling a Bank Account

The steps in reconciling a bank account are outlined below.

1 Have the following records available:
   a. the bank statement and related vouchers received from the bank;
   b. the bank reconciliation statement for the previous month;
   c. the general ledger Bank account;
   d. the cash receipts journal;
   e. the cash payments;
   f. the general journal.

2 Write the heading "Bank Reconciliation Statement" and the date on a sheet of paper. Then divide the page down the middle. Write the heading "Company's Record" on one side. Write the heading "Bank's Record" on the other side.

3 Enter the ending balance from the bank statement on the side of the page headed Bank's Record. Enter the ending balance from the general ledger Bank account on the side of the page headed Company's Record.

4 Search for and identify all of the "discrepancy items," that is, the items causing the two balances to differ. This is the most difficult and the most important part of the reconciliation. It involves an item-by-item comparison of the bank's record with the business's record. Search for items that are not recorded equally in both sets of records. Locating the discrepancy items involves a well-organized and skillful search. The techniques for doing this are explained below.

5 Record the discrepancy items on the reconciliation statement, adding or subtracting them as necessary until the two balances are shown to be equal. This step is explained on the next page. The reconciliation is not complete until a balance is reached.

Locating the Discrepancy Items

The following suggestions will be helpful to you in searching out the discrepancy items.

1. When comparing the two sets of records, it is never necessary to go back in the records beyond one month. The previous reconciliation statement will show any differences that originated before then.

2. The bank's record must be compared item by item with the business's record. When individual items are found to correspond exactly, mark them with a coloured pen or pencil. After this is done, the items without coloured marks beside them are the discrepancy items.

3. The most common discrepancy item is the quantity of uncashed cheques, commonly known as the outstanding cheques. An **outstanding cheque** is a cheque that is issued and recorded by the company, but not cashed by the bank during the period covered by the bank statement. Recall that when a cheque is issued by a business, it is recorded promptly in the books of the business. But it is not recorded in the records of the bank until it is presented to them for payment. In many cases, this may be after several days or even weeks have passed.

4. Another common discrepancy item is the late deposit. A **late deposit** is a deposit that is made and recorded in the books of the business on the last day (usually) of the period covered by the bank statement, but which does not appear on the statement because of a processing delay at the bank. The late deposit usually appears as the first item on the bank statement for the following period.

5. Several other discrepancy items may occur. For example, a bank employee or a company employee might make an error, such as recording an amount incorrectly. Another example might be a bank service charge that the company had not yet learned of.

6. When comparing the records, it is important to deal with items from the previous reconciliation statement. Most of those items will be cleared up during the current month. However, there are usually some that do not get cleared up in the current month. They must be carried forward to the new reconciliation statement. For example, consider a cheque that was outstanding on the reconciliation statement for April 30. This cheque would be outstanding as of May 31 if it was not cashed during the month of May. It would have to go on the reconciliation statement for May 31. On the other hand, if the cheque was cashed during the month of May, it would no longer be an outstanding cheque and would be marked off as being cleared.

Recording the Discrepancy Items

Discrepancy items are recorded on the bank reconciliation statement.

1 Include all discrepancy items. It is customary to group items of a similar nature, such as outstanding cheques.

2 Record each item on one side of the reconciliation statement only, either on the bank side or on the company side. Always choose the side for which the item has not shown up as of the reconciliation date. For example, record an outstanding cheque on the bank's side because it represents an item not seen by the bank. Similarly, record a bank service charge on the company's side because it represents an item not seen in the company's records.

3 Each item represents either an increase or a decrease to the balance. Common sense should tell you which it is. Just decide what effect the item has on the bank balance and act accordingly. For example, cheques and service charges represent decreases to the bank balance; therefore treat them as deductions. Similarly, deposits increase the bank balance; therefore, treat them as additions.

4 The two final totals on the reconciliation statement will be the same if all discrepancy items are found and entered properly. If the totals are not equal, repeat the process until a balance is reached.

Bringing the Accounts Up to Date

The discrepancy items on the company's side of the reconciliation statement are the reasons why the Bank account is not currently up to date. These particular items must be journalized and posted to bring the Bank account up to date. For the reconciliation statement in Figure 13.13 the following two journal entries are necessary.

		DR	CR
Mar. 31	Miscellaneous Expense	$ .90	
	Bank		$ .90
	To correct error on cheque #697		
31	Bank Charges	$13.50	
	Bank		$13.50
	To record bank charges for March		

Personal Bank Reconciliation

Individuals, as well as businesses, should reconcile their bank accounts regularly. One cannot be certain of the accuracy of personal bank records unless they are reconciled. A reconciliation for a personal account is simpler than one for a business. Usually, there are fewer transactions, and only the one personal record (the personal record book) to compare with the bank statement. Still, it is a task requiring care and perseverence.

SECTION REVIEW QUESTIONS

1. Define "internal control."
2. Why is internal control not necessary for a one-person business?
3. When does internal control become necessary?
4. Describe what is meant by "separation of duties" with respect to internal control.
5. What is the purpose of having an independent audit?
6. Why should responsibilities be firmly established?
7. Why is cash control extremely important?
8. Explain what is meant by the phrase, "depositing funds intact."
9. What is a bank reconciliation?
10. Why is a bank reconciliation necessary?
11. What is a discrepancy item?
12. What is an outstanding cheque?
13. What is a late deposit?
14. What does it mean to bring the accounts up to date, with respect to a bank reconciliation?

SECTION EXERCISES

1. **Analyze each of the following mini-cases and prepare a brief report taking into consideration such things as:**
   Is there dishonesty or theft?
   Is there income tax evasion?
   Are there poor hiring practices?
   Who benefits? the owner? the employee?
   Who loses? the owner? the public?

Identify weaknesses in internal control.
Identify or speculate upon internal control strengths.
State what steps could be taken to improve the system.

1. The Doggie Salon is a very small family operation in the business of washing and grooming dogs. The work is done for cash and the money is collected when the dog is picked up. There is no paper work. The owner pockets the cash.

2. Phil Baker is negotiating with a contractor to have his driveway paved. After a price is unofficially agreed upon, Phil tells the contractor that the job is hers if she is willing to take cash under the table at a 15 per cent discount. The contractor agrees because she needs the work.

3. Mary Gozzard drives a delivery van for Excel Electrical Supply. She is allowed to take the van home at night so that she can make deliveries on her way to and from work. Mary usually manages to slip some materials for herself into the van. She drops these off at her home where she either uses them herself or sells them to others.

4. Karen Ion has a position of authority with the Exact Company. She arranges for a major repair to be performed on her home and for the repair bill to be sent to her employer. Karen intercepts the bill when it arrives, approves it for payment, and has it processed through the company.

5. Fran Boyko has a responsible position with Apex Company. She arranges with a supplier of goods to the company to charge a higher than normal price for them. Fran later approves these inflated bills for payment. Fran receives a percentage.

6. Super Sand and Gravel is engaged by Crown Road Builders to deliver loads of stone to the site of a road building project. The stone costs $500 a load. Jim Cox, foreman at the site, signs for each load as it is delivered. The signed slips form the basis for the invoice sent by Super Sand and Gravel to Crown Road Builders. Jim Cox has a friend who is building a house not far from the job site. The house needs a lot of stone for the large driveway, basement, and garage. Jim diverts a number of loads from the job site to the home of his friend, and signs for them as if they had been delivered to the project. Jim is rewarded by his friend for the favour.

7. Valley Forest is a ski resort with an extensive network of cross-country ski trails. The fee for cross-country skiing is six dollars a day, paid at the main chalet. Many people do not bother to pay for the cross-country skiing but merely drive to remote sections of the course and enter and exit freely.

8. A friend of yours works as a waitress in a local restaurant. One evening you are dining at the restaurant at a time when your friend is on duty. You suggest to her that it would be nice if you could have a free dinner. Your friend replies that she would be sure to be caught.

9. Joanne Lake is the accounts receivable clerk for a large company. On many occasions customers come personally to the company to pay their accounts in cash. Joanne, who is often short of money, keeps the cash for her own use with the intention of paying it back later. She is far behind in paying back the money.

10. Stephanie Chabot is a roofing contractor. She has a hired crew that does all of the roofing. Stephanie makes the contacts and does the estimating. She never loses any materials. Her workers find it impossible to work for anyone else on the sly, without Stephanie's knowledge.

11. Eric and Thelma together own a butcher shop and grocery store. Whenever they need food for their family, they just take it home out of the store. There is no bookkeeping involved.

12. Mario Tremblay is a carpenter. He is building a new bathroom in his home and requires some plumbing work. Andrew Carmichael is a plumber. He is building an addition onto his house and needs some carpentry work. The two men agree to exchange services free of charge.

2. The following are the personal chequing account record and the bank statement for the account of Paul Swartz for the month of June. Paul Swartz's bank reconciliation statement for May is also shown.

1. From these records, using the form in the Workbook, reconcile the bank account of Paul Swartz as of June 30.

2. State what entry or entries are necessary to bring the personal record to the true bank balance.

A. Paul Swartz's previous reconciliation.

Paul Swartz
Bank Reconciliation
May 31, 19—

Personal Record		Bank Statement		
Latest Balance	1 200.75	Latest Balance		1 450.75
		Deduct:		
		Outstanding cheques		
		#44	100—	
		#45	150—	250—
True Balance	1 200.75	True Balance		1 200.75

B. Paul Swartz's personal record.

CHEQUE NO.	DATE	CHEQUE ISSUED TO	AMOUNT OF CHEQUE		√	AMOUNT OF DEPOSIT		BALANCE FORWARD 1 200 75	
46	Jun 2	Rowlands Garage	237	50				963	25
47	4	Joanne's Clothes	92	50				870	75
48	9	Provincial Treasurer	9	–				861	75
49	15	Rockway Gardens	7	73				854	02
50	20	The Examiner	5	50				848	52
51	20	Daily Times	6	30				842	22
	27	Salary				740	–	1682	22
52	30	Marigold Apartments	275	–				1 407	22

C. Bank statement sent to Paul Swartz.

GENERAL BANK

STATEMENT OF ACCOUNT WITH   PAUL SWARTZ

CHEQUES		DEPOSITS	DATE		BALANCE
Balance forward			May	31	1 450.75
100.00			June	1	1 350.75
150.00			June	4	1 200.75
237.50			June	9	963.25
92.50	9.00		June	16	861.75
7.73			June	20	854.02
		740.00	June	27	1 594.02
5.50			June	30	1 588.52
S.C. 1.75			June	30	1 586.77

S.C. Service Charge

3. **Workbook Exercise: Additional bank reconciliation exercise.**

4. **Answer the following questions about J. C. Waters's bank reconciliation statement as shown below.**

J.C. WATERS		
BANK RECONCILIATION STATEMENT		
MARCH 31, 19—		
Balance per bank statement		$2 046.75
Add late deposit, March 31		271.50
		$2 318.25
Less outstanding cheques		
#418	$ 62.80	
#522	103.40	
#523	41.90	208.10
True balance		$2 110.15
Balance per Cash account		$2 186.85
Less bank charges	$ 5.40	
NSF cheque — Walker	71.30	76.70
True balance		$2 110.15

1. Does the $2 046.75 represent the bank balance at the beginning or at the end of the month?
2. Why do you think the March 31 deposit was not included in the bank balance?
3. How does Waters know that there are three cheques outstanding? Why are they subtracted?
4. Is $2 186.85 the cash balance at the beginning or at the end of the month?
5. What is an NSF cheque? Why is it subtracted from the balance per books?
6. A certified cheque for $200 payable to R. Smit is still outstanding. Why is it not part of the outstanding cheques on the bank reconciliation statement?

13.5 PETTY CASH FUND

The most common way of paying for expenditures is by cheque. However, it is not always convenient to issue a cheque, and payment in cash is often expected. Consider the following transactions.

• The custodian needs some electrical fuses. During her lunch hour she purchases some electrical fuses from the hardware store with her own money. She then submits the cash register slip to the accounting department so that she may be repaid.

• Two salaried employees are asked to work overtime in order to complete a special job. They are each given $12 for supper money.
• An express company delivers a parcel for which express charges of $12.50 must be paid immediately.

The usual way to pay for small expenditures of this type is with cash from a petty cash fund. A **petty cash fund** is a small quantity of cash, usually no more than $200, that is kept in the office for small expenditures.

Establishing a Petty Cash Fund

To establish a petty cash fund, a small sum ($100 to $200) is withdrawn from the bank account and put in the care of someone in the office. More precisely, a cheque is issued (usually made out to Petty Cash) and given to the person selected to be in charge of the petty cash. This person cashes the cheque and brings the money (in the form of small bills and coins) back to the office to be kept in a metal cash box (with a lock). This is known as the imprest system. The **imprest method for petty cash** is a system for handling small expenditures in which a certain amount of cash is entrusted to an individual.

The accounting entry to establish a petty cash fund is shown by the following example.

TRANSACTION **It is decided to establish a petty cash fund of $100. A cheque in the amount of $100 is made out to Petty Cash and is given to the person chosen to keep the petty cash. The cheque is cashed and the money put in a petty cash box.**

The accounting entry to establish the petty cash fund is the following:

	DR	CR
Petty Cash	$100	
Bank		$100

When this accounting entry is posted, the petty cash box will contain $100 in cash and will be in agreement with the Petty Cash account.

Operating the Petty Cash Fund

The keeper of the petty cash fund is authorized to make small payments out of the fund as necessary. Every amount paid out of the fund must be replaced by a bill for the expenditure (submitted by the person receiving the money). If a bill is not available, the recipient of the money must fill out a petty cash voucher such as the one shown in Figure 13.14. A **petty cash voucher** is a form that is filled out when money is paid out of the petty cash fund and no bill for the expenditure is available.

The bill or petty cash voucher is then placed in the box. A supply of unused petty cash vouchers (also known as petty cash slips) is kept with the petty cash fund.

At any time, the total of the bills, vouchers, and cash in the petty cash box should be equal to the amount of the petty cash fund. The keeper of the fund is responsible for seeing that this is so.

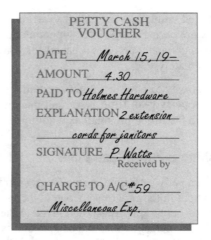

Figure 13.14 A petty cash voucher.

Accounting for this aspect of petty cash is easy because no accounting entries are made. It is one of those accounting situations in which it is convenient to allow the records to become temporarily inexact.

Replenishing the Petty Cash Fund

The cash in the petty cash box decreases as bills and vouchers are paid. A point is reached when there may not be enough cash in the fund to pay for the next bill or voucher to be presented. To prevent this, a lower limit is usually placed on the fund. When the lower limit for the petty cash fund is reached, the fund must be replenished. **Replenishing petty cash** is the procedure by which the petty cash fund is renewed when it reaches an already-determined lower limit.

To show the accounting for replenishing petty cash, let us work with a petty cash fund of $100 having a lower limit of $10. Assume that the contents of the petty cash box are:

Cash	$ 7.15
Bills and vouchers	92.85
Total	$100.00

Assume further that the bills and vouchers contained in the petty cash box are the following:

No.	Account Charged	Amount
1	Miscellaneous Expense	$12.59
2	Postage	10.00
3	Miscellaneous Expense	13.75
4	Building maintenance	11.56
5	Donations	5.00
6	Building Maintenance	4.75
7	Truck Expense	15.15
8	Miscellaneous Expense	5.30
9	Postage	5.70
10	Supplies	9.05
		$92.85

The petty cash fund must be replenished because the petty cash box contains less cash than the lower limit of $10. The steps to be followed are:

1 The keeper of the fund prepares a summary by account of the charges from the bills and vouchers in the box. There is no definite form in which the summary must be prepared. The summary might be drawn up like the one in Figure 13.15. The bills and vouchers from which the summary is prepared must be attached to the summary;

		Petty Cash Fund			
		Summary of Charges			
		October 2, 19—			
		Building Maintenance		16 31	
		Donations		5 —	
		Miscellaneous Expense		31 64	
		Postage		15 70	
		Supplies		9 05	
		Truck Expense		15 15	
				92 85	

Figure 13.15   A summary of charges from a petty cash fund.

2 The petty cashier submits the summary, together with the bills and vouchers, to the person or department that issues cheques;

3 A cheque, usually made out to Petty Cash for an amount equal to the total on the summary (in this case $92.85), is obtained in exchange for the vouchers. The summary and the supporting documents are accepted as the source document for the cheque;

4 The cheque is cashed by the petty cashier and the money is added to the total ($7.15) in the petty cash box. The fund has been restored to its original amount of $100. The petty cash fund is then ready to begin another cycle;

5 An accounting entry must be made for the cheque to replenish the petty cash. In our example, the accounting entry is:

	DR	CR
Building Maintenance	$16.31	
Donations	5.00	
Miscellaneous Expense	31.64	
Postage	15.70	
Supplies	9.05	
Truck Expense	15.15	
Bank		$92.85
	Debits taken from summary	Credit taken from cheque

We have seen that only two accounting entries are involved in petty cash transactions:

1. the entry to establish the fund. A similar entry is used to increase the fund;
2. the entry to replenish the fund.

SECTION REVIEW QUESTIONS

1. What does "cash" mean in its narrow sense?
2. What does "cash" mean in its broad sense?
3. Where does a business keep most of its cash?
4. What is the commonest method of making payment for expenditures?
5. What is the purpose of a petty cash fund?
6. When is a petty cash voucher used?
7. Describe the contents of the petty cash box.
8. How can the contents of the petty cash box be checked for correctness?
9. When is the petty cash fund replenished?
10. What happens to the vouchers in the petty cash box?

SECTION EXERCISES

1. On January 15, Mary Market issues a cheque in the amount of $200 to establish a petty cash fund. **Give the accounting entry in general journal form to establish the petty cash fund.** You will find a form in the Workbook.

2. On February 20, Seneca Sales Company issues a cheque to increase the petty cash fund from $100 to $150. **Give the accounting entry in general journal form to increase the petty cash fund.** You will find a form in the Workbook.

3. On March 16, 19—, after a bill of $12.16 is paid, the contents of a petty cash fund with a lower limit of $10 are as follows:

Cash	$7.68
Bills and Vouchers	
Supplies	10.00
Miscellaneous Expense	6.04
Miscellaneous Expense	1.25
Sales Promotion	8.50
Building Maintenance	10.50
C. Parkes, Drawings	12.00
Car Expense	8.17
Postage	8.50
Miscellaneous Expense	2.05
Postage	9.00
Miscellaneous Expense	4.15
Building Maintenance	12.16

1. **Prepare the summary of charges necessary to replenish the fund.**
2. **In general journal form, write out the accounting entry necessary to replenish the fund.**

You will find forms in the Workbook.

---

4. On June 10, 19—, a petty cash fund with a lower limit of $12 is in the following condition:

Cash	$8.25
Bills and Vouchers	
Delivery Expense	15.00
Wages	10.00
Office Expense	15.02
Supplies	10.75
Advertising	12.00
Supplies	11.79
Advertising	15.00
Wages	12.50
Office Expense	12.14
P. Martin, Drawings	10.00
Office Expense	4.20
Office Expense	2.00
Supplies	11.35

1. **Prepare the summary of charges necessary to replenish the fund.**
2. **In general journal form, write out the required accounting entry to replenish the fund.**

You will find forms in the Workbook.

---

5. **Indicate whether each of the following statements is true or false by placing a "T" or an "F" in the space indicated in your Workbook. Explain the reason for each "F" response in the space provided.**

1. The Petty Cash account in the general ledger must never change.
2. A petty cash voucher must be prepared for every payment out of the fund.
3. The petty cash fund is used for the purpose of cutting down on the number of cheques issued.
4. The accounting entry to replenish the petty cash fund is made by the keeper of the fund.
5. The petty cash box is locked and put away in a safe place outside business hours.
6. The keeper of the petty cash fund must never borrow from it.
7. The petty cash summary is organized by general ledger accounts.
8. A payment out of petty cash can only be charged to an expense account or an asset account.
9. The keeper of the fund is expected to make up any shortage in the petty cash fund.
10. If an auditor were to check the petty cash fund, the procedure would be to total all of the cash and vouchers in the box and check this total against the balance in the Petty Cash account.

13.6   ACCOUNTING CONTROLS FOR EXPENDITURES

You have seen how internal control is essential in a good accounting system. In this section you will learn about accounting controls for cash expenditures—that is, the spending of money for goods and services.

The Voucher System

The **voucher system** is a common method for processing expenditure transactions. Essentially, it is a system designed to ensure that all expenditure transactions are right and proper, and that the business papers pertaining to such expenditures are all present and correct.

A voucher system controls expenditures through a rigid set of procedures. The documents supporting the transactions are "vouched" (seen to be correct), payment of the debt is approved, and the transaction is properly recorded. Every bill received for goods or services, whether it is to be paid right away or some time in the future, must be validated according to this set of procedures. With only a few exceptions, the business does not issue cheques unless they represent a payment for a validated expenditure. A **voucher** is any document used in the voucher system as part of the verification process. The basic features of a voucher system are described below.

The Voucher Approval Form

An important feature of the voucher system is the **voucher jacket**, also called the voucher approval cover or voucher approval jacket. This is either a page or a file folder with information preprinted on it A voucher jacket is shown in Figure 13.16.

VOUCHER APPROVAL FORM

Supplier	Sailrite Incorporated	Voucher No.	403
Address	431 Beech Road	Purchase Order Checked	
	Chicago, Illinois	Description	MP
	14737	Price	MP
Invoice Date	Aug. 7, 19–	Terms	MP
Invoice Amount	1 734.50	Goods or Service Rec'd	RF
Discount	34.69	Calculations Checked	S
Net Amount	1 699.81	Accounting Distribution	J
Payment Date	August 27, 19–	Approved for Payment	GB

ACCOUNTING DISTRIBUTION

Debits	Purchases	1 734 50
	Supplies	

Cheque No.   1376
Cheque Date   August 27, 19–

Credit	Vouchers Payable	1 734 50

Figure 13.16   A voucher jacket (approval form).

As they arrive, the vouchers for every expenditure are stapled to the cover page or placed inside the file folder.

The Verification Steps

The flowchart in Figure 13.17 describes the steps performed to verify an expenditure and make it ready for journalizing and for payment. The system makes it very difficult to get money out of the company fraudulently. It would take several employees working together (collusion) to commit a fraud.

Observe in particular that three separate source documents must be matched against each other. The three source documents, along with the voucher jacket, form the basis for the journal entry. If anything is missing, the documents are given to an accounting clerk for special attention.

SECTION REVIEW QUESTIONS

1. Describe the voucher system.
2. Explain what is meant by "the documents are vouched."
3. What is a voucher?
4. What type of information is preprinted on the voucher approval jacket or cover?
5. Name the three documents that must be matched.
6. The verification steps described in this section involve a number of employees. Why is this a good control feature?

SECTION EXERCISES

1. **Complete each of the following statements by writing in your Workbook the appropriate word or phrase from the list below.**

    1. Poor accounting controls can result in the payment of bills that were _____ sent to the business.
    2. The voucher system is a method of processing _____.
    3. The _____ is effective because it controls expenditures through a rigid set of verification procedures.
    4. Any document used in the voucher system as part of the verification process is a _____.
    5. The purchasing department formally orders goods when it issues a _____.
    6. A _____ contains detailed information about goods received from suppliers.
    7. The _____ is a combination file folder and voucher approval form.

    List of Words and Phrases

expenditure transactions	voucher
fraudulently	voucher jacket
purchase order	voucher system
receiving report	

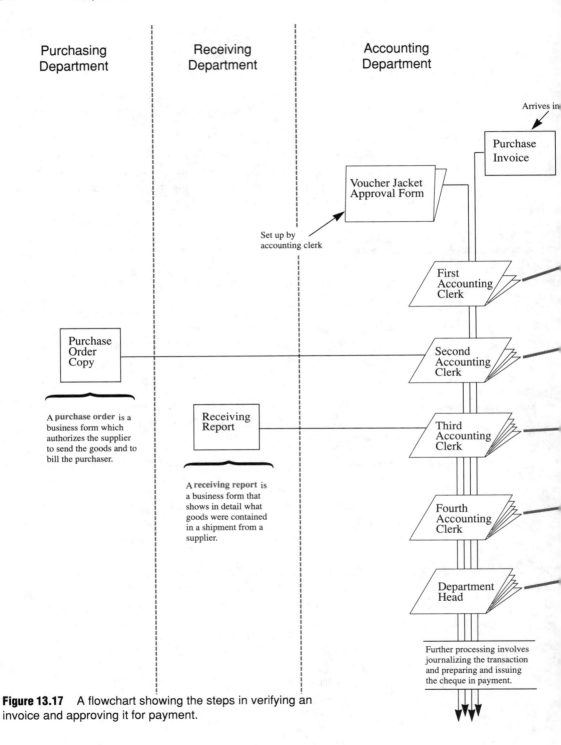

Figure 13.17 A flowchart showing the steps in verifying an invoice and approving it for payment.

As soon as a purchase invoice (or a batch of purchase invoices) is received from the supplier, a voucher jacket is set up. The first seven items of information are recorded on it. Calculations on the purchase invoice are checked. The clerk initials the "Calculations Checked" box. The invoice is placed inside the voucher jacket.

Note: A request for a cheque to meet the payroll would be initiated by a memorandum signed by the paymaster. A request for a cheque for the owner's personal use would be initiated by a memorandum from the owner. Neither of these two transactions would have any other supporting documents, but a voucher jacket would be set up for them.

The purchase order is compared to the purchase invoice to see that the goods were properly ordered and that the two documents match in respect to description, price, and terms of sale. The purchase order copy is placed inside the voucher jacket. The clerk initials the "Purchase Order Checked" boxes.

The receiving report is compared to the purchase invoice to ensure that the goods are received and that they are correct in terms of quantity, quality, and description. The receiving report (if there is one) is placed inside the voucher jacket. The clerk initials the "Goods or Services Received" box.

Note: The invoice may involve a purchase of a service rather than goods such as a telephone bill or a lawyer's bill. In such cases, someone within the organization must attest to the validity of the charge by writing on the bill something such as "Service received OK" and by signing the bill.

The accounting entry is worked out and recorded on the voucher jacket. A clerk initials the "Distribution" box.

Before approval for payment is given, the voucher jacket and its contents are examined to ensure that all of the verification steps have been fully completed and that all documentation is present and in order. Then the "Approved for Payment" box is initialed.

2. Using the flowcharts on pages 514 and 515 as a help, answer the following questions:

1. In which department does the purchase order originate?

2. Who in the accounting department receives the purchase order copy?

3. In which department does the receiving report originate?

4. Who in the accounting department receives the receiving report copy?

5. What is a purchase invoice?

6. Describe the voucher jacket.

7. What information is put on the voucher jacket by the clerk who sets it up?

8. What use is made of the purchase order copy by the second accounting clerk?

9. What happens to the purchase order copy?

10. What use is made of the receiving report copy by the third accounting clerk?

11. How many clerks initial the voucher jacket before the department head receives it?

12. What does the department head do with the jacket and the vouchers before giving approval for payment?

3. 1. For the purchase invoice shown below, set up the initial information on the voucher jacket that appears in the Workbook. The next consecutive voucher jacket number is 403.

2. Complete the accounting distribution section, and initial the voucher jacket in the appropriate box.

BOX 100 CROWN HILL L4M 4Y8	**The Chronicle** CROWN HILL ONTARIO	PHONE 577-2140
SOLD TO 　Crown Hill Supply 　Crown Hill, Ontario 　L4M 4Y8		DATE　May 9, 19-- TERMS 2/10,n/30

DESCRIPTION	DLY RATE	AMOUNT
Quarter page ad (copy attached) Run Thursday May 4 to Sunday May 7 　　Four days	$150	$600
		NO. 3874

4. You are employed by Mayfair Manufacturing as an "expediter" in the payables section. Your job is to work with business papers that for some reason have become a problem. Some of them don't match, while others have errors or omissions on them. You must check out all aspects of problem transactions and resolve difficulties so that the papers can be processed. Most of your company's suppliers can be reached by local telephone.

The three business documents below and on page 518 have come to your desk for resolution. **Examine these documents and answer the following questions.**

1. Why do these business papers present a problem? Be specific.
2. What details would you check out?
3. What solution would you propose?

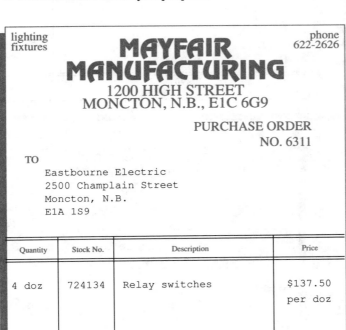

lighting fixtures	**MAYFAIR MANUFACTURING**	phone 622-2626

1200 HIGH STREET
MONCTON, N.B., E1C 6G9

PURCHASE ORDER
NO. 6311

TO

Eastbourne Electric
2500 Champlain Street
Moncton, N.B.
E1A 1S9

Quantity	Stock No.	Description	Price
4 doz	724134	Relay switches	$137.50 per doz

Date Ordered	Date Required	Terms
May 30, 19--	June 15, 19--	2%, 15/ n, 60

Ship By	Destination	Sales Tax Exempt
Truck	FOB 1200 High St.	No. 14876

EASTBOURNE ELECTRIC

Phone 701-7010
2500 Champlain Street
Moncton, N.B. E1A 1S9

SOLD TO:

Mayfair Manufacturing
1200 High Street
Moncton, N.B.
E1C 6C9

SHIP TO:

Same

QUANTITY	STOCK NO.	DESCRIPTION	PRICE	AMOUNT
48	724134	Relay Switches	$137.50	$550.00
		Sales Tax		27.50
		Total		$577.50

DATE	TERMS	P.O. NO.	INV. NO.
June 12, 19--	Net 60	6311	**1764**

RECEIVING REPORT
MAYFAIR MANUFACTURING

No. 906

Date goods received	*June 14, 19–*	Purchase order number	*6311*

RECEIVED FROM

Eastbourne Electric

2500 Champlain Street

Moncton, N.B.

Quantity	Stock No.	Description	Price
4 pkgs 10 to a pkg	*724 104*	*relay switches*	*137.50*

No. Packages	Weight	Delivered by	Received by
4	*10 #*	*C.N.*	*J.X.*

13.7 COMPUTERS IN ACCOUNTING: DESIGNING SPREADSHEETS

To get the most out of a spreadsheet model the user should be able to quickly produce information time and time again. Having to adjust formulas and other cell contents each time a model is used would be a waste of time. If a spreadsheet model is carefully planned, time will be used most efficiently.

A useful and recommended method of design is the use of the split screen. As its name suggests this feature splits the screen into two areas commonly referred to as windows. The split screen can be put to a number of uses. In this chapter, the split screen is used to allow one area to be used as a work area and the other area to view final results.

A bank reconciliation is a good application for the split screen. Figure 13.18 shows a programmed spreadsheet for a bank reconciliation. You can call this up on your screen by loading the file named CH13. Observe that this model is clean, in that it has no data in it. This is the best way to design and save your spreadsheet models for use again and again.

As you can see, the spreadsheet cannot all be viewed at one time. The final line of this spreadsheet, the one that shows the true bank balance figures, cannot be seen most of the time. It would be ideal to be able to view this line at all times as you enter bank reconciliation data so that you can see when the true bank balance figures are the same. This can be achieved by using the *window* option explained below.

To split the screen, move the cell pointer to line 48, which is where you want the screen to be split. Call up the command line for your spreadsheet, or pull down the appropriate menu, and carry out the split screen command.

Immediately, you will see the screen split horizontally before line 48. In effect, there are now two window panes. At this time the cell pointer is in the upper pane but it can be moved back and forth between the two areas by toggling the F6 function key.

Place the cell pointer in the upper area and begin to enter the reconciliation data. As you do this you have the true bank balance figures in view at all times. When the two figures are the same, in all likelihood, the bank account has been reconciled. Then, your results can be saved and printed out as you choose.

Before attempting a reconciliation exercise let us practise on the spreadsheet model by using the data from Figure 13.13 for Boxwell and Company on page 499 of your text. If you enter the data correctly, you should obtain a balanced reconciliation and experience the benefit of using a split screen.

	A	B	C	D	E	F	G	H
1	Bank Reconciliation							
2	Company Name							
3	Date							
4								
5	Bank Records		$		Business Records		$	
6	——————				——————			
7	Statement Balance:				Ledger Balance:			
8								
9	Add: Late Deposits				Deduct: Bank Charges			
10		$				$		
11	1				Interest			
12	2				Serv. Charges			
16	Deduct: O/S Cheques							
17	#	$			Deduct: (−) Error or			
18					Omission			
19					1			
20					2			
21					Total	0.00		
22					Add: (+) Error or			
23					Omission			
24					$			
25					1			
26					2			
27					Total	0.00		
28	Total Cheques		0.00					
29	Add: (+) Error or							
30	Omission							
31	Deduct: (−) Error or							
32	Omission							
33	True Bank Balance		0.00		True Bank Balance		0.00	

Figure 13.18   Programmed spreadsheet for a bank reconciliation.

SPREADSHEET EXERCISES

1. In the spreadsheet model CH13 for a bank reconciliation you will see a number of places where 0.00 appears. These represent seven cells which contain a formula or function. **Identify each of these cells and give the formula or function associated with each one.**

2. **Use the spreadsheet model CH13 to reconcile exercise 4 on page 524 in your textbook.**

COMPUTER REVIEW QUESTIONS

1. Explain the main advantage of designing a spreadsheet model with a split screen.
2. Why would one want to split a spreadsheet window into different panes?
3. Explain how your spreadsheet program permits you to move the cell pointer from one window to another.

Communicate It

After working with your bank reconciliation spreadsheet model for some time, you are unable to get the January 31 statement balanced. Finally, after checking the cancelled cheques, you find that bank personnel have made an encoding error. They mistakenly entered cheque #221 for $31.09 as $31.90. **Prepare a business letter dated February 4 to inform them of their error and to outline the action that you want taken.**

CHAPTER HIGHLIGHTS

Now that you have completed Chapter 13, you should:

1. know the purpose of a petty cash fund;
2. know how to establish, operate, and replenish a petty cash fund;
3. know the accounting entries for establishing and for replenishing a petty cash fund;
4. know the basic services, accounts, documents, and statements of chartered banks;
5. know what is meant by the terms NSF cheque, certified cheque, and post-dated cheque;
6. be able to do the accounting for bank credit card transactions;
7. appreciate the place of cash registers in a modern computerized system;
8. understand the purpose of, and be able to interpret, the detailed audit strip;
9. be able to prove the cash and prepare the bank deposit and related accounting summaries;
10. be able to account for cash short or over;
11. know the features of a current bank account;
12. understand the meaning of internal control;
13. know the specific control features associated with cash;
14. be able to reconcile a bank statement for a business or an individual;
15. be able to perform the accounting entries that result from a bank reconciliation;
16. understand the need for accounting controls over expenditures;
17. know how the voucher system works.

ACCOUNTING TERMS

audit strip
bank reconciliation
bank reconciliation statement
cash short or over

certified cheque
change fund
current bank account
daily interest savings account

float

imprest method for petty cash

internal control

late deposit

NSF cheque

outstanding cheque

petty cash fund

petty cash voucher

point-of-sale terminal

post-dated cheque

proving the cash

purchase order

receiving report

replenishing petty cash

restrictive endorsement

voucher

voucher jacket

voucher system

CHAPTER EXERCISES

Using Your Knowledge

1. You are the keeper of the petty cash fund for Graphic Art Supplies. Since the fund is very low, you are in the process of preparing the petty cash summary to be used to obtain the replenishing cheque.

   Below left is a listing of the vouchers in the petty cash box, giving a description of the nature of the payment for each. Below right is the chart of accounts for Graphic Art Supplies.

   Prepare the petty cash summary for the purpose of obtaining the replenishing cheque.

PETTY CASH VOUCHERS

1. Owner's parking receipt	$ 9.00
2. Paint for building	13.50
3. New broom for janitor	12.75
4. Typewriter ribbons	8.35
5. Supper money for employee	7.50
6. Postage stamps	15.00
7. New window pane	20.00
8. Telegram charge	10.50
9. Donation to Boy Scouts	10.00
10. Payment to student for cleaning up the grounds	10.50
11. Mileage to employee for using personal car for business	17.50
12. Coffee and doughnuts brought in for a business meeting	24.35
13. Dog licence for watchdog	10.00
14. Parking receipt of owner	7.00
15. Supper money for employee	7.50
16. Postage for parcel delivery	15.00

CHART OF ACCOUNTS

101 Bank

105 Accounts Receivable

110 Merchandise Inventory

115 Supplies

120 Equipment

125 Automobile

201 Bank loan

205 Accounts Payable

305 Judi Mavar, Capital

310 Judi Mavar Drawings

405 Sales

505 Purchases

510 Freight-in

515 Advertising

520 Bank Charges

525 Building Maintenance

530 Car Expense

535 Delivery Expense

540 Donations Expense

545 Light and Heat Expense

550 Miscellaneous Expense

555 Telephone Expense

560 Wages Expense

2. **This exercise also appears in your Workbook.**
   From the audit strip given below:
   1. compute the summary totals that would be produced by the machine;
   2. work out the accounting entry for these totals if the Paid Out is for supplies.

		137.00	MDS
		9.59	TAX
		146.59	TOTL
		150.00	CASH
CASL	166	3.41	CHNG
		175.00	MDS
		12.25	TAX
VISA	167	187.25	TOTL
		100.00	RECD
RECD	168	100.00	TOTL
		356.25	MDS
		24.94	TAX
VISA	169	381.19	TOTL
	REFUND		
		128.00–	MDS
		8.96–	TAX
		136.96–	TOTL
CASL	170	136.96–	CASH
		50.00	P.O.
P.O.	171	50.00	TOTL
		150.00	MDS
		10.50	TAX
		160.50	TOTL
		170.00	CASH
CASL	172	9.50	CHNG
		70.00	MDS
		4.90	TAX
CHRG	173	74.90	TOTL

SUMMARY

CASL	174	_____	(CASH SALES INCL. TAX)
RECD	175	_____	(VISA SALES INCL. TAX)
P.O.	176	_____	(PAID OUTS)
CHRG	177	_____	(CHRG SALES INCL. TAX)
RECD	178	_____	(RECEIVED ON ACCOUNT)
CRDT	179	_____	(RETURN FOR CREDIT)
TAX	180	_____	(NET SALES TAX)
MDS	181	_____	(SALES LESS RETURNS)
CASH	182	_____	(NET CASH RECEIVED)

3. **Workbook Exercise: Completing a chart about bank reconciliations.**

4. Shown below are all of the records that you will need to reconcile the current bank account of Proctor & Kemp at July 31, 19—.

(**Note:** Normally the bank returns all of the "paid" cheques to the business along with the bank statement. This cannot be done in a textbook. Instead, on the bank statement in brackets beside each amount in the Cheques column is either an explanation of the charge or the cheque number.)

A. Bank reconciliation statement for the previous month's end, shown below.

	Proctor & Kemp				
	Bank Reconciliation Statement				
	June 30, 19—				
Balance per Bank			*Balance per General*		
Statement	1 4 0 6 03		*Ledger*		7 7 3 28
Add: Late Deposit	5 5 1 00		*Deduct Bank Charge*		
	1 9 5 7 03		*not entered in books*		
Deduct Outstanding			*of company*		
Cheques			*(1) Service charge $16.50*		
#83 *$5.10*			*(2) Loan Interest 33.50*		5 0 00
780 *71.03*					
828 *400.00*					
846 *96.02*					
852 *123.50*					
860 *15.00*					
871 *16.01*					
873 *17.50*					
881 *33.60*					
886 *121.47*					
889 *60.00*					
890 *170.00*					
891 *31.94*					
892 *27.61*					
894 *13.82*					
898 *12.50*					
899 *18.65*	1 2 3 3 75				
True Balance	7 2 3 28		*True Balance*		7 2 3 28

B. Bank Debit column of cash receipts journal for July, page 14.

$ 262.75
312.70
274.19
161.40
700.20
265.92
400.61
396.21
316.40
$3 090.38

C. July general journal entry affecting "Bank," page 9.

Bank	5.10	
Miscellaneous Income		5.10
To cancel outstanding cheque		
No. 83 issued June 19—		

D. Excerpts from cash payments journal for July, page 18.

Explanation	Chq. No.	Bank Credit
	900	$ 100.00
	901	171.31
	902	142.19
Loan Interest, June		33.50
Service Charge, June		16.50
	903	16.41
	904	17.50
	905	10.00
	906	12.40
	907	19.61
	908	31.40
	909	76.39
	910	65.20
	911	500.00
	912	216.75
	914	8.21
	915	2.60
	916	9.40
	917	50.00
	918	50.00
	919	33.19
	920	29.33
	921	65.00
	922	25.00
	923	25.00
	924	419.63
	925	372.60
	926	900.00
		$3 419.12

E. Partial general ledger Bank account.

BANK							No. 1
Date	Particulars	P.R.	Debit	Credit	Balance	DR CR
19–						
June 30					773.28	DR
July 31		CR14	3090.38			
July 31		CP18		3419.12		
July 31		J9	5.10		449.64	DR

F. July bank statement.

Cheques				Deposits	Date	Balance
					June 30	1 406.03
18.65	(899)	31.94	(891)	551.00	July 2	1 906.44
121.47	(886)				3	1 784.97
100.00	(900)	96.02	(846)	262.75	5	1 851.70
12.50	(898)				5	1 839.20
71.03	(780)	27.61	(892)		6	1 740.56
142.19	(902)				6	1 598.37
400.00	(828)			312.70	8	1 511.07
15.00	(860)	13.82	(894)		9	1 482.25
16.01	(871)	171.31	(901)		10	1 294.93
17.50	(904)				10	1 277.43
10.00	(905)			274.19	11	1 541.62
500.00	(911)				12	1 041.61
33.60	(N.S.F. cheque of R.C. Jones)			161.40	15	1 169.42
50.00	(913)				16	1 119.42
170.00	(890)	12.40	(906)		17	937.02
76.39	(909)				19	860.63
31.40	(908)			700.20	22	1 529.43
9.40	(916)	19.61	(907)		23	1 500.42
2. 60	(915)				23	1 497.82
				265.92	25	1 763.74
33.19	(919)			400.61	26	2 131.16
17.50	(873)				27	2 113.66
50.00	(917)			396.21	30	2 459.87
25.00	(922)	419.63	(924)		31	2 015.24
165.00	Visa discount fee				31	1 850.24
29.00	(Interest on Loan)				31	1 821.24
12.60	(Service Charge)				31	1 808.64

Reconcile the bank account and make the necessary accounting entries in the books of the company. Cheque no. 913 is for supplies. You will find forms in the Workbook.

5. **Workbook Exercise: Additional bank reconciliation exercise.**

6. **Workbook Exercise: Additional bank reconciliation exercise.**

7. **For each of the following groups, indicate which statement is NOT true by recording the appropriate letter in the space indicated in your Workbook.**

1. **a.** Cash means dollar bills and coins only.
   b. The principal objective of a business is to earn a profit.
   c. The usual method of establishing a petty cash fund is to issue a cheque made out to Petty Cash.
   d. The imprest system of petty cash involves entrusting the cash to an individual.
   e. The vouchers and the cash in the petty cash box should add up to the balance of the Petty Cash account.

2. **a.** The cheque made out to Petty Cash is usually handed over to the person responsible for the petty cash fund.
   b. Outside of office hours the petty cash box is usually kept in the company safe.
   c. For every expenditure out of the petty cash fund there must be a bill or sales slip from a store.
   d. When a payment is being made out of the petty cash fund, no accounting entries are made immediately.
   e. The petty cash fund must be replenished when the amount of cash in the box gets low.

3. **a.** The first step to replenishing the petty cash fund is to prepare a summary of the vouchers in the petty cash box.
   b. The petty cashier submits the summary of charges, together with the bills and vouchers, in order to obtain a cheque.
   c. The summary and the vouchers together are accepted as the source document for the replenishing cheque.
   d. The accounting entry to record the replenishing cheque is: debit Petty Cash; credit Bank.
   e. The accounting entry to replenish the petty cash fund is one of the two accounting entries that affect petty cash.

4. **a.** Banks provide essential services for both businesses and individuals.
   b. The processing of cheques and bank credit card vouchers is known as the electronic transfer of funds.
   c. Banks are able to meet the needs of most customers by having a variety of accounts and services.
   d. The interest rate for a daily interest savings account is higher than it is for a pure savings account.
   e. You must put some money in a bank account to "open" it.

5. a. The bank statement given to the customer once a month is identical to the bank's own record.
   b. Except for breakdowns, electronic tellers may be used at any time.
   c. It is difficult to borrow money if your credit rating is poor.
   d. Writing cheques that bounce can be damaging to your credit rating.
   e. The true bank balance is the one shown by the bank's record.

6. a. Placing only your signature on the back of a cheque made out to you is an "open" endorsement.
   b. Banks require the payee (the person to whom the cheque is issued) to guarantee the cheque by signing it on the back.
   c. If the balance in the issuer's account is not large enough to cover the amount of a cheque, the bank will dishonour it.
   d. A cheque that has not bounced is a dishonoured cheque.
   e. The bank has the right to take the amount of a dishonoured cheque out of your account without contacting you.

7. a. The accounting entry to record a dishonoured cheque is the exact opposite of the accounting entry that was made when the cheque was deposited.
   b. You must phone the bank to find out if a cheque that you received is certified.
   c. You can be sure of a cheque not bouncing if it is certified.
   d. The funds to pay a certified cheque are taken out of the bank account at the time the cheque is certified.
   e. A post-dated cheque is one that is dated for some time in the future.

8. a. The usual reason for issuing a post-dated cheque is to meet a series of payments such as for a mortgage.
   b. A certified cheque is marked GUARANTEED by the bank.
   c. A cheque written on January 15 but dated for March 1 is a post-dated cheque.
   d. You should ask for a certified cheque when you are dealing with a stranger and when the amount of money is large.
   e. The bank does not cash cheques bearing a future date.

9. a. Bank credit cards can be obtained from large department stores and similar chains.
   b. Most smaller retail outlets do not offer their own company credit cards.
   c. Visa and Mastercard are bank credit cards sponsored by major banks.
   d. The consumer is usually given 21 days from the statement date to make payment.
   e. Bank credit cards may be used to obtain a cash advance.

10. a. A listing of cheques received in the mail is prepared because the cheques have to be deposited in the bank.
   b. The listing of the cheques in part **a** is prepared by a member of the accounting department who knows the system.
   c. Sales slips are prenumbered so that all slips can be accounted for.
   d. In a business where there are "cash" receipts, it is necessary to prove the cash at the end of the day.
   e. There is a greater chance for a cash shortage than there is for a cash overage.

11. **a.** A point-of-sale terminal is a stand-alone electronic cash register.
    b. A "float" is a small sum of money set aside to be used as a starting fund for the cash register each day.
    c. The detailed audit tape is locked inside the cash register.
    d. At the end of each day the cash register can be made to produce summary totals for the day.
    e. A modern cash register can itself produce most of the figures needed to prove the cash.

12. **a.** At the end of each day the cash, vouchers, and daily balance form are forwarded to the accounting department.
    b. A cash shortage is entered as a debit to an expense account.
    c. A current bank account is one designed especially for the use of businesses.
    d. With a current account the paid cheques are returned to the depositor at the end of each month.
    e. Cash is said to be proved when there is no shortage or overage.

13. **a.** Businesses endorse all cheques FOR DEPOSIT ONLY.
    b. All cheques for deposit must be endorsed.
    c. For businesses, deposit slips are prepared in duplicate.
    d. Every business requires internal control to ensure accuracy and honesty.
    e. The person who records transactions or prepares accounting records should not also be the one to control or handle the assets physically.

14. **a.** Cash is the single item most likely to be stolen.
    b. The total cash receipts for the day should be deposited on that day and intact.
    c. Since both the bank and the business keep a record of the same funds, the two balances should always agree unless an error has been made.
    d. Every bank account should be reconciled once a month.
    e. An outstanding cheque is a cheque that is issued and recorded by the company but not cashed by the bank.

For Further Thought

8. Briefly answer the following questions.

1. You have a pure savings account in a local bank which pays interest every six months on the minimum balance for the six months. Except for one day, on which your balance dipped to $49, you have maintained a balance in your account of $3 500 for the latest six-month period. On what balance will you be paid interest? Comment on this.

2. For emergency use only you acquired a card that permits you to use the automatic tellers for your bank. You have never had to use the service until now, when you find yourself out of town and without money. However, you cannot remember your personal identification number which is necessary to operate the machines. When seeking help from a nearby bank branch, you are told that there is no way for them to help you get your number. Comment on this predicament.

3. PQ company has a petty cash fund but it is not under any one employee's specific control. Why is this undesirable?

4. The auditor of a company, when checking the petty cash fund, finds a number of employees' I.O.U.s in the fund. However, the fund totals correctly with the I.O.U.s included. What course of action should the auditor take?

5. You are the custodian of the petty cash fund. An employee presents you with a legitimate bill to be paid from the fund, but there is not enough cash in the fund to pay it. What will you do?

6. You accepted a cheque for a debt from a friend because you knew with certainty that sufficient funds were in the bank to cover it. However, there were not sufficient funds in the account when you presented the cheque for payment five days later. How could this be possible?

7. You accept a cheque drawn on a bank in a nearby town. You drive to the nearby town to cash the cheque right away. The bank there will not cash the cheque for you but does certify it. Why would they follow this procedure?

8. You are about to write a cheque for $4 500 to pay for a new computer. While you are waiting, another customer pays for an identical purchase with a Visa card. You know that the merchant will only receive about $4 365 for the Visa sale because of the Visa discount. You change your mind and offer the merchant a cheque for $4 365. Will the merchant accept your offer? Comment on this.

9. Assume that Bill Wallingford, a local businessperson, neither rolls coins nor arranges currency by denomination when he is making up his daily deposit. Assuming that the bank accepts Bill's deposit in this state, what effect will it have on the bank teller and the people in the line-up behind Bill?

CASE STUDIES

CASE 1 *Service Charges: Are They Always Fair?*

Sarah Hurtig and her husband Irwin have two bank accounts: a savings account and a chequing account. Each of the two accounts is a joint account, meaning that either of the partners can independently use the accounts in all respects.

The two partners keep a personal record of each account and do attempt to keep them up to date. However, it is not always easy to do this, particularly with the chequing account, which gets a lot of use. Both partners cannot have the personal register at the same time, which would let them make the appropriate updating entries. Still, each one often needs to write a cheque at a time when the other partner has the register. When this happens, the one without the register tries to remember to make a note of the cheque or cheques written. These notes are supposed to be used to bring the register up to date as quickly as possible.

In theory this sounds simple enough, but it does not always work in practice. During one particular Christmas rush neither Sarah nor Irwin took the register at a time when both were writing lots of cheques. And because they were either tired or busy or distracted, they failed to update the register for several days. Each assumed that there was plenty of money in the account.

However, on this occasion, the balance in the chequing account was overspent and the account was overdrawn. This means that the balance in the account became a minus balance. In effect, this is a bank loan. In such a case, the bank takes action to cover the overdraft. It looks to see if there are any funds available in other accounts owned by the same depositor. If there are, it transfers sufficient funds to cover the overdraft, allowing the cheque to be honoured. The Hurtigs had a healthy balance in their savings account and the transfer was made. The bank charged $3.50 for the service.

Unfortunately, in this case, the Hurtigs had written several cheques and each one put the account into a new overdraft position. Each time, the bank followed the same procedure including the $3.50 service charge. Since there were 14 such cheques, the total charge was $49.00.

The Hurtigs did not learn of the overdraft situation until they received their bank statement in the mail. When they saw what had happened, they were annoyed.

Questions

1. In your opinion, why were the Hurtigs annoyed?
2. In your opinion, were the Hurtigs justified in being annoyed? Explain.
3. Why do you think the bank acted in the manner it did?
4. What can the Hurtigs do to ensure that their personal register is kept up to date in the future? Explain.

CASE 2   *Trials of a Young Entrepreneur*

Garn Mennell, a student, started up a summer business as a small contractor. Garn was regarded as being "handy with tools" and was proficient at building decks, garages, and so on; he could also do a nice job of re-roofing houses.

The funds with which to start his business came from the following sources: a newly acquired inheritance of $5 000, a low-interest loan of $10 000 from his brother, and a $3 000 non-interest-bearing loan from a chartered bank (part of a government program to help youth employment). With these funds Garn purchased a used truck for $7 000, ladders and equipment for $1 000, and other tools for $500. The remaining funds were placed in a business bank account.

Garn was quite good at attending to the numerous details associated with starting up a new business. As well, Garn did a thorough job of looking after the banking records and of obtaining and filing vouchers for all expenditures. He also designed first-rate estimating sheets and contracts to help him in pricing and ensuring a solid legal base for each job. However, Garn had absolutely no knowledge of accounting, and he completely neglected this aspect of running the business.

During the first season of business, Garn was able to get a number of jobs, but not enough to keep him busy all the time. He bought construction materials on credit and was able to pay his trade debts when they became due. At the end of the season he had no trade debts, had repaid the bank loan, and had paid back one-half of the principal (but no interest) on the loan from his brother. He was satisfied that things were going well. He had lots of spending money, was enjoying himself thoroughly, and had a truck to drive around in. As well, he took pleasure in owning his own business, and could hold his head high among his friends.

The second season was much the same as the first except that jobs were fewer. Although Garn's work was of good quality, he was not very good at acquiring new business. He felt awkward about knocking on doors looking for work and relied on newspaper advertisements and the yellow pages. As a consequence, Garn had fewer contracts and was able to enjoy more free time as well as his status as a businessman. Towards the end of the season, however, he began to suspect that all was not well. He was beginning to experience difficulty in paying his trade bills on time and this made him uneasy. At the end of the season, he was concerned enough to ask the help of a family friend who was an accountant. The first suggestion he received was to make a list of the assets and liabilities of the business, which he did. The list showed the following:

Assets		Liabilities	
Bank balance	$150	Bank Loan	$2 000
Truck (Market Value)	5 500	Loan from brother	5 000
Total	$5 650	2 years interest	950
		Trade debts	2 000
		Total	$9 950

For two seasons Garn had been confident that he was operating a profitable business. He was absolutely certain that he had made a profit on every individual job. But now he was shaken by the picture presented by the list of assets and liabilities.

Questions

1. How much cash did Garn have in the bank to begin with, after purchasing the major assets?
2. What is Garn's present equity figure?
3. Is it possible to determine Garn's profit or loss? Explain.
4. Is it possible to determine how much money Garn withdrew for personal use? Explain.
5. How could the above situation develop without Garn's being aware of it?
6. Outline briefly the reasons for Garn's predicament.
7. What is meant by "spending capital"?
8. What is the best course of action for Garn to take now?

CASE 3   *The Good Life on Plastic Money*

Kevin and Jean Ross grew up during the age of credit cards. It is not surprising then that they have lots of them. Kevin, in particular, likes to show off his wallet full of credit cards. They include: Sears, The Bay, Eaton's, Canadian Tire, Visa, Mastercard, Imperial Oil, Esso, Petro-Can, American Express, Air Canada, and En Route.

Kevin and Jean saw no reason to worry about using credit cards. They were both university graduates with high-paying jobs and lots of common sense and ability. But they also liked the good life and denied themselves very little. They bought an expensive house with fine furnishings. They ate out two or three times a week. They loved to travel and took at least one overseas vacation a year.

When they were in their twenties and living in an apartment, their lifestyle was easy to maintain. They found no difficulty in making payments on time and avoided any interest charges.

When they were in their thirties (with two children) and had moved into their nice home, their use of credit cards had changed. They seemed to have lost sight of the "account balance" amount and could only see the figure for the "minimum payment required." In most cases, this was the amount that they paid.

Now, Kevin and Jean are in their forties. To their surprise, they are often having difficulty paying even the minimum payment required. Several times now, they have received letters from creditors requesting them to reduce the balance of their account. Without really understanding it all, Kevin and Jean have realized that they are in a financial hole and need help. For assistance, they turn to the Metropolitan Credit Counselling Service.

Questions

1. Explain the chain of circumstances that led up to the situation that Kevin and Jean find themselves in.
2. In your opinion, how common is Kevin's and Jean's situation? Explain.
3. When credit limits are established, designed to keep spending within reason, how can a situation like Kevin's and Jean's develop?
4. What will the advice of the credit counselling service probably be? Explain fully.
5. Will Kevin and Jean be able to continue their lifestyle?

CASE 4   *Is Opportunity Knocking?*

Frances Wywrot, a widow, is physically handicapped and has stopped working. Her only source of income is from $200 000 of long-term government bonds. These bonds were purchased from her own savings and from life insurance proceeds that she received when her husband died. The bonds are not guaranteed, provide for interest at 12 per cent, and have a market value of $96 for each $100 of face value.

In recent years Frances has found it increasingly difficult to maintain a decent standard of living. She has let it be known among her friends that she is looking for ways to increase her income.

A local entrepreneur who is building apartment buildings approaches Frances with a business proposal. The entrepreneur claims that Frances will receive a 25 per cent return on an investment in apartment buildings if she can put up a minimum of $120 000 cash. There is no guarantee, but a severe shortage of apartment units does exist in the community and the risk is considered to be minimal.

Frances is seriously considering the proposal and comes to you for advice. She is fearful of disposing of the bonds because the income from them is assured. Nevertheless, she feels that she must do something in order to improve her lot. She is considering the following three options:

a. sell all of the bonds, and invest the entire proceeds;

b. sell $125 000 of the bonds to produce the minimum investment of $120 000 cash, and keep $75 000 in bonds;

c. keep all of the bonds, and borrow $120 000 from the bank to invest.

Using the additional information given below, work out the net income from each of the three proposals over a two-year period. Advise Frances on the option that she should choose.

Additional Information

1. Income tax is calculated according to the following schedule:
   - on income between $20 001 and $30 000, 32 per cent;
   - on income between $30 001 and $40 000, 36 per cent;
   - on income over $40 001, 40 per cent.

   Ignore any special income tax exemptions and conditions.
2. Personal capital losses are not chargeable as an expense of the venture.
3. Bank interest is chargeable as an expense of the venture. The current rate of bank interest is 15 per cent.

CAREER
David Nagashima / Regional Manager

David Nagashima was first exposed to accounting in his high school classes at Campbellton High School in Campbellton, New Brunswick.

In 1975, after graduating with a Bachelor of Commerce degree from the University of New Brunswick, he started his banking career as a management trainee with Canada Trust. During this period, David gained experience in all the offices of the company's accounting system. He learned, for example, how to process loans, keep ledgers, handle many types of bank accounts, calculate interest, and exchange foreign currency.

As his career progressed, David joined the Canadian Imperial Bank of Commerce as an account executive and service product manager. He was promoted to senior product manager, and his duties included developing personal lines of credit and marketing the services offered by the bank. As part of this marketing, he prepared radio advertisements to promote the bank's services; keeping abreast of the competition was important. David was also responsible for preparing the advertising budget. He presided over regular meetings on budget estimates.

Seeking broader horizons, David went to the Bank of Montreal where his first job was project manager responsible for personal loans at the bank's fully automated branch (with computerized bank statements).

David's specific tasks were to recommend interest rates on loans, report rates to senior executives, stage conferences to promote better ways to market loans, and, again, be responsible for budget estimates and budget submissions. He was then given responsibility for opening and subsequently managing a Bank of Montreal in a shopping mall. Later still, his responsibilities as bank manager for consumer marketing in New Brunswick included giving direct market assistance to 150 branches. David decided whether or not to open, close, or relocate branches; he also monitored each bank's trends in profits, loans, deposits, and revenues and expenses.

Because of the nature of the banking industry, David understood that he might be called on to change locations at any time.

David is now regional manager responsible for profitability, customer relations, and corporate liaison for 14 branches of the Bank of Montreal in the Campbellton area of New Brunswick. As regional manager, his duties include the hiring of branch managers and the preparation of budgets which must be approved by the regional vice-president. The qualities David looks for in applicants for branch manager are maturity, problem-solving ability, a marketing background, and accounting and computer experience. David also analyzes the profits of each bank in the region and recommends ways to increase profits and cut costs. In his position as regional manager, David is involved in

community relations work. He speaks to service groups and schools, organizes activities in the community, and appears on television and radio shows to discuss various banking topics. David realizes the importance of communication skills.

Because he knew that practical experience was valuable, David worked his way up through the branch banking system. He enjoyed branch banking affairs so much that he has remained in this field rather than seeking a role in head office.

David is now 32 years old, and his hope is to become a vice-president in charge of 11 bank areas.

DISCUSSION

1. Make a chart illustrating David's education and career advancements. In the first column, list David's past positions, what he does now, and what he hopes to do in the future. In the next column, place a check mark after each job that requires a basic knowledge of accounting skills. In a third column, next to the appropriate positions, list the educational programs David has completed and those he will have to complete to attain his career goals.
2. What are the qualities David looks for when he is hiring a branch manager?
3. Prepare an advertisement for the "Canadian Northern Bank" setting out reasons why your bank can provide better service than your competitors.
4. What do you regard as a "significant cash shortage"? How would David help his staff keep cash discrepancies to a minimum?
5. What is meant by the branch banking system in Canada?
6. Using the business section of the newspaper, make a chart showing each of the following for a period of one month:
   a. interest rates on loans
   b. mortgage rates
   c. interest rates on deposits.
   Use the figures from three banks and three trust companies of your choice.
7. Prepare a report on the four-year Bachelor of Commerce degree at a university of your choice. Find out the qualifications needed to enrol, the number of courses required for graduation, how many accounting courses must be taken, what other business courses are offered, and the average needed for graduation.

Supplementary Exercise

Green Thumb Garden Centre

Introductory Information

The Green Thumb Garden Centre is a business owned and operated by Mr. G. O. Emms. It is a seasonal business which the owner closes down each year during the winter months. During the season that the business is open, the business is operated seven days a week.

The Green Thumb Garden Centre sells a variety of trees and shrubs and all of the common garden and landscaping materials. All goods and services are subject to a seven per cent government sales tax.

Mr. Emms employs a number of workers. Most of these are hired on a part-time basis as they are needed. Once each week, Mr. Emms withdraws from the bank (by means of a cheque made out to Cash) sufficient cash to pay the employees.

Most of the sales of the business are on a cash or Visa basis. As a result, the accounting system of the business is geared toward the cash register. There are only a few charge customers. All sales transactions and receipts from customers are processed through the cash register.

The system uses the three special journals that follow:

Purchases Journal

							page 77
Date	Name	Other Accounts Dr.	Truck Expense Dr.	Soil Prep. & Mtce. Dr.	Equipment Expense Dr.	Purchases Dr.	Accounts Payable Cr.

Cash Payments Journal

								Page 47
Date	Name	Other Accounts Dr.	Wages Dr.	G.O.E Drawings Dr.	Soil Prep. & Mtce. Dr.	Discounts Earned Cr.	Accounts Payable Dr.	Bank Cr.

Cash Receipts Journal

								Page 65
Date	Name	Other Accounts Cr.	Cash Short & Over Dr.	Discounts Allowed Dr	Sales Tax Payable Cr.	Sales Cr.	Accounts Receivable Cr.	Bank Dr.

At the close of each day's business, a cash register balancing procedure is performed and an accounting summary is prepared. A bank deposit is made each day by using a night depository service.

Small expense items are not paid for out of the cash register funds. Mr. Emms maintains a petty cash fund of $100 for this purpose.

The business uses the periodic inventory system.

The three ledgers of the Green Thumb Garden Centre as of May 31, 19— are set up in the Workbook and the trial balances are shown below. The Workbook also contains the cash receipts journal (page 65), the cash payments journal (page 47), and the purchases journal (page 77).

GREEN THUMB GARDEN CENTRE
GENERAL LEDGER TRIAL BALANCE
MAY 31, 19—

No.	Accounts	DR	CR
105	Petty Cash	$ 100.00	
110	Bank	3 527.24	
115	Accounts Receivable	1 925.18	
120	Merchandise Inventory	75 746.53	
125	Supplies	595.00	
130	Land	48 000.00	
135	Buildings	65 500.00	
145	Trucks and Tractors	40 500.00	
205	Bank Loan		$ 20 000.00
210	Accounts Payable		7 861.87
215	Sales Tax Payable		2 195.45
220	Mortgage Payable		45 500.00
305	G. O. Emms, Capital		176 415.91
310	G. O. Emms, Drawings	15 654.60	
405	Sales		45 042.19
505	Bank Charges	547.53	
510	Building Repairs	146.51	
515	Cash Short and Over	10.50	
520	Discounts Allowed	95.75	
525	Discounts Earned		54.70
530	Equipment Expense	506.86	
535	Freight-in	856.60	
540	Light, Heat & Power	1 306.75	
545	Miscellaneous Expense	192.45	
550	Purchases	30 001.05	
555	Soil Preparation and Maintenance	4 858.25	
560	Telephone	519.42	
565	Trucks Expense	2 104.40	
570	Wages	4 375.50	
		$297 070.12	$297 070.12

GREEN THUMB GARDEN CENTRE
ACCOUNTS RECEIVABLE TRIAL BALANCE
MAY 31, 19—

Customer	Usual Terms	Invoice Date	Invoice Number	Amount
F. Carson & Sons	2/10,n/30	May 30	408	$ 541.80
C. Swinton	2/10,n/30	May 26	407	1 094.63
Varga Brothers	2/10,n/30	May 24	402	288.75
				$1 925.18

GREEN THUMB GARDEN CENTRE
ACCOUNTS PAYABLE TRIAL BALANCE
MAY 31, 19—

Supplier	Terms	Inv. No.	Inv. Date	Inv. Amount	Account Balance
Acorn Seed	2/15,n/30	654	May 18	$147.00	
		672	May 21	317.10	$ 464.10
Clay Ceramic Co.	Net 45	1701	Apr 24		540.75
Canada Products	Net 30	B160	May 4	58.80	
		B188	May 12	98.91	
		B249	May 30	35.91	193.62
Kemp Haulage	1/10,n/30	747	May 23	52.50	
		754	May 23	52.50	
		760	May 23	52.50	
		772	May 27	52.50	
		795	May 31	78.75	288.75
M. & M. Chemicals	Net 60	1046	Apr 9		1 932.00
Poplar Finance	Per contract				2 560.00
Sylvester Concrete	Net 30	446	May 5		783.51
Triangle Sod	Net 30	374	May 22		1 099.14
					$7 861.87

1. Journalize the following transactions. Post daily to the subsidiary ledgers, directly from the source documents.

Transactions

June 1   *Cash Register Summary*

LINE NO.	ACCOUNTS			DR	CR
1	Cash	169	20		
2	Visa	33	70	500 90	
3	Accounts Rec'l (Charge Sales)				
4	Asset or Expense				
5	Asset or Expense				
6	Asset or Expense				
7	Cash Short or Over			2 —	
8	Accounts Rec'l (Rec'd on A/c)				
9	Accounts Rec'l (Ret'd for Cr.)				
10	Sales				470 —
11	Sales Tax Payable				32 90
12	Cash Short or Over				
	BALANCING TOTALS			502 90	502 90

CASHIER'S SIGNATURE   *C. Deng*

Purchase Invoice
From Canada Products, No. B261, $372.75, dated May 31, terms Net 30, for fertilizer for resale.

June 2   *Cash Register Summary*

LINE NO.	ACCOUNTS			DR	CR
1	Cash	443	47		
2	Visa	33	70	775 17	
3	Accounts Rec'l (Charge Sales)				
4	Asset or Expense *Discounts Allowed*			5 78	
5	Asset or Expense				
6	Asset or Expense				
7	Cash Short or Over				
8	Accounts Rec'l (Rec'd on A/c)				288 75
9	Accounts Rec'l (Ret'd for Cr.)				
10	Sales				460 —
11	Sales Tax Payable				32 20
12	Cash Short or Over				
	BALANCING TOTALS			780 95	780 95

CASHIER'S SIGNATURE   *C. Deng*

"Received" Voucher
Voucher No. 416 made out to Varga Brothers for $282.97 in payment of invoice No. 402, less the two per cent discount.

Purchase Invoice
   From Triangle Sod, No. 406, $312.90, dated June 1, terms
   Net 30, for sod for resale.
Cheque Copies
   No. 661, to Acorn Seed Company, $?, paying invoice 654 less the two
   per cent discount.
   No. 662, to Kemp Haulage, $?, paying invoices 747, 754, and 760 less the
   one per cent discount.

June 3   *Cash Register Summary*

LINE NO.	ACCOUNTS		DR	CR
1	Cash	276 06	573 52	
2	Visa	297 46		
3	Accounts Rec'l (Charge Sales)			
4	Asset or Expense			
5	Asset or Expense			
6	Asset or Expense			
7	Cash Short or Over			
8	Accounts Rec'l (Rec'd on A/c)			
9	Accounts Rec'l (Ret'd for Cr.)			
10	Sales			536 —
11	Sales Tax Payable			37 52
12	Cash Short or Over			
	BALANCING TOTALS		573 52	573 52

CASHIER'S SIGNATURE   *C. May*

Cheque Copy
   No. 663, to Petty Cash, $?, to reimburse the petty cash fund for the fol-
   lowing petty cash expenditures:

PETTY CASH SUMMARY JUNE 3, 19--	
Building Repairs	$14.10
Equipment Expense	2.50
Soil Preparation and Maintenance	35.50
Truck Expense	17.70
Miscellaneous Expense	26.75

June 4   *Cash Register Summary*

LINE NO.	ACCOUNTS	ACCOUNTING ENTRY	DR	CR
1	Cash 53 50			
2	Visa 299 60		353 10	
3	Accounts Rec'l (Charge Sales)		337 05	
4	Asset or Expense _____			
5	Asset or Expense _____			
6	Asset or Expense _____			
7	Cash Short or Over			
8	Accounts Rec'l (Rec'd on A/c)			
9	Accounts Rec'l (Ret'd for Cr.)			
10	Sales			645 -
11	Sales Tax Payable			45 15
12	Cash Short or Over			
	BALANCING TOTALS		690 15	690 15

CASHIER'S SIGNATURE   *C. May*

"Charge" Voucher

Voucher No. 417 made out to Varga Brothers for the sale of merchandise, $315.00 plus seven per cent sales tax, terms 2/10,n/30, total $337.05.

Purchase Invoices

From Clay Ceramic Co., No 1916, $1 003.80, dated June 3, terms Net 45, for flower pots and ornamental garden items for resale.

From M. & M. Chemicals, No. 1193, $784.00, dated June 3, terms Net 60, for insecticides for resale.

Cheque Copies

No. 664, to Sylvester Concrete, $?, paying invoice No. 446.

No. 665, to Public Utilities Commission, $44.85, for electricity for the month of May. (Cheque No. 665 was issued as soon as this bill was received.)

Bank Statement and Vouchers

The bank statement and related vouchers and paid cheques for May arrived from the bank. Included in the vouchers was a debit note for bank charges in the amount of $41.50 for May. This was the first notice of these charges.

At this time, the following reconciliation statement was prepared. You will need this statement in order to prepare a reconciliation statement at the end of June.

Green Thumb Garden Centre					
Bank Reconciliation Statement					
May 31, 19--					
Balance per Bk Statement	3 4 0 6 15	Balance per General Ledger		3 5 2 7 24
Add Outstanding Deposit	5 1 6 31	Deduct Bank Interest and Service Charge		4 1 50
	3 9 2 2 46			
Deduct Outstanding Cheques				
#641 $74.00				
#650 36.50				
#654 29.12				
#655 116.26				
#657 37.40				
#658 42.15				
#659 95.14				
#660 6.15	4 3 6 72			
True Balance	3 4 8 5 74	True Balance		3 4 8 5 74

June 5   *Cash Register Summary*

LINE NO.	ACCOUNTING ENTRY			
	ACCOUNTS		DR	CR
1	Cash	1 292 44		
2	Visa	438 70	1 731 14	
3	Accounts Rec'l (Charge Sales)			
4	Asset or Expense *Discounts Allowed*		21 89	
5	Asset or Expense			
6	Asset or Expense			
7	Cash Short or Over		5 -	
8	Accounts Rec'l (Rec'd on A/c)			1 094 63
9	Accounts Rec'l (Ret'd for Cr.)			
10	Sales			620 -
11	Sales Tax Payable			43 40
12	Cash Short or Over			
	BALANCING TOTALS		1 758 03	1 758 03
CASHIER'S SIGNATURE *C. Deng*				

"Received" Voucher

Voucher No. 418, made out to C. Swinton for $1 072.74 in payment of invoice No. 407 less the two per cent cash discount.

Cheque Copies

No. 666, to Cash, $604.16, for wages for the week.

No. 667, to G. O. Emms, $440.00, for personal drawings of the owner.

No. 668, to Acorn Seed Company, $?, paying invoice No. 672 less the two per cent cash discount.

June 6   *Cash Register Summary*

LINE NO.	ACCOUNTS	ACCOUNTING ENTRY DR	CR
1	Cash 347 75		
2	Visa 165 85	513 60	
3	Accounts Rec'l (Charge Sales)	552 19	
4	Asset or Expense _____		
5	Asset or Expense _____		
6	Asset or Expense _____		
7	Cash Short or Over		
8	Accounts Rec'l (Rec'd on A/c)		
9	Accounts Rec'l (Ret'd for Cr.)		
10	Sales		996 07
11	Sales Tax Payable		69 72
12	Cash Short or Over		
	BALANCING TOTALS	1 065 79	1 065 79
CASHIER'S SIGNATURE	*C. Deng*		

"Charge" Voucher

Voucher No. 419, made out to C. Swinton, $516.07 plus seven per cent sales tax, for sale of merchandise, terms 2/10,n/30, total $552.19.

Purchase Invoices

From Equipment Repair and Supply, No. 21, $157.50, dated June 5, terms Net 30, for repairs to equipment.

From Canada Products, No. B295, $997.50, dated June 4, terms Net 30, for fertilizers and chemicals to be charged as follows: Purchases, $871.50; Soil Preparation and Maintenance, $126.00.

Cheque Copies

No. 669, to Clay Ceramic Co., $540.75, paying invoice No. 1701.

No. 670, to Kemp Haulage, $?, paying invoice No. 772 less the one per cent cash discount.

No. 671, to Canada Products, $58.80, paying invoice No. B160.

June 7   *Cash Register Summary*

LINE NO.	ACCOUNTS		DR	CR
		ACCOUNTING ENTRY		
1	Cash	481 50	989 75	
2	Visa	508 25		
3	Accounts Rec'l (Charge Sales)			
4	Asset or Expense _____			
5	Asset or Expense _____			
6	Asset or Expense _____			
7	Cash Short or Over			
8	Accounts Rec'l (Rec'd on A/c)			
9	Accounts Rec'l (Ret'd for Cr.)			
10	Sales			925 -
11	Sales Tax Payable			64 75
12	Cash Short or Over			
	BALANCING TOTALS		989 75	989 75
	CASHIER'S SIGNATURE	*C. Deng*		

Cheque Copy

No. 672, to Public Utilities Commission, $97.50, cash payment of water bill (charged to Soil Preparation and Maintenance).

June 8   *Cash Register Summary*

LINE NO.	ACCOUNTS		DR	CR
		ACCOUNTING ENTRY		
1	Cash	648 66	728 91	
2	Visa	80 25		
3	Accounts Rec'l (Charge Sales)			
4	Asset or Expense *Discounts Allowed*		10 84	
5	Asset or Expense _____			
6	Asset or Expense _____			
7	Cash Short or Over			
8	Accounts Rec'l (Rec'd on A/c)			541 80
9	Accounts Rec'l (Ret'd for Cr.)			185 -
10	Sales			12 95
11	Sales Tax Payable			
12	Cash Short or Over			
	BALANCING TOTALS		739 75	739 75
	CASHIER'S SIGNATURE	*C. Deng*		

"Received" Voucher

Voucher No. 420 made out to F. Carson & Sons for $530.96 in payment of invoice No. 408 less the two per cent cash discount.

Cheque Copies
No. 673, to M. & M. Chemicals, $1 932.00, paying invoice No. 1046.
No. 674, to Poplar Finance, $275.00, regular monthly payment on truck.

June 9   *Cash Register Summary*

LINE NO.	ACCOUNTS		DR		CR	
1	Cash	119 84				
2	Visa	230 05	349	89		
3	Accounts Rec'l (Charge Sales)					
4	Asset or Expense					
5	Asset or Expense					
6	Asset or Expense					
7	Cash Short or Over					
8	Accounts Rec'l (Rec'd on A/c)					
9	Accounts Rec'l (Ret'd for Cr.)					
10	Sales				327	-
11	Sales Tax Payable				22	89
12	Cash Short or Over					
	BALANCING TOTALS		349	89	349	89

CASHIER'S SIGNATURE   *C. Deng*

Purchase Invoices
From City Gas & Oil, No. 1651, $135.68, dated June 8, terms Net 30, for gasoline and oil used in the trucks and equipment as follows: Trucks, $94.67; Equipment, $41.01.
From Kemp Haulage, No. 822, $231.00, dated June 7, terms 1/10,n/30, for topsoil for resale.

June 10   *Cash Register Summary*

LINE NO.	ACCOUNTS		DR		CR	
1	Cash	225 77				
2	Visa	53 50	279	27		
3	Accounts Rec'l (Charge Sales)					
4	Asset or Expense					
5	Asset or Expense					
6	Asset or Expense					
7	Cash Short or Over					
8	Accounts Rec'l (Rec'd on A/c)					
9	Accounts Rec'l (Ret'd for Cr.)					
10	Sales				261	-
11	Sales Tax Payable				18	27
12	Cash Short or Over					
	BALANCING TOTALS		279	27	279	27

CASHIER'S SIGNATURE   *C. May*

Cheque Copies
No. 675, to Northwestern Telephone Company, $45.20, cash payment of telephone bill.
No. 676, to Kemp Haulage, $?, paying invoice No. 795 less the one per cent cash discount.

June 11 *Cash Register Summary*

LINE NO.	ACCOUNTS	ACCOUNTING ENTRY		DR		CR	
1	Cash	26	75				
2	Visa	267	50	294	25		
3	Accounts Rec'l (Charge Sales)						
4	Asset or Expense _____						
5	Asset or Expense _____						
6	Asset or Expense _____						
7	Cash Short or Over						
8	Accounts Rec'l (Rec'd on A/c)						
9	Accounts Rec'l (Ret'd for Cr.)						
10	Sales					275	–
11	Sales Tax Payable					19	25
12	Cash Short or Over						
	BALANCING TOTALS			294	25	294	25
CASHIER'S SIGNATURE	*C May*						

Purchase Invoice
From M. & M. Chemicals, No. 1221, $781.90, dated June 10, terms Net 60, to be charged to Soil Preparation and Maintenance.
Cheque Copy
No. 677, to Canada Products, $98.91, paying invoice No. B188.

June 12   *Cash Register Summary*

LINE NO.	ACCOUNTS			DR		CR	
			ACCOUNTING ENTRY				
1	Cash	102	–				
2	Visa	96	30	198	30		
3	Accounts Rec'l (Charge Sales)			283	55		
4	Asset or Expense _____						
5	Asset or Expense _____						
6	Asset or Expense _____						
7	Cash Short or Over			5	–		
8	Accounts Rec'l (Rec'd on A/c)						
9	Accounts Rec'l (Ret'd for Cr.)						
10	Sales					455	–
11	Sales Tax Payable					31	85
12	Cash Short or Over						
	BALANCING TOTALS			486	85	486	85
CASHIER'S SIGNATURE *C. Deng*							

"Charge" Voucher

Voucher No. 421 made out F. Carson & Sons for the sale of merchandise, terms 2/10,n/30, $265.00 plus seven per cent sales tax, total $283.55.

Cheque Copies

No. 678, to Cash, $705.19 for the wages for the week.

No 679, to G. O. Emms, $350.00, for owner's personal drawings.

No. 680, to Foster Bros., $44.21, for the cash purchase of miscellaneous items to be charged to Miscellaneous Expense.

June 13   *Cash Register Summary*

LINE NO.	ACCOUNTS			DR		CR	
			ACCOUNTING ENTRY				
1	Cash	150	50				
2	Visa	486	85	637	35		
3	Accounts Rec'l (Charge Sales)						
4	Asset or Expense _____						
5	Asset or Expense _____						
6	Asset or Expense _____						
7	Cash Short or Over			10	–		
8	Accounts Rec'l (Rec'd on A/c)						
9	Accounts Rec'l (Ret'd for Cr.)						
10	Sales					605	–
11	Sales Tax Payable					42	35
12	Cash Short or Over						
	BALANCING TOTALS			647	35	647	35
CASHIER'S SIGNATURE *C. Deng*							

Purchase Invoice
>   From Acorn Seed Company, No. 756, $82.43, dated June 12, terms
>   2/15,n/30, for the purchase of merchandise for resale.

June 14   *Cash Register Summary*

LINE NO.	ACCOUNTS			DR		CR	
	ACCOUNTING ENTRY						
1	Cash	779	71				
2	Visa	192	60	972	31		
3	Accounts Rec'l (Charge Sales)						
4	Asset or Expense *Discounts Allowed*			6	74		
5	Asset or Expense						
6	Asset or Expense						
7	Cash Short or Over						
8	Accounts Rec'l (Rec'd on A/c)					337	05
9	Accounts Rec'l (Ret'd for Cr.)						
10	Sales					600	–
11	Sales Tax Payable					42	–
12	Cash Short or Over						
	BALANCING TOTALS			979	05	979	05
CASHIER'S SIGNATURE *C. Deng*							

"Received" Voucher
>   Voucher No. 422 made out to Varga Brothers, $330.31, in payment of
>   invoice No. 417 less the two per cent cash discount.

Purchase Invoice
>   From Triangle Sod, No. 452, $787.50, dated June 12, terms Net 30, for
>   the purchase of sod for resale.

Bank Debit Advice
>   This debit note from Central Bank stated that $2 000 had been deducted
>   from the business bank account for the purpose of reducing the bank loan.
>   Mr. Emms had instructed the bank to make the deduction.

June 15   *Cash Register Summary*

LINE NO.	ACCOUNTS		ACCOUNTING ENTRY DR	CR
1	Cash	33 70		
2	Visa	101 65	433 35	
3	Accounts Rec'l (Charge Sales)			
4	Asset or Expense _____			
5	Asset or Expense _____			
6	Asset or Expense _____			
7	Cash Short or Over			
8	Accounts Rec'l (Rec'd on A/c)			
9	Accounts Rec'l (Ret'd for Cr.)			
10	Sales			405 –
11	Sales Tax Payable			28 35
12	Cash Short or Over			
	BALANCING TOTALS		433 35	433 35
CASHIER'S SIGNATURE	*C. Deng*			

Cheque Copies

No. 681, to Provincial Treasurer, $?, paying the sales tax for the previous month.

No. 682, to Proud Insurance Company, $378.50, paying the regular monthly mortgage payment.

June 16   *Cash Register Summary*

LINE NO.	ACCOUNTS		ACCOUNTING ENTRY DR	CR
1	Cash	203 30		
2	Visa	331 70	535 –	
3	Accounts Rec'l (Charge Sales)			
4	Asset or Expense _____			
5	Asset or Expense _____			
6	Asset or Expense _____			
7	Cash Short or Over			
8	Accounts Rec'l (Rec'd on A/c)			
9	Accounts Rec'l (Ret'd for Cr.)			
10	Sales			500 –
11	Sales Tax Payable			35 –
12	Cash Short or Over			
	BALANCING TOTALS		535 –	535 –
CASHIER'S SIGNATURE	*C. Deng*			

Cheque Copies

No. 683, to Central Supply, $89.38, for the cash purchase of supplies.

No. 684, to Mainline Express, $105.85, for the cash payment of express charges to be charged to Freight-in.

June 17   *Cash Register Summary*

LINE NO.	ACCOUNTS	ACCOUNTING ENTRY	DR	CR
1	Cash 760 50			
2	Visa 374 50		1 135 –	
3	Accounts Rec'l (Charge Sales)			
4	Asset or Expense _Discounts Allowed_		11 04	
5	Asset or Expense			
6	Asset or Expense			
7	Cash Short or Over			
8	Accounts Rec'l (Rec'd on A/c)			552 19
9	Accounts Rec'l (Ret'd for Cr.)			
10	Sales			555 –
11	Sales Tax Payable			38 85
12	Cash Short or Over			
	BALANCING TOTALS		1 146 04	1 146 04
CASHIER'S SIGNATURE	*C. May*			

"Received" Voucher

Voucher No. 423 made out to C. Swinton for $541.15 in payment of invoice No. 419 less the two per cent cash discount. Although the payment arrived after the discount date, it was decided to allow the discount.

Purchase Invoices

From Equipment Repair and Supply, No. 40, $201.60, dated June 15, terms Net 30, for truck repairs.

From Kemp Haulage, No. 856, $211.05, dated June 16, terms 1/10,n/30, for topsoil and fertilizer to improve the condition of the soil on the business's property, to be charged to Soil Preparation and Maintenance.

Cheque Copy

No. 685, to Kemp Haulage, $?, paying invoice No. 822 less the cash discount.

June 18   *Cash Register Summary*

LINE NO.	ACCOUNTS			DR		CR	
1	Cash	144	45				
2	Visa	331	70	476	15		
3	Accounts Rec'l (Charge Sales)			428	–		
4	Asset or Expense						
5	Asset or Expense						
6	Asset or Expense						
7	Cash Short or Over						
8	Accounts Rec'l (Rec'd on A/c)						
9	Accounts Rec'l (Ret'd for Cr.)						
10	Sales					845	–
11	Sales Tax Payable					59	15
12	Cash Short or Over						
	BALANCING TOTALS			904	15	904	15

CASHIER'S SIGNATURE   *C. May*

"Charge" Voucher
  Voucher No. 424 made out to Varga Brothers for the sale of merchandise, terms 2/10,n/30, $400.00 plus seven per cent sales tax, total $428.00.

Cheque Copy
  No. 686, to The Business House, $35.75, for the cash purchase of items to be charged to Miscellaneous Expense.

June 19   *Cash Register Summary*

LINE NO.	ACCOUNTS			DR		CR	
1	Cash						
2	Visa	330	63	330	63		
3	Accounts Rec'l (Charge Sales)						
4	Asset or Expense						
5	Asset or Expense						
6	Asset or Expense						
7	Cash Short or Over						
8	Accounts Rec'l (Rec'd on A/c)						
9	Accounts Rec'l (Ret'd for Cr.)						
10	Sales					309	–
11	Sales Tax Payable					21	63
12	Cash Short or Over						
	BALANCING TOTALS			330	63	330	63

CASHIER'S SIGNATURE   *C. Deng*

Purchase Invoice

From Sylvester Concrete, No. 491, $1 236.25, dated June 17, terms Net 30, for patio stones for resale.

Cheque Copies

No. 687, to Cash, $567.25, for the wages for the week.

No. 688, to G. O. Emms, $400.00, for owner's personal drawings.

June 20   *Cash Register Summary*

LINE NO.	ACCOUNTS		DR	CR
1	Cash	160 50		
2	Visa	342 40	502 90	
3	Accounts Rec'l (Charge Sales)			
4	Asset or Expense _____			
5	Asset or Expense _____			
6	Asset or Expense _____			
7	Cash Short or Over			
8	Accounts Rec'l (Rec'd on A/c)			
9	Accounts Rec'l (Ret'd for Cr.)			53 50
10	Sales			420 -
11	Sales Tax Payable			29 40
12	Cash Short or Over			
	BALANCING TOTALS		502 90	502 90

ACCOUNTING ENTRY

CASHIER'S SIGNATURE   *C. Deng*

"Credit Note" Voucher

Voucher No. 425 made out to Varga Brothers for the return of unsatisfactory merchandise, $50.00 plus seven per cent sales tax, total $53.50.

Purchase Invoice

From Triangle Sod, No. 474, $558.08, dated June 19, terms Net 30, for purchase of sod for resale.

June 21   *Cash Register Summary*

LINE NO.	ACCOUNTS		DR		CR	
		ACCOUNTING ENTRY				
1	Cash	428 14				
2	Visa	421 58	849 72			
3	Accounts Rec'l (Charge Sales)					
4	Asset or Expense					
5	Asset or Expense					
6	Asset or Expense					
7	Cash Short or Over		2 -			
8	Accounts Rec'l (Rec'd on A/c)					
9	Accounts Rec'l (Ret'd for Cr.)					
10	Sales				796 -	
11	Sales Tax Payable				55 72	
12	Cash Short or Over					
	BALANCING TOTALS		851 72		851 72	

CASHIER'S SIGNATURE   *C. Deng*

Cheque Copies

No. 689, to Petty Cash, $?, to replenish the petty cash fund for the following expenditures:

PETTY CASH SUMMARY
JUNE 21, 19--

Soil Preparation and Maintenance	$26.15
Truck Expense	36.75
Miscellaneous Expense	35.01

No. 690, to Triangle Sod, paying invoice No. 374.

June 22   *Cash Register Summary*

LINE NO.	ACCOUNTS			DR		CR	
	ACCOUNTING ENTRY						
1	Cash	397	72				
2	Visa	240	75	638	47		
3	Accounts Rec'l (Charge Sales)			2 200	56		
4	Asset or Expense *Discounts Allowed*			5	67		
5	Asset or Expense						
6	Asset or Expense						
7	Cash Short or Over						
8	Accounts Rec'l (Rec'd on A/c)					283	55
9	Accounts Rec'l (Ret'd for Cr.)						
10	Sales					2 393	60
11	Sales Tax Payable					167	55
12	Cash Short or Over						
	BALANCING TOTALS			2 844	70	2 844	70

CASHIER'S SIGNATURE   *C. Deng*

"Charge" Voucher

Voucher No. 426 made out to C. Swinton for the sale of merchandise, terms 2/10,n/30, $2 156.60 plus seven per cent sales tax, total $2 200.56.

"Received" Voucher

Voucher No. 427 made out to F. Carson & Sons for $277.88 paying invoice No. 421 less the two per cent cash discount.

June 23   *Cash Register Summary*

LINE NO.	ACCOUNTS			DR	CR
			ACCOUNTING ENTRY		
1	Cash	42	80		
2	Visa	537	14	579 94	
3	Accounts Rec'l (Charge Sales)				
4	Asset or Expense				
5	Asset or Expense				
6	Asset or Expense				
7	Cash Short or Over				
8	Accounts Rec'l (Rec'd on A/c)				
9	Accounts Rec'l (Ret'd for Cr.)				
10	Sales				542 -
11	Sales Tax Payable				37 94
12	Cash Short or Over				
	BALANCING TOTALS			579 94	579 94
	CASHIER'S SIGNATURE *C. Deng*				

June 24   *Cash Register Summary*

LINE NO.	ACCOUNTS			DR	CR
			ACCOUNTING ENTRY		
1	Cash	208	15		
2	Visa	283	55	491 70	
3	Accounts Rec'l (Charge Sales)				
4	Asset or Expense				
5	Asset or Expense				
6	Asset or Expense				
7	Cash Short or Over			50	
8	Accounts Rec'l (Rec'd on A/c)				
9	Accounts Rec'l (Ret'd for Cr.)				
10	Sales				460 -
11	Sales Tax Payable				32 20
12	Cash Short or Over				
	BALANCING TOTALS			492 20	492 20
	CASHIER'S SIGNATURE *C. May*				

Purchase Invoices

From Acorn Seed Company, No. 801, $813.75, dated June 23, terms 2/15,n/30, for merchandise for resale.

From Clay Ceramic Co., No. 2016, $136.50, dated June 22, terms Net 45, for merchandise for resale.

June 25   *Cash Register Summary*

LINE NO.	ACCOUNTS			DR		CR	
			ACCOUNTING ENTRY				
1	Cash	98	44				
2	Visa	299	60	398	04		
3	Accounts Rec'l (Charge Sales)						
4	Asset or Expense _____						
5	Asset or Expense _____						
6	Asset or Expense _____						
7	Cash Short or Over						
8	Accounts Rec'l (Rec'd on A/c)						
9	Accounts Rec'l (Ret'd for Cr.)						
10	Sales					372	–
11	Sales Tax Payable					26	04
12	Cash Short or Over						
	BALANCING TOTALS			398	04	398	04
CASHIER'S SIGNATURE *C. May*							

Cheque Copy
   No. 691, to Poplar Finance Co., $182.00, for regular finance payment on tractor.

June 26   *Cash Register Summary*

LINE NO.	ACCOUNTS			DR		CR	
			ACCOUNTING ENTRY				
1	Cash	188	25				
2	Visa	230	05	418	30		
3	Accounts Rec'l (Charge Sales)						
4	Asset or Expense _____						
5	Asset or Expense _____						
6	Asset or Expense _____						
7	Cash Short or Over						
8	Accounts Rec'l (Rec'd on A/c)						
9	Accounts Rec'l (Ret'd for Cr.)						
10	Sales					390	–
11	Sales Tax Payable					27	30
12	Cash Short or Over					1	–
	BALANCING TOTALS			418	30	418	30
CASHIER'S SIGNATURE *C. Deng*							

Cheque Copies
   No. 692, to Acorn Seed Co., $?, paying invoice No. 756 less the two per cent cash discount.
   No. 693, to Cash, $505.60, for the wages for the week.
   No. 694, to G. O. Emms, $400.00, for the owner's personal drawings.

June 27   *Cash Register Summary*

LINE NO.	ACCOUNTS		DR		CR	
	ACCOUNTING ENTRY					
1	Cash	768 26				
2	Visa	454 75	1 223 01			
3	Accounts Rec'l (Charge Sales)					
4	Asset or Expense *Discounts Allowed*		7 49			
5	Asset or Expense					
6	Asset or Expense					
7	Cash Short or Over					
8	Accounts Rec'l (Rec'd on A/c)				374 50	
9	Accounts Rec'l (Ret'd for Cr.)					
10	Sales				800 —	
11	Sales Tax Payable				56 —	
12	Cash Short or Over					
	BALANCING TOTALS		1 231 50		1 231 50	
	CASHIER'S SIGNATURE *C. Deng*					

"Received" Voucher
Voucher No. 428 made out to Varga Brothers for $367.01 in payment of Voucher No. 424 and No. 425 less the two per cent cash discount.

Purchase Invoice
From Canada Products, No. B340, $330.75, dated June 25, terms Net 30, for merchandise for resale.

June 28   *Cash Register Summary*

LINE NO.	ACCOUNTS		DR		CR	
	ACCOUNTING ENTRY					
1	Cash	146 59				
2	Visa	354 17	500 76			
3	Accounts Rec'l (Charge Sales)					
4	Asset or Expense					
5	Asset or Expense					
6	Asset or Expense					
7	Cash Short or Over					
8	Accounts Rec'l (Rec'd on A/c)					
9	Accounts Rec'l (Ret'd for Cr.)					
10	Sales				468 —	
11	Sales Tax Payable				32 76	
12	Cash Short or Over					
	BALANCING TOTALS		500 76		500 76	
	CASHIER'S SIGNATURE *C. Deng*					

June 29 *Cash Register Summary*

LINE NO.	ACCOUNTS			DR	CR
			ACCOUNTING ENTRY		
1	Cash	242	89		
2	Visa	218	28	461 17	
3	Accounts Rec'l (Charge Sales)				
4	Asset or Expense _____				
5	Asset or Expense _____				
6	Asset or Expense _____				
7	Cash Short or Over				
8	Accounts Rec'l (Rec'd on A/c)				
9	Accounts Rec'l (Ret'd for Cr.)				
10	Sales				431 –
11	Sales Tax Payable				30 17
12	Cash Short or Over				
	BALANCING TOTALS			461 17	461 17
	CASHIER'S SIGNATURE *C. Deng*				

Cheque Copies

No. 695, to Canada Products, $35.91, paying invoice No. B249.

No. 696, to First-Rate Repair Service, $233.10, cash payment to be charged to Equipment Expense.

Credit Note Received

From Triangle Sod, No. 509, $183.75, with respect to defective goods shipped on invoice No. 474.

June 30 *Cash Register Summary*

LINE NO.	ACCOUNTS			DR	CR
			ACCOUNTING ENTRY		
1	Cash	26	75		
2	Visa	444	05	470 80	
3	Accounts Rec'l (Charge Sales)				
4	Asset or Expense _____				
5	Asset or Expense _____				
6	Asset or Expense _____				
7	Cash Short or Over				
8	Accounts Rec'l (Rec'd on A/c)				
9	Accounts Rec'l (Ret'd for Cr.)				
10	Sales				440 –
11	Sales Tax Payable				30 80
12	Cash Short or Over				
	BALANCING TOTALS			470 80	470 80
	CASHIER'S SIGNATURE *C. Deng*				

2. Balance the journals and post to the general ledger.
3. Balance the general ledger, and the two subsidiary ledgers.
4. On June 3, the bank statement and related vouchers for June arrive in the mail. The bank statement is shown below. **Reconcile the bank account for Green Thumb Garden Centre as of June 30.**

THE CENTRAL BANK

In Account With

Green Thumb Garden Centre
Concord Highway

Cheques and Debits				Deposits	Date		Balance
		Balance Brought Forward			May	31	3 406.15
(#650)	36.50	(#660)	6.15	516.31	June	1	3 879.81
(#659)	95.14			500.90	June	2	4 285.57
(#661)	144.06			775.17	June	3	4 916.68
				573.52	June	4	5 490.20
(#662)	155.92	(#663)	96.55	353.10			
(#665)	44.85				June	5	5 545.98
(#657)	37.40			1 731.14			
				513.60			
				989.75	June	8	8 743.07
(#666)	604.16			728.91	June	9	8 867.82
				349.89	June	10	9 217.71
(#667)	440.00	(#668)	310.76	279.27	June	11	8 746.22
(DM)	2 000.00	(Loan Reduction)		294.25	June	12	7 040.47
(#658)	42.15	(#669)	540.75	198.30			
(#681)	2 195.45			637.35			
				972.31	June	15	6 070.08
				433.35	June	16	6 503.43
(#641)	74.00	(#670)	51.97	535.00	June	17	6 912.46
(#671)	58.80	(#677)	98.91	1 135.00	June	18	7 889.75
(#682)	378.50	(#685)	228.69	476.15	June	19	7 758.71
(#655)	116.26	(#686)	35.75	330.63			
				502.90			
				849.72	June	22	9 289.95
(#673)	1 932.00	(#684)	105.85	638.47	June	23	7 890.57
(#675)	45.20	(#678)	705.19	579.94	June	24	7 720.12
(#679)	350.00	(#687)	567.25	491.70	June	25	7 294.57
(#676)	77.96			398.04	June	26	7 614.65
(#654)	29.12			418.30			
				1 223.01			
				500.76	June	29	9 727.60
(#688)	450.00	(#691)	182.00	461.17			
(#690)	1 099.14						
(DM)	210.00	(Bank Interest)			June	30	8 247.63

14 Payroll Accounting

The term **payroll** refers to that part of the accounting process that deals with salaries, wages, and commissions paid to employees. Payroll may seem simple to the worker who receives money in return for his time and effort. It is, however, a complex process, and the person in charge of it has a great deal of responsibility. The paymaster must be well informed about numerous government rules, regulations, and other related matters.

Both federal and provincial governments have passed legislation that greatly affects payroll procedures. Examples include the Income Tax Act, the Unemployment Insurance Act, the Canada Pension Plan Act, and various provincial hospitalization acts. These acts set out regulations that employers, by law, must follow. The regulations are many and often complex, and take a great deal of study. Revenue Canada supplies booklets outlining all of the federal rules and regulations.

The minimum requirements an employer must follow are:

1. to make appropriate deductions from the earnings of employees, according to the regulations;
2. to know what income and other benefits (such as the use of an automobile, travel allowances, etc.) are taxable;
3. to keep up with changes in the regulations;
4. to keep detailed payroll records as required and to permit these records to be checked when asked to do so;
5. to send to the government, or other agencies, the amounts withheld from the employees, together with the employer's own contribution where required.

This chapter covers only the most basic aspects of payroll preparation.

14.1   GROSS PAY

Gross pay is the amount of an employee's earnings before any deductions are made from it. There are three different methods of determining gross pay: salaries, wages, and commissions.

Salaries

Salaries are paid to office workers, teachers, supervisors, executives, and many civil servants. A **salary** is a fixed sum of money paid to an employee on a regular basis over a period of time (usually one year). A person on salary is allowed a certain number of sick days without any loss of pay.

Consider the case of Harold Evans, who is employed by Nor-Can Grocers Limited, a food wholesaler. Mr. Evans receives an annual salary of $31 200 and is paid every two weeks, or biweekly. (There are 26 biweekly pay periods in a year.) His gross pay for each biweekly pay period is calculated as follows:

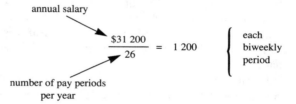

Wages

Wages are payments to workers for their labour, on an hourly, daily, or weekly basis, or by the piece. Payment by the piece means that the workers are paid according to the quantity of goods they produce (piecework). Some businesses pay a certain minimum hourly rate plus a piecework bonus for quantities produced over and above a stated amount per day or week.

Time Clocks and Timecards

Timecards are often used by workers who are paid by the hour. A **timecard** is a card on which a time clock records the times that the employee starts and finishes work each day. Timecards are used by the payroll department to calculate the total hours worked by each employee for each pay period. A time clock is illustrated in Figure 14.1.

When a timecard is inserted into a time clock, the clock automatically imprints the time at which the employee is entering or leaving work. This is referred to as "punching in" and "punching out." Time clocks are normally located near the employees' entrance to the plant, and placed so that they can be seen by a foreman or supervisor to prevent improper use. A timecard for a one-week period is shown in Figure 14.2. The times are automatically printed by the clock in one of six columns: Morning In, Morning Out, Afternoon In, Afternoon Out, Extra In, Extra Out.

Figure 14.1 A time recorder. Courtesy of Simplex International Time Equipment Company Ltd.

Time Card

Week Ended   September 14   19 __

Social Ins. No. 603 456 667

Name   **Burns, Joseph**

Day	Morning In	Morning Out	Afternoon In	Afternoon Out	Extra In	Extra Out	Total Hours
M	7:58	12:01	12:59	5:01			*8*
T	7:56	12:01	12:58	5:02			*8*
W	8:03	12:00	12:58	5:01			*7 3/4*
T	7:58	12:01	12:59	5:01			*8*
F	7:59	12:01	12:57	5:00	5:57	7:02	*8 1/1*
S	7:59	12:02					*1/4*
S							

	Hours	Rate	Earnings
Regular Time	*39 3/4*	*12.00*	*477.00*
Overtime	*5*	*18.00*	*90.00*
Gross Pay			*567.00*

Figure 14.2 A completed time card.

Completing the Timecard

At the end of each pay period the payroll department completes the timecards, such as the one shown in Figure 14.2, for all employees who receive wages. For each card, a payroll clerk must perform the steps outlined below.

1 Calculate the number of hours worked each day. Regular hours and overtime hours are shown separately.
2 Total the number of regular hours.
3 Total the number of overtime hours.
4 Complete the bottom section of the card. There is space provided to multiply the regular hours by the regular rate, and the overtime hours by the overtime rate. Then add the regular earnings and the overtime earnings together to obtain the gross earnings for the employee.

Notes

For the calculations in this text, the rules below are used. But the actual rules used in business will vary from company to company.

a. The regular work week consists of a five-day week of eight hours per day for a total of 40 hours. Any time worked after 5:00 P.M., or on Saturday or Sunday, is considered overtime.
b. Employees who are late arriving for work are penalized as follows:
   • Fifteen minutes, if they are late by one to 15 minutes;
   • Thirty minutes, if they are late by 16 to 30 minutes, and so on.
c. The rate of pay for overtime is one-and-a-half times the regular rate.

Commissions

Commissions are paid to salespersons and sales agents. When the sales representative makes a sale, he or she gets a percentage of the dollar value, called a **commission**. In most cases, however, a basic salary is paid in addition to the commission to provide the employee with at least a minimum income during difficult periods.

Consider the case of Rod Ferguson, a salesman for Nor-Can Grocers Limited, who receives $250 per week and a commission equal to one-half of one per cent of the net sales he makes. During the last two weeks Mr. Ferguson sold $59 000 worth of merchandise.

Rod Ferguson's pay is calculated as follows:

Basic salary (two weeks × $250)	=	$500
Commission (1/2 × 1% × $59 000)	=	295
Total earnings for two weeks	=	$795

SECTION REVIEW QUESTIONS

1. Define payroll.
2. Why does the person in charge of payroll have a responsible position?
3. Name three government Acts that affect payroll.
4. How does one obtain the details of government regulations regarding payroll?
5. Describe the five most basic payroll requirements imposed on an employer.
6. What is gross pay?
7. What is a salary?
8. What are wages?
9. Explain the purpose of the timecard.
10. Explain the rule to be used in this textbook in regard to overtime hours.
11. Explain the rule to be used in this textbook in regard to late arrival for work.
12. What is the overtime rate to be used in this text?
13. What are commissions?
14. Why would someone on commission also get a salary?

SECTION EXERCISES

(**Note:** Use the rules set out on page 564 where necessary.)

1. **Complete the following schedule in your Workbook.**

Annual Salary	Payroll Period	Gross Pay Per Period
$39 000	Weekly	
	Weekly	$800
$22 750	Biweekly	
	Biweekly	$1 250
$36 000	Semi-monthly	
	Semi-monthly	$1 800
$30 000	Monthly	
	Monthly	$3 200

2. Phyllis Marshall earns a salary of $35 000 per year. **In the Workbook calculate the gross pay she would receive under each of the payroll periods given.**

Payroll Period	Gross Pay
a. Weekly	
b. Biweekly	
c. Semi-monthly	
d. Monthly	

3. Complete the following schedule in your Workbook.

Total Hours	Regular Rate	Regular Hours	Overtime Hours	Regular Pay	Overtime Pay	Gross Pay
46	$11.50					
43	$14.50					
44 1/2	$12.00					
54	$21.00					
47 1/4	$13.75					

4. Grace Fung works in a factory assembling radio components. She is paid $50 a day ($25 for a half day) plus $4 for each component that she completes. **In the Workbook, calculate Grace's gross pay for one week based on the production figures given.**

Day	Number of Units Completed	Salary	Piecework Earnings	Gross Pay
Monday	10			
Tuesday	9			
Wednesday (1/2)	5			
Thursday	11			
Friday	10			
TOTALS				

5. The timecards for two employees are given below and in your Workbook.

Time Card

Week Ended   July 23   19 --
Social Ins. No. 642 393 438
Name   Frank Windsor

Day	Morning In	Morning Out	Afternoon In	Afternoon Out	Extra In	Extra Out	Total Hours
M	7:58	12:01	12:58	5:01			
T	8:07	12:00	12:57	5:02			
W	7:56	12:03	12:59	5:00			
T	7:59	12:02	1:01	5:03			
F	7:57	12:02	12:59	5:01			
S							
S							

	Hours	Rate	Earnings
Regular Time		14.00	
Overtime			
Gross Pay			

Time Card

Week Ended   July 23   19 --
Social Ins. No. 643 461 217
Name   Ray Peterson

Day	Morning In	Morning Out	Afternoon In	Afternoon Out	Extra In	Extra Out	Total Hours
M	7:58	12:01	1:00	5:02			
T	7:59	12:00	12:58	5:01	5:59	8:55	
W	7:57	12:01	12:59	5:02			
T	7:56	12:01	12:58	5:03			
F	7:59	12:01	12:59	5:01			
S	7:58	12:01					
S							

	Hours	Rate	Earnings
Regular Time		12.20	
Overtime			
Gross Pay			

1. **Determine and write in the total number of regular hours and overtime hours worked each day for each employee.**
2. **Calculate and write in the regular and the overtime earnings for each employee.**
3. **Calculate and write in the gross pay for each employee.**

6. The Greenfield Real Estate Company pays its salespeople a basic salary of $325 per month plus a two per cent commission on their sales. **In your Workbook, complete the schedule shown below.**

Sales Person	Sales for Month	Salary	Commission	Gross Earnings
Mary Hunt	$90 000			
Anna Mocha	$122 000			
Bob Rennie	$75 000			
Fay Savard	$316 000			
Paul Thors	$50 000			
Gloria Unich	$70 000			
Gladys Wilson	$26 000			

14.2   PAYROLL DEDUCTIONS AND NET PAY

Employees are hired with the understanding that they will be paid a certain amount per hour, week, or year. However, certain deductions are made before the employee is actually paid.

As we have seen, Harold Evans receives an annual salary of $31 200 payable every two weeks in equal portions of $1 200. This amount is his gross pay. When Evans receives his cheque, however, it is made out for only $836.36. Harold Evans was not shortchanged the difference of $363.64. The $363.64 is the total amount deducted from his pay. The amount that Harold Evans receives, $836.36, is his net pay. The **net pay** is the amount of pay remaining after all deductions have been made.

The payroll equation is:

GROSS PAY minus DEDUCTIONS equals NET PAY

For Harold Evans:

$1 200.00 minus $363.64   equals $836.36

Payroll Journal

The calculations that are needed in order to arrive at the net pay for Harold Evans are recorded in a special journal. The **payroll journal**, or **payroll register**, is a columnar journal designed especially for recording payroll calculations and figures. The payroll journal used by Nor-Can Grocers Ltd. is shown in Figure 14.3. For Harold Evans the first amount recorded in the journal is his gross pay of $1 200.00.

Payroll Journal   For the two weeks ended Jan. 28 19 --

| Employee | Net Claim Code | Earnings | | | R.P.P. | Union Dues | Income Tax | | C.P.P. | U.I. | Health Insce. | Group Life | Total Deductions | Net Pay |
		Regular	Extra	Gross			Taxable Earnings	Tax Deduction						
Harold Evans	3	1 200 —		1 200 —										

Figure 14.3   A payroll journal form with gross pay recorded.

Social Insurance Number

An employer must withhold certain amounts from an employee's pay. These deductions include Canada Pension Plan or Quebec Pension Plan contributions, personal income taxes, and unemployment insurance premiums. To ensure that employees get proper credit for their contributions, the federal government requires all employees to have a social insurance number, recorded on a social insurance card.

The social insurance number system enables Canada to permanently identify every citizen of the country. The government uses the number to direct information correctly to an individual's account or file. The federal government will not pay out any benefits unless the claimant has a social insurance number. The social insurance card for Harold Evans, with its nine-digit number, is shown in Figure 14.4.

Figure 14.4   A social insurance card.

Registered Pension Plan Deduction

Employees are often enrolled in private "registered" pension plans through their workplaces. A **registered pension plan (R.P.P.)** or a **registered retirement savings plan (R.R.S.P.)** is a private pension plan approved by the government for income tax purposes. The amount paid into a registered plan (up to an allowed limit) may be deducted by the employees when calculating their income taxes.

Usually, both the employee and the employer contribute an amount which is a set percentage of the employee's gross pay. Nor-Can Grocers Ltd. has a registered pension plan. Both the employees and the employer contribute to the plan at the rate of five per cent of gross pay.

The deduction for Harold Evans is five per cent of $1 200, which is $60.00. This is recorded in the R.P.P. column of the payroll journal as shown in Figure 14.5. The company contributes an equal amount. You will see how this is handled later.

Payroll Journal   For the two weeks ended Jan. 28 19 --

Employee	Net Claim Code	Earnings			R.P.P.	Union Dues	Income Tax		C.P.P.	U.I.	Health Insce.	Group Life	Total Deductions	Net Pay
		Regular	Extra	Gross			Taxable Earnings	Tax Deduction						
Harold Evans	3	1 200 –		1 200 –	60 –									

Figure 14.5   Payroll journal with R.P.P. deduction recorded.

Union Dues Deduction

The employees of many businesses are organized in labour unions. Union dues are often deducted by the employer and paid periodically to the union. This obligation of the employer is usually part of the contract negotiated between the employer and the employees' union.

The amount that is deducted from the employees' pay is set by the union. The union to which Harold Evans belongs requires a deduction of $10.00 each pay period from every union member. Figure 14.6 shows this amount recorded correctly in the payroll journal.

Payroll Journal   For the two weeks ended Jan. 28 19 --

Employee	Net Claim Code	Earnings			R.P.P.	Union Dues	Income Tax		C.P.P.	U.I.	Health Insce.	Group Life	Total Deductions	Net Pay
		Regular	Extra	Gross			Taxable Earnings	Tax Deduction						
Harold Evans	3	1 200 –		1 200 –	60 –	10 –								

Figure 14.6   Payroll journal with union dues deduction recorded.

Income Tax Deduction

According to Canadian income tax laws, employers must make a deduction from the earnings of each employee for personal income tax. The amount is based on two factors:

1. the total of the employee's personal exemptions;
2. the amount of the employee's taxable earnings.

Personal Exemption/The Net Claim Code

Every employee is required to fill out a Tax Exemption Return form known as the TD1. A completed TD1 form for Harold Evans is shown in Figure 14.7. This form is used to determine the employee's total personal exemption. The **total personal exemption** is the amount that a person may earn in a year without being taxed. The amount varies, depending on the employee's marital status, the number of dependent children, and other factors including family allowance benefits. This form is completed by every employee once a year, and when an employee changes jobs, begins a new job, or when an event, such as the birth of a baby, changes the employee's personal exemption status.

Figure 14.7 shows that Harold Evans has a total personal exemption figure of $8 825.24 and, consequently, a net claim code of 3. The net claim code figure is used when referring to the income tax deduction tables.

Taxable Earnings

The most recent government publication regarding income tax deductions reads as follows:

Once you have determined the gross remuneration ... you must subtract the following amounts before determining the tax to withhold at source:

(a) the employee's contributions to a registered pension fund or plan,
(b) union dues,
(c) deduction for residing in a prescribed area,
(d) the employee's contributions to a registered retirement savings plan, and
(e) other amounts authorized by the district taxation office (i.e. alimony and maintenance payments).

Items (c), (d) and (e) are not common deductions and are ignored in the payrolls developed in this chapter. For our purposes, items (a) and (b) are the only items considered. On this basis, the calculation necessary to obtain the taxable earnings figure can be seen below, as it is worked out for Harold Evans.

Gross pay		$1 200.00
Less: Registered pension plan deduction	$60.00	
Union dues deduction	10.00	70.00
Taxable earnings		$1 130.00

The taxable earnings figure for Harold Evans is recorded in the payroll journal as shown in Figure 14.8.

◼◆ Revenue Canada   Revenu Canada
Taxation   Impôt

page 1.

TD1 (E)
Rev. 1989

1989 PERSONAL TAX CREDIT RETURN

FAMILY NAME (Please Print)	USUAL FIRST NAME AND INITIALS	EMPLOYEE NUMBER
EVANS	*HAROLD J.*	*12650*

ADDRESS	For NON-RESIDENTS ONLY Country of Permanent Residence	SOCIAL INSURANCE NUMBER
2000 5TH ST.		*609 | 779 | 152*

CASTLEGAR , B. C.   Postal Code *VIN 2E9*

DATE OF BIRTH
Day *28* | Month *04* | Year *60*

Instructions

- Please fill out this form so your employer or payer will know how much tax to deduct regularly from your pay. Regular deductions will help you avoid having to pay when you file your income tax return.
- **You must complete this form if you receive** • salary, wages, commissions or any other remuneration;
    • pension plan benefits or annuity payments (under registered retirement income funds and registered retirement savings plans);
    • Unemployment Insurance benefits including training allowances.
- Give the completed form to your employer or payer. Otherwise, you will be allowed **only** the basic personal amount of $6,066.
- All amounts on this form should be rounded to the nearest dollar.
- **Need Help?** If you need help to complete this form, you may ask your employer or payer, or call the Source Deductions Section of your local Revenue Canada district taxation office. Before you do this, please refer to the additional information on page 2 under "Notes to Employees and Payees."

---

1. **Are you a non-resident of Canada?** (see note 1 on page 2). If so, and less than 90 per cent of your 1989 total world income will be included when calculating taxable income earned in Canada, enter 0 in the box on line 17 and sign the form. If you are a resident of Canada, go to item 2.

2. **Basic personal amount.** (everyone may claim $6,066) ▶ $6,066   2.

3. (a) **Are you married and supporting your spouse?** (see notes 4 and 5 on page 2)
    or
    (b) **Are you single, divorced, separated or widowed and supporting a relative who lives with you who is either your parent or grandparent, OR who is under 19 at the end of 1989, OR 19 or older and infirm?** (see notes 2, 3 and 4 on page 2)
    Note: A spouse or dependant claimed here cannot be claimed again on lines 4 or 5.
    If you answered yes to either (a) or (b) and your spouse's or dependant's 1989 net income will be

	$ 5,561	(c)
Minus: spouse or dependant's net income	*2800*	(d)
Claim (c minus d)	*2761*	(e)

    • under $506, CLAIM $5,055
    • between $506 and $5,561, CLAIM (e) →
    • over $5,561, CLAIM $0   ▶ *2761*   3.

4. **Do you have any dependants who will be under 19 at the end of 1989?** (see notes 2 and 4 on page 2). If so, and your 1989 net income will be **higher** than your spouse's, calculate the amount to claim for **each** dependant. If you are not married, please refer to notes 2, 3 and 4 on page 2.
    Note: If you have three or more dependants who will be under 19 years old at the end of the year, you do not have to claim them in the order they were born. You may claim them in the **most** beneficial order. For example, a dependant who is 16 years old with a net income of $3,500 could be claimed as the first dependant (claim 0) while the other two, with no income, could be claimed as second and third dependants.

    First and second dependant:
    If your dependant's 1989 net income will be
    • under $2,528, CLAIM $392
    • between $2,528 and $2,920, CLAIM (e) →
    • over $2,920, CLAIM $0

Minus:	$ 2,920	(c)
dependant's net income	_____	(d)
Claim (c minus d)	_____	(e)

    1st dependant *392*
    2nd dependant *392*

    Third and each additional dependant:
    If your dependant's 1989 net income will be
    • under $2,528, CLAIM $784
    • between $2,528 and $3,312, CLAIM (e) →
    • over $3,312, CLAIM $0

Minus:	$ 3,312	(c)
dependant's net income	_____	(d)
Claim (c minus d)	_____	(e)

    3rd dependant _____
    4th dependant _____
    5th dependant _____

    Total *784* ▶ *784*   4.

5. **Do you have any infirm dependants who will be 19 or older at the end of 1989?** (see notes 2 and 4 on page 2). If so, and your dependant's net income will be
    • under $2,528, CLAIM $1,487
    • between $2,528 and $4,015, CLAIM (e)
    • over $4,015, CLAIM $0 →

Minus:	$ 4,015	(c)
dependant's net income	_____	(d)
Claim (c minus d)	_____	(e)

    1st dependant _____
    2nd dependant _____
    3rd dependant _____

    Total ══ ▶ _____   5.

6. **Do you receive eligible pension income?** (see note 6 on page 2). If so, claim this amount or $1,000, **whichever is less.** ▶ _____   6.

7. **Will you be 65 or older at the end of 1989?** If so, claim $3,272. ▶ _____   7.

8. **Are you disabled?** (see note 7 on page 2). If so, claim $3,272. ▶ _____   8.

9. **Are you a student?** If so, claim
    • **tuition fees** paid for courses you take in 1989 to attend either a university, college or a certified educational institution. If you receive any scholarships, fellowships or bursaries in 1989, subtract the amount over $500 from your tuition fees before you claim them.
    • $60 for each month in 1989 that you will be in **full-time attendance** in a qualifying program, at either a university, college or a school offering job re-training courses.

    Total _____ ▶ _____   9.

10.   Total (add lines 2 to 9 - please enter this amount on line 11 on page 2) *9611*   10.

Figure 14.7a   An employee's TD1 form, front.

page 2.

11.   Total (from line 10 on page 1) _96 11 –_ 11.

12. Are you claiming any transfers of unused pension income, age, disability, tuition fees and education amounts from your spouse and/or dependants? (see note 10 below)

- If your **spouse receives eligible pension income**, you may claim any unused balance to a maximum of $1,000 (see note 6 below).
- If your **spouse will be 65 or older** in 1989, you may claim any unused balance to a maximum of $3,272.
- If your **spouse and/or dependants are disabled**, you may claim any unused balance to a maximum of $3,272 for each (see note 7 below).
- If you **are supporting a spouse and/or dependants who are attending either a university, college or a certified educational institution**, you may be entitled to claim the unused balance to a maximum of $3,529 for each (see item 9 on page 1).

                                                              Total _____ ▶ _____ 12.

13. Total Claim Amount - Add lines 11 and 12.   ▶ _96 11 –_ 13.

14. Will you or your spouse receive family allowance (baby bonus) payments in 1989? If so, and your 1989 net income will be **higher** than your spouse's, enter the amount of family allowance payments you will receive in 1989. If you are not married, see note 3 below. _392.88 X 2_   ▶ _785.76_ 14.

15. NET CLAIM AMOUNT - Line 13 minus line 14.   ▶ _8825.24_ 15.

16. Is your estimated total income for 1989 (excluding family allowance payments) **less than your net claim amount on line 15?** If so, enter E in the box on line 17 and tax will **not** be deducted from your pay. Otherwise, go to line 17.

17. NET CLAIM CODE - Match your net claim amount from line 15 with the net claim code table below to determine your net claim code, and enter this code in the box. If you already have a code in the box, go to line 18. | _3_ | 17.

18. Do you want to increase the amount of tax to be deducted from your salary or from other amounts paid to you such as pensions, **commissions** etc.? (see note 8 below) If so, state the amount of additional tax you wish to have deducted from each payment. The amount must be a multiple of $5, for example, 5, 10, 15, 20 etc.   ▶ _____ 18.

19. Will you live in the Yukon, Northwest Territories or another prescribed area for more than six months in a row beginning or ending in 1989? If so, claim $225 for each 30-day period that you live in a prescribed area, or if you maintain a "self-contained domestic establishment" in a prescribed area and you are the only person within that establishment claiming this deduction, claim $450 for each 30-day period. You **cannot** claim more than 20 per cent of your net income for 1989 (see note 9 below). ▶ _____ 19.

I HEREBY CERTIFY that the information given in this return is correct and complete.

Signature _Harold Evans_   Date _January 4, 19 –_

Complete a new return within seven days of any change in your claim. It is an offence to make a false return.

NOTES TO EMPLOYEES AND PAYEES

1. If you are in doubt about your **non-resident** status, please contact the Source Deductions Section of your local district taxation office. If you are a **non-resident and 90 per cent or more** of your 1989 total world income will be included in determining your taxable income earned in Canada, you are entitled to claim certain personal amounts. Again for more information contact your district taxation office.

2. A dependant is an individual who is dependent on you for support and is either under 19 years old, OR 19 or older and physically or mentally infirm. This includes a child, grandchild, parent, grandparent, brother, sister, aunt, uncle, niece or nephew (including in-laws). Except in the case of a child or grandchild, this individual must also be resident in Canada.

3. Except for married individuals, the recipient of the **family allowance** must report the benefits and claim the amount for the child or children. Whoever claims the dependant for an equivalent-to-married amount must also report the family allowance for that dependant regardless of who receives the family allowance benefits.

4. Your spouse's or dependant's **net income**, for tax withholding purposes, is the total annual income from all sources including salary, pensions, Old Age Security, UI benefits, worker's compensation and social assistance (welfare) payments **minus** annual deductions for registered pension plan and registered retirement savings plan contributions.

5. If you marry during the year, your spouse's net income will include the income before and during marriage.

6. **Eligible pension income** includes pension payments received from a pension plan **or fund** as a life annuity and foreign pension payments. It does not include payments from Canada or Quebec Pension plans, Old Age Security, guaranteed income supplement and lump-sum withdrawals from a pension fund.

7. To claim a **disability**, you must be severely impaired (mentally or physically) in 1989 and have a Disability Credit Certificate. Such an impairment must markedly restrict you in your daily living activities. The impairment must have lasted or be expected to last for a continuous period of at least 12 months.

8. Line 18 on the form replaces the TD3 form. You may find it convenient to deduct tax here for other income you receive that has little or no tax deducted from it. For example, UI benefits, investment or rental income.

9. "**Self-contained domestic establishment**" means the dwelling house, apartment or similar place where you sleep and eat. It does NOT include a bunkhouse, dormitory, hotel room or rooms in a boarding house. For further information, including the list of prescribed areas, see the "Northern Residents Deductions Tax Guide" which is available at our district taxation office.

10. Your spouse and/or dependants **must** first use their pension income, age, disability, tuition fees and education amounts as applicable to reduce their federal tax to zero before they can transfer any unused balance of these amounts to you.

1989 NET CLAIM CODES	
net claim amount	claim code
NO claim amount	0
$ 0 - 6,066	1
6,067 - 7,552	2
7,553 - 9,038	3
9,039 - 10,525	4
10,526 - 12,011	5
12,012 - 13,497	6
13,498 - 14,983	7
14,984 - 16,469	8
16,470 - 17,955	9
17,956 - 19,442	10
19,443 and over	X
NO tax withholding required	E

Cette formule est disponible en français.

Figure 14.7b An employee's TD1 form, back.

Payroll Journal   For the two weeks ended Jan. 28 19 --

Employee	Net Claim Code	Earnings					Deductions									
		Regular	Extra	Gross	R.P.P.	Union Dues	Income Tax		C.P.P.	U.I.	Health Insce.	Group Life		Total Deductions	Net Pay
							Taxable Earnings	Tax Deduction							
Harold Evans	3	1 200	–	1 200	–	60	–	10	–	1 130	–								

Figure 14.8 Payroll journal showing taxable income.

Employee Contributions

Revenue Canada Taxation provides a booklet of deduction tables for personal income taxes. A page from the section of the booklet dealing with biweekly pay periods is given at the end of this section. The column along the left side shows the biweekly pay brackets. Along the top are 10 column headings representing the net claim codes.

The amount to deduct for income tax is found where the correct "pay bracket" line intersects with the correct "net claim code" column. Harold Evans's taxable earnings fall within the range 1120.–1136. His net claim code is 3. Figure 14.9 shows that the figure at the intersection of this row and column is $210.20.

	BI-WEEKLY TAX DEDUCTIONS Basis — 26 Pay Periods per Year			TABLE 2		RETENU Base —
BI-WEEKLY PAY Use appropriate bracket *PAIE DE* *DEUX SEMAINES* *Utilisez le palier approprié*	IF THE EMPLOYEE'S "NET CLAIM C *SI LE CODE DE DEMANDE NETTE DE L'EMPLOY*					
	0	1	2	3	4	5
From · *De* Less than *Moins que*	DEDUCT FROM EACH PAY — *RETE*					
896.– 912.	238.20	167.65	160.10	145.05	130.00	114.90
912.– 928.	242.40	171.70	164.15	149.10	134.05	118.95
928.– 944.	246.65	175.75	168.20	153.15	138.10	123.00
944.– 960.	250.85	179.80	172.25	157.20	142.15	127.05
960.– 976.	255.05	183.85	176.30	161.25	146.15	131.10
976.– 992.	259.30	187.90	180.30	165.30	150.20	135.15
992.– 1008.	263.50	191.95	184.35	169.35	154.25	139.20
1008.– 1024.	267.70	196.00	188.40	173.40	158.30	143.25
1024.– 1040.	271.95	200.05	192.45	177.45	162.35	147.25
1040.– 1056.	276.15	204.10	196.50	181.50	166.40	151.30
1056.– 1072.	280.35	208.10	200.55	185.55	170.45	155.35
1072.– 1088.	286.00	213.70	206.10	191.10	176.00	160.95
1088.– 1104.	292.45	220.05	212.50	197.45	182.40	167.30
1104.– 1120.	298.90	226.40	218.85	203.85	188.75	173.65
1120.– 1136.	305.35	232.80	225.20	210.20	195.10	180.05
1136.– 1152.	311.80	239.15	231.60	216.55	201.50	186.40
1152.– 1168.	318.25	245.50	237.95	222.90	207.85	192.75
1168.– 1184.	324.70	251.90	244.30	229.30	214.20	199.10

Figure 14.9 A section of the income tax deductions booklet showing the deduction for Harold Evans.

The deduction of $210.20 for Harold Evans is recorded in the payroll journal as shown below in Figure 14.10. An employee's income tax is paid entirely by the employee.

Payroll Journal   For the two weeks ended Jan. 28 19 --

| Employee | Net Claim Code | Earnings | | | R.P.P. | Union Dues | Income Tax | | C.P.P. | U.I. | Health Insce. | Group Life | Total Deductions | Net Pay |
		Regular	Extra	Gross			Taxable Earnings	Tax Deduction						
Harold Evans	3	1 200	—	1 200	—	60	—	10	—	1 130	—	210 20								

Figure 14.10   Payroll journal with income tax deduction recorded.

Canada Pension Plan Deduction

The federal government instituted a pension plan for Canadian workers which became effective January 1, 1966. This plan is called the Quebec Pension Plan in Quebec, and the Canada Pension Plan (C.P.P.) in the rest of the country.

The Canada Pension Plan booklet provides many details about the plan. In particular it states:

> Employers must deduct the required Canada Pension Plan contribution from the remuneration of every employee who meets all three (3) criteria below.
> • who is eighteen years of age and has not reached seventy years of age, and
> • who is employed in pensionable employment during the year, and
> • who is not receiving a Canada or a Quebec Pension Plan retirement or disability pension.

Employee Contributions

The simplest way of determining C.P.P. deductions is by using the deduction tables provided in the government booklet. A page from this booklet is included at the end of this section. The booklet contains a set of deduction tables for every possible payroll period. Each set of tables gives a series of possible figures for earnings and their corresponding pension contributions.

To determine the deduction for an employee, look down the column headed "Remuneration" until you find the range containing the employee's gross pay figure. Observe the C.P.P. deduction figure to the immediate right. This is shown in Figure 14.11 for Harold Evans, whose gross pay is $1 200.

The C.P.P. deduction for Harold Evans is $23.04. It is recorded in the C.P.P. column of the payroll journal opposite Harold Evans's name. This is shown in Figure 14.12.

Remuneration Rémunération		C.P.P. R.P.C.	Remuneration Rémunération		C.P.P. R.P.C.
From-*de*	To-*à*		From-*de*	To-*à*	
1063.61 –	1064.07	20.16	1735.99 –	1745.98	34.38
1064.08 –	1064.55	20.17	1745.99 –	1755.98	34.59
1064.56 –	1065.03	20.18	1755.99 –	1765.98	34.80
1065.04 –	1065.50	20.19	1765.99 –	1775.98	35.01
1065.51 –	1065.98	20.20	1775.99 –	1785.98	35.22
1065.99 –	1075.98	20.31	1785.99 –	1795.98	35.43
1075.99 –	1085.98	20.52	1795.99 –	1805.98	35.64
1085.99 –	1095.98	20.73	1805.99 –	1815.98	35.85
1095.99 –	1105.98	20.94	1815.99 –	1825.98	36.06
1105.99 –	1115.98	21.15	1825.99 –	1835.98	36.27
1115.99 –	1125.98	21.36	1835.99 –	1845.98	36.48
1125.99 –	1135.98	21.57	1845.99 –	1855.98	36.69
1135.99 –	1145.98	21.78	1855.99 –	1865.98	36.90
1145.99 –	1155.98	21.99	1865.99 –	1875.98	37.11
1155.99 –	1165.98	22.20	1875.99 –	1885.98	37.32
1165.99 –	1175.98	22.41	1885.99 –	1895.98	37.53
1175.99 –	1185.98	22.62	1895.99 –	1905.98	37.74
1185.99 –	1195.98	22.83	1905.99 –	1915.98	37.95
1195.99 –	1205.98	23.04	1915.99 –	1925.98	38.16
1205.99 –	1215.98	23.25	1925.99 –	1935.98	38.37

Figure 14.11 A section from the C.P.P. tables showing the deduction figure for Harold Evans.

Payroll Journal   For the two weeks ended Jan. 28 19 --

Figure 14.12 Payroll journal with C.P.P. deduction recorded.

(**Note:** There is a maximum limit on the amount to be paid in one year. In 1989 the amount was $525. It is the employer's responsibility to keep track of the total deducted for every employee. Once the maximum figure is reached, no further deductions will be made in that calendar year.)

Employer's Contribution

The employer as well as the employee is required to contribute to the C.P.P. fund. You will be shown how this is handled in a later section.

Unemployment Insurance Deduction

In Canada, employed workers pay a portion of their earnings into an unemployment insurance fund. These payments are in the form of deductions made by the employer from the employees' pay cheques. If a worker who has made sufficient contributions to the fund becomes unemployed while willing and able to accept employment, that worker is entitled to receive payments out of the fund.

Employee Contributions

The unemployment insurance premium deductions are found in the same government booklet as the C.P.P. contributions. The tables read in the same way as the C.P.P. tables, but there are two important differences:

1. There is only one set of U.I. deduction tables, to be used for all payroll periods.
2. There is a maximum deduction figure for each different payroll period. You can see the maximums in Figure 14.13. The maximum deductions for each of the various pay periods are given at the bottom of each page and are also highlighted within the tables themselves.

Harold Evans's deduction figure is in Figure 14.13 below. Observe that the maximum deduction for biweekly payrolls is $23.60.

Remuneration From – To	U.I. Premium	Remuneration From – To	U.I. Premium
1198.72 – 1199.23	23.38	1235.65 – 1236.15	24.10
1199.24 – 1199.74	23.39	1236.16 – 1236.66	24.11
1199.75 – 1200.25	23.40	1236.67 – 1237.17	24.12
1200.26 – 1200.76	23.41	1237.18 – 1237.69	24.13
1200.77 – 1201.28	23.42	1237.70 – 1238.20	24.14
1201.29 – 1201.79	23.43	1238.21 – 1238.71	24.15
1201.80 – 1202.30	23.44	1238.72 – 1239.23	24.16
1202.31 – 1202.82	23.45	1239.24 – 1239.74	24.17
1202.83 – 1203.33	23.46	1239.75 – 1240.25	24.18
1703.34 – 1203.84	23.47	1240.26 – 1240.76	24.19
1703.85 – 1204.35	23.48	1240.77 – 1241.28	24.20
1204.36 – 1204.87	23.49	1241.29 – 1241.79	24.21
1204.88 – 1205.38	23.50	1241.80 – 1242.30	24.22
1205.39 – 1205.89	23.51	1242.31 – 1242.82	24.23
1205.90 – 1206.41	23.52	1242.83 – 1243.33	24.24
1206.42 – 1206.92	23.53	1243.34 – 1243.84	24.25
1206.93 – 1207.43	23.54	1243.85 – 1244.35	24.26
1207.44 – 1207.94	23.55	1244.36 – 1244.87	24.27
1207.95 – 1208.46	23.56	1244.88 – 1245.38	24.28
1208.47 – 1208.97	23.57	1245.39 – 1245.89	24.29
1208.98 – 1209.48	23.58	1245.90 – 1246.41	24.30
1209.49 – 1209.99	23.59	1246.42 – 1246.92	24.31
1210.00 – 1210.51	23.60	1246.93 – 1247.43	24.32
1210.52 – 1211.02	23.61	1247.44 – 1247.94	24.33

Figure 14.13 A section of the unemployment insurance tables showing the deduction for Harold Evans.

The unemployment insurance deduction for Harold Evans is $23.40. This deduction is recorded in the U.I. column of the payroll journal as shown in Figure 14.14.

Payroll Journal   For the two weeks ended Jan. 28 19 --

Employee	Net Claim Code	Earnings			Deductions												
		Regular	Extra	Gross	R.P.P.	Union Dues	Income Tax Taxable Earnings	Income Tax Tax Deduction	C.P.P.	U.I.	Health Insce.	Group Life		Total Deductions	Net Pay	
Harold Evans	3	1 200 –		1 200 –	60 –	10 –	1 130 –	210 20	23 04	23 40						

Figure 14.14   Payroll journal with U.I. deduction recorded.

Employer's Contribution

The employer is also required to contribute to the unemployment insurance fund. The employer's contribution is 1.4 times that contributed by the employees. You will see how this is handled in a later section.

Health Insurance Deduction

Most provinces operate a universal health insurance program. The basic plan generally covers both doctors' fees and hospital expenses. Employers are authorized to deduct from the employees' pay the amount of the premiums that is set by the provincial governments. The premium for a single person is less than that for a married person or one who has dependent children. The rates to be used in this text are:

BIWEEKLY HEALTH INSURANCE RATES	
1. Single Person	$24.00
2. Married Person	$48.00

In recent years, health insurance plans have been developed that provide additional benefits not included in the basic health plans operated by the provinces. Such programs as extended health care and dental health care are now quite common.

Employers often pay a portion, or in some cases the entire cost, of the premium for the health care programs for their employees. In this text, assume that the employer pays 75 per cent of the cost.

For Harold Evans, who is married, the biweekly premium is $48.00. His employer pays three-quarters of this amount, or $36.00. Harold Evans pays one-quarter, or $12.00. Figure 14.15 shows this amount recorded properly in the payroll journal.

Payroll Journal   For the two weeks ended Jan. 28 19 --

Employee	Net Claim Code	Earnings			R.P.P.	Union Dues	Income Tax		C.P.P.	U.I.	Health Insce.	Group Life	Total Deductions	Net Pay
		Regular	Extra	Gross			Taxable Earnings	Tax Deduction						
Harold Evans	3	1200 -		1200 -	60 -	10 -	1130 -	210 20	23 04	23 40	12 -			

Figure 14.15   Payroll journal with health insurance deduction recorded.

Group Life Insurance Deduction

Some firms make it possible for their employees to enrol in a group life insurance plan. Premiums for this plan are handled as payroll deductions. Premiums are negotiated between the insurance company and the employees' group or the company. Usually, the premium depends on the amount of insurance coverage selected.

For the purposes of this text the insurance premium rate is as shown below. The maximum coverage is $100 000. The employees pay the full premium.

> **GROUP LIFE INSURANCE BIWEEKLY PREMIUM RATE**
>
> $0.50 for each $1 000 of coverage

Harold Evans has $50 000 of group life insurance coverage. His premium is $0.50 × 50 = $25.00. Figure 14.16 shows this amount recorded correctly in the payroll journal.

Payroll Journal   For the two weeks ended Jan. 28 19 --

Employee	Net Claim Code	Earnings			R.P.P.	Union Dues	Income Tax		C.P.P.	U.I.	Health Insce.	Group Life	Total Deductions	Net Pay
		Regular	Extra	Gross			Taxable Earnings	Tax Deduction						
Harold Evans	3	1200 -		1200 -	60 -	10 -	1130 -	210 20	23 04	23 40	12 -	25 -		

Figure 14.16   Payroll journal with group life deduction recorded.

Other Deductions

Other deductions may be made from an employee's earnings if authority is granted by the employee. They are handled in a manner similar to those deductions already discussed. Some of these other deductions include extended health care, a dental plan, the United Way, Canada Savings Bonds, and disability insurance.

Calculating Net Pay

At this point, the last deduction has been made for Harold Evans. There are two steps remaining. First, the deductions are totaled and the total is entered in the column headed Total Deductions. Second, the total deductions figure ($363.64) is subtracted from the gross pay figure ($1 200), giving the net pay figure ($836.36). This is entered in the Net Pay column. These two final amounts are shown entered in the payroll journal in Figure 14.17.

Payroll Journal · For the two weeks ended Jan. 28 19 --

Employee	Net Claim Code	Earnings Regular	Extra	Gross	R.P.P.	Union Dues	Income Tax Taxable Earnings	Tax Deduction	C.P.P.	U.I.	Health Insce.	Group Life	Total Deductions	Net Pay
Harold Evans	3	1 200 –		1 200 –	60 –	10 –	1 130 –	210 20	23 04	23 40	12 –	25 –		363 64	836 36

Figure 14.17 Payroll journal showing total deductions and net pay.

Completing the Payroll Journal

The procedure that has been discussed and illustrated for Harold Evans is repeated for each of the employees in the company. One line of the payroll journal is used for each employee. All the payroll details for every employee are entered in the journal. The final step in preparing the payroll journal is adding all the money columns and cross balancing the journal. The completed payroll journal for Nor-Can Grocers Ltd. is shown in Figure 14.18.

Payroll Journal · For the two weeks ended Jan. 28 19 --

Employee	Net Claim Code	Earnings Regular	Extra	Gross	R.P.P.	Union Dues	Income Tax Taxable Earnings	Tax Deduction	C.P.P.	U.I.	Health Insce.	Group Life	Total Deductions	Net Pay
Harold Evans	3	1 200 –		1 200 –	60 –	10 –	1 130 –	210 20	23 04	23 40	12 –	25 –	363 64	836 36
Ronald Fell	4	1 110 –		1 110 –	55 50	10 –	1 044 50	166 40	21 15	21 65	12 –	10 –	296 70	813 30
Robert Funston	3	1 300 –		1 300 –	65 –	10 –	1 225 –	248 45	25 14	25 35	12 –	50 –	435 94	864 06
Dennis Murray	3	1 250 –		1 250 –	62 50	10 –	1 177 50	229 30	24 09	24 38	6 –	20 –	376 27	873 73
Les Williams	5	1 200 –		1 200 –	60 –	10 –	1 130 –	180 05	23 04	23 40	12 –	50 –	358 49	841 51
		6 060 –		6 060 –	303 –	50 –	5707 –	1 034 40	116 46	118 18	54 –	155 –	1 831 04	4 228 96

Figure 14.18 A completed payroll journal.

Proving the Accuracy of the Payroll Journal

There are three steps taken to prove the accuracy of the payroll journal. Ensure that:

1 the Regular Earnings column + the Extra Earnings column = the Gross Earnings column;
2 the sum of all of the deductions columns = the Total Deductions column;
3 the Gross Earnings column – the Total Deductions column = the Net Pay column.

CANADA PENSION PLAN CONTRIBUTIONS   **COTISATIONS AU RÉGIME DE PENSIONS DU CANADA**

BI-WEEKLY PAY PERIOD — *PÉRIODE DE PAIE DE DEUX SEMAINES*

926.46 — 1063.60

Remuneration / Rémunération (From-de / To-à)	C.P.P. R.P.C.	Remuneration / Rémunération (From-de / To-à)	C.P.P. R.P.C.	Remuneration / Rémunération (From-de / To-à)	C.P.P. R.P.C.	Remuneration / Rémunération (From-de / To-à)	C.P.P. R.P.C.
926.46 - 926.93	17.28	960.75 - 961.22	18.00	995.04 - 995.50	18.72	1029.32 - 1029.79	19.44
926.94 - 927.41	17.29	961.23 - 961.69	18.01	995.51 - 995.98	18.73	1029.80 - 1030.26	19.45
927.42 - 927.88	17.30	961.70 - 962.17	18.02	995.99 - 996.45	18.74	1030.27 - 1030.74	19.46
927.89 - 928.36	17.31	962.18 - 962.64	18.03	996.46 - 996.93	18.75	1030.75 - 1031.22	19.47
928.37 - 928.83	17.32	962.65 - 963.12	18.04	996.94 - 997.41	18.76	1031.23 - 1031.69	19.48
928.84 - 929.31	17.33	963.13 - 963.60	18.05	997.42 - 997.88	18.77	1031.70 - 1032.17	19.49
929.32 - 929.79	17.34	963.61 - 964.07	18.06	997.89 - 998.36	18.78	1032.18 - 1032.64	19.50
929.80 - 930.26	17.35	964.08 - 964.55	18.07	998.37 - 998.83	18.79	1032.65 - 1033.12	19.51
930.27 - 930.74	17.36	964.56 - 965.03	18.08	998.84 - 999.31	18.80	1033.13 - 1033.60	19.52
930.75 - 931.22	17.37	965.04 - 965.50	18.09	999.32 - 999.79	18.81	1033.61 - 1034.07	19.53
931.23 - 931.69	17.38	965.51 - 965.98	18.10	999.80 - 1000.26	18.82	1034.08 - 1034.55	19.54
931.70 - 932.17	17.39	965.99 - 966.45	18.11	1000.27 - 1000.74	18.83	1034.56 - 1035.03	19.55
932.18 - 932.64	17.40	966.46 - 966.93	18.12	1000.75 - 1001.22	18.84	1035.04 - 1035.50	19.56
932.65 - 933.12	17.41	966.94 - 967.41	18.13	1001.23 - 1001.69	18.85	1035.51 - 1035.98	19.57
933.13 - 933.60	17.42	967.42 - 967.88	18.14	1001.70 - 1002.17	18.86	1035.99 - 1036.45	19.58
933.61 - 934.07	17.43	967.89 - 968.36	18.15	1002.18 - 1002.64	18.87	1036.46 - 1036.93	19.59
934.08 - 934.55	17.44	968.37 - 968.83	18.16	1002.65 - 1003.12	18.88	1036.94 - 1037.41	19.60
934.56 - 935.03	17.45	968.84 - 969.31	18.17	1003.13 - 1003.60	18.89	1037.42 - 1037.88	19.61
935.04 - 935.50	17.46	969.32 - 969.79	18.18	1003.61 - 1004.07	18.90	1037.89 - 1038.36	19.62
935.51 - 935.98	17.47	969.80 - 970.26	18.19	1004.08 - 1004.55	18.91	1038.37 - 1038.83	19.63
935.99 - 936.45	17.48	970.27 - 970.74	18.20	1004.56 - 1005.03	18.92	1038.84 - 1039.31	19.64
936.46 - 936.93	17.49	970.75 - 971.22	18.21	1005.04 - 1005.50	18.93	1039.32 - 1039.79	19.65
936.94 - 937.41	17.50	971.23 - 971.69	18.22	1005.51 - 1005.98	18.94	1039.80 - 1040.26	19.66
937.42 - 937.88	17.51	971.70 - 972.17	18.23	1005.99 - 1006.45	18.95	1040.27 - 1040.74	19.67
937.89 - 938.36	17.52	972.18 - 972.64	18.24	1006.46 - 1006.93	18.96	1040.75 - 1041.22	19.68
938.37 - 938.83	17.53	972.65 - 973.12	18.25	1006.94 - 1007.41	18.97	1041.23 - 1041.69	19.69
938.84 - 939.31	17.54	973.13 - 973.60	18.26	1007.42 - 1007.88	18.98	1041.70 - 1042.17	19.70
939.32 - 939.79	17.55	973.61 - 974.07	18.27	1007.89 - 1008.36	18.99	1042.18 - 1042.64	19.71
939.80 - 940.26	17.56	974.08 - 974.55	18.28	1008.37 - 1008.83	19.00	1042.65 - 1043.12	19.72
940.27 - 940.74	17.57	974.56 - 975.03	18.29	1008.84 - 1009.31	19.01	1043.13 - 1043.60	19.73
940.75 - 941.22	17.58	975.04 - 975.50	18.30	1009.32 - 1009.79	19.02	1043.61 - 1044.07	19.74
941.23 - 941.69	17.59	975.51 - 975.98	18.31	1009.80 - 1010.26	19.03	1044.08 - 1044.55	19.75
941.70 - 942.17	17.60	975.99 - 976.45	18.32	1010.27 - 1010.74	19.04	1044.56 - 1045.03	19.76
942.18 - 942.64	17.61	976.46 - 976.93	18.33	1010.75 - 1011.22	19.05	1045.04 - 1045.50	19.77
942.65 - 943.12	17.62	976.94 - 977.41	18.34	1011.23 - 1011.69	19.06	1045.51 - 1045.98	19.78
943.13 - 943.60	17.63	977.42 - 977.88	18.35	1011.70 - 1012.17	19.07	1045.99 - 1046.45	19.79
943.61 - 944.07	17.64	977.89 - 978.36	18.36	1012.18 - 1012.64	19.08	1046.46 - 1046.93	19.80
944.08 - 944.55	17.65	978.37 - 978.83	18.37	1012.65 - 1013.12	19.09	1046.94 - 1047.41	19.81
944.56 - 945.03	17.66	978.84 - 979.31	18.38	1013.13 - 1013.60	19.10	1047.42 - 1047.88	19.82
945.04 - 945.50	17.67	979.32 - 979.79	18.39	1013.61 - 1014.07	19.11	1047.89 - 1048.36	19.83
945.51 - 945.98	17.68	979.80 - 980.26	18.40	1014.08 - 1014.55	19.12	1048.37 - 1048.83	19.84
945.99 - 946.45	17.69	980.27 - 980.74	18.41	1014.56 - 1015.03	19.13	1048.84 - 1049.31	19.85
946.46 - 946.93	17.70	980.75 - 981.22	18.42	1015.04 - 1015.50	19.14	1049.32 - 1049.79	19.86
946.94 - 947.41	17.71	981.23 - 981.69	18.43	1015.51 - 1015.98	19.15	1049.80 - 1050.26	19.87
947.42 - 947.88	17.72	981.70 - 982.17	18.44	1015.99 - 1016.45	19.16	1050.27 - 1050.74	19.88
947.89 - 948.36	17.73	982.18 - 982.64	18.45	1016.46 - 1016.93	19.17	1050.75 - 1051.22	19.89
948.37 - 948.83	17.74	982.65 - 983.12	18.46	1016.94 - 1017.41	19.18	1051.23 - 1051.69	19.90
948.84 - 949.31	17.75	983.13 - 983.60	18.47	1017.42 - 1017.88	19.19	1051.70 - 1052.17	19.91
949.32 - 949.79	17.76	983.61 - 984.07	18.48	1017.89 - 1018.36	19.20	1052.18 - 1052.64	19.92
949.80 - 950.26	17.77	984.08 - 984.55	18.49	1018.37 - 1018.83	19.21	1052.65 - 1053.12	19.93
950.27 - 950.74	17.78	984.56 - 985.03	18.50	1018.84 - 1019.31	19.22	1053.13 - 1053.60	19.94
950.75 - 951.22	17.79	985.04 - 985.50	18.51	1019.32 - 1019.79	19.23	1053.61 - 1054.07	19.95
951.23 - 951.69	17.80	985.51 - 985.98	18.52	1019.80 - 1020.26	19.24	1054.08 - 1054.55	19.96
951.70 - 952.17	17.81	985.99 - 986.45	18.53	1020.27 - 1020.74	19.25	1054.56 - 1055.03	19.97
952.18 - 952.64	17.82	986.46 - 986.93	18.54	1020.75 - 1021.22	19.26	1055.04 - 1055.50	19.98
952.65 - 953.12	17.83	986.94 - 987.41	18.55	1021.23 - 1021.69	19.27	1055.51 - 1055.98	19.99
953.13 - 953.60	17.84	987.42 - 987.88	18.56	1021.70 - 1022.17	19.28	1055.99 - 1056.45	20.00
953.61 - 954.07	17.85	987.89 - 988.36	18.57	1022.18 - 1022.64	19.29	1056.46 - 1056.93	20.01
954.08 - 954.55	17.86	988.37 - 988.83	18.58	1022.65 - 1023.12	19.30	1056.94 - 1057.41	20.02
954.56 - 955.03	17.87	988.84 - 989.31	18.59	1023.13 - 1023.60	19.31	1057.42 - 1057.88	20.03
955.04 - 955.50	17.88	989.32 - 989.79	18.60	1023.61 - 1024.07	19.32	1057.89 - 1058.36	20.04
955.51 - 955.98	17.89	989.80 - 990.26	18.61	1024.08 - 1024.55	19.33	1058.37 - 1058.83	20.05
955.99 - 956.45	17.90	990.27 - 990.74	18.62	1024.56 - 1025.03	19.34	1058.84 - 1059.31	20.06
956.46 - 956.93	17.91	990.75 - 991.22	18.63	1025.04 - 1025.50	19.35	1059.32 - 1059.79	20.07
956.94 - 957.41	17.92	991.23 - 991.69	18.64	1025.51 - 1025.98	19.36	1059.80 - 1060.26	20.08
957.42 - 957.88	17.93	991.70 - 992.17	18.65	1025.99 - 1026.45	19.37	1060.27 - 1060.74	20.09
957.89 - 958.36	17.94	992.18 - 992.64	18.66	1026.46 - 1026.93	19.38	1060.75 - 1061.22	20.10
958.37 - 958.83	17.95	992.65 - 993.12	18.67	1026.94 - 1027.41	19.39	1061.23 - 1061.69	20.11
958.84 - 959.31	17.96	993.13 - 993.60	18.68	1027.42 - 1027.88	19.40	1061.70 - 1062.17	20.12
959.32 - 959.79	17.97	993.61 - 994.07	18.69	1027.89 - 1028.36	19.41	1062.18 - 1062.64	20.13
959.80 - 960.26	17.98	994.08 - 994.55	18.70	1028.37 - 1028.83	19.42	1062.65 - 1063.12	20.14
960.27 - 960.74	17.99	994.56 - 995.03	18.71	1028.84 - 1029.31	19.43	1063.13 - 1063.60	20.15

Table 14.1   Canada Pension Plan contributions schedule.

CANADA PENSION PLAN CONTRIBUTIONS — COTISATIONS AU RÉGIME DE PENSIONS DU CANADA

BI-WEEKLY PAY PERIOD — *PÉRIODE DE PAIE DE DEUX SEMAINES*

1063.61 — 3805.98

Remuneration / Rémunération From-de — To-à	C.P.P. R.P.C.	Remuneration / Rémunération From-de — To-à	C.P.P. R.P.C.	Remuneration / Rémunération From-de — To-à	C.P.P. R.P.C.	Remuneration / Rémunération From-de — To-à	C.P.P. R.P.C.
1063.61 – 1064.07	20.16	1735.99 – 1745.98	34.38	2455.99 – 2465.98	49.50	3175.99 – 3185.98	64.62
1064.08 – 1064.55	20.17	1745.99 – 1755.98	34.59	2465.99 – 2475.98	49.71	3185.99 – 3195.98	64.83
1064.56 – 1065.03	20.18	1755.99 – 1765.98	34.80	2475.99 – 2485.98	49.92	3195.99 – 3205.98	65.04
1065.04 – 1065.50	20.19	1765.99 – 1775.98	35.01	2485.99 – 2495.98	50.13	3205.99 – 3215.98	65.25
1065.51 – 1065.98	20.20	1775.99 – 1785.98	35.22	2495.99 – 2505.98	50.34	3215.99 – 3225.98	65.46
1065.99 – 1075.98	20.31	1785.99 – 1795.98	35.43	2505.99 – 2515.98	50.55	3225.99 – 3235.98	65.67
1075.99 – 1085.98	20.52	1795.99 – 1805.98	35.64	2515.99 – 2525.98	50.76	3235.99 – 3245.98	65.88
1085.99 – 1095.98	20.73	1805.99 – 1815.98	35.85	2525.99 – 2535.98	50.97	3245.99 – 3255.98	66.09
1095.99 – 1105.98	20.94	1815.99 – 1825.98	36.06	2535.99 – 2545.98	51.18	3255.99 – 3265.98	66.30
1105.99 – 1115.98	21.15	1825.99 – 1835.98	36.27	2545.99 – 2555.98	51.39	3265.99 – 3275.98	66.51
1115.99 – 1125.98	21.36	1835.99 – 1845.98	36.48	2555.99 – 2565.98	51.60	3275.99 – 3285.98	66.72
1125.99 – 1135.98	21.57	1845.99 – 1855.98	36.69	2565.99 – 2575.98	51.81	3285.99 – 3295.98	66.93
1135.99 – 1145.98	21.78	1855.99 – 1865.98	36.90	2575.99 – 2585.98	52.02	3295.99 – 3305.98	67.14
1145.99 – 1155.98	21.99	1865.99 – 1875.98	37.11	2585.99 – 2595.98	52.23	3305.99 – 3315.98	67.35
1155.99 – 1165.98	22.20	1875.99 – 1885.98	37.32	2595.99 – 2605.98	52.44	3315.99 – 3325.98	67.56
1165.99 – 1175.98	22.41	1885.99 – 1895.98	37.53	2605.99 – 2615.98	52.65	3325.99 – 3335.98	67.77
1175.99 – 1185.98	22.62	1895.99 – 1905.98	37.74	2615.99 – 2625.98	52.86	3335.99 – 3345.98	67.98
1185.99 – 1195.98	22.83	1905.99 – 1915.98	37.95	2625.99 – 2635.98	53.07	3345.99 – 3355.98	68.19
1195.99 – 1205.98	23.04	1915.99 – 1925.98	38.16	2635.99 – 2645.98	53.28	3355.99 – 3365.98	68.40
1205.99 – 1215.98	23.25	1925.99 – 1935.98	38.37	2645.99 – 2655.98	53.49	3365.99 – 3375.98	68.61
1215.99 – 1225.98	23.46	1935.99 – 1945.98	38.58	2655.99 – 2665.98	53.70	3375.99 – 3385.98	68.82
1225.99 – 1235.98	23.67	1945.99 – 1955.98	38.79	2665.99 – 2675.98	53.91	3385.99 – 3395.98	69.03
1235.99 – 1245.98	23.88	1955.99 – 1965.98	39.00	2675.99 – 2685.98	54.12	3395.99 – 3405.98	69.24
1245.99 – 1255.98	24.09	1965.99 – 1975.98	39.21	2685.99 – 2695.98	54.33	3405.99 – 3415.98	69.45
1255.99 – 1265.98	24.30	1975.99 – 1985.98	39.42	2695.99 – 2705.98	54.54	3415.99 – 3425.98	69.66
1265.99 – 1275.98	24.51	1985.99 – 1995.98	39.63	2705.99 – 2715.98	54.75	3425.99 – 3435.98	69.87
1275.99 – 1285.98	24.72	1995.99 – 2005.98	39.84	2715.99 – 2725.98	54.96	3435.99 – 3445.98	70.08
1285.99 – 1295.98	24.93	2005.99 – 2015.98	40.05	2725.99 – 2735.98	55.17	3445.99 – 3455.98	70.29
1295.99 – 1305.98	25.14	2015.99 – 2025.98	40.26	2735.99 – 2745.98	55.38	3455.99 – 3465.98	70.50
1305.99 – 1315.98	25.35	2025.99 – 2035.98	40.47	2745.99 – 2755.98	55.59	3465.99 – 3475.98	70.71
1315.99 – 1325.98	25.56	2035.99 – 2045.98	40.68	2755.99 – 2765.98	55.80	3475.99 – 3485.98	70.92
1325.99 – 1335.98	25.77	2045.99 – 2055.98	40.89	2765.99 – 2775.98	56.01	3485.99 – 3495.98	71.13
1335.99 – 1345.98	25.98	2055.99 – 2065.98	41.10	2775.99 – 2785.98	56.22	3495.99 – 3505.98	71.34
1345.99 – 1355.98	26.19	2065.99 – 2075.98	41.31	2785.99 – 2795.98	56.43	3505.99 – 3515.98	71.55
1355.99 – 1365.98	26.40	2075.99 – 2085.98	41.52	2795.99 – 2805.98	56.64	3515.99 – 3525.98	71.76
1365.99 – 1375.98	26.61	2085.99 – 2095.98	41.73	2805.99 – 2815.98	56.85	3525.99 – 3535.98	71.97
1375.99 – 1385.98	26.82	2095.99 – 2105.98	41.94	2815.99 – 2825.98	57.06	3535.99 – 3545.98	72.18
1385.99 – 1395.98	27.03	2105.99 – 2115.98	42.15	2825.99 – 2835.98	57.27	3545.99 – 3555.98	72.39
1395.99 – 1405.98	27.24	2115.99 – 2125.98	42.36	2835.99 – 2845.98	57.48	3555.99 – 3565.98	72.60
1405.99 – 1415.98	27.45	2125.99 – 2135.98	42.57	2845.99 – 2855.98	57.69	3565.99 – 3575.98	72.81
1415.99 – 1425.98	27.66	2135.99 – 2145.98	42.78	2855.99 – 2865.98	57.90	3575.99 – 3585.98	73.02
1425.99 – 1435.98	27.87	2145.99 – 2155.98	42.99	2865.99 – 2875.98	58.11	3585.99 – 3595.98	73.23
1435.99 – 1445.98	28.08	2155.99 – 2165.98	43.20	2875.99 – 2885.98	58.32	3595.99 – 3605.98	73.44
1445.99 – 1455.98	28.29	2165.99 – 2175.98	43.41	2885.99 – 2895.98	58.53	3605.99 – 3615.98	73.65
1455.99 – 1465.98	28.50	2175.99 – 2185.98	43.62	2895.99 – 2905.98	58.74	3615.99 – 3625.98	73.86
1465.99 – 1475.98	28.71	2185.99 – 2195.98	43.83	2905.99 – 2915.98	58.95	3625.99 – 3635.98	74.07
1475.99 – 1485.98	28.92	2195.99 – 2205.98	44.04	2915.99 – 2925.98	59.16	3635.99 – 3645.98	74.28
1485.99 – 1495.98	29.13	2205.99 – 2215.98	44.25	2925.99 – 2935.98	59.37	3645.99 – 3655.98	74.49
1495.99 – 1505.98	29.34	2215.99 – 2225.98	44.46	2935.99 – 2945.98	59.58	3655.99 – 3665.98	74.70
1505.99 – 1515.98	29.55	2225.99 – 2235.98	44.67	2945.99 – 2955.98	59.79	3665.99 – 3675.98	74.91
1515.99 – 1525.98	29.76	2235.99 – 2245.98	44.88	2955.99 – 2965.98	60.00	3675.99 – 3685.98	75.12
1525.99 – 1535.98	29.97	2245.99 – 2255.98	45.09	2965.99 – 2975.98	60.21	3685.99 – 3695.98	75.33
1535.99 – 1545.98	30.18	2255.99 – 2265.98	45.30	2975.99 – 2985.98	60.42	3695.99 – 3705.98	75.54
1545.99 – 1555.98	30.39	2265.99 – 2275.98	45.51	2985.99 – 2995.98	60.63	3705.99 – 3715.98	75.75
1555.99 – 1565.98	30.60	2275.99 – 2285.98	45.72	2995.99 – 3005.98	60.84	3715.99 – 3725.98	75.96
1565.99 – 1575.98	30.81	2285.99 – 2295.98	45.93	3005.99 – 3015.98	61.05	3725.99 – 3735.98	76.17
1575.99 – 1585.98	31.02	2295.99 – 2305.98	46.14	3015.99 – 3025.98	61.26	3735.99 – 3745.98	76.38
1585.99 – 1595.98	31.23	2305.99 – 2315.98	46.35	3025.99 – 3035.98	61.47	3745.99 – 3755.98	76.59
1595.99 – 1605.98	31.44	2315.99 – 2325.98	46.56	3035.99 – 3045.98	61.68	3755.99 – 3765.98	76.80
1605.99 – 1615.98	31.65	2325.99 – 2335.98	46.77	3045.99 – 3055.98	61.89	3765.99 – 3775.98	77.01
1615.99 – 1625.98	31.86	2335.99 – 2345.98	46.98	3055.99 – 3065.98	62.10	3775.99 – 3785.98	77.22
1625.99 – 1635.98	32.07	2345.99 – 2355.98	47.19	3065.99 – 3075.98	62.31	3785.99 – 3795.98	77.43
1635.99 – 1645.98	32.28	2355.99 – 2365.98	47.40	3075.99 – 3085.98	62.52	3795.99 – 3805.98	77.64
1645.99 – 1655.98	32.49	2365.99 – 2375.98	47.61	3085.99 – 3095.98	62.73		
1655.99 – 1665.98	32.70	2375.99 – 2385.98	47.82	3095.99 – 3105.98	62.94		
1665.99 – 1675.98	32.91	2385.99 – 2395.98	48.03	3105.99 – 3115.98	63.15		
1675.99 – 1685.98	33.12	2395.99 – 2405.98	48.24	3115.99 – 3125.98	63.36		
1685.99 – 1695.98	33.33	2405.99 – 2415.98	48.45	3125.99 – 3135.98	63.57		
1695.99 – 1705.98	33.54	2415.99 – 2425.98	48.66	3135.99 – 3145.98	63.78		
1705.99 – 1715.98	33.75	2425.99 – 2435.98	48.87	3145.99 – 3155.98	63.99		
1715.99 – 1725.98	33.96	2435.99 – 2445.98	49.08	3155.99 – 3165.98	64.20		
1725.99 – 1735.98	34.17	2445.99 – 2455.98	49.29	3165.99 – 3175.98	64.41		

"For remuneration in excess of the above amount refer to "Employee's Contribution — Calculation Method"."

"Si la rémunération dépasse le montant ci-dessus se reporter à la rubrique «Cotisation de l'employé — Méthode par le calcul.»"

Table 14.1 cont'd   Canada Pension Plan contributions schedule.

UNEMPLOYMENT INSURANCE PREMIUMS / PRIMES D'ASSURANCE-CHÔMAGE

For minimum and maximum insurable earnings amounts for various pay periods see Schedule II. For the maximum premium deduction for various pay periods see bottom of this page.

Les montants minimum et maximum des gains assurables pour diverses périodes de paie figurent en annexe II. La déduction maximale de primes pour diverses périodes de paie figure au bas de la présente page.

Rémunération From-de	To-à	Prime d'a.-c.	Rémunération From-de	To-à	Prime d'a.-c.	Rémunération From-de	To-à	Prime d'a.-c.	Rémunération From-de	To-à	Prime d'a.-c.
886.42	886.92	17.29	923.34	923.84	18.01	960.26	960.76	18.73	997.18	997.69	19.45
886.93	887.43	17.30	923.85	924.35	18.02	960.77	961.28	18.74	997.70	998.20	19.46
887.44	887.94	17.31	924.36	924.87	18.03	961.29	961.79	18.75	998.21	998.71	19.47
887.95	888.46	17.32	924.88	925.38	18.04	961.80	962.30	18.76	998.72	999.23	19.48
888.47	888.97	17.33	925.39	925.89	18.05	962.31	962.82	18.77	999.24	999.74	19.49
888.98	889.48	17.34	925.90	926.41	18.06	962.83	963.33	18.78	999.75	1000.25	19.50
889.49	889.99	17.35	926.42	926.92	18.07	963.34	963.84	18.79	1000.26	1000.76	19.51
890.00	890.51	17.36	926.93	927.43	18.08	963.85	964.35	18.80	1000.77	1001.28	19.52
890.52	891.02	17.37	927.44	927.94	18.09	964.36	964.87	18.81	1001.29	1001.79	19.53
891.03	891.53	17.38	927.95	928.46	18.10	964.88	965.38	18.82	1001.80	1002.30	19.54
891.54	892.05	17.39	928.47	928.97	18.11	965.39	965.89	18.83	1002.31	1002.82	19.55
892.06	892.56	17.40	928.98	929.48	18.12	965.90	966.41	18.84	1002.83	1003.33	19.56
892.57	893.07	17.41	929.49	929.99	18.13	966.42	966.92	18.85	1003.34	1003.84	19.57
893.08	893.58	17.42	930.00	930.51	18.14	966.93	967.43	18.86	1003.85	1004.35	19.58
893.59	894.10	17.43	930.52	931.02	18.15	967.44	967.94	18.87	1004.36	1004.87	19.59
894.11	894.61	17.44	931.03	931.53	18.16	967.95	968.46	18.88	1004.88	1005.38	19.60
894.62	895.12	17.45	931.54	932.05	18.17	968.47	968.97	18.89	1005.39	1005.89	19.61
895.13	895.64	17.46	932.06	932.56	18.18	968.98	969.48	18.90	1005.90	1006.41	19.62
895.65	896.15	17.47	932.57	933.07	18.19	969.49	969.99	18.91	1006.42	1006.92	19.63
896.16	896.66	17.48	933.08	933.58	18.20	970.00	970.51	18.92	1006.93	1007.43	19.64
896.67	897.17	17.49	933.59	934.10	18.21	970.52	971.02	18.93	1007.44	1007.94	19.65
897.18	897.69	17.50	934.11	934.61	18.22	971.03	971.53	18.94	1007.95	1008.46	19.66
897.70	898.20	17.51	934.62	935.12	18.23	971.54	972.05	18.95	1008.47	1008.97	19.67
898.21	898.71	17.52	935.13	935.64	18.24	972.06	972.56	18.96	1008.98	1009.48	19.68
898.72	899.23	17.53	935.65	936.15	18.25	972.57	973.07	18.97	1009.49	1009.99	19.69
899.24	899.74	17.54	936.16	936.66	18.26	973.08	973.58	18.98	1010.00	1010.51	19.70
899.75	900.25	17.55	936.67	937.17	18.27	973.59	974.10	18.99	1010.52	1011.02	19.71
900.26	900.76	17.56	937.18	937.69	18.28	974.11	974.61	19.00	1011.03	1011.53	19.72
900.77	901.28	17.57	937.70	938.20	18.29	974.62	975.12	19.01	1011.54	1012.05	19.73
901.29	901.79	17.58	938.21	938.71	18.30	975.13	975.64	19.02	1012.06	1012.56	19.74
901.80	902.30	17.59	938.72	939.23	18.31	975.65	976.15	19.03	1012.57	1013.07	19.75
902.31	902.82	17.60	939.24	939.74	18.32	976.16	976.66	19.04	1013.08	1013.58	19.76
902.83	903.33	17.61	939.75	940.25	18.33	976.67	977.17	19.05	1013.59	1014.10	19.77
903.34	903.84	17.62	940.26	940.76	18.34	977.18	977.69	19.06	1014.11	1014.61	19.78
903.85	904.35	17.63	940.77	941.28	18.35	977.70	978.20	19.07	1014.62	1015.12	19.79
904.36	904.87	17.64	941.29	941.79	18.36	978.21	978.71	19.08	1015.13	1015.64	19.80
904.88	905.38	17.65	941.80	942.30	18.37	978.72	979.23	19.09	1015.65	1016.15	19.81
905.39	905.89	17.66	942.31	942.82	18.38	979.24	979.74	19.10	1016.16	1016.66	19.82
905.90	906.41	17.67	942.83	943.33	18.39	979.75	980.25	19.11	1016.67	1017.17	19.83
906.42	906.92	17.68	943.34	943.84	18.40	980.26	980.76	19.12	1017.18	1017.69	19.84
906.93	907.43	17.69	943.85	944.35	18.41	980.77	981.28	19.13	1017.70	1018.20	19.85
907.44	907.94	17.70	944.36	944.87	18.42	981.29	981.79	19.14	1018.21	1018.71	19.86
907.95	908.46	17.71	944.88	945.38	18.43	981.80	982.30	19.15	1018.72	1019.23	19.87
908.47	908.97	17.72	945.39	945.89	18.44	982.31	982.82	19.16	1019.24	1019.74	19.88
908.58	909.48	17.73	945.90	946.41	18.45	982.83	983.33	19.17	1019.75	1020.25	19.89
909.49	909.99	17.74	946.42	946.92	18.46	983.34	983.84	19.18	1020.26	1020.76	19.90
910.00	910.51	17.75	946.93	947.43	18.47	983.85	984.35	19.19	1020.77	1021.28	19.91
910.52	911.02	17.76	947.44	947.94	18.48	984.36	984.87	19.20	1021.29	1021.79	19.92
911.03	911.53	17.77	947.95	948.46	18.49	984.88	985.38	19.21	1021.80	1022.30	19.93
911.54	912.05	17.78	948.47	948.97	18.50	985.39	985.89	19.22	1022.31	1022.82	19.94
912.06	912.56	17.79	948.98	949.48	18.51	985.90	986.41	19.23	1022.83	1023.33	19.95
912.57	913.07	17.80	949.49	949.99	18.52	986.42	986.92	19.24	1023.34	1023.84	19.96
913.08	913.58	17.81	950.00	950.51	18.53	986.93	987.43	19.25	1023.85	1024.35	19.97
913.59	914.10	17.82	950.52	951.02	18.54	987.44	987.94	19.26	1024.36	1024.87	19.98
914.11	914.61	17.83	951.03	951.53	18.55	987.95	988.46	19.27	1024.88	1025.38	19.99
914.62	915.12	17.84	951.54	952.05	18.56	988.47	988.97	19.28	1025.39	1025.89	20.00
915.13	915.64	17.85	952.06	952.56	18.57	988.98	989.48	19.29	1025.90	1026.41	20.01
915.65	916.15	17.86	952.57	953.07	18.58	989.49	989.99	19.30	1026.42	1026.92	20.02
916.16	916.66	17.87	953.08	953.58	18.59	990.00	990.51	19.31	1026.93	1027.43	20.03
916.67	917.17	17.88	953.59	954.10	18.60	990.52	991.02	19.32	1027.44	1027.94	20.04
917.18	917.69	17.89	954.11	954.61	18.61	991.03	991.53	19.33	1027.95	1028.46	20.05
917.70	918.20	17.90	954.62	955.12	18.62	991.54	992.05	19.34	1028.47	1028.97	20.06
918.21	918.71	17.91	955.13	955.64	18.63	992.06	992.56	19.35	1028.98	1029.48	20.07
918.72	919.23	17.92	955.65	956.15	18.64	992.57	993.07	19.36	1029.49	1029.99	20.08
919.24	919.74	17.93	956.16	956.66	18.65	993.08	993.58	19.37	1030.00	1030.51	20.09
919.75	920.25	17.94	956.67	957.17	18.66	993.59	994.10	19.38	1030.52	1031.02	20.10
920.26	920.76	17.95	957.18	957.69	18.67	994.11	994.61	19.39	1031.03	1031.53	20.11
920.77	921.28	17.96	957.70	958.20	18.68	994.62	995.12	19.40	1031.54	1032.05	20.12
921.29	921.79	17.97	958.21	958.71	18.69	995.13	995.64	19.41	1032.06	1032.56	20.13
921.80	922.30	17.98	958.72	959.23	18.70	995.65	996.15	19.42	1032.57	1033.07	20.14
922.31	922.82	17.99	959.24	959.74	18.71	996.16	996.66	19.43	1033.08	1033.58	20.15
922.83	923.33	18.00	959.75	960.25	18.72	996.67	997.17	19.44	1033.59	1034.10	20.16

Maximum Premium Deduction for a Pay Period of the stated frequency.
Déduction maximale de prime pour une période de paie d'une durée donnée.

Weekly - Hebdomadaire	11.80	
Bi-Weekly - Deux semaines	23.60	
Semi-Monthly - Bi-mensuel	25.56	
Monthly - Mensuellement	51.12	
10 pp per year - 10 pp par année	61.35	
13 pp per year - 13 pp par année	47.19	
22 pp per year - 22 pp par année	27.89	

Table 14.2   Unemployment insurance premiums schedule.

UNEMPLOYMENT INSURANCE PREMIUMS		PRIMES D'ASSURANCE-CHÔMAGE	
For minimum and maximum insurable earnings amounts for various pay periods see Schedule II. For the maximum premium deduction for various pay periods see bottom of this page.		Les montants minimum et maximum des gains assurables pour diverses périodes de paie figurent en annexe II. La déduction maximale de primes pour diverses périodes de paie figure au bas de la présente page.	

Remuneration / Rémunération From-de To-à	U.I. Premium / Prime d'a.-c.	Remuneration / Rémunération From-de To-à	U.I. Premium / Prime d'a.-c.	Remuneration / Rémunération From-de To-à	U.I. Premium / Prime d'a.-c.	Remuneration / Rémunération From-de To-à	U.I. Premium / Prime d'a.-c.
1034.11 - 1034.61	20.17	1071.03 - 1071.53	20.89	1107.95 - 1108.46	21.61	1144.88 - 1145.38	22.33
1034.62 - 1035.12	20.18	1071.54 - 1072.05	20.90	1108.47 - 1108.97	21.62	1145.39 - 1145.89	22.34
1035.13 - 1035.64	20.19	1072.06 - 1072.56	20.91	1108.98 - 1109.48	21.63	1145.90 - 1146.41	22.35
1035.65 - 1036.15	20.20	1072.57 - 1073.07	20.92	1109.49 - 1109.99	21.64	1146.42 - 1146.92	22.36
1036.16 - 1036.66	20.21	1073.08 - 1073.58	20.93	1110.00 - 1110.51	21.65	1146.93 - 1147.43	22.37
1036.67 - 1037.17	20.22	1073.59 - 1074.10	20.94	1110.52 - 1111.02	21.66	1147.44 - 1147.94	22.38
1037.18 - 1037.69	20.23	1074.11 - 1074.61	20.95	1111.03 - 1111.53	21.67	1147.95 - 1148.46	22.39
1037.70 - 1038.20	20.24	1074.62 - 1075.12	20.96	1111.54 - 1112.05	21.68	1148.47 - 1148.97	22.40
1038.21 - 1038.71	20.25	1075.13 - 1075.64	20.97	1112.06 - 1112.56	21.69	1148.98 - 1149.48	22.41
1038.72 - 1039.23	20.26	1075.65 - 1076.15	20.98	1112.57 - 1113.07	21.70	1149.49 - 1149.99	22.42
1039.24 - 1039.74	20.27	1076.16 - 1076.66	20.99	1113.08 - 1113.58	21.71	1150.00 - 1150.51	22.43
1039.75 - 1040.25	20.28	1076.67 - 1077.17	21.00	1113.59 - 1114.10	21.72	1150.52 - 1151.02	22.44
1040.26 - 1040.76	20.29	1077.18 - 1077.69	21.01	1114.11 - 1114.61	21.73	1151.03 - 1151.53	22.45
1040.77 - 1041.28	20.30	1077.70 - 1078.20	21.02	1114.62 - 1115.12	21.74	1151.54 - 1152.05	22.46
1041.29 - 1041.79	20.31	1078.21 - 1078.71	21.03	1115.13 - 1115.64	21.75	1152.06 - 1152.56	22.47
1041.80 - 1042.30	20.32	1078.72 - 1079.23	21.04	1115.65 - 1116.15	21.76	1152.57 - 1153.07	22.48
1042.31 - 1042.82	20.33	1079.24 - 1079.74	21.05	1116.16 - 1116.66	21.77	1153.08 - 1153.58	22.49
1042.83 - 1043.33	20.34	1079.75 - 1080.25	21.06	1116.67 - 1117.17	21.78	1153.59 - 1154.10	22.50
1043.34 - 1043.84	20.35	1080.26 - 1080.76	21.07	1117.18 - 1117.69	21.79	1154.11 - 1154.61	22.51
1043.85 - 1044.35	20.36	1080.77 - 1081.28	21.08	1117.70 - 1118.20	21.80	1154.62 - 1155.12	22.52
1044.36 - 1044.87	20.37	1081.29 - 1081.79	21.09	1118.21 - 1118.71	21.81	1155.13 - 1155.64	22.53
1044.88 - 1045.38	20.38	1081.80 - 1082.30	21.10	1118.72 - 1119.23	21.82	1155.65 - 1156.15	22.54
1045.39 - 1045.89	20.39	1082.31 - 1082.82	21.11	1119.24 - 1119.74	21.83	1156.16 - 1156.66	22.55
1045.90 - 1046.41	20.40	1082.83 - 1083.33	21.12	1119.75 - 1120.25	21.84	1156.67 - 1157.17	22.56
1046.42 - 1046.92	20.41	1083.34 - 1083.84	21.13	1120.26 - 1120.76	21.85	1157.18 - 1157.69	22.57
1046.93 - 1047.43	20.42	1083.85 - 1084.35	21.14	1120.77 - 1121.28	21.86	1157.70 - 1158.20	22.58
1047.44 - 1047.94	20.43	1084.36 - 1084.87	21.15	1121.29 - 1121.79	21.87	1158.21 - 1158.71	22.59
1047.95 - 1048.46	20.44	1084.88 - 1085.38	21.16	1121.80 - 1122.30	21.88	1158.72 - 1159.23	22.60
1048.47 - 1048.97	20.45	1085.39 - 1085.89	21.17	1122.31 - 1122.82	21.89	1159.24 - 1159.74	22.61
1048.98 - 1049.48	20.46	1085.90 - 1086.41	21.18	1122.83 - 1123.33	21.90	1159.75 - 1160.25	22.62
1049.49 - 1049.99	20.47	1086.42 - 1086.92	21.19	1123.34 - 1123.84	21.91	1160.26 - 1160.76	22.63
1050.00 - 1050.51	20.48	1086.93 - 1087.43	21.20	1123.85 - 1124.35	21.92	1160.77 - 1161.28	22.64
1050.52 - 1051.02	20.49	1087.44 - 1087.94	21.21	1124.36 - 1124.87	21.93	1161.29 - 1161.79	22.65
1051.03 - 1051.53	20.50	1087.95 - 1088.46	21.22	1124.88 - 1125.38	21.94	1161.80 - 1162.30	22.66
1051.54 - 1052.05	20.51	1088.47 - 1088.97	21.23	1125.39 - 1125.89	21.95	1162.31 - 1162.82	22.67
1052.06 - 1052.56	20.52	1088.98 - 1089.48	21.24	1125.90 - 1126.41	21.96	1162.83 - 1163.33	22.68
1052.57 - 1053.07	20.53	1089.49 - 1089.99	21.25	1126.42 - 1126.92	21.97	1163.34 - 1163.84	22.69
1053.08 - 1053.58	20.54	1090.00 - 1090.51	21.26	1126.93 - 1127.43	21.98	1163.85 - 1164.35	22.70
1053.59 - 1054.10	20.55	1090.52 - 1091.02	21.27	1127.44 - 1127.94	21.99	1164.36 - 1164.87	22.71
1054.11 - 1054.61	20.56	1091.03 - 1091.53	21.28	1127.95 - 1128.46	22.00	1164.88 - 1165.38	22.72
1054.62 - 1055.12	20.57	1091.54 - 1092.05	21.29	1128.47 - 1128.97	22.01	1165.39 - 1165.89	22.73
1055.13 - 1055.64	20.58	1092.06 - 1092.56	21.30	1128.98 - 1129.48	22.02	1165.90 - 1166.41	22.74
1055.65 - 1056.15	20.59	1092.57 - 1093.07	21.31	1129.49 - 1129.99	22.03	1166.42 - 1166.92	22.75
1056.16 - 1056.66	20.60	1093.08 - 1093.58	21.32	1130.00 - 1130.51	22.04	1166.93 - 1167.43	22.76
1056.67 - 1057.17	20.61	1093.59 - 1094.10	21.33	1130.52 - 1131.02	22.05	1167.44 - 1167.94	22.77
1057.18 - 1057.69	20.62	1094.11 - 1094.61	21.34	1131.03 - 1131.53	22.06	1167.95 - 1168.46	22.78
1057.70 - 1058.20	20.63	1094.62 - 1095.12	21.35	1131.54 - 1132.05	22.07	1168.47 - 1168.97	22.79
1058.21 - 1058.71	20.64	1095.13 - 1095.64	21.36	1132.06 - 1132.56	22.08	1168.98 - 1169.48	22.80
1058.72 - 1059.23	20.65	1095.65 - 1096.15	21.37	1132.57 - 1133.07	22.09	1169.49 - 1169.99	22.81
1059.24 - 1059.74	20.66	1096.16 - 1096.66	21.38	1133.08 - 1133.58	22.10	1170.00 - 1170.51	22.82
1059.75 - 1060.25	20.67	1096.67 - 1097.17	21.39	1133.59 - 1134.10	22.11	1170.52 - 1171.02	22.83
1060.26 - 1060.76	20.68	1097.18 - 1097.69	21.40	1134.11 - 1134.61	22.12	1171.03 - 1171.53	22.84
1060.77 - 1061.28	20.69	1097.70 - 1098.20	21.41	1134.62 - 1135.12	22.13	1171.54 - 1172.05	22.85
1061.29 - 1061.79	20.70	1098.21 - 1098.71	21.42	1135.13 - 1135.64	22.14	1172.06 - 1172.56	22.86
1061.80 - 1062.30	20.71	1098.72 - 1099.23	21.43	1135.65 - 1136.15	22.15	1172.57 - 1173.07	22.87
1062.31 - 1062.82	20.72	1099.24 - 1099.74	21.44	1136.16 - 1136.66	22.16	1173.08 - 1173.58	22.88
1062.83 - 1063.33	20.73	1099.75 - 1100.25	21.45	1136.67 - 1137.17	22.17	1173.59 - 1174.10	22.89
1063.34 - 1063.84	20.74	1100.26 - 1100.76	21.46	1137.18 - 1137.69	22.18	1174.11 - 1174.61	22.90
1063.85 - 1064.35	20.75	1100.77 - 1101.28	21.47	1137.70 - 1138.20	22.19	1174.62 - 1175.12	22.91
1064.36 - 1064.87	20.76	1101.29 - 1101.79	21.48	1138.21 - 1138.71	22.20	1175.13 - 1175.64	22.92
1064.88 - 1065.38	20.77	1101.80 - 1102.30	21.49	1138.72 - 1139.23	22.21	1175.65 - 1176.15	22.93
1065.39 - 1065.89	20.78	1102.31 - 1102.82	21.50	1139.24 - 1139.74	22.22	1176.16 - 1176.66	22.94
1065.90 - 1066.41	20.79	1102.83 - 1103.33	21.51	1139.75 - 1140.25	22.23	1176.67 - 1177.17	22.95
1066.42 - 1066.92	20.80	1103.34 - 1103.84	21.52	1140.26 - 1140.76	22.24	1177.18 - 1177.69	22.96
1066.93 - 1067.43	20.81	1103.85 - 1104.35	21.53	1140.77 - 1141.28	22.25	1177.70 - 1178.20	22.97
1067.44 - 1067.94	20.82	1104.36 - 1104.87	21.54	1141.29 - 1141.79	22.26	1178.21 - 1178.71	22.98
1067.95 - 1068.46	20.83	1104.88 - 1105.38	21.55	1141.80 - 1142.30	22.27	1178.72 - 1179.23	22.99
1068.47 - 1068.97	20.84	1105.39 - 1105.89	21.56	1142.31 - 1142.82	22.28	1179.24 - 1179.74	23.00
1068.98 - 1069.48	20.85	1105.90 - 1106.41	21.57	1142.83 - 1143.33	22.29	1179.75 - 1180.25	23.01
1069.49 - 1069.99	20.86	1106.42 - 1106.92	21.58	1143.34 - 1143.84	22.30	1180.26 - 1180.76	23.02
1070.00 - 1070.51	20.87	1106.93 - 1107.43	21.59	1143.85 - 1144.35	22.31	1180.77 - 1181.28	23.03
1070.52 - 1071.02	20.88	1107.44 - 1107.94	21.60	1144.36 - 1144.87	22.32	1181.29 - 1181.79	23.04

Maximum Premium Deduction for a Pay Period of the stated frequency. Déduction maximale de prime pour une période de paie d'une durée donnée		
Weekly - Hebdomadaire	11.80	10 pp per year - 10 pp par annee .61.35
Bi-Weekly - Deux semaines	23.60	13 pp per year - 13 pp par annee 47.19
Semi-Monthly - Bi-mensuel	25.56	22 pp per year - 22 pp par annee 27.89
Monthly - Mensuellement	51.12	

Table 14.2 cont'd Unemployment insurance premiums schedule.

UNEMPLOYMENT INSURANCE PREMIUMS   PRIMES D'ASSURANCE-CHÔMAGE

For minimum and maximum insurable earnings amounts for various pay periods see Schedule II. For the maximum premium deduction for various pay periods see bottom of this page.

Les montants minimum et maximum des gains assurables pour diverses périodes de paie figurent en annexe II. La déduction maximale de primes pour diverses périodes de paie figure au bas de la présente page.

Remuneration / Rémunération From-de – To-à	U.I. Premium / Prime d'a.-c.	Remuneration / Rémunération From-de – To-à	U.I. Premium / Prime d'a.-c.	Remuneration / Rémunération From-de – To-à	U.I. Premium / Prime d'a.-c.	Remuneration / Rémunération From-de – To-à	U.I. Premium / Prime d'a.-c.
1181.80 – 1182.30	23.05	1218.72 – 1219.23	23.77	1255.65 – 1256.15	24.49	1292.57 – 1293.07	25.21
1182.31 – 1182.82	23.06	1219.24 – 1219.74	23.78	1256.16 – 1256.66	24.50	1293.08 – 1293.58	25.22
1182.83 – 1183.33	23.07	1219.75 – 1220.25	23.79	1256.67 – 1257.17	24.51	1293.59 – 1294.10	25.23
1183.34 – 1183.84	23.08	1220.26 – 1220.76	23.80	1257.18 – 1257.69	24.52	1294.11 – 1294.61	25.24
1183.85 – 1184.35	23.09	1220.77 – 1221.28	23.81	1257.70 – 1258.20	24.53	1294.62 – 1295.12	25.25
1184.36 – 1184.87	23.10	1221.29 – 1221.79	23.82	1258.21 – 1258.71	24.54	1295.13 – 1295.64	25.26
1184.88 – 1185.38	23.11	1221.80 – 1222.30	23.83	1258.72 – 1259.23	24.55	1295.65 – 1296.15	25.27
1185.39 – 1185.89	23.12	1222.31 – 1222.82	23.84	1259.24 – 1259.74	24.56	1296.16 – 1296.66	25.28
1185.90 – 1186.41	23.13	1222.83 – 1223.33	23.85	1259.75 – 1260.25	24.57	1296.67 – 1297.17	25.29
1186.42 – 1186.92	23.14	1223.34 – 1223.84	23.86	1260.26 – 1260.76	24.58	1297.18 – 1297.69	25.30
1186.93 – 1187.43	23.15	1223.85 – 1224.35	23.87	1260.77 – 1261.28	24.59	1297.70 – 1298.20	25.31
1187.44 – 1187.94	23.16	1224.36 – 1224.87	23.88	1261.29 – 1261.79	24.60	1298.21 – 1298.71	25.32
1187.95 – 1188.46	23.17	1224.88 – 1225.38	23.89	1261.80 – 1262.30	24.61	1298.72 – 1299.23	25.33
1188.47 – 1188.97	23.18	1225.39 – 1225.89	23.90	1262.31 – 1262.82	24.62	1299.24 – 1299.74	25.34
1188.98 – 1189.48	23.19	1225.90 – 1226.41	23.91	1262.83 – 1263.33	24.63	1299.75 – 1300.25	25.35
1189.49 – 1189.99	23.20	1226.42 – 1226.92	23.92	1263.34 – 1263.84	24.64	1300.26 – 1300.76	25.36
1190.00 – 1190.51	23.21	1226.93 – 1227.43	23.93	1263.85 – 1264.35	24.65	1300.77 – 1301.28	25.37
1190.52 – 1191.02	23.22	1227.44 – 1227.94	23.94	1264.36 – 1264.87	24.66	1301.29 – 1301.79	25.38
1191.03 – 1191.53	23.23	1227.95 – 1228.46	23.95	1264.88 – 1265.38	24.67	1301.80 – 1302.30	25.39
1191.54 – 1192.05	23.24	1228.47 – 1228.97	23.96	1265.39 – 1265.89	24.68	1302.31 – 1302.82	25.40
1192.06 – 1192.56	23.25	1228.98 – 1229.48	23.97	1265.90 – 1266.41	24.69	1302.83 – 1303.33	25.41
1192.57 – 1193.07	23.26	1229.49 – 1229.99	23.98	1266.42 – 1266.92	24.70	1303.34 – 1303.84	25.42
1193.08 – 1193.58	23.27	1230.00 – 1230.51	23.99	1266.93 – 1267.43	24.71	1303.85 – 1304.35	25.43
1193.59 – 1194.10	23.28	1230.52 – 1231.02	24.00	1267.44 – 1267.94	24.72	1304.36 – 1304.87	25.44
1194.11 – 1194.61	23.29	1231.03 – 1231.53	24.01	1267.95 – 1268.46	24.73	1304.88 – 1305.38	25.45
1194.62 – 1195.12	23.30	1231.54 – 1232.05	24.02	1268.47 – 1268.97	24.74	1305.39 – 1305.89	25.46
1195.13 – 1195.64	23.31	1232.06 – 1232.56	24.03	1268.98 – 1269.48	24.75	1305.90 – 1306.41	25.47
1195.65 – 1196.15	23.32	1232.57 – 1233.07	24.04	1269.49 – 1269.99	24.76	1306.42 – 1306.92	25.48
1196.16 – 1196.66	23.33	1233.08 – 1233.58	24.05	1270.00 – 1270.51	24.77	1306.93 – 1307.43	25.49
1196.67 – 1197.17	23.34	1233.59 – 1234.10	24.06	1270.52 – 1271.02	24.78	1307.44 – 1307.94	25.50
1197.18 – 1197.69	23.35	1234.11 – 1234.61	24.07	1271.03 – 1271.53	24.79	1307.95 – 1308.46	25.51
1197.70 – 1198.20	23.36	1234.62 – 1235.12	24.08	1271.54 – 1272.05	24.80	1308.47 – 1308.97	25.52
1198.21 – 1198.71	23.37	1235.13 – 1235.64	24.09	1272.06 – 1272.56	24.81	1308.98 – 1309.48	25.53
1198.72 – 1199.23	23.38	1235.65 – 1236.15	24.10	1272.57 – 1273.07	24.82	1309.49 – 1309.99	25.54
1199.24 – 1199.74	23.39	1236.16 – 1236.66	24.11	1273.08 – 1273.58	24.83	1310.00 – 1310.51	25.55
1199.75 – 1200.25	23.40	1236.67 – 1237.17	24.12	1273.59 – 1274.10	24.84	1310.52 – 1311.02	25.56
1200.26 – 1200.76	23.41	1237.18 – 1237.69	24.13	1274.11 – 1274.61	24.85	1311.03 – 1311.53	25.57
1200.77 – 1201.28	23.42	1237.70 – 1238.20	24.14	1274.62 – 1275.12	24.86	1311.54 – 1312.05	25.58
1201.29 – 1201.79	23.43	1238.21 – 1238.71	24.15	1275.13 – 1275.64	24.87	1312.06 – 1312.56	25.59
1201.80 – 1202.30	23.44	1238.72 – 1239.23	24.16	1275.65 – 1276.15	24.88	1312.57 – 1313.07	25.60
1202.31 – 1202.82	23.45	1239.24 – 1239.74	24.17	1276.16 – 1276.66	24.89	1313.08 – 1313.58	25.61
1202.83 – 1203.33	23.46	1239.75 – 1240.25	24.18	1276.67 – 1277.17	24.90	1313.59 – 1314.10	25.62
1203.34 – 1203.84	23.47	1240.26 – 1240.76	24.19	1277.18 – 1277.69	24.91	1314.11 – 1314.61	25.63
1203.85 – 1204.35	23.48	1240.77 – 1241.28	24.20	1277.70 – 1278.20	24.92	1314.62 – 1315.12	25.64
1204.36 – 1204.87	23.49	1241.29 – 1241.79	24.21	1278.21 – 1278.71	24.93	1315.13 – 1315.64	25.65
1204.88 – 1205.38	23.50	1241.80 – 1242.30	24.22	1278.72 – 1279.23	24.94	1315.65 – 1316.15	25.66
1205.39 – 1205.89	23.51	1242.31 – 1242.82	24.23	1279.24 – 1279.74	24.95	1316.16 – 1316.66	25.67
1205.90 – 1206.41	23.52	1242.83 – 1243.33	24.24	1279.75 – 1280.25	24.96	1316.67 – 1317.17	25.68
1206.42 – 1206.92	23.53	1243.34 – 1243.84	24.25	1280.26 – 1280.76	24.97	1317.18 – 1317.69	25.69
1206.93 – 1207.43	23.54	1243.85 – 1244.35	24.26	1280.77 – 1281.28	24.98	1317.70 – 1318.20	25.70
1207.44 – 1207.94	23.55	1244.36 – 1244.87	24.27	1281.29 – 1281.79	24.99	1318.21 – 1318.71	25.71
1207.95 – 1208.46	23.56	1244.88 – 1245.38	24.28	1281.80 – 1282.30	25.00	1318.72 – 1319.23	25.72
1208.47 – 1208.97	23.57	1245.39 – 1245.89	24.29	1282.31 – 1282.82	25.01	1319.24 – 1319.74	25.73
1208.98 – 1209.48	23.58	1245.90 – 1246.41	24.30	1282.83 – 1283.33	25.02	1319.75 – 1320.25	25.74
1209.49 – 1209.99	23.59	1246.42 – 1246.92	24.31	1283.34 – 1283.84	25.03	1320.26 – 1320.76	25.75
1210.00 – 1210.51	23.60	1246.93 – 1247.43	24.32	1283.85 – 1284.35	25.04	1320.77 – 1321.28	25.76
1210.52 – 1211.02	23.61	1247.44 – 1247.94	24.33	1284.36 – 1284.87	25.05	1321.29 – 1321.79	25.77
1211.03 – 1211.53	23.62	1247.95 – 1248.46	24.34	1284.88 – 1285.38	25.06	1321.80 – 1322.30	25.78
1211.54 – 1212.05	23.63	1248.47 – 1248.97	24.35	1285.39 – 1285.89	25.07	1322.31 – 1322.82	25.79
1212.06 – 1212.56	23.64	1248.98 – 1249.48	24.36	1285.90 – 1286.41	25.08	1322.83 – 1323.33	25.80
1212.57 – 1213.07	23.65	1249.49 – 1249.99	24.37	1286.42 – 1286.92	25.09	1323.34 – 1323.84	25.81
1213.08 – 1213.58	23.66	1250.00 – 1250.51	24.38	1286.93 – 1287.43	25.10	1323.85 – 1324.35	25.82
1213.59 – 1214.10	23.67	1250.52 – 1251.02	24.39	1287.44 – 1287.94	25.11	1324.36 – 1324.87	25.83
1214.11 – 1214.61	23.68	1251.03 – 1251.53	24.40	1287.95 – 1288.46	25.12	1324.88 – 1325.38	25.84
1214.62 – 1215.12	23.69	1251.54 – 1252.05	24.41	1288.47 – 1288.97	25.13	1325.39 – 1325.89	25.85
1215.13 – 1215.64	23.70	1252.06 – 1252.56	24.42	1288.98 – 1289.48	25.14	1325.90 – 1326.41	25.86
1215.65 – 1216.15	23.71	1252.57 – 1253.07	24.43	1289.49 – 1289.99	25.15	1326.42 – 1326.92	25.87
1216.16 – 1216.66	23.72	1253.08 – 1253.58	24.44	1290.00 – 1290.51	25.16	1326.93 – 1327.43	25.88
1216.67 – 1217.17	23.73	1253.59 – 1254.10	24.45	1290.52 – 1291.02	25.17	1327.44 – 1327.94	25.89
1217.18 – 1217.69	23.74	1254.11 – 1254.61	24.46	1291.03 – 1291.53	25.18	1327.95 – 1328.46	25.90
1217.70 – 1218.20	23.75	1254.62 – 1255.12	24.47	1291.54 – 1292.05	25.19	1328.47 – 1328.97	25.91
1218.21 – 1218.71	23.76	1255.13 – 1255.64	24.48	1292.06 – 1292.56	25.20	1328.98 – 1329.48	25.92

Maximum Premium Deduction for a Pay Period of the stated frequency. Déduction maximale de prime pour une période de paie d'une durée donnée.		
Weekly - Hebdomadaire	11.80	
Bi-Weekly - Deux semaines	23.60	10 pp per year - 10 pp par année 61.35
Semi-Monthly - Bi-mensuel	25.56	13 pp per year - 13 pp par année 47.19
Monthly - Mensuellement	51.12	22 pp per year - 22 pp par année 27.89

Table 14.2 cont'd   Unemployment insurance premiums schedule.

BI-WEEKLY TAX DEDUCTIONS   **TABLE 2**   **RETENUES D'IMPÔT DE DEUX SEMAINES**
Basis — 26 Pay Periods per Year   Base — 26 périodes de paie par année

BI-WEEKLY PAY Use appropriate bracket — PAIE DE DEUX SEMAINES Utilisez le palier approprié		IF THE EMPLOYEE'S "NET CLAIM CODE" ON FORM TD1 IS *SI LE CODE DE DEMANDE NETTE DE L'EMPLOYÉ SELON LA FORMULE TD1 EST DE*										
From - De	Less than Moins que	0	1	2	3	4	5	6	7	8	9	10
		DEDUCT FROM EACH PAY — *RETENEZ SUR CHAQUE PAIE*										
896.-	912.	238.20	167.65	160.10	145.05	130.00	114.90	99.90	84.80	69.80	54.70	39.60
912.-	928.	242.40	171.70	164.15	149.10	134.05	118.95	103.95	88.85	73.80	58.75	43.65
928.-	944.	246.65	175.75	168.20	153.15	138.10	123.00	108.00	92.90	77.85	62.80	47.70
944.-	960.	250.85	179.80	172.25	157.20	142.15	127.05	112.00	96.95	81.90	66.85	51.75
960.-	976.	255.05	183.85	176.30	161.25	146.15	131.10	116.05	101.00	85.95	70.90	55.80
976.-	992.	259.30	187.90	180.30	165.30	150.20	135.15	120.10	105.05	90.00	74.90	59.85
992.-	1008.	263.50	191.95	184.35	169.35	154.25	139.20	124.15	109.05	94.05	78.95	63.90
1008.-	1024.	267.70	196.00	188.40	173.40	158.30	143.25	128.20	113.10	98.10	83.00	67.95
1024.-	1040.	271.95	200.05	192.45	177.45	162.35	147.25	132.25	117.15	102.15	87.05	72.00
1040.-	1056.	276.15	204.10	196.50	181.50	166.40	151.30	136.30	121.20	106.20	91.10	76.00
1056.-	1072.	280.35	208.10	200.55	185.55	170.45	155.35	140.35	125.25	110.25	95.15	80.05
1072.-	1088.	286.00	213.70	206.10	191.10	176.00	160.95	145.90	130.80	115.80	100.70	85.65
1088.-	1104.	292.45	220.05	212.50	197.45	182.40	167.30	152.25	137.20	122.15	107.10	92.00
1104.-	1120.	298.90	226.40	218.85	203.85	188.75	173.65	158.65	143.55	128.55	113.45	98.35
1120.-	1136.	305.35	232.80	225.20	210.20	195.10	180.05	165.00	149.90	134.90	119.80	104.75
1136.-	1152.	311.80	239.15	231.60	216.55	201.50	186.40	171.35	156.30	141.25	126.20	111.10
1152.-	1168.	318.25	245.50	237.95	222.90	207.85	192.75	177.75	162.65	147.65	132.55	117.45
1168.-	1184.	324.70	251.90	244.30	229.30	214.20	199.10	184.10	169.00	154.00	138.90	123.85
1184.-	1200.	331.15	258.25	250.70	235.65	220.55	205.50	190.45	175.40	160.35	145.30	130.20
1200.-	1216.	337.60	264.60	257.05	242.00	226.95	211.85	196.85	181.75	166.75	151.65	136.55
1216.-	1232.	344.05	271.05	263.50	248.45	233.40	218.30	203.25	188.20	173.15	158.10	143.00
1232.-	1248.	350.50	277.50	269.95	254.90	239.80	224.75	209.70	194.65	179.60	164.55	149.45
1248.-	1264.	356.95	283.95	276.40	261.35	246.25	231.20	216.15	201.10	186.05	171.00	155.90
1264.-	1280.	363.40	290.40	282.80	267.80	252.70	237.65	222.60	207.55	192.50	177.40	162.35
1280.-	1296.	369.85	296.85	289.25	274.25	259.15	244.10	229.05	214.00	198.95	183.85	168.80
1296.-	1312.	376.30	303.30	295.70	280.70	265.60	250.55	235.50	220.45	205.40	190.30	175.25
1312.-	1328.	382.75	309.75	302.15	287.15	272.05	257.00	241.95	226.85	211.85	196.75	181.70
1328.-	1344.	389.20	316.20	308.60	293.60	278.50	263.45	248.40	233.30	218.30	203.20	188.15
1344.-	1360.	395.65	322.65	315.05	300.05	284.95	269.90	254.85	239.75	224.75	209.65	194.60
1360.-	1376.	402.10	329.10	321.50	306.50	291.40	276.30	261.30	246.20	231.20	216.10	201.05
1376.-	1392.	408.55	335.55	327.95	312.95	297.85	282.75	267.75	252.65	237.65	222.55	207.50
1392.-	1408.	415.00	342.00	334.40	319.40	304.30	289.20	274.20	259.10	244.10	229.00	213.95
1408.-	1424.	421.45	348.45	340.85	325.85	310.75	295.65	280.65	265.55	250.55	235.45	220.35
1424.-	1440.	427.90	354.90	347.30	332.30	317.20	302.10	287.10	272.00	257.00	241.90	226.80
1440.-	1456.	434.35	361.30	353.75	338.75	323.65	308.55	293.55	278.45	263.45	248.35	233.25
1456.-	1472.	440.75	367.75	360.20	345.20	330.10	315.00	300.00	284.90	269.90	254.80	239.70
1472.-	1488.	447.20	374.20	366.65	351.65	336.55	321.45	306.45	291.35	276.35	261.25	246.15
1488.-	1504.	453.65	380.65	373.10	358.05	343.00	327.90	312.90	297.80	282.80	267.70	252.60
1504.-	1520.	460.10	387.10	379.55	364.50	349.45	334.35	319.35	304.25	289.25	274.15	259.05
1520.-	1536.	466.55	393.55	386.00	370.95	355.90	340.80	325.80	310.70	295.70	280.60	265.50
1536.-	1552.	473.00	400.00	392.45	377.40	362.35	347.25	332.25	317.15	302.10	287.05	271.95
1552.-	1568.	479.45	406.45	398.90	383.85	368.80	353.70	338.70	323.60	308.55	293.50	278.40
1568.-	1584.	485.90	412.90	405.35	390.30	375.25	360.15	345.15	330.05	315.00	299.95	284.85
1584.-	1600.	492.35	419.35	411.80	396.75	381.70	366.60	351.55	336.50	321.45	306.40	291.30
1600.-	1616.	498.80	425.80	418.25	403.20	388.15	373.05	358.00	342.95	327.90	312.85	297.75
1616.-	1632.	505.25	432.25	424.70	409.65	394.60	379.50	364.45	349.40	334.35	319.30	304.20
1632.-	1648.	511.70	438.70	431.15	416.10	401.00	385.95	370.90	355.85	340.80	325.75	310.65
1648.-	1664.	518.15	445.15	437.60	422.55	407.45	392.40	377.35	362.30	347.25	332.20	317.10
1664.-	1680.	524.60	451.60	444.00	429.00	413.90	398.85	383.80	368.75	353.70	338.60	323.55
1680.-	1696.	531.05	458.05	450.45	435.45	420.35	405.30	390.25	375.20	360.15	345.05	330.00
1696.-	1712.	537.50	464.50	456.90	441.90	426.80	411.75	396.70	381.65	366.60	351.50	336.45
1712.-	1728.	543.95	470.95	463.35	448.35	433.25	418.20	403.15	388.05	373.05	357.95	342.90
1728.-	1744.	550.40	477.40	469.80	454.80	439.70	424.65	409.60	394.50	379.50	364.40	349.35
1744.-	1760.	556.85	483.85	476.25	461.25	446.15	431.10	416.05	400.95	385.95	370.85	355.80
1760.-	1776.	563.30	490.30	482.70	467.70	452.60	437.50	422.50	407.40	392.40	377.30	362.25

Table 14.3 Biweekly tax deductions schedule.

SECTION REVIEW QUESTIONS

1. What is "gross pay"?
2. What is "net pay"?
3. What is the payroll equation?
4. Where are the payroll calculations made?
5. Explain the purpose of the social insurance number.
6. What is the simplest way to determine the deductions for the C.P.P.?
7. Explain how to find the deduction figure for the C.P.P.
8. Explain how to find the deduction figure for unemployment insurance.
9. Where does a person see what the maximum deduction figure is for unemployment insurance?
10. What is an R.R.S.P.?
11. Explain why it is more difficult to determine the deduction for income tax than it is for the Canada Pension Plan.
12. Where does one encounter the "total personal exemption" figure?
13. Where is the net claim code used?
14. On what two things does the income tax deduction depend?
15. What is a TD1 form?
16. Explain how taxable earnings are determined.
17. Explain how to read the income tax deduction tables.
18. Explain how to complete the payroll journal.
19. Describe three balances that can be performed to test the accuracy of the payroll journal.

SECTION EXERCISES

1. **1. In your Workbook, complete the schedule that appears below. Use Tables 14.1, 14.2, and 14.3 where necessary.**

Employee	Biweekly Gross Pay	C.P.P. Deduction	U.I.. Deduction	R.P.P.(5%) Deduction
F. Mazur	$930			
C. Koch	$950			
P. Parsons	$1 100			
G. Vittelli	$1 050			
Y. Van Del	$1 300			

2. For V. Van Del how many deductions for C.P.P. will be made during the year? What will be the amount of the final deduction?

2. Complete the following schedule in the Workbook. The payroll period is biweekly.

Net Claim Code	Gross Earnings	R.P.P. Deduction 6%	Union Dues	Taxable Earnings	Income Tax Deduction	C.P.P. Deduction	U.I. Deduction
10	1 150 –		15 –				
8	1 275 –		15 –				
5	1 325 –		15 –				
1	1 180 –		15 –				
2	1 230 –		15 –				
TOTALS							

3. In your Workbook, complete the line shown below. J. Bell is single, does not belong to a union, and has $100 000 of group life insurance coverage and full health insurance coverage. The rate of R.P.P. contribution is five per cent. The employer pays three-quarters of the health insurance and one-half of the group life.

Payroll Journal   For the two weeks ended June 10 19 --

Employee	Net Claim Code	Earnings			Deductions										
		Regular	Extra	Gross	R.P.P.	Union Dues	Taxable Earnings	Tax Deduction	C.P.P.	U.I.	Health Insce.	Group Life	Total Deductions	Net Pay
J. Bell	8	1310 –		1310 –										

4. Complete each of the following statements by writing in your Workbook the appropriate word or phrase from the list below.

a. An amount kept back from an employee's gross pay is known as a _____.

b. The amount of pay remaining after all deductions have been made is known as _____.

c. Payroll calculations are summarized in a book known as the _____.

d. Keeping back an amount from an employee's pay is called _____ it.

e. Certain payroll deductions are made on behalf of the federal government. The _____ system is used to keep track of all these deductions for all of the citizens of the country.

f. The deductions in question e. above are for _____, _____, and _____.

g. To assist employers in making the deductions in question f., above, the government provides _____.

h. The Canada Pension Plan deduction and the Unemployment Insurance deduction are based on the _____ figure.

i. For the Canada Pension Plan, there is a _____ figure after which no further deductions will be made for the year.

j. Employers, as well as employees, must _____ to the Canada Pension Plan and Unemployment Insurance funds.

k. A payroll made every two weeks is known as a _____ payroll.

l. The maximum unemployment insurance deduction for a _____ payroll period is $23.60.

m. A private pension plan that is approved by the government is known as a _____ pension plan.

n. An employee fills out a TD1 form in order to determine the _____ figure.

o. The _____ number is based on the figure arrived at in question n. above.

p. The deduction for income tax is not based on gross earnings. It is based on (estimated) _____ earnings.

q. The figure in question p. above is found by making deductions from the gross pay figure. These deduction are allowed by _____.

r. Most provinces operate a _____.

s. The payroll journal is a _____ journal and therefore must be _____.

List of Words and Phrases

biweekly	income tax	social insurance number
Canada Pension Plan	maximum	taxable
columnar	net claim code	total exemptions
contribute	net pay registered	unemployment insurance
cross balanced	payroll deduction	withholding
deduction tables	payroll journal	
gross pay	Revenue Canada	
health insurance plan	semi-monthly	

14.3   RECORDING THE PAYROLL

Once the payroll journal has been prepared and balanced, the payroll is recorded in the books of account. The following aspects of payroll must be considered:

1. the totals from the payroll journal;
2. the *employer's* contribution to the Canada Pension Plan;
3. the *employer's* contribution to the unemployment insurance fund;
4. the *employer's* contribution to the registered pension plan (if any);
5. the *employer's* contribution to health insurance (if any).

The accounting entries to record each of the above five aspects of payroll are explained on pages 590 and 591.

The Accounting Entries

1. The Totals from the Payroll Journal

Figure 14.19 shows the totals taken from the payroll journal of Nor-Can Grocers on p. 580, recorded in the form of a general journal entry.

		GENERAL JOURNAL			PAGE 43	
DATE		PARTICULARS	PR	DEBIT	CREDIT	
May¹⁹	24	Salaries Expense		6060 —		← The gross pay
		Reg. Pension Plan Payable			303 —	
		Union Dues Payable			50 —	Each of the credit items is a column total and represents a liability to be paid in the near future.
		Employees' Income Tax Payable			1034 40	
		Canada Pension Plan Payable			116 46	
		Unemployment Insurance Payable			118 18	
		Health Insurance Payable			54 —	
		Group Life Insurance Payable			155 —	
		Payroll Payable			4228 96	
		To record payroll totals for May 24, 19—				

Figure 14.19 Totals from the payroll journal recorded in the general journal.

2. The Employer's Contribution to the Canada Pension Plan

The government booklet about the Canada Pension Plan states, "Every employer is also required to make a contribution on behalf of employees equal to the contributions deducted from their remuneration." The payroll journal for Nor-Can Grocers Ltd. shows that the employees contributed $116.46 through payroll deductions. The employer must contribute an equal amount. Figure 14.20 shows the accounting entry for this recorded in the general journal. Observe the two aspects of this accounting entry:

1. There is an expense because the business has to pay out of its own funds;
2. There is a liability because the business owes the money. It has not been paid yet.

May	24	Canada Pension Plan Expense		116 46	
		Canada Pension Plan Payable			116 46
		Employer's C.P.P. contribution			

Figure 14.20 General journal entry to record employer's C.P.P. contribution.

3. The Employer's Contribution to Unemployment Insurance

The government booklet on Unemployment Insurance states, "Calculate the employer's premium at 1.4 times the employee's premium." The payroll journal for

Nor-Can Grocers Ltd. shows that the employees contributed $118.18 through payroll deductions. The employer must contribute this amount multiplied by 1.4; that is, $118.18 × 1.4 = $165.45. Figure 14.21 shows the accounting entry for this recorded in the general journal. Note the two aspects: the expense, and the liability.

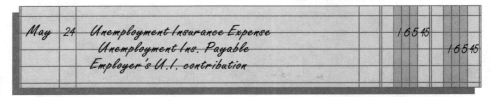

Figure 14.21   General journal entry to record employer's U.I. contribution.

4. The Employer's Contribution to the Registered Pension Plan

The agreement between Nor-Can Grocers Ltd. and its employees states that both the employees and the employer shall contribute equally to the registered pension plan. The payroll journal for Nor-Can Grocers Ltd. shows that the employees paid $303 to the registered pension plan through payroll deductions. The employer, therefore, is liable for an equal amount. Figure 14.22 shows the accounting entry for this recorded in the general journal.

May	24	Registered Pension Plan Expense	303 –	
		Reg'd Pension Plan Payable		303 –
		Employer's R.P.P. contribution		

Figure 14.22   General journal entry for employer's R.P.P. contribution.

5. The Employer's Contribution to Health Insurance

Nor-Can Grocers Ltd. and its employees agreed that the employer pays three-quarters and the employees pay one-quarter of the cost of health insurance. Thus the employer pays three times as much as the employees. The payroll journal for Nor-Can Grocers Ltd. shows that the employees paid $54.00 for health insurance through payroll deductions. Therefore, the employer must pay 3 × $54.00 = $162.00. Figure 14.23 shows the accounting entry for this recorded in the general journal.

May	24	Health Insurance Expense	162 00	
		Health Insurance Payable		162 00
		Employer's health insurance		
		contribution		

Figure 14.23   General journal entry for employer's health insurance contribution.

The Effect in the Accounts

Each of the five accounting entries in the previous section is posted to the accounts in the general ledger. Figure 14.24 shows the effect of these five accounting entries in the accounts involved.

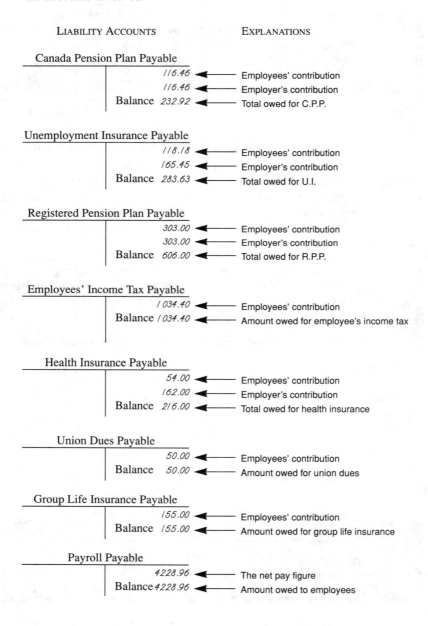

LIABILITY ACCOUNTS   EXPLANATIONS

Canada Pension Plan Payable

	116.46	◄——— Employees' contribution
	116.46	◄——— Employer's contribution
Balance	232.92	◄——— Total owed for C.P.P.

Unemployment Insurance Payable

	118.18	◄——— Employees' contribution
	165.45	◄——— Employer's contribution
Balance	283.63	◄——— Total owed for U.I.

Registered Pension Plan Payable

	303.00	◄——— Employees' contribution
	303.00	◄——— Employer's contribution
Balance	606.00	◄——— Total owed for R.P.P.

Employees' Income Tax Payable

| | 1 034.40 | ◄——— Employees' contribution |
| Balance | 1 034.40 | ◄——— Amount owed for employee's income tax |

Health Insurance Payable

	54.00	◄——— Employees' contribution
	162.00	◄——— Employer's contribution
Balance	216.00	◄——— Total owed for health insurance

Union Dues Payable

| | 50.00 | ◄——— Employees' contribution |
| Balance | 50.00 | ◄——— Amount owed for union dues |

Group Life Insurance Payable

| | 155.00 | ◄——— Employees' contribution |
| Balance | 155.00 | ◄——— Amount owed for group life insurance |

Payroll Payable

| | 4228.96 | ◄——— The net pay figure |
| Balance | 4228.96 | ◄——— Amount owed to employees |

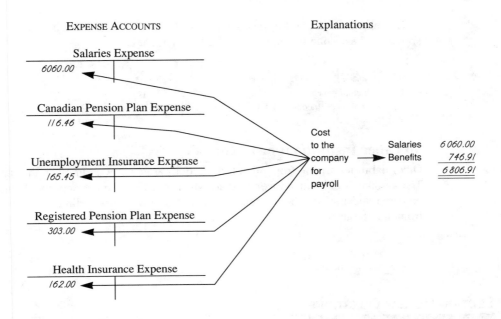

Figure 14.24   General ledger accounts with payroll entries recorded.

Payment of Payroll Liabilities

To the Federal Government

The amounts withheld from employees in any month for the federal government are to be paid by the 15th day of the following month. For example, deductions made in August are due by September the 15th, and so on. This regulation applies to the Canada Pension Plan, unemployment insurance, and personal income taxes. Cheques sent to the government of Canada are made out to the Receiver General for Canada.

A special two-part form, PD7AR (Tax Deduction—Canada Pension Plan—Unemployment Insurance Remittance Return), accompanies the payment. The upper portion is submitted along with the cheque. The lower portion is retained for the employer's own records. The payment may be made at a branch of a bank or sent to the appropriate taxation centre.

To determine the amount of the cheque, add the balances *for the month just ended* for the accounts shown below. Assume the amounts shown are the month-end balances.

Canada Pension Plan Payable	465.84
Unemployment Insurance Payable	567.26
Employees' Income Tax Payable	2 068.80
Total	3 101.90

One cheque is drawn for the combined amount of $3101.90 and is paid to the government. The accounting entry to record the payment is:

	DR	CR
Canada Pension Plan Payable	465.84	
Unemployment Insurance Payable	567.26	
Employees' Income Tax Payable	2068.80	
Bank		3101.90

To Other Institutions or Agencies

Other liabilities arising from payroll deductions are dealt with in much the same way. The amount is determined from the accounts. A cheque to the appropriate agency is prepared and issued. The accounting entry, as shown below, eliminates the liability from the accounts.

	DR	CR
Liability	$$$$	
Bank		$$$$

SECTION REVIEW QUESTIONS

1. Give five aspects of payroll that require accounting entries.
2. Not all of the columns in the payroll journal are used to work out the accounting entry. Explain why.
3. How much C.P.P. does the employer have to pay, relative to the employees?
4. How much U.I. does the employer have to pay, relative to the employees?
5. If the deduction from employees for U.I. is $100, how much will the employer have to pay?
6. Explain why there are liability accounts involved in payroll.
7. Explain why there is more than one expense account involved in payroll.
8. To whom is the cheque to the federal government made out?
9. Explain how the amount of the cheque to the federal government is calculated.
10. What form is prepared to accompany the above cheque?
11. In what two ways can one pay the federal government?
12. When is the cheque to the government due?

SECTION EXERCISES

1. The illustration on page 595 shows the final column totals from the payroll of Hudson Fisheries for the semi-monthly pay period ended October 15.

   1. **Given that the employer matches the employees' contributions for R.P.P. and pays 75 per cent of the health insurance, prepare the general journal entries to record this payroll.**
   2. **Post the journal entries for the above payroll to the T-accounts provided in the Workbook.**

Payroll Journal   For the 1/2 month ended October 15 19 --

Employee	Net Claim Code	Earnings			R.P.P.	Union Dues	Income Tax		C.P.P.	U.I.	Health Insce.	Group Life	Total Deductions	Net Pay
		Regular	Extra	Gross			Taxable Earnings	Tax Deduction						
TOTALS		9965 –	3225 90	13190 90	659 54	168 –	12363 36	2554 44	180 52	186 86	81 –	317 –	4147 36	9043 54

3. Journalize and post the accounting entry to pay the employees.

4. Given that the payroll for the next period is identical to the one above, post the second payroll for October to the T-accounts (all entries).

5. Journalize and post the accounting entry to pay the employees.

6. Answer the following questions.

   a. How much is owed to the federal government for the month of October?

   b. How much is owed to the health insurance agency for the month of October?

   c. Give the accounting entry for the payment in question a. above.

   d. Give the accounting entry for the payment in question b. above.

---

2. **Workbook Exercise: Answering questions with regard to payroll accounts.**

---

3. **Briefly answer each of the following questions.**

   1. The first pay period in February ends on the 14th. One of the payroll journal entries is the following:

	DR	CR
C.P.P. Expense	$184.00	
C.P.P. Payable		$184.00

   How much was deducted from the employees' pay for the Canada Pension Fund?

   2. In this same pay period the journal entry for unemployment insurance is the following:

	DR	CR
U.I. Expense	$212.80	
U.I. Payable		$212.80

   How much was deducted from the employees' pay for unemployment insurance?

   3. Assume that the payroll data for the second pay period in February is the same as the first. What will be the balances at the end of the month in each of the following accounts?

   a. Unemployment Insurance Expense

   b. Unemployment Insurance Payable

   c. Canada Pension Fund Expense

   d. Canada Pension Fund Payable

4. For the second payroll in February one of the journal entries was the following:

	DR	CR
Health Insurance Expense	$288.00	
Health Insurance Payable		$288.00

a. What was the amount of the employees' contribution for health insurance for the month if the insurance plan is as described in the text?

b. What will be the balances at the end of the month in each of the following accounts?

> Health Insurance Expense
> Health Insurance Payable

5. Using the group life insurance rates given in the text, calculate the insurance coverage for an employee from whom a payroll deduction of $37.50 was made in the second pay period.

14.4 PAYMENT TO EMPLOYEES

Paying by Cash

A few small companies still pay their employees with cash. When employees are paid in cash, the right number of bills and coins must be obtained to fill the envelopes. The first step is to prepare a currency requisition form such as that shown in Figure 14.25.

PAYROLL CURRENCY REQUISITION										PAY PERIOD ENDED May 24 19—
EMPLOYEE	NET PAY	$20	$10	$5	$1	25¢	10¢	5¢	1¢	
Harold Evans	833 65	41	1		3	2	1	1		
Ronald Fell	810 48	40	1			1	2		3	
Robert Funston	863 25	43			3	1				
Dennis Murray	871 95	43	1		1	3	2			
Les Williams	838 30	41	1	1	3	1		1		
NUMBER OF COINS OR BILLS		208	4	1	10	8	5	2	3	
DOLLAR VALUE	4217 63	4160	40	5	10	2	.50	.10	.03	

Figure 14.25   A completed payroll currency requisition form.

The completed currency requisition form is given to the bank together with a cheque made out for the total amount of the payroll. In return, the company receives cash in the denominations shown on the form and equalling the amount of the cheque. The accounting entry to record the cheque is:

	DR	CR
Payroll Payable	$$$$	
Bank		$$$$

The effect of this entry is to eliminate the liability in the Payroll Payable account.

The currency requisition form is also used when preparing the pay envelopes. The pay envelopes are filled with the bills and coins indicated on the form. Included with each pay envelope is a statement showing the employee's earnings, deductions, and net pay. This statement may be a separate statement or may be printed on the outside of the envelope. The employee's signature is obtained at the time of remuneration as proof of payment.

Paying by Cheque

Many businesses, especially firms with a large number of employees, prefer to pay by cheque rather than by cash. This eliminates the problem of having large sums of money around. Also, the cancelled cheques serve as evidence that the employees did receive their pay.

The cheques for the employees may be drawn from the company's regular bank account or from a special payroll bank account established for payroll cheques only.

Regular Bank Account

A separate cheque, drawn on the regular bank account, is issued to each employee. The accounting entry for each cheque, when recorded in the cash payments journal, is:

	DR	CR
Payroll Payable	$$$$	
Bank		$$$$

The sum of all of the individual payroll cheques issued will be equal to the total of the Net Pay column of the payroll journal. Since each cheque results in a debit to the Payroll Payable account, they will effectively eliminate the credit balance in this liability account.

Special Payroll Bank Account

To allow the payroll department to independently issue its own payroll cheques, many businesses set up a separate payroll bank account.

Under this method, only one cheque is drawn on the regular bank account each pay period for the amount of the total net pay. In the cash payments journal the accounting entry to record the cheque is:

	DR	CR
Payroll Payable	$$$$	
Bank		$$$$

This cheque is given to the payroll department. It is cashed by depositing it in the special payroll bank account. This provides the funds for the payroll department to meet its obligations for one pay period.

The payroll department then issues its own payroll cheques to the employees. No accounting entries are required for these payroll cheques. When they are all cashed, the balance in the payroll bank account will be reduced to zero.

However, some employees are slow to cash their cheques. Often, before all of the cheques are cashed, a new payroll cycle begins with the deposit for the next payroll. Thus the payroll bank account might never actually reach the stage where it has a zero balance.

Paying by Bank Transfer

A business can arrange with the bank to pay its employees by bank transfer. With this method, the bank deducts the amount of the total payroll from the company's account and transfers the amounts of the individual pays to the accounts of the firm's employees. The company will supply the bank with the bank account data of its employees and, for each pay period, a list of their individual earnings and the total payroll figure. Naturally, the business is charged for the service.

The accounting entry to record the payment is the same as for paying by cash:

	DR	CR
Payroll Payable	$$$$	
Bank		$$$$

SECTION REVIEW QUESTIONS

1. What are two uses for the currency requisition form?
2. Explain how the currency requisition form is balanced.
3. When paying employees by cash, what is it important to obtain in return?
4. Why do most businesses prefer to pay their employees by cheque or bank transfer?
5. Most businesses who pay their employees by cheque prefer to set up a special "payroll" bank account. Why would they prefer this method?
6. No accounting entries are required for payroll cheques issued on a special payroll bank account. Explain why.

SECTION EXERCISES

1. **Workbook Exercise: Preparing a currency requisition form.**

2. Shown below and on page 600, and in your Workbook are certain records of Central Supply House of Altona, Manitoba. These records pertain to the company's payroll bank account.

A. The reconciliation statement for the payroll bank account as at February 28, 19—.

CENTRAL SUPPLY HOUSE
BANK RECONCILIATION
PAYROLL ACCOUNT
FEBRUARY 28, 19—

Balance per bank statement			$3 269.42
Deduct outstanding cheques			
	#1201	$502.16	
	#1210	372.42	
	#1237	906.16	
	#1242	726.42	
	#1243	316.20	
	#1244	446.06	3 269.42
True bank balance			nil

B. Payroll cheques issued during the month of March.

PAY PERIOD ENDED MARCH 14,19—			PAY PERIOD ENDED MARCH 28, 19—	
No.	*Amount*		*No.*	*Amount*
1245	$530.72		1258	$512.36
1246	602.17		1259	614.50
1247	741.02		1260	854.23
1248	600.00		1261	745.19
1249	375.16		1262	725.32
1250	475.02		1263	651.32
1251	550.12		1264	845.71
1252	615.18		1265	245.16
1253	705.19		1266	258.94
1254	695.00		1267	865.34
1255	712.99		1268	258.78
1256	232.16		1269	896.54
1257	312.13		1270	358.56
Total	$7 146.86		Total	$7 831.95

C. Payroll account bank statement for the month of March 19—.

Cheques and Charges			Deposits	Date	Balance
CENTRAL BANK Downtown Centre Winnipeg, Manitoba					
In account with: Central Supply House					
Balance Forward					$3 269.42
(#1210) 372.42	(#1237)	906.16		Mar 3	
(#1242) 726.42	(#1201)	502.16		Mar 3	$ 762.29
(#1244) 446.06				Mar 6	$ 316.20
			7 146.86	Mar 14	$7 463.06
(#1245) 530.72	(#1248)	600.00		Mar 15	
(#1246) 602.17	(#1249)	375.16		Mar 15	
(#1247) 741.02	(#1251)	550.12		Mar 15	$4 063.87
(#1253) 705.19	(#1254)	695.00		Mar 16	
(#1255) 712.99				Mar 16	$1 950.69
(#1243) 316.20				Mar 21	$1 634.49
(#1256) 232.16				Mar 25	$1 402.33
(#1250) 475.02			7 831.95	Mar 28	$8 759.26
(#1258) 512.36	(#1259)	614.50		Mar 31	
(#1262) 725.32	(#1265)	245.16		Mar 31	
(#1267) 865.34	(#1269)	896.54		Mar 31	$4 900.04

Prepare a bank reconciliation statement for the above as of March 31, 19—.

---

3. A simplified payroll is given below.

Employee	Gross Pay	Deductions					Net Pay
		CPP	UI	RPP	Tax	Union	
Mary Aduono	500	10	12	50	56	6	366
Beth Demitrio	550	11	13	55	60	6	405
Joan Pasquale	480	9	11	48	50	6	356
Bruno Wyotick	540	10	12	54	62	6	376
	2 070	40	48	227	228	24	1503

Briefly answer each of the following questions regarding the above payroll.

1. How much would be deducted from the bank to cover this payroll if it were paid in cash?

2. Give the accounting entry to record the payment of this payroll if it were paid in cash.

3. Give the accounting entry to record the payment of this payroll if it were paid by cheques drawn on a special payroll bank account.

4. Give the accounting entry to record the payment of this payroll if it were paid by bank transfer.
5. Why is a cheque for payroll drawn on the general bank account if the payroll is paid for by means of special payroll cheques?
6. What is the amount of the cheque in question 4 above?

14.5 BASIC PAYROLL RECORDS

You are aware by now of the importance of written records in the accounting process. There are a number of important records produced by the payroll department. Three of these are:

1. the payroll journal;
2. the payroll cheque, or payroll cash statement;
3. the employee's earnings record.

Payroll Journal

You are familiar with the payroll journal. It is shown in Figure 14.18. It is prepared for each pay period and used to accumulate all of the figures for each pay period.

The Payroll Journal as a Book of Original Entry

So far, the payroll journal has been used as a summary sheet. As a result, it has been necessary to journalize the totals from the payroll journal into the general journal.

Some business firms use the payroll journal as a book of original entry. Certain column totals are posted directly from the payroll journal to the general ledger. When this system is used, it is still necessary to process payroll entries 2, 3, 4, and 5 as described in section 14.3, Recording the Payroll. These entries record the employer's share of employee benefits. There is no standard way of handling this. The method used is left to the discretion of the accountant.

Payroll Cheques or Payroll Cash Statements

Most businesses pay their employees by cheque. Attached to each cheque is a tear-off portion that shows the employee's gross pay, the various deductions, and the net pay. A payroll cheque is shown in Figure 14.26.

Businesses that prefer to pay their employees by cash use a payroll cash statement. It serves the same purpose as the voucher portion of the payroll cheque. It indicates the earnings, the various deductions, and the net pay. When payment is made by cash, a signature must be obtained from each employee.

NAME	1200.00		120.00	60.00	10.00	210.20	23.04	23.40	12.00	25.00	363.64	836.36
DETACH AND RETAIN THIS STATEMENT OF YOUR EARNINGS AND DEDUCTIONS FOLD BEFORE DETACHING	Regular Earnings	Extra Earnings	GROSS PAY	R.P.P	UNION DUES	Income Tax	C.P.P.	U.I.	HEALTH INSCE	GROUP LIFE	TOTAL DEDUC.	NET PAY

NOR-CAN GROCERS LIMITED
3880-5th St , Castlegar, B.C V1N 2E9

PAYROLL   1371

Date *Jan.28*   19*89*

Miscellaneous
Deductions

PAY TO THE ORDER OF _Harold Evans_ $ *836.36*

THE SUM OF *Eight Hundred & Thirty-six and* ————— *36/100* Dollars

NATIONAL BANK OF CANADA

NOR-CAN GROCERS LIMITED

Harold Evans

A._____

B._____

C._____

0:162410000400:   0455000083003000

Figure 14.26   A payroll cheque for Harold Evans.

Employee's Earnings Record

The employer must keep track of many details with respect to each employee's earnings. The **employee's earnings record** form is used to accumulate payroll details every payday, individually by employee. This form is illustrated in Figure 14.27.

NAME Evans, *Harold J.*   SIN *609 779 152*   EXEMPTION CODE *3*   DATE OF BIRTH *Feb 9,19- MARITAL*

ADDRESS   MARITAL STATUS *M*   DEPENDANTS *2*   DEPARTMENT

2000 5th St.

Castlegar B.C.   DATE STARTED: May 10,19-

V1N 2E9   DATE LEFT

PHONE *1-604* *444-4444*

	DATE	STANDARD EARNINGS		STANDARD DEDUCTIONS							
	Jan.4	1200	1200	60-	10-	210.20	23.04	23.04	12-	25-	

		1	2	3	4	5	6	7	8	9	10	11	12	13	14	15	16
		NET CLAIM	EARNINGS			DEDUCTIONS											INSURED
DATE	EMPLOYEE	CODE	REGULAR	EXTRA	GROSS	R.P.P.	Union Dues	Tax	C.C.P.	U.I.	Health Insce	Group Life	TOTAL DEDUC'S	NET PAY	CHQ NO	C.P.P. TO DATE	EARNINGS TO DATE
1/14	*Evans HJ*	3	1200		1200	60-	10-	210.20	23.04	23.40	12-	25-	363.64	836.36	1291	23.04	1200
1/28	*Evans HJ*	3	1200		1200	60-	10-	210.20	23.04	23.04	12-	25-	363.64	836.36	1371	46.08	2400
2/11	*Evans HJ*	3	1200		1200	60-	10-	210.20	23.04	23.04	12-	26-	363.64	836.64	1452		3600

Figure 14.27   An earnings record form for Harold Evans.

At the end of the calendar year, the column totals of the employee's earnings record provide the information necessary for the T4 slips. A T4 slip must be prepared for every employee, and represents a summary of the employee's earnings and deductions for one year. This form is required for income tax purposes. Copies of the T4 slips are sent to Revenue Canada, and given to the employees.

A T4 slip is shown in Figure 14.28.

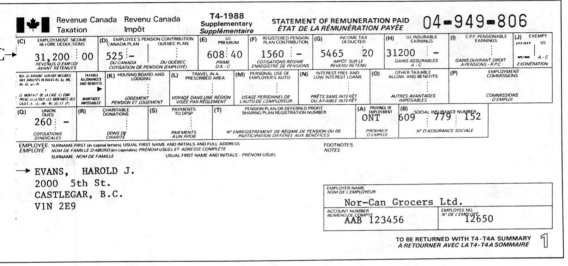

Figure 14.28   A T4 slip for Harold Evans.

SECTION REVIEW QUESTIONS

1. Name the three important payroll records discussed in this section.
2. Explain how the payroll journal can be used as a book of original entry.
3. How do employees who are paid in cash learn of the details of their pay?
4. How do employees who are paid by cheque learn of the details of their pay?
5. What is an employee's earnings record?
6. What is the purpose of the employee's earnings record?
7. What is the purpose of the T4 slip?
8. Three parties obtain copies of the T4 slip. Who are they?

SECTION EXERCISES

1. Mary Watson started work with the Empire Company of Medicine Hat, Alberta, on January 1 at a salary of $1 125 for every two weeks. Mary received two $100 pay raises during the year. The first took place after 20 weeks. The second took place after 40 weeks. Part of Mary's employee's earnings record card is shown below.

Date	Employee	Net Claim Code	Earnings			Deductions							Net Pay
			Reg	Extra	Gross	Pension	Union	Income Tax	CPP	UI	Health Insce	United Appeal	
Jan 14	Mary Watson	4	1125.00		1125.00	56.25	10.00	170.45	21.36	21.94	24.00	5.00	816.00
June 3	Mary Watson	4	1225.00		1225.00	61.25	10.00	207.85	23.46	23.60	24.00	5.00	869.84
Oct 21	Mary Watson	4	1325.00		1325.00	66.25	10.00	246.25	25.56	23.60	24.00	5.00	924.34

1. Calculate the following yearly totals for Mary Watson:
   a. gross pay;
   b. Canada Pension Plan;
   c. unemployment insurance;
   d. registered pension plan;
   e. income tax.
2. For which pay period was the last C.P.P. deduction for the year made? What was the amount of this last deduction?
3. Why did the deduction for unemployment insurance not increase when Mary received her third raise?

---

2. Given on page 605 is the employee's earnings record for Carol Mann for the period from January 1 to December 31, 19—.

1. From this record determine the figures that would be entered on the T4 slip in the following boxes.
   a. Box C   Employment Income Before Deductions
   b. Box D   Employee's Pension Contribution Canada Plan
   c. Box E   U.I. Premium
   d. Box F   Registered Pension Plan Contribution
   e. Box G   Income Tax Deducted
2. Explain why the CPP deductions were changed starting in the month of August.

NAME Carol Mann		S.I.N.	723 852 487				
Date	Gross Pay	CPP	UI	RPP	Inc Tax	Other	Net Pay
Jan 31	3 500.00	68.85	61.35	175.00	611.70	125.56	2 457.54
Feb 28	3 500.00	68.85	61.35	175.00	611.70	125.56	2 457.54
Mar 31	3 500.00	68.85	61.35	175.00	611.70	125.56	2 457.54
Apr 30	3 500.00	68.85	61.35	175.00	611.70	125.56	2 457.54
May 31	3 500.00	68.85	61.35	175.00	611.70	125.56	2 457.54
Jun 31	3 500.00	68.85	61.35	175.00	611.70	125.56	2 457.54
Jul 31	3 500.00	68.85	61.35	175.00	611.70	125.56	2 457.54
Aug 31	3 500.00	43.05	61.35	175.00	611.70	125.56	2 483.34
Sep 30	4 000.00		61.35	200.00	803.55	125.56	2 809.54
Oct 31	4 000.00		61.35	200.00	803.55	125.56	2 809.54
Nov 30	4 000.00		61.35	200.00	803.55	125.56	2 809.54
Dec 31	4 000.00		61.35	200.00	803.55	125.56	2 809.54

CHAPTER HIGHLIGHTS

Now that you have completed Chapter 14, you should:

1. understand the nature of accounting for payroll;
2. know the three most common methods of paying employees and how to make the calculations for each method;
3. be able to determine common payroll deductions and read government tables of deductions for income tax, unemployment insurance, and the Canada Pension Plan;
4. understand the purpose of the TD1 form;
5. know how to determine the employer's contribution for unemployment insurance, Canada Pension Plan, and other employee benefits;
6. know how to prepare basic payroll records: the payroll, the payroll cheque or cash statement, and the employee's earnings record;
7. know the accounting entries to record a complete payroll;
8. understand that employees' deductions out of payroll, and the employer's obligatory contributions, are to be remitted to the appropriate government department or other organization;
9. understand how the T4 slip is prepared from the employee's earnings record.

ACCOUNTING TERMS

commission	registered pension plan (R.P.P.)
employee's earnings record	registered retirement savings plan (R.R.S.P.)
gross pay	salary
net pay	timecard
payroll	total personal exemption
payroll journal	T4 slip
payroll register	wages

CHAPTER EXERCISES

Using Your Knowledge

1. A blank payroll journal for this exercise appears in the Workbook.

   1. **Prepare the payroll journal from the data given below for the two weeks ending August 12, 19—. Use rates and rules as given in the text if not stated otherwise.**

      a.

Employee	Hours Worked Wk.1	Wk.2	Net Claim Code	Hourly Rate	Health Insurance Coverage	Life Insurance Coverage
Axelson, A.	40	48	9	$12.00	Family	$ 50 000
Jones, P.	40	40	1	15.00	Single	100 000
Koehler, M.	40	40	3	14.00	Family	50 000
Peterson, S.	46	46	5	13.00	Family	100 000
Sauve, R.	40	40	4	14.50	Single	75 000

      b. Each employee is enrolled in the registered pension plan with contributions set at four per cent of the gross pay. The employer matches the employees' contributions.

      c. Union dues are set at $8.00 for each employee per pay period.

      d. The employer pays 75 per cent of health insurance coverage.

   2. **Total the columns of the payroll journal and perform the steps to ensure its accuracy.**

   3. **Journalize the accounting entries to record the five aspects of the payroll and to pay the employees by means of one cheque to the payroll bank account.**

2. Workbook Exercise: Additional payroll calculation exercise.

3. A blank payroll journal for this exercise appears in the Workbook.

   1. **Prepare the payroll journal from the data given below for the two weeks ending January 20, 19—. Use rates and rules as given in the text except where stated otherwise.**

a. Each of the employees listed below is employed by E-Z Trading Company. They are paid every two weeks. Those in the warehouse are paid on an hourly basis. The sales people are paid a salary plus commission.

For the warehouse workers, a regular work week is 40 hours. They belong to the IAM union and pay union dues of $10 each pay period. Overtime is paid at the rate of time and a half.

The salespeople are paid a basic salary of $350 per pay period. They also receive a commission of two per cent of their sales for the period. Salespeople do not belong to the union.

Employee	Net Claim Code	Hours	Hourly Rate	Net Sales	Health Insurance Status	Group Insurance Coverage
Cower, I.	4	80	15.00		Single	$100 000
Durand, D.	6	84	15.00		Married	$100 000
Hansen, W.	8	87	14.00		Married	$50 000
Kuchma, E.	2	86	14.00		Single	$75 000
Milani, M.	5			40 500	Married	$100 000
Nyman, G.	3			47 000	Married	$90 000
Sutherland, T.	9			42 500	Married	$80 000

b. The rate of contribution to the registered pension plan for employees is five per cent of gross pay. The employer contributes one and a half times the amount paid by the employees.

c. The employer pays two-thirds of the health insurance costs.

d. Group life insurance is paid for entirely by the employees at the rate of 35 cents for each $1 000 of coverage.

2. Complete and balance the payroll journal.

3. Journalize the accounting entries to record the five aspects of the payroll and to pay the employees by means of one cheque made out to the payroll bank account. Wages and salaries are kept in separate accounts.

Comprehensive Exercises

4. Karen Paquette of Carman, Manitoba, has been in business for several years. Given on p. 608 are selected ledger accounts for her business. Shown in these accounts are all of the accounting entries affecting payroll for the month of February.

Answer the following questions regarding the accounting entries.

1. What is the total cost related to payroll for the month of February?
2. Explain the credit entry of $3 050 in the bank account.
3. What is the length of the payroll period?
4. Explain the debit entry of $750 in the Hospital Insurance Payable account.
5. What fraction of the total cost of hospital insurance does the company pay?
6. To what extent does the employer contribute to the employees' pension fund?
7. How often is payment made by the company for hospital insurance?
8. Give the amount of the cheque that will be sent to the federal government in March.

Bank	
8 225	
3 050	
8 680	
750	
2 010	

C.P.P. Payable	
740	190
	190
	200
	200

Wages Expense	
10 000	
10 500	

U.I. Payable	
920	210
	294
	230
	322

C.P.P. Expense	
190	
200	

R.P.P. Payable	
2 010	500
	500
	505
	505

U.I. Expense	
294	
322	

Income Tax Payable	
1 390	750
	760

R.P.P. Expense	
500	
505	

Hospital Insurance Payable	
750	125
	250
	125
	250

Hospital Insurance Expense	
250	
250	

Payroll Payable	
8 225	8 225
8 680	8 680

---

5. Shown below are the summary figures for the first four payrolls for Precision Company. These are followed by additional information.

Payroll Summaries

Pay Date	Gross Pay	C.P.P.	U.I.	R.P.P.	Income Tax	Health	Union	Net Pay
Jan 14	5 700	98	101	285	560	75	50	4 531
Jan 28	5 400	90	97	270	520	75	50	4 298
Feb 11	5 800	99	103	290	570	75	50	4 613
Feb 25	5 900	100	105	295	580	75	50	4 695

Additional Information

1. Use the rules set out in the chapter. Round off to the nearest dollar where necessary.
2. The company matches the R.P.P. contribution and pays three-quarters of the health insurance.
3. Payment for health insurance is made on the 15th of the following month.
4. Payments for R.P.P. and Union are made at the end of every second month.
5. Assume that the bank balance always has sufficient funds on hand to make the payments.
6. The accounts needed for this exercise are those shown below. They are set up for you in the Workbook.

Bank	Payroll Payable
Canada Pension Plan Payable	Wages Expense
Unemployment Insurance Payable	Canada Pension Plan Expense
Registered Pension Plan Payable	Unemployment Insurance Expense
Employees' Income Tax Payable	Registered Pension Plan Expense
Health Insurance Payable	Health Insurance Expense
Union Dues Payable	

1. **Record all accounting entries for these four payrolls for the period from January 1 to March 15. Record these entries directly into the T-accounts in your Workbook without using a journal. Record the entries in their correct order.**
2. **Calculate the total expense of these four payrolls. Show that this total expense figure is equal to the total paid out in cash.**

For Further Thought

6. Briefly answer each of the following questions.

1. In the government booklet for the Canada Pension Plan there is a summary of types of employment and benefits that are subject to C.P.P. contributions. What steps would you take to resolve a doubt you had about a certain kind of employment?
2. Give one definite advantage of being paid by the hour.
3. Usually there is at least a one-week delay in paying employees. What do you think is the reason for this?
4. From the employee's point of view, are payroll deductions all negative things? Explain.
5. With insurance in general, the greater the risk you are, the more you pay. For example, if you have a number of speeding convictions, your car insurance premium increases. In some cases, your insurance might be cancelled. In view of the above, is it right to regard unemployment insurance as "insurance"? Explain.
6. The unemployment insurance booklet states that the premium rate for employees is 1.95 per cent. The employer pays 1.4 times the amount paid by the employee. What is the employer's true rate?

7. Why do you think there are registered pension plans when there is already the Canada Pension Plan?

8. Income taxes are deducted from each pay during the year on an estimated basis. How does the government eventually get the right amount from each person?

9. Management and unions are often adversaries. Why would management agree to deduct union dues for the benefit of a union which it considers to be an opponent?

10. Explain why the true balance of a payroll bank account is theoretically zero.

11. Matt Cook's T4 slip indicates that his employer has withheld $5 260 for income tax from his earnings for the year. When Matt prepares his income tax return, he discovers that the total tax he has to pay is only $4 830. How can this happen?

12. Maxwell Company's payroll is due to be paid this afternoon. The payroll amounts to $22 565 but Maxwell Company has only $14 275 in its general bank account. Should Maxwell Company be concerned about this, and to what degree? Explain. What steps should Maxwell Company be taking in regard to this situation?

CASE STUDIES

CASE 1   *Comparing Wage Increases*

The following salaries and wages are paid by the Magic Tape Company.

Employee		*Salary or Wage*
General Manager:	P. Sanderson	$180 000
Plant Workers:	M. Bailey	18 000
	B. Dorst	19 000
	N. Gehrals	28 000
	V. Ripley	35 000

The owner of this company, P. Epps, grants a 10 per cent pay raise to the plant employees to cover a 10 per cent rise in the cost of living. Sanderson, the general manager, argues that what applies to the plant employees also applies to him, and he puts in a request for a 10 per cent pay increase.

Questions

1. Comment on Sanderson's request, using some simple calculations or figures.

2. Are percentages a fair way to compare earnings?

CASE 2   *Wage Increase—How Much Can Be Offered?*

You are the proprietor of Brite Cleaners. The following data are extracted from your most recent income statement.

Revenue:	Cleaning	$134 900
	Storage	5 974
	Tailoring	30 500
		$171 374
Expenses:	Rent	$ 4 800
	Delivery	2 930
	Wages	104 300
	Supplies used	3 250
	General expense	1 975
	Depreciation	7 560
	Power	4 250
		$129 065
	Net Income	$ 42 309

The employees have requested a 20 per cent increase in wages.

Questions
1. Assuming that no other expense is affected, how much would the wage increase cost the company?
2. Can you grant this request and still make a profit, based on the above statement?
3. How much would the net income be if the increase were granted?
4. You want to make at least $30 000 per year from the business, and you expect an increase of $5 000 in revenue for the coming year. Calculate the maximum increase that you can grant to your employees, expressed in dollars and as a percentage. Assume there is no increase in other expenses.

CASE 3   *Dummy Employees on the Payroll*

Armco is a very large developer of homes in the Toronto area. At the present time, the company is engaged in the building of several large subdivisions in five different locations. The company has several hundred field workers on its payroll.

Because they work on the sites, the field workers rarely have occasion to visit the head office. Also, there is considerable turnover of staff in this industry. Consequently, to the payroll department, the field workers are just names, not faces.

The field workers are paid by the hour but do not punch a time clock. Their hours are kept on individual time sheets by the supervisors on the various jobs. Once a week, the supervisors bring the time sheets to head office and give them directly to Pat Pasco, the paymaster.

Pat Pasco is technically a very good paymaster. She has a lot of experience and knows all there is to know about payroll. She keeps absolute control over everything that happens in her department and sees to it that the department is run smoothly and efficiently.

The time sheets received by Pat from the supervisors are turned over to payroll clerks to be processed. However, before handing them over, Pat slips in a couple of phony timesheets. These phony timesheets show fictitious names, addresses, social insurance numbers, etc. The payroll department processes the phony sheets along with all of the legitimate ones. When the payroll is completed and the cheques ready, they are all given to Pat for her signature.

Pat signs the cheques and forwards them to the supervisors who in turn distribute them to the workers. Of course, the two phony cheques are removed by Pat for herself. Pat is smart enough to have established a way of cashing the cheques, adjusting the payments to the government, and so on. She also sees to it that from time to time the phony employees leave and new ones begin working for Armco. She seems to have all the bases covered.

Questions

1. In your opinion, is this scheme possible? Give reasons why you think so.
2. If you answered "Yes" to question 1, how long do you think the scheme could go undetected? In your opinion, how might it be detected?

CASE 4   *A Profit-Sharing Proposal*

A.

You are the accountant for Sayers & Company, a successful and growing company. The company has just completed its sixth fiscal year of operation. Its income statement for 19-6 is shown below in abbreviated form.

Sayers & Company
Income Statement
Year Ended December 31, 19–6
(Figures in thousands)

Revenue		$2 000
Operating Expenses		
Wages	$ 400	
Other Expenses	1 280	
Total Expenses		1 680
Net Income		$ 320

The company is presently engaged in wage negotiations with its union. There have been persistent difficulties between the union and the company, resulting in one strike and several other disruptions. At the present time, the union is demanding a 10 per cent wage increase retroactive to the beginning of the 19-6 year.

The owner is frustrated by the union versus management confrontations. She hopes to eliminate them by introducing a plan which ties employees' wages to company profits.

She makes the following proposal to the employees.

> *Sayers & Company*
> *Profit-Sharing Plan*
>
> Item 1. The employees will terminate their connection with the union.
> Item 2. There will be no more wage negotiations.
> Item 3. The total wages figure for every fiscal year will be fixed — at 60 per cent of the *income before wages figure* (net income plus wages).
> Item 4. The plan will be retroactive to January 1, 19–6.
> Item 5. The plan is expected to foster harmony, increase productivity, and keep the number of employees to a minimum. It is to the employees' benefit to keep their numbers as low as they can.

Questions

1. From the income statement on p. 612, calculate the wages as a percentage of the *income before wages* figure.
2. Prepare a revised income statement for 19-6 based on the owner's profit-sharing formula.
3. **a.** Give the increase in wages for 19-6 if the employees accept the profit-sharing proposal.
   b. Calculate the percentage wage increase for 19-6.
4. Explain the employer's claim that the employees will benefit if they keep their numbers down.

B.

As part of the discussions with the employees, the owner reveals the company's forecasts for the next three years. These are as follows:

	19-7	19-8	19-9
Revenue	2 100	2 200	2 500
Other Expenses (excluding wages)	1 320	1 400	1 580

Questions

5. Using the above data, prepare a schedule showing the projected income statements side by side for the years 19-6, 19-7, 19-8, and 19-9 on the assumption that the profit-sharing plan is accepted.
6. Based on the projected data, show the percentage wage increases for 19-7, 19-8, and 19-9. This is done by using the following calculation:

$$\frac{\text{increase in wages for the year}}{\text{wages figure for prior year}} \times 100$$

7. Calculate the average percentage increase for the three years 19-7, 19-8, and 19-9.

8. In terms of wage increases only, explain why employees should or should not accept the profit-sharing proposal.

C.

Assume that the employees did accept the owner's profit-sharing proposal. Also, assume that the years 19-7, 19-8, and 19-9 have been concluded and the actual figures for these years are now known. Some of these figures are given below.

	19-7	19-8	19-9
Revenue	2 150	2 280	2 350
Other Expenses	1 320	1 390	1 400

Questions

9. Complete a side-by-side schedule of the income statements for the years 19-6, 19-7, 19-8, and 19-9 based on the actual data.

10. Comparing this data with the projected data worked out previously, give your opinion as to whether the profit-sharing plan has been a financial success. Consider both the employees' and the employer's point of view. In your analysis include a calculation of the average percentage increase in wages for 19-7, 19-8, and 19-9. Also, investigate some of the benefits that unions provide workers. Take these into account before making an overall recommendation concerning the proposal.

CASE 5 *Employee's Wages—How Much?*

The Cycle and Sports Centre is the foremost repair centre for bicycles in the community. There is never a shortage of repair work, and there is always a large backlog of repair work waiting to be done. The Centre depends on this repair work for a substantial portion of its revenue.

One summer, the business hires George Sumac, a university student, to repair bicycles on a part-time basis. George suggests that he and the owners split the repair bills on a 50-50 basis. This will not include any charges for the bicycle parts that the store supplies. The owners, a father and son, agree to the suggestion.

This arrangement works fine in the first season. George turns out to be an exceptional worker. He repairs bicycles quickly and thoroughly. Customers rarely complain about his work. As George becomes more experienced, however, he begins to turn out a greater volume of work. The more work that George turns out, the more he earns in wages. George earns $14 000 in his second year, and $17 000 in his third. The owners, particularly the father, become increasingly concerned. They are not used to paying part-time workers $17 000 in a season.

The owners meet with George to discuss the situation. The father insists that George is overpaid and will have to take a smaller percentage. George argues that he actually works on a piecework basis. He may earn good money, but his work merits it. The more he earns, the more the company earns as well.

The father is unable to accept George's arguments. George refuses to take a cut and gives up his job.

Questions

1. Is the father justified in his claim that the amount paid for part-time work is excessive?
2. Is George right to refuse to take a cut in pay?
3. What will the owners have to do now that George is gone?
4. What factors are the store owners ignoring?
5. Can the store make more money without George's services?

CAREER
Thu Vinh Lan / Senior Payroll Supervisor

Thu Vinh Lan arrived in Canada with his family when he was 11 years old. While in high school, he decided that a business education would improve his chances of a successful career in his new country. Thu began preparing for a business career by taking a number of accounting courses. After graduating from high school, he continued this preparation by completing a three-year business administration diploma at a local community college.

After college, Thu worked for a General Motors dealership. There, his duties included the control of the general ledger and the preparation of the financial statements.

For the past five years, Thu has been employed by Suburban Metal Industries, a medium-sized manufacturing company, as the senior payroll supervisor.

Each week, Thu prepares the payroll for salaried personnel. On each

employee's master sheet, he records days worked, vacation pay, rate changes, hospitalization charges, sick leave, changes in personal income tax exemptions, and so on. All this information is then summarized and fed into the computer so that salary cheques can be issued. Two other payroll clerks, under Thu's supervision, prepare the payroll in an identical manner for employees who are paid hourly wages.

Thu is responsible for a payroll of 220 employees who work on salary. In addition, he prepares the confidential payrolls for the executive officers of the company at the head and regional offices. Thu also calculates the commissions earned by the salespeople and sales agents, and supervises the typing and mailing of the commission statements.

Each month, he arranges payroll deductions for the Canada Pension Plan, unemployment insurance, income tax, union dues, hospitalization, and the company pension plan. At the end of each month, Thu determines the total wages, salaries, and commissions paid during the month and sends these figures to the accounting department for entry in the general journal. Finally, at the end of each year, he sees that T4 slips are typed and sent to all employees.

In the computerized payroll system for Suburban Metal Industries, the entries for pay and deductions are based on the employee's classification, such as mechanic, assembly line, or maintenance worker, and so on. For each employee, the number of regular and overtime hours is keyed into the computer. This input is automatically sorted by means of employee number and department. The computer prints out the total amount of the cheques issued so that Thu can transfer the proper amount of money to the special payroll account.

As supervisor of payroll, Thu coordinated the changeover from a manual to a computerized payroll system, and redesigned his department to take full advantage of the computer. This was a great challenge for him, and he considers today an exciting time to be an accountant.

DISCUSSION

1. List the information that Thu records on each employee's master sheet. Is this sheet similar to an employee's earnings record?
2. What is the purpose of a special payroll account?
3. Why are the payroll records for the executive officers of a company usually confidential?
4. Describe and state the importance of a T4 slip.
5. As senior payroll supervisor, Thu has the responsibility over all the payroll accounts. Prepare a payroll chart of accounts for Suburban Metal Industries and classify each account. Your chart should contain at least 10 accounts.

15

End-of-Period Accounting

15.1 Accountability
15.2 Adjusting for Depreciation
15.3 Adjusting for Doubtful Accounts
15.4 Adjusting for Accrued Expenses
15.5 Reversing Entries

In Chapter 9 you learned about the process of making adjustments at the end of a fiscal period for prepaid expenses and for late-arriving invoices. As well, you learned how to complete an eight-column work sheet and the classified financial statements.

In this chapter you will learn how to handle some additional adjustment situations. Further, you will learn how management has an obligation to provide proof of its performance.

15.1 ACCOUNTABILITY

Accounting data are used in many ways. Perhaps the most important use is to provide the information for the financial statements. It is through the financial statements that managers of companies carry out an important function known as accountability. **Accountability** is the company officers' obligation to show how well they have been managing the company. Management must provide evidence of its performance. This is required by law, agreement, or custom.

Users of Financial Statements

There are five groups who are the most common users of financial statements. The groups are:

1. Managers Managers probably use the financial statements more than any other group. They carefully study the statements in order to improve results and efficiency, and to eliminate weaknesses. The statements help them make key business decisions.

2. *Owners*   Many owners are not directly involved in managing their companies. They use financial statements to evaluate the performance of the people who run the company for them, as well as to learn about company activities in general.

3. *Creditors*   Creditors, particularly bankers, ask for financial statements regularly. They use them to stay informed about a company's progress, and its ability to meet its loan obligations. Bankers make sure that they are ready to act swiftly to protect their loans.

4. *Shareholders*   The law requires that corporations provide their shareholders with financial statements regularly. The shareholders are the real owners of the company. They must be made aware of its progress.

5. *Investors and brokers*   Shares of public corporations are traded by stockbrokers through stock exchanges. The employees of stock brokerage companies, and potential investors, stay informed about the affairs of corporations by reading their financial reports.

Quality of Financial Statements

As was pointed out above, accounting statements are very important to various groups of individuals. Naturally, these groups will expect statements that are accurate, complete, up-to-date, and reliable. It is for this reason that the accounting profession has established the body of accounting standards known as generally accepted accounting principles. These standards play an important part in the accountability process. The reader of financial statements—absentee owner, banker, shareholder, or other—should be able to read the statements with confidence. To make sure that the standards are being met, most companies are required to have an independent audit. An **audit** is a critical review by a public accountant of the internal controls and accounting records of a company. The audit makes it possible to evaluate the fairness of a company's financial statements.

Before you can produce top-notch financial statements, there are additional generally accepted accounting principles that you must learn.

GAAP—The Consistency Principle

The **consistency principle** requires that **accountants must use the same methods and procedures from period to period**. If they change a method from one period to another they must say so clearly on the financial statements. The readers of financial statements have the right to assume that consistency has been applied unless they are notified of some change in procedure.

The consistency principle prevents people from manipulating figures on financial statements by changing methods of accounting. For example, consider the case of a contracting company that records revenue when payments are received, not when invoices are issued. If this company has a bad year, it would be wrong to make the results look better by including some revenue for invoices issued but not paid for.

GAAP—The Materiality Principle

The **materiality principle** provides that **accountants must follow generally accepted accounting principles except when to do so would be expensive, or difficult, and where it makes no real difference if the rules are ignored**. If a rule is temporarily ignored, the net income of the company must not be significantly affected, nor should the reader's ability to judge the financial statements be impaired.

For example, suppose that an invoicing error for $50 was discovered by a company that had just received its financial statements from the printer. Assume also that the error affected the net income of approximately $350 000 shown on the financial statements. In this case, no effort would be made to correct the error because the $50 is not significant in relation to the net income figure of $350 000.

GAAP—The Full Disclosure Principle

The **full disclosure principle** provides that **all information needed for a full understanding of the company's financial affairs be included in the financial statements**. Some items may not affect the ledger accounts directly. These would be included in the form of accompanying notes.

For example, suppose that a chemical company was being sued for millions of dollars by employees claiming that their health was ruined by working for the company, which had assured them that no danger existed. Assume also that the company would suffer seriously if it lost the lawsuit. This information must be revealed to the reader of the financial statements by means of an accompanying note.

Other examples of items that might require an accompanying note are tax disputes and company takeovers.

SECTION REVIEW QUESTIONS

1. What is probably the most important use for accounting data?
2. What is meant by accountability?
3. Give reasons why managers require financial statements.
4. Name five groups of individuals who use financial statements.
5. Why would an absentee owner want financial statements for his or her business?
6. Why do bankers insist on financial statements from businesses to which they lend money?
7. Why do corporations provide their shareholders with financial reports?
8. Why do stockbrokers obtain copies of financial reports of public companies?
9. Why are users of financial statements able to rely on them?
10. Give another expression for "accounting standards."
11. What is an audit? What is its purpose?
12. What two things does the auditor seek to do when performing an audit?
13. Explain the consistency principle.
14. Explain the materiality principle.
15. Explain the full disclosure principle.

SECTION EXERCISE

1. Briefly answer the following questions.

1. Who is required by law to provide financial statements as evidence of account-ability?
2. Who would provide financial statements as evidence of accountability even though not legally required to do so?
3. Give three ways that management would use data from the financial statements. Do not include normal daily routines.
4. What can an absentee owner do if he or she is not satisfied with the results of the business as shown on the financial statements?
5. How else (besides reading the financial reports) could an absentee owner stay informed of company activities?
6. Banks sometimes take swift action to protect a loan that they believe has gone bad. What action do you think that they would take?
7. Usually banks obtain "security" before giving a loan. What does this mean?
8. If a bank loan is secured, why is it sometimes still necessary to take swift action?
9. What might banks insist on so as to be sure they have been given reliable financial statements?
10. What can a shareholder who is not happy with the progress of a corporation do about it?
11. Compare what can be done in question 10 above with what can be done in question 4 above.
12. Assume that you lost a large sum of money in a business deal. Assume further that you relied on information from audited financial statements, some of which proved to be misleading. What might you do about this?

15.2 *ADJUSTING FOR DEPRECIATION*

The Nature of Depreciation

Assets that are bought, not to resell but to use to produce revenue over several fiscal periods, are known as "fixed assets." Assets of this type are also known as "long-lived assets," "capital equipment," and "plant and equipment."

With the exception of land, every fixed asset is expected to be used up in the course of time and activity. Thus it decreases or depreciates in value. *Depreciation* normally refers to the decrease in value of an asset over time.

The following example shows how depreciation works: Assume that a person pur-chases a new truck at a cost of $24 000 in order to begin a delivery business. After operating for five years, the business is closed down. As part of closing down the business, the owner sells the truck (now used) for $1 500. Clearly, over the five-year period, the truck cost the business $22 500 ($24 000 – $1 500). Just as clearly, the truck was needed to carry on the business.

The $22 500 cost of the truck cannot be ignored. It is part of the true profit picture of the business. Theoretically, the $22 500 must be considered an expense of the business at the rate of $4 500 ($22 500/5) for each of the five years. The profit picture of the company over its five-year life might then look like this:

	19-1	19-2	19-3	19-4	19-5
Revenues	$57 560	$65 250	$68 354	$65 270	$59 230
Expenses					
Depreciation Truck	$ 4 500	$ 4 500	$ 4 500	$ 4 500	$ 4 500
Other Expenses	36 750	38 256	39 954	42 570	45 320
Total Expenses	$41 250	$42 756	$44 454	$47 070	$49 820
Net Income	$16 310	$22 494	$23 900	$18 200	$ 9 410

The schedule shows that the $22 500 net cost of the truck has been spread evenly over its five-year life. This is how depreciation works. Each year that the company benefited from the truck's use has been charged with $4 500, an equal portion of its cost. **Depreciation** can be thought of as allocating a part of the cost of an asset as an expense for each accounting period during which the business uses that asset.

Calculating Depreciation

It is not possible to calculate depreciation exactly until the end of the asset's life. Only then can you say how many years it was used, and what its final worth was. But accountants and business people cannot wait until then. The depreciation must be included on every income statement. So depreciation must be estimated while the asset is still in use.

Straight-line Depreciation

The simplest way of estimating depreciation is the straight-line method. The **straight-line method of depreciation** divides up the net cost of the asset equally over the years of the asset's life. For this method, the following formula is used:

$$\text{Straight-line depreciation for one year} = \frac{\text{Original cost of asset} \;\; \text{less} \;\; \text{Estimated salvage value}}{\text{Estimated number of periods in the life of the asset}}$$

The following two examples show how the calculation works.

1. Tip Top Trucking purchased $78 000 of automotive equipment on January 1, 19-2. It estimated that the assets would be useful for six years. At the end of that time, the equipment would have a market value of $7 800.

   Applying the formula to these data gives the following calculation:

   $$\text{Estimated annual depreciation} = \frac{\$78\ 000 - \$7\ 800}{6} = \$11\ 700$$

This gives an estimated annual depreciation figure of $11 700 for Automotive Equipment. The figure is the same each year.

2. Tip Top Trucking purchased $5 120 of furniture and equipment on January 1, 19-2. The company estimated that the assets would be useful for 10 years, at which time they would have a market value of $500.

Applying the formula to these data gives the following calculation:

$$\text{Estimated annual depreciation} \quad = \quad \frac{\$5\ 120 \quad - \quad \$500}{10} \quad = \quad \$462$$

This gives an estimated annual depreciation figure of $462 for Furniture and Equipment. The figure is the same each year.

Depreciation for Part Year   The above calculations were for a full year. Sometimes an asset is used for only part of a year. Then further calculation is necessary. This can happen if the asset is purchased or disposed of during the year. It may also happen if the fiscal period being reported on is shorter than one year.

Consider the following example. The Edwards Company purchases a building on May 1, 19-5 for $120 000. The building is expected to be used for 30 years, after which it will be worth $30 000. The Edwards Company prepares quarterly financial statements (that is, it issues statements every three months).

The annual depreciation for the above building is ($120 000 – $30 000)/30, which is $3 000. The quarterly depreciation is $3 000/4 or $750. However, in the first statement period after the purchase of the asset, it had only been in use for two months. Therefore, depreciation for only two months can be charged to this period. This amount is $500.

Declining-Balance Method of Depreciation

There is more than one way of calculating depreciation. The declining-balance method is common because the government of Canada requires it on statements that are submitted for income tax purposes. A company that does not use the declining-balance method must modify the financial statement that it sends to the government.

The **declining-balance method of depreciation** calculates the annual depreciation by multiplying the remaining undepreciated cost of the asset by a fixed percentage. In the first year, the undepreciated cost is equal to the purchase price (capital cost). The percentage figures set by the government are shown in the table below.

GOVERNMENT OF CANADA RATES OF DEPRECIATION		
Class	*Description*	*Rate*
3	Buildings of brick, stone, or cement	5%
6	Buildings of frame, log, or stucco	10%
8	Office furniture and equipment	20%
10	Trucks, tractors and automotive equipment	30%
29	Manufacturing and processing equipment	50%

To see how declining-balance depreciation is calculated, assume that a truck is purchased on January 1, 19-1 for $22 000. The table on page 623 shows that the rate to be used is 30 per cent.

Year 1

For the 19-1 fiscal year the depreciation = $22 000 × 30% = $6 600.

Summary:	Undepreciated cost before depreciation	$22 000
	Less depreciation for 19-1	6 600
	Undepreciated cost at end of 19-1	$15 400

Year 2

For the 19-2 fiscal year the depreciation = $15 400 × 30% = $4 620

Summary:	Undepreciated cost before depreciation	$15 400
	Less depreciation for 19-2	4 620
	Undepreciated cost at end of 19-2	$10 780

Year 3

For the 19-3 fiscal year, the depreciation = $10 780 × 30% = $3 234

Summary:	Undepreciated cost before depreciation	$10 780
	Less depreciation for 19-3	3 234
	Undepreciated cost at end of 19-3	$ 7 546

The annual calculations continue in this way until the truck is sold, or until its remaining (undepreciated) cost equals its estimated scrap value.

Comparison of the Two Methods

The two schedules below show how the depreciation for the above asset would be calculated under the straight-line and the declining-balance methods. Assume the truck was expected to last for eight years and have an ending value of $2 000.

Straight-line method		
Year	**Depreciation**	**Undepreciated Cost**
Original cost		$22 000
1	$2 500	19 500
2	2 500	17 000
3	2 500	14 500
4	2 500	12 000
5	2 500	9 500
6	2 500	7 000
7	2 500	4 500
8	2 500	2 000

Declining-balance method		
Year	**Depreciation**	**Undepreciated Cost**
Original cost		$22 000
1	$6 600	15 400
2	4 620	10 780
3	3 234	7 546
4	2 264	5 282
5	1 585	3 697
6	1 109	2 588
7	776	1 812
8	544	1 268

The straight-line method produces depreciation figures that are the same each year. Over the estimated life of the asset its book value is gradually reduced until it reaches its estimated final value. Only one calculation is necessary.

The declining-balance method produces depreciation figures that are larger in the early years and smaller in the later years. Estimated final value is ignored when using this method. A new calculation is necessary every year.

The Adjusting Entry for Depreciation

The adjusting entry for depreciation has two aims. These are:

1. to reduce the asset account by the amount of the depreciation;
2. to set up the depreciation figure in a depreciation expense account.

However, this is not done in the manner you would expect. The reduction in the value of the asset is not made in the asset account. Rather, it is made in a separate "accumulated depreciation" account known as a contra account. A **contra account** is one that must be considered along with a given asset account in order to show the true book value of the asset account. A contra account is also known as a "valuation" account. A contra account always has a type of balance (debit or credit) that is opposite to the account it is associated with.

The following sequence shows how the accumulated depreciation account is used together with the asset account. The data in the straight-line table on page 624 are used in the example.

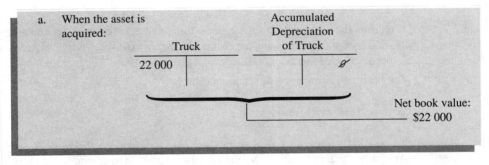

a. When the asset is acquired:

Truck: 22 000

Accumulated Depreciation of Truck: 0̸

Net book value: $22 000

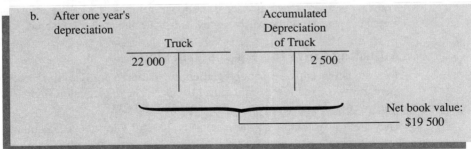

b. After one year's depreciation

Truck: 22 000

Accumulated Depreciation of Truck: 2 500

Net book value: $19 500

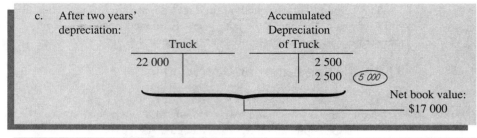

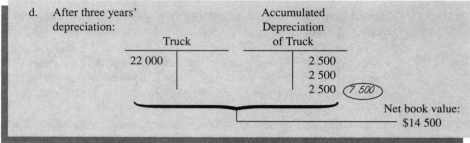

This pattern continues.

The adjusting entry for depreciation:

1. records the depreciation for the period in a depreciation expense account;
2. increases the appropriate depreciation account for the asset. This reduces the net book value of the asset.

The basic adjusting entry for depreciation is:

	DR	CR
Depreciation Expense	$$$$	
Accumulated Depreciation (of Asset)		$$$$

As you will recall, adjusting entries are first recorded on the work sheet. To demonstrate how to handle the adjusting entries for this chapter, the work sheet of Tip Top Trucking is used. This work sheet is shown in Figure 15.1. The adjusting entries for prepaid expenses and late-arriving invoices have already been entered.

Adjusting Entry for Tip Top Trucking

Two adjusting entries for depreciation are required for Tip Top Trucking because there are two fixed assets on the trial balance. The depreciation figures for these two items were calculated previously on page 622 and 623.

They are: for Automotive Equipment, $11 700; for Furniture and Equipment, $462.

The adjusting entries to record the depreciation for Tip Top Trucking are:

	DR	CR
1. Depreciation of Automotive Equipment	$11 700	
Accumulated Depreciation—Automotive Equipment		$11 700
2. Depreciation of Furniture and Equipment	$462	
Accumulated Depreciation—Furniture and Equipment		$462

Tip Top Trucking	Work Sheet						Year Ended Dec. 31, 19-4	
ACCOUNTS	TRIAL BALANCE		ADJUSTMENTS		INCOME STATEMENT		BALANCE SHEET	
	DR.	CR.	DR.	CR.	DR.	CR.	DR.	CR.
Bank	1575.07							
Accounts Receivable	28316.40							
Allowance for Doubtful Debts		56.05						
Supplies	1725.50			① 1200.50			525—	
Prepaid Insurance	3895—			② 2647—			1248—	
Furniture and Equipment	5120—							
Accum. Deprec. Furn. & Equip.		924—						
Automotive Equipment	78000—							
Accum. Deprec. Auto. Equip.		23400—						
Accounts Payable		4675.10		③ 643.50				5318.60
Loan Payable - 10%		25000—						
R. Hansen, Capital		41256.64						
R. Hansen, Drawings	48000—							
Revenue		226742.90						
Interest Expense	625—							
Light, Heat, Water	3820—							
Miscellaneous Expense	1974—		③ 127.50		2101.50			
Rent	24000—							
Telephone	2165—							
Truck Expense	52631.12		③ 516—		53147.12			
Wages	70207.60							
	322054.69	322054.69						
Supplies Used			① 1200.50		1200.50			
Insurance Expense			② 2647—		2647—			

Figure 15.1   The partially completed work sheet for Tip Top Trucking, with the adjusting entries for prepaid expenses and late-arriving invoices already entered.

You can see these recorded (coded 4) on the work sheet for Tip Top Trucking in Figure 15.2.

Depreciation on the Financial Statements

The financial statements for Tip Top Trucking appear on pages 646 and 647. Look ahead to these statements and you will see:

1. depreciation expense on the income statement;
2. accumulated depreciation deducted from its respective asset account to show the net book value of the asset.

Tip Top Trucking	Work Sheet						Year Ended Dec. 31, 19-4	
ACCOUNTS	TRIAL BALANCE		ADJUSTMENTS		INCOME STATEMENT		BALANCE SHEET	
	DR.	CR.	DR.	CR.	DR.	CR.	DR.	CR.
Bank	1575.07							
Accounts Receivable	28316.40							
Allowance for Doubtful Debts		56.05						
Supplies	1725.50			(1) 1200.50			525 —	
Prepaid Insurance	3895 —			(2) 2647 —			1248 —	
Furniture and Equipment	5120 —							
Accum. Deprec. Furn. & Equip.		924 —		(4) 462 —				1386 —
Automotive Equipment	78000 —							
Accum. Deprec. Auto. Equip.		23400 —		(4) 11700 —				35100 —
Accounts Payable		4675.10		(3) 643.50				5318.60
Loan Payable - 10%		25000 —						
R. Hansen, Capital		41256.64						
R. Hansen, Drawings	48000 —							
Revenue		226742.90						
Interest Expense	625 —							
Light, Heat, Water	3820 —							
Miscellaneous Expense	1974 —		(3) 127.50		2101.50			
Rent	24000 —							
Telephone	2165 —							
Truck Expense	52361.12		(3) 516 —		53147.12			
Wages	70207.60							
	323054.69	323054.69						
Supplies Used			(1) 1200.50		1200.50			
Insurance Expense			(2) 2647 —		2647 —			
Depreciation Furn. & Equip.			(4) 462 —		462 —			
Depreciation Auto & Equip.			(4) 11700 —		11700 —			

Figure 15.2 Work sheet for Tip Top Trucking showing adjusting entries for depreciation.

SECTION REVIEW QUESTIONS

1. Define depreciation.
2. What is the purpose of depreciation from an accountant's point of view?
3. Why is it not possible to make a precise calculation of depreciation until the end of the asset's useful life?
4. What is the simplest depreciation method?
5. What depreciation method is required by Revenue Canada for income tax purposes?
6. Give the formula for calculating straight-line depreciation.
7. Describe how to calculate declining-balance depreciation.
8. How is depreciation for partial years handled?

9. Give the basic adjusting entry for depreciation.
10. How is a depreciable asset represented in the ledger accounts?
11. What is a contra account?

SECTION EXERCISES

1. **In your Workbook, for each of the following situations, allocate the total cost to the proper fiscal periods. Assume a company that commenced business on January 1, 19-1 and has a fiscal year-end of December 31.**

   1. A truck was purchased on January 1, 19-1 for $18 000. It was expected to last for five full years at the end of which it would have a trade-in value of $3 000. Use the straight-line method of depreciation.

19-1	19-2	19-3	19-4	19-5

   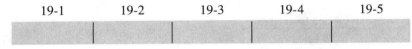

   2. A used vehicle was bought on November 1, 19-1 for $5 800. It was expected to last for four full years, at the end of which it would have a resale value of $1 000. Use the straight-line method of depreciation.

19-1	19-2	19-3	19-4	19-5

   3. A building was purchased on May 1, 19-2 for the sum of $113 000. It was expected to last for 25 years, at which time it would have a resale value of $5 000. Use the straight-line method of depreciation.

19-1	19-2	19-3	19-4	19-5

   4. A new machine was bought on January 1, 19-1 for $54 000. It is depreciated using the declining-balance method at the rate of 20 per cent.

19-1	19-2	19-3	19-4	19-5

   5. A new building was bought on July 1, 19-1 for $282 000. It is depreciated using the declining-balance method at the rate of five per cent.

19-1	19-2	19-3	19-4	19-5

2. A company purchases equipment costing $100 000 which it expects to last for seven years and have a salvage value of $5 500.

    1. For the use of management, prepare a depreciation schedule for the first five years of the asset's life showing depreciation calculated on a straight-line basis.

    2. Prepare a depreciation schedule for the first five years of the asset's life showing depreciation calculated on a declining-balance basis at the government rate of 20 per cent.

3. This exercise appears in your Workbook.
The general ledger of Salk Company of Banff, Alberta, at the end of its annual fiscal period appears below.

    1. Using the additional information that is provided, record the year-end adjusting entries directly in the T-accounts.

    2. Prepare an adjusted trial balance.

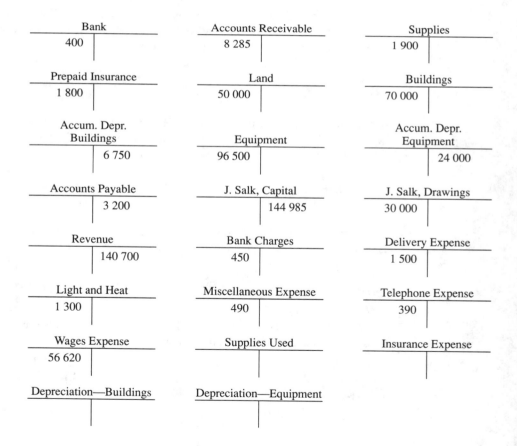

Bank		Accounts Receivable		Supplies	
400		8 285		1 900	

Prepaid Insurance		Land		Buildings	
1 800		50 000		70 000	

Accum. Depr. Buildings		Equipment		Accum. Depr. Equipment	
	6 750	96 500			24 000

Accounts Payable		J. Salk, Capital		J. Salk, Drawings	
	3 200		144 985	30 000	

Revenue		Bank Charges		Delivery Expense	
	140 700	450		1 500	

Light and Heat		Miscellaneous Expense		Telephone Expense	
1 300		490		390	

Wages Expense		Supplies Used		Insurance Expense	
56 620					

Depreciation—Buildings		Depreciation—Equipment	

Additional Information:

1. Inventory of supplies at the year-end is $850.
2. Unexpired insurance at the year-end is $625.
3. Depreciation is calculated on a straight-line basis. The building is expected to last 40 years, at which time it will be worth $25 000. The equipment is expected to last 15 years, after which it will be worth $6 500.

---

4. **Workbook Exercise: Recording adjusting entries directly into T-accounts.**

---

5. The following work sheet also appears in your Workbook. It contains a number of errors. **Locate the errors, correct them, and balance the work sheet.**

Pinnacle Company — Work Sheet — Year Ended Dec. 31, 19-

ACCOUNTS	TRIAL BALANCE DR.	TRIAL BALANCE CR.	ADJUSTMENTS DR.	ADJUSTMENTS CR.	INCOME STATEMENT DR.	INCOME STATEMENT CR.	BALANCE SHEET DR.	BALANCE SHEET CR.
Bank	3170 -							
Accounts Receivable	19473 -							
Supplies	1850 -			1200 -			1850 -	
Prepaid Insurance	4795 -			3130 -			7925 -	
Land	70000 -							
Building	90750 -						90750 -	
Accumulated Depreciation Bldg.		12943 22		3890 34				16833 56
Office Equipment	17350 -						17350 -	
Accumulated Depreciation O.E.		8466 80		1776 64				10243 44
Automotive Equipment	38429 50						38429 50	
Accumulated Deprec. Auto. Eq.		25248 18		3954 40				3954 40
Accounts Payaable		7216 10		362 -				7216 10
Bank Loan		15000 -				15000 -		
Mortgage Payable		100000 -				100000 -		
S. Bloom, Capital		62483 40						62483 40
S. Bloom, Drawings	25000 -					25000 -		
Sales		99374 10				99374 10		
Bank Charges	1640 30				1640 -			
Car Expenses	7316 50		157 -		7473 50			
Light, Heat & Water	6017 -				6017 -			
Miscellaneous Expense	1536 -		95 -		1631 -			
Property Taxes	2250 -				2250 -			
Telephone	1847 -		110 -		1957 -			
Wages	39307 50				39703 50			
	330731 80	330731 80						
Supplies Used			1200 -					
Insurance Expense			3130 -					
Deprec. Office Equipment			1776 64					
Deprec. Auto Equipment			3954 40					
					58672 -	239374 10	156367 50	100730 90
					180702 10			155636 60
					239374 10	239374 10	156367 50	156367 50

6. **From the trial balance and additional information shown below, complete the work sheet in the Workbook for the year ended September 30, 19-4 for Karen Denby, proprietor of a real estate business in Gimli, Manitoba.**

KAREN DENBY, REAL ESTATE
TRIAL BALANCE
SEPTEMBER 30, 19-4

Bank	$ 3 800	
Accounts Receivable	10 000	
Supplies	500	
Prepaid Insurance	1 000	
Prepaid Licences	400	
Land	50 000	
Building	70 000	
Accumulated Depreciation—Building		$ 5 600
Furniture and Equipment	15 000	
Accumulated Depreciation—Furniture and Equipment		4 000
Automotive Equipment	17 000	
Accumulated Depreciation—Automotive Equipment		6 300
Accounts Payable		400
Bank Loan		100 000
Karen Denby, Capital		40 000
Karen Denby, Drawings	30 000	
Commissions Revenue		96 600
Advertising Expense	4 700	
Bank Charges	8 600	
Car Expenses	8 000	
Commissions Expense	18 000	
Light and Heat Expense	2 200	
Miscellaneous Expense	200	
Postage Expense	600	
Telephone Expense	900	
Wages Expense	12 000	
	$252 900	$252 900

Additional Information:

1. The supplies inventory at September 30 is $200.
2. The prepaid insurance schedule shows a value of $300 for prepaid insurance.
3. The prepaid licences figure in the trial balance represents a licence fee of $200 each for two cars. These fees are for the calendar year.
4. Depreciation is calculated on a straight-line basis.

   The building is expected to have a useful life of 50 years after which its value will be $5 000.

   The furniture and equipment are expected to have a useful life of 15 years after which they will have a value of $900.

   The automobiles are expected to have a useful life of five years after which they will have a value of $1 250.

7. Tom Michaud is in the plastering business under the name of Tom's Plastering. **From the following trial balance and additional information, prepare the work sheet and the financial statements in your Workbook for Tom's Plastering for the year ended October 31, 19-1.**

TOM'S PLASTERING
TRIAL BALANCE
OCTOBER 31, 19-1

	DR	CR
Bank	$ 1 412.01	
Accounts Receivable	8 025.00	
Supplies	1 416.70	
Small Tools	1 903.00	
Prepaid Insurance	2 107.80	
Equipment	9 500.00	
Accumulated Depreciation—Equipment		$ 3 200.00
Truck	19 500.00	
Accumulated Depreciation—Truck		8 000.00
Accounts Payable		2 407.35
Bank Loan		10 000.00
Tom Michaud, Capital		18 212.28
Tom Michaud, Drawings	35 534.00	
Revenue		120 365.00
Bank Interest and Charges	1 325.15	
Materials Used	25 369.20	
Miscellaneous Expense	756.32	
Rent Expense	6 000.00	
Telephone Expense	864.32	
Truck Expense	8 325.40	
Utilities Expense	4 563.26	
Wages Expense	35 582.47	
	$162 184.63	$162 184.63

Additional Information:

1. Office supplies on hand at October 31 are valued at $360.
2. Unexpired insurance at October 31 is calculated at $510.95.
3. Depreciation is calculated using the straight-line method. All assets were on hand for the entire year.

    The equipment cost $9 500 and was expected to last for 10 years. It was estimated that it would be worth $1 500 at that time.

    The truck cost $19 500 and was expected to last for five years. It was estimated that it would be worth $3 500 at that time.
4. Late bills pertaining to the 19-1 year were as follows:

Supplies	$ 56.20
Miscellaneous Expense	26.85
Truck Expense	563.85
Total	$646.90

5. The small tools at October 31 are valued at $350. The tools represented by the difference between the $350 figure and the trial balance figure have been lost, stolen, or used up.

6. Of the $25 369.20 shown on the trial balance under Materials Used, $2 850 is still on hand and unused.

15.3 ADJUSTING FOR DOUBTFUL ACCOUNTS

Businesses that sell on credit take a certain risk. No matter how carefully the customers' credit ratings are checked out, there are always some customers who cannot or do not pay. Business people are quite aware of this, and yet they continue to sell on credit. Overall, there must be a net benefit or they would not do so. The gain from increased sales must be greater than the loss resulting from failure to collect.

A customer's account is first seen as doubtful if it becomes overdue. A **doubtful account**, or **doubtful debt**, is one that the business does not feel certain it will collect. The longer an account is overdue, the less likely it is to be collected, and therefore the more doubtful it is.

A business must decide what to do with doubtful accounts when preparing its financial statements. There are two reasons for this.

1. The business must show any losses from doubtful accounts as expenses in the same period as the sale was recorded. This is required by the matching principle.

2. The business probably will not collect some of the accounts in its accounts receivable ledger. These *doubtful* accounts should not be included in the total of accounts receivable for the balance sheet. The business must deduct them to arrive at the estimated true value of accounts receivable for the balance sheet. This is required by the principle of conservatism.

For example, assume that a business owner hears that a customer may be going bankrupt. He examines the accounts receivable ledger and discovers that the customer owes $2 000. He realizes that he may recover only a small portion of this sum. When the statements are prepared, the accountant will show the $2 000 as a doubtful debt.

Accounts Receivable Aging Schedule

At the end of each accounting period, an accounts receivable aging schedule is prepared. An **accounts receivable aging schedule** is a breakdown of customers' accounts showing how long the balances have been unpaid. It can be prepared by hand or by computer. The doubtful accounts figure comes from this schedule. An example of an aging schedule is shown in Figure 15.3.

The Allowance for Doubtful Debts Account

At the end of every accounting period an adjusting entry is necessary for the doubtful accounts. This adjustment causes the accounts to reflect the estimated true value of the accounts receivable. It is done by setting up the doubtful accounts figure as a credit balance in a *contra* account called Allowance for Doubtful Debts. The estimated true value of the accounts receivable is shown by the Accounts Receivable account and the Allowance for Doubtful Debts account taken together. This is shown below for Tip Top Trucking based on the doubtful accounts figure from the schedule in Figure 15.3.

Accounts Receivable		Allowance for Doubtful Debts	
28 316.40			1 430.00

The estimated true value of accounts receivable of
$26 886.40 is shown by these two accounts together.

TIP TOP TRUCKING	ACCOUNTS RECEIVABLE AGING SCHEDULE						DEC. 31, 19-4
CUSTOMER	ACCOUNT BALANCE	1-30 DAYS	31-60 DAYS	61-91 DAYS	OVER 90 DAYS	REMARKS	DOUBTFUL ACCOUNTS
ADVANCE ASSOCIATES	1 056 50	5 16 30	3 17 -	2 23 20		Will be OK	
BATH BOUTIQUE	3 746 10	2 6 12 -	1 1 10 10	24 -		Will be OK	
CANWEST INDUSTRIES	460 -	460 -				AOK	
DAVE'S AUTO PARTS	740 -	450 -	290 -			AOK	
EDGEMONT FURNITURE	350 -				350 -	Disputed item In lawyer's hands	350 -
FLEET LINE DISTRIBUTORS	5 63 40	420 -	1 43 40			AOK	
GASTOWN PRODUCTS	2 16 -		2 16 -			AOK	
HEALTH SCIENCES	300 -	300 -				AOK	
HURDLE, W.	946 -	8 10 -			1 36 -	Item requires clarification. Customer is expected to pay.	
JAMES, A.	3 75 -				3 75 -	Customer is in bankruptcy.	3 75 -
KEM MANUFACTURING	2 646 30	9 06 10	8 40 30	492 -	4 07 90	Customer is slow but sure. A good customer for over 10 years	
SEVEN SEAS FISH COMPANY	1 056 10	6 40 30	4 15 80				
VALLEY SERVICES	834 -	834 -					
	28 3 16 40	12 373 20	8 8 49 20	5 3 09 -	1 7 80 -		1 430 -

Figure 15.3 An aging schedule for Tip Top Trucking.

You may wonder why the figure for doubtful debts is not credited directly to the Accounts Receivable account. There is a very good reason for this. Just because an account is doubtful is no reason to stop trying to collect it. In fact it is a good reason for using more aggressive collection methods. As long as there is hope of collecting the account, it is kept in the subsidiary ledger. And if it remains in the subsidiary ledger, then it also remains in the control account. For it is a cardinal rule of accounting that the subsidiary ledger and the control account remain equal.

The Adjusting Entry for Doubtful Debts

Once the aging schedule is completed, the figure for doubtful debts is known and the adjusting entry can be made. There are two aspects to this adjusting entry:

1. **The accounts**   The accounts involved are always the same.
   The adjusting entry is always:

	DR	CR
Bad Debts Expense	$$$$	
Allowance for Doubtful Debts		$$$$

2. **The amount**   The adjustment will be for the amount needed to bring the Allowance for Doubtful Debts account up from its existing balance to the figure shown on the aging schedule. As is explained in a later section, the Allowance account will have a small balance. This should not present you with a problem when making the adjustment. Just remember that the amount of the adjustment must cause the balance in the Allowance account to be equal to the figure arrived at on the aging schedule.

Adjusting Entry for Tip Top Trucking

The trial balance for Tip Top Trucking shows a $56.05 credit balance in the Allowance for Doubtful Debts account. The aging schedule shows that the doubtful debts are really $1 430. Therefore, an adjusting entry in the amount of $1 373.95 ($1 430 minus $56.05) is needed. The adjusting entry is the following:

	DR	CR
Bad Debts Expense	$1 373.95	
Allowance for Doubtful Debts		$1 373.95

This adjusting entry (coded 5) is shown on the work sheet in Figure 15.4. Observe that since it is a contra asset, the Allowance for Doubtful Debts figure is extended to the credit side of the Balance Sheet column.

Allowance for Doubtful Debts on the Balance Sheet

The financial statements for Tip Top Trucking are shown as Figures 15.8 and 15.9 on pages 646 and 647. Look ahead to these statements and you will see how the estimated true value of accounts receivable is presented on the balance sheet. The allowance for doubtful debts figure is deducted from the accounts receivable figure on the balance sheet to arrive at the estimated true value of accounts receivable.

Tip Top Trucking	Work Sheet						Year Ended Dec. 31, 19-4	
ACCOUNTS	**TRIAL BALANCE**		**ADJUSTMENTS**		**INCOME STATEMENT**		**BALANCE SHEET**	
	DR.	CR.	DR.	CR.	DR.	CR.	DR.	CR.
Bank	1675.07							
Accounts Receivable	28316.40							
Allowance for Doubtful Debts		56.05		⑤ 1373.95				1430.—
Supplies	1725.50			① 1200.50			525.—	
Prepaid Insurance	3895.—			② 2647.—			1248.—	
Furniture and Equipment	5120.—							
Accum. Deprec. Furn. & Equip		924.—		④ 462.—				1386.—
Automotive Equipment	78000.—							
Accum. Deprec. Auto. Equip.		23400.—		④ 11700.—				35100.—
Accounts Payable		4675.10		③ 643.50				5318.60
Loan Payable - 10%		25000.—						
R. Hansen, Capital		41256.64						
R. Hansen, Drawings	48000.—							
Revenue		226742.90						
Interest Expense	625.—							
Light, Heat, Water	3820.—							
Miscellaneous Expense	1974.—		③ 127.50		2101.50			
Rent	24000.—							
Telephone	2165.—							
Truck Expense	52361.12		③ 516.—		53147.12			
Wages	70207.60							
	322054.69	322054.69						
Supplies Used			① 1200.50		1200.50			
Insurance Expense			② 2647.—		2647.—			
Depreciation Furn. & Equip			④ 462.—		462.—			
Depreciation Auto & Equip			④ 11700.—		11700.—			
Bad Debts Expense			⑤ 1373.95		1373.95			

Figure 15.4 Work sheet for Tip Top Trucking showing the adjusting entry for doubtful debts.

Writing Off a Bad Debt

A doubtful account becomes a bad debt when there is no longer any chance of collecting it. At this point, the account balance is written off, that is, taken out of the books by means of an accounting entry. The entry to write off a bad debt is:

	DR	CR
Allowance for Doubtful Debts	$$$$	
Accounts Receivable (R. Jones)		$$$$

This accounting entry is recorded in the general journal. The posting to Accounts Receivable must be made twice: once in the general ledger, and once in the subsidiary ledger. The accounts receivable clerk will have to be informed by memo because this information would not appear in a normal source document.

Observe that the Allowance account is debited (reduced) whenever an account is written off. The balance in this account decreases, therefore, with the passing of time. At the end of each accounting period, there will be a small balance remaining in the account. This is because the total of the accounts written off never quite agrees with the figure from the previous aging schedule that was set up in the accounts. If the accounts written off were for less than the aging schedule figure, the Allowance account will end up with a credit balance. However, if the accounts written off were for more than the aging schedule figure, the Allowance account will end up with a debit balance.

Recovering a Bad Debt

Sometimes a business is lucky enough to collect an account that it has written off. Before such a collection can be recorded in the usual manner, the write-off must be reversed. Otherwise the customer would continue to suffer from a poor credit rating.

The following entries illustrate this type of transaction.

1. Writing off the account:

   On March 3, the account of Rex Brooks, in the amount of $75, is written off as uncollectible. The following accounting entry records the write-off.

	DR	CR
Allowance for Doubtful Debts	$75	
Accounts Receivable (Rex Brooks)		$75
To write off the account of Rex Brooks.		

2. Recovering the account:

   On August 5, a cheque is received from Rex Brooks paying his account in full. The following two accounting entries are necessary to record this collection.

   a. To reverse the write-off

	DR	CR
Accounts Receivable (Rex Brooks)	$75	
Allowance for Doubtful Debts		$75
Reversing account previously written off.		

   b. To record the collection

	DR	CR
Bank	$75	
Accounts Receivable (Rex Brooks)		$75
To record the collection of an account previously written off.		

Showing that the account was paid has the effect of preserving the customer's credit rating.

SECTION REVIEW QUESTIONS

1. What risk is involved for businesses that sell on credit?
2. Why do businesses continue to sell on credit despite the risk of losing some accounts?
3. When is a customer's account first seen as doubtful?
4. Explain how the matching principle applies to doubtful debts.
5. Explain how the principle of conservatism applies to doubtful debts.
6. What is the purpose of an aging schedule?
7. Explain the purpose of the Allowance for Doubtful Debts account.
8. What kind of account is the Allowance for Doubtful Debts?
9. In the ledger, how is the estimated true value of accounts receivable found?
10. Explain why the credit for doubtful debts is not made directly to the Accounts Receivable account.
11. In general terms, give the adjusting entry for doubtful debts.
12. How is the amount for the above entry determined?
13. Explain how the accounts receivable are presented on a balance sheet.
14. When does a doubtful debt become a bad debt?
15. Give the accounting entry to write off a bad debt.
16. What circumstances would cause the Allowance for Doubtful Debts account to end the period with a credit balance? A debit balance?
17. Give the accounting entry to recover a bad debt.
18. When a bad debt is recovered, why is the customer's account set up again and then shown as collected in the usual manner?

SECTION EXERCISES

1. **Complete each of the following statements by writing in your Workbook the appropriate word or phrase from the list on page 640.** A word may be used more than once.

   1. No matter how carefully the customers' _____ are checked out, there are always some customers who cannot or do not pay.
   2. A customer's account is first seen as doubtful if it becomes _____.
   3. The _____ requires than any losses from doubtful accounts be shown as expense in the same period as the sales were recorded.
   4. The _____ requires that doubtful accounts not be included in the real value of accounts receivable shown on the balance sheet.
   5. An _____ is a breakdown of customers' accounts showing how long the balances have been unpaid.
   6. The Allowance for Doubtful Debts account is a _____ account.
   7. Because an account is _____ is a good reason for trying harder to collect it.
   8. As long as there is hope of collecting the account, it is kept in the _____.
   9. The adjustment for doubtful debts always involves a _____ to the Allowance account.

10. On the balance sheet the allowance for doubtful debts is deducted from the accounts receivable to show their _____.
11. A doubtful account becomes a _____ when there is no longer any chance of collecting it.
12. The Allowance account is _____ whenever an account is written off.
13. If the accounts written off were for _____ than the previous aging schedule figure, the Allowance account will end up with a credit balance.
14. If the accounts written off were for _____ than the previous aging schedule figure, the Allowance account will end up with a debit balance.
15. When a bad debt is recovered, the write-off must be _____.

List of Words and Phrases

aging schedule	less
bad debt	matching principle
contra	more
credit	overdue
credit ratings	principle of conservatism
debited	reversed
estimated true value	subsidiary ledger

2. **Workbook Exercise: Completing a chart about the allowance for doubtful accounts.**

3. **Workbook Exercise: Completing simplified work sheets involving the adjustment for bad debts.**

4. **In your Workbook, journalize the following transactions.**

TRANSACTIONS

19-6

Feb. 2	Write off the account of J. Lohre, $175.
Apr. 16	Write off the account of F. Padula, $360.
May 12	Write off the account of K. Stamer, $450.
Aug. 24	Write off the account of W. Vanderveen, $120.
Oct. 5	Recover the account of F. Padula, $360.
Dec. 20	Write off the account of P. Knopp, $120.

In your Workbook, post from the journal entries for the above to the Allowance for Doubtful Debts account provided. The account had a beginning balance (January 1, 19-6) of $850 credit. **Work out the new account balance.**

15.4   *Adjusting for Accrued Expenses*

Accrued Interest Expense

The easiest way to learn about accrued expense is by looking at an example involving interest expense on a loan payable.

> On February 1, 19-1, Modern Industries, owned by G. Nagy, borrows $100 000 from a loan company. The loan agreement states that interest is at 10 per cent to be paid annually on February 28, and that the loan principal is to be repaid in full on February 1, 19-6.

The accounting entry to record this loan is a debit to Bank and a credit to Loan Payable in the amount of $100 000.

The interest on this loan amounts to $27.40 per day. Theoretically, an accounting entry for this amount, debiting Interest Expense and crediting Interest Payable should be made in the account daily. But it is common practice to ignore these entries during the fiscal period. This is one of those situations where it is not necessary to maintain the accounting records perfectly accurately.

At statement time, however, the situation is looked at quite differently. The matching principle dictates that the interest expense be recorded in its proper fiscal period. Therefore, an adjusting entry must be made for the interest that has built up over the 10 months — $100 000 \times 10\% \times 10/12 = \$8 333.33$. This is known as accrued interest expense, or accrued interest payable. An **accrued expense** is one that has built up during the accounting period, has not been recorded in the accounts, and is not yet due. In general, the adjusting entry required for accrued interest is:

	DR	CR
Interest Expense	$$$$	
Accrued Interest Payable		$$$$

Accrued Interest for Tip Top Trucking

On the work sheet for Tip Top Trucking there is an item, Loan Payable — 10%, $25 000. Tip Top Trucking took out this loan a few years previously on March 31. Interest on the loan is paid annually every March 31. The interest figure of $625 on the work sheet represents the expense for the period from January 1 to March 31.

Interest was last paid on this loan on March 31, 19-4. It is clear that interest has accrued on this loan for nine months. The accrued interest amounts to $25 000 \times 10\% \times 9/12 = \$1 875$. The adjusting entry necessary to record the accrued interest for Tip Top Trucking is:

	DR	CR
Interest Expense	$1 875	
Accrued Interest Payable		$1 875

You can see this adjusting entry (coded 6) recorded on the work sheet for Tip Top Trucking in Figure 15.5. Observe that this adjustment, together with the balance already in the Interest Expense account, produces the correct interest expense figure of $2 500 for the year.

Observe also that accrued interest payable is extended to the Balance Sheet credit column because it represents a liability.

ACCOUNTS	TRIAL BALANCE DR.	CR.	ADJUSTMENTS DR.	CR.	INCOME STATEMENT DR.	CR.	BALANCE SHEET DR.	CR.
Bank	1 575 07							
Accounts Receivable	28 316 40							
Allowance for Doubtful Debts		56 05		(5) 1 373 95				1 430 -
Supplies	1 725 50			(1) 1 200 50			525 -	
Prepaid Insurance	3 895 -			(2) 2 647 -			1 248 -	
Furniture and Equipment	5 120 -							
Accum. Deprec. Furn. & Equip.		924 -		(4) 462 -				1 386 -
Automotive Equipment	78 000 -							
Accum. Deprec. Auto. Equip.		23 400 -		(4) 11 700 -				35 100 -
Accounts Payable		4 675 10		(3) 643 50				5 318 60
Loan Payable - 10%		25 000 -						
R. Hansen, Capital		41 256 64						
R. Hansen, Drawings	48 000 -							
Revenue		226 742 90						
Interest Expense	625 -		(6) 1 875 -		2 500 -			
Light, Heat, Water	3 820 -							
Miscellaneous Expense	1 974 -		(3) 127 50		2 101 50			
Rent	24 000 -							
Telephone	2 165 -							
Truck Expense	52 301 12		(3) 516 -		53 147 12			
Wages	70 207 60							
	322 054 69	322 054 69						
Supplies Used			(1) 1 200 50		1 200 50			
Insurance Expense			(2) 2 647 -		2 647 -			
Depreciation Furn. & Equip.			(4) 462 -		462 -			
Depreciation Auto & Equip.			(4) 11 700 -		11 700 -			
Bad Debts Expense			(5) 1 373 95		1 373 95			
Accrued Interest Payable				(6) 1 875 -				1 875 -

Tip Top Trucking — Work Sheet — Year Ended Dec. 31, 19-4

Figure 15.5 The work sheet for Tip Top Trucking showing the adjusting entry for accrued interest.

Recording the Interest Payment

As part of the year-end accounting activity, the interest expense account of $2 500 will be closed out. But the liability for accrued interest payable of $1 875 will sit untouched until the next payment date of March 31, 19-5. On that day a cheque for one year's interest, that is $2 500, will be issued. From an accounting point of view, this cheque is in payment of the $1 875 liability already on the books together with

$625 interest for the period from January 1 to March 31, 19-5. The accounting entry to record the cheque is as follows:

	DR	CR
Interest Expense	$625	
Accrued Interest Payable	$1 875	
Bank		$2 500

The effect of this accounting entry is to eliminate the balance in the Accrued Interest Payable account and to set up the interest expense for the first three months of the new fiscal period. This is the situation that will remain until December 31, 19-5, at which time the cycle will repeat itself.

Accrued Wages Expense

A regularly occurring expense, such as wages, is normally accounted for only on the day that payment for it is made. From one payment date to the next, the liability for such an expense gradually builds up. But not until the payment is actually made is the transaction accounted for by means of an accounting entry such as the following:

	DR	CR
Wages Expense	$$$$	
Bank		$$$$

Generally, the date of payment for wages does not coincide with the date of the end of the fiscal period. For example, consider Figure 15.6.

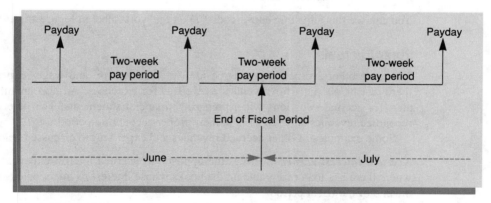

Figure 15.6   A two-week pay period straddling the end of the fiscal period.

The illustration shows that one of the two-week pay periods straddles the year-end. In other words, the date of the end of the fiscal period falls between two paydays.

This situation poses a problem when preparing financial statements. At the end of the accounting period, some unrecorded wages expense must be accounted for according to the matching principle.

Accrued Wages for Tip Top Trucking

To calculate the accrued wages for Tip Top Trucking, wait until after completing the payroll for the pay period straddling the year-end. Then compute the portion of the total that belongs to the fiscal period just ended.

First, take the total wages for the two-week period (assume $2 961.20 in this case). The employer's share of pension, unemployment insurance, and other deductions is usually ignored, unless it is quite large. Second, calculate the number of working days (of the two-week period) that fell before January 1 (assume six in this case). Then compute the accrued wages according to the following formula:

$$\frac{\text{In the last pay period, the number of working days before the year-end}}{\text{In the last pay period, the total number of working days}} \times \text{Total wages for the pay period}$$

That is, $\dfrac{6}{10} \times \$2\,961.20 = \$1\,776.72$

Once the accrued wages figure is calculated, an adjusting entry is made on the work sheet. For Tip Top Trucking, the adjusting entry is:

	DR	CR
Wages Expense	$1 776.72	
Accrued Wages Payable		$1 776.72

You can see this adjusting entry (coded 7) on the work sheet in Figure 15.7.

Other Accruals

There are other accrued expenses besides interest expense and wages expense. And there can be accruals for revenues as well as for expenses. An accountant must be alert for accrual situations when preparing financial statements. The objective is to recognize revenues and expenses in their proper accounting period.

Some examples of other accrued revenues and expenses are discussed below:

Accrued interest earned This is the opposite of accrued interest expense. It occurs where there is a loan receivable on the books whose interest payment date is later than the end of the fiscal period.

Accrued rent (revenue or expense) Sometimes rent is paid (or received) every two months or every three months. Where the payment date for this rent does not coincide with the end of the fiscal period, an adjustment for accrued rent is necessary.

Accrued management fees (revenue or expense) A business may enter into a contract to provide, or receive, maintenance services for a specified period of time, for which payment is made at the end of that time. If the payment date does not coincide with the end of the fiscal period, an adjustment is necessary for the accrued management fees.

Tip Top Trucking			Work Sheet			Year Ended Dec. 31, 19-4		
ACCOUNTS	TRIAL BALANCE		ADJUSTMENTS		INCOME STATEMENT		BALANCE SHEET	
	DR.	CR.	DR.	CR.	DR.	CR.	DR.	CR.
Bank	1575.07						1575.07	
Accounts Receivable	28316.40						28316.40	
Allowance for Doubtful Debts		56.05		(5) 1373.95				1430.-
Supplies	1725.50			(1) 1200.50			525.-	
Prepaid Insurance	3895.-			(2) 2647.-			1248.-	
Furniture and Equipment	5120.-						5120.-	
Accum. Deprec. Furn. & Equip.		924.-		(4) 462.-				1386.-
Automotive Equipment	78000.-						78000.-	
Accum. Deprec. Auto. Equip.		23400.-		(4) 11700.-				35100.-
Accounts Payable		4675.10		(3) 643.50				5318.60
Loan Payable – 10%		25000.-						25000.-
R. Hansen, Capital		41256.64						41256.64
R. Hansen, Drawings	48000.-						48000.-	
Revenue		226742.90				226742.90		
Interest Expense	625.-		(6) 1875.-		2500.-			
Light, Heat, Water	3820.-				3820.-			
Miscellaneous Expense	1974.-		(3) 127.50		2101.50			
Rent	24000.-				24000.-			
Telephone	2165.-				2165.-			
Truck Expense	52361.12		(3) 516.-		53147.12			
Wages	70207.60		(7) 1776.72		71984.32			
	322054.69	322054.69						
Supplies Used			(1) 1200.50		1200.50			
Insurance Expense			(2) 2647.-		2647.-			
Depreciation Furn. & Equip			(4) 462.-		462.-			
Depreciation Auto & Equip			(4) 11700.-		11700.-			
Bad Debts Expense			(5) 1373.95		1373.95			
Accrued Interest Payable				(6) 1875.-				1875.-
Accrued Wages Payable				(7) 1776.72				1776.72
			21678.67	21678.67	177101.39	226742.90	162784.47	113142.96
Net Income					49641.51			49641.51
					226742.90	226742.90	162784.47	162784.47

Figure 15.7 The completed work sheet for Tip Top Trucking showing the adjustment for accrued wages.

Accrued salaries (bonus)   This occurs where the business agrees to pay a bonus to an employee (usually an executive). The amount is based on the sales figure or the net income figure which is not known until the end of the fiscal period. Then an adjustment is needed for accrued salaries.

Accrued Workers' Compensation   In Canada, most employers are required to pay into the Workers' Compensation fund a fee based on their total wages paid for the year. The payments must be made in instalments. But the employer cannot calculate the final figure until the end of the fiscal period, when the final wages figure is known. Then an adjustment is needed for accrued workers' compensation expense.

Financial Statements for Tip Top Trucking

In Chapter 8 you learned that the work sheet is designed to assist the accountant to organize the data needed to prepare the financial statements. In this chapter you have seen the additional adjustments that may be needed to ensure that the data for the financial statements is correct and up to date.

Keep in mind that the only source of information for the financial statements should be the work sheet. All of the information needed to prepare the Income Statement can be found in the Income Statement columns of the work sheet. Similarly, all of the information needed to prepare the balance sheet can be found in the Balance Sheet columns of the work sheet. It is unnecessary to look anywhere else.

The income statement and the balance sheet for Tip Top Trucking are shown in Figures 15.8 and 15.9. The data for these two statements came from the work sheet shown in Figure 15.7 on page 645.

TIP TOP TRUCKING
INCOME STATEMENT
YEAR ENDED DECEMBER 31, 19-4

REVENUE		
Trucking Revenue		$226 742.90
OPERATING EXPENSES		
Interest Expense	$ 2 500.00	
Light, Heat, and Water	3 820.00	
Miscellaneous Expense	2 101.50	
Rent	24 000.00	
Telephone	2 165.00	
Truck Expense	53 147.12	
Wages	71 984.32	
Supplies Used	1 200.50	
Insurance Expense	2 647.00	
Depreciation — Furniture and Equipment	462.00	
Depreciation — Automotive Equipment	11 700.00	
Bad Debts Expense	1 373.95	
Total Expenses		177 101.39
Net Income		$ 49 641.51

Figure 15.8   The income statement for Tip Top Trucking.

Adjusting and Closing Entries

You learned about the adjusting and closing entries for a proprietorship in Chapter 9. The several additional adjusting entries discussed in this chapter do not change the adjusting and closing entry process. Be sure to review and follow the procedures laid down in Chapter 9.

TIP TOP TRUCKING
BALANCE SHEET
DECEMBER 31, 19-4

ASSETS

Current Assets

Bank		$ 1 575.07	
Accounts Receivable	$28 316.40		
Less Allowance for Doubtful Debts	1 430.00	26 886.40	$28 461.47

Prepaid Expenses

Supplies		$ 525.00	
Prepaid Insurance		1 248.00	1 773.00

Plant and Equipment

Furniture and Equipment	$ 5 120.00		
Less Accumulated Depreciation	1 386.00	$ 3 734.00	
Automotive Equipment	$78 000.00		
Less Accumulated Depreciation	35 100.00	42 900.00	46 634.00
			$76 868.47

LIABILITIES AND OWNER'S EQUITY

Current Liabilities

Accounts Payable		$5 318.60	
Accrued Interest Payable		1 875.00	
Accrued Wages Payable		1 776.72	$8 970.32

Long Term Liability

Loan Payable — 10% — Due 19–8			25 000.00

R. Hansen, Capital

Balance, January 1		$41 256.64	
Net Income	$49 641.51		
Drawings	48 000.00		
Increase in Capital		1 641.51	
Balance, December 31			42 898.15
			$76 868.47

Figure 15.9   The balance sheet for Tip Top Trucking.

Accountant's Working Papers

When financial statements are prepared, numerous inventories, schedules, calculations, and so on must be made to adjust the work sheet figures and the financial statements. All papers and calculations related to the preparation of the financial statements are usually collected in one file. This file of papers is known as the accountant's working papers.

SECTION REVIEW QUESTIONS

1. Why is it common practice to ignore certain accounting entries during the accounting period?
2. What is an accrued expense?
3. Give the accounting entry to record accrued interest on a loan payable.
4. Give the accounting entry to record accrued interest on a loan receivable.
5. Explain why an accrual for wages is usually necessary.
6. Give the accounting entry to record accrued wages.
7. Explain how to calculate accrued wages.
8. Give the accounting entry to record accrued rent (payable).
9. Give the accounting entry to record accrued management fees (receivable).
10. Give the accounting entry to record an accrued salary bonus.

SECTION EXERCISES

1. **Workbook Exercise: Recording adjusting entries for accrued items on simplified work sheets.**

2. Avery Company has a September 30th year-end. At September 30, 19-6, the following items appeared on the trial balance for Avery Company.

Loan Payable, eight per cent	$60 000
Interest Expense	$2 400
Wages Expense	$1 575 020
Workers' Compensation Expense	$18 000

Using the additional information given below, work out the necessary adjusting entries for accruals.

Additional Information
1. The loan was borrowed on March 31, 19-0. The date for payment of interest is March 31 annually.
2. The payroll period (10 working days) ending on Friday, October 3 amounted to $60 580.
3. The workers' compensation rate is set at 1.5 per cent of the total wages figure for the year (including accrued wages).

3. **This exercise also appears in your Workbook.**

Morrow Company has a June 30th year-end. Shown on p. 649 is the work sheet for the year ended June 30, 19-9 with the trial balance figures (simplified) entered.

Morrow Company			Work Sheet				Year Ended June 30, 19-9			
Accounts	Trial Balance		Adjustments		Income Statmt		Balance Sheet			
	Dr	Cr	Dr	Cr	Dr	Cr	Dr	Cr		
Bank	5 000									
Loan Receivable — 12%	100 000									
Other Assets	300 000									
Liabilities		121 000								
Morrow, Capital		186 000								
Morrow, Drawings	50 000									
Sales		300 000								
Interest Revenue		10 000								
Rent Expense	5 000									
Salaries	102 000									
Other Expenses	55 000									
	617 000	617 000								

Work out the adjusting entries from the additional information given below, and complete the work sheet. Assume that there are no other adjustments.

Additional Information

1. The loan was originally granted on April 30, 19-0. Interest is due annually on April 30.
2. The executives are to receive a salary bonus equal to two per cent of the sales figure.
3. Rent, at the rate of $500 per month, is paid every three months. The next rent payment is due on July 31.

---

4. **Workbook Exercise: Completing a simplified work sheet involving accruals.**

Fonda Company has an April 30th year-end. Shown on page 650 is the work sheet for the year ended April 30, 19-7 with the trial balance figures (simplified) entered.

Work out the adjusting entries from the additional information given below, and complete the work sheet. Assume that there are no other adjustments.

Additional Information

1. The loan anniversary date and interest payment date is October 31.
2. Rent is paid half-yearly on February 28 and August 31 at the rate of $800 per month.
3. The wages for the five working days ended May 1 amounted to $3 000.
4. The executives are to receive a salary bonus equal to three per cent of sales.

Fonda Company			Work Sheet					Year Ended April 30, 19-7	
Accounts	Trial Balance		Adjustments		Income Statmt		Balance Sheet		
	Dr	Cr	Dr	Cr	Dr	Cr	Dr	Cr
Bank	5 000							
Other Assets	410 000							
Loan Payable — 15%		70 000						
Other Liabilities		152 625						
Fonda, Capital		169 625						
Fonda, Drawings	50 000							
Sales		400 000						
Interest Expense	5 250							
Rent Expense	8 000							
Salaries Expense	80 000							
Wages Expense	140 000							
Other Expenses	94 000							
	792 250	792 250						

5. The completed work sheet for General Lighting is shown (in part) on page 651 for the year ended December 31, 19-5.

Prepare the financial statements for General Lighting for the year ended December 31, 19-5.

General Lighting — Work Sheet	Year Ended December 31, 19–5			
ACCOUNTS	INCOME STATEMENT		BALANCE SHEET	
	DEBIT	CREDIT	DEBIT	CREDIT
Bank			4 326 12	
Accounts Receivable			31 205 16	
Allowance for Doubtful Debts				2 750 00
Merchandise Inventory	31 650 00	33 500 00	33 500 00	
Supplies			1 250 00	
Prepaid Insurance			3 040 00	
Furniture and Equipment			37 305 00	
Accum. Depr. Furn. & Equip.				14 400 00
Automotive Equipment			52 400 00	
Accum. Depr. Auto. Equip.				30 000 00
Accounts Payable				2 900 00
Bank Loan				52 000 00
Sales Tax Payable				1 102 16
R. Brooks, Capital				51 564 73
R. Brooks, Drawings			48 000 00	
Sales		290 306 40		
Bank Charges	9 232 32			
Car Expenses	14 713 04			
Light, Heat, and Water	3 702 00			
Miscellaneous Expense	2 036 00			
Postage	756 20			
Purchases	126 124 07			
Rent	12 000 00			
Telephone	2 416 70			
Wages	50 278 27			
Bad Debts Expense	1 675 80			
Supplies Expense	1 215 70			
Insurance Expense	2 174 19			
Depreciation of Furn. & Equip.	2 400 00			
Depreciation of Auto. Equip.	10 000 00			
Accrued Interest Payable				715 16
Accrued Wages Payable				2 162 12
	270 374 29	323 806 40	211 026 28	157 594 17
Net Income	53 432 11			53 432 11
	323 806 40	323 806 40	211 026 28	211 026 28

15.5 REVERSING ENTRIES

Reversing Entry for Late Purchase Invoices

You learned about late purchase invoices in Chapter 9. These are purchase invoices for a fiscal period that are not received until after that fiscal period has ended. An adjusting entry must be made in the financial statements to record these late purchase invoices in their proper accounting period. This adjusting entry for the late purchase invoices of Tip Top Trucking is recorded in the accounts as shown below. The adjustment can be seen on the work sheet illustrations in this chapter.

	DR	CR
Miscellaneous Expense	$127.50	
Truck Expense	516.00	
Accounts Payable		$643.50

Once the adjusting entry for late purchase invoices is made (in the previous period), the purchase invoices themselves are inserted into the accounting system in the new period. They are then processed by the accounting clerks in the usual manner. The usual routine is followed because the invoices must be checked against the purchase orders and the receiving reports, posted to the subsidiary ledgers, and so on. But one of the results of this process is that the accounting entries are recorded in the accounts a second time, this time in the new accounting period.

This problem is corrected by means of another accounting entry, called a reversing entry. A **reversing entry** cancels out the double effect created when something is recorded in one accounting period by an adjusting entry and also in the next accounting period by the accounting routines. A reversing entry is the exact opposite of the adjusting entry. It is made early in the new period.

For Tip Top Trucking the reversing entry is shown below beneath the adjusting entry.

a. The adjusting entry

	DR	CR
Miscellaneous Expense	$127.50	
Truck Expense	516.00	
Accounts Payable		$643.50

b. The reversing entry

	DR	CR
Accounts Payable	$643.50	
Miscellaneous Expense		$127.50
Truck Expense		516.00

It is clear from the above that the reversing entry is the exact opposite of the adjusting entry.

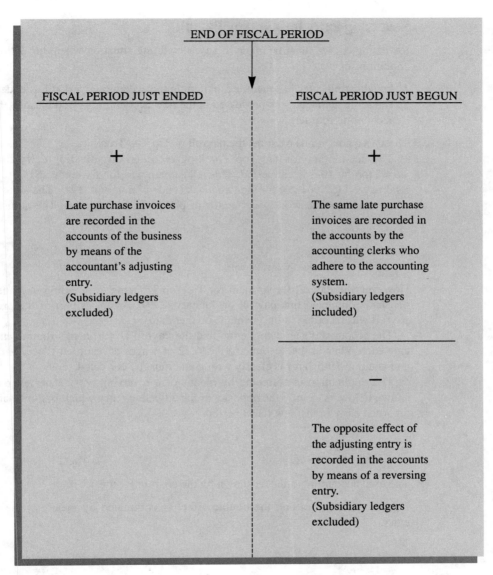

Figure 15.10   A chart showing the overall effect of accounting for late purchase invoices.

Figure 15.10, which illustrates the effect of all the accounting entries, shows that the double effect is eliminated by the reversing entry in the new accounting period.

Reversing Entry for Accrued Payroll

Reversing entries must be made in any accounting situation where the following two conditions exist:

1. An adjusting entry has recorded an item in the accounting period just ended.
2. The same item has been processed in the new accounting period through the regular accounting routines.

These two conditions exist for the payroll of Tip Top Trucking.

The accountant for Tip Top Trucking recorded an adjusting entry for accrued wages for the 19-4 fiscal period. This adjustment was for six-tenths ($1 776.72) of the total payroll ($2 961.20) for the two weeks ended January 4, 19-5. The adjusting entry was entered on the work sheet and later posted in the accounts. The adjusting entry was as follows:

	DR	CR
Wages Expense	$1 776.72	
Accrued Wages Payable		$1 776.72

However, the Payroll Department for Tip Top Trucking, proceeding in its usual manner, had completed this payroll on January 4, 19-5. And, as part of the process, the payroll was recorded in the accounts on that date.

The accountant's adjusting entry and the Payroll Department's routine entry duplicate each other in the accounts. $1 776.72 of wages is recorded twice, once in 19-4 and again in 19-5. This is clearly wrong and must be corrected.

The duplication is corrected by means of a reversing entry. The reversing entry, shown below, is exactly the opposite of the adjusting entry which is shown above. It is recorded early in the new fiscal period.

	DR	CR
Accrued Wages Payable	$1 776.72	
Wages Expense		$1 776.72

The total accounting effect is shown by the chart in Figure 15.11.

Figure 15.11 shows that the double effect is eliminated by means of the reversing entry.

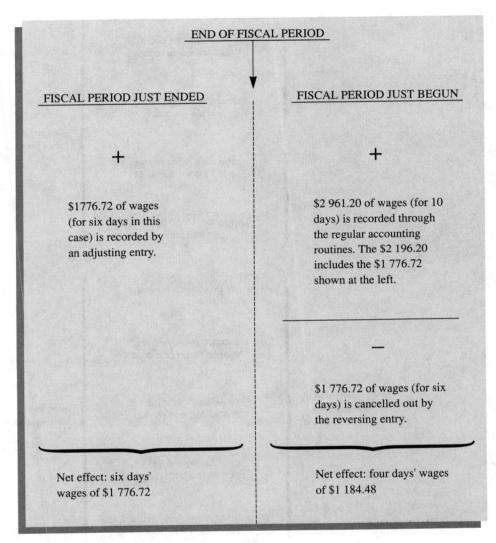

END OF FISCAL PERIOD

FISCAL PERIOD JUST ENDED

+

$1776.72 of wages
(for six days in this
case) is recorded by
an adjusting entry.

FISCAL PERIOD JUST BEGUN

+

$2 961.20 of wages (for 10
days) is recorded through
the regular accounting
routines. The $2 196.20
includes the $1 776.72
shown at the left.

−

$1 776.72 of wages (for six
days) is cancelled out by
the reversing entry.

Net effect: six days'
wages of $1 776.72

Net effect: four days' wages
of $1 184.48

Figure 15.11   A chart showing the total effect of adjusting and reversing entries concerning payroll.

The Accounting Cycle

The inclusion of the adjusting entries and the reversing entries is the final stage in developing the accounting cycle. Figure 15.12 shows the steps in the accounting cycle in its final form.

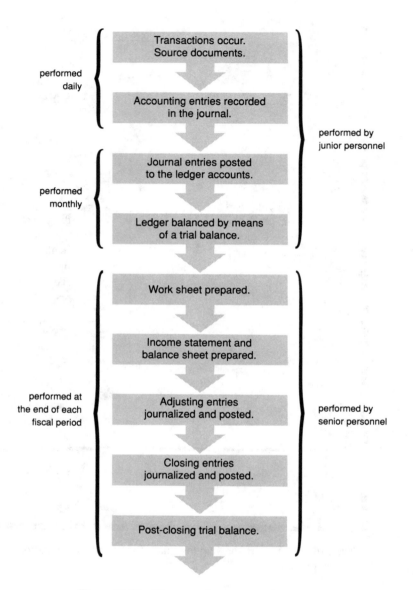

Figure 15.12 The complete accounting cycle.

SECTION REVIEW QUESTIONS

1. What are late purchase invoices?
2. Give the adjusting entry for late purchase invoices.
3. What happens to the late invoices once the adjusting entry is made?

4. Explain why a reversing entry is necessary for late purchase invoices.
5. Give the reversing entry for late purchase invoices.
6. Explain the effect of a reversing entry.
7. Explain why a reversing entry is necessary for accrued payroll.
8. Give the adjusting entry and the reversing entry for accrued payroll.
9. Give the 10 steps in the complete accounting cycle.

SECTION EXERCISES

1. 1. **Based on the following information, calculate the amount of the accrued pay on September 30 and give the adjusting entry for it.**
   a. The fiscal year-end is September 30.
   b. The payroll is calculated on a biweekly basis with 10 working days.
   c. The first payday in October falls on Friday, October 4th.
   d. The amount of the first pay in October is $48 306.18.
   Give the reversing entry for the above. Show the date.

   2. **Based on the following information, calculate the amount of the accrued pay on March 31, and give the adjusting entry for it.**
   a. The fiscal year-end is March 31.
   b. The payroll is calculated on a weekly basis with five working days.
   c. The first payday in April falls on Friday, April 2nd.
   d. The amount of the first pay in April is $120 784.17.
   Give the reversing entry for the above. Show the date.

2. The accountant for Polz Company is in the process of preparing the work sheet for the year ended December 31, 19-2. She has just gathered together all of the purchase invoices during the first three weeks of January, 19-3. Her objective is to work out the adjusting entry for late-arriving purchase invoices.

   The purchase invoices for the three-week period are listed below.

Date	Amount	Reason	Date goods or services received
January 2	$ 315.24	Car expenses	December 19-2
2	1 015.20	Merchandise for resale	December 19-2
3	95.40	Miscellaneous expense	December 19-2
3	102.36	Telephone	December 19-2
3	26.32	Supplies	November 19-2
4	1 036.28	Merchandise for resale	December 19-2
4	345.65	Merchandise for resale	December 19-2
7	75.89	Car repairs	December 19-2
7	42.50	Gas and oil	December 19-2
8	125.87	Heating fuel	December 19-2
8	187.36	Hydro	December 19-2
9	352.12	Repairs for building	December 19-2
10	85.25	Freight-in	January 19-3
10	54.37	Lawyer's bill	January 19-3
11	7.30	Postage	January 19-3

11	19.63	Supplies	December 19-2
11	333.57	Insurance	January 19-3
14	55.25	Freight-in	December 19-2
14	235.89	Miscellaneous expense	January 19-3
15	11 025.74	New car	January 19-3
15	338.85	Undercoating for new car	January 19-3
15	279.46	Merchandise for resale	January 19-3
16	144.21	Miscellaneous expense	December 19-2
17	145.68	Supplies	January 19-3
17	457.39	Merchandise for resale	January 19-3
18	906.88	Merchandise for resale	January 19-3
18	1 366.54	Repairs to building	January 19-3
18	225.52	Postage	January 19-3

1. **Analyze the above list of purchase invoices and work out the adjusting entry for late-arriving purchase invoices.**
2. **Give the reversing entry required as a result of the above adjusting entry. Show the proper date.**

3. **This exercise appears in your Workbook.**
   Shown below and on page 659 are the T-account ledger and the work sheet for Kisik Company at the end of the 19-4 fiscal period.

T-account Ledger

Bank	Other Assets	Accounts Payable
1 000	10 000	1 500

Capital	Drawings	Revenue	Expense A
7 500	5 000	20 000	2 000

Expense B	Wages	Accrued Wages Payable	Income Summary
3 000	8 000		

| Kisik Company | Work Sheet | | | | | | Year Ended December 31, 19-4 | |
| Accounts | Trial Bal | | Adj Entries | | Inc Statmt | | Bal Sheet | |
	Dr	Cr	Dr	Cr	Dr	Cr	Dr	Cr
Bank	1000 –						1000 –	
Other Assets	10000 –						10000 –	
Accs Payable		1500 –		(1)400 –				1900 –
Capital		7500 –						7500 –
Drawings	5000 –						5000 –	
Revenue		20000 –				20000 –		
Expense A	2000 –		(1)50 –		2050 –			
Expense B	3000 –		(1)350 –		3350 –			
Wages	8000 –		(2)900 –		8900 –			
	29000 –	29000 –						
Accrued Wages Payable				(2)900 –				900 –
			1300 –	1300 –	14300 –	20000 –	16000 –	10300 –
Net Income					5700 –			5700 –
					20000 –	20000 –	16000 –	16000 –

1. Journalize the adjusting entries for late invoices and for accrued payroll.
2. Post the above entries (informally) to the T-accounts.
3. Journalize and post the closing entries.
4. Take off a post-closing trial balance.
5. Act as the invoice-processing department: journalize and post the late invoices in 19-5.
6. Act as the payroll department: journalize and post the first payroll ($1 500) on January 5.
7. Act as the accountant: journalize and post the two reversing entries.
8. Study the accounts to ensure that the expenses have been recorded in their proper accounting period.

4. **Workbook Exercise: Completing a chart related to the fiscal period.**

CHAPTER HIGHLIGHTS

Now that you have completed Chapter 15, you should:

1. know the meaning of accountability;
2. know the five common groups who use financial statements;
3. know three additional GAAPs: the consistency principle, the materiality principle, and the full disclosure principle;
4. be able to calculate depreciation using both the straight-line and the declining-balance methods;
5. be able to perform the accounting for depreciation;
6. be able to perform the accounting for doubtful accounts, writing off a bad debt, and recovering a bad debt;
7. be able to perform the accounting for accrued expenses and accrued revenues;
8. be able to prepare classified financial statements;
9. understand reversing entries and be able to do the accounting for reversing entries;
10. know the steps in the full accounting cycle.

ACCOUNTING TERMS

accountability
accounts receivable aging schedule
accrued expense
audit
consistency principle
contra account
declining-balance method of depreciation
depreciation

doubtful account
doubtful debt
full disclosure principle
materiality principle
reversing entry
straight-line method of depreciation

CHAPTER EXERCISES

Using Your Knowledge

1. Dictating Systems Company of Burnaby, B.C., started business on January 1, 19-3. During its first year, it purchased the following insurance policies.

Company	Policy Date	Term	Premium
Atlantic	March 1, 19-3	1 year	$216.00
Pacific	Sept. 1, 19-3	1 year	468.00

1. **What is the balance in the Prepaid Insurance account on December 31, 19-3 before any adjusting entries?**
2. **Calculate the correct prepaid insurance figure as at December 31, 19-3.**
3. **Give the adjusting entry for the 19-3 year-end.**
4. **Prove the insurance expense figure for 19-3.**

During the 19-4 year, Dictating Systems purchased the following insurance policies.

Company	Policy Date	Term	Premium
Indian	June 1, 19-4	1 year	$252.00
Arctic	June 30, 19-4	2 years	360.00

5. **What is the balance in the Prepaid Insurance account on December 31, 19-4 before any adjusting entries?**
6. **Calculate the correct prepaid insurance figure as at December 31, 19-4.**
7. **Give the adjusting entry for the 19-4 year-end.**
8. **Prove the insurance expense figure for 19-4.**

During the 19-5 year, Dictating Systems purchased or renewed insurance policies as follows.

Company	Policy Date	Term	Premium
Superior	Feb. 1, 19-5	2 years	$336
Indian	June 1, 19-5	1 year	264
Huron	Nov. 1, 19-5	1 year	396

9. **What is the balance in the Prepaid Insurance Account on December 31, 19-5 before any adjusting entries?**
10. **Calculate the correct prepaid insurance figure as at December 31, 19-5.**
11. **Give the adjusting entry for the 19-5 year-end.**
12. **Prove the insurance expense figure for 19-5.**

2. During the first three years of a company's life, it purchased or renewed insurance policies as shown in the chart below. The company has a December 31 year-end.

Year	Company	Date	Term	Premium
19-1	Ace	February 1	1 year	$120
	Star	April 30	2 years	300
	Galaxy	September 30	1 year	672
19-2	Beneficial	January 31	2 years	288
	Ace	February 1	1 year	132
	Guardian	May 1	1 year	168
	Empire	December 1	2 years	576
19-3	Ace	February 1	1 year	156
	Provincial	July 1	2 years	240
	Dominion	October 1	1 year	168

Complete the following summary in your Workbook.

Year	Insurance Expense for Year	Value of Prepaid Insurance at Year-end
19-1		
19-2		
19-3		

3. A company purchases a truck at a cost of $25 000 which it expects to last six years and have a salvage value of $3 500.

   Prepare two depreciation schedules as follows:
   a. A six-year schedule showing depreciation calculated on a straight-line basis.
   b. A six-year schedule showing depreciation calculated on a declining-balance basis at the government rate of 30 per cent.

4. **Workbook Exercise: Completing a chart apportioning cost of insurance to a series of accounting periods.**

5. **For each of the following groups, indicate which statement is not true by recording the appropriate letter in your Workbook.**

   1. **a.** Accounting data provide the information for the preparation of the financial statements.
      b. Accountability refers to the responsibility to show evidence of the quality of performance.
      c. Managers study the financial statements very carefully looking for ways to make improvements.
      d. Absentee owners have little use for financial statements because they rely on hired managers.
      e. Bankers use financial statements to be informed about the business affairs of their debtors.
   2. **a.** Readers of financial reports require statements that can be relied on with confidence.
      b. The accounting profession has developed a set of accounting standards.
      c. An audit is a critical review of the internal controls and accounting records.
      d. A one-person business is never called upon to have an audit.
      e. The consistency principle requires that accountants use the same procedures from period to period.

3. a. Accountants are required to follow generally accepted accounting principles except when to do so would be expensive, or difficult, and where it makes no real difference if the rules are ignored.
  b. All information needed for a full understanding of the company's financial affairs should be included in the financial statements.
  c. Assets that are expected to be used over several periods to produce revenue are known as capital equipment.
  d. Depreciation is the decrease in value of an asset over time.
  e. Depreciation must be exact and be included on every income statement.
4. a. The simplest method of calculating depreciation is the declining-balance method.
  b. The government of Canada requires the use of the declining-balance method of depreciation when reporting for income tax purposes.
  c. Under the declining-balance method of depreciation, in the first year the purchase price is equal to the undepreciated cost figure.
  d. The straight-line method of depreciation requires the use of estimates.
  e. The straight-line method of depreciation produces depreciation figures that are the same each year.
5. a. One of outcomes of the adjusting entry for depreciation is a direct reduction of the asset account.
  b. A contra account is one that must be considered along with a given asset account.
  c. The asset account together with the contra account gives the estimated true value of the asset.
  d. A contra account is also known as a valuation account.
  e. Accumulated depreciation appears on the balance sheet as a deduction from the asset.
6. a. Businesses continue to sell on credit despite the fact that they cannot always collect from their customers.
  b. A customer's account is first seen as doubtful if it becomes overdue.
  c. Doubtful accounts are written off as soon as they become doubtful.
  d. Both the matching principle and the principle of conservatism are factors in dealing with doubtful debts on financial statements.
  e. At the end of the accounting period, an accounts receivable aging schedule is prepared.
7. a. The doubtful accounts figure is set up in a contra account.
  b. The fact that an account is doubtful is a good reason for using more aggressive collection methods.
  c. As long as there is hope of collecting the account it is kept in the subsidiary ledger.
  d. The amount of the adjustment for doubtful debts is equal to the total figure for doubtful accounts shown on the aging schedule.
  e. The Allowance for Doubtful Debts account is reduced whenever an account is written off.

8. a. The total of the accounts written off rarely agrees in total with the accounts that were "allowed for."

  b. An account cannot be collected once it is written off.

  c. Accrued expenses are a factor to consider only when preparing financial statements.

  d. An accrued expense and an accrued liability are closely related.

  e. At the end of each accounting period there usually exist some unrecorded expenses which must be taken into consideration.

9. a. Accruals can involve revenues as well as expenses.

  b. Accrued items affect both the balance sheet and the income statement.

  c. All of the papers and calculations related to the preparation of the financial statements are known as the accountant's working papers.

  d. The adjusting entry for late purchase invoices always affects accounts payable.

  e. Late purchase invoices are not processed by the accounting clerks because they will already have been recorded as an adjusting entry by the accountant.

10. a. A reversing entry is always exactly the opposite of a previously made adjusting entry.

  b. A reversing entry is always made early in the new accounting period.

  c. The effect of a reversing entry is to eliminate any doubling effect created by an adjusting entry and the regular accounting procedures.

  d. The adjusting entry for late purchase invoices does not affect any accounts in the subsidiary ledger.

  e. The last step in the complete accounting cycle is the post-closing trial balance.

Challenge Exercise

6. Shown below and on page 665 is the adjusted trial balance of ABC Company arranged alphabetically as of December 31, 19-6.

Examine the trial balance carefully and answer the questions that follow. Round off figures to the nearest dollar.

ABC COMPANY

TRIAL BALANCE

DECEMBER 31, 19-6

	DR	CR
Accounts Payable		$ 15 364
Accounts Receivable	$ 18 500	
Accumulated Depreciation—Automotive Equipment		28 321
Accumulated Depreciation—Buildings		14 042
Accumulated Depreciation—Office Equipment		4 930
Advertising Expense	2 750	
Automotive Equipment	37 270	
Bank	1 800	
Bank Charges and Interest	3 250	
Bank Loan		20 000
Buildings	75 700	
Depreciation of Automotive Equipment	3 835	
Depreciation of Building	3 245	

Depreciation of Office Equipment	855	
Drawings	50 000	
Gasoline and Oil Expense	11 437	
Insurance Expense	3 275	
J. Scott, Capital, January 1		57 155
Land	50 000	
Light and Heat Expense	12 070	
Miscellaneous Expense	350	
Mortgage Payable		65 000
Office Equipment	8 350	
Prepaid Insurance	2 750	
Revenue		124 276
Supplies	1 075	
Supplies Used	1 250	
Telephone Expense	950	
Wages	40 376	
	$329 088	$329 088

1. **Given that the current portion of the mortgage payable is $2 500, calculate the totals of each classification on the balance sheet.**
2. **Is this company in a good position to pay its debts? Explain.**
3. **Does the company have an increase or decrease in capital over the year? How much is the increase or decrease?**
4. **Given that the fixed assets were all purchased on January 1, and are depreciated on the declining balance method at government rates, calculate exactly when they were purchased.**
5. **Is this a profitable business in terms of the percentage of net income compared to the owner's investment? What is the percentage figure?**
6. **Calculate the percentage of net income compared to total revenue.**
7. **In percentage terms, how much of this company is owned by the owner, and how much by the creditors?**

---

7. **Examine each of the following situations carefully. In each case, decide if an adjusting entry is necessary. If you decide one is not, give an explanation. If you decide one is, give the adjusting entry. Also, state the accounting principles involved in making your decision.**

In each case you are dealing with a company that has a December 31 year-end. You are employed by the company either as an auditor or as an accountant.

1. The company is a paving company. It keeps on hand (Paving Materials account) a supply of materials which it needs for the type of work it performs. During the course of preparing the work sheet, you are handed $12 500 of "materials used slips" which should have been given to you before December 31. All of these slips pertained to jobs completed before December 31.
2. The company owns a building which has become unnecessary. It rents the building at a monthly rental fee of $1 000. The renter provides 12 post-dated cheques for the rent in advance. During the course of your audit you discover

that the rent cheques for the last four months of the year were not deposited. The employee who had attended to this had terminated her employment and the replacement had not known about the rental arrangements. The cheques were found in an envelope in the company safe and were deposited in January.

3. Last March 1, the company that you work for borrowed $20 000 from a close friend of the owner. The agreement was that the principle would be paid back in five years, and that the loan would carry interest at the rate of 15 per cent to be paid annually on March 1. The loan was recorded but no entries were made for the interest.

4. During the course of your audit you discover that the owner of the company has had a $17 500 automobile charged to Truck Expense. The automobile was purchased on September 1. The company uses the declining-balance method of depreciation at government rates.

5. While performing the audit of a movie theatre, you uncover the following situation. During November and December the movie house conducted a promotion of the sale of books of theatre tickets. These were intended as gift ideas for the Christmas season. The promotion was a success. $32 500 was taken in and was credited to Ticket Revenue. Your investigation revealed that none of the tickets had been used in the year just ended.

6. During the course of your audit for a lawyer you discover that she had engaged in a barter transaction that was never recorded in the company books. The lawyer had done legal work for a construction company which had built a recreation room for the lawyer in full payment. The contractor, when contacted by you, said that the amount involved was $25 000.

7. The company which you work for has a biweekly pay system with a one week holdback. In other words, employees are not paid until one week after a pay period is completed. You find out that the total payroll of $27 500 for the two weeks which ended on December 31 was recorded one week later, in the month of January.

8. You are engaged in auditing a major company with a net income in the range of $4 000 000. During the course of your audit you discover that the company neglected to depreciate a $100 000 brick building which had an undepreciated cost of $73 509.19. The company has already had its financial statements printed.

9. The company you are auditing usually records revenue when the jobs are completed. You discover that a job worth $72 000 was recorded on January 5, after the year-end. Your inquiries reveal that the job was entirely completed before the year-end but that it took a few days to get the invoice prepared.

10. During the course of your audit you find that $2 500 of this January's sales were recorded in the books in December last. Your questions reveal that the owner had requested this be done to improve the income statement for the period just ended.

8. **If the following errors are not corrected, state in each case whether the net income will be understated or overstated and by how much.**

   1. The $4 200 cost of installing a new machine in a factory was charged to Repair Expense.
   2. $135.00 was credited to Discounts Allowed instead of to Discounts Earned.
   3. A journal entry in the amount of $1 500 was posted as a $150 debit to Furniture and Fixtures and as a $150 credit to Accounts Payable.

9. The Sutton Hardware store takes inventory only at December 31, the end of its fiscal year. The gross profit of the business is stable and has averaged 40 per cent over the last five years. As of January 31 the ledger of the business showed the following balances:

Merchandise Inventory (at cost)	$ 51 920
Sales	103 850
Purchases	65 920

   Complete the schedule below to estimate the value of the merchandise inventory at January 31.

Sales		$ _____
Cost of Goods Sold		
Inventory January 1	$ _____	
Purchases	_____	
Goods Available for Sale	$ _____	
Less: Inventory January 31	_____	
Cost of Goods Sold		_____
Gross Profit		$ _____

10. During a physical inventory at December 31, 19—, certain merchandise which cost $2 500 was counted and included twice. The inventory was therefore overstated by $2 500.

    1. **What is the effect of this error on the cost of goods sold figure?**
    2. **What is the effect of this error on the net income figure?**
    3. **What is the effect of this error on the total assets?**

11. Given below is the general ledger trial balance of Marlin Marine of Halfmoon Bay, B.C., at December 31, 19-5, the end of the fiscal year.

MARLIN MARINE
TRIAL BALANCE
DECEMBER 31, 19-5

	DR	CR
Bank	$ 3 642.09	
Accounts Receivable	26 319.04	
Allowance for Doubtful Accounts		$ 179.15
Merchandise Inventory	170 209.41	
Supplies	2 655.00	
Prepaid Insurance	2 956.00	
Land	90 000.00	
Buildings (Brick)	120 309.00	
Accumulated Depreciation—Buildings		17 159.06
General Equipment	56 237.50	
Accumulated Depreciation—General Equipment		27 443.90
Automotive Equipment	48 962.11	
Accumulated Depreciation—Automotive Equipment		32 168.11
Accounts Payable		39 374.17
Sales Tax Payable		2 389.60
Bank Loan		148 000.00
M. McIvor, Capital		242 541.10
M. McIvor, Drawings	40 000.00	
Sales		425 931.20
Bank Charges Expense	18 026.19	
Building Repairs	3 751.70	
Car and Truck Expense	26 491.30	
Freight-in	4 976.21	
Light, Heat, and Water	2 627.48	
Miscellaneous Expense	1 924.30	
Purchases	216 307.06	
Telephone	2 497.60	
Wages	97 294.30	
	$935 186.29	$935 186.29

1. Using the additional information given below, complete the work sheet for the year ended December 31, 19-5.

Additional Information

a. Purchase invoices received subsequent to the year-end but pertaining to the fiscal period just ended were as follows:

Supplier	Explanation	Amount
Jack's Hardware	Paint for building	$ 192.50
King Oil Company	Gasoline for truck	365.10
Dominion Boats	Boat for resale	1 565.00
Best Marine Limited	Merchandise for resale	1 750.00
Handy Cable	Merchandise for resale	230.45

b. Depreciation is calculated with the declining-balance method using government rates of 5%, 20%, and 30% respectively.

c. The accounts receivable aging schedule showed a total for doubtful accounts at the year-end in the amount of $1 376.45.

d. Inventories taken at December 31, 19-5 were as follows:

| Merchandise | $184 292.00 |
| Supplies | 1 255.00 |

e. Prepaid insurance at December 31 was calculated at $1 432.

f. Wages for the two-week period ended Friday, January 5, 19-6 were $1 875.06. The employees work a five-day week.

g. Bank interest for the month of September is unrecorded. The interest rate is 12 per cent.

2. Prepare the balance sheet and the income statement.
3. Journalize the adjusting and closing entries.
4. Journalize the reversing entries.

12. **Workbook Exercise: Completing a Work Sheet and Performing End-of-Period Accounting.**

13. **Workbook Exercise: Completing a Work Sheet and Performing End-of-Period Accounting.**

14. **Workbook Exercise: Completing a Work Sheet and Performing End-of-Period Accounting.**

For Further Thought

15. **Briefly answer each of the following questions.**

1. Accountability does not always refer to financial statements. Give an example of another accountability situation.

2. Which group of users of financial statements is in the best position to manipulate them? Explain.

3. Is accountability a factor in a business owned and operated by one person? Explain.

4. What is the principal measure of a banker's performance? Explain.

5. Assume that Mrs. Smith is a shareholder in the Coca-Cola Company which has millions of shares outstanding. Mrs. Smith owns 50 shares. She disapproves of certain actions of the company. What can she do about it? What influence will she have?

6. Assume that no reversing entry is made regarding the adjustment for late purchase invoices of a company. Will the accountant have any problem when next attempting to balance the accounts payable ledger? Explain.

7. An auditor might confidently give an opinion on the fairness of the financial statements of a company even though only two or three weeks were spent actually auditing the company's books. On what does the auditor rely to sign the statements with confidence?

8. The text states that "inexact" does not mean "inaccurate." Explain.

9. Explain how the value of the first four columns of a work sheet is determined. In your answer show that there are several possible debit and credit combinations.

10. The general ledger can be counted on to show the estimated true value of accounts receivable only for a short period after the year-end. Explain.

11. How accurate should one be when calculating prepaid insurance? Explain.

12. Depreciation to an accountant does not mean the same thing as it does to the ordinary person. What does it mean to the ordinary person? What factors affect or cause depreciation in the normal sense?

13. Straight-line depreciation requires the making of estimates in advance. How would one obtain reasonably good estimates for an automobile?

14. You are told that the net book value of Trucks is $22 500. What does this information not tell you?

CASE STUDIES

CASE 1 *Comparing Depreciation*

John Franks, a businessman, seeks your advice in regard to the depreciation method that he should use in his business. To help you explain the two methods, complete the following table in your Workbook.

John's only depreciable asset is automotive equipment costing $100 000, expected to last eight years, and to have a salvage value of $5 000.

Year	Net Income Before Depreciation	Declining-Balance at 30%			Straight-Line			Income Tax Gain (or Loss)
		Depreciation for Year	Net Income for Year	Income Tax at 40%	Depreciation For Year	Net Income For Year	Income Tax at 40%	
1	75 000 –							
2	75 000 –							
3	80 000 –							
4	82 000 –							
5	85 000 –							
6	85 000 –							
7	90 000 –							
8	90 000 –							

Questions

1. Under which method is depreciation higher in the earlier years?
2. Which method provides a tax advantage in the early years?
3. What is the net tax advantage or disadvantage after eight years?
4. Why would a businessperson choose the government declining-balance method?
5. Give an advantage or disadvantage of the straight-line method.

CASE 2   *Banker Beware*

You are the manager of a Corner Brook, Newfoundland, bank that has loaned $25 000 to Eunice Freeman, the owner of Ace Consulting Services. You have become concerned about the loan. Eunice has not been cooperative about reducing the loan even when she seems to have money available.

Eunice has provided you with the latest financial statements for the year ended December 31, 19-5. You have just placed these beside the statements for the previous year. The two sets of statements, side by side, appear as follows:

Balance Sheet Year 19-4 ASSETS		Balance Sheet Year 19-5 ASSETS	
Cash	$ 9 000	Cash	$ 2 000
—	—	Accounts Receivable	12 000
Equipment	21 000	Equipment	21 000
Total	$30 000	Total	$35 000
LIABILITIES AND EQUITY		**LIABILITIES AND EQUITY**	
Bank Loan	$25 000	Bank Loan	$25 000
Capital	5 000	Capital	10 000
Total	$30 000	Total	$35 000
Income Statement Year Ended December 31, 19-4		Income Statement Year Ended December 31, 19-5	
Revenues	$59 000	Revenues	$51 000
Expenses	24 000	Expenses	26 000
Net Income	$35 000	Net Income	$25 000

Study the above statements as if you were the banker. Then answer the following questions.

1. What significant new item appears on the 19-5 statement?
2. Give two specific pieces of data that suggest the company is experiencing financial difficulties.
3. Assume that Eunice has used the cash basis of accounting prior to 19-5. This means that revenue was recognized when (and not until) the cash was received for services rendered. In 19-5, however, the balance sheet included the item Accounts Receivable

in the amount of $12 000. Clearly, Eunice has changed to a system that recognizes revenue when it is billed (accrual basis). Suggest a reason why this was done.

4. Redo the statements for 19-5 to be consistent with prior years.

5. What principle has been violated by Eunice?

6. Eunice comes to you to inform you that the revenue for 19-5 should be greater by $200 because of a bookkeeping error. What effect will this have on your evaluation of her company? What principle is at work here?

CASE 3   *Meeting the Deadline*

Stetsko and Company performs all of its own accounting up to the trial balance stage. Then Lu and Company, a firm of chartered accountants from the big city, prepares the adjusting entries and the financial statements.

You are an auditor with Lu and Company, which has just completed the financial statements for Stetsko. You have just driven 500 miles to deliver these statements for an important business meeting that day, and to begin some other audit work.

When you open your files, you find that your working papers have been tampered with. Most important, the balance sheet, the work sheet, and the list of adjusting entries for Stetsko are missing. Only the income statement is present.

The important meeting is only two hours away. Working only with the client's preadjustment trial balance and the income statement, prepare an up-to-date balance sheet in time for the meeting. In addition, prepare a list of the adjusting entries that would have been on the work sheet.

STETSKO AND COMPANY
PRE-ADJUSTED TRIAL BALANCE
JUNE 30, 19—

	DR	CR
Bank	$ 4 172.50	
Accounts Receivable	27 421.00	
Supplies	1 365.00	
Prepaid Insurance	2 280.00	
Furniture and Equipment	12 596.00	
Accumulated Depreciation—Furniture and Equipment		$ 2 500.00
Automotive Equipment	24 800.00	
Accumulated Depreciation—Automotive Equipment		6 500.00
Accounts Payable		6 521.92
Bank Loan		20 000.00
Sales Tax Payable		560.00
I. Stetsko, Capital		25 558.20
I. Stetsko, Drawings	15 000.00	
Sales		58 072.50
Bank Charges	1 132.10	
Automotive Expense	4 547.52	
Miscellaneous Expense	761.50	
Rent	2 600.00	
Telephone	1 712.00	
Wages	21 325.00	
	$119 712.62	$119 712.62

```
                     STETSKO AND COMPANY
                       INCOME STATEMENT
                 SIX MONTHS ENDED JUNE 30, 19—

Revenue
   Sales                                                        $58 072.50
Operating Expenses
   Automotive Expense                          $ 4 997.52
   Bank Charges                                   1 132.10
   Depreciation — Furniture and Equipment          500.00
   Depreciation — Automotive Equipment            1 250.00
   Insurance Expense                              1 580.00
   Miscellaneous Expense                            851.50
   Rent                                           2 600.00
   Supplies Used                                    955.00
   Telephone                                      1 822.00
   Wages                                         21 325.00      37 013.12

Net Income                                                     $21 059.38
```

CASE 4 *Declining-Balance versus Distance-Used*

The company you work for depreciates its trucks using the declining-balance method at government rates. Your boss suggests to you that this does not fairly charge the cost of the truck to the years of its use. It is her opinion that the cost of the truck should be charged over the years on the basis of actual use, that is, on the basis of kilometres travelled. You agree that it is worth considering and decide to make a comparison.

In your investigation you select one truck that was recently sold and for which you have full and complete records. The truck was bought on January 1, 19-1 at a cost of $35 000, had no major repairs, and lasted until December 31, 19-8 at which time it was sold for $3 500. Your records also show that the truck travelled the distances in the following table.

Year	Distance
19-1	21 468 km
19-2	35 698 km
19-3	42 654 km
19-4	45 965 km
19-5	40 365 km
19-6	35 632 km
19-7	27 526 km
19-8	16 201 km
Total	265 509 km

Prepare two depreciation schedules for the above truck to compare the declining-balance method with the distance-used method. With the distance-used method, the depreciation for the first year is calculated as follows: 21 468/265 509 × (35 000–3 500).

Discuss the merits of your boss's proposal.

ENTREPRENEUR
Sonia Jones / Chairman, Peninsula Farm Ltd.

In business, nothing succeeds like a good plan. Occasionally, however, sheer hard work and determination can make a business succeed even when experience and planning are missing. The story of a cow named Daisy, who inspired middle-aged Spanish professor Sonia Jones to plunge into the yogurt industry, is not an illustration of success through careful planning.

Sonia Jones, whose Peninsula Farm Ltd. now sells more than $2 million worth of yogurt a year to nearly 300 food stores in Atlantic Canada, never had anything remotely resembling a plan when she began. Her business started as a kitchen hobby, took over her house, survived her marketing igno-

rance, and threatened her family with bankruptcy. At last — more by hard work, grit, and luck than by design — it became Nova Scotia's prime example of "the little industry that could."

Peninsula Farm came into being "all because we made the mistake of buying a cow," according to Sonia Jones, now its chairman and chief executive officer. In 1972 Sonia was accepted for a teaching position by the Spanish department at Dalhousie University. Her husband, Gordon Jones, who ran a management consulting business on Park Avenue in New York City, sold his business. He was happy to move to Nova Scotia to begin a new life. The Joneses bought a farm on the South Shore of Nova Scotia near Lunenburg, with nearly a kilometre of coastline, a farmhouse, and a barn.

A neighbour advised the Joneses to obtain animals to "gnaw off" the land, and prevent it from being overtaken by bush. After investing in a tractor to cut the hay, a herd of 11 beef cattle to "gnaw," a Jersey cow named Daisy for milk, new fences for the cattle, and chickens to eat the insects, the Joneses found that their country home had become a farming operation, which required a great deal of time to run. In addition, the milk cow, Daisy, produced 24 litres a day of uncommonly rich milk. Since the Joneses were unable to get a licence to sell milk, they started to make what thousands of Atlantic residents would come to regard as "the freshest, creamiest, and tastiest yogurt this side of heaven."

For three years, Sonia's testing laboratory and factory was her home. After many tries, she established a successful technique for incubating gallons of yogurt-inoculated milk in styrofoam picnic baskets. Gordon bought six pigs to eat her mistakes. Soon, the yogurt operation took over the kitchen, dining room, and living room. Sonia recalls, "Our daughters grew up thinking that a house was a kind of gigantic igloo lined with enormous styrofoam blocks." As Sonia's superb yogurt and ice cream became locally famous, visitors flocked to the farm, and, thanks to the pigs, the Joneses were ready for them with ham sandwiches.

It has been difficult to balance the costs of production, including the purchase of automated equipment, against the price they could ask for their yogurt and the volume they could produce and sell. They must also compete with large established yogurt manufacturers from other parts of the country. Their hard work and dedication to quality have paid off, however. Behind their house, the Joneses have built a modern factory. Peninsula Farm Ltd. now makes more than 700 000 litres of yogurt a year, as well as dips and ice cream. They employ 35 people, have their own fleet of trucks, and sell to every major food chain in the region, as well as to small chains and independent stores.

In addition to her success in the food industry, Sonia wrote of her experiences in a best-selling book, *It All Began with Daisy* (E.P. Dutton, 1987). A condensed version in *Reader's Digest* has reached millions of people in five languages, among them actress Tyne Daly, who played Sonia in a TV film based on the book. The publicity from the written material and the film has brought steady streams of visitors to Peninsula Farm and encouraged non-yogurt eaters to try their product.

DISCUSSION

1. How did the Joneses succeed in business with no initial planning?
2. Why did Sonia Jones become a yogurt manufacturer?
3. How did the Joneses manage to live within their means in the early stages of business?
4. How do you think the publicity from Sonia's book and the TV movie might help the sales of Peninsula Farm yogurt?

16 Partnership

16.1 **Partnership: General Information**
16.2 **Accounting for Simple Partnership Formations**
16.3 **Apportionment of Net Income or Net Loss for a Partnership**
16.4 **Financial Statements for a Partnership**
16.5 **Computers in Accounting   Spreadsheets and Decision-Making**

So far you have studied only one type of business organization, the single proprietorship, which is a business owned by one person. The basic concepts and skills of accounting have been introduced in as simple a setting as possible. The single proprietorship, however, is not the only type of business organization. Partnerships and corporations are other types of organization that are very common in the business world. The largest volume of business is done by corporations, which are presented in Chapter 17.

16.1   PARTNERSHIP: GENERAL INFORMATION

A **partnership** is a legal arrangement in which two or more persons (called partners) join together in a business and share in its profits and losses. A company's name often indicates if it is a partnership. Names such as H. Gregg and Sons, Siwicki and Associates, and Lem and Kato are typical.

Each province in Canada has its own Partnership Act to govern the operations of partnerships within its boundaries. There is little difference in the partnership acts of the various provinces.

Partnership Accounts

The main difference between accounting for a partnership and for a single proprietorship occurs in the capital and drawings accounts. A single proprietorship is owned by one person. It has one capital account and one drawings account. A partnership is owned by two or more persons. Each of the owners needs a Capital account and a Drawings account. Therefore, a partnership has more than one capital account and more than one drawings account.

Figure 16.1 offers a simple, graphic comparison of the books for a single proprietorship and those for a partnership with three partners. Observe that the main difference between the two forms of business organization is reflected in the capital and drawings accounts.

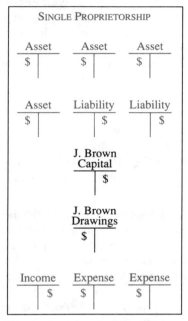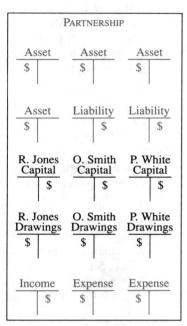

Figure 16.1   A comparison of the accounts for a single proprietorship and for a partnership.

Most of the day-to-day accounting for a partnership is the same as for a single proprietorship. The one aspect of partnership accounting that is new concerns the partners' capital accounts. The partners' capital accounts represent their respective stakes in the business. They must be maintained accurately and in accordance with the wishes of the partners. Their wishes will be stated in the partnership agreement. You will encounter this new aspect of accounting at the end of the fiscal period. At that time the partnership net income or net loss is calculated and divided among the partners.

Reasons for Partnerships

Partnership is a common and convenient form of business organization. To understand why partnerships develop, consider the following simple case histories.

Case 1

Joan O'Brien has wanted her own business for some time but has lacked the courage to start on her own. She has been afraid of the financial risk and the heavy responsibility that she would have to bear alone. Then Joan meets Bob James who agrees to go into business with her. With someone to share the burdens and risks of ownership, Joan finds the courage she needs to change the direction of her career.

Case 2

For several years Bill Salino has been the general manager of a large building firm. Bill knows the business thoroughly and is anxious to go into business for himself. Unfortunately, the nature of the business requires much more capital than Bill can raise alone. Bill is frustrated until he meets Bruno Moro who has the needed capital and is looking for a business opportunity. The two men agree to enter business as partners. By combining their individual resources, they are able to achieve a goal that neither could reach alone.

Case 3

Over the years, J. R. Hall has built up a profitable and expanding business. Mr. Hall sees a good future in the business for his son, Edward. He persuades Edward to join him in the partnership of J. R. Hall and Son. The partnership is a convenient way for father and son to share ownership and keep the business in the family.

These simplified case histories demonstrate that:

1. Partnership allows two or more persons to pool their financial resources to put together funds that could not be raised by any of them separately.
2. Partnership allows two or more persons to bring different resources—money, expertise, personal connections, talent, or experience—together in a business venture.
3. Partnership provides a simple, convenient way for members of a family to operate or continue a family business.
4. Partnership allows two or more persons to give each other the emotional strength needed to undertake a business venture while decreasing the financial risk to any one of them.

Advantages and Disadvantages of a Partnership

Advantages

1. Compared to a corporation, a partnership is simple to organize. It is usually only necessary to register the firm with the provincial government and pay a nominal fee required in the regulations.
2. A partnership lets the business owners bring together greater financial resources and more varied abilities than does a single proprietorship.
3. A partnership is not taxed twice, as are the shareholders of a corporation. A corporation pays annual income tax. In addition, the shareholders of the corporation must pay personal income tax on the dividends the corporation pays them from its after-tax income.

Disadvantages

1. A partnership has a limited life. If any partner dies, goes bankrupt, or becomes mentally ill, the partnership is terminated by law. The remaining partners must arrange to buy out the departed partner's share of the firm. They must also register a new partnership to carry on the business.

2. Partners have unlimited liability. Every partner is liable for the debts of the partnership. This means that an unpaid creditor may sue any partner personally, to recover the money. If the creditor wins the lawsuit, the partner must pay the creditor. The partner may have to sell off personal property, causing financial hardship. This partner in turn has the legal right to recover the money from the other partners. But this may be time-consuming, costly, and inconvenient. Since the creditor will likely choose to sue the partner with the most funds, the other partners may not be able to pay. In that case the sued partner is an unfortunate victim.

3. Partners have "mutual agency." This means that all of the partners are bound by the actions of any one of them, as long as these actions are within the normal scope of the firm's business activities. If one of the partners happens to make a poor business decision, the others cannot say that they are not responsible.

Partnership Agreement

Forming a partnership is not a simple matter. As you have seen, partnerships are formed for various reasons. This means that there is a variety of ownership situations.

No one should enter into a partnership without first obtaining legal advice. A lawyer will see that the firm is registered, provide professional advice to safeguard the interest of the individual partners, and prepare the partnership agreement. The **partnership agreement** is a legal contract that sets forth the terms and conditions of the partnership. The agreement helps the partners to have harmonious relationships from the very beginning. This means that the partnership has a better chance for success and survival.

The following details are included in a partnership agreement:

1. The firm's name and address.
2. The partners' name and addresses.
3. The date on which the partnership is formed.
4. The nature of the partnership business.
5. The duties of the individual partners and the amount of time that they agree to devote to business activities.
6. The amount of capital to be contributed by each of the partners.
7. The salaries (if any) to be paid to each of the partners.
8. The rate of interest (if any) to be paid on the partners' capital account balances.
9. How net income or net loss will be shared.
10. The procedure to be followed in case the partnership ends suddenly because of the death or bankruptcy of a partner.

Partnership Acts

The Partnership Acts of the various provinces protect, in a general way, persons who have entered into partnerships. The terms of these acts, however, cannot take individual cases into account. In particular, the laws state that **if there is no partnership agreement, profits and losses are to be divided equally**. This may be unfair in many instances. Some partners may have contributed more than others to a business.

Partners who have no agreement are bound by the terms of a provincial partnership act, whether it is fair or not. Thus they have a strong reason for ensuring that there is an effective partnership agreement.

SECTION REVIEW QUESTIONS

1. Define *partnership*.
2. Give two examples of a partnership name.
3. What is the main difference between the accounts of a partnership and a proprietorship?
4. How many capital accounts does a partnership have?
5. Why is it important to maintain the partners' capital accounts accurately?
6. Give four reasons why business persons would choose the partnership form of business organization.
7. Give three advantages of the partnership form of business organization.
8. Give three disadvantages of the partnership form of business organization.
9. Explain the purpose of the partnership agreement.
10. In your opinion, what are the three most important items contained in a partnership agreement?
11. Why is it advisable for a partnership to have a formal agreement?

SECTION EXERCISE

1. **Complete each of the following statements by writing in your Workbook the appropriate word or phrase from the list on page 681.**

   1. The partners of a business share in its _____ and _____.
   2. There is a separate _____ account and _____ account for each partner.
   3. You can usually tell if a business is a _____ from its name. You can also tell by examining its _____.
   4. The day-by-day accounting for a partnership is no different than for a _____.
   5. Accounting for the partners' _____ is the principal new aspect of partnership accounting.
   6. The capital accounts of a partnership must be maintained in agreement with the terms of the _____.
   7. Persons may pool their _____ when forming a partnership.
   8. Persons may bring together _____ when forming a partnership.
   9. Partnership provides a convenient way to keep a business in the _____.
   10. Partners often give each other _____ support in regard to running a business.
   11. A partnership is simple to _____.
   12. A partnership is not subject to _____.
   13. According to the law, a partnership is terminated by the _____, _____, or _____ of any partner.
   14. There is no _____ in regards to partnership debts.
   15. _____ means that the partners are legally bound by the actions of any one of them.

16. The partnership agreement should be worked out with the help of a _____.

17. The _____ of the various provinces come into play where there is no partnership agreement and a dispute arises.

List of Words and Phrases

capital accounts	lawyer
capital	ledger
death	limited liability
different resources	losses
double taxation	mutual agency
drawings	organize
emotional support	partnership acts
family	partnership agreement
financial resources	partnership
incapacity	profits
insolvency	proprietorship

16.2 ACCOUNTING FOR SIMPLE PARTNERSHIP FORMATIONS

There is no simple set of rules to be followed in setting up the accounts of a partnership. Circumstances vary greatly and each case must be considered separately.

To introduce you to accounting for partnerships, and to add to your understanding of partnerships in general, the formation of a number of partnerships is described below. These are simplified cases so they are not typical. They are meant to show the general accounting treatment of partnerships without any of the legal complexities.

Case 1   A new business is formed by investment of cash.

Frank Henderson and Charles Wright have been long-time senior employees of Paper Products Company. The two men were dismissed from their positions when the company was taken over by a large corporation. Both men had worked in the paper products business since leaving high school and had no other skills or experience.

For several reasons, they decide to establish a paper products business of their own. They agree to form a partnership in which both are equal partners. To establish the business, $200 000 is needed to lease a suitable building and obtain the necessary furniture and equipment. They each raise $100 000 by means of a mortgage on their homes.

The $200 000 is put in the bank, the necessary legal and accounting advice is obtained, and the partnership of Henderson Wright Paper Products is born. The first accounting entry, to establish the partnership, is:

	DR	CR
Bank	$200 000	
F. Henderson, Capital		$100 000
C. Wright, Capital		$100 000

After the above entry is posted, the accounts of the business are as follows:

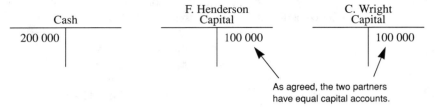

	F. Henderson	C. Wright
Cash	Capital	Capital
200 000	100 000	100 000

As agreed, the two partners have equal capital accounts.

In this case, the following conditions apply.

1. There is no existing business.
2. An entirely new business is formed.
3. New capital in the form of cash is introduced into the business.
4. No money changes hands privately.

Case 2   *Buying into an existing business at book value. Payment is made directly to the owner.*

Debbie Harris is the owner of a well-established and profitable business. She has an equity in the business of $80 000. The books of her business (simplified) are as shown below.

		D. Harris
Bank	Equipment	Capital
20 000	60 000	80 000

Debbie's work load is extremely heavy. She is looking for someone to help her who can handle a lot of responsibility. Jack Soo, a bright young engineer, agrees to go into business with Debbie and to provide the much-needed assistance. The two form a partnership with the following terms and conditions.

1. Jack Soo is to pay $40 000 to Debbie Harris personally for a one-half interest in the business.
2. Net income or net loss of the business is to be shared equally.
3. Jack Soo is to gradually assume an equal share of the work load.

The partnership arrangements are concluded and the $40 000 is paid directly to Debbie Harris. The following accounting entry is made in the books of the existing business to establish it as a partnership.

	DR	CR
D. Harris, Capital	$40 000	
Jack Soo, Capital		$40 000

The accounting entry converts the books from a single proprietorship to a partnership, as shown on page 683.

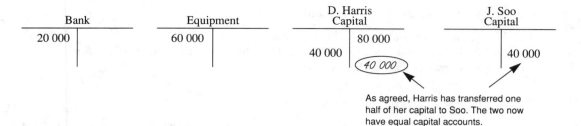

As agreed, Harris has transferred one half of her capital to Soo. The two now have equal capital accounts.

In this case, the following conditions apply.

1. There is already an existing business.
2. No new money is introduced into the business.
3. The money that changes hands between the two partners does so privately, outside of the business.

Case 3   A partner invests cash and other assets in an existing business.

T. Wolfe has a small prosperous business which is growing rapidly. Assume that the accounts of her business, in which she has an equity of $150 000, are as follows:

Bank	Equipment	T. Wolfe Capital
20 000	130 000	150 000

The business needs more facilities and equipment, but Ms. Wolfe does not have the funds to finance the expansion. She has therefore agreed to enter into partnership with R. Hulf. He agrees to contribute land valued at $25 000 cash and a building valued at $75 000 for a full 40 per cent interest in the business. The accounting entry to record the incoming partner's investment is made in the existing books as follows:

	DR	CR
Land	$25 000	
Building	$75 000	
R. Hulf, Capital		$100 000

After the above entry is recorded in the accounts, the business becomes a partnership. Its ledger shows this, as follows:

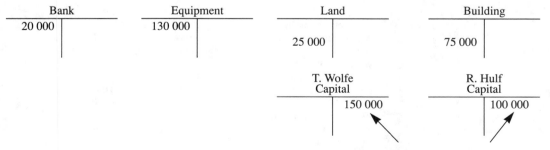

The two partners now have capital accounts in the agreed ratio of 60:40.

In this case, the following conditions apply.

1. There is already an existing business.
2. New capital in the form of land and a building is introduced into the business.
3. No money changes hands privately.

Case 4   Two existing business join together.

F. Malchuk and J. Romback each own a small drugstore. Their stores are located within a few blocks of each other. Their small business operations are threatened by a proposed large shopping centre which will include a branch of a national drugstore chain.

Rather than risk financial failure, the two men decide to join together to lease and operate the new drugstore in the shopping centre. To prepare for the move, they arrange to have their businesses evaluated by an independent appraiser.

The move to the new store is to take place on July 1, 19—. On that day, the new business will assume the assets and accounts payable of the former businesses at the appraised values as shown below.

	Malchuk	*Romback*
Accounts Receivable	$ 20 000	$ 24 000
Merchandise Inventory	100 000	76 000
Supplies	2 000	1 400
Store and Office Equipment	30 000	32 800
Delivery Equipment	16 000	19 200
Total Assets	$168 000	$153 400
Accounts Payable	$50 000	$40 000
Owners' Equity	$118 000	$113 400

The partners agree to the following.

1. Each of them is free to sell or dispose of any business property other than what is listed above.
2. Romback is to bring his equity up to the value of Malchuk's by contributing $4 600 in cash to the partnership. Observe that he does not pay this money to Malchuk privately. It becomes part of the assets of the business.

The accounting entries to set up the partnership in a new set of books are as follows:

		DR	CR
July 1	Accounts Receivable	$ 20 000	
	Merchandise Inventory	100 000	
	Supplies	2 000	
	Store and Office Equipment	30 000	
	Delivery Equipment	16 000	
	Accounts Payable		$ 50 000
	F. Malchuk, Capital		118 000
	To record the appraised		
	assets and accounts payable		
	of F. Malchuk.		

July 1	Bank	$ 4 600	
	Accounts Receivable	24 000	
	Merchandise Inventory	76 000	
	Supplies	1 400	
	Store and Office Equipment	32 800	
	Delivery Equipment	19 200	
	Accounts Payable		$ 40 000
	J. Romback, Capital		118 000
	To record the appraised		
	assets and accounts payable		
	of J. Romback.		

After the above entries are posted, the accounts of the business are as follows:

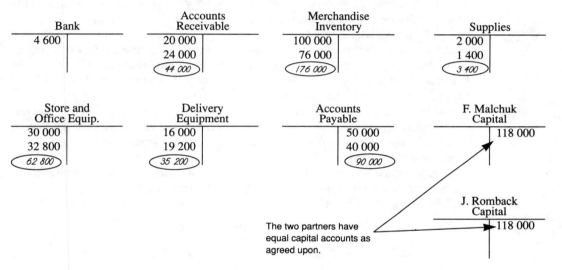

Bank	Accounts Receivable	Merchandise Inventory	Supplies
4 600	20 000	100 000	2 000
	24 000	76 000	1 400
	44 000	*176 000*	*3 400*

Store and Office Equip.	Delivery Equipment	Accounts Payable	F. Malchuk Capital
30 000	16 000	50 000	118 000
32 800	19 200	40 000	
62 800	*35 200*	*90 000*	

J. Romback Capital
118 000

The two partners have equal capital accounts as agreed upon.

In this case, the following conditions apply

1. Two existing businesses are joined together.
2. A new business is formed which takes over most of the assets and accounts payable of the individual proprietorships.
3. No money changes hands privately between the partners.

Note: Cases 1 to 4 describe very simple partnership formations. But partnership formations are seldom simple. The following three cases are more complex.

Case 5   Buying a part interest in an existing business from the owner at a price greater than book value.

John DeLuca is the sole owner of the only commercial licence to operate a taxi business in the small town of Royston, B.C. As a result, his taxi business has thrived.

Mr. DeLuca's investment in the business is $120 000 as reflected in the ledger accounts below.

Bank	Automobiles	Equipment	Building	J. DeLuca Capital
4 000	56 000	24 000	36 000	120 000

The net income figures for the last three years are $90 000, $96 000, and $100 000, respectively. Profits are expected to continue to grow.

Because Mr. DeLuca is nearing retirement age, he is trying to sell a one-half interest in the business. The sale would give him cash for his personal use and reduce his direct involvement. George Blackburn has expressed an interest in a partnership, but the two men have not made a deal.

DeLuca tells Blackburn that the business is expected to earn $100 000 a year or more. As an equal partner, Blackburn would earn a minimum of $50 000 a year. Therefore, DeLuca argues that Blackburn should pay in the range of $400 000 or more for a half share of the business.

The book value of a one-half interest in the business is only $60 000. However, Blackburn is smart enough to know that he cannot expect to buy into the business at book value. He knows that the price for a business depends more on its earning power than on any other factor.

Eventually, the two men agree to a partnership in which Blackburn acquires a full one-half interest in the business by directly paying DeLuca $360 000.

The following accounting entry establishes the business as an equal partnership.

	DR	CR
J. DeLuca, Capital	$60 000	
G. Blackburn, Capital		$60 000

After the above entry is posted, the accounts of the business are as follows:

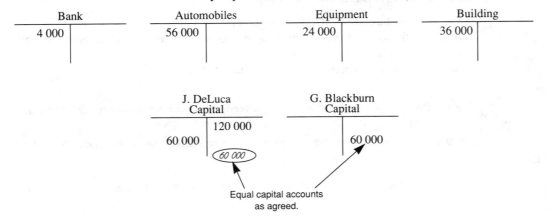

Equal capital accounts
as agreed.

In this case, the following conditions apply.

1. There is an existing business.
2. No new capital is introduced into the business.
3. Money changes hands between the partners privately, outside the business.
4. Part of the business is sold for more than its book value.

Notice that this case is the same as case 2 except that the price paid is more than the book value. This case shows that a business is worth more than its book value when it enjoys above-average profits. These may be the result of good management, superior location, or some other factor.

The introduction of a new partner or the sale of a business can involve payments for goodwill. **Goodwill** is the amount paid for a business in excess of its book value. In the case of DeLuca and Blackburn there was goodwill in the amount of $300 000. The introduction of a new partner could also involve bonus payments (see cases 6 and 7).

Case 6   Introduction of a new partner who invests cash into the business and agrees to pay a capital bonus to the existing partner.

Jerry Mathews is the proprietor of Provincial Developers, a relatively new company in the business of building homes. Although the company is earning above-average profits, it is short of cash because of heavy costs in a number of long-term projects. These projects are expected to bring in substantial profits, but not for two or three years.

When exploring sources of additional funds, Mathews meets Mary Rego. Rego has money available and is anxious to become a full partner in the business. She agrees to contribute $200 000 in cash to the business for a 50 per cent interest.

Mathews's present equity of $100 000 is reflected in the following T-accounts:

Bank	Other Assets	J. Mathews Capital
2 000	98 000	100 000

The first step to admit Rego as a partner is to record her cash contribution. The accounting entry is:

	DR	CR
Bank	$200 000	
M. Rego, Capital		$200 000

After posting, the ledger is as follows:

Bank	Other Assets	J. Mathews Capital	M. Rego Capital
2 000	98 000	100 000	
200 000			200 000
202 000			

Total Capital $300 000

The ledger on page 687 shows that Rego has a capital investment of two-thirds of the total. This is not the agreed ratio. To be correct, each of the partners should have a capital balance of one-half of $300 000, or $150 000. Therefore, an adjustment must be made to transfer $50 000 from Rego's capital account to Mathews's capital account. The accounting entry is:

	DR	CR
M. Rego, Capital	$50 000	
J. Mathews, Capital		$50 000

After posting, the ledger is as shown below:

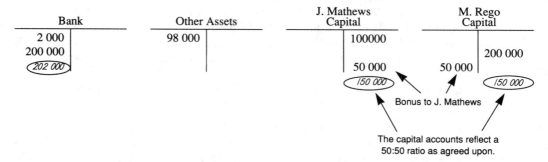

The ledger now reflects an equity section in which the balance in M. Rego's capital account is 50 per cent of the total capital.

Case 7   Introduction of a new partner who is given a capital bonus for agreeing to invest in the business.

Sheri Ludwig owns a small computer business with an equity of $90 000. Sheri manages the business and is a very effective sales person. However, Gayle Perez, a hired employee, possessed the technical competence in computers. When Gayle left the business to accept a better position elsewhere, Sheri was left with a big hole to fill.

Sheri found it impossible to replace Gayle with a hired employee. To attract someone into the business, she had to offer a partnership. Eventually, Susan Ward agreed to join the firm and invest $30 000 for a 40 per cent interest.

Assume that the ledger of the business, immediately before taking in the new partner, is:

Bank	Other Assets	S. Ludwig Capital
16 000	74 000	90 000

The first accounting entry necessary must record Susan Ward's cash contribution. The accounting entry is:

	DR	CR
Bank	$30 000	
S. Ward, Capital		$30 000

After posting, the ledger is as follows:

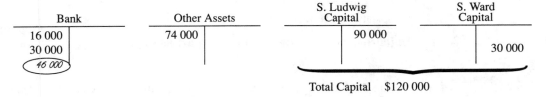

Total Capital $120 000

It can be seen from the above that Susan Ward's capital is $30 000 and the total capital is $120 000. As it stands, Susan Ward's capital is only 25 per cent of the total, not the 40 per cent that was agreed to. Susan Ward's capital must be $48 000 to be correct. Therefore, an adjustment must transfer $18 000 from Sheri Ludwig's capital account to Susan Ward's capital account as shown below.

	DR	CR
S. Ludwig, Capital	$18 000	
S. Ward, Capital		$18 000

After posting, the ledger is as shown below:

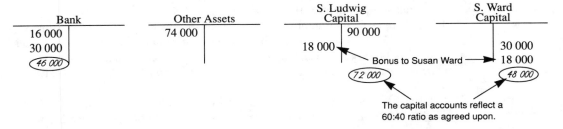

The ledger now reflects an equity section in which the balance in Susan Ward's capital account is 40 per cent of the total capital.

SECTION EXERCISES

1. Eight small scenarios for partnership formation are presented below.

   For each scenario:
   1. In your Workbook complete the chart pertaining to the following questions.
      a. Is there an existing business? Yes or no?
      b. If yes, state the amount of its capital.
      c. Is a new business being started? Yes or no?
      d. Is new capital being put into the business? Yes or no?
      e. If yes, state the amount.
      f. Is money changing hands privately? Yes or no?
      g. If yes, state the amount.
      h. State the total capital of the new firm.

i. Give the final capital ratios for the new firm.
j. Is a bonus to a partner involved? Yes or no?
k. If yes, state how much and to whom.

2. **Give the journal entry to establish the new partnership.**

Scenarios
1. Poulin and Sitch decide to go into the tree and shrub nursery business together. They each invest $50 000 cash with which to begin purchasing the necessary land, stock, facilities, and equipment.
2. Voutt, Gabriel, and Lacosse decide to establish a new dry cleaning business in a small town. They plan to open the business as a partnership and agree to contribute cash in the amounts of $60 000, $60 000, and $20 000 respectively. When the cash is deposited, the partners begin to acquire the facilities needed for the new business.
3. Legrange, Murray, and Remus form a partnership to start a business in the art and graphics field. The partners contribute capital to the firm as follows:
    Legrange—Land, $40 000; Building, $60 000
    Murray—Cash, $100 000
    Remus—Equipment, $50 000.
4. Torma is the sole proprietor of a small car repair business with a capital investment of $75 000. The business is badly in need of expanded facilities to serve its customers but Torma does not have the funds. He agrees to take Cooper in as a partner for a cash contribution to the business of $50 000. Cooper receives a 40% interest in the business.
5. Leblanc is a veterinarian firmly established in a sole proprietorship in a large centre. The capital investment in her business is $200 000. To reduce her work load, she agrees to take in Pella as a partner. Pella is to pay Leblanc $50 000 privately for a one-quarter interest in the business.
6. Carter is the owner of a clothing store for men in which he has invested $100 000. To bring additional capital into the business, he agrees to take in Aspenwall as a partner. Aspenwall is to contribute $25 000 into the business for a 20 per cent interest in the business.
7. Rausch is proprietor of a brick and block business with a total capital of $200 000. Zarba joins the firm as a partner with a cash contribution to the firm of $100 000 for a one-quarter interest in the business.
8. MacLeod and Larson are partners in a fruit and vegetable business. Their capital investments are $85 000 and $65 000 respectively. They share profits and losses equally. Krouse joins the firm as a partner by contributing $60 000 of much-needed cash to the business. Krouse receives a one-third interest in the business.

16.3 APPORTIONMENT OF NET INCOME OR NET LOSS FOR A PARTNERSHIP

In a one-owner business, net income, net loss, and drawings are handled in the accounts in a straightforward manner. In a partnership, the process is more complex. Net income must be properly credited to the individual partners' equity accounts. For the reasons set out below, this requires careful attention.

1. Interest may be paid to the partners based on the balance in their capital accounts.
2. If the partnership is terminated, the net assets of the partnership are distributed to the partners in the same ratio as their capital account balances.
3. Income tax law assumes that the net income of a partnership is earned by the individual partners on the last day of the fiscal period. The way the net income is divided up, therefore, affects the calculation of the partners' individual income taxes.

Factors affecting the Apportionment of Net Income or Net Loss

The following three factors help you decide how to divide up the net income or net loss.

1. *Salaries*   A partner's share of net income (or net loss) often includes some payment for active involvement in running the business. For example, one partner may help manage the business full time and another may not participate at all. Clearly, the partner who participates should be rewarded for the extra time and effort. This is generally referred to as *salary*.
2. *Interest*   A partner's share of net income (or net loss) may include payment for his or her investment in the business. For example, assume that one partner's investment in the business is $100 000 and another's is $20 000. An agreement to pay interest at, say, 10 per cent would reward the partners with $10 000 and $2 000 respectively. The payment of interest rewards the partners in proportion to how much they have invested.
3. *Income- or loss-sharing ratio*   Individual partners expect to receive extra compensation if they bring special talent, business connections, or experience to the partnership. For example, a partner may have some special ability or family connections that will bring additional business to the company.
    These special factors are taken into account when the income- or loss-sharing ratio is decided on. The income- or loss-sharing ratio is the percentages in which the net income or net loss is apportioned to the partners, after salaries and interest are deducted.

> **Note:** Salaries and interest are given preference when apportioning net income or net loss. In other words, salaries and interest are decided first. The remaining net income or net loss is then divided in the income- or loss-sharing ratio.

Statement of Distribution of Net Income

The net income for a partnership is determined in the usual way by means of a work sheet. Once the net income is known, the amount that goes to each partner can be calculated. The factors involved in the calculation, discussed in the previous section, can be found in the partnership agreement.

> **Note:** In the absence of a partnership agreement, income and loss are divided equally in accordance with statute law. Such an equal division does not take into consideration any special contributions of individual partners and may not be fair in all circumstances.

To show how the net incomes of the individual partners are calculated, a formal statement is prepared. The **statement of distribution of net income** shows in detail how the net income is apportioned to the partners.

Case 1   Net income greater than salaries and interest together.

Morris and Graves are partners. Their capital accounts are $100 000 and $40 000 respectively. Their partnership agreement states the following:

1. Graves is allowed a salary of $22 000, and Morris a salary of $10 000.
2. Interest is allowed on the balances in the capital accounts at the rate of 10 per cent.
3. After allowing for salaries and interest, the balance of the net income is divided equally.

At December 31, 19—, the end of their fiscal year, the partnership net income was $130 624.16. The net income is divided according to the calculation shown in Figure 16.2 below.

	Morris	Graves	Total
1. Allocate salaries to partners:	10 000 –	22 000 –	32 000 –
2. Allocate interest to partners	10 000 –	4 000 –	14 000 –
Morris – 10% of $100 000 = $10 000			
Graves – 10% of $40 000 = $4 000			
Subtotals	20 000 –	26 000 –	46 000 –
3. Determine balance of			
net income:			
$130 624.16			
less 46 000 –			
$84 624.16 divided equally	42 312 08	42 312 08	84 624 16
Totals to Partners	62 312 08	68 312 08	130 624 16

Figure 16.2   A rough calculation of the apportionment of net income where the net income is greater than the combined total of salaries and interest.

This calculation is presented by means of the formal statement of distribution of net income as shown in Figure 16.3 below.

MORRIS AND GRAVES
STATEMENT OF DISTRIBUTION OF NET INCOME
YEAR ENDED DECEMBER 31, 19—

	Morris's Share	Graves's Share	Total
Net Income available for distribution			$130 624.16
Salary allowed to Graves	$10 000.00	$22 000.00	$ 32 000.00
Interest at 10 percent allowed on Capital account balances	10 000.00	4 000.00	14 000.00
Morris: 10% of $100 000 = $10 000			
Graves: 10% of $40 000 = $4 000			
Balance of net income divided equally	42 312.08	42 312.08	84 624.16
Totals	$62 312.08	$68 312.08	$130 624.16

Figure 16.3   A statement of distribution of net income where the net income is greater than the salaries and interest combined.

Case 2   Net income less than salaries and interest together.

On June 30, 19—, the partnership of Watts, Tate, and Barlow completed a fiscal year with a net income of $40 152.16. The partnership agreement specifies that net income or net loss is to be allocated according to the following terms.

1. The following salaries are allowed: Watts, $18 000; Tate, $9 000; Barlow, nil.
2. Interest is allowed on capital account balances at eight per cent. The partners' capital account balances are: Watts, $80 000; Tate, $100 000; Barlow, $200 000.
3. The remaining net income or net loss is to be divided as follows: Watts, 25 per cent; Tate, 25 per cent; Barlow, 50 per cent.

The distribution of net income calculation is shown on page 694 in Figure 16.4. Note that in this particular case the total of the salaries and interest is greater than the net income figure. This requires special handling when making the calculation.

	Watts	Tate	Barlow	Total
1. Allocate salaries to partners	18 000 —	9 000 —	—	27 000 —
2. Allocate interest to partners	6 400 —	8 000 —	16 000 —	30 400 —
Watts — 8% of $80 000 = $6 400				
Tate — 8% of $100 000 = $8 000				
Barlow — 8% of $200 000 = $16 000				
Subtotals	24 400 —	17 000 —	16 000 —	57 400 —
3. Deduct Net Income Deficiency				
$57 400 —				
Less 40 152.16				
$17 247.84 divided on				
ratio of 1:1:2	4 311 96	4 311 96	8 623 92	17 247 84
Totals to Partners	20 088 04	12 688 04	7 376 08	40 152 16

Figure 16.4   A rough calculation of the apportionment of net income where the net income is less than the combined total of salaries and interest.

This calculation is presented formally on the statement of distribution of net income as shown in Figure 16.5 below.

WATTS, TATE, AND BARLOW
STATEMENT OF DISTRIBUTION OF NET INCOME
YEAR ENDED JUNE 30, 19—

	Watts's Share	Tate's Share	Barlow's Share	Total
Net Income available for distribution				$40 152.16
Salaries allowed to partners	$18 000.00	$9 000.00		$27 000.00
Interest allowed on Capital accounts				
at 8 per cent	6 400.00	8 000.00	16 000.00	30 400.00
Watts: 8% of $80 000 = 6 400				
Tate: 8% of $100 000 = 8 000				
Barlow: 8% of $200 000 = 16 000				
Subtotals	$24 400.00	$17 000.00	$16 000.00	$57 400.00
Deduct: Net Income deficiency				
in ratio of 1:1:2	4 311.96	4 311.96	8 623.82	17 247.84
Total	$20 088.04	$12 688.04	$7 376.08	$40 152.16

Figure 16.5   A statement of distribution of net income where net income is less than salaries and interest combined.

Accounting for Salaries, Interest, and Drawings in a Partnership

Salaries and Interest

According to the law, a partner participates in a partnership for a share of the earnings of the business, not for a salary or for interest on investment. Therefore, salaries and interest are only used as mathematical factors when dividing net income. Salaries and interest are used in the calculation at the end of the fiscal period. They are then distributed to the partners as part of their share of the net income. But they are not entered into the accounts as salaries and interest.

Drawings

The partners usually need to receive money from the business during the year. Any such payments are considered to be drawings and are debited to the partners' respective drawings accounts. The partners should know roughly how well the business is doing. They can draw money based on their anticipated share of the profits. In some businesses, the amount of the drawings is fixed by formal agreement.

The partners' drawings accounts and their respective shares of the net income are transferred to their capital accounts as part of the closing entry process. This process is explained in the next section.

SECTION REVIEW QUESTIONS

1. Explain, in general, why there is more to the process of handling net income (or loss) and drawings for a partnership than for a sole proprietorship.
2. Give three reasons why it is important to account for partners' capital accounts accurately.
3. How are the net assets of a partnership distributed to the partners if the partnership is terminated?
4. State how the net income of a partnership (or a proprietorship) is looked upon by the income tax department.
5. Three factors affect the calculation of the distribution of net income or net loss to the partners. Name them.
6. What is the usual way to reward a partner who puts more time and effort into the business?
7. What is the usual way to reward a partner who has a greater investment in the business?
8. What is the usual way to reward a partner who brings greater talent, experience, or business connections to the business?
9. What are the two prior charges when apportioning the net income or net loss?
10. How is the net income of a partnership arrived at?
11. How is net income or net loss apportioned in the absence of a partnership agreement?
12. Give the name of the financial statement that shows the apportionment of net income or net loss.
13. Explain if and how salaries and interest are recorded in the accounts.

14. Explain how the partners' drawings are recorded during the fiscal period.
15. How do the partners know how much (approximately) to take out of the business during the fiscal period?

SECTION EXERCISES

1. **This exercise appears in your Workbook.**

   Three partnership situations are described below. **For each one, complete the chart to show how you would arrange for the partnership profits to be apportioned.**

   1. A and B operate a partnership in which:
      — the two partners maintain equal capital account balances,
      — both partners work full time in the business,
      — neither partner has any special background or experience.

   Complete the chart.

Give a salary to a partner or partners?	Y or N?	
If yes, which one(s)?		
Give interest on capital balances?	Y or N?	
Divide balance of net income equally?	Y or N?	
If N, ratio to favour which partner?		

   2. A and B form a partnership in which:
      — A invests $200 000 in cash,
        B invests $20 000 in cash.
      — A does not participate at all in running the business,
        B works full time in the business.
      — A has many profitable business connections,
        B has a great deal of experience and talent in the industry.

   Complete the chart.

Give a salary to a partner or partners?	Y or N?	
If yes, which one(s)?		
Give interest on capital balances?	Y or N?	
Divide balance of net income equally?	Y or N?	
If N, ratio to favour which partner?		

3. A, B, and C form a partnership in which:
  — A invests $500 000 cash in the business,
    B invests $100 000 cash in the business,
    C makes no financial investment.
  — A and B do not work in the business in any way,
    C works full time in the business.
  — A and B have no experience, talent, or connections,
    C is experienced, talented, and has connections.

Complete the chart.

Give a salary to a partner or partners?	Y or N?	
If yes, which one(s)?		
Give interest on capital balances?	Y or N?	
Divide balance of net income equally?	Y or N?	
If N, ratio to favour which partners?		

2. **In your Workbook, for each of the following situations, informally prepare the calculation of apportionment of net income.**

	a.		b.		c.		d.			e.		f.		
Partners	A	B	A	B	A	B	A	B	C	A	B	A	B	C
Capital account balances	50 000	50 000	25 000	150 000	100 000	100 000	20 000	20 000	25 000	100 000	10 000	10 000	20 000	80 000
Rate of interest on capital	nil		nil		nil		8%			10%		10%		
Salaries	nil		nil		10 000	25 000	20 000	nil	nil	nil	15 000	nil	12 000	8 000
Remaining income- or loss-sharing ratio	3:2		capital accounts		1:1		4:3:2			1:2		5:3:1		
Net income or loss	$60 000		$72 800		$90 000		$135 000			$86 600		$130 000		

3. **In your Workbook for each of the following situations, informally prepare the calculation of apportionment of net income or net loss.**

	a.		b.		
Partners	A	B	A	B	C
Capital account balances	50 000	100 000	20 000	30 000	40 000
Rate of interest on capital	8%		12%		
Salaries remaining	20 000	25 000	10 000	12 000	14 000
Income- or loss-sharing ratio	1 : 1		3 : 2 : 1		
Net profit or loss	profit $13 000		loss $48 000		

16.4 FINANCIAL STATEMENTS FOR A PARTNERSHIP

Financial statements for a partnership include more than the balance sheet and the income statement. A partnership also requires a statement of distribution of net income, which you have just studied, and a statement of partners' capital, which is described in this section.

The financial statements of a partnership consist of the following:

Statement No.1. Balance Sheet
Statement No. 2. Income Statement
Statement No. 3. Statement of Distribution of Net Income
Statement No. 4. Statement of Partners' Capital

The financial statements for a partnership have to be prepared in a certain order. This is because information from one statement is needed to complete another. The statements of a partnership are prepared in the following order:

1. Income Statement
2. Statement of Distribution of Net Income.
3. Statement of Partners' Capital.
4. Balance Sheet.

The preparation of the four statements for a partnership is studied below. The sample statements are based on the simplified work sheet for Jones, Ross, and Warner shown in Figure 16.6.

Jones, Ross, & Warner	Work Sheet				Year Ended Dec 31, 19—			
Accounts	Trial Balance		Adjustments		Income Statement		Balance Sheet	
	Dr.	Cr.	Dr.	Cr.	Dr.	Cr.	Dr.	Cr.
Petty Cash	100 —						100 —	
Bank	3700 —						3700 —	
Accounts Receivable	37461 —						37461 —	
Allow. for Doubtful Debts		1956 —		102 —				2058 —
Supplies	1500 —			625 —			875 —	
Prepaid Insurance	900 —			484 —			416 —	
Investment in Property	20000 —						20000 —	
Furniture and Equipment	7000 —						7000 —	
Accum. Depr. Furn. & Equip.		3490 —		702 —				4192 —
Automobiles	12000 —						12000 —	
Accum. Depr. Automobiles		4875 —		2137 50				7012 50
Accounts Payable		5962 —		175 —				6137 —
M. Jones, Capital		19452 12						19452 12
M. Jones, Drawings	18500 —						18500 —	
G. Ross, Capital		15137 09						15137 09
G. Ross, Drawings	14000 —						14000 —	
A. Warner, Capital		25410 79						25410 79
A. Warner, Drawings	22396 —						22396 —	
Sales		82940 —				82940 —		
Advertising	3000 —				3000 —			
Automobile Expense	4600 —				4600 —			
General Expense	350 —		175 —		525 —			
Light, Heat, and Water	600 —				600 —			
Rent	2400 —				2400 —			
Telephone	1290 —				1290 —			
Wages	9426 —		110 —		9536 —			
	159223 —	159223 —						
Bad Debts Expense			102 —		102 —			
Supplies Expense			625 —		625 —			
Insurance Expense			484 —		484 —			
Deprec. Furn. & Equip.			702 —		702 —			
Deprec. Automobiles			2137 50		2137 50			
Accrued Wages Payable				110 —				110 —
			4335 50	4335 50	26001 50	82940 —	136448 —	79509 50
Net Income					56938 50			56938 50
					82940 —	82940 —	136448 —	136448 —

Figure 16.6 The work sheet for Jones, Ross, and Warner.

Income Statement (Statement 1)

The income statement is prepared in the usual way from information on the work sheet. Figure 16.7 shows the income statement for Jones, Ross, and Warner.

		Statement 1
JONES, ROSS, AND WARNER		
INCOME STATEMENT		
YEAR ENDED DECEMBER 31, 19—		

Income
Sales		$82 940.00

Operating Expenses
Advertising	$3 000.00	
Bad Debts	102.00	
Automotive Expense	4 600.00	
Depreciation of Automobiles	2 137.50	
Depreciation of Furniture and Equipment	702.00	
General Expense	525.00	
Insurance	484.00	
Light, Heat, and Water	600.00	
Rent	2 400.00	
Supplies	625.00	
Telephone	1 290.00	
Wages	9 536.00	26 001.50
Net Income		$56 938.50

Figure 16.7 The income statement for Jones, Ross, and Warner.

Statement of Distribution of Net Income (Statement 2)

The net income figure of $56 938.50 to be distributed to the partners is picked up from the work sheet. Additional information needed to complete the statement is found in the partnership agreement. In this case,

1. G. Ross and A. Warner are to receive annual salaries of $5 000 each.
2. Interest is allowed on capital at the rate of 10 per cent.
3. After allowing for salaries and interest, the balance of net income or net loss is apportioned in the ratio of 2:1:2 to Jones, Ross, and Warner respectively.

You are already familiar with the statement of distribution of net income. For Jones, Ross, and Warner, the statement is shown below in Figure 16.8 on page 701.

Statement of Partners' Capital (Statement 3)

The statement of partners' capital shows the changes in the partners' capital accounts for the fiscal period. It is shown on a separate statement because there is not enough room on the balance sheet for more than one proprietor.

The statement begins with the capital account balances carried forward from the previous period's statement. The increases from profits and the decreases from drawings are then summarized. The statement ends with the current end-of-period balances.

Statement 2

JONES, ROSS, AND WARNER
STATEMENT OF DISTRIBUTION OF NET INCOME
YEAR ENDED DECEMBER 31, 19—

Net income available for distribution $56 938.50

	M. Jones	G. Ross	A. Warner	Total
Salaries allowed to partners		$ 5 000.00	$ 5 000.00	$10 000.00
Interest on Capital accounts	$ 1 945.21	1 513.71	2 541.08	6 000.00
M. Jones $19 452.12 at 10%				
G. Ross $15 137.09 at 10%				
A. Warner $25 410.79 at 10%				
Balance of net income divided in ratio of 2:1:2	16 375.40	8 187.70	16 375.40	40 938.50
Total distribution to partners	$18 320.61	$14 701.41	$23 916.48	$56 938.50

Figure 16.8   The statement of distribution of net income for Jones, Ross, and Warner.

The information for this statement is picked up from the work sheet and the statement of distribution of net income. The only exception to this occurs if a partner has increased his or her capital investment with a cash contribution. This piece of information can be picked up from the partner's capital account.

For Jones, Ross, and Warner, the statement of partners' capital is shown in Figure 16.9.

Statement 3

JONES, ROSS, AND WARNER
STATEMENT OF PARTNERS' CAPITAL
YEAR ENDED DECEMBER 31, 19—

	M. Jones	G. Ross	A. Warner	Total
Capital Balances January 1	$19 452.12	$15 137.09	$25 410.79	$60 000.00
Add: Share of Net Income for Year (Statement 2)	18 320.61	14 701.41	23 916.48	56 938.50
	$37 772.73	$29 838.50	$49 327.27	$116 938.50
Deduct: Drawings for Year	18 500.00	14 000.00	22 396.00	54 896.00
Capital Balances December 31	$19 272.73	$15 838.50	$26 931.27	$62 042.50

Figure 16.9   The statement of partners' capital for Jones, Ross, and Warner.

Balance Sheet (Statement 4)

The balance sheet of a partnership is the same as for a sole proprietorship, except for the equity section. The final capital figures are taken from statement 3, the statement of partners' capital. The balance sheet for Jones, Ross, and Warner appears in Figure 16.10.

Statement 4

JONES, ROSS, AND WARNER
BALANCE SHEET
DECEMBER 31, 19—

ASSETS

Current Assets			
Petty Cash		$ 100.00	
Bank		3 700.00	
Accounts Receivable	$37 461.00		
Less Allowance for Doubtful Accounts	2 058.00	35 403.00	$39 203.00
Prepaid Expenses			
Supplies		$ 875.00	
Insurance		416.00	1 291.00
Investment			
Property — at cost			20 000.00
Fixed Assets			
Furniture and Equipment	$7 000.00		
Less Accumulated Depreciation	4 192.00	$ 2 808.00	
Automobiles	$12 000.00		
Less Accumulated Depreciation	7 012.00	4 987.50	7 795.50
			$68 289.50

LIABILITIES

Current Liabilities		
Accounts Payable	$ 6 137.00	
Accrued Wages	110.00	$6 247.00

PARTNERS' EQUITY

Partners' Capital (Statement 3)		
M. Jones	$19 272.73	
G. Ross	15 838.50	
A. Warner	26 931.27	62 042.50
		$68 289.50

Figure 16.10   The balance sheet for Jones, Ross, and Warner.

Adjusting and Closing Entries for a Partnership

You have already learned how to make the adjusting and closing entries for a proprietorship. For a partnership, the concept is the same. However, a slight change in the process is required for a partnership because there is more than one capital account and more than one drawings account.

The steps in making the adjusting and closing entries for a partnership are outlined below. Again, the partnership of Jones, Ross, and Warner is used as the example.

1 **Journalize the adjusting entries that appear in the Adjustments column of the work sheet.** These are shown below for Jones, Ross, and Warner.

Dec	31	General Expense	175 –	
		Accounts Payable		175 –
	31	Bad Debts Expense	102 –	
		Allow. for Doubtful Accounts		102 –
	31	Supplies Expense	625 –	
		Supplies		625 –
	31	Insurance Expense	484 –	
		Prepaid Insurance		484 –
	31	Deprec. Furniture & Equipment	702 –	
		Accum. Deprec. Furn. & Equip.		702 –
	31	Depreciation Automobiles	2 137 50	
		Accum. Deprec. Automobiles		2 137 50
	31	Wages Expense	110 –	
		Accrued Wages Payable		110 –
		Adjusting entries for year		

2 **Make an accounting entry that debits each item appearing in the credit column of the Income Statement section of the work sheet, and credits the Income Summary account with the column total.** For Jones, Ross, and Warner, the entry is:

Dec	31	Sales	829 40 –	
		Income Summary		829 40 –
		To close out Income Section		
		credits to Income Summary		
		account.		

3 **Make an accounting entry that credits each item that appears in the debit column of the Income Statement section of the work sheet, and debits the Income Summary account with the column total.** For Jones, Ross, and Warner, the entry is:

Dec	31	Income Summary	26 00 1 50		
		Advertising		3 00 0 —
		Automobile Expense		4 60 0 —
		General Expense		5 25 —
		Light, Heat, and Water		6 00 —
		Rent		2 40 0 —
		Telephone		1 29 0 —
		Wages		9 53 6 —
		Bad Debts Expense		1 02 —
		Supplies Expense		6 25 —
		Insurance Expense		4 84 —
		Deprec. Furn. & Equip.		7 02 —
		Deprec. Automobiles		2 1 3 7 50
		To close out Income Section debits		
		to Income Summary account.		

At this point all of the revenue and expense accounts are closed out, all accounts requiring an adjustment are adjusted, and the Income Summary account has a balance equal to the net income or the net loss.

4 **Close out the Income Summary account to the partners' capital accounts.** The figures needed to do this are found on the final line of the statement of distribution of net income (see page 701). For Jones, Ross, and Warner, the entry is:

Dec	31	Income Summary	56 93 8 50		
		M. Jones, Capital		18 32 0 61
		R. Ross, Capital		14 70 1 41
		A. Warner, Capital		23 9 1 6 48
		To apportion net income to partners.		

The Income Summary account is now closed out and the partners' capital accounts have been increased by their respective shares of the net income. The capital accounts for Jones, Ross, and Warner at this stage are as follows:

M. Jones, Capital

Date	Particulars	Debit	Credit	Balance
Balance	Forwarded			19 452.12 Cr
Dec 31			18 320.61	37 772.73 Cr

G. Ross, Capital

Date	Particulars	Debit	Credit	Balance
Balance	Forwarded			15 137.09 Cr
Dec 31			14 701.41	29 838.50 Cr

A. Warner, Capital

Date	Particulars	Debit	Credit	Balance
Balance	Forwarded			25 410.79 Cr
Dec 31			23 916.48	49 327.27 Cr

5 **For the final closing entry, close out the partners' drawings accounts to their respective capital accounts.** The amounts are picked up from the work sheet. For Jones, Ross, and Warner, these entries are as follows:

Dec	31	M. Jones, Capital	18 500	—		
		G. Ross, Capital	14 000	—		
		A. Warner, Capital	22 396	—		
		M. Jones, Drawings			18 500	—
		R. Ross, Drawings			14 000	—
		A. Warner, Drawings			22 396	—
		To close out Drawings accounts				
		to capital				

When this five-step procedure is completed, the ledger accounts will be adjusted and closed out as necessary. The partners' capital accounts will then reflect the proper balances as at the fiscal year-end. For the partnership of Jones, Ross, and Warner, the capital accounts at this stage are as follows:

M. Jones, Capital

Date	Particulars	Debit	Credit	Balance
Balance	Forwarded			19 452.12 Cr
Dec 31			18 320.61	37 772.73 Cr
Dec 31		18 500.00		19 272.73 Cr

G. Ross, Capital

Date	Particulars	Debit	Credit	Balance
Balance	Forwarded			15 137.09 Cr
Dec 31			14 701.41	29 838.50 Cr
Dec 31		14 000.00		15 838.50 Cr

A. Warner, Capital

Date	Particulars	Debit	Credit	Balance
Balance	Forwarded			25 410.79 Cr
Dec 31			23 916.48	49 327.27 Cr
Dec 31		22 396.00		26 931.27 Cr

The partners' capital accounts at this point agree with the statement of partners' capital (page 701) and with the equity section of the balance sheet (page 702).

SECTION REVIEW QUESTIONS

1. Name the two common financial statements for any business.
2. There are two additional financial statements for a partnership. Name them.
3. Give the order in which to prepare the financial statements of a partnership.
4. Explain the difference, if any, in determining the net income for a partnership.
5. Once the net income figure is known, what additional information is needed in order to make the apportionment to the partners?
6. Why is there a statement of partners' capital?
7. Describe the statement of partners' capital.
8. Describe how the balance sheet for a partnership differs from that for a proprietorship.
9. Explain why there is a difference in closing the books of a partnership.
10. Explain the effect of closing out the Income Summary account to the partners' capital accounts.
11. Explain the effect of closing out the partners' drawings accounts.
12. After closing the accounts the capital balances will appear in three places. Explain.

SECTION EXERCISES

1. Given below are data extracted from the work sheet of Li and Ahu, who are partners in business.

Li and Ahu *Work Sheet*	*Year Ended December 31, 19–8*	
	Balance Sheet	
Accounts	Debit	Credit
P. Li, Capital		116 240
P. Li, Drawings	38 500	
S. Ahu, Capital		204 760
S. Ahu, Drawings	59 300	
	836 495	736 170
Net Income		100 325
	836 495	836 495

Using the additional information given below, prepare:
1. a statement of distribution of net income,
2. a statement of partners' capital.

Additional Information

1. Neither partner receives a salary.
2. Interest at 10 per cent is allowed on capital.
3. The income-sharing ratio is 2:3 for Li and Ahu respectively.

2. Given below is a simplified work sheet for General Associates, owned in partnership by H. Hacio, J. Jaako, and S. Saasto.

General Associates	Work Sheet						Year Ended December 31, 19—0	
	Trial Balance		Adjustments		Inc Statement		Bal Sheet	
Accounts	Dr.	Cr.	Dr.	Cr.	Dr.	Cr.	Dr.	Cr.
Bank	500						500	
Mdse. Inventory	8 000				8 000	9 000	9 000	
Equipment	4 000			500			3 500	
Accounts Payable		2 000						2 000
Hacio, Capital		5 000						5 000
Hacio, Drawings	8 000						8 000	
Jaako, Capital		3 000						3 000
Jaako, Drawings	4 000						4 000	
Saasto, Capital		1 000						1 000
Saasto, Drawings	4 000						4 000	
Sales		45 000				45 000		
Purchases	12 000				12 000			
General Expense	500				500			
Rent	2 500				2 500			
Wages	12 500				12 500			
	56 000	56 000						
Deprec. Equip.			500		500			
			500	500	36 000	54 000	29 000	11 000
Net Income					18 000			18 000
					54 000	54 000	29 000	29 000

Using the additional information given below, prepare:
1. a statement of distribution of net income;
2. a statement of partners' capital;
3. a simple balance sheet;
4. the closing entries.

Additional Information
1. Interest at 20 per cent is allowed on capital.
2. Salaries are given to : Jaako, $4 200; Saasto, $4 000.
3. The income-sharing ratio is 2:1:1 for Hacio, Jaako, and Saasto respectively.

16.5   COMPUTERS IN ACCOUNTING: SPREADSHEETS AND DECISION-MAKING

In business today spreadsheets are not much used for routine bookkeeping activities. Procedures such as journalizing and posting would not be verifiable on a spreadsheet because cell contents can too easily be erased or altered. Using a spreadsheet to record debits and credits would be similar to using a pencil with an eraser nearby.

Why then are spreadsheets so popular with accountants? Accountants are decision-makers and spreadsheets are decision-making tools. In this chapter, you will use a new function that will increase your appreciation of the role of spreadsheets in making decisions.

The Lookup Function

Before you use the **lookup** function to help make decisions, let us look at an application that you are already familiar with. When you completed payroll calculations in Chapter 14, you used tables to determine deductions for the Canada Pension Plan, unemployment insurance, and income tax. To refresh your memory, suppose that you wanted to find the payroll deduction for the Canada Pension Plan for Lynn Coburn. Her biweekly salary is $1 710. To find the amount of her required contribution, you would look it up in the booklet of deduction tables. A section of the tables is shown below in Figure 16.11.

Salary = $1710

Canada Pension Plan Contributions Table (Partial)

From		To	C.P.P.
1692.54	—	1702.53	28.82
1702.54	—	1712.53	29.00
1712.54	—	1722.53	29.18

Figure 16.11   Manual lookup table.

Using the manual method, you would run your finger down the "From" column until you reached the first number greater than $1 710. At that point ($1 712.54), you would back up one row and move across to locate the amount of the deduction: $29.

A spreadsheet can do precisely the same thing. Consider the spreadsheet in Figure 16.12.

First of all, observe that the spreadsheet is split into two distinct areas — the payroll calculation area and the C.P.P. lookup table area. Second, be aware that the figures in the C.P.P. column of the payroll are derived by the spreadsheet from the lookup table. This is done by using the **lookup** function.

	A	B	C	D	M	N	
1	EMPLOYEE	GROSS PAY	C.P.P.	U.I.			
2	C. Abbott	1710.00	29.00				
3	G. Barry	1700.00	28.82				
4	D. Coutts	1800.00	29.18				
5	P. Edie	1702.00	28.82		C.P.P. Lookup Table		
6					1692.54	28.82	
7					1702.54	29.00	
8					1712.54	29.18	
9							
10							
11							
12							
13							

Figure 16.12   A split-screen spreadsheet showing a work area and a lookup table.

Each of the cells in column C of the spreadsheet contains a lookup function. These lookup functions are shown in the table below.

Cell	Function
C2	@VLOOKUP(B2,M6..N8,1)
C3	@VLOOKUP(B3,M6..N8,1)
C4	@VLOOKUP(B4,M6..N8,1)
C5	@VLOOKUP(B5,M6..N8,1)

Let us now study this function more carefully by examining the contents of cell C2 in detail. The contents of cell C2 are interpreted as shown below.

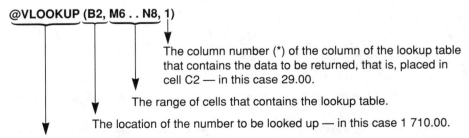

@VLOOKUP (B2, M6 .. N8, 1)

The column number (*) of the column of the lookup table that contains the data to be returned, that is, placed in cell C2 — in this case 29.00.

The range of cells that contains the lookup table.

The location of the number to be looked up — in this case 1 710.00.

The name of the function, meaning to look up a table of data arranged vertically.

Note: The columns of the table are numbered from the left starting at 0. Therefore, the second column of the table is column 1.

To carry out the lookup function, the spreadsheet follows the same logic that you did when you used the manual method. It locates the amount of the salary from cell B2; it runs its electronic finger down the lookup table (M6..N8) until it finds an amount bigger than 1 710.00; it backs up one row; and finally, it moves across to the appropriate column of the table to pick up the amount of the C.P.P. deduction, 29.00, at N7. The 29.00 is returned to C2 for display.

This spreadsheet function increases your ability to make decisions in accounting. The exercises below will give you practice with this new function.

SPREADSHEET EXERCISES

1. **1. Load the spreadsheet model named CH16-1.** The detail from Figure 16.12 will come into view.

   Add three or four more employees of your own choosing to column A. Give them short names so as to stay within one column. Decide on and enter their salaries in column B. Enter the lookup functions in column C. Check out your work to see that the figures returned to Column C are correct.

2. **Load the spreadsheet model named CH16-2.** A work area comes into view which contains the statement of distribution of net income for Morris and Graves who are partners. A new profit-sharing agreement has been worked out by the partners. Graves is to be given a bonus because she is doing most of the work. Once the profit of the partnership reaches $100 000, the bonus arrangement comes into effect. The bonus schedule is given below.

Morris and Graves
Bonus Schedule

Profit	Bonus Percentage
$100 000 — $149 999	5
$150 000 — $199 999	10
$200 000 — $249 999	15
$250 000 — $299 999	20
$300 000 and over	25

Modify the spreadsheet to take into account the new bonus arrangement.

a. Split your spreadsheet window so that you can see both the scratch pad area and the statement area which begins on row 22. Examine the contents of each cell in the statement area until you understand how the model works.

b. Move the cell pointer to A50. A lookup table has already been entered. Carefully read the bonus schedule and see that it corresponds to the lookup table.

c. Move the cell pointer to A15 and enter "Income Bonus" as a label. Then, enter the proper lookup function at C15. The net income figure to be "looked up" is at G6. If you are successful, 5% should be displayed.

d. Adjust the statement by adding the label "Income Bonus" at A31. At E31, the amount of the bonus will be found by multiplying C15 (the bonus percentage) by a cell that contains the net income. To complete the statement, the formulas on row 35 must also be adjusted.

e. **What If?** The "what if capacity" is a term used to describe the power of the spreadsheet to return useful information speedily. Your model now shows the distribution of net income under the new proposal when the net income is $130 624.16. What if the net income is $175 000? $225 000? Or more? The spreadsheet can produce this information easily so that it can be evaluated.

To find the answers to the above questions, all you have to do is change the contents of one cell: G6. To see how this works, change the net income six times so that a different net income bonus percentage is produced by each change. If your model is working properly, cell G37 should always show the correct amount of net income.

Challenge Exercise

3. **Prepare a new proposal for Morris and Graves that uses different income bonus percentages based on different net incomes.** A new lookup table will be necessary. **Start it at A60.**

After you have finished, test your model under different net income conditions. Use a filename other than CH16-2 to save your work.

Communicate It

Prepare a report to Graves that explains the different effects that the bonus proposal may have on the distribution of net income. Graphs would be extremely helpful. **Comment on the soundness of the proposal. End the report with your recommendations.**

COMPUTER REVIEW QUESTIONS

1. Why are spreadsheets inappropriate for use in routine bookkeeping procedures?
2. Explain why the name "lookup" was chosen for the function in this chapter.
3. What does the V in VLOOKUP mean?
4. What would the H in HLOOKUP mean?

CHAPTER HIGHLIGHTS

Now that you have completed Chapter 16 you should:

1. be able to define "partnership";
2. know the purposes of the partnership form of business organization;
3. understand how the equity section of a partnership differs from that of a proprietorship;
4. know the advantages and disadvantages of a partnership;
5. know the essential features of a partnership agreement;
6. know that each of the provinces has a Partnership Act;
7. be able to do the accounting for simple partnership formations;
8. be able to perform the calculations to apportion partnership net income or net loss;
9. be able to prepare the four financial statements for a partnership;
10. be able to prepare the adjusting and closing entries for a partnership.

ACCOUNTING TERMS

goodwill
income- or loss-sharing ratio
partnership agreement

partnership
statement of partners' capital
statement of distribution of net income

CHAPTER EXERCISES

Using Your Knowledge

1. I. James, W. Walsh, and P. Norris are sole proprietors working independently as public accountants. They decide to join together in partnership so that each can specialize in a different aspect of accounting, and jointly purchase a new office building.

   The partnership is to begin on June 1, 19—. At that time, the appraised assets and liabilities of the individual firms are to be transferred to a new set of books for the partnership. It is agreed that capital balances are to be brought up to the level of the partner with the largest equity by the direct contribution of cash to the partnership.

   The appraised values of the assets and liabilities on June 1 are as follows:

Assets	I. James	W. Walsh	P. Norris
Bank	$ 1 500	$ 1 200	$ 800
Accounts Receivable	4 700	3 800	4 200
Supplies	740	630	315
Office Equipment	1 100	3 000	1 500
Automobiles	5 000	4 200	5 500
Total Assets	$13 040	$12 830	$12 315

Liabilities			
Accounts Payable	$ 1 350	$ 1 700	$ 950
Owner's Equity	$11 690	$11 130	$11 365

Give the accounting entries to set up the new partnership.

---

2. Johnson and Anderson are partners in a prosperous business. They have capital balances of $60 000 and $50 000 respectively, and they share income or loss in the ratio of 3:2.

   Campbell is admitted to the partnership on the condition that she contributes $70 000 cash for a one-third capital interest.

   Record the accounting entries necessary to admit Campbell into the partnership.

---

3. The partnership of Franks, Morris, and Shane has been experiencing financial difficulties. The capital balances of Franks, Morris, and Shane are $75 000, $75 000, and $30 000 respectively. They share income or loss in the ratio of 3:3:2.

   The partners persuade Walker, a management expert, to join the firm. Because of Walker's special skills, the partners agree to give her a one-quarter interest in the firm for only $20 000.

   Record the accounting entries to introduce the new partner into the business.

---

4. C. Fredericks is the sole proprietor of a dry-cleaning business. Her equity is $70 000. M. Masters and T. Fritz agree to become partners in the business. Each agrees to contribute $50 000 in cash for a one-quarter interest.

   Record the journal entry or entries to establish the partnership, continuing the same set of books.

---

5. Adams and Suarez are partners who share profits or losses in the ratio of 1:2. They have capital account balances of $40 000 and $50 000 respectively. Because the business needs additional funds, a third partner, Simms, is admitted. Simms agrees to contribute $54 000 cash for a one-third interest in capital.

   Record the accounting entry or entries to admit Simms to the partnership.

---

6. A. Hicks is a sole proprietor with an equity of $73 000. To expand her business, Hicks agrees to take in B. McDoal and T. Wilks as partners. McDoal will pay $125 000 and Wilks will pay $135 000 into the partnership. All three partners will have an equal interest in the business.

   Record the accounting entries to establish the partnership.

---

7. C. Lemaire, R. Kennedy, B. Henning, and S. Dudley are lawyers in partnership. They have just completed their December 31, 19— fiscal year with a net income figure of $126 040.28. Their partnership agreement stipulates that Lemaire and

Kennedy, the senior partners, are to receive salaries of $12 500 before distributing the remainder of net income equally.
Calculate the net income of each of the partners. Show your calculations.

8. Allen and Associates is a loan company with four partners: R. Allen, M. Hamilton, R. Cooper, and T. Cavanaugh. Their respective capital account balances are $12 000, $24 000, $18 000, and $30 000. Their partnership agreement states that net income or net loss is to be divided in the ratio of their capital account balances.
Calculate how the partners would divide a net income of $110 040. Show your calculations.

9. A. Barnes, W. Doby, and S. Barnes are partners who share income and loss in the ratio of 4:4:3 respectively. Their partnership agreement further stipulates that S. Barnes receives a salary of $10 000 while the others receive none, and that interest is to be allowed at nine per cent on the capital account balances held throughout the year. The capital account balances have been $20 000, $35 000, and $5 500 for A. Barnes, W. Doby, and S. Barnes, respectively.
Prepare a statement of distribution of net income for the year ended April 30, 19—. The net income was $87 199.21.

10. For the year ended June 30, 19—, Expert Investors had a net income of $19 640.40. **Using the additional information shown below, prepare the statement of distribution of net income for Expert Investors.**

Additional Information
1. The partners are J. Hunter and C. Lamont.
2. The balances in the partners' capital accounts are: Hunter, $12 000; Lamont, $30 000.
3. Hunter is to receive a salary of $15 000; Lamont, $7 500.
4. Interest is allowed on capital account balances at the rate of eight per cent.
5. The balance of net income or net loss is divided equally.

11. For the year ended June 30, 19—, Industrial Suppliers, owned by Farago and George, had a net income of $37 130. **Using the additional information below, prepare the statement of distribution of net income.**

Additional Information
1. The capital balances are: Farago, $68 000; George, $17 000.
2. No interest is allowed on capital.
3. Farago is to receive a salary of $25 000; George, $20 000.
4. The balance net income or net loss is divided in the ratio of the partners' capital account balances.

12. Given below is the work sheet for Frame Brothers for an annual fiscal period. Additional information appears on p. 716.

ACCOUNTS	TRIAL BALANCE DR.	TRIAL BALANCE CR.	ADJUSTMENTS DR.	ADJUSTMENTS CR.	INCOME STATEMENT DR.	INCOME STATEMENT CR.	BALANCE SHEET DR.	BALANCE SHEET CR.
Frame Brothers	**Work Sheet**						*Year Ended Dec. 31, 19—*	
Petty Cash	100 –						100 –	
Bank	625 40						625 40	
Accounts Receivable	1881 4 32						1881 4 32	
Allow. for Doubtful Accs		630 –		(2) 130 –				760 –
Merchandise Inventory	541 1 0 –				541 1 0 –	571 50 –	571 50 –	
Supplies	1480 –			(3) 830 –			650 –	
Prepaid Insurance	632 –			(4) 408 –			224 –	
Furniture & Equipment	3814 6 –						3814 6 –	
Accum. Depr. Furn. & Equip.		981 4 40		(5) 5666 32				1548 0 72
Automobiles	5328 5 80						5328 5 80	
Accum. Depr. Automobiles		2274 6 24		(6) 916 1 86				3190 8 10
Bank Loan		10000 –						10000 –
Accounts Payable		1144 2 30		(1) 179 8 54				1324 0 84
Sales Tax Payable		1 583 20						1 583 20
Employees' Income Tax Payable		804 20						804 20
S. Frame, Capital		40000 –						40000 –
S. Frame, Drawings	211 6 6 12						211 6 6 12	
G. Frame, Capital		40000 –						40000 –
G. Frame, Drawings	211 3 3 40						211 3 3 40	
Sales		2711 4 0 540				2711 4 0 540		
Bank Charges	900 –				900 –			
Canada Pension Plan Exp	750 –				750 –			
Light, Heat, & Water	1940 40				1940 40			
Miscellaneous Expense	384 40				384 40			
Purchases	9462 4 40		(1) 168 3 20		9630 7 60			
Rent	2400 0 –				2400 0 –			
Telephone	1200 –		(1) 115 34		131 5 34			
Unemployment Insce. Exp.	293 50				293 50			
Wages	7484 0 –				7484 0 –			
	4084 2 5 74	4084 2 5 74						
Bad Debts Expense			(2) 130 –		130 –			
Supplies Expense			(3) 830 –		830 –			
Insurance Expense			(4) 408 –		408 –			
Deprec. Furn. & Equipment			(5) 5666 32		5666 32			
Deprec. Automobiles			(6) 916 1 86		916 1 86			
			1799 4 72	1799 4 72	2711 0 3742	3285 5 5 40	2112 9 504	1537 7 7 06
Net Income					575 1 7 98			575 1 7 98
					3285 5 5 40	3285 5 5 40	2112 9 504	2112 9 504

Additional Information
1. S. Frame receives a salary of $20 000, G. Frame receives a salary of $16 000.
2. S. Frame and G. Frame divide the remainder of net income in the ratio of 2:1 respectively.

Required:
1. Prepare the statement of distribution of net income.
2. Prepare the statement of partners' capital.
3. Prepare the balance sheet.
4. Prepare the closing entries.

---

13. The work sheet for Childs, Fogh, and Hedman for an annual fiscal period is on page 717.

Additional Information
1. Each partner receives an annual salary of $36 000.
2. Interest is allowed on capital account balances at the rate of eight per cent.
3. The remainder of net income is divided in the ratio of 3:2:2 to Childs, Fogh, and Hedman respectively.

Required:
1. Prepare the statement of distribution of net income.
2. Prepare the statement of partners' capital.
3. Prepare the balance sheet.
4. Prepare the closing entries.

---

14. **In your Workbook, for each of the following, indicate which statement is not true.**

1. a. In terms of volume of business, corporations are by far the most significant type of business.
   b. A partnership exists where two or more persons called partners join together in a business venture and share in its profits or losses.
   c. Lem and Kato could be the name of a partnership.
   d. Arnold Felic, Carpenter, could be the name of a partnership.
2. a. The province of Alberta does not have a Partnership Act.
   b. The main difference in accounting for a partnership and for a proprietorship is in respect to the capital and the drawings accounts.
   c. A proprietorship has only one Capital account and one Drawings account.
   d. Each owner of a partnership needs a Capital account and a Drawings account.
3. a. The partners' capital accounts represent their respective stakes in the business.
   b. The partnership net income or net loss is divided among the partners as part of the end-of-period accounting activity.
   c. The information needed to work out the split of net income or net loss is found in the Partnership Act.

d. A person might go into partnership to ease the financial risk involved in a business venture.

Childs, Fogh, and Hedman — Work Sheet — Year Ended June 31, 19-5	TRIAL BALANCE DR.	TRIAL BALANCE CR.	ADJUSTMENTS DR.	ADJUSTMENTS CR.	INCOME STATEMENT DR.	INCOME STATEMENT CR.	BALANCE SHEET DR.	BALANCE SHEET CR.
ACCOUNTS								
Petty Cash	300 –						300 –	
Bank	4496.22						4496.22	
Accounts Receivable	39857.64						39857.64	
Allow. for Doubtful Accs		73.50		(2) 1764.63				1838.13
Supplies	1238.10			(2) 290.85			947.25	
Prepaid Insurance	2412.30			(4) 1029.30			1383 –	
Investment in Property	21000.00						21000.00	
Furniture and Equipment	17568 –						17568 –	
Accum. Deprec. Furn. & Equ.		5840.70		(5) 2345.46				8186.16
Automobiles	48218.52						48218.52	
Accum. Deprec. Autos		21180.63		(6) 8111.37				29292 –
Accounts Payable		4694.91		(1) 435 –				5129.91
Employees Inc. Tax Payable		255 –						255 –
C.P.P. Payable		92.25						92.25
K. Childs, Capital		105000 –						105000 –
K. Childs, Drawings	45600.93						45600.93	
R. Fogh, Capital		105000 –						105000 –
R. Fogh, Drawings	45286.05						45286.05	
B. Hedman, Capital		60000 –						60000 –
B. Hedman, Drawings	30027.90						30027.90	
Fees Earned		218310.78				218310.78		
C.P.P. Expense	687.48				687.48			
Car Expenses	10227.21		(1) 270 –		10497.21			
Light, Heat, and Water	3051.45				3051.45			
Miscellaneous Expense	982.89		(1) 165 –		1147.89			
Postage	2893.38				2893.38			
Rent	14400 –				14400 –			
Telephone	1899.87				1899.87			
Unemp. Insce Expense	441.63				441.63			
Wages	40858.20		(7) 1500 –		42358.20			
	520447.77	520447.77						
Bad Debts, expense			(2) 1764.63		1764.63			
Supplies Expense			(2) 290.85		290.85			
Insurance Expense			(4) 1029.30		1029.30			
Deprec. Furn. & Equip.			(5) 2345.46		2345.46			
Deprec. Automobiles			(6) 8111.37		8111.37			
Accrued Wages Payable				(7) 1500 –				1500 –
			15476.61	15476.61	90918.72	218310.78	44368.55	31629.45
Net Income					127392.06			127392.06
					218310.78	218310.78	44368.55	44368.55

4. **a.** A partnership allows for the pooling of financial and other resources.

   b. J. R. Hall and Daughter could be the name of a partnership.

   c. Mary Smith and Father could be the name of a partnership.

   d. A partnership is subject to double taxation.

5. **a.** The net income of a partnership is eventually paid out in the form of dividends.

   b. A partnership has *limited life*.

   c. A partnership has *unlimited liability*.

   d. A partnership has *mutual agency*.

6. **a.** A disadvantage of a partnership is the procedure to be followed in the event that one of the partners dies.

   b. In case of a partnership bankruptcy, creditors must sue all of the partners personally.

   c. If one partner makes a stupid decision in the course of partnership business, the other partners are stuck with it.

   d. There should be a partnership agreement for every partnership.

7. **a.** The partners' names and addresses are included in the partnership agreement.

   b. In the absence of a partnership agreement, income or loss is shared equally.

   c. The best procedure to be followed in the case of the unforeseen termination of a partnership is found in the provincial Partnership Act.

   d. A person can become a partner in a business without contributing any cash or other asset.

8. **a.** Tutt has a proprietorship with an equity of $50 000. Koster agrees to join the firm for a full one-half interest without contributing any assets. Tutt's equity will become $25 000.

   b. Copp owns a business with an equity of $50 000. Kent agrees to join the firm for a full one-quarter interest and contributes $50 000 to the partnership. Copp's equity will become $75 000.

   c. Aaron owns a business with an equity of $50 000. Kapp agrees to join the firm for a full one-third interest and contributes $40 000 to the partnership. Aaron's equity will become $60 000.

   d. Boyko owns a business with an equity of $50 000. Lysak agrees to join the firm for a full one-fifth interest and makes no financial contribution to the firm. Boyko's equity will remain at $50 000.

9. A, B, and C are partners in a business. The net income of the business for the year just completed is $60 000. The partnership agreement provides for no salaries or interest. The net income is divided among the partners as follows: $5 000, $20 000, and $35 000 respectively.

   The income-sharing ratio is:

   a. 5:20:35

   b. 1:4:7

   c. 1/12:4/12:7/12

   d. none of the above.

10. A and B are partners. The net income for their business for the fiscal period just completed is $100 000. The two partners each get $50 000.

    a. The income-sharing ratio could have been 50:50.

b. A could have received a salary of $25 000.

c. The income-sharing ratio could have been 1:2.

d. A could have received a salary of $60 000, and B a salary of $40 000.

11. a. According to the law, a partner earns a share of the profits and not interest or salary.

b. The use of salaries and interest in apportioning net income or net loss serves no useful purpose.

c. The partners' drawings accounts are closed out to their capital accounts.

d. The statement of partners' capital is necessary because of lack of room on the balance sheet.

CASE STUDIES

CASE 1 *Keeping a Key Employee*

D. R. Johnson is a lawyer with a well-established and highly profitable practice. He built up the practice alone over a period of 20 years. In the past few years, the demands of the business have been exceptionally heavy, forcing him to work many more hours than normal. He has not been able to spend much time with his family nor enjoy much time at the summer home.

To help relieve the work load, Johnson hired Lorna Fox, a law student. At first, Lorna worked during the summer months when her classes were not in session and in the evenings during the school term. Later, she joined the firm on a full-time basis for one year's required work experience. Lorna proved to be talented and energetic and of considerable value to the business.

Lorna acquired the experience that she needed, and Johnson benefited by the reduced workload. But, now Lorna's graduation is approaching. She will be fully qualified in her own right and will be free to open her own office or to seek employment with a more prestigious firm.

Johnson is faced with the unpleasant prospect of losing Lorna. He is very happy with her performance and, above all, does not want a return to the long, arduous working days.

Questions

1. Why did Lorna join Johnson's firm?

2. How well has Lorna performed in the business?

3. What is the most prized benefit to Johnson of the present arrangement?

4. What event is about to take place that will change the relationship between Lorna and Mr. Johnson?

5. Explain how this relationship will be changed.

6. Devise a plan whereby Mr. Johnson could entice Lorna to stay with his firm. Be prepared to explain your plan to your classmates.

CASE 2   *A Way out of a Cash Squeeze*

Fred Norris is the sole owner of Hilltop Ski Area which he has developed over the last 10 years. The ski area has excellent hills and very reliable snow conditions. Since its beginning, the business has been increasingly profitable. In the most recent fiscal year the business earned $110 000.

Over the years, Fred has used the profits of the business to pay off the large debts incurred for the original property and equipment. As a result, the position of the business is regarded as sound, with property presently valued at $1 500 000, and no large debts. Unfortunately, however, the equipment is either completely worn out or obsolete.

If the ski area is to remain popular, Fred must obtain new lifts and hill-grooming equipment. The new equipment would cost $1 200 000 and would last for a minimum of 20 years. Neither Fred nor the business has that kind of money available. Bank financing is available at an interest rate of 12 1/2 per cent, on the condition that the bank loan be reduced by $50 000 annually. The bank interest would amount to $150 000 in the first year. Fred estimates that the new equipment would attract additional skiers to the area and produce an annual net income in earnings of $180 000 in the first year and more in subsequent years.

Fred receives an offer from Harry Watson, a man with great confidence in the future of skiing. Harry offers to put up the $1 200 000 for the new equipment on the condition that he receive a half interest in the business.

Questions

1. **On the assumption that Fred Norris proceeds with the improvements, and obtains the needed funds from the bank, answer the following questions.**

   1. State the amount of last year's net income.
   2. State the amount of the expected increase in revenue.
   3. State the amount of the increase in expense as a result of bank interest.
   4. State the amount of the increase in expense as a result of additional depreciation.
   5. Calculate the expected net income for this year.
   6. State the amount that must be repaid to the bank.
   7. State the amount of net income that remains for Fred Norris personally.

2. **On the assumption that Fred Norris proceeds with the improvements and obtains the needed funds from Harry Watson, answer the following questions.**

   1. State the amount of last year's net income.
   2. State the amount of the expected increase in revenue.
   3. State the amount of the increase in expense as a result of interest.
   4. State the amount of the increase in expense as a result of additional depreciation.
   5. Calculate the expected net income for this year.
   6. State Fred Norris's share of the net income figure.
   7. State the amount of net income that remains for Fred Norris personally.

3. In your opinion, what choice should Fred Norris make? **Keep in mind that if he chooses to take in a partner, he must give up one half of his equity in the ski area.**

CASE 3 A Problem of Sudden Termination

R. Iwasko and G. Nashimo have been partners in the business of importing goods from Japan and other Pacific countries. The business has been very profitable. But the two partners have had to draw heavily on their personal resources to get the business started and to cope with rapid growth.

On January 31, 19—, the balance sheet of the business is as shown below. The equity figure of $90 496 does not represent the true worth of the business which is estimated to be in the neighbourhood of $300 000.

IWASKO AND NASHIMO
BALANCE SHEET
JANUARY 31, 19—

ASSETS

Current Assets			
Cash		$ 438	
Accounts Receivable (Net)		13 072	
Merchandise Inventory		125 000	
Prepaid Insurance		415	
Supplies		1 432	$140 357
Plant and Equipment			
Land		$ 35 000	
Buildings	$145 000		
Less Accumulated Depreciation	32 075	112 925	
Furniture and Equipment	$72 000		
Less Accumulated Depreciation	48 456	23 544	
Automobiles	$22 473		
Less Accumulated Depreciation	15 903	6 570	178 039
			$318 396

LIABILITIES AND OWNERS' EQUITY

Current Liabilities		
Accounts Payable	$112 500	
Bank Loan	50 000	$162 500
Mortgage Payable		65 400
Owners' Equity		
R. Iwasko, Capital	$ 45 248	
G. Nashimo, Capital	45 248	90 496
		$318 396

On February 1, Nashimo is killed in an automobile accident. Lawyers for the estate of the deceased inform Iwasko that Nashimo's death legally terminates the partnership. Further, the family is taking the legal steps necessary to obtain Nashimo's share of the worth of the business.

Iwasko is fully aware that he will have to comply with the law. However, he has his own future to think about. He hopes to be able to continue to operate the business because it has proven to be profitable and satisfying.

Questions

1. What does partnership law state regarding the death of a partner?
2. What is Nashimo's equity in the business?
3. What is the estimated worth of the business?
4. How much should Nashimo's family get out of the business?
5. What problem does this present for Iwasko?
6. What would be the most straightforward way for Iwasko to resolve the problem suggested in 5 above?
7. Give one undesirable aspect and one desirable aspect of this course of action.
8. Give an alternative course of action, one involving participation in the business by Nashimo's family.
9. Give an undesirable aspect of this course of action.
10. What must happen if Iwasko can neither borrow money nor make a deal with Nashimo's family?
11. What additional hardship would this involve?
12. How could insurance be used to avoid difficulties of sudden termination?

CASE 4   *Partnership Agreement Unnecessary?*

Hutton and Inman hastily formed a partnership which was expected to last for only two or three years. They intended to buy and sell metric supplies in order to take advantage of the changeover to the metric system of measurement.

Hutton was an expert on metrication. He had lived and worked for several years in a country that used the metric system. Inman knew nothing of the metric system but agreed to study it and become expert in it.

Prior to officially registering the partnership, the two partners discussed a tentative income-sharing plan. Each partner was to be compensated according to his contribution of capital, time, and talent. However, because Hutton quickly became very busy, the two men never got together to make an official agreement. The business was operated without one.

In the process of establishing the business, Inman could raise only $16 000 of the $30 000 that he had promised. As well as coming up with his own $30 000 share, Hutton came up with the $14 000 balance of Inman's share.

The business did well financially, thanks to the efforts of Hutton, who did most of the work. Inman never could master the metric system of measurement. He was of little help except to unpack and pack goods for shipment. Inman also took off a lot of time for golf in the summer and curling in the winter.

At the end of the first year of operation, the business netted a tidy profit of $76 000. When it came time to discuss the profit split, Inman told Hutton that the Partnership Act stated that profits have to be divided equally. Inman claimed to be sorry but there was nothing either of them could do about it.

Questions

1. Is Inman correct in his claim that the profits of the business must be divided evenly?

2. What serious business error was made by Hutton?

3. If you were Hutton, what action would you take at the end of the first year?

4. If the partnership were terminated, would the net assets of the business be divided equally? Explain.

ENTREPRENEUR
Peggy Cole / Mmmarvellous Mmmuffins

Peggy Cole grew up during a time when many people felt a woman's place was in the home. Accepting the social values of her time, Peggy spent most of her life "performing her duty" as a wife, mother, and homemaker. As attitudes changed, Peggy's changed as well, and in her mid-fifties she did a remarkable thing. At an age when many people are set in their ways, looking ahead to retirement, Peggy opened her own business.

Her first venture was a small shop selling wooden products. The attempt failed because the supplier of the merchandise did not deliver the goods as promised. The failure was disappointing but not without benefit. It provided good experience for Peggy since she discovered inner qualities that would help her succeed in the business world. She had good health and tireless energy, and wasn't afraid of change. Although at first she worried about her lack of formal education, she found it wasn't a handicap. She was a good organizer, she could learn, and she could handle details.

Peggy kept her eyes open for another business opportunity. A relative who had a muffin outlet advised her to look at a franchising operation. With a successful franchising chain, the extensive research and planning is already done so the chance for success is far greater. Having a relative already established in the business gave her access to important information that made her decision easier. However, there were obstacles to overcome. The cash investment of nearly $200 000 was too much for her alone. As well, an outlet demanded a lot of owner participation; this would mean long hours. It was intimidating, to say the least.

At this time Tom Bullock came into the picture. Tom, a member of the family circle, was also interested in owning a small business. He agreed to join Peggy in applying for a muffin outlet that they would own in partnership. Having a partner made the business a lot easier for both of them. First, it gave them a broader financial base from which to approach the bank for the needed initial investment. Second, they could split the duties. Peggy, who disliked paperwork, would run the store. Tom would look after the banking, payroll, accounting, and the extensive reporting that was required by head office. They would split the investment equally, but because Peggy's workload would be heavier than Tom's, she would receive a larger share of the earnings. On this basis they applied for and obtained a "mmmarvellous mmmuffins" franchise in the Georgian Mall in Barrie, Ontario.

Peggy and Tom have been operating their franchise now for over three years. The profits are not on a grand scale; wages and bank interest take a big chunk. There is the nuisance of staff turnover to deal with. And the hours are long. Baking starts at seven in the morning and the outlet closes at nine in the evening. Peggy has to be there so much of the time that she regularly puts in 70-hour weeks. Because she is tied down by the business it has been quite some time since she had a vacation.

Despite the downside, Peggy feels good about the business. It gives her an important focus in her life and has a positive effect on her self-image. "It's mine," she says with great pride.

What about the future? Peggy and Tom are committed to a 10-year lease on the premises. When the lease expires, they will reevaluate their plans. What they decide to do will depend on many things, not the least of which will be Peggy's energy as she reaches her sixties. An interesting possibility is the sale of the business at a good profit. But that is a long way down the road. For now, it is business as usual.

DISCUSSION

1. Name three personal qualities that were an advantage to Peggy in business.
2. How did having a partner help Peggy overcome obstacles of starting the business?
3. Why did Peggy receive a higher share of the earnings?
4. What is one of the biggest disadvantages that Peggy encounters in owning a muffin franchise?
5. What is a plus factor for Peggy in owning her own business?
6. How can Tom and Peggy make a good profit over and above the regular earnings of the business?

Corporations

17.1 General Information
17.2 Accounts of a Corporation
17.3 Dividends
17.4 Accounting for the Issue of Shares and for Organization Costs
17.5 Types of Preferred Shares
17.6 Equity Section of the Balance Sheet for a Corporation
17.7 Income Tax for Corporations

The corporation is a very common form of business organization. Since most large businesses and industries are corporations, they do more business in terms of dollars than partnerships and proprietorships put together.

17.1 GENERAL INFORMATION

A **corporation** is a company which the law considers to be separate and distinct from its owners. Its capital is divided into shares which are held by shareholders.

You can recognize a corporation by its name. According to the laws of Canada and the provinces, a corporation name must include

1. the word *Limited* (which may be abbreviated "Ltd.") or
2. the word *Incorporated* (which may be abbreviated as "Inc." or "Corp.")

Accounting for corporations, particularly for large companies, can be very complex. This chapter does not go into advanced or specialized accounting theory. Rather, it explains the basic concepts of accounting for corporations, so that you will understand how this prominent form of business organization differs from a proprietorship or partnership.

Original Purpose of Corporations

Corporations were originally set up to raise large amounts of capital for risky and costly ventures. The easiest way to obtain funds for a risky venture was from many small investors. The potential effect of a loss for any one investor was thereby reduced. Each investor was able to participate with a relatively small amount of money for a share in the anticipated profits.

726

For example, assume that a capital investment of $2 000 000 is required to put a new mine into operation. This capital would be difficult to raise from only a few people. It is much easier to raise it from a large number of persons. If there were 200 000 contributors they would have to pay only $10 each. Each contributor would receive a **share certificate** (also known as a stock certificate) indicating the amount of that person's share in the venture. A person who owns shares in a company is a **shareholder** or **stockholder**. The shareholder's share of the company's profits is the same proportion as his or her shares in the company.

Characteristics of Corporations

1. A corporation may have different kinds of shares, as will be explained later. However, only the *common shareholders* have voting rights. The controlling owners of a corporation are its **common shareholders**. A small private corporation may have only one shareholder, but a large public corporation usually has many. Each common share in a corporation carries one vote at any shareholders' meeting. A shareholder who owns 50 common shares of a corporation is entitled to 50 votes, whereas one who owns 10 common shares is entitled to 10 votes.

2. An incorporated company is a separate legal entity in the eyes of the law. It is an artificial legal being, separate from those who own it. Even if only one person owns the corporation, it is still a separate legal being from that person. Its existence continues regardless of anything that may happen to any of its shareholders. It has the following rights and obligations of a real person.

   1. It can buy or sell property in its own name.
   2. It can sue or be sued in its own name.
   3. It can enter into legal contracts in its own name.
   4. It must pay its own income tax.

3. The shareholders are financially liable for any actions of the corporation only up to the fully paid value for their shares. They thus have what is known as **limited liability**. In this respect, the corporation is quite different from the single proprietorship and partnership, where the business owners have *unlimited* liability.

4. For the protection of shareholders and prospective shareholders, corporations are subject to government control. The federal government laws concerning corporations are found in the Canada Business Corporations Act. Each of the provinces has a similar act.

   The federal and provincial acts lay down the numerous rules and regulations that must be followed strictly in forming and operating limited companies (corporations). If a company operates across Canada, it will usually choose to operate under the federal act. If a company's operations are within a particular province, it will likely choose to operate under the corporations act for that province. Unfortunately, company law is complex; parts of it are difficult to read and understand.

5. Company policy is not decided by the shareholders as a group but by a committee of the shareholders called a **board of directors**. Directors are elected by the shareholders at the annual meeting. Control of the company is usually in the hands of a few shareholders who have large holdings of the company's shares. They are able

to vote themselves in as directors. Directors do not run the day-to-day operations of the company. But they control the affairs of the company by passing by-laws and making major policy decisions.

6. The board of directors passes by-laws to establish the executive positions of a company. These are the positions of president, vice-president(s), (executive) secretary, treasurer, general manager, and so on. The daily operations of the company are controlled by these hired company officers, or executives.

7. In theory, to control a corporation one must own 50 per cent of the shares, plus one. In fact, a corporation can be effectively controlled through a much smaller percentage of shares. This is because shares are widely distributed and most shareholders do not participate in policy decisions.

Procedure To Incorporate a Company

To incorporate a company, one or more petitioners makes a formal request to the government. Those persons must be directly involved in the formation of the new company. If permission is granted, the government will issue a document called a **charter**, or **letters patent**. The charter contains the following information:

1. the name of the company;
2. the purpose of the company;
3. the address of the head office of the company;
4. the amount of capital authorized. The *authorized* capital is the maximum amount of capital that the charter allows the company to raise. At a later time, the company may wish to increase the authorized capital. It must then apply for permission, which may be given in the form of *supplementary letters patent*.
5. the number of shares authorized;
6. the names, addresses, and occupations of the petitioners for the formation of the company and the number of shares to be taken by each;
7. the number of directors.

Public and Private Corporations

Public Corporations

Business corporations can be either public corporations or private corporations. A **public corporation** obtains its capital partly by the sale of shares to the general public. A public corporation has no limit on the number of its shareholders. Most large corporations are of this type.

Private Corporations

A **private corporation** must meet certain special conditions. The number of shareholders cannot exceed 50. The corporation must raise funds privately and is not allowed to advertise the sale of shares to the public. Most private corporations are small or medium-sized businesses. They have been incorporated by the owners to allow them to retain control of the business while obtaining the benefit of limited liability to protect their personal assets.

Advantages and Disadvantages of Corporations

Advantages

1. In case of a lawsuit or bankruptcy, the liability of shareholders is limited to the full amount that they agree to pay for their shares of the company.
2. The power of the directors is controlled by government regulations.
3. Large investments of capital can be assembled more easily.
4. The company continues to exist despite the death, insolvency, or incapacity of any of its shareholders.
5. New capital can be brought into the business by selling additional shares up to the authorized limit.
6. Shares of a public company may easily be bought or sold through a stockbroker.
7. A person can enjoy ownership in a company without having the responsibility of management.

Disadvantages

1. Most individual shareholders have no influence in the life of the corporation. The board of directors that controls the corporation is elected by the shareholders at the annual meeting. A shareholder has only one vote per share. Those with the most shares have the most votes. It is this group (called majority shareholders) which controls the corporation because they decide who is to be elected to the board of directors.
2. A corporation pays its own income tax, usually at a high rate. In addition, when the profits of the company are distributed to the shareholders, the shareholders are required to include these as income on their personal income tax return. In effect, this is double taxation.
3. Government controls are quite strict. In addition, corporate law is often difficult to read and understand.
4. The fees and legal expenses for incorporating a company are usually substantial.

The Prospectus

In general, a corporation (or person) who wants to sell shares (or bonds) to the public to raise money must prepare a prospectus. It must be made available to potential investors.

A **prospectus** usually takes the form of a brochure. It contains a lot of information about the company. It also describes in considerable detail how the funds the company is raising will be used.

A prospectus forces the corporation to provide true and complete information about its intentions. Members of the public can then more surely make an intelligent investment decision about buying the company's shares.

Included in any prospectus are financial statements. Existing companies seeking additional capital would include financial statements showing their performance for the past several years. New companies would have to include projected statements showing the expected results of future operations.

SECTION REVIEW QUESTIONS

1. Which form of business organization is the most dominant in our economy?
2. In a legal sense, what is special about a corporation?
3. What does the owner of a corporation receive to show that he or she has ownership in the company?
4. What are the owners of a corporation called?
5. How does one know if a company is a corporation?
6. Explain the original purpose of corporations. Give an example of the benefits to one of the owners.
7. Explain what a *common* shareholder is.
8. Give the four ways in which a corporation has the rights and obligations of a real person.
9. Explain what is meant by *limited liability*.
10. Name the federal government act that controls the actions of corporations.
11. How is the board of directors selected?
12. What are the responsibilities of the board of directors?
13. What is the difference between a director and a company officer or executive?
14. What document gives a company the authority to function as a corporation?
15. Explain the difference between a public and a private corporation.
16. Give four advantages of the corporate form of business organization that you believe are the most important ones.
17. Give two serious disadvantages of the corporate form of business organization.

SECTION EXERCISES

1. **In your Workbook, in a numbered column, write down the word or phrase that corresponds to each of the following definitions.** A list of words and phrases is given below.

   1. A corporation that does not obtain its capital from the general public.
   2. The true owners of a corporation.
   3. One of the principal persons involved in obtaining the charter of a corporation.
   4. A company which by law has an existence separate and distinct from its owners.
   5. The restricted responsibility for the debts of a corporation.
   6. A certificate indicating how much ownership a person has in a corporation.
   7. The group of shareholders who are elected to control the operations of the company.
   8. A person who owns shares in a company.

   List of Words and Phrases

board of directors	private corporation
common shareholders	shareholder
corporation	share certificate
limited liability	
petitioner	

2. **Complete each of the following statements by writing in your Workbook the appropriate word or phrase from the list below.**

1. A corporation's capital is divided into _____ which are held by the shareholders.
2. The name of a corporation includes the word _____ or _____, or an accepted abbreviation of one of them.
3. Corporations were originally used for the purpose of raising large amounts of _____.
4. Each owner of a corporation receives a _____ or _____.
5. Only the _____ shares carry the privilege of ownership. Each one carries the right to one _____.
6. An incorporated company is a _____ in the eyes of the law.
7. In certain respects a corporation has the _____ and _____ of a real person.
8. The shareholders have no responsibility for _____ of the corporation beyond the amount required to pay for their shares. This is known as _____.
9. If the scope of a company's operations is within a particular province, it will likely choose to operate under the _____ for that province.
10. The _____ is a committee of shareholders elected to manage the affairs of the company.
11. The day-by-day operations of a corporation are controlled by hired _____.
12. Permission to establish a corporation is given by the government in the form of a _____ or _____.
13. A _____ obtains its capital from the sale of bonds or shares to the general public.
14. A _____ cannot have more than _____ shareholders.
15. The _____ of a corporation continues despite anything that happens to individual shareholders.
16. Shares of a public corporation may be easily acquired or disposed of through a _____.
17. The board of directors is elected at the _____.
18. A corporation must pay its own _____. Thus the shareholders are subject to _____.

List of Words and Phrases

annual meeting	letters patent
board of directors	limited liability
capital	limited
charter	private corporation
common	privileges
Corporations Act	public corporation
debts	rights
double taxation	separate legal entity
executives	share certificate
existence	shares
fifty	stock certificate
income tax	stockbroker
incorporated	vote

3. **For each of the following groups, indicate which statement is NOT true by recording the appropriate letter in your Workbook.**

1. **a.** Most large businesses are corporations.
   b. A corporation has an existence separate and distinct from its owners.
   c. A company is not a corporation if it does not have the word "Limited" in its name.
   d. The corporate form of business reduces the potential loss for any one shareholder.
   e. Corporations allow persons who do not have large sums of money to participate in business ventures.

2. **a.** Each shareholder receives a share certificate that shows the number of shares purchased.
   b. A shareholder who owns a share certificate that reads "Fifty Shares" is entitled to 50 votes.
   c. The true owners of a corporation are its "common" shareholders.
   d. A small private corporation may have only one shareholder.
   e. If a majority shareholder (one who owns more shares than all other shareholders together) dies, the corporation's life is terminated.

3. **a.** A corporation can buy or sell property in its own name.
   b. A corporation can sue or be sued in its own name.
   c. A corporation can suspend a shareholder for misconduct.
   d. A corporation can enter into legal contracts in its own name.
   e. A corporation must pay its own income tax.

4. **a.** The limited liability of a shareholder is given in the company's charter.
   b. Shareholders have no financial responsibility to the company if their shares are paid for.
   c. Corporations are subject to government controls.
   d. The "Acts" which regulate corporations are complex and can be difficult to understand.
   e. Major company policy of a corporation is decided by the board of directors.

5. **a.** All corporations in Canada operate under the Canada Business Corporations Act.
   b. Directors are elected by the shareholders at the annual meeting.
   c. The daily operations of a corporation are carried out by hired executives and other employees.
   d. To have absolute control of a company, a shareholder must own 50 per cent of the shares plus one.
   e. The company charter is a formal document issued by the government.

6. **a.** A public corporation has no limit on the number of its shareholders.
   b. A public corporation obtains all of its capital from the sale of bonds to the public.
   c. A private corporation cannot have more than 50 shareholders.
   d. Most private corporations are small to medium-sized companies.
   e. The main reason that an individual incorporates a business is to have limited liability.

7. **a.** Shares of a public corporation can be easily disposed of through the services of a stockbroker.
   b. Most individual shareholders have no influence in the life of the corporation.
   c. A shareholder with only one share could become a director.
   d. A corporation pays a high rate of income tax.
   e. A corporation pays its own income tax and therefore, when its profits are distributed to its shareholders, they are tax free.

17.2 ACCOUNTS OF A CORPORATION

The accounts of a corporation differ in one major respect from those of a proprietorship or a partnership. The accounts of a proprietorship or partnership have Capital and Drawings accounts. The accounts of a corporation have neither. In their place, the total capital of all of the shareholders together is recorded in two accounts, a Capital Stock account, and a Retained Earnings account.

The **Capital Stock account** is the capital invested by the shareholders when they purchase company shares.

The **Retained Earnings account** is the capital that comes from company profits which have not yet been paid out to shareholders.

These two new accounts are shown in Figure 17.1.

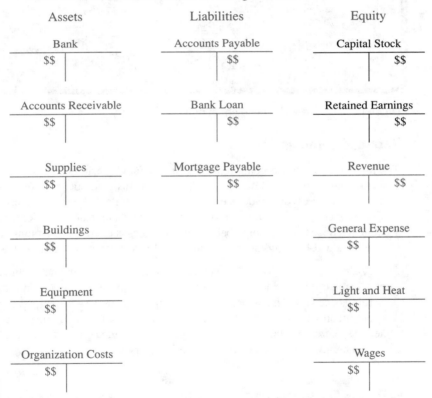

Figure 17.1 A simple general ledger of a small corporation showing the shareholders' equity in two accounts.

Simple Balance Sheet of a Corporation

A simplified balance sheet of a corporation is given in Figure 17.2. The illustration shows the two components of the shareholders' equity—Capital Stock and Retained Earnings.

```
                        CROWN INDUSTRIES LIMITED
                              BALANCE SHEET
                               JUNE 30, 19—

              ASSETS                              LIABILITIES

   Current Assets                        Current Liabilities
   Bank                      $10 500      Accounts Payable           $ 17 800
   Accounts Receivable        25 350
   Merchandise Inventory      20 742
                             $56 592
                                             SHAREHOLDERS' EQUITY
                                         Capital Stock
   Fixed Assets                          Authorized and Issued
   Land                      $ 35 000     10 000 Common Shares       $100 000
   Plant and Equipment         75 000     Retained Earnings          $ 51 292
                             $110 000                                $151 292

   Organization Costs        $  2 500
   TOTAL                     $169 092     TOTAL                      $169 092
```

Figure 17.2   A simple balance sheet of a corporation.

Retained Earnings

The Retained Earnings account represents a company's accumulation of profits over the years, less any profits paid out to shareholders. Profits paid out are known as *dividends*. As profits (or losses) are made, they are put into the Retained Earnings account. As these profits are paid out in the form of dividends to the shareholders, the Retained Earnings account is reduced. The account balance that remains is the retained earnings to that date.

The Retained Earnings account is affected by two types of accounting activity.

1. *Net Income or Net Loss*   At the end of each fiscal period, the net income or net loss of a company is transferred out of the Income Summary account into the Retained Earnings account. This is part of the closing entry process for corporations (p. 760). A net income increases the Retained Earnings account and is entered as a credit. A net loss decreases the Retained Earnings account and is entered as a debit.

    If a net income is earned the accounting entry is:

	DR	CR
Income Summary	$$$$	
Retained Earnings		$$$$

2. *Dividends*   The shareholders of a company are its owners. They expect to receive some of the company's profits in the form of dividends. The directors have the power to declare a dividend. That means they vote a payment to shareholders out of the accumulated net profits in the the Retained Earnings account. A dividend declared reduces the credit balance in the Retained Earnings account. The accounting entries for this are explained in the next section.

Normally, the Retained Earnings account has a credit balance, which is the accumulated net income from years in which a profit was made. It is possible, however, for the account to have a debit balance—a state of negative retained earnings. This usually follows a severe loss or a series of losses. A Retained Earnings account with a debit balance is known as a **deficit**.

SECTION REVIEW QUESTIONS

1. In what major respect do the accounts of a corporation differ from those of a proprietorship?
2. What does the Capital Stock account represent?
3. What does the Retained Earnings account represent?
4. What items are contained in the equity section of a corporation's balance sheet?
5. What item causes retained earnings to increase?
6. Is the increase in question 5 above recorded as a debit or a credit to the Retained Earnings account?
7. What two items cause retained earnings to decrease?
8. Are the decreases in question 7 above recorded as debits or credits to the Retained Earnings Account?
9. At what time are profits or losses transferred to retained earnings?
10. Who decides whether or not there will be a dividend?
11. What type of balance does the Capital Stock account have?
12. What type of balance does the Retained Earnings account usually have?
13. What would cause a negative balance of retained earnings?
14. What is a negative balance of retained earnings called?

SECTION EXERCISES

1. **This exercise appears in your Workbook.**
   A corporation began business on January 1, 19-1. Over the next seven years it made profits and paid out dividends as shown in the chart below.

   Complete the Retained Earnings column of the chart.

Year	Profits (Losses)	Dividends Paid	Retained Earnings at Year-end
1	($45 000)	nil	
2	($20 000)	nil	
3	$25 000	nil	
4	$48 000	nil	
5	$110 000	$50 000	
6	$156 000	$100 000	
7	$227 000	$120 000	

Answer the following questions.

1. Why were no dividends paid in the first three years?
2. Could a dividend have been paid in year 4?
3. In your opinion, why was a dividend not paid in year 4?
4. All of the retained earnings were not paid out in dividends. Give reasons why this would be the case.

2. Mandrell Limited has 10 000 common shares authorized and issued. The trial balance of the company as of December 31, 19-6, is given below.

Prepare a simple balance sheet for Mandrell Limited as of December 31.

TRIAL BALANCE
DECEMBER 31, 19-6

	DR	CR
Bank	$ 500.25	
Accounts Receivable	7 858.35	
Merchandise Inventory	25 326.00	
Supplies	450.00	
Land	50 000.00	
Buildings	275 000.00	
Equipment	116 125.40	
Accounts Payable		$ 23 125.60
Bank Loan		50 000.00
Mortgage Payable		212 325.40
Capital Stock (10 000 Common Shares)		100 000.00
Retained Earnings		89 809.00
	$475 260.00	$475 260.00

3. In your Workbook, in a numbered column, write down the word or phrase that corresponds to each of the following definitions.

1. The funds invested by shareholders in respect to their purchase of company shares.
2. The capital acquired from company profits not paid out to shareholders.
3. Profits paid out to shareholders.
4. A debit balance in the Retained Earnings account.

17.3 DIVIDENDS

A **dividend** is an amount paid to the shareholders out of company profits. Each share of the company receives an equal dividend. The amount paid (if any) is decided (declared) by the board of directors at a directors' meeting.

As was seen in the previous section, the Retained Earnings account is the company's net earnings available to distribute to the shareholders. Therefore dividends may be thought of as coming out of the Retained Earnings account.

Whether a dividend is distributed or not depends on the directors. Only the directors have the power to declare a dividend. They may decide not to declare a dividend, but to use the retained earnings for some other purpose—for example, company expansion. The ordinary shareholder has no direct say in the matter.

Normally, dividends are not declared unless a company is earning satisfactory profits on a regular basis.

Declaring the Dividend

The board of directors meets on an agreed date to decide whether to declare a dividend. If the board of directors declares a dividend, it decides to pay all the shareholders who own their shares on a certain future date. These are the shareholders of record. It also decides the date for which the cheques will be issued. Therefore, there are three important dates associated with dividends.

1. *The date of declaration*   This is the day on which the directors meet and vote for the dividend.
2. *The date of record*   The shareholders who own the shares on this day will be the ones who receive the dividends. Because company shares may change hands frequently (usually through the stock market), a good system is necessary for keeping stock records up to date and accurate.
3. *The date of payment*   This is the date the dividend cheques are to be issued. It is usually a few weeks after the date of record, to give the accounting department time to make the proper calculations and to get the cheques ready for the mail.

Dividends are usually stated at so much a share; for example, a dividend may be $.50 per share for the quarter (a three-month period). Once the board of directors has declared a dividend, the payment becomes a legal obligation of the company. If the company fails to make the payment, the shareholders can sue in the courts.

The various companies acts protect the interests of shareholders. Dividends may only be declared if the following two requirements can be met.

1. Enough cash is available to make the payment.
2. The credit balance in the Retained Earnings account must be large enough that paying the dividend will not create a deficit.

Accounting for Dividends

Accounting for dividends is usually done in two stages as follows.

1. When the board of directors declares a dividend, the liability is set up in a Dividends Payable account. The Retained Earnings account is reduced by the same amount.

   For example, Apex Limited is incorporated with 100 000 shares. Its retained earnings balance is $95 500. On January 10, 19—, the directors of Apex Limited declare a dividend of 50 cents a share to be paid to shareholders of record on January 31. Payment will be made on February 15.

The accounting entry to record the declaration on January 10 is:

	DR	CR
Retained Earnings	$50 000	
Dividends Payable		$50 000

On February 15, when the dividend is paid, the accounting entry to record the payment is:

	DR	CR
Dividends Payable	$50 000	
Bank		$50 000

SECTION REVIEW QUESTIONS

1. What is a dividend?
2. Explain the basis upon which dividends are distributed to the shareholders.
3. Who decides if there is to be a dividend?
4. Give two reasons why a dividend might not be declared.
5. Under what conditions are dividends normally declared?
6. Explain how a dividend is created.
7. Explain how it is determined who is to receive dividends.
8. Explain why the payment date is a few weeks after the date of record.
9. What can the shareholders do if a declared dividend is not paid?
10. What conditions are necessary before a dividend can be declared?
11. Give the accounting entry (ignore amounts) to record the declaration of a dividend.
12. Give the accounting entry (ignore amounts) to record the payment of a dividend.

SECTION EXERCISES

1. **In your Workbook, in a numbered column, write down the word or phrase that corresponds to each of the following definitions.** A list of words and phrases is given below.

   1. An amount of earnings declared by the board of directors to be distributed to the shareholders of a corporation in proportion to their holdings of shares.
   2. The day on which the directors meet and vote for the dividend.
   3. The day as of which it is determined who owns the company shares and therefore who is to receive the dividends.
   4. The account used to show the liability for dividends.

   List of Words and Phrases
   date of declaration
   date of record
   dividend
   dividend payable

2. **Complete each of the following statements by writing in your Workbook the appropriate word or phrase from the list below.**

   1. A dividend is distributed to the _____ in proportion to the number of shares held.
   2. Retained Earnings represents the company's net _____ of earnings.
   3. Only the _____ has the power to declare a dividend.
   4. When dividends are declared they are declared to _____ on a certain date.
   5. A good system is necessary for keeping _____ up to date and accurate.
   6. _____ are usually stated at so much a share.
   7. Once declared, a dividend becomes a _____ of the company.
   8. The Retained Earnings account normally has a _____ balance.
   9. When a dividend is declared, it is set up in a _____ account.
   10. When a dividend is declared, the _____ account is reduced.

   List of Words and Phrases

accumulation	number
board of directors	Retained Earnings
credit	shareholders' records
Dividends Payable	shareholders of record
dividends	shareholders
legal liability	

3. **In your Workbook, complete the schedule shown below for a company whose fiscal year ends on December 31.**

Year	Number of Shares Sold	Cumulative Number of Shares Issued	Income for Year	Dividend Declared Dec. 15	Total Dividend for Year	Retained Earnings Dec. 31
1	10 000		$52 500	$1.00		
2	12 000		$50 250	$1.50		
3	12 500		$60 750	$1.60		
4	15 000		$75 200	$1.75		
5	20 000		$95 050	$1.85		

4. Precision Tools Limited is a company incorporated with 220 000 common shares outstanding. On March 1, 19— the board of directors of the company declared a dividend of 25 cents a share to be paid on March 31 to shareholders of record on March 15.

   Answer the following questions in your Workbook.

   1. **Calculate the total dividend to be paid.**
   2. **Journalize the accounting entry to record the declaration of the dividend.**
   3. **Journalize the accounting entry to record the payment of the above dividend.**

17.4   ACCOUNTING FOR THE ISSUE OF SHARES AND FOR ORGANIZATION COSTS

Company Shares

When company shares are sold for cash, the proceeds from the sale are credited to an account called Capital Stock. The simplest accounting entry to record the sale of shares is the following.

	DR	CR
Bank	$$$$	
Capital Stock		$$$$

The Capital Stock account has a credit balance. It represents the sum of the proceeds from all sales of shares made directly by the company to its shareholders.

Organization Costs

Incorporating a company can be expensive. Initial costs include the fee to obtain the charter from the government, legal fees to company lawyers, and costs for miscellaneous items such as the company seal. Large issues of shares are often sold through an investment dealer, who charges a commission.

Initial costs of incorporation are debited to a "deferred expense" account called **Organization Costs**. On the balance sheet the Organization Costs account appears as an asset. The usual practice is to write off the balance in the Organization Costs account over a period of a few years.

If organization expenses are paid for in cash, the accounting entry to record them is:

	DR	CR
Organization Costs	$$$$	
Bank		$$$$

Often these initial organizational services are not paid for in cash. Instead, they are paid for with shares equal in value to the cost of the services received. When this happens, the accounting entry is:

	DR	CR
Organization Costs	$$$$	
Capital Stock		$$$$

Common Stock (Common Shares)

A corporation's basic class of stock is known as **common stock**. The rights of the holders of common stock include the following:

1. The right to vote at shareholders' meetings. Each share of common stock carries the right to one vote.
2. The right to receive any common dividends in proportion to the number of shares held.
3. The right to share in the assets that remain after creditors have been paid if the corporation is liquidated.

Preferred Stock (Preferred Shares)

A corporation may issue more than one class of stock. Each class of capital stock must be kept in a separate account.

Figure 17.3 shows a simplified general ledger with more than one capital stock account. The accounting entries are the same for each class of stock.

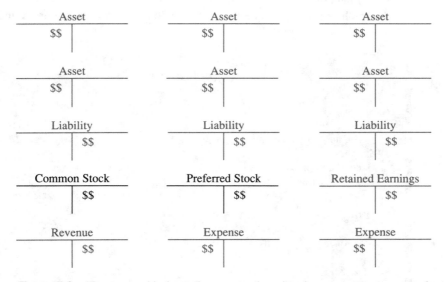

Figure 17.3   The general ledger of a corporation showing separate accounts for two classes of shares.

Preferred stock means shares that have a special privilege when it comes to the payment of dividends. A disadvantage of preferred shares is that they normally do not carry voting rights. The common shareholders usually issue preferred stock so that they can acquire additional capital funds from outsiders without having to give up any control of the company.

If a company issues preferred stock, the preferred shareholders receive dividends first, before anything is given to the common shareholders. This is explained more fully later. Also, if a corporation is liquidated, the preferred shareholders recover their equity before the common shareholders.

Preferred stock can be recognized by the way the company describes it. The following examples show how preferred stock may be described.

1. *8% preferred stock, $100 par value* (a preferred stock with a dividend per share of eight per cent of $100, or $8).
2. *$8 preferred stock, $100 par value* (a preferred stock with a dividend of $8 a share).
3. *$5 preferred stock, no par value* (a no par value preferred stock carrying a dividend of $5 a share).

As is fully explained later, the dividend for preferred shares is limited to a fixed amount. But the amount of common shares dividend is limited only by the earning capacity of the company. In a very profitable year it is possible for the common stock-holders to receive a very large dividend while the preferred stockholders are restricted to their fixed amount.

Preferred shareholders do not necessarily receive dividends every year. If a corpo-ration is not in a position to pay dividends, then the preferred shareholders may be no better off than the common stockholders.

A simplified balance sheet of a corporation having both preferred and common shares is shown in Figure 17.4.

DELTA CORPORATION
BALANCE SHEET
DECEMBER 31, 19–3

ASSETS		
Bank		$ 1 200
Accounts Receivable		35 236
Supplies		1 800
General Equipment		46 588
Automotive Equipment		20 239
		$105 063
LIABILITIES		
Accounts Payable		$ 12 563
Bank Loan		20 000
		$ 32 563
SHAREHOLDERS' EQUITY		
Capital Stock — Common		
5 000 Shares, no par value	$50 000	
Capital Stock — Preferred $2		
1 000 shares, no par value	10 000	
Retained Earnings	12 500	72 500
		$105 063

Figure 17.4   A simplified balance sheet showing both preferred and common shares.

Par Value Shares

Before issuing shares, the board of directors may decide to establish a *preset* value per share known as the **par value**. This value is printed right on the share certificate. Common figures chosen for par value are round amounts such as $10, $25, or $100.

The par value of a share is the suggested selling price at the time it is issued. However, depending on many factors, the shares may be sold 1) at par, 2) for more than par (at a premium), or 3) for less than par (at a discount). This creates accounting complications that are a nuisance. For this reason, the sale of par value shares is now uncommon.

No Par Value Shares

In recent times it has become common practice to issue shares without a par value. This kind of share is known as a **no par value share** .

Corporations which use this type of share avoid the accounting nuisance of discounts and premiums on the sale of shares. Shares of no par value can be sold by the company at any price established from time to time by the board of directors. Provided that they are of the same class, shares of equal rank may sell for different prices at different times.

Accounting Entries for No Par Value Shares

The accounting for the issue of no par value shares is simple because no discount or premium situations exist. Consider the following series of share transactions.

1. *Example:* 1 000 no par value common shares are issued for cash at $9 a share on February 2.

   Accounting entry:

		DR	CR
Feb. 2	Bank	9 000	
	Capital Stock		9 000
	Sale of 1 000 no par value		
	shares at $9 for cash		

2. *Example:* 5 000 no par value common shares are issued for cash at $8.50 on June 15.

   Accounting entry:

		DR	CR
Jun. 15	Bank	42 500	
	Capital Stock		42 500
	Sale of 5 000 no par value		
	shares at $8.50 for cash		

3. *Example:* 500 no par value common shares are issued in exchange for equipment valued at $5 000 on August 20.

   Accounting entry:

		DR	CR
Aug. 20	Equipment	5 000	
	Capital Stock		5 000
	Sale of 500 no par value		
	shares for equipment		
	valued at $5 000		

4. *Example:* 100 no par value common shares are issued on September 1 to pay for $1 250 in legal fees of incorporation.

   Accounting entry:

		DR	CR
Sep. 1	Organization Costs	1 250	
	Capital Stock		1 250
	Issue of 100 shares to pay		
	for legal fees of		
	incorporation		

5. *Example:* 5 000 shares are sold through an investment dealer on September 15 at a price of $12.50. Of these, 4 750 are sold to the public for $59 375 and 250 are kept by the investment dealer to pay for his or her services.

Accounting entry:

		DR	CR
Sep. 15	Bank	59 375	
	Organization Costs	3 125	
	Capital Stock		62 500
	Issue of 4 750 shares to the public and 250 to the investment dealer, all at $12.50		

SECTION REVIEW QUESTIONS

1. What is the simplest transaction regarding the sale of shares of a corporation?
2. What kind of account is the Capital Stock account?
3. What are organization costs?
4. Are organization costs always paid for in cash? Explain.
5. Give the name for the basic class of stock of a corporation.
6. Give the name for the second class of stock of a corporation.
7. What is the usual advantage associated with preferred stock?
8. Explain the meaning of the *par value* of a share.
9. Give the name for a share that does not have a par value.

SECTION EXERCISES

1. **In your Workbook, in a numbered column, write down the word or phrase that corresponds to each of the following definitions.** A list of words and phrases is given below.

   1. Initial costs of incorporation.
   2. A corporation's basic class of stock.
   3. Shares that carry a special privilege in regard to dividends.
   4. A predetermined value that is printed on the share certificate.
   5. A share that does not have a par value.

   List of Words and Phrases
   common stock
   no par value share
   organization costs
   par value
   preferred shares

2. **In your Workbook, indicate whether each of the following statements is true or false by entering a "T" or "F" beside the corresponding statement number. Explain the reason for each "F" response.**

1. The proceeds from the sale of shares are credited to a Capital Stock account.
2. A corporation is allowed to have only one Capital Stock account.
3. The legal fees paid to a lawyer for services in setting up the corporation are an organization cost.
4. Organization costs are debited directly to an expense account.
5. Every share certificate of a corporation carries the right to one vote.
6. Each class of capital stock must be kept in a separate account.
7. At the annual meeting preferred shareholders vote before the common shareholders.
8. Preferred stock is issued so that common shareholders can retain their control of the corporation.
9. Usually, a preferred dividend is limited to a specific amount.
10. Preferred dividends are paid annually without fail.
11. The par value of a share is the amount it must be sold for.
12. It is now common practice to issue shares that have no par value.

---

3. OPRA Corporation is started with authorized capital stock of 200 000 common shares of no par value.

1. In your Workbook, journalize the following initial transactions of OPRA Corporation.

TRANSACTIONS

Feb. 19-6

3   10 000 shares are sold for cash to each of the three petitioners at a price of $10 a share.

8   25 000 shares are sold to some investors at the price of $15, cash.

10 The lawyer accepts 100 shares in exchange for services in organizing the company. The lawyer's services were valued at $1 500.

15 The government fee for incorporation is paid in cash, $100.

18 10 000 shares are sold to an investor at the price of $18 each.

20 5 000 shares are exchanged for land valued at $40 000 and a building valued at $60 000.

22 5 000 shares are sold to an investor for cash at the price of $20.

2. Post the journal entries to the T-accounts provided in the Workbook. Answer the following questions for the date of February 22.
a. What is the balance in the Capital Stock account?
b. What is the balance in the Retained Earnings account?
c. How many shares have been issued?
3. Prepare the balance sheet for OPRA Corporation as of February 22.

4. Wonder World Limited, an amusement park, is a newly incorporated company authorized to issue 100 000 common shares of no par value and 100 000 eight per cent preferred shares having a par value of $100. Five organizing petitioners agree to take 1 000 common shares each at a value of $25 a share.

   1. Journalize the following transactions.

   ### TRANSACTIONS

   May
   6   The five petitioners pay cash for and receive one half of the agreed-upon shares.
   15   Theresa Nyzuk, a lawyer, is given 20 common shares in payment for legal work done in respect to incorporating the company. The work is valued at $500.
   21   5 000 preferred shares are sold through an investment dealer at par. Of these, 4 900 are sold to the general public and 100 are kept by the investment dealer in payment for his services valued at $10 000.
   26   Legal and other incorporation expenses of $200 are paid for in cash.
   29   The petitioners agree to accept the balance of their agreed-upon shares as payment for services rendered in incorporating the company.

   June
   5   Land is purchased for $120 000 cash.
   10   Plant and equipment are purchased for $200 000 cash.
   30   2 000 preferred shares are sold privately for cash at par.

   2. Post the above transactions to the T-accounts provided in the Workbook and prepare a simple balance sheet as at June 30.

5. Regus Corporation is started with authorized capital stock of 10 000 common shares of no par value and 100 000 $5 preferred shares of no par value.

   1. In the T-accounts provided in the Workbook, post the accounting entries for the following transactions for the first year of operation.

   ### TRANSACTIONS

   1. 10 000 shares deemed to be worth $20 000 are taken by the petitioner for her services in establishing the corporation.
   2. 10 000 preferred shares are sold to the general public at $50 a share.
   3. $5 000 cash is paid to the investment dealer for selling the shares above.
   4. Land ($100 000) and a building ($200 000) are purchased for cash.
   5. A net income of $88 000 is earned for the year. (Debit Other Assets and credit Retained Earnings.)
   6. The preferred dividend is declared.

   2. Prepare a simple balance sheet for Regus Corporation after transaction 6.

17.5   *TYPES OF PREFERRED SHARES*

Numerous conditions may be attached to preferred shares. These conditions are important to the shareholder because they can greatly affect the amount of dividends received over the years. Only the most common conditions are discussed here.

The following three conditions are common to holders of most preferred shares.

- They have no voting rights.
- They have a first claim to dividends.
- The dividend is stated as a percentage of the par value or at so much a share.

In addition to the above, preferred shares are usually one of the following three types.

- Non-cumulative
- Cumulative
- Fully participating.

Non-Cumulative Preference Shares

Non-cumulative preference shares are ones where, if the preferred dividend is not paid in any year, the preferred stockholders lose their right to that particular dividend in that year. Remember too that the common shareholders are not entitled to a dividend either in any year that the preferred dividend is not paid.

Sample Calculation of Non-Cumulative Dividends

To understand how non-cumulative dividends work, assume the following data:

1. Common stock, no par value, 100 000 shares, $250 000.
2. Preferred stock 50¢, no par value, 50 000 shares, $500 000 (The normal preferred dividend is $25 000 per year.)
3. Total dividends paid in years 1 through 4:

Year 1	$30 000
Year 2	nil
Year 3	$50 000
Year 4	$120 000
Total	$200 000

The distribution of dividends will be as shown on page 748 (the first figure) if the preferred shares are non-cumulative.

Cumulative Preference Shares

With **cumulative preference shares**, if the preferred dividend is not paid in any year, the unpaid dividend (known as the *arrears* of dividends) must be made up in following years. This must be done before any dividends can be paid to the common shareholders.

Year	Total Dividend	To Preferred	To Common
1	$30 000	$25 000	$5 000
2	nil	nil	nil
3	$50 000	$25 000	$25 000
4	$120 000	$25 000	$95 000
Totals	$200 000	$75 000	$125 000

Note: 1. In any year that a dividend is paid, the preferred dividend is satisfied first.
2. The preferred shareholders lose their right to the dividend in any year that it is not declared.

Sample Calculation of Cumulative Preference Shares

To see how cumulative dividends work assume the same situation as given above for non-cumulative dividends. The distribution of dividends will be as shown below if the preferred shares are cumulative.

Year	Total Dividend	To Preferred	To Common
1	$30 000	$25 000	$5 000
2	nil	nil	nil
3	$50 000	$50 000	nil
4	$120 000	$25 000	$95 000
Totals	$200 000	$100 000	$100 000

Note: In year 3 the preferred dividend is $50 000; $25 000 for year 3, and $25 000 for the dividend missed the previous year.

Fully Participating Cumulative Preference Shares

Fully participating preference shares are ones where the annual dividend paid to the common shareholders is limited. The ratio of the common dividend to the preferred dividend may not be higher than the ratio of the value of the Common Stock account to the value of the Preferred Stock account. Thus the preferred shareholders are protected against the common shareholders' voting themselves an excessive dividend.

Sample Calculation of Fully Participating Preference Shares

To explain fully participating shares, assume the following data:

1. There are no arrears of dividends.
2. Total dividend of $100 000 is declared.

3. Capital stock is as follows:

		Ratio
Fully participating preferred 6%	$1 000 000	4
Common	$ 250 000	1
Total	$1 250 000	

The dividend can be thought of as being distributed in two stages: 1) a basic dividend, and 2) an extra dividend. In this example, the distribution of the dividend between the two groups is calculated as follows:

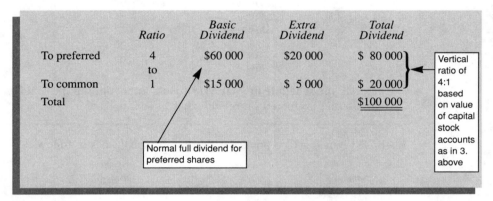

	Ratio	Basic Dividend	Extra Dividend	Total Dividend	
To preferred	4	$60 000	$20 000	$ 80 000	Vertical ratio of 4:1 based on value of capital stock accounts as in 3. above
	to				
To common	1	$15 000	$ 5 000	$ 20 000	
Total				$100 000	

Normal full dividend for preferred shares

SECTION REVIEW QUESTIONS

1. Give the three conditions that are common to most preferred shares.
2. Explain what is meant by a *non-cumulative* preferred share.
3. Explain what is meant by a *cumulative* preferred share.
4. Explain how fully participating dividends are calculated.
5. If preferred shares are fully participating, the preferred shareholders are protected. Explain.

SECTION EXERCISES

1. ABC Limited is incorporated with paid-up capital stock as follows:

Common Stock—no par value—25 000 shares
$1 *Non-cumulative* Preferred Stock—no par value—100 000 shares

Over a seven-year period ABC Limited declared and paid out dividends as follows:

Year	Total Dividend
1	nil
2	$100 000
3	$100 000
4	nil
5	$ 50 000
6	$120 000
7	$150 000

Complete the schedule in your Workbook, apportioning the dividends between common and preferred shareholders.

---

2. PQ Limited is incorporated with paid-up capital stock as follows:

Common Stock—no par value—2 000 shares
$2 *Cumulative* Preferred stock—no par value—10 000 shares

Over a five-year period PQ Limited declared and paid out dividends as follows:

Year	Total Dividend	Common	Preferred
1	$50 000		
2	$70 000		
3	nil		
4	$50 000		
5	$70 000		

Complete the schedule in your Workbook, apportioning the dividend between common and preferred shareholders.

---

3. ABCD Limited is incorporated with paid-up capital stock as follows:

	Account Balance
Common	
No par value, 50 000 shares	$ 500 000
Preferred $1 cumulative, fully participating	
No par value, 100 000 shares	$1 000 000

Over a five-year period the company declared and paid out dividends as follows:

Year	Total Dividend	Common	Preferred
1	$150 000		
2	$150 000		
3	$210 000		
4	$240 000		
5	$270 000		

Complete the schedule in your Workbook, apportioning the dividends between the common and preferred shareholders.

---

4. XYZ Limited is incorporated with paid-up capital stock as follows:

	Account Balance
Common	
No par value, 10 000 shares	$ 400 000
Preferred $7\frac{1}{2}$% Cumulative	
Par value $120, 10 000 shares	$1 200 000

Over a 10-year period XYZ Limited declared and paid out dividends as follows:

Year	Total Dividend
1	$ 90 000
2	$ 80 000
3	nil
4	$190 000
5	$120 000

6	$140 000
7	$148 000
8	nil
9	$250 000
10	$240 000

Complete the schedule in your Workbook, apportioning the dividends between common and preferred shareholders where

1. the preferred shares are non-participating.
2. the preferred shares are fully participating.

17.6 EQUITY SECTION OF THE BALANCE SHEET FOR A CORPORATION

Two typical examples of the equity sections of a balance sheet are shown below in Figure 17.5. These examples were taken from the published reports of public corporations. They show clearly that all of the details of equity are presented. They also show the following common practices:

1. The figures for the current year and the previous year are printed side by side.
2. Large amounts are rounded off to the nearest dollar, or in some cases, the nearest thousand dollars.

(In thousands of dollars)	19-5	19-6
SHAREHOLDERS' EQUITY		
Share Capital		
Common Shares		
Authorized 500 000 no par value shares		
Issued and Outstanding 2 132 151 shares	$ 8 451*	$ 8 373
Retained Earnings	10 865	8 574
	$19 316	$16 947

*These figures represent thousands of dollars. They are rounded off to the nearest thousand.

	19–7	19–8
SHAREHOLDERS' EQUITY		
Common Stock		
Authorized		
4 251 880 Class A common shares		
without par value		
4 000 000 Class B common shares		
without par value		
Issued		
4 251 880 Class A shares	$14 564 045	$ 14 951 670
Contributed Surplus	73 720	73 720
Retained Earnings	22 340 595	18 168 714
	$36 978 360	$33 194 104

Figure 17.5 Two examples of the equity section from published balance sheets.

Contributed Surplus

An equity item called *contributed surplus* occurs frequently in the published reports of public companies. **Contributed surplus** means primarily the following:

1. gifts of plant or property from outsiders,
2. donations of stock or assets from shareholders.

The above items are put into various accounts in the equity section of the ledger when they are received. On financial statements they are usually totaled together and shown as one item called Contributed Surplus.

Appropriations

A substantial credit balance in the Retained Earnings account raises the shareholders' hopes of receiving dividends. However, the directors may decide against declaring dividends. They may decide that it is in the best interests of the company to use available funds for some other purpose. The most common purpose is to expand the company. The company can save on interest expense by using money raised through profits rather than borrowing from outsiders. Also, the directors can retain control of the company if they do not have to sell additional shares in order to raise funds.

To achieve this goal, the directors can reduce the balance in the Retained Earnings account. They can transfer a portion of the retained earnings into a special-purpose account called an *appropriation account*. An **appropriation account** is one to which a portion of retained earnings is transferred so that they won't be seen as being available for dividends.

For example, the directors of Dartco Limited intend to use accumulated company profits to pay for a new building that will cost $250 000. To make their intention clear to the ordinary shareholders, the board of directors meet on June 5 and vote to appropriate $250 000 to pay for the new building. The appropriation is entered in the accounts in the following way:

		DR	CR
June 5	Retained Earnings	$250 000	
	Appropriation for New Building		$250 000
	To record resolution of board of		
	directors, date June 4, 19-2		

Figure 17.6 shows the equity section of the company's balance sheet 1) with no appropriation and 2) after making the appropriation.

1. Without appropriation		2. With appropriation	
Shareholders' Equity		*Shareholders' Equity*	
Common Stock	$100 000	Common Stock	$100 000
Retained Earnings	285 000	Retained Earnings	35 000
Total Equity	$385 000	Appropriation for	
		Expansion	250 000
		Total Equity	$385 000

Figure 17.6   The equity section of a balance sheet as it would appear if 1) no appropriation were made, and 2) an appropriation were made.

When the shareholders read the information from the Balance Sheet they will see a balance of only $35 000 available for dividends, not $285 000. The appropriation has then achieved its purpose of altering the shareholders' perception of retained earnings.

Eventually, the new building will be completed and paid for. The funds for the building will have come from company profits rather than from borrowing. At this point the Appropriation account is no longer needed. When the building is completed and paid for, the balance of the Appropriation account is returned to the Retained Earnings account. The accounting entry is the reverse of the one which made the appropriation in the first place:

In our example

	DR	CR
Appropriation for New Building	$250 000	
Retained Earnings		$250 000

Statement of Retained Earnings

A statement of retained earnings is a part of each set of financial statements of a corporation. The details for this new statement are obtained from the Retained Earnings account for the fiscal period.

A sample statement of retained earnings is shown in Figure 17.7.

STATEMENT OF RETAINED EARNINGS For the year ended December 31, 19-3		
	19-3	*19-2*
Balance at Beginning of Year	$ 301 000	$107 000
Add Net Income for Year	993 000	742 000
	$1 294 000	$849 000
Deduct Dividends Paid	561 000	548 000
Balance at End of Year	$ 733 000	$301 000

Figure 17.7   A statement of retained earnings.

Market Value of Company Shares

Shares of a public corporation may be bought or sold on the open market. A buyer and a seller simply agree on a price and make the transaction. The share certificate is transferred to the new owner.

Public companies must, however, obey the rules of the stock exchange. Shares of these companies are bought and sold ("traded") with the help of stockbrokers. The services of stockbrokers can be obtained for a commission.

The sales data of all transactions on each of the stock exchanges are listed daily in the financial pages of the larger newspapers, as shown in Figure 17.8.

STOCK PRICES Pages 26-35

Your guide for week ending March 10, 1989
An exclusive single record of final weekly quotations of all four Canadian Stock Exchanges: Montreal, Toronto, Alberta and Vancouver.

INDUSTRIAL AND RESOURCE STOCKS

52 Week High	52 Week Low	Stock	Div Rate	High	Low	Cls or Latest	Net Chge	Vol 100s	Yield %	P/E Ratio	Fiscal Period	Eps
						A						
140	35	A&A Foods	....	110	100	100	−10	138 V	....	....	.....	.....
126	25	AAA Stamp Coin	..47	45	45	−5		60 V	....	.....	.....	.....
20	5	AAI Inds	..10	$7\frac{1}{2}$	10	+1		240 C	....	.....	.....	.....
165	60	AAO Aquaculture	..80	80	80	unch		30 V	....	.....	.....	.....
100	8	ABC Technologies	..12	8	10	+1		190 V	....		.....	.....
125	25	ACDS Graphic Sys	..39	31	33	−2		201 M	....	.....	.....	.....
31	17	ACSI Biorex	..19	17	18	−1		808 M	....	.....	.....	.....
150	70	ADS Associates	..80	79	79	−1		40 M	7.9	.....	1988 Jan	.02
....	....	ADT Limited $US	L	19Jan88	265	....	nil	....	....	.....	.....	.....
$\$9\frac{1}{8}$	$5\frac{1}{2}$	AGF Mgmt B pf	0.44	$\$7\frac{1}{8}$	$6\frac{7}{8}$	$7\frac{1}{8}$	unch	449 T	6.2	9.1	1987 Nov	1.26
345	75	AHA Automotive	..125	110	110	-10		162 T	....	....	1987 Dec	.28
$\$6\frac{3}{4}$	325	AMCA Intl	up0.12$\frac{1}{2}$	480	460	465	-15	4453 T	3.2	....	1987 Dec	du6.04
$25	$23\frac{3}{8}$	AMCA Intl pf A	2.21	$\$24\frac{3}{4}$	$24\frac{5}{8}$	$24\frac{5}{8}$	unch	56 T	9.0	....	1986 Dec	.....
$\$24\frac{7}{8}$	$18\frac{1}{2}$	AMCA Intl pf B	2.37$\frac{1}{2}$	$23	$22\frac{3}{4}$	23	$-\frac{1}{8}$	66 T	10.3	....	1986 Dec	.....
$25	$22\frac{1}{2}$	AMCA Intl pf C	2.31$\frac{1}{4}$	$\$24\frac{5}{8}$	$24\frac{1}{2}$	$24\frac{1}{2}$	$-\frac{1}{8}$	159 T	9.4	....	1986 Dec	.....
185	100	AME Limited	0.05	165	160	160	-15	11 M	3.1	14.5	1986 Dec	.11
80	20	APP Applied Poly	..20	20	20	-10		5 V	....	.....	.....	.....
$\$5\frac{3}{4}$	325	ARC Intl	..$\$5\frac{1}{8}$	5	5	+10		70 T	....	.....	1988 Apr	.14
60	26	Aabbax Intl	..45	45	45	unch		40 V	....	.....	.....	.....
20	3	Aabco Ventures	L	28Feb89	4	....	nil	....	....	.....	.....	.....
15	4	Aard Ri Intl	..5	5	5	-3		10 C	....	.....	.....	.....
250	45	Abbey Woods	..121	120	121	-4		7 V	....	.....	.....	.....
60	17	ABDA Intl Hldg	..60	52	55	-2		250 C	....	.....	.....	.....
$\$25\frac{1}{2}$	$18\frac{1}{2}$	Abitibi Price	1.00	$20	$19\frac{5}{8}$	$19\frac{5}{8}$	$-\frac{1}{4}$	1008 T	5.1	7.5	1987 Dec	1.70
$49	46	Abitibi Price A pf	3.75	$\$46\frac{3}{8}$	$46\frac{3}{8}$	47	unch	z60 T	8.0	....	1987 Dec	x15.52
465	55	Abitibi Price wts	..60	55	57	-3		472 T	....	.....	.....	.....
101	30	Absorptive Tech	..75	60	75	+10		209 V	....	.....	.....	.....
185	45	Accugraph Corp A	..105	90	90	-15		48 T	....		1988 Aug	d.69
41	20	Ace Developments	L	27Feb89	20	....	nil	....	....	.....	.....	.....
285	160	Acier Leroux	..175	175	175	unch		32 M	5.3	.....	1987 Oct	.34
25	9	Acies Properties	..9	9	9	unch		275 C	....	.....	.....	.....
$\$16\frac{3}{4}$	$13\frac{3}{4}$	Acklands	..$\$14\frac{1}{8}$	14	$14\frac{1}{8}$	$+\frac{1}{8}$		209 T	....	26.2	1987 Nov	.64
147	100	Actidev Inc	..125	110	120	-5		101 M	6.3	.....	1986 Jun	.06
68	11	AcuVision Sys	..50	35	45	+10		1470 V	....	.....	.....	.....
25	3	Ad Com Mktg	..6	5	6	+1		453 V	....	.....	.....	.....
11	5	Advance Sports	L	18Jan89	5	....	nil	....	....	.....	.....	.....
121	50	Advanced Gravis	..116	101	114	+10		411 V	....	.....	.....	.....
25	5	Advanced Growth	L	3Mar89	11	....	nil	....	....	.....	.....	.....
156	125	Advantage Etnmt	..150	150	150	unch		72 V	....	.....	.....	.....
100	60	Adventure Vehicle	..75	70	70	-2		45 V	....	.....	.....	.....
19	3	Advent Vehicle wts	L	1Mar89	13	....	nil	....	....	.....	.....	.....
125	50	Aerolift Inc	..57	51	54	-1		210 V	....	.....	.....	.....
$\$23\frac{1}{2}$	$22\frac{1}{2}$	Aetna Life Ins 1 pf	1.9063	$\$22\frac{1}{2}$	$22\frac{1}{2}$	$22\frac{1}{2}$	$-\frac{1}{2}$	50 T	8.5	....	.....	.....
$\$20\frac{3}{4}$	$11\frac{3}{8}$	Agnico Eagle	up0.30	$\$12\frac{3}{4}$	$12\frac{3}{8}$	$12\frac{1}{2}$	unch	253 T	2.9	....	1987 Dec	.69
$\$8\frac{1}{8}$	6	Agra Inds A	0.10	$\$7\frac{3}{8}$	$7\frac{1}{4}$	$7\frac{1}{4}$	unch	13 T	1.4	72.5	1988 Jul	.46
$\$7\frac{7}{8}$	$6\frac{1}{4}$	Agra Inds B	0.12	$\$7\frac{3}{8}$	$7\frac{1}{4}$	$7\frac{3}{8}$	$+\frac{1}{8}$	474 T	1.6	73.8	988 Jul	.46
405	250	Agra Inds wts	L	21Feb89	300	....	nil	....	....	.....	.....	.....
120	50	Agromex Inc	..54	51	52	+1		154 M	....	.....	1988 Aug	d.06
110	30	Aigner Holdings	..55	50	50	-8		150 V	....	.....	.....	.....
175	30	Aim Safety Co	..175	85	175	+115		224 V	....	.....	.....	.....
69	20	AIMS Biotech	..30	25	30	+3		429 V	....	.....	.....	.....
$\$12\frac{1}{2}$	7	Air Canada	..$\$12\frac{3}{8}$	$\$11\frac{3}{4}$	12	$+\frac{1}{8}$		3309 T	....	6.0	1987	1.12

Figure 17.8 Part of a financial page showing transactions of stock exchanges.

The price of the last sale of any stock is generally regarded as its current *market price*. The market price of a stock is not a fixed figure but may change when a new transaction takes place.

Investors tend to bid up the price of a stock that they find attractive. A bad news report on a stock will almost certainly cause its market price to drop.

There is no direct relationship between the issue price of a stock, as reflected in the company's records, and the market price of that stock. The issue price is a one-time price, fixed at the time of issue. The market price changes from day to day according to market forces. Generally, if a company is profitable, the market price of its stock will be steady or rising. If it is not profitable, the market price of its stock will fall.

The fact that shareholders can sell or give away their shares is an important feature of corporations. Corporate record-keeping requires up-to-date information about all shareholders, so that information notices, dividend cheques, and financial reports can be sent out to the right people. The share records of a small company are kept by the company treasurer. Larger companies, whose shares are traded on the stock market, have share records kept by other companies which specialize in that field. These specialized firms' computers are connected to the stock exchange's computer.

SECTION REVIEW QUESTIONS

1. Describe the two common practices used when presenting financial reports of public corporations.
2. Name the two most common items contained in contributed surplus.
3. Why would directors prefer to use funds generated from net income rather than funds borrowed from lending institutions?
4. What is an appropriation?
5. Give the accounting entry (ignore dollars) to make an appropriation.
6. Explain the effect of an appropriation.
7. Give the accounting entry (ignore dollars) to reverse an appropriation.
8. What does the statement of retained earnings show?
9. What is the market value of a share?
10. Where can a person find the market value for a stock?
11. Describe the types of things that affect market value.
12. Why is it necessary to be concerned about shareholders' records?

SECTION EXERCISES

1. AKO Corporation is incorporated with authorized capital of 50 000 no par value common shares. On March 31, 19-2 the equity section of AKO's ledger was as shown on page 756.

   In your Workbook, write up the equity section of the balance sheet for AKO Corporation as of March 31, 19-2.

Capital Stock

Date	Particulars	Debit	Credit	Balance	
19-2					
Mar. 31	(50 000 shares)			250 000.00	Cr

Retained Earnings

Date	Particulars	Debit	Credit	Balance	
19-2					
Mar. 31	(balance)			172 463.10	Cr

2. Mainmast Limited is incorporated with authorized capital as follows:

Common Stock, No Par Value—50 000 shares
$4 Cumulative Preferred Stock, No Par Value—200 000 shares

The equity section of the ledger of Mainmast Limited as of December 31, 19-4 is shown below.

Common Stock

Date	Particulars	Debit	Credit	Balance	
19-4					
Dec. 31	(15 000 shares)			157 500.00	Cr

$4 Preferred Stock

Date	Particulars	Debit	Credit	Balance	
19-4					
Dec. 31	(200 000 shares)			1 900 000.00	Cr

Retained Earnings

Date	Particulars	Debit	Credit	Balance	
19-4					
Dec. 31	(Balance)			632 184.19	Cr

In your Workbook, write up the equity section of the balance sheet for Mainmast Limited as of December 31, 19-4.

3. The equity section of the balance sheet of LeBrun Corporation as of December 31, 19-5 is given below.

SHAREHOLDERS' EQUITY

Capital Stock

Common, No Par Value, 20 000 shares	$ 400 000
$5 Preferred, Cumulative, No Par Value, 75 000 shares	1 875 000
Retained Earnings	752 365
Total Shareholders' Equity	$3 027 365

On January 2, 19-6 the directors pass a resolution to transfer $700 000 into an Appropriation for Land Acquisition account.

Required:
1. **Give the accounting entry to record the appropriation transfer.**
2. **Prepare the equity section of the balance sheet as it would appear after recording the above transaction. Assume that there are no other transactions.**

---

4. The Retained Earnings account for Wood Products Limited is shown below.

Retained Earnings

Date	Particulars	Debit	Credit	Balance	
19-7					
Dec. 31	Balance Brought Forward			178 426.10	Cr
19-8					
Dec. 31	Income Summary		105 320.64	283.746.74	Cr
31	Dividend Declaration	85 400.00		198 346.74	Cr

In your Workbook, prepare a statement of retained earnings in proper form.

17.7 *INCOME TAX FOR CORPORATIONS*

Corporations, by law, must pay income tax on their earnings at a fairly high rate. The income tax rate in Canada has been as high as 52 per cent. At the present time the rate is 38 per cent. Therefore, income tax is an important expense item for a corporation.

The federal law requires a corporation to estimate its income tax in advance and to pay it throughout the corporate fiscal year. The procedure for estimating the income tax for any year is set out in government regulations. Before the last day of each month of each fiscal year, a corporation must pay the Receiver General for Canada 1/12 of its estimated income tax for that year. The corporation must also finalize its tax return and settle its account for its fiscal year within the first three months of its next fiscal period.

To illustrate, assume that Superior Products Limited is incorporated on January 1. Its fiscal year ends on the following December 31. Assume further that its estimated income tax for the year is $30 000. The required monthly instalment is 1/12 of this, that is $2 500.

By December 31, the fiscal year-end, the company has made 12 instalment payments. The Income Tax expense account will have a debit balance of $30 000 as shown in Figure 17.9.

INCOME TAX EXPENSE					
Date	Particulars	Debit	Credit	Balance	
Jan 31		2 500		2 500	Dr
Feb 28		2 500		5 000	Dr
Mar 31		2 500		7 500	Dr
Apr 30		2 500		10 000	Dr
May 31		2 500		12 500	Dr
Jun 30		2 500		15 000	Dr
Jul 31		2 500		17 500	Dr
Aug 31		2 500		20 000	Dr
Sep 30		2 500		22 500	Dr
Oct 31		2 500		25 000	Dr
Nov 30		2 500		27 500	Dr
Dec 31		2 500		30 000	Dr

Figure 17.9   The Income Tax Expense account for Superior Products Limited showing the monthly income tax payments.

Income Tax Adjustment on the Worksheet

First, remember that a corporation must pay income tax and will therefore have an Income Tax Expense account. You can see the Income Tax expense figure of $30 000 on the partially completed work sheet of Superior Products Limited in Figure 17.10.

Also, remember that the $30 000 figure represents an *estimate* of the company's income tax and is not the true income tax figure. The true income tax figure is still to be calculated, based on the company's *net income before tax.*

Completing the Work Sheet

To complete a work sheet for a corporation a methodical step-by-step approach is necessary, as follows:

1 Except for the Income Tax line, complete the work sheet (making all necessary adjustments) to the point of taking column totals. This is the state of the work sheet in Figure 17.10.
2 Total each of the two columns in the Income Statement section. Use a printout calculator so that the figures can be double-checked. The totals are: debit column, $351 516.52; credit column: $433 733.00.
3 Find the difference between the two figures in step 2. This result is the *net income before tax* figure; in our example, $82 216.48.
4 Based on the net income before tax figure in step 3 above, complete the income tax return according to government rules and regulations. Determine the company's actual income tax expense. In our example, assume that the income tax for the year is 40 per cent of the net income before tax, that is, 40% of $82 216.48, which is $32 886.59.

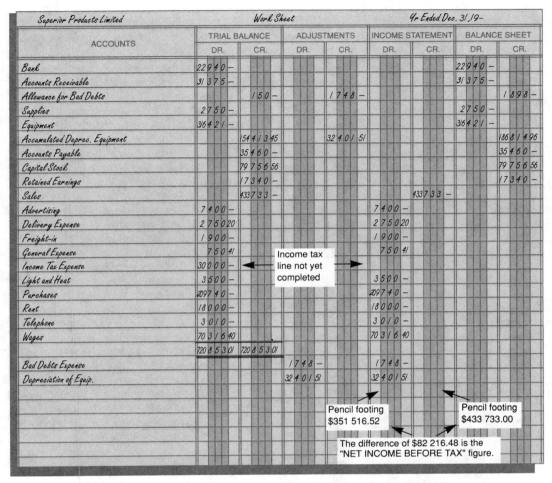

ACCOUNTS	TRIAL BALANCE DR.	TRIAL BALANCE CR.	ADJUSTMENTS DR.	ADJUSTMENTS CR.	INCOME STATEMENT DR.	INCOME STATEMENT CR.	BALANCE SHEET DR.	BALANCE SHEET CR.
Superior Products Limited		Work Sheet					Yr Ended Dec. 31, 19–	
Bank	22 940 –						22 940 –	
Accounts Receivable	31 375 –						31 375 –	
Allowance for Bad Debts		150 –		1 748 –				1 898 –
Supplies	2 750 –						2 750 –	
Equipment	316 421 –						316 421 –	
Accumulated Deprec. Equipment		154 413 45		32 401 51				186 814 96
Accounts Payable		35 460 –						35 460 –
Capital Stock		79 756 56						79 756 56
Retained Earnings		17 340 –						17 340 –
Sales		433 733 –				433 733 –		
Advertising	7 400 –				7 400 –			
Delivery Expense	2 750 20				2 750 20			
Freight-in	1 900 –				1 900 –			
General Expense	750 41				750 41			
Income Tax Expense	30 000 –							
Light and Heat	3 500 –				3 500 –			
Purchases	209 740 –				209 740 –			
Rent	18 000 –				18 000 –			
Telephone	3 010 –				3 010 –			
Wages	70 316 40				70 316 40			
	720 853 01	720 853 01						
Bad Debts Expense			1 748 –		1 748 –			
Depreciation of Equip.			32 401 51		32 401 51			

Income tax line not yet completed

Pencil footing $351 516.52

Pencil footing $433 733.00

The difference of $82 216.48 is the "NET INCOME BEFORE TAX" figure.

Figure 17.10   A partial work sheet showing the income tax expense figure.

5 Now that the true figure for income tax is known, an adjusting entry for income tax can be made on the work sheet. The effect of this entry is:

a. To adjust the income tax expense line on the work sheet to reflect the true income tax expense—in this case, $32 886.59.

b. To set up an account for the balance of tax either owing to or owing from the tax department—in this case, $2 886.59 payable. This is arrived at by comparing the true tax figure ($32 886.59) with the tax paid in instalments ($30 000).

6 Complete the work sheet in the usual manner. The total expense figure will change. The completed work sheet for Superior Products Limited is shown in Figure 17.11.

Superior Products Limited	Work Sheet				Year Ended Dec. 31, 19-			
ACCOUNTS	TRIAL BALANCE		ADJUSTMENTS		INCOME STATEMENT		BALANCE SHEET	
	DR.	CR.	DR.	CR.	DR.	CR.	DR.	CR.
Bank	22940 —						22940 —	
Accounts Receivable	31375 —						31375 —	
Allowance for Bad Debts		150 —		1748 —				1898 —
Supplies	2750 —						2750 —	
Equipment	36421 —						36421 —	
Accumulated Deprec. Equipment		154413 45		32401 51				186814 96
Accounts Payable		35460 —						35460 —
Capital Stock		79756 56						79756 56
Retained Earnings		17340 —						17340 —
Sales		43373 3				43373 3 —		
Advertising	7400 —				7400 —			
Delivery Expense	2750 20				2750 20			
Freight-in	1900 —				1900 —			
General Expense	750 41				750 41			
Income Tax Expense	30000 —		2886 59		32886 59			
Light and Heat	3500 —				3500 —			
Purchases	20974 —				20974 —			
Rent	18000 —				18000 —			
Telephone	3010 —				3010 —			
Wages	70316 40				70316 40			
	720853 01	720853 01						
Bad Debts Expense			1748 —		1748 —			
Depreciation of Equip.			32401 51		32401 51			
Income Tax Payable				2886 59				2886 59
			37036 10	37036 10	38440 3 11	43373 3 —	37348 6 —	32415 6 11
Net Income					49329 89			49329 89
					43373 3 —	43373 3 —	37348 6 —	37348 6

True income tax figure

Income tax adjustment

Balance of tax owing

Net income after tax figure

Figure 17.11 Completed work sheet of Superior Products Limited showing income tax accounts.

An example of income tax on an income statement is shown in Figure 17.12.

Adjusting and Closing Entries for a Corporation

There are no individual owners' Capital or Drawings accounts in a corporation. Therefore, the process of adjusting and closing the books is slightly different. Step 4 on page 761 is the one which is different for a corporation. The following four accounting entries are required.

1 Record all and only those adjusting entries that appear in the Adjustments section of the work sheet.

2 Close out the balances on the credit side of the Income Statement section of the work sheet to the Income Summary account.

3 Close out the balances on the debit side of the Income Statement section of the work sheet to the Income Summary account.

4 Close out the Income Summary account to the Retained Earnings account.

ROBIN HOOD MINES LIMITED

Statement of Income

For the year ended December 31, 19-3

	19–3	*19–2*
Revenue		
Bullion production	$3 271 000	$1 988 000
Interest	55 000	15 000
	3 326 000	2 003 000
Expense		
Development	285 000	187 000
Mining	367 000	296 000
Milling	198 000	138 000
Fees and charges for the use of underground facilities of parent company	348 000	290 000
Mine management, office and general	161 000	122 000
Head office administration and general	71 000	36 000
Marketing	15 000	9 000
Provision for tax under the Mining Tax Act, Ontario	198 000	131 000
	1 643 000	1 209 000
Operating Income	1 683 000	794 000
Other Expense		
Amortization of deferred development and administrative expenditures	163 000	136 000
Provision for depreciation of buildings, machinery, and equipment	21 000	6 000
	184 000	142 000
Income Before Income Taxes	1 499 000	652 000
Income taxes	506 000	222 000
Net Income for the Year	$ 993 000	$ 430 000

Figure 17.12   The income statement of Robin Hood Mines Limited showing income tax expense.

SECTION REVIEW QUESTIONS

1. What expense item does a corporation have that a proprietorship or partnership do not have?
2. Describe briefly the manner in which a corporation remits its income tax.
3. What does the Income Tax Expense figure in the Trial Balance section of the work sheet represent?
4. On what figure is the true income tax expense figure based?
5. Describe how to find the figure asked for in question 4 above.
6. Is it possible for a corporation to overpay its income tax? Explain.
7. What circumstances would produce a balance in an Income Tax Payable account? Would it be a debit or a credit balance?
8. What circumstances would produce a balance in an Income Tax Receivable account? Would it be a debit or a credit balance?
9. Describe how the income statement of a corporation differs from that of a proprietorship.
10. Describe the significant differences in the closing entries for a corporation.

SECTION EXERCISES

1. **This exercise appears in your Workbook.**

   A simple work sheet is completed below except for the income tax. **Given that the corporate rate of income tax is 38 per cent, finish off the work sheet.**

Little Company Limited	Work Sheet				Year Ended Dec. 31,19–		
ACCOUNTS	TRIAL BALANCE		ADJUSTMENTS		INCOME STATEMENT		BALANCE SHEET
	DR.	CR.	DR.	CR.	DR.	CR.	DR.	CR.
Asset A	50 –						50 –	
Asset B	100 –						100 –	
Asset C	1000 –						1000 –	
Asset D	10000 –						10000 –	
Liability A		500 –						500 –
Liability B		1000 –						1000 –
Capital Stock		5000 –						5000 –
Retained Earnings		2150 –						2150 –
Revenue		10000 –				10000 –		
Expense A	1000 –				1000 –			
Expense B	3000 –				3000 –			
Expense C	2000 –				2000 –			
Income Tax Exp.	1500 –							
	18650 –	18650 –						
Inc. Tax Payl								
Net Income								

2. Shown below is the partially completed work sheet for Giant Company Limited. The trial balance figures are already entered.

ACCOUNTS	TRIAL BALANCE DR.	TRIAL BALANCE CR.	ADJUSTMENTS DR.	ADJUSTMENTS CR.	INCOME STATEMENT DR.	INCOME STATEMENT CR.	BALANCE SHEET DR.	BALANCE SHEET CR.
Bank	4 003							
Accs Receivable	40 201							
Supplies	941							
Equipment	63 666							
Acc Depr Equip		18 356						
Accs Payable		1 241						
Capital Stock		20 000						
Retained Earnings		33 091						
Revenue		119 044						
Advertising	3 742							
Bank Charges	1 502							
Income Tax Exp	18 000							
Light and Heat	4 016							
Misc. Expense	1 240							
Rent	16 000							
Telephone	2 519							
Wages	35 902							
	191 732	191 732						
Deprec Equip								
Supplies Used								
Inc. Tax Recl								
Net Income								

Giant Company Limited   Work Sheet   Year Ended Dec. 31, 19-8

1. **Complete the work sheet given the following:**
   a. Equipment is depreciated at 20 per cent of its net book value.
   b. The value of supplies on hand at the year-end is $200.
   c. The corporate rate of income tax is 40 per cent.
2. **Journalize the adjusting and closing entries.**

CHAPTER HIGHLIGHTS

Now that you have completed Chapter 17, you should:

1. understand that a corporation has a number of owners called shareholders;
2. understand how the accounts of a corporation differ from those of a proprietorship or a partnership;
3. know the difference between common and preferred shares and between par value and no par value shares;
4. be able to give four reasons why a corporation is considered to be a separate legal entity from its owners;
5. explain what limited liability means;
6. know that a corporation is governed by strict rules and regulations;
7. know what a director is and what the board of directors does;
8. know the difference between a public corporation and a private corporation;
9. know the main advantages and disadvantages of a corporation;
10. understand the items in the equity section of a corporation's ledger and be able to prepare a simple balance sheet for a corporation;
11. understand the factors affecting retained earnings and be able to prepare a statement of retained earnings;
12. know the accounting entries for the formation of a corporation;
13. understand what a dividend is and the three dates associated with dividends;
14. be able to calculate a dividend and to prepare the accounting entries for dividends;
15. understand the items contained in contributed surplus;
16. be able to prepare the accounting entries for appropriations;
17. understand that a corporation must pay income tax and be able to complete a work sheet for a corporation, including income tax.

ACCOUNTING TERMS

appropriation account
board of directors
Capital Stock account
charter
common shareholder
common stock
contributed surplus
corporation
cumulative preference share
deficit
dividend
fully participating preference shares
letters patent

limited liability
no par value share
non-cumulative preference share
Organization Costs account
par value share
preferred stock
private corporation
public corporation
Retained Earnings account
share certificate
shareholder
stockholder

CHAPTER EXERCISES

Using Your Knowledge

1. Parks Company Limited is a newly incorporated company with authorized capital stock of 10 000 no par value common shares.

1. Journalize the following transactions of Parks Company Limited.

Year 1
1. The three organizers each take 1 000 shares valued at $25 a share in payment for their services in organizing the company.
2. 5 000 shares are sold through an investment dealer at $30 a share for cash.
3. $2 000 of legal expenses of incorporation are paid in cash.
4. The investment dealer's commission of three per cent is paid in cash.
5. $100 000 is borrowed from the bank.
6. Cash is paid for the following: Land, $30 000; Buildings, $70 000; and Equipment, $75 000.
7. A net income of $18 000 is recorded (assume in cash and credited to Income Summary).
8. The Income Summary account is closed out to Retained Earnings.

Year 2
9. 2 000 shares are sold through the investment dealer at $35 a share for cash.
10. The investment dealer's commission of three per cent is paid in cash.
11. A net income of $52 000 is recorded (assume in cash).
12. The Income Summary account is closed out.

Year 3
13. A dividend of $2 a share is declared by the board of directors.
14. The above dividend is paid in cash.

2. Prepare a trial balance for Parks Company Limited after transaction 14.

2. Sentra Loan Corporation receives its charter authorizing the issue of capital stock as follows:

Common Stock—no par value—50 000 shares
$5 Preferred Stock—no par value—10 000 shares

1. Journalize the following transactions of Sentra Loan Corporation.

Year 1
1. 30 000 common shares are sold for cash at $5 each through an investment dealer who withholds the commission of four per cent.
2. Each of the five organizers takes 100 common shares valued at $5 each as payment for their initial efforts in getting the company started.
3. Each of the five organizers purchases 3 000 common shares for cash at a price of $5 per share.

4. $1 500 of legal expenses of incorporation are paid for in cash.
5. Land, $70 000; Buildings, $90 000; and Equipment, $45 000 are purchased for cash.
6. A net loss of $12 000 from business operations is incurred (assume in cash and debited to Income Summary).
7. The Income Summary account is closed out.

Year 2
8. 2 000 preferred shares are sold at $50 for cash through the services of an investment dealer who withholds the commission of four per cent.
9. 2 000 preferred shares are sold at $51 for cash through the services of an investment dealer who withholds the commission of four per cent.
10. 4 000 preferred shares are sold at $52 for cash through the services of an investment dealer who withholds the commission of four per cent.
11. A net income of $95 000 is earned and recorded (assume in cash).
12. The Income Summary account is closed out.

Year 3
13. The regular preferred dividend is declared.
14. The above dividend is paid.
15. A net income of $250 000 is earned and recorded (assume in cash).
16. The Income Summary account is closed out.

Year 4
17. The regular preferred dividend is declared.
18. A common dividend of $3 a share is declared.
19. The above dividends are paid.

2. Prepare a trial balance for Sentra Loan Company after transaction 19.

---

3. The issued capital stock of Marwell Limited is as follows:

   a. No par value common shares, 76 700 shares.
   b. Six per cent preferred shares, par value $10, 27 500 shares.

   1. Calculate the total dividend on the preferred stock.
   2. Calculate the total dividend on the common stock if the rate is to be 26 cents per share.
   3. Show the journal entries necessary to record the declaration of both of the above dividends. Date of declaration is April 12.
   4. Show the journal entries necessary to record the payment of the above dividends. Date of payment is April 30.

---

4. The issued capital stock of EFG Co. Ltd. has remained as shown below for several years.

   a. Common Stock, no par value, 10 000 shares.
   b. Preferred Stock, par value $25, six per cent cumulative, 40 000 shares.

For the last few years the net income of the company has been too small to fully pay the preferred dividends. Dividend payments on the preferred shares have been as follows: 19-2, $50 000; 19-3, $25 000; 19-4, $16 000. 19-5 has been a profitable year, with the company earning a net income of $154 000. It has been proposed that the entire year's profit be paid out in dividends.

If this is done, how much per share will the common shareholders receive? Show your calculations.

5. At December 31, 19-7, the end of a fiscal year, Vintage Products Limited has fully paid capital stock as shown below:

a. Common Stock 500 000 shares of no par value.
b. Preferred Stock, five per cent cumulative, 100 000 shares, par value of $25 per share.

Dividends on preferred shares are fully paid up to December 31, 19-5. No preferred dividends have been paid since that time.

1. **Calculate the total amount of dividends on preferred shares that must be paid before any dividends can be paid on the common shares.**
2. On December 31, 19-7, the balance of the Retained Earnings account is $900 000 Cr. and the balance in the Bank account is $700 000 Dr. **Calculate the greatest dividend per share that can be paid on the common shares without borrowing money.**
3. The dividends calculated in both cases above are declared by the directors on January 3, 19-8. **Give the accounting entries to record them.**
4. The dividends above are paid on January 15, 19-8. **Give the accounting entries to record the payment.**

6. A company has the following capital stock:

a. Common Stock, authorized and fully paid for, 50 000 shares of no par value.
b. Preferred Stock, authorized and fully paid for, 25 000 shares, eight per cent, non-participating, $10 par value.

The company has paid dividends as follows:

Year	Amount
1	$70 000
2	nil
3	40 000
4	5 000
5	55 000
6	80 000
7	15 000
8	45 000

Complete the schedule in your Workbook showing the dividends to be paid to each class of shares where the preferred share are non-cumulative and where the preferred share are cumulative.

7. E-Z Limited is incorporated with paid-up capital stock as follows:

	Account Balance
Common	
No par value; 10 000 shares	$250 000
Preferred 6%, Cumulative	
Par value $50; 20 000 shares	$1 000 000

Over a 10-year period E-Z Limited declared and paid out dividends as follows:

Year	*Total Dividend*
1	$60 000
2	$ 75 000
3	nil
4	$120 000
5	$180 000
6	nil
7	$135 000
8	$90 000
9	$100 000
10	$150 000

Complete the schedule in your Workbook apportioning the dividends between common and preferred shareholders where:

a. the preferred shares are non-participating;
b. the preferred shares are fully participating.

---

8. The shareholders' equity of Alpine Products Limited is comprised of the following:

Common Stock
Authorized, 10 000 shares; no par value;
issued and fully paid, 10 000 shares; book
value of issued shares, $94 216

Retained Earnings
$26 412
Appropriation
For land acquisition, $50 000

Prepare the Shareholders' Equity section of the balance sheet.

---

9. The shareholders' equity of Kingston Investments Limited consists of the following:

Common Stock
Authorized, 5 000 shares; no par value;
issued and fully paid, 5 000 shares; book
value of issued shares, $54 260

Preferred Stock
six per cent cumulative preferred;
par value $25; authorized, issued,
and fully paid; 20 000 shares

Contributed Surplus
$40 000

Retained Earnings
$157 206

Prepare the Shareholders' Equity section of the balance sheet.

---

10. The accountant for Sesco Limited is in the midst of the year-end activity of preparing the work sheet, making the income tax calculation, preparing the financial statements, and recording the adjusting and closing entries. The accountant's partially finished work appears on page 770 and in your Workbook.

Required

1. a. **Calculate the income tax expense for the year.** The tax rate is 40 per cent, based on net income before tax.

   b. **Complete the income tax line of the work sheet and complete and balance the work sheet.**

2. **Complete the income statement and the balance sheet.** Sesco is authorized to sell 25 000 shares with a par value of $10. 10 000 shares have been sold and are fully paid for.

3. **Journalize the adjusting and closing entries.**

---

11. **This exercise also appears in your Workbook.**

    The partially completed work sheet for Alice Harper and Associates Limited appears on page 771. The trial balance columns have been entered for you.

    Using the additional information provided below, complete the work sheet for the year ended December 31, 19-5.

    Additional Information

    1. The allowance for doubtful accounts should be $850 at the year-end.
    2. The year-end supplies inventory is $850.
    3. The prepaid insurance figure at the year-end is $500.
    4. The depreciation figures for the year are:
       Buildings   — $3 000
       Furniture and Equipment — $2 500
       Automotive Equipment   — $7 000
    5. Accrued wages at the year-end amounted to $900.
    6. $700 is to be written off the Organization Costs account.
    7. The income tax rate is 40 per cent.

Sesco Limited	Work Sheet						Yr. Ended Dec. 31, 19-
	TRIAL BALANCE		ADJUSTMENTS		INCOME STATEMENT		BALANCE SHEET
ACCOUNTS	DR.	CR.	DR.	CR.	DR.	CR.	DR.	CR.
Petty Cash	100-						100-	
Bank	1462-						1462-	
Accounts Receivable	29053 74						29053 74	
Allow. Doubtful Accs.		750 80		652 20				1403-
Merchandise Inventory	21416-				21416-	28331 50	28331 50	
Supplies	1470-			864-			606-	
Prepaid Insurance	2798-			1562-			1236-	
Land	42200 46						42200 46	
Buildings	95900-						95900-	
Accum. Depr. Buildings		13677 74		4111 11				17788 85
Furniture & Equipment	42750-						42750-	
Accum. Depr. Furn. & Eq.		20862-		4377 60				25239 60
Automotive Equipment	29750-						29750-	
Accum. Depr. Auto. Eq.		19545 75		3061 28				22607 03
Accounts Payable		46315 15		3072 40				49387 55
Bank Loan		11000-						11000-
Sales Tax Payable		1032 01						1032 01
Capital Stock		100000-						100000-
Retained Earnings		26225 42						26225 42
Sales		196917 62				196917 62		
Bank Charges	915-				915-			
Building Maintenance	1206-				1206-			
Car Expenses	1815 70				1815 70			
Duty	3741 11		1057-		4798 11			
Freight-in	1707-		916-		2623-			
Income Tax	24000-							
Light, Heat, Water	1946 70				1946 70			
Miscellaneous Expense	315 77		75-		390 77			
Purchases	75647-		1024 40		76671 40			
Telephone Expense	1217 81				1217 81			
Wages	56914 20				56914 20			
	436326 49	436326 49						
Bad Debts Expense			652 20		652 20			
Supplies Used			864-		864-			
Insurance Expense			1562-		1562-			
Depreciation Buildings			4111 11		4111 11			
Depr. Furn. & Equip.			4377 60		4377 60			
Depr. Auto. Equip.			3061 28		3061 28			
Income Tax Receivable								
Net Income								

Alice Harper and Associates Limited		Work Sheet				Yr. Ended Dec. 31, 19-5		
ACCOUNTS	TRIAL BALANCE		ADJUSTMENTS		INCOME STATEMENT		BALANCE SHEET	
	DR.	CR.	DR.	CR.	DR.	CR.	DR.	CR.
Bank	900 —							
Accounts Receivable	24 400 —							
Allow. for Doubtful Debts		200 —						
Supplies	1 475 —							
Prepaid Insurance	1 260 —							
Land	95 690 —							
Buildings	120 000 —							
Accum. Depr. Buildings		24 000 —						
Furniture & Equipment	38 000 —							
Accum. Depr. Furn. & Eq.		20 000 —						
Automotive Equipment	38 000 —							
Accum. Depr. Auto. Eq.		14 000 —						
Organization Costs	4 200 —							
Accounts Payable		15 700 —						
Sales Tax Payable		938 —						
Capital Stock — Common		25 000 —						
Capital Stock — 8% Pref.		100 000 —						
Retained Earnings		7 287 —						
Revenue		160 800 —						
Advertising	1 850 —							
Bank Charges	2 750 —							
C.P.P. Expense	750 —							
Income Tax Expense	5 600 —							
Light, Heat, Water,	1 650 —							
Miscellaneous Expense	175 —							
Postage	500 —							
Telephone	1 025 —							
U.I. Expense	300 —							
Wages	29 400 —							
	367 925 —	367 925 —						
Bad Debts Expense								
Supplies Used								
Insurance Expense								
Depreciation Buildings								
Depreciation Furn. & Equip.								
Depreciation Auto Equipment								
Accrued Wages Payable								
Organization Costs Written Off								
Income Tax Payable								

12. The balance sheet of Rollins Limited as of December 31, 19-8 appears below. **Study the balance sheet and answer the questions that follow.**

ROLLINS LIMITED
BALANCE SHEET
DECEMBER 31, 19–8

Assets		*Liabilities*	
Bank	$ 3 750	Bank Loan	$150 000
Accounts Receivable	42 906	Accounts Payable	49 601
Merchandise Inventory	70 374		$199 601
Plant and Equipment	505 061	*Shareholders' Equity*	
		Capital Stock	
		25 000 Common Shares	250 000
		Retained Earnings	172 490
	$622 091		$622 091

Answer the following questions in your Workbook.

1. How much equity was raised by the sale of common shares?

2. How much equity was generated by company profits?

3. Assuming that all shares were sold for the same price, for how much each were the shares sold?

4. Is this company in a good position to pay out dividends? Yes or no? Explain.

13. ABC Company is incorporated on January 1, 19-1 with 100 000 common shares issued and fully paid for. On December 31, 19-6, the company's Retained Earnings account appeared as shown below.

Retained Earnings

19–1	Dec.	31		42 700	42 700	Cr
19–2	Dec.	31		57 600	100 300	Cr
19–3	Jan.	31	50 000		50 300	Cr
	Dec.	31		76 400	126 700	Cr
19–4	Jan.	31	100 000		26 700	Cr
	Dec.	31	16 209		10 491	Cr
19–5	Dec.	31	27 402		-16 911	Dr
19–6	Dec.	31		37 240	20 329	Cr

In your Workbook, answer the following questions regarding the above account.

1. In what two years (most likely) were dividends paid?

2. In how many years did the company earn a net income?

3. What was the total amount of the above net incomes?

4. In how many years did the company suffer a net loss?

5. In which years did the company suffer a net loss?

6. What was the total amount of the net losses?

7. Break down the account balance of $20 329 into the three components below.

Total Net Incomes

Total Net Losses

Total Dividends

8. How much was the dividend per share in 19-3?

9. How much was the dividend per share in 19-4?

10. Give the accounting entry for the transaction on December 31, 19-6.

11. Give the accounting entry for the transaction on January 31, 19-4.

12. Give the accounting entry for the transaction on December 31, 19-4.

---

14. W. Murray, M. Walters, and F. Stevens operate a partnership in which they share income and loss and maintain their Capital accounts in the ratio of 3:3:2 respectively. The three have applied for and received letters patent to incorporate their business under the name Master Products Limited, effective June 30, 19—. The letters patent authorize capital stock of 48 000 no par value common shares.

After closing the books at June 30, the trial balance of the partnership is as follows:

MURRAY, WALTERS, AND STEVENS

POST-CLOSING TRIAL BALANCE

JUNE 30, 19—

	DR	CR
Bank	$ 10 250	
Accounts Receivable	28 450	
Allowance for Doubtful Debts		$ 2 881
Supplies	1 516	
Prepaid Insurance	2 008	
Land	60 000	
Buildings	235 000	
Accumulated Depreciation of Buildings		92 000
Furniture and Equipment	87 250	
Accumulated Depreciation of Furniture and Equipment		40 000
Automobiles	57 845	
Accumulated Depreciation of Automobiles		20 000
Bank Loan		29 000
Accounts Payable		18 438
W. Murray, Capital		105 000
M. Walters, Capital		105 000
F. Stevens, Capital		70 000
	$482 319	$482 319

The partners have agreed to revalue the land and the buildings and to adjust these accounts to the appraised values immediately prior to incorporation. Any gains or losses on appraisal, and any expenses of appraisal or incorporation, are to be accumulated in a Gain or Loss on Incorporation account. This account is to be closed out to the partners' capital accounts in the income-sharing ratio. It is also agreed that the books of the partnership will continue and become the books of the corporation.

1. **On June 30, journalize the effect of the revaluation of the land and buildings.** Land is appraised at $120 000 and buildings at $300 000. The Accumulated Depreciation of Buildings account is to remain unchanged.
2. **Journalize the payments by cheque on June 30 for the following: the appraiser's fee, $3 752; and the incorporation and legal costs, $5 000.**
3. **Convert the partnership books into those of the new limited company by**
   a. **closing out the gain or loss on appraisal to the partners' capital accounts,**
   b. **closing out the partners' adjusted capital accounts to a common stock account.**
4. All of the authorized shares are to be distributed to the partners. The distribution is to be made in the ratio of their final capital account balances as partners.
   a. Calculate the number of shares that each partner will receive.
   b. Calculate the value per share to be recorded in the company's minute book.
5. **Prepare a trial balance of the ledger of the corporation.**

For Further Thought

15. 1. Corporate law is quite complex. What would be a good initial step if you were considering setting up a corporation?
    2. Ajax Corporation is a small corporation with authorized capital of 100 000 shares of common stock. The only shareholder is John Smith, who owns all of the 10 000 shares that have been issued. Suggest a way for John Smith to acquire desperately needed cash for the corporation without giving up any control.
    3. Limited liability is an advantage for persons willing to invest in business ventures. Give an example of a situation where it could be a disadvantage to someone doing business with a corporation.
    4. The text states that a corporation can be effectively controlled without having 50 per cent of the shares plus one, in fact with a much smaller percentage. Explain how this can be true.
    5. Suppose a large chemical-producing corporation was responsible for the deaths of many people and was ordered by the courts to pay out several millions in compensation. The shareholders of the corporation are protected by limited liability. How would they be affected?
    6. The ordinary shareholders of a corporation can benefit financially from their ownership of the shares in two ways. What are these two ways?
    7. Merla Jones is the majority shareholder of Fomex Corporation. The ordinary shareholders of Fomex Corporation have received no dividends for several years. Their complaints at the annual meetings of the company have gone unheeded. Explain what is probably happening in this case.
    8. A dividend is *declared* on March 1, 19-2 by the directors of Power Limited. On that date you own 50 shares of Power Limited. You are sure to receive the dividend. True or false? Explain.

9. A dividend is *paid* on March 31, 19-5 by Quantum Corporation. On that date you own 50 shares of Quantum Corporation. You are sure to receive the dividend. True or false? Explain.

10. Mesa Company Limited declared a dividend on January 10, 19-3 to shareholders of record on January 31 to be paid on February 15. You sold all of your shares in Mesa Company Limited on January 29. However, shortly after February 15, you receive a cheque for the dividend. What must have happened?

11. In the initial stages of getting established, a corporation was having trouble paying its expenses because of a cash shortage. Suggest an alternative way that the company could pay these expenses.

12. A corporation had used the *appropriation* technique to influence its shareholders to wait for a dividend. Explain what this technique is.

CASE STUDIES

CASE 1   *Should Dividends Be Declared?*

The board of directors of Grover Contracting Limited is meeting on January 10, 19-4 to consider the payment of dividends to shareholders. The following data have been collected for the meeting to help the directors in their discussion:

Net income, year ended December 31, 19-3	$150 000
Cash on hand, January 10, 19-4	95 000
Retained earnings, January 10, 19-4	156 750
Total current assets, January 10, 19-4	99 000
Total current liabilities, January 10, 19-4	104 000

Capital Stock
   Common: 50 000 shares, no par value, issued and fully paid.
   Preferred, 6% cumulative, 150 000 shares, issued and fully paid, par value $1 500 000.

Dividends:
   The last common dividend, in the amount of $100 000, was for the year 19-2.
   The last preferred dividend, in the amount of $90 000, was for the year 19-2.

Questions
1. Is the company profitable?
2. For what year were dividends last paid?
3. Are there any arrears of preferred dividends?
4. For what year are dividends being considered?
5. Give the amount of one full year's dividend on the preferred shares.
6. Is there a sufficient balance in the Retained Earnings account to support the payment of the preferred dividend?
7. Is there a sufficient cash balance to support the payment of the preferred dividend?
8. Would there be any bad effects resulting from paying the preferred dividend?
9. Based on the above information, what decision should the directors make? Give your reasons.

CASE 2 Buy the Shares or the Assets?

Jane Church, the owner of a corporation, has decided to get out of the glass and mirror business. She has put the 10 000 company shares up for sale at the very fair price of $750 000.

Cynthia Pollock is anxious to purchase the business and has made an offer to Jane for the full asking price. However, her offer is for the assets of the business, not for the shares. She is concerned about the fact that the merchandise inventory of $300 000 is shown on the financial statements at $50 000.

Questions

1. What could Jane Church have gained by showing the inventory incorrectly on the financial statements?
2. If the inventory were misrepresented on the financial statements, Cynthia was not responsible for it. Why, then, would she be concerned about it?
3. Why is it to Jane's advantage to sell the shares of the company rather than just the assets?
4. Why is it to Cynthia's advantage to buy the assets of the company and not the shares?

CASE 3 Control of a Corporation

An acquaintance of yours, Mr. Farmer, offers to sell you some shares that he owns in a medium-sized and very profitable company. He acquired these shares some time ago as an investment. Mr. Farmer claims that he is selling them because he needs cash to take advantage of another investment opportunity.

Mr. Farmer shows you the following breakdown of the shareholdings of the company:

Mrs. Adams	30 shares	She is a widow who inherited her shares upon the death of her husband. She has shown no interest whatever in the company affairs, and is quite satisfied that it must be an excellent company because she receives a dividend cheque regularly.
R. Baker	40 shares	He acquired his shares from a third person in settlement of a debt. He attends the company meetings regularly and is highly critical of the management. Whenever he suggests a change, however, he is always voted down.
S. Clarke	65 shares	He is the secretary-treasurer of the company, a position that he has held for 15 years. He is also one of the three company directors.
M. Dunn	100 shares	She is the general manager, president, and a director of the company, which she started 15 years ago.
C. Everett	10 shares	He had his shares given to him. He does not know anything about the company and is not interested. He would be willing to sell his shares for a fair price.

Mr. Farmer	150 shares	
Mrs. Greig	35 shares	Mrs. Greig is a wealthy lady who travels a great deal. She has had no known direct involvement in any affairs of the company. It is not known how she acquired her shares.
H. Harris	70 shares	He has been the vice-president for the last 10 years, is the brother-in-law of the president, and is also a director.

Mr. Farmer believes that the company could earn substantially higher profits with new management. By acquiring his shares, you would become the shareholder with the largest individual holdings. You would stand a good chance of gaining control of the company by getting the support or acquiring the shares of the four small shareholders.

Mr. Farmer is asking $50 000 for his shares. This is a fair price. You have the management skills, the technical expertise, and the experience to handle the company.

Questions

1. How many shares are there in total?
2. Which shareholders control the corporation? Give their names and the total number of shares held by them.
3. If you were to buy Farmer's shares, who could you count on for sure support?
4. How many additional shares would you need on your side to get certain control?
5. What do you think of your chances of getting the needed shares? Give reasons.
6. What would the controlling shareholders likely do to prevent you from acquiring a controlling interest?
7. Decide on a course of action and give reasons for your answer.

CAREER
Kim Brady / Financial Analyst

Encouraged by an older brother who is a public accountant, Kim Brady enrolled in the Certified General Accounting (CGA) program while still at high school in Vancouver, British Columbia. She graduated from high school with an average of 80 per cent and won several academic awards.

The following year, Kim enrolled in Business Administration at Simon Fraser University, and during her four-year honours program she again earned high marks. She was able to obtain 10 course exemptions for her CGA program. After she graduated, Kim had to complete only six of the 16 courses to earn her CGA title.

Kim's first employer was Barry Demers, a Certified Management Accountant (CMA). Kim worked as a senior accounting clerk, keeping the clients' books and performing all accounting work up to the taking of the trial balance for the general ledger. While working for Demers, Kim completed her six remaining courses and became a Certified General Accountant.

Kim now works as a financial analyst for Sterling Drugs, a leading manufacturer of drugs and household items which employs more than

300 people. Kim's is a highly responsible position. She analyzes all the figures on the income statement and the balance sheet and presents her findings to management. She examines current ratios and quick ratios and conducts trend analyses for a number of successive periods. She continually monitors and analyzes the profit figures and investigates any figures that vary from those of the previous month or previous year. This process is called "analytical analysis" and is used by external auditors when comparing current account balances with those of the previous year.

Further analysis of the financial statements leads Kim to compare budgeted expenses with actual costs to review accounts to see if they are out of line. She prepares monthly journal entries and makes adjustments for expenses from previous and for future accounting periods. She also supervises the preparation of fixed asset schedules, manufacturing costs, and inventory costs.

At Sterling Drugs, Kim is responsible for analyzing four distinct financial topics: costs, budgets, financial analysis systems, and plant and payroll accounting.

In the area of financial analysis and planning, Kim uses the computer to simulate different situations. She is then able to provide management with a chance to see potential trouble spots and evaluate the probable results of proposed activities. She calls this process "model building." Some examples of the models Kim provides for management include short-range forecasts, new product analyses, ratios analyses by sales area and product line, cash flow analyses and financial ratio analyses.

Kim firmly believes that the future of accounting and financial analysis will centre on the computer. Because of her interest in computer programming, Kim attends many company-sponsored training programs to further her knowledge and skills in this important field.

DISCUSSION

1. What is meant by "analytical analysis"?
2. **a.** How was Kim able to earn 10 course exemptions in her CGA program?
   b. What is the minimum mark she had to achieve in each of her university courses in order to receive this exemption?
3. Describe Kim's duties as a financial analyst for Sterling Drugs.
4. What is the purpose of a budget?
5. How do you think Kim's accounting courses helped her to achieve her present position as a financial analyst?
6. How does Kim employ the computer as a management tool for analysis?

Analyzing
Financial Statements

18.1 Users of Financial Statements
18.2 Comparing Financial Data
18.3 Simple Ratios and Percentages
18.4 Additional Ratios, Percentages, and Statistics
18.5 Computers in Accounting   Linking Accounting Software
    with Spreadsheets

The set of financial statements for a company shows its financial position simply and clearly. However, financial statements alone do not satisfy the needs of all readers. Many people are interested in special information which goes beyond that found on standard financial statements.

18.1 USERS OF FINANCIAL STATEMENTS

Financial statements may be used by many different persons, groups, companies, and agencies. Those who are interested fall into two groups.

Insiders

The insiders of a company are its owners and its executive and management group. The management of a company studies the financial statements most thoroughly. They apply a number of tests to the data and use the results to make special calculations. They are looking for danger signals and unfavourable trends. They want to get rid of the company's weak points and encourage its strengths. The management group has a lot at stake. Their careers usually depend on the continued success of their company.

At one time managers had to wait until the end of an accounting period to obtain much of the information they needed. This has all changed in the age of the computer. It is possible now to obtain most information as soon as it is needed. Managers must pay attention to results on a daily basis, or risk losing out to a competitor who does.

The owners of a company are keenly interested in the progress of the business. In many cases they depend on the income from the business for their livelihood. Profits are usually related to the quality of the management. Profitability, therefore, will be a major factor in deciding if a change in management is advisable.

In other cases, the owners view the company strictly as an investment, and evaluate its performance in comparison with other investment possibilities.

Outsiders

The outsiders of a company include bankers and other creditors, prospective investors, shareholders, and government agencies such as Revenue Canada.

Bankers, when asked to lend money to a business, normally request financial statements covering several years of operation. Bankers analyze these statements to evaluate the borrower's ability to repay the loan. In particular, they look at two things. One of these is the company's ability to make a profit. The other is the worth and marketability of the company's assets in case they have to be sold to repay the loan.

Investors and prospective investors in a company are interested in the trend of the company's earnings. Investors are always looking for companies that are growing and profitable. They are also anxious to sell any interest they have in companies that seem to be heading for trouble.

SECTION REVIEW QUESTIONS

1. Why do standard financial statements not satisfy the needs of all readers?
2. Name the two major groups who are interested in financial statements.
3. Who are the "insiders"?
4. Who are the "outsiders"?
5. Which group of people studies the financial statements most thoroughly?
6. In general terms, what is the group in question 5 above looking for?
7. Describe two uses to which the owners put the financial statements.
8. What does a banker look for in the financial statements of a company to which the bank has just lent money?
9. Why are investors interested in a company's financial statements?

18.2 COMPARING FINANCIAL DATA

A number of techniques of analysis can help us evaluate a company. The most common of these are discussed in this section.

Trend Analysis

A useful technique for examining financial statements is the trend analysis. A trend analysis presents financial data for a number of consecutive periods. We can see tendencies that are not evident from the dollar figures alone. Trend analyses are used primarily to see how the company is performing over several periods.

There are three ways to present data for a number of periods. These are discussed on page 782.

1. Selected data can be presented in dollars for a number of periods as shown in Figure 18.1.

WESTWIND COMPANY LIMITED, SELECTED INCOME STATEMENT DATA 19-1 to 19-5					
	19-1	*19-2*	*19-3*	*19-4*	*19-5*
Sales	$65 000	$68 000	$58 000	$69 000	$81 000
Cost of Goods Sold	32 000	33 000	28 000	35 000	39 500
Gross Profit	$33 000	$35 000	$30 000	$34 000	$41 500

Figure 18.1 A schedule of income statement data for a five-year period.

2. These data can also be presented in the form of percentages. The percentages for each line are calculated using the first year's figures as the base (denominator). For example, the sales figure of 104.6% for year 2 in Figure 18.2 is calculated as follows:

$$\frac{\text{(Sales for year 2)}}{\text{(Sales for year 1)}} \quad \frac{\$68\ 000}{\$65\ 000} \times 100 = 104.6\%$$

Observe how Westwind Company is performing again, in Figure 18.2, this time in percentages instead of dollars.

WESTWIND COMPANY LIMITED SELECTED INCOME STATEMENT DATA 19-1 to 19-5					
	19-1	*19-2*	*19-3*	*19-4*	*19-5*
Sales	100.0	104.6	89.2	106.2	124.6
Cost of Goods Sold	100.0	103.1	87.5	109.4	123.4
Gross Profit	100.0	106.1	90.9	103.0	125.8

Figure 18.2 Income statement data presented in a percentage chart.

3. Another popular way to present financial data uses a line chart or bar graph. The selected data from Figure 18.1 are used again to illustrate a line chart, Figure 18.3, and a bar graph, Figure 18.4.

The percentage chart and graphs show tendencies more clearly than the dollar amounts alone would. For example:

• Sales have increased over the years.
• A dip in sales occurred in year 3.
• An exceptional rise in sales occurred in year 5.
• There was very little growth in gross profit until year 5, which experienced a big increase.

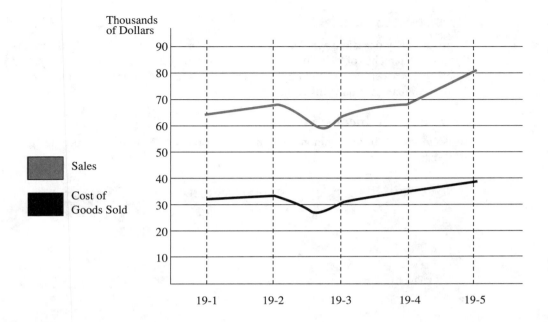

Figure 18.3   Selected data presented in a line chart.

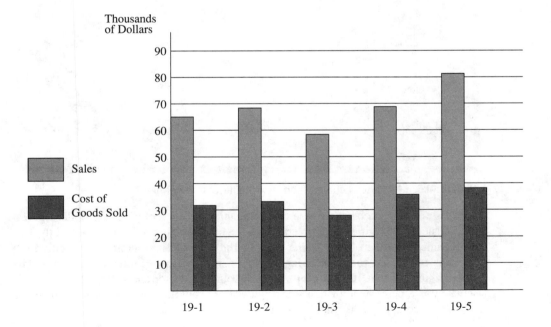

Figure 18.4   Selected data presented in a bar graph.

Common-Size Financial Statements

There are many occasions when someone, usually an investor, wishes to compare the financial statements of two different companies. Comparing common-size financial statements is a very useful technique, especially in situations where the dollar size of the two companies is quite different.

Common-Size Income Statement

To begin the study of common-size financial statements, examine the income statement data shown in Figure 18.5.

COMPARATIVE FINANCIAL DATA FOR COMPANY A AND COMPANY B		
	Company A	*Company B*
Sales	$72 051	$232 508
Cost of Goods Sold		
Opening Inventory	$ 6 600	$ 26 500
Purchases	39 830	113 005
Cost of Goods Available	$46 430	$139 505
Less Closing Inventory	6 800	27 900
Cost of Goods Sold	$39 630	$111 605
Gross Profit	$32 421	$120 903
Operating Expenses		
Advertising	$ 1 500	$ 2 500
Depreciation	2 875	7 200
Interest	5 010	28 500
Wages	13 402	55 370
Other	1 528	2 153
Total Expenses	$24 315	$ 95 723
Net Income	$ 8 106	$ 25 180

Figure 18.5   A financial comparison of two different companies.

It is not easy to compare these two companies just by looking at the dollar figures. It is easier if the figures are converted to percentages. This can be done so that the two companies appear to be the same size. **In the case of the income statement, each item is converted to a percentage figure using the sales figure as the base.** The sales figure is set at 100 per cent. All of the other figures in the same column are calculated as a percentage of that sales figure. For example, the gross profit percentage figure for company A is calculated this way:

$$\frac{\text{gross profit}}{\text{sales}} \quad \frac{32\,421}{72\,051} \quad \times \quad 100 = 45\%$$

All of the other percentages are calculated using the same base of $72 051. Figure 18.6 shows the previous illustration modified by the addition of the percentages.

YEAR ENDED DECEMBER 31, 19—
COMPANY A AND COMPANY B
COMMON-SIZE INCOME STATEMENT

	Company A		Company B		
	$	%	$	%	Sales figure is the base figure, or denominator, for each item converted to a %.
Sales	$72 501	100.0	$232 508	100.0	
Cost of Goods Sold					
Opening Inventory	$ 6 600	9.1	$ 26 500	11.4	
Purchases	39 830	55.3	113 005	48.6	
Cost of Goods Available	$46 430	64.4	$139 505	60.0	
Less Closing Inventory	6 800	9.4	27 900	12.0	
Cost of Goods Sold	$39 630	55.0	$111 605	48.0	
Gross Profit	$32 421	45.0	$120 903	52.0	
Operating Expenses					
Advertising	$ 1 500	2.1	$ 2 500	1.1	
Depreciation	2 875	4.0	7 200	3.1	
Interest	5 010	6.9	28 500	12.3	
Wages	13 402	18.6	55 370	23.8	
Other	1 528	2.1	2 153	.9	
Total Expenses	$24 315	33.7	$95 723	41.2	
Net Income	$ 8 106	11.3	$25 180	10.8	

Figure 18.6   A common-size income statement.

Looking at the percentages makes it appear as if the companies are the same size. This is why such statements are called common-size financial statements. A **common-size financial statement** is one that includes the figures for two companies as percentages. This makes it easier to compare the two companies. This technique is also used frequently to compare the same company over a period of two or more years.

The percentage analysis reveals information not easily seen with a straight comparison of dollar figures. For example, in Figure 18.6:

- Company B earns a seven per cent higher gross profit, yet produces a half per cent lower net income;
- Company B has a much higher percentage of interest charges and wages than Company A;
- neither company has a very good profit percentage figure when compared to the sales figure.

Common-Size Balance Sheet

For a common-size balance sheet, the base figure for making the calculations is the total assets figure. The merchandise inventory percentage for Company P is calculated as follows:

$$\frac{\text{Merchandise Inventory}}{\text{Total Assets}} \quad \frac{\$\ 27\ 550}{\$226\ 450} = 12.2\%$$

All other calculations are made in the same manner. Figure 18.7 shows a common-size balance sheet.

COMPANY P AND COMPANY Q
COMMON-SIZE BALANCE SHEET
DECEMBER 31, 19—

	Company P		Company Q	
	$	%	$	%
ASSETS				
Current Assets				
Bank	$ 5 000	2.2	$ 3 000	.3
Accounts Receivable	22 400	9.9	74 270	8.0
Merchandise Inventory	27 550	12.2	101 350	10.9
Total Current Assets	$54 950	24.3	$178 620	19.2
Plant and Equipment				
Land	$ 49 000	21.6	$150 000	16.2
Buildings	70 000	30.9	275 000	29.6
Equipment	52 500	23.2	325 000	35.0
Total Plant and Equipment	$171 500	75.7	$750 000	80.6
Total Assets	$226 450	100.0	$928 620	100.0
LIABILITIES AND OWNER'S EQUITY				
Current Liabilities				
Accounts Payable	$19 200	8.5	$ 94 300	10.1
Bank Loan	—	—	100 000	10.8
Total Current Liabilities	$19 200	8.5	$194 300	20.9
Owner's Equity				
Capital, January 1	$198 750	87.5	$721 950	77.7
Add Net Income	60 500	26.7	57 370	6.2
	$259 250	114.5	$779 320	83.9
Deduct Drawings	52 000	23.0	45 000	4.8
Capital, December 31	$207 250	91.5	$734 320	79.1
Total Liabilities and Equity	$226 450	100.0	$928 620	100.0

Total Assets figure is the base figure, or denominator, for each item converted to a %.

Figure 18.7   A common-size balance sheet.

The most significant fact revealed by this common-size balance sheet is the difference in the net income percentage. Based on its assets, Company P earns 26.7 per cent, whereas Company Q earns only 6.2 per cent. These figures are highlighted in Figure 18.7.

Comparative Financial Statements

A common technique for analyzing financial data is to compare financial statements over two years or a number of years. A **comparative financial statement** presents the figures for successive years side by side in columns. Comparative financial statements are illustrated below for Apollo Corporation in Figures 18.8 and 18.9. Highlighted items are explained later.

The comparative balance sheet in Figure 18.9 shows the book values of the individual balance sheet items in the first and second columns. The dollar increases or decreases are shown in the third column. The percentage increases or decreases are shown in the fourth column. This format is used again for the comparative income statement in Figure 18.9.

When analyzing comparative financial statements, one looks first for items showing unusual change. These could signal difficult situations. Items showing unusual change are investigated to find out if corrective action is needed.

There are times when no change is also considered a bad thing. For example, suppose management advertises heavily in an effort to increase sales substantially. In this case, no change in sales would be a serious disappointment and a major concern.

Changes that are favourable are naturally encouraged and applied in other areas. Changes that are unfavourable receive special attention in order to correct or eliminate them. Sometimes the solution involves changing the people in management. At other times it is necessary to change the way things are done.

You can see from the comparative financial statements of Apollo Corporation that some items have changed significantly and would require investigation. These items are summarized below.

| | | | Increase or | |
SUMMARY OF ITEMS SHOWING MOST SIGNIFICANT DEGREE OF CHANGE	19-2	19-1	Decrease	% Change
BALANCE SHEET				
Accounts Receivable	$42 100	$17 500	$24 600	140.6
Merchandise Inventory	45 300	22 600	22 700	100.0
Bank Loan	20 000	10 000	10 000	100.0
Accounts Payable	36 700	19 050	17 650	92.7
INCOME STATEMENT				
Net Sales	333 723	319 802	13 921	4.4
Net Purchases	200 318	173 619	26 699	15.4
Insurance Expense	1 050	1 350	−300	−22.2
Interest and Bank Charges	2 800	1 400	1 400	100.0
Wages and Salaries	46 600	41 560	5 040	12.1

APOLLO CORPORATION
COMPARATIVE BALANCE SHEET
DECEMBER 31, 19-2 and 19-1

	19-2	19-1	Increase or Decrease	% Change
ASSETS				
Current Assets				
Bank	$ 7 220	$ 3 611	$ 3 609	99.9
Accounts Receivable	42 100	17 500	24 600	140.6
Merchandise Inventory	45 300	22 600	22 700	100.4
Prepaid Expenses	2 050	2 100	−50	−2.4
	$96 670	$45 811	$50 859	111.2
Plant and Equipment (Net)				
Land	$ 40 000	$ 40 000	—	—
Buildings	57 500	60 000	−$ 2 500	−4.2
General Equipment	41 750	47 500	− 5 750	−12.1
Automotive Equipment	49 900	61 900	− 12 000	−19.4
	$189 150	$209 400	−$20 250	−9.7
Total Assets	$285 820	$255 211	$30 609	12.0
LIABILITIES AND OWNER'S EQUITY				
Current Liabilities				
Bank Loan	$20 000	$10 000	$10 000	100.0
Accounts Payable	36 700	19 050	17 650	92.7
	$56 700	$29 050	$27 650	95.2
Shareholder's Equity				
Common Stock				
12 000 Shares, No Par Value	$120 000	$120 000	—	—
Retained Earnings	109 120	106 161	$ 2 959	2.8
	$229 120	$226 161	$ 2 959	1.3
Total Liabilities and Equity	$285 820	$255 211	$30 609	12.0

Figure 18.8 A comparative balance sheet for Apollo Corporation.

APOLLO CORPORATION
COMPARATIVE INCOME STATEMENT
YEAR ENDED DECEMBER 31, 19-2 and 19-1

	19-2	19-1	Increase or Decrease	% Change
Revenue				
Net Sales	$333 723	$319 802	$ 13 921	4.4
Cost of Goods Sold				
Inventory, January 1	$ 22 600	$ 20 400	$ 2 200	10.8
Net Purchases	200 318	173 619	26 699	15.4
Goods Available for Sale	$222 918	$194 019	$ 28 899	14.9
Less Inventory, December 31	45 300	22 600	22 700	100.4
Cost of Goods Sold	$177 618	$171 419	$ 6 199	3.6
Gross Profit	$156 105	$148 383	$ 7 722	5.2
Operating Expenses				
Advertising	$ 5 500	$ 5 750	–$ 250	–4.3
Car Expense	18 010	17 450	560	3.2
Depreciation — Building	2 500	2 500		
Depreciation — Office Equip.	5 750	5 750		
Depreciation — Automotive Equip.	12 000	12 000		
Insurance	1 050	1 350	–300	–22.2
Interest and Bank Charges	2 800	1 400	1 400	100.0
Miscellaneous Expense	310	300	10	3.3
Light, Heat, and Power	1 340	1 210	130	10.7
Supplies Used	1 400	1 475	– 75	– 5.1
Telephone	1 475	1 462	13	.9
Wages and Salaries	46 600	41 560	5 040	12.1
	$ 98 735	$ 92 207	$ 6 528	7.1
Net Income before Income Tax	$ 57 370	$ 56 176	$ 1 194	2.1
Income Tax	$ 17 211	$ 16 852	$ 359	2.1
Net Income	$ 40 159	$ 39 324	$ 835	2.1

Figure 18.9   A comparative income statement for Apollo Corporation.

Management would look into these items very carefully because they signal potential trouble. They would hope to find good reasons for the changes, but would be mentally prepared for the worst and ready to take corrective action. Their analysis would centre on the following items.

Item	The Concern	Questions To Be Considered
Accounts Receivable	Any unusual increase in accounts receivable is undesirable. In this case the receivables have more than doubled. This is a worrisome increase, considering that there has been no corresponding increase in sales.	Are there some large uncollectable accounts? Is the credit department doing a satisfactory job? Has there been an ill-advised change in the credit-granting policy? Does the collection policy of the company need to be strengthened?
Sales	There is only a modest increase in sales. A company strives to increase its sales every year.	Has there been a real increase in the number of units sold, or is it the result of increased prices brought on by inflation?
Closing Inventory and Purchases	Businesses try to keep their inventory as low as possible. It takes money to buy and store inventory. There is always the danger of a big loss if the goods become obsolete or out of fashion. In this case, the inventory has doubled, a disturbing increase. It looks as if the increase in purchases did not result in increased sales but in a larger ending inventory.	Are there unsaleable goods on hand? Were purchases made at prices that were too high? Did the company buy more than it should have? Did the company buy on a large scale to get a special price?
Accounts Payable and Bank Loan	Businesses try to avoid any increase in debt because it represents an obligation that will use up funds in the future. It may involve additional interest charges. In this case the interest expense has doubled.	Is the increase in debt caused by the increase in merchandise inventory?
Insurance	The business must be sure that its insurance coverage is adequate. At a time when costs are rising, why has insurance expense decreased?	Has there been a decrease in insurance coverage, and if so, why? Have some insurance policies lapsed? Has there been a reduction or discount on insurance costs?
Wages	Business tries to keep its wages down but must expect increases from time to time. In this case, the increase is fairly large.	Has there been a recent wage settlement? Are the employees working below their potential? Is more overtime being worked than necessary? Are there more employees than necessary?
Net Income	Net income has only increased slightly. There is always pressure for healthy increase.	Is a more aggressive management style needed? Should the company be looking for new opportunities?

SECTION REVIEW QUESTIONS

1. What is the purpose of a trend analysis?
2. Describe the three ways of presenting data for several periods.
3. What is the base figure for a percentage chart?
4. What is the objective of a common-size financial statement?
5. What is the base figure for a common-size balance sheet?
6. What is the base figure for a common-size income statement?
7. A common-size analysis reveals information not readily seen from a straight comparison of dollar figures. Explain.
8. Describe a comparative financial statement.
9. What is one looking for when using the comparative statements approach to analyzing data?
10. There are times when no change is considered to be a bad sign. Explain.
11. Why is an item that shows extraordinary change looked at carefully?
12. What course of action is followed if an item is thought to show unfavourable change?

SECTION EXERCISES

1. Income statement data for Gorry and Associates are given below.

GORRY AND ASSOCIATES
INCOME STATEMENT DATA
19-1 TO 19-5

	Year 1	Year 2	Year 3	Year 4	Year 5
Sales	$120 000	$124 500	$125 000	$120 500	$131 000
Cost of Goods Sold	65 000	66 000	68 000	65 500	71 000
Gross Profit	$ 55 000	$ 58 500	$ 57 000	$ 55 000	$ 60 000
Operating Expenses	30 000	31 000	32 000	33 000	35 000
Net Income	$ 25 000	$ 27 500	$ 25 000	$ 22 000	$ 25 000

1. **Prepare a percentage chart.**
2. **Comment on the performance of this company.**

---

2. Income statement data for Surrey Industries are given below.

SURREY INDUSTRIES
INCOME STATEMENT DATA
19-1 TO 19-5

	Year 1	Year 2	Year 3	Year 4	Year 5
Sales	$120 000	$135 000	$145 000	$160 000	$175 000
Net Income	$ 20 000	$ 27 000	$ 29 000	$ 32 000	$ 40 000

1. **Prepare a line chart of the above data.**
2. **Comment on the performance of this company.**

3. The current assets and the current liabilities of Goodenough Company for a five-year period are given below.

GOODENOUGH COMPANY
BALANCE SHEET DATA

	19-1	19-2	19-3	19-4	19-5
Current Assets	$50 000	$55 500	$59 500	$64 000	$68 500
Current Liabilities	35 000	38 000	40 000	42 500	45 000
Working Capital*					

* Working capital is found by subtracting current liabilities from current assets.

1. **Complete the above schedule by calculating the working capital figures for the five years.**
2. **Convert the above data into a percentage chart.**
3. **Show the above data in the form of a bar graph.**

4. Shown below and on page 793 are the condensed financial statements for Rose Company and Lily Company.

1. **In your Workbook, convert these figures to common-size form.**

ROSE COMPANY AND LILY COMPANY
COMPARATIVE BALANCE SHEETS
DECEMBER 31, 19-6

	Rose Company	Lily Company
ASSETS		
Bank	$ 41 474	$ 34 971
Accounts Receivable	44 371	24 008
Merchandise Inventory	106 780	42 464
Plant & Equipment	183 538	26 725
Automobiles	25 675	8 390
Total Assets	$401 838	$136 558
LIABILITIES AND EQUITY		
Accounts Payable	$ 86 480	$ 13 940
Bank Loan	50 000	
Mortgage Payable	120 000	
Total Liabilities	$256 480	$13 940
Owner's Equity		
Beginning Capital	$114 728	$118 539
Net Income	105 630	29 079
	$220 358	$147 618
Drawings	75 000	25 000
Ending Capital	$145 358	$122 618
Total Liabilities and Equity	$401 838	$136 558

ROSE COMPANY AND LILY COMPANY
COMPARATIVE INCOME STATEMENTS
YEAR ENDED DECEMBER 31, 19–6

	Rose Company	%	Lily Company	%
Sales	$767 830		$332 879	
Costs of Goods Sold				
Beginning Inventory	$ 98 200		$ 44 224	
Purchases	561 280		208 740	
Costs of Goods Available	$659 480		$252 964	
Less Ending Inventory	106 780		42 464	
Costs of Goods Sold	$552 700		$210 500	
Gross Profit	$215 130	28%	$122 379	37%
Operating Expenses				
Bank Interest	$ 7 000		$1 000	
Mortgage Interest	11 250			
Depreciation — Equipment	5 500		6 600	
Depreciation — Automobiles	10 000		3 500	
Rent			24 000	
Wages	35 750		47 500	
Other Expenses	40 000		10 700	
Total Expenses	$109 500		$ 93 300	
Net Income	$105 630	13.8%	$ 29 079	8.7%

2. Answer the following questions.

    a. Lily Company has the higher gross profit percentage but the lower net income percentage. **Explain why this is so.**

    b. Comment on the difference in the equity of the two companies. Explain the effect of this on the income statements.

5. Shown on page 794 is the partially completed comparative balance sheet for Playfair Company.

    1. Complete the statement for Playfair Company in your Workbook.

    2. Identify the four most significant changes. For each, say whether the change has been good or bad.

PLAYFAIR COMPANY
COMPARATIVE BALANCE SHEET
DECEMBER 31, 19-4 AND 19-3

	19-4	19-3	Increase or Decrease (—)	% Change
ASSETS				
Current Assets				
Bank	$ 9 090	$ 5 500	_____	•
Accounts Receivable	65 220	35 700	_____	•
Merchandise Inventory	67 096	42 100	_____	•
Prepaid Expenses	3 540	3 500	_____	•
Total Current Assets	$144 946	$ 86 800	_____	•
Fixed Assets				
Land	$ 50 000	$ 50 000	_____	•
Buildings (Net)	135 000	138 000	_____	•
Equipment (Net)	141 000	160 000	_____	•
Automobiles (Net)	25 000	30 000	_____	•
Total Fixed Assets	$351 000	$378 000	_____	•
Total Assets	$495 946	$464 800	_____	•
LIABILITIES AND OWNER'S EQUITY				
Current Liabilities				
Accounts Payable	$ 97 936	$ 52 750	_____	•
Bank Loan	50 000	50 000	_____	•
Total Current Liabilities	$147 936	$102 750	_____	•
Long-Term Liability				
Mortgage Payable	$ 70 000	$ 75 000	_____	•
Total Liabilities	$217 936	$177 750	_____	•
T. Jennings, Capital				
Capital, January 1	$287 050	$277 700	_____	•
Net Income	90 960	84 350	_____	•
	$378 010	$362 050	_____	•
Drawings	100 000	75 000	_____	•
Capital, December 31	$278 010	$287 050	_____	•
Total Liabilities & Equity	$495 946	464 800	_____	•

18.3   SIMPLE RATIOS AND PERCENTAGES

A number of ratios and percentages may be worked out to make it easier to see what the financial statements have to say about a business. Simple calculations can be made for specific aspects of the statements.

These figures are not very meaningful by themselves. They should be used with other pertinent information, and compared with figures for the industry as a whole.

In general, there are two aspects to accounting ratios and percentages—liquidity and profitability. **Liquidity ratios** (also called **solvency ratios**) are used to decide how easily a company can pay its debts. **Profitability percentages** are used to evaluate a company's ability to earn a profit. They are usually compared to the results of other years, other companies, or other investment opportunities.

Several specific ratios are described in this and the next section. The financial statements for Apollo Corporation which appear on pages 788 and 789 are used for the calculations.

Current Ratio or Working Capital Ratio

The formula:

$$\text{current ratio} = \frac{\text{total current assets}}{\text{total current liabilities}}$$

The data:

	19-2	19-1
Total Current Assets	$96 670	$45 811
Total Current Liabilities	$56 700	$29 050

The computations:

		19-2	19-1
current ratio	=	$\frac{96\,670}{56\,700}$	$\frac{45\,811}{29\,200}$

The results:

		19-2	19-1
current ratio	=	1.7	1.6

Interpretation   The **current ratio** measures a business's ability to pay its debts in the normal course of business operations. This is an important consideration because a business that is unable to pay its debts can be closed down by its creditors.

The general standards for interpreting current ratios are shown in the following table.

Current Ratio	Interpretation
2.5	very good
2.0	good
1.5	fair
1.0	poor*
less than 1.0	precarious

* Except in regard to certain specialized industries such as public utilities.

Apollo Corporation's current ratio is not good. Its ability to pay its debts on time is not assured. The company should seek to improve this ratio.

The current ratio is also referred to as the working capital ratio. The **working capital** of a business is found by subtracting the total current liabilities from the total current assets. The working capital for Apollo Corporation for the second year is $96 670 – $56 700 = $39 970.

Quick Ratio or Acid-Test Ratio

The formula:

$$\text{quick ratio} = \frac{\text{total current assets (less inventory and prepaid expenses)}}{\text{total current liabilities}}$$

The data:

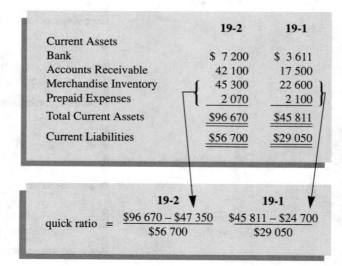

	19-2	19-1
Current Assets		
Bank	$ 7 200	$ 3 611
Accounts Receivable	42 100	17 500
Merchandise Inventory	45 300	22 600
Prepaid Expenses	2 070	2 100
Total Current Assets	$96 670	$45 811
Current Liabilities	$56 700	$29 050

The computations:

19-2	19-1
quick ratio = $\dfrac{\$96\ 670 - \$47\ 350}{\$56\ 700}$	$\dfrac{\$45\ 811 - \$24\ 700}{\$29\ 050}$

The results:

	19-2	19-1
current ratio =	.87	.73

Interpretation   The calculation of the quick ratio includes only quick assets, those that can be converted into cash quickly. Therefore, the quick ratio or acid-test ratio measures a business's ability to pay its debts within a short period of time, say two months. It would be used by someone who was concerned about whether the business could continue operating. A quick-ratio figure of less than one is undesirable, but not uncommon.

Debt/Equity Percentages

The formulas:

$$\text{debt ratio} = \frac{\text{total liabilities}}{\text{total assets}}$$

$$\text{equity ratio} = \frac{\text{total equity}}{\text{total assets}}$$

The data:

	19-2	19-1
Total Liabilities	$ 56 700	$ 29 050
Total Equity	$229 120	$226 161
Total Assets	$285 820	$255 211

The computations:

	19-2	19-1
debt ratio =	$\frac{56\ 700}{285\ 820} \times 100$	$\frac{29\ 050}{255\ 211} \times 100$

	19-2	19-1
equity ratio =	$\frac{229\ 120}{285\ 820} \times 100$	$\frac{226\ 161}{255\ 211} \times 100$

The results:

		19-2	19-1
debt ratio	=	19.8%	11.4%
equity ratio	=	80.2%	88.6%

Interpretation   The debt ratio shows what proportion of the total assets has been bought using borrowed money. The equity ratio shows what proportion of the total assets has been bought using the owner's money. The two percentages are complementary, which means that they add up to 100.

Creditors and prospective creditors are interested in these two ratios. They like to see a high proportion of owner's money in a business. Owners with a high stake in the business are strongly committed to its success.

Creditors of Apollo Corporation would undoubtedly view the ratios favourably. If the two figures were reversed, so that the owners had the small 11- to- 20 per cent share in the business, creditors would view the situation with caution.

Rate of Return on Net Sales

The formula:

$$\text{rate of return on net sales} = \frac{\text{net income}}{\text{net sales}} \times 100$$

The data:

	19-2	19-1
Net Income	$ 40 159	$ 39 324
Net Sales	$333 723	$319 802

The computations:

	19-2	19-1
rate of return =	$\frac{40\,159}{333\,732} \times 100$	$\frac{39\,324}{319\,802} \times 100$

The results:

	19-2	19-1
rate of return =	12.0%	12.3%

Interpretation   The **rate of return on net sales** measures the dollars that remain after all expenses are deducted from net sales. Comparing this figure with other years gives an indication of how well a company is performing. In Apollo Corporation's case, the rate of return has dropped slightly. This would be a disappointment.

It is important to look at the rate of return figure as well as the net income figure in dollars. As shown by the schedule below, a business can have an increase in net income dollars and still have a drop in the net income percentage.

	Year 2	Year 1
Sales	$525 000	$500 000
Net Income	$ 50 500	$ 50 000
Net Income %	9.6%	10.0%

Rate of Return on Owner's Equity

The formula:

$$\text{return on owners' equity} = \frac{\text{net income}}{\text{owners' average equity}} \times 100$$

The data:

	19-2	19-1
Net Income	$ 40 159	$ 39 324
Beginning Capital	$226 161	$224 637*
Ending Capital	$229 120	$226 161

*Would be picked up from previous year's statement.

The computation:

	19-2	19-1

$$\text{return on owners' equity} = \frac{40\ 159}{\dfrac{226\ 161 + 229\ 120}{2}} \times 100 \qquad \frac{39\ 324}{\dfrac{224\ 637 + 226\ 161}{2}} \times 100$$

The results:

	19-2	19-1
return on owners' equity =	17.6%	17.4%

Interpretation   The **return on owner's equity** measures how well the business is doing compared with other investments the owner might make, using the capital. In particular, the owner would be interested in knowing how much the equity could earn in interest if it could be loaned out. However, the capital of a business cannot just be taken out. A buyer must be found first. But, of course, if the owner wants to sell out because the business is a poor investment, he or she may have trouble finding a buyer. In other words, the capital invested in a business is not always available to be invested in other ways.

The owner of Apollo Corporation would be quite happy with the above return on investment figures. They are higher than current interest rates.

SECTION REVIEW QUESTIONS

1. Name the ratios and percentages described in this section.
2. What are the two aspects of accounting ratios and percentages?
3. What is the purpose of working out simple ratios and percentages?
4. Explain the purpose served by a liquidity ratio.
5. Explain the purpose served by a profitability percentage.

SECTION EXERCISES

1. Given below and on page 801 are the income statement and the balance sheet for Schooner Company for the year ended December 31, 19-2.

SCHOONER COMPANY
INCOME STATEMENT
YEAR ENDED DECEMBER 31, 19-2

Revenue		
Sales		$141 900
Cost of Goods Sold		
Inventory, January 1	$ 32 000	
Purchases	74 000	
Costs of Goods Available for Sale	$106 000	
Less Inventory, December 31	35 000	
Cost of Goods Sold		71 000
Gross Profit		$ 70 900
Operating Expenses		
Interest	$1 000	
Depreciation	7 000	
General	4 000	
Wages	20 300	
Utilities	4 400	
Total Expenses		36 700
Net Income		$ 34 200

1. **Calculate each of the following.**
   a. current ratio
   b. quick ratio
   c. debt/equity ratios
   d. rate of return on net sales
   e. rate of return on owner's equity.

2. **Comment on each of the above figures, explaining why they are favourable or unfavourable.**

SCHOONER COMPANY
BALANCE SHEET
DECEMBER 31, 19-2

ASSETS

Current Assets

Bank	$ 1 500	
Accounts Receivable	17 000	
Merchandise Inventory	35 000	
Prepaid Expenses	1 000	$54 500

Plant and Equipment

Equipment	$18 000	
Automobiles	17 000	35 000
Total Assets		$89 500

LIABILITIES AND OWNER'S EQUITY

Current Liabilities

Bank Loan	$10 000	
Accounts Payable	3 000	$13 000

J. Morrow, Capital

Balance, January 1		$72 300
Net Income	$34 200	
Drawings	30 000	
Increase in Capital		4 200
Balance, December 31		76 500
Total Liabilities and Equity		$89 500

2. Given on page 802 are the income statement and the balance sheet for The Cloverdale Company for the year ended December 31, 19-8.

   1. Calculate each of the following.
      a. current ratio
      b. quick ratio
      c. debt/equity ratios
      d. rate of return on net sales
      e. rate of return on owner's equity.

   2. Comment on each of the above figures, explaining why they are favourable or unfavourable.

THE CLOVERDALE COMPANY
INCOME STATEMENT
YEAR ENDED DECEMBER 31, 19-8

Revenue

Sales		$208 900
Cost of Goods Sold		
Inventory, January 1	$ 32 500	
Purchases	142 650	
Cost of Goods Available for Sale	$175 150	
Less Inventory, December 31	25 400	
Cost of Goods Sold		149 750
Gross Profit		$ 59 150
Operating Expenses		
Bank Interest	$ 2 500	
Depreciation	8 400	
General	3 750	
Wages	27 000	
Utilities	4 800	
Total Expenses		46 450
Net Income		$12 700

THE CLOVERDALE COMPANY
BALANCE SHEET
DECEMBER 31, 19-8

ASSETS

Current Assets		
Bank	$ 700	
Accounts Receivable	15 200	
Merchandise Inventory	25 400	
Prepaid Expenses	1 000	$42 300
Plant and Equipment		
Land	$100 000	
Equipment	12 000	
Automobiles	20 000	132 000
Total Assets		$174 300

LIABILITIES AND OWNER'S EQUITY

Current Liabilities			
Bank Loan		$25 000	
Accounts Payable		17 500	$42 500
P. Potts, Capital			
Balance, January 1		$128 100	
Net Income	$12 700		
Drawings	9 000		
Increase in Capital		3 700	
Balance, December 31			131 800
Total Liabilities and Equity			$174 300

3. Given below are selected data for two comparable companies.

	Company A	Company B
Total current assets	$47 500	$50 000
Total quick assets	22 000	30 000
Total assets	195 000	166 000
Total current liabilities	30 000	45 000
Total liabilities	100 000	110 000
Beginning equity	90 000	51 000
Ending equity	95 000	56 000
Net sales	145 000	210 000
Net income	15 700	32 000

1. Calculate the following six ratios and percentages for each company.
   a. current ratio
   b. quick ratio
   c. debt ratio
   d. equity ratio
   e. rate of return on net sales
   f. rate of return on owner's equity.

2. Which of the two companies would you prefer to own? Give reasons for your choice.

18.4 ADDITIONAL RATIOS, PERCENTAGES, AND STATISTICS

The following calculations can also be used to evaluate the health of a business.

Collection Period

The formula:

$$\text{collection period} = \frac{\text{accounts receivable}}{\text{average charge sales per day}}$$

The data:

	19-2	19-1
Accounts Receivable	$ 42 100	$ 17 500
Sales*	$333 732	$319 802

*Assume that all sales are charge sales.

The computations:

		19-2	19-1
collection period	=	$\dfrac{42\,100}{333\,723/365}$	$\dfrac{17\,500}{319\,802/365}$

The results:

		19-2	19-1
collection period (in days)	=	46	20

Interpretation   The **collection period** or **accounts receivable turnover** figure gives an indication of how many days it takes the business to collect an account receivable. The lower the number, the better it is. The meaning of the figure depends on the business's usual terms of sale and its discount policy. A rule of thumb is that the figure should be less than one and a half times the usual credit period. If a discount for prompt payment is offered, the figure should be lower.

Apollo Corporation's collection period figure for 19-1 is exceptionally low. The figure for 19-2 is more normal.

Inventory Turnover

The formula:

$$\text{inventory turnover} = \frac{\text{cost of goods sold}}{\text{average merchandise inventory}}$$

The data:

	19-2	19-1
Cost of Goods Sold	$177 618	$171 419
Beginning Inventory	$ 22 600	$ 20 400
Ending Inventory	$ 45 300	$ 22 600

The computations:

	19-2	19-1
inventory turnover =	$\dfrac{177\,618}{\dfrac{22\,600 + 45\,300}{2}}$	$\dfrac{171\,419}{\dfrac{20\,400 + 22\,600}{2}}$

The results:

		19-2	19-1
inventory turnover	=	5.2	8.0

Interpretation   The **inventory turnover** figure represents the number of times a business has been able to sell and replace its inventory in one year. An inventory turnover of 8.0 means that the business has been able to sell and replace its goods eight times a year or every month and a half. To be most useful, this figure must be compared with other years, or with other companies in the same line of business. Not all lines of business have the same rate of turnover.

Apollo Corporation shows a marked decrease in the turnover figure from its first year to its second. This is further evidence that Apollo Corporation is carrying too much inventory.

Times Interest Earned Ratio

The formula:

$$\text{times interest earned} = \frac{\text{net income}}{\text{interest expense}}$$

The data:

	19-2	19-1
Net Income	$40 159	$39 324
Interest Expense	$ 2 800	$ 1 400

The computations:

	19-2	19-1
times interest earned =	$\dfrac{\$ 40\ 159}{\$ 2\ 800}$	$\dfrac{\$ 39\ 324}{\$ 1\ 400}$

The results:

	19-2	19-1
times interest earned =	14.3	28.1

Interpretation   The **times interest earned ratio** measures the company's ability to cover its interest expense. The figures for Apollo Corporation are extremely favourable. This indicates that Apollo Corporation can handle its interest charges very easily. However, a company that had a low figure, five, for example, would have to express some concern over interest charges. The higher the ratio the better. Creditors would be very cautious in dealing with a company with a low figure.

Basic Earnings per Share
(Corporations with simple capital structures only)

The formula:

$$\text{earnings per share} = \frac{\text{net income (after income tax)}}{\text{number of common shares outstanding}}$$

The data:

	19-2	19-1
Net Income (after tax)	$ 40 159	$ 39 324
number of common shares	12 000	12 000

The computations:

		19-2	19-1
earnings per share	=	$\dfrac{\$\,40\,159}{12\,000}$	$\dfrac{\$\,39\,324}{12\,000}$

The results:

		19-2	19-1
earnings per share	=	$ 3.35	$ 3.28

Interpretation

The **earnings per share** figure is used to measure the performance of a corporation and its executive officers. The figure is used by shareholders and prospective investors. The earnings per share figure may be used in two ways.

1. It can be used to compare earning power over a number of periods to determine trends and stability.
2. It can be compared against the same ratio for other companies to evaluate each as a potential investment.

Public corporations usually give their earnings per share figures in their published reports.

Price Earnings Ratio (Public corporations only)

The formula:	price earnings ratio $= \dfrac{\text{market price per share}}{\text{earnings per share}}$

The data:		19-2	19-1
	market price (assumed)	$ 54	$ 47
	earnings per share	$ 3.35	$ 3.28

The computations:		19-2	19-1
	price earnings ratio $=$	$\dfrac{\$\ 54}{\$\ 3.35}$	$\dfrac{\$\ 47}{\$\ 3.28}$

The results:		19-2	19-1
	price earnings ratio $=$	16	14

Interpretation

The **price earnings ratio** tells how outside investors feel about the company. The stock market quotation reflects their confidence in the shares of the company.

The price earnings ratio of a company is used to help compare alternative investment opportunities, and is of little value by itself. Suppose, for example, that Company A and Company B manufacture the same item, are equal in all other ways, and have price earnings ratios of 14 and 19 respectively. This is like saying that you can spend $14 to buy a share of Company A that will earn $1, or you can spend $19 for a share of Company B that will earn $1. Clearly, the $14 stock would be the better buy.

Note: Price earnings ratio figures should not be confused with the market price of a stock. Market price is what you must pay to obtain the share. The price earnings ratio helps you determine if it is a good buy.

SECTION REVIEW QUESTIONS

1. What is a ratio or statistic as applied in accounting?
2. Ratios should not be analyzed apart from other data. Explain.
3. What is the formula for the collection period statistic?
4. What does the collection period statistic mean?
5. How is the inventory turnover calculated?
6. What does the inventory turnover figure mean?

7. Explain the reason for the difference between the turnover figure for a fruit market and the figure for a gift store.
8. How is the times interest earned statistic calculated?
9. In what two ways may the earnings per share figure be used?
10. How is the price earnings ratio used?

SECTION EXERCISES

1. The balance sheet and income statement for Saturn Sales Company are shown below and on page 809. **Assume all sales are made on account.**

SATURN SALES COMPANY
BALANCE SHEET
DECEMBER 31, 19-5

ASSETS

Current Assets

Bank	$ 3 400	
Accounts Receivable	33 070	
Merchandise Inventory	27 400	$ 63 870

Prepaid Expenses

Supplies		1 500

Plant and Equipment

Land	$ 50 000	
Buildings	125 000	
Equipment	69 000	244 000
Total Assets		$309 370

LIABILITIES AND EQUITY

Current Liabilities

Bank Loan	$ 25 000	
Accounts Payable	17 970	$42 970

Long-Term Liability

Mortgage Payable		65 700

Owner's Equity

P. Shawn, Capital, January 1		$194 895
Net Income	$30 805	
Withdrawals	25 000	
Increase in Capital		5 805
P. Shawn, Capital, December 31		200 700
Total Liabilities and Equity		$309 370

SATURN SALES COMPANY
INCOME STATEMENT
YEAR ENDED DECEMBER 31, 19-5

Revenue

Sales		$343 342
Cost of Goods Sold		
Merchandise Inventory, January 1	$ 26 500	
Purchases	226 500	
Merchandise Available for Sale	$253 000	
Less: Merchandise Inventory, December 31	27 400	225 600
Gross Profit		$117 742
Operating Expenses		
Interest Expense	$ 8 256	
Depreciation of Building	6 250	
Depreciation of Equipment	6 900	
Power	2 800	
Miscellaneous Expense	350	
Telephone	425	
Car Expense	4 940	
Wages	57 016	86 937
Net Income		$30 805

Calculate the following to one decimal place. Give your opinion as to whether each ratio is poor, fair, good, etc. A schedule is provided in your Workbook.

1. **current ratio**
2. **quick ratio**
3. **collection period**
4. **inventory turnover**
5. **net income percentage**
6. **rate of return on owner's investment**
7. **debt ratio**
8. **equity ratio**
9. **times interest earned.**

2. The following data apply to Calvino Company.
   a. The collection period is 36.5.
   b. The current ratio is 1.3.
   c. The net-income percentage is 12.5.
   d. The debt ratio is 15.
   Use these data to fill in the missing information on the partially completed financial statements in your Workbook. You will find copies of these statements on page 810.

INCOME STATEMENT
YEAR ENDED DECEMBER 31, 19-8

Revenue
Sales $170 000

Cost of Goods Sold
  Opening Inventory
  Purchases $128 500
  Goods Available for Sale
  Closing Inventory
  Cost of Goods Sold $129 000

Gross Profit $ _____

Operating Expenses $ _____

Net Income $ _____

BALANCE SHEET
DECEMBER 31, 19-8

ASSETS

Current Assets
  Bank $ 3 700
  Accounts Receivable
  Merchandise Inventory   10 500
  Total Current Assets $ _____

Plant and Equipment
  Land $ 35 000
  Buildings and Equipment
  Total Plant and Equipment $ _____
  Total Assets $ _____

LIABILITIES AND OWNER'S EQUITY

Current Liabilities
  Bank Loan $ 15 000
  Accounts Payable
  Total Current Liabilities $ _____

Owner's Equity
  Beginning Capital $134 750
  Add: Net Income
  Deduct: Drawings $ _____
  Ending Capital $ _____
  Total Liabilities and Owner's Equity $ _____

3. Shown below side by side are the simplified financial statements of Pluto Company and Neptune Company. These two companies are in the same line of business. Pluto Company is considering expanding its business by purchasing Neptune Company. Neptune Company has been having financial difficulties recently. A schedule is provided in your Workbook.

BALANCE SHEETS
DECEMBER 31, 19—

	PLUTO	NEPTUNE
Current Assets		
Bank	$ 5 000	$ 10 000
Accounts Receivable	80 000	72 000
Merchandise Inventory	52 000	40 000
Supplies	1 800	2 500
	$138 800	$124 500
Plant and Equipment		
Land	$ 70 000	—
Buildings	125 000	—
Equipment	85 000	$142 000
Automobiles	62 000	92 000
	$342 000	$234 000
Total Assets	$480 800	$358 500
Current Liabilities		
Bank Loan	$ 30 000	$ 90 000
Accounts Payable	32 000	30 000
	$ 62 000	$120 000
Mortgage Payable	$ 60 000	—
Total Liabilities	$122 000	$120 000
Owner's Equity		
Beginning Capital	$320 300	$226 700
Net Income	$142 630	$ 52 000
Drawings	104 130	40 200
Increase in Capital	$ 38 500	$ 11 800
Ending Capital	$358 800	$238 500
Total Liabilities and Equity	$480 800	$358 500

INCOME STATEMENTS
YEAR ENDED DECEMBER 31, 19--

	PLUTO	NEPTUNE
Sales	$921 630	$570 000
Cost of Goods Sold		
Beginning Inventory	$ 48 000	$ 42 000
Purchases	609 000	304 100
Goods Available for Sale	$657 000	$346 100
Less: Ending Inventory	52 000	40 000
Cost of Goods Sold	$605 000	$306 100
Gross Profit	$316 630	$263 900
Operating Expenses		
Depreciation	$ 33 500	$ 55 000
Gas and Oil	42 600	47 200
Interest	15 000	20 000
Power	7 500	6 000
Miscellaneous	1 900	1 500
Rent		24 000
Telephone	1 500	1 200
Wages	72 000	57 000
Total Expenses	$174 000	$211 900
Net Income	$142 630	$ 52 000

1. **Work out all of the key ratios and statistics for the two companies. Assume that all sales are on account.**
2. **Comment on any of the above ratios that are unfavourable. Is the situation serious? Can it be overcome? How?**
3. **Decide whether Pluto Company should proceed with the purchase of Neptune Company. If you decide it should not, explain why.**

4. This exercise also appears in your Workbook.

   1. **For each of the following situations work out the earnings per share figure and the price earnings ratio to one decimal place.**

Corporation	A	B	C	D
Net income for year	$172 647	$2 350 700	$85 362	$312 062
Number of shares	100 000	1 200 000	10 000	500 000
Market value per share	$ 32.50	$ 23.50	$125	$5
Earnings per share				
Price earnings ratio				

Corporation	E	F	G	H
Net income for year	$1 250 000	$257 680	$102 000	$569 251
Number of shares	126 500	350 000	250 000	100 000
Market value per share	$100	$18	$8	$50
Earnings per share				
Price earnings ratio				

2. **On the basis of your calculations, which company's shares appear to be the best buy?**

5. **Complete the following schedule in your Workbook by filling in the blanks with the correct values.**

	a	b	c	d	e
Number of shares	50 000	120 000	25 000	30 000	8 000
Net Income	$130 000	$180 000	$125 000	$75 000	$72 000
Earnings per Share			$ 5.00	$ 2.50	$ 9.00
Market Value	$ 52	$ 18			$ 45
Price earnings ratio			8	16	

18.5 COMPUTERS IN ACCOUNTING: LINKING ACCOUNTING SOFTWARE WITH SPREADSHEETS

Computer Applications

You now have had lots of practice with spreadsheets in accounting situations. You should be ready to build your own programs, save them on disk, and use them again and again.

Spreadsheets are ideal for performing analytical work in accounting. The assignments below will give you an opportunity to test your ability to develop useful spreadsheets.

Linking Accounting Software with Spreadsheets

The two main financial statements that Bedford produces are the income statement and the balance sheet. A feature of the Bedford system is that the formats of the statements cannot be changed. The formats that are built in are not suitable for every business, however.

There is a way to get around this. The Bedford system allows its financial statements to be *exported*. The files for the financial statements can be saved as files of other software such as Lotus 123 or Wordperfect. These other software packages have greater formatting capability, and the files can be rearranged as needed.

Exporting with a Macintosh System

With the Macintosh version of Bedford, after you display the statement that you want to export, you simply choose EXPORT from the FILE menu. This allows you to create a separate "text" file which will contain all of the figures and words in the statement.

Once the file has been created, Bedford is finished with it. Now it is up to the Macintosh spreadsheet program to IMPORT the file. Virtually all spreadsheets have the capability to do this. Also, if you wish to use the text file in a report you can use a word processing program to import it.

Exporting With IBM and Compatible Systems

There are two paths to be followed if an IBM system is being used.

1 Follow the path SYSTEM, Default, Export to produce the menu in Figure 18.10 on page 815.

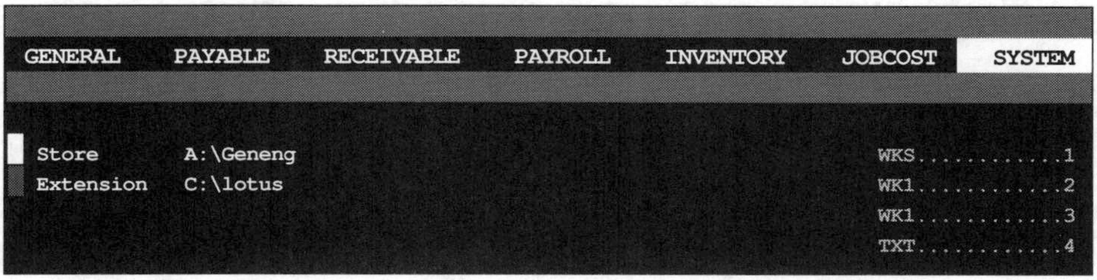

GENERAL	PAYABLE	RECEIVABLE	PAYROLL	INVENTORY	JOBCOST	SYSTEM

Store   A:\Geneng   WKS...........1
Extension C:\lotus   WK1...........2
                                                        WK1...........3
                                                        TXT...........4

Figure 18.10   Defaults for exporting.

The Store option allows you to name the disk drive and the directory where you want the file to be stored. The Extension option allows you to select one of four file extensions for your file names. Pick WKS if the file is to be used by Lotus 123 or MS Works. Pick Text if the file is to be used by a word processing program.

2 Return to the Module menu. Follow the path GENERAL, Export to produce the menu shown below in Figure 18.11.

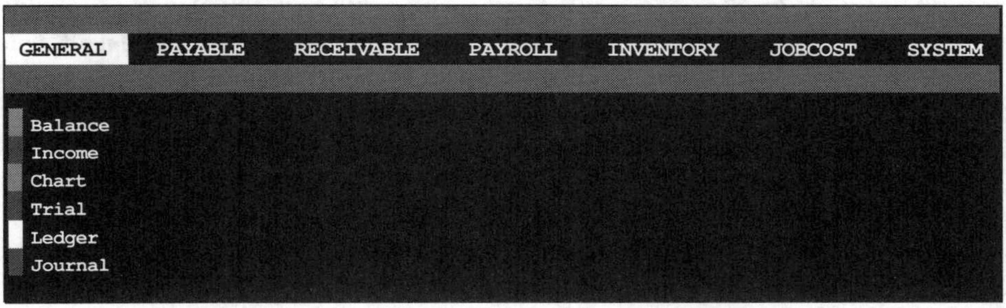

GENERAL	PAYABLE	RECEIVABLE	PAYROLL	INVENTORY	JOBCOST	SYSTEM

Balance
Income
Chart
Trial
Ledger
Journal

Figure 18.11   Screen menu showing the export options.

You can export one or all of the files shown. They will be saved in the directory specified by you in step 1. They will be named Balance.WKS or Balance.TXT, Income.WKS or Income.TXT and so on.

The most common choice is to export the statements as spreadsheet files. An exported spreadsheet file automatically puts mathematical functions in certain cells. For example, after transferring an income statement, the cell containing Total Expenses will contain a SUM function.

COMPUTER EXERCISES

1. Given below is a spreadsheet application program for a trend analysis. The data are taken from Figures 18.1 and 18.2 for Westwind Company Limited. The program is designed so that the top section will show the raw data in dollar amounts and the bottom section will show the data converted to percentages. The hidden formulas are given in faint print.

	A	B	C	D	E	F	G
1	WESTWIND COMPANY LIMITED						
2	COMPARATIVE INCOME STATEMENT						
3	19-1 TO 19-5						
4							
5			19-1	19-2	19-3	19-4	19-5
6	SALES						
7	COST OF GOODS						For raw data
10							
11							
12			19-1	19-2	19-3	19-4	19-5
13	SALES		100	D6/C6*100	E6/C6*100	F6/C6*100	G6/C6*100
14	COST OF GOODS SOLD		100	D7/C7*100	E7/C7*100	F7/C7*100	G7/C7*100
15	GROSS PROFIT		100	D8/C8*100	E8/C8*100	F8/C8*100	G8/C8*100
16							
17							
18							

a. **Load your spreadsheet software. Then build the above program into the spreadsheet. Round off to even amounts. Save the program before entering any data so that it can be used for other applications.**

b. **Enter the raw data from Figure 18.1. When finished, turn the calculator on. Compare the results with Figure 18.2. Print out the results if you wish.**

c. **Change some of the raw data in the example and observe the results on the screen.**

d. **Use the program again to do exercise 1 on page 791.**

2. The computer spreadsheet is exceptionally good for calculating accounting ratios and statistics. You will see this if you complete the following exercise.

1. **Use the spreadsheet outline on page 817 as a guide to preparing a program on the accounting spreadsheet. Do all calculations to two decimal places. Save the program before you enter any data.** The hidden formulas are shown in faint print.

2. **Load the above program into the computer. In the space for the raw data, enter the data from the financial statements for Apollo Corporation which appear on pages 788, 789 and 799. After the computer makes the calculations, compare your results with the calculations made with these data throughout the chapter.**

3. **Use your program to work out the ratios for question 1 of Section 18.3 on page 800.**

3. Given on page 817 is a spreadsheet program outline to produce common-size statements. The program is based on the data in Figure 18.7 on page 786. The hidden formulas are given in faint print.

1. **Prepare the program and save it before entering any raw data.**

For Exercise 2   A spreadsheet program outline to produce key ratios and statistics.

	A	B	C	D
1	FINANCIAL STATEMENT ANALYSIS			
2				
3	RAW DATA		YEAR 1	YEAR 2
4	TOTAL CURRENT ASSETS			
5	TOTAL QUICK ASSETS			
6	TOTAL CURRENT LIABILITIES			
7	TOTAL ACCOUNTS RECEIVABLE			
8	TOTAL CHARGE SALES			
9	BEGINNING INVENTORY			
10	ENDING INVENTORY		For raw data	For raw data
11	COST OF GOODS SOLD			
12	TOTAL ASSETS			
13	TOTAL LIABILITIES			
14	BEGINNING EQUITY			
15	ENDING EQUITY			
16	NET INCOME			
17	INTEREST EXPENSE			
18	NET SALES			
19				
20	KEY RATIOS AND STATISTICS			
21	WORKING CAPITAL		C4-C6	D4-D6
22	CURRENT RATIO		C4/C6	D4/D6
23	QUICK RATIO		C5/C6	D5/D6
24	COLLECTION PERIOD		C7/C8*365	D7/D8*365
25	INVENTORY TURNOVER		C11/(C9+C10)*2	D11/(D9+D10)*2
26	DEBT RATIO		C13/C12*100	D13/D12*100
27	EQUITY RATIO		C15/C12*100	D15/D12*100
28	TIMES INTEREST EARNED RATIO		C16/C17	D16/D17
29	RATE OF RETURN ON NET SALES		C16/C18*100	D16/D18*100
30	RATE OF RETURN ON OWNER'S EQUITY		C16/(D14+C15)*200	D16/(D14+D15)*200

For Exercise 3   A spreadsheet program outline to produce a common-size balance sheet.

	A	B	C	D	E	F
1	COMMON-SIZE BALANCE SHEET					
2	COMPANY P AND COMPANY Q					
3	DECEMBER 31, 19-					
4						
5	ASSETS		$	%	$	%
6	CURRENT ASSETS					
7	BANK			C7/C16*100		E7/E16*100
8	ACCOUNTS RECEIVABLE			C8/C16*100		E8/E16*100
9	MERCHANDISE INVENTORY		Raw data	C9/C16*100	Raw data	E9/E16*100
10	TOTAL CURRENT ASSETS			C10/C16*100		E10/E16*100
11	PLANT AND EQUIPMENT			C11/C16*100		E11/E16*100
12	LAND			C12/C16*100		E12/E16*100
13	BUILDINGS			C13/C16*100		E13/E16*100
14	EQUIPMENT			C14/C16*100		E14/E16*100
15	TOTAL PLANT & EQUIPMENT			C15/C16*100		E15/E16*100
16	TOTAL ASSETS			100.00		100.00
17	LIABILITIES AND EQUITY		$	%	$	%
18	CURRENT LIABILITIES			C18/C16*100		E18/E16*100
19	ACCOUNTS PAYABLE			C19/C16*100		E19/E16*100
20	BANK LOAN			C20/C16*100		E20/E16*100
21	TOTAL CURRENT LIABS			C21/C16*100		E21/E16*100
22	OWNER'S EQUITY		Raw data	C22/C16*100	Raw data	E22/E16*100
23	CAPITAL, JANUARY 1			C23/C16*100		E23/E16*100
24	NET INCOME			C24/C16*100		E24/E16*100
25	DRAWINGS			C25/C16*100		E25/E16*100
26	CAPITAL, DECEMBER 31			C26/C16*100		E26/E16*100
27	TOTAL LIABS AND EQUITY			C27/C16*100		E27/E16*100
28						100.00

2. **Enter the data from the balance sheets for Companies P and Q in the spaces reserved for raw data. After the computer makes the calculations, compare the results with those in the textbook.**
3. **Use the above program as a guide in order to do the first part of question 4 for Rose Company and Lily Company on page 792.**

---

4. On your data disk, you will find a directory or folder named GENENGX, which means General Engineering Export. It is the completed version of a Bedford exercise assigned in Chapter 12. In this exercise, you will transfer financial statements to a spreadsheet program where they will be reformatted and analyzed.

   1. **Load the GENENGX Bedford files and check the SYSTEM defaults for exporting. Make sure you specify the disk drive and directory the files will be exported to, and make sure the files will have WKS extensions (not necessary for Macintosh users).**
   2. **Select GENERAL, Export. Export the income statement for General Engineering, then quit the Bedford program.**
   3. **Check your data disk to confirm the location of the exported file. Once you have found it, load your spreadsheet program.**
   4. If the exported file has a WKS extension, and your spreadsheet is either MS Works or Lotus 1-2-3, you can load the file in the normal fashion. **Otherwise, check your spreadsheet menus for IMPORT commands and carry them out.**
   5. **Once the General Engineering figures appear in your spreadsheet, arrange them so they are all contained in Column C. See Figure 18.12 on page 819 for a reference.** To get your figures to look like the ones in Figure 18.12, you may have to delete rows, clear cell contents, and move cell contents.
   6. Column D will contain forecasted figures for October. Pat Schelling, the owner, expects income statement items to increase by the following percentages:

Service Revenue	15%
Wages Expense	8%
Rent Expense	10%
All other expenses	5%

      Record these percentages in a scratch pad area somewhere below the income statement.
   7. **Develop formulas in Column D that use the September figures and the scratch pad percentages in order to produce the dollar projections for October. Since you will copy the formulas in column D later, make sure references to scratch pad cells are made absolute.**
   8. **If you are successful in producing the projected income statement for October, and you have formatted it to your satisfaction, try preparing statements for November, December, January, and February.** This is accomplished by copying Column D to Columns E, F, G, and H. **Remember to add a brief heading to each statement.**
   9. **Use SUM functions in Column I to produce projected totals for the six months ended February 28.**

10. Print your model of projected income statements for General Engineering.
11. WHAT IF the owner has been too optimistic with the forecasted percentage for Service Revenue? **Change the figure in the scratch pad area to 10%. Print the revised model.**
(**Note:** Assume that all the Service Revenue for General Engineering is generated on a credit basis.)

Challenge Exercise
5. Repeat the exporting process for the balance sheet of General Engineering. Once the figures are in a spreadsheet file, copy them to blank cells in the file that already contains the income statement data.

Once the balance sheet and income statement figure are in the same spreadsheet file, you can use some of the analytical skills you learned in this chapter. These may include creating common-size statements and calculating ratios. Charts will also be meaningful, and the projected income statements lend themselves well to trend analyses and line graphs.

Communicate It

You have a good deal of information about General Engineering. **Prepare a report of Pat Schelling, the owner, that examines the current condition of the company and the outlook for the first six months of business. If possible, use a word processing package and attempt to transfer figures and graphs from the spreadsheet file to the word processing file.**

COMPUTER REVIEW QUESTIONS

1. What are text files? Why are they used?
2. With Bedford's IBM and IBM-compatible version, what are the reasons for checking the system defaults for exporting files?

	A	B	C	D	E
1			Shantz and Company		
2			Income Statement		
3					
4			September	October	
5	Revenue:				
6	Service Revenue		$5 600		
7					
8	Operating Expenses:				
9	Automobile Expense		884		
10	Bank Charges		258		
11	Rent Expense		880		
12	Wages Expense		1 200		
13					
14	Total Expenses		$3 222		
15					
16	Net Income		$2 378		

Figure 18.12   Income statement with figures in a single column.

CHAPTER HIGHLIGHTS

Now that you have completed Chapter 18 you should:

1. know who analyzes financial statements and for what reasons;
2. be able to prepare and interpret comparative financial statements;
3. be able to prepare and interpret common-size financial statements;
4. be able to prepare and interpret trend analyses;
5. be able to calculate and interpret the following liquidity ratios and statistics: current ratio; quick ratio; collection period; inventory turnover; debt/equity ratios; times interest earned ratio;
6. be able to calculate and interpret the following profitability percentages: rate of return on net sales; rate of return on owner's equity; earnings per share; price earnings ratio.

ACCOUNTING TERMS

accounts receivable	outsiders
acid-test ratio	price earnings ratio
collection period	profitability percentage
common-size financial statement	quick ratio
comparative financial statement	rate of return on net sales
current ratio	return on owner's equity
debt ratio	solvency ratio
earnings per share	times interest earned ratio
equity ratio	trend analysis
insiders	working capital
inventory turnover	working capital ratio
liquidity ratio	

CHAPTER EXERCISES

Using Your Knowledge

1. **This exercise also appears in your Workbook.**

The condensed financial statements of Magnus Company for the years 19-5 and 19-6 are shown on page 821.

1. **Complete the Net Change column of the comparative balance sheet.**
2. **Complete the Per cent columns of the comparative income statement.**

MAGNUS COMPANY
COMPARATIVE BALANCE SHEET
DECEMBER 31, 19-5 and 19-6

	19-5	19-6	Net Change
ASSETS			
Bank	$ 13 000	$ 960	$
Accounts Receivable	29 500	35 200	
Merchandise Inventory	37 450	38 950	
Prepaid Expenses	3 700	2 600	
Land	64 500	64 500	
Buildings	90 000	166 500	
Equipment	75 000	146 400	
Automobiles	30 000	21 000	
	$343 150	$476 110	$
LIABILITIES AND EQUITY			
Bank Loan	$ 40 000	$200 000	$
Accounts Payable	26 500	18 700	
Mortgage Payable	125 300	112 770	
Owner's Equity	151 350	144 640	
	$343 150	$476 110	$

MAGNUS COMPANY
COMPARATIVE INCOME STATEMENT
YEARS ENDED DECEMBER 31, 19-5 AND 19-6

	19-5 Amount	19-5 Per Cent	19-6 Amount	19-6 Per Cent
Sales	$289 500	•	$309 120	•
Cost of Goods Sold	142 750	•	155 700	•
Gross Profit	$146 750	•	$153 420	•
Operating Expenses				
Advertising	$ 1 500	•	$ 1 500	•
Car Expense	4 000	•	4 050	•
Depreciation of Building	4 250	•	8 500	•
Depreciation of Equipment	18 000	•	29 280	•
Depreciation of Automobiles	9 000	•	9 000	•
Power	3 500	•	3 950	•
Interest and Bank Charges	16 530	•	36 530	•
Supplies Used	1 000	•	1 100	•
Wages	36 700	•	38 900	•
Total Operating Expenses	$ 94 480	•	$132 810	•
Net Income	$ 52 270	•	$ 20 610	•

3. Answer the following questions related to the income statement:
   a. By how many dollars have sales increased?
   b. By how many dollars has net income decreased?
   c. Do the percentages indicate that the profit decline is caused by the cost of goods sold or the operating expenses?
   d. State the three operating expenses that show the greatest increases.
4. State the three balance sheet items that show the greatest increases.
5. From the above data write a brief explanation describing the factors that caused the profit decline. Explain also, with reasons, whether you believe this condition is permanent.

---

2. **This exercise appears in your Workbook.**
   The following is the partially completed common-size comparative income statement for two companies in the same line of business. You are preparing this analysis with a view to making an investment in one of the two companies.

COMMON-SIZE COMPARATIVE INCOME STATEMENT
YEAR ENDED DECEMBER 31, 19-3

	Dollars		Percentage of Sales	
	Co. A	Co. B	Co. A	Co. B
Sales	$200 000	$150 000	•	•
Cost of Goods Sold				
Opening Inventory	$ 50 000	$ 25 000	•	•
Purchases	123 000	81 200	•	•
Goods Available for Sale	$173 000	$106 200	•	•
Less Closing Inventory	57 000	24 000	•	•
Cost of Goods Sold	$116 000	$ 82 200	•	•
Gross Profit	$ 84 000	$ 67 800	•	•
Operating Expenses				
Advertising	$ 5 000	$ 4 000	•	•
Bank Interest	900	10 000	•	•
Depreciation Building	10 000	—	•	•
Depreciation Equipment	4 500	3 000	•	•
General Expense	1 900	1 500	•	•
Insurance	500	400	•	•
Postage	750	350	•	•
Property Tax	2 000	—	•	•
Rent	—	18 000	•	•
Telephone	450	300	•	•
Wages	13 740	9 500	•	•
Total Expenses	$ 39 740	$ 47 050	•	•
Net Income	$ 44 260	$ 20 750	•	•

1. **Complete the common-size income statement. (Calculations to one decimal place.)**
2. **Answer the following questions.**
   a. Which company has the larger net income?
   b. Which company has the larger percentage net income?
   c. Which company has the larger investment in inventory?
   d. Which company has the larger gross income percentage?
   e. Which company does not own its own building?
   f. What are the three clues to question e?
   g. If the owners' average equities are $80 000 for Company A, and $30 000 for Company B, calculate the respective returns on owners' investment.
   h. Which company gives the greater return on owners' investment?
   i. Which company has the greater interest-bearing debt?
   j. How much is Company B disadvantaged by not owning its own building?
   k. Listed below are factors that favour Company A or Company B. For each one, indicate **in your Workbook** the company favoured.

	Favours Co. A	Favours Co. B
i. greater net income		
ii. higher gross income percentage		
iii. greater return on owners' investment		
iv. more established, owns own building		
v. lower inventory		
vi. lower expense		
vii. greater potential to reduce expenses		
viii. greater share of market (sales)		
ix. fewer interest-bearing debts.		

   l. In which company would you choose to invest? **Give reasons.**

3. The following data apply to Sparta Company.
   a. The inventory turnover figure is 8.5.
   b. The collection period figure is 40.
   c. The rate of return on average equity is 25%.

   Use these data to fill in the missing figures on the partially completed financial statements that appear in your Workbook. You will find copies of these statements on page 824.

SPARTA COMPANY
INCOME STATEMENT
YEAR ENDED DECEMBER 31, 19-3

Sales		$
Cost of Goods Sold		
Beginning Inventory	$	
Purchases		
Goods Available for Sale	$	
Less Ending Inventory	21 000	
Cost of Goods Sold	$ 170 000	
Gross Profit	$	
Operating Expenses	$ 114 375	
Net Income	$	

SPARTA COMPANY
BALANCE SHEET
DECEMBER 31, 19-3

ASSETS
Current Assets

Bank	$
Accounts Receivable	35 000
Merchandise Inventory	21 000
Total Current Assets	$

Fixed Assets

Land	$ 50 000
Plant and Equipment	
Total Fixed Assets	$ 120 000
Total Assets	$

LIABILITIES AND EQUITY
Current Liabilities

Accounts Payable	$
Bank Loan	20 000
Total Current Liabilities	$ 32 000

Owner's Equity

Beginning Capital	$ 130 000
Net Income	
	$
Drawings	
Ending Capital	$
Total Liabilities and Equity	$

4. Certain financial data pertaining to Anson Company are given below and on page 826. **Assume that all sales are for cash.**

ITEM 1

ANSON COMPANY
STATEMENT OF OWNER'S EQUITY
YEAR ENDED DECEMBER 31, 19-8

Beginning Balance	$542 000
Add: Net Income from Operations	83 000
Profit on Sale of Land	200 000
	$825 000
Deduct: Drawings for Year	50 000
Ending Balance	$775 000

ITEM 2

ANSON COMPANY
INCOME STATEMENT
YEAR ENDED DECEMBER 31, 19-8

Revenue		$700 000
Cost of Goods Sold		475 000
Gross Profit		$225 000
Expenses		
Operating Expenses (except depreciation)		120 000
Profit before Depreciation		$105 000
Depreciation		
Buildings	$ 4 000	
Equipment	18 000	$ 22 000
Net Income		$ 83 000

1. In your Workbook, complete the Net Change column of the balance sheet.

2. Answer the following questions.
   a. What caused the decrease in Buildings?
   b. What caused the decrease in Equipment?
   c. What caused the decrease in Land?
   d. Does Anson Company sell on credit? Explain.
   e. How much did the company make on the sale of the land?
   f. For how much was the land sold?

ITEM 3

ANSON COMPANY
COMPARATIVE BALANCE SHEET
YEARS ENDED DECEMBER 31, 19-7 AND 19-8

	19-7	19-8	Net Change
ASSETS			
Current Assets			
Bank	$ 4 000	$509 000	$
Merchandise Inventory	50 000	50 000	
	$ 54 000	$559 000	$
Fixed Assets			
Land	$380 000	$ 80 000	$
Buildings	80 000	76 000	
Equipment	90 000	72 000	
	$550 000	$228 000	$
Total Assets	$604 000	$787 000	$
LIABILITIES AND EQUITY			
Current Liabilities			
Bank Loan	$ 20 000	—	$
Accounts Payable	42 000	$ 12 000	
	$ 62 000	$ 12 000	$
Owner's Equity			
R. Anson, Capital	$542 000	$775 000	$
Total Liabilities and Equity	$604 000	$787 000	$

Challenge

g. The bank balance increased by $505 000. **Prepare a schedule that shows the increases to bank and the decreases to bank that resulted in the net increase of $505 000.**

Increases 1.
          2.

                    Total Increases   _____

Decreases 1.
          2.
          3.

                    Total Decreases   _____
                    Net Increase   _____

5. You are given the following limited information about a company by a client.

Sales (approximate)	$300 000
Long-term debt	nil
Current ratio	1.7
Quick ratio	.8
Collection period	63 days
Inventory turnover	2.9
Debt ratio	.56
Times interest earned	11.2
Net income as a percentage of equity	7.6

Discuss the meanings of these ratios and statistics in a small group. Prepare a report about the company and be ready to present the results of your discussion to the class.

6. On the financial statements of Phoenix Company an inventory turnover figure of 9.1 is shown. This is based on the following information.

Cost of goods sold	$100 000
Beginning inventory	$ 10 000
Ending inventory	$ 12 000

The calculation made by the company is:

$$\frac{100\ 000}{\dfrac{10\ 000 + 12\ 000}{2}} = 9.1$$

You feel that the average inventory is really much higher. You show that the inventories shown on an end-of-month basis are:

January	$ 10 000
February	11 000
March	13 000
April	15 000
May	17 000
June	20 000
July	22 000
August	23 000
September	20 000
October	15 000
November	14 000
December	12 000
Total	$192 000

The total of $192 000 divided by 12 gives a figure of $16 000. Using this figure in the calculation produces an inventory turnover figure of 6.3.

Is the $16 000 figure the real average inventory? Is the 6.3 the real inventory turnover figure? Explain.

7. **Using the stock prices given in Figure 17.8 on page 754, answer the following questions:**

   1. Name a stock that has a 52-week high price of $9 $\frac{1}{8}$ and a 52-week low price of $5 $\frac{1}{2}$.
   2. Name a stock that has a price earnings ratio of 26.2.
   3. Give the earnings per share figure for Abitibi Price.
   4. How many shares of Adventure Vehicle could be purchased for $2 500 as of the listing date (ignore stockbroker's commission)?
   5. Give the price earnings ratio and the earnings per share figures for Air Canada. In your opinion, do these figures suggest that Air Canada stock is a good buy? Explain.

For Further Thought

8. **Briefly answer the following questions.**

   1. Bankers, when approached for a loan, will look primarily at two aspects of a company. What are these?
   2. When comparing financial statements from year to year, it is important that the data be prepared consistently. Why? Give an example.
   3. Company A's sales figure showed a 10 per cent drop which was considered unfavourable. Company B's sales figure showed no change. Explain whether Company B's status is favourable or not.
   4. Why is it advisable to keep inventories as low as possible? Give reasons.
   5. Do you agree that common-size statements make two companies appear to be of the same size? Explain.
   6. Would a trend analysis be suitable for a display on a chart? Explain.
   7. A company with a high inventory turnover is able to operate on a low per-item profit margin. A company with a low inventory turnover cannot survive on a low margin. Explain why.
   8. A company with an equity ratio of eight per cent is seeking to purchase goods from you on credit. Explain the danger of dealing with this company. What could you do to protect yourself?
   9. A company with a high debt ratio probably also has a low figure for times interest earned. Why?
   10. Your banker is concerned about your current ratio, which is calculated from the following data.

Current Assets	
Bank	$ 150
Accounts Receivable	9 052
Merchandise Inventory	22 540
Prepaid Expenses	800
Marketable Securities—at cost	80 000
	$112 542

Current Liabilities	
Accounts Payable	$ 75 256
Bank Loan	100 000
	$175 256

Why is the banker concerned about this current ratio? You are able to show that the marketable securities have a market value of $125 000. How does this change the picture?

11. The collection period of a company is gradually increasing. What could be causing this? Give two possibilities.

12. The assets of a company are based on their cost prices and therefore many of the assets are undervalued in terms of current market prices. If the assets are undervalued, so is the equity because the two are mathematically related. How does this affect the debt/equity ratio? The rate of return on owner's equity?

13. It becomes necessary for you to evaluate two companies very quickly. You decide to use only five ratios. Which five ratios would you select and why?

14. If you were allowed to use only one ratio to evaluate a company, which one would you use? Explain your choice.

15. The current ratio for your company is calculated as follows:

$$\frac{152\ 630}{82\ 603} = 1.8$$

The auditor of your company discovers that $42 000 of obsolete merchandise is included in the inventory figure. How should this be handled? How will it affect the current ratio?

CASE STUDIES

CASE 1 *Owning Your Own Business: A Blessing or a Curse?*

Part A

Ausma Ozolins is a high school teacher earning over $40 000 a year. Recently, she inherited $50 000 on the death of a relative. Her husband, George Ozolins, has worked in the payroll department of a large corporation for a number of years. His present salary is $28 000. He sees no hope of promotion because he is not a qualified accountant. Ausma and George consider investment opportunities for the inherited money. Eventually, they decide that they want to open a men's clothing shop. In this way, they hope to do better than just earn interest and to provide a way for George to improve his earnings.

They learn of a men's clothing store for sale in a popular shopping centre and begin negotiations with the owner. The owner provides them with a set of audited financial statements to help them evaluate the business. These statements are shown on page 830 and page 831.

COMPARATIVE BALANCE SHEET

	19-3	19-4	19-5
ASSETS			
Current Assets			
Bank	$ 3 000	$ 6 300	$ 11 400
Inventory	35 000	45 000	42 000
Supplies	2 000	1 900	2 000
Total Current Assets	$ 40 000	$ 53 200	$ 55 400
Fixed Assets			
Store Equipment	$ 80 000	$ 72 000	$ 64 000
Total Assets	$120 000	$125 200	$119 400
LIABILITIES AND EQUITY			
Current Liability			
Accounts Payable	$ 20 000	$ 22 450	$ 21 450
Long Term Liability			
Personal Loan (12%)	$ 60 000	$ 60 000	$ 45 000
Owner's Equity			
Beginning Capital	$ 48 000	$ 40 000	$ 42 750
Net Income	52 000	57 750	65 200
	$ 90 000	$ 97 750	$107 950
Drawings	50 000	55 000	55 000
Ending Capital	$ 40 000	$ 42 750	$ 52 950
Total Liabilities and Equity	$120 000	$125 200	$119 400

1. The Ozolins are not skilled in accounting. They hire you, a qualified accountant, to assist them in evaluating the financial statements. Study the above statements and work out ratios for 19-4 and 19-5. Look for significant trends, and make a statement about the strengths and weaknesses of the business.

COMPARATIVE INCOME STATEMENT

	19-4	19-5
Revenue		
Sales	$245 000	$260 000
Cost of Goods Sold		
Beginning Inventory	$ 35 000	$ 45 000
Purchases and Freight	150 000	142 000
Cost of Goods Available	$185 000	$187 000
Less Closing Inventory	45 000	42 000
Cost of Goods Sold	$140 000	$145 000
Gross Profit	$105 000	$115 000
Operating Expenses		
Advertising	$ 3 500	$ 4 000
Depreciation — Equipment	8 000	8 000
Interest	7 200	7 200
Miscellaneous	2 100	2 900
Rent ($5 000 + 1% of Sales)	7 450	7 600
Utilities	4 000	4 100
Wages	15 000	16 000
Total Expenses	$ 47 250	$ 49 800
Net Income	$ 57 750	$ 65 200

Part B (Challenge)

The Ozolins decide to buy the business. They pay book value for the store. They also agree to pay off the personal loan of $45 000. They have the cash to purchase the owner's equity. But they have to take out a bank loan, at 15% to pay off the personal loan. The Ozolins put up their house as security for the bank loan.

It is decided between them that George will leave his present job in order to manage the store, and Ausma will continue with her teaching and help out in the store.

The results of their first full year of operation are shown by the financial statements on page 832 and page 833.

OZOLINS MEN'S WEAR
BALANCE SHEET
DECEMBER 31, 19-6

ASSETS
Current Assets

Bank	$ 1 000
Accounts Receivable	25 000
Inventory	64 000
Supplies	1 400
Total Current Assets	$ 91 400

Fixed Assets

Store Equipment	$ 56 000
Total Assets	$147 400

LIABILITIES AND EQUITY
Current Liabilities

Accounts Payable	$ 30 100
Bank Loan	45 000
Total Current Liabilities	$ 75 100

Owner's Equity

Beginning Capital	$ 52 950
Net Income	39 350
	$ 92 300
Drawings	20 000
Ending Capital	$ 72 300
Total Liabilities and Equity	$147 400

2. The Ozolins come to you again for assistance. It is your task to size up the financial situation accurately and to be in a position to answer any questions that they may have. To help you in this respect: **a)** complete comparative financial statements for 19-5 and 19-6; **b)** work out any accounting ratios to help you. (Charge sales were $75 000.)

3. Prepare some brief notes to help you in your discussion with the Ozolins. Be prepared to answer questions regarding the following:
   a. net income
   b. inventory
   c. bad debts
   d. favourable or unfavourable trends
   e. favourable or unfavourable ratios.

4. Be prepared to recommend a course of action for the Ozolins. Decide whether they should sell or continue in business. Give reasons for your recommendations.

OZOLINS MEN'S WEAR
INCOME STATEMENT
YEAR ENDED DECEMBER 31, 19-6

Revenue

Sales	$230 000

Cost of Goods Sold

Beginning Inventory	$ 42 000
Purchases and Freight	160 000
Cost of Goods Available	$202 000
Less Closing Inventory	64 000
Cost of Goods Sold	$138 000
Gross Profit	$ 92 000

Operating Expenses

Advertising	$ 1 000
Bad Debts	15 000
Depreciation — Equipment	8 000
Interest	6 750
Miscellaneous	2 400
Rent ($5 000 + 1% of Sales)	7 300
Utilities	4 200
Wages	8 000
Total Expenses	$ 52 650
Net Income	$ 39 350

CASE 2   *Is the Manager Competent?*

Ki Hanna has owned and operated an importing business for several years. Last year he retired and hired Sue Ans as the new manager at an annual salary of $30 000. Sue promised to expand the business and to increase profits. Mr. Hanna left on a world cruise for a year, and Sue was given a free hand to run the business.

Upon his return, Mr. Hanna is eager to see how the business has done under Sue Ans's management. He anxiously compares the most recent statement, reflecting Sue's work, with the statement of the previous year, when he was manager. At first glance, Mr. Hanna is disappointed with the results. He must now decide whether to retain Sue as manager or seek someone else.

Income statements for the two most recent years appear on page 834, as well as additional data. Analyze this information and answer the questions that follow.

HANNA IMPORTING
INCOME STATEMENT

	19-1 (Hanna)	19-2 (Ans)
Sales	$315 000	$480 000
Cost of Goods Sold		
Opening Inventory	$ 80 000	$ 85 000
Purchases	195 000	285 000
Goods Available for Sale	$275 000	$370 000
Less Closing Inventory	85 000	55 000
Cost of Goods Sold	$190 000	$315 000
Gross Profit	$125 000	$165 000
Operating Expenses		
Advertising	$ 2 000	$ 7 000
Bad Debts	300	2 500
Bank Interest	10 000	5 000
Car Expense	3 000	3 100
Depreciation of Car	1 500	1 500
Delivery Expense	9 000	8 000
Depreciation of Delivery Truck	3 600	—
Light and Heat	1 700	2 000
Miscellaneous Expense	300	350
Rent	13 000	16 500
Telephone	400	500
Wages and Salaries	24 500	55 000
Loss on Sale of Truck		2 000
Total Expenses	$ 69 300	$103 450
Net Income	$ 55 700	$ 61 550

Additional Information:

The following policy changes were made by Sue Ans:

a. More money was spent on advertising in an attempt to increase sales.

b. Credit was granted more freely in an attempt to increase sales.

c. The size of the inventory was reduced, but not the number or the variety of products.

d. The delivery equipment was sold and an outside trucking firm was hired to make the deliveries.

e. Neither the plant nor the facilities were expanded.

1. Complete a comparative income statement.

2. Calculate all of the ratios for which the necessary figures are available.

3. Answer the following questions.

1. What two factors are the probable cause of the increase in sales?
2. Identify a direct monetary gain caused by the reduction in inventory.
3. Did a monetary saving result from the change in the method of delivery?
4. If you answered "yes" to question 3 above, how much was the saving?
5. Why did wages and salaries increase so much?

4. **Prepare a list of the expense items over which Sue Ans has little control.**
5. **Acting as if you were Sue Ans, convince Mr. Hanna that you managed the business competently in his absence. Back up your claim with appropriate figures and calculations.**

CASE 3   *To Lend or Not To Lend*

Part A

In the city of Kempenfelt, population 150 000, Gary Maw owns the most popular store for stereo and electronic equipment. Gary's store is extremely modest, but the location is ideal. There is good access to Gary's store from anywhere in the city. Gary has built up an excellent reputation for quality merchandise, low prices, and excellent service.

Gary Maw's improving financial position is shown by the comparative financial statements shown below and on page 836.

1. **Complete a schedule of key ratios for 19-6, 19-7, and 19-8. Assume that one-half of all sales are credit sales.**
2. **Provide a general statement about this business, giving your opinion of its profitability, efficiency, weaknesses, and so on.**

COMPARATIVE BALANCE SHEET				
	19-5	*19-6*	*19-7*	*19-8*
ASSETS				
Cash	$ 3 040	$ 1 814	$ 8 680	$ 6 180
Accounts Receivable	37 820	39 000	45 500	49 600
Merchandise Inventory	22 200	23 400	25 600	35 000
Store Equipment	11 950	9 950	8 350	7 150
Total Assets	$75 010	$74 164	$88 130	$97 930
LIABILITIES AND EQUITY				
Bank Loan	$20 000	$20 000	$30 000	$30 000
Accounts Payable	24 794	26 198	24 684	31 074
Owner's Equity	30 216	27 966	33 446	36 856
Total Liabilities and Equity	$75 010	$74 164	$88 130	$97 930

COMPARATIVE INCOME STATEMENT

	19-6	19-7	19-8
Sales	$180 000	$210 000	$240 000
Cost of Goods Sold	89 200	100 000	121 550
Gross Profit	$ 90 800	$110 000	$118 450
Operating Expenses			
Depreciation	$ 2 000	$ 1 600	$ 1 200
Interest	3 000	3 000	4 500
Other Expenses	37 000	45 000	49 300
Total Expenses	$ 42 000	$ 49 600	$ 55 000
Net Income	$ 48 800	$ 60 400	$ 63 450
Drawings	$ 50 000	$ 55 000	$ 60 000

Part B

Gary Maw has learned recently that a national chain of electronics and stereo specialists is opening a branch store within a year in a large new downtown mall. To meet this competition, Gary believes that he will have to restructure his store to provide greater room, variety, and convenience in more modern surroundings.

Gary intends to acquire the empty property next door to his store and to build a modern store with plenty of parking. He has found out the following facts.

1. The property will cost $80 000 and the building $170 000, for a total of $250 000.
2. The bank rate is 12 per cent.
3. Current mortgage rates are nine per cent and a mortgage loan in the amount of $210 000 is available if he decides to go ahead.
4. $10 000 of additional equipment will be needed.

Gary has no outside savings. He realizes that he will have to obtain an additional bank loan of $50 000. He knows that he will have to reduce his drawings by about half until the new store is firmly established and profitable. He is determined to become much more aggressive in collecting accounts receivable. He intends to do some serious research into advertising.

Gary has had a preliminary discussion with the bank manager in regard to borrowing the additional $50 000. The bank manager wants to see a set of estimated financial statements for the coming year as if the expansion had taken place.

3. **Acting as the accountant for Gary Maw, prepare the estimated income statement. Use the additional information given below.**

   Additional Information
   1. Allow 10 per cent growth in sales (a conservative figure).
   2. Assume that the gross profit will be 50 per cent (a conservative figure).
   3. Take into account a full year's bank interest on a new, increased bank loan.
   4. Take into account a full year's interest on the mortgage.
   5. Depreciate the new building at the rate of five per cent.
   6. Depreciate all of the equipment at the rate of 20 per cent.
   7. Other expenses are estimated to be $60 900.

4. **Challenge: Prepare the estimated balance sheet as at the end of the coming year. Use the additional information given below.**

   Additional Information
   1. All but $40 000 of accounts receivable were collected.
   2. All but $30 000 of accounts payable were paid.
   3. Ending merchandise inventory, $50 000.
   4. Owner withdrew $25 000 for personal use.

5. **Challenge: Acting as the bank manager, decide whether or not you would grant the increased bank loan. Give reasons for your decision.**

ENTREPRENEUR
Steven Syme / Designer and Builder of Custom Homes

From an early age Steven was fanatic about building forts and cabins — some in the family backyard, others out in the woods. He gathered packing crates, old nails and wood, and other items from construction sites in new subdivisions. On more than one occasion, his parents had to appease an irate house builder over missing materials. He was still building a fort when he was 16 years old. But by then, it was quite elaborate, with a brick fireplace, stairs to a second storey, and a peaked, shingled roof.

His high school marks were ordinary. His father, a teacher, wished that his son had been more studious. But school didn't turn him on, so that he studied only as much as he had to. His most notable project in high school was a French Provincial table made in woodworking class. Steven's table was a work of art which attracted a lot of attention and demonstrated his natural talent for working with wood.

The year Steven graduated from high school his family moved to Barrie, Ontario. Steven decided to remain in Thunder Bay and live on his own. Over the next four years, he supported himself surprisingly well by working at a number of seasonal and part-time jobs. He financed a new sports car and two complete years of engineering at Lakehead University.

For a few years Steven was seriously involved in free-style skiing and hang-gliding. Whenever there was a local competition he was usually the one in charge. This meant that he accepted responsibility for schedules, personnel, food, accommodation, and communication systems. Because he could speak easily on television, he handled publicity too. It was at one of these events that Steven's father came to recognize that his son had "executive ability."

In 1979 Steven met Karen. They married soon after and pooled their resources to purchase a starter home. Steven decided then to go into business for himself as a contractor and roofer, since he felt that he could do superior work to much of what he saw around him. So the sports car was sold in order to purchase a used half-ton truck, some ladders, and other equipment. Steven began by roofing houses, and building decks, garages, and small additions to houses. He began renovating their starter home in order to sell it. Karen's job as a nurse helped pay their way.

In the early 1980s the Arab oil crisis created fear that North American oil supplies would be severely reduced. Therefore there was a great deal of concern over the cost of heating homes in Canada. The Ontario government sponsored a contest among home-builders to encourage the design of energy-efficient houses. Each competitor first had to design a home; then, if the design was one of those chosen, the home had to be built in order to collect the grant of $10 000. Steven entered the competition and, without ever having built a house before, won the award for his region. He didn't hesitate for a moment to sell the starter home in order to finance the construction of the contest house. He benefited from a great deal of local publicity, with the result that his company, Northern Contracting, and his career as a home-builder were launched in 1981.

From its beginning Northern Contracting grew steadily. From decks and renovations, the company moved on to custom-designed, energy-efficient homes. Gross revenues grew from $15 000 in 1981 to approximately $1 500 000 in 1988, which meant that Steven was close to being a millionaire.

There are a number of reasons why Steven was a successful entrepreneur.

1. He was capable and intelligent, despite his school record.

2. He loved his work and had special aptitude for it. Without hesitation, he could say that he would sooner build houses than do anything else.
3. He dealt with people easily and was well liked.
4. He insisted on quality workmanship and efficiency from all who worked on his homes. He was known personally as a good craftsperson.
5. He became a complete home-builder, knowledgeable in all aspects of home construction. He designed homes and did his own blueprinting, a service that gave him an advantage over other builders.
6. He was committed to hard work, but had the good sense to relax during the off-season to maintain his health and energy.
7. He believed in himself. It took courage to enter a provincial contest in home-building and design when he had yet to build his first house.

Steven's story is not uncommon. He was a youngster whose personality didn't fit the expected mold. He didn't shine as a student and wasn't the one expected to be a big success. Because of this, his abilities were hidden for a long time. However, when it counted, they were there. Those who knew Steven as a young businessman held him in awe. They saw in him a perfect example of a seemingly ordinary person achieving a breakthrough in business. He made people think about what it takes to be a success.

It will never be known to what heights Steven might have risen. He was killed in a plane crash in Dryden, Ontario, on March 10, 1989.

DISCUSSION

1. Steven had a natural aptitude from which he developed a career. Give two examples of this aptitude from his youth.
2. Discuss the factors that indicated that he would be a financially independent person.
3. On what occasion did his father first realize that Steven had abilities that he hadn't shown before.
4. Give two examples of small sacrifices made for the purpose of reaching a larger goal.
5. Give an example of how Steven took advantage of a world event affecting the economy.
6. Give an example of how Steven demonstrated confidence in himself.
7. Explain how Steven was a good role model for the ordinary citizen.

Appendix — GAAPS

Generally Accepted Accounting Principles, Concepts, and Conventions

The Business Entity Concept

The business entity concept provides that the accounting for a business or organization be kept separate from the personal affairs of its owner, or from any other business or organization. This means that the owner of a business should not place any personal assets on the business balance sheet. The balance sheet of the business must reflect the financial position of the business alone. Also, when transactions of the business are recorded, any personal expenditures of the owner are charged to the owner and are not allowed to affect the operating results of the business.

The Continuing Concern Concept (Also, the Going Concern Concept)

The continuing concern concept assumes that a business will continue to operate, unless it is known that such is not the case. The values of the assets belonging to a business that is alive and well are straightforward. For example, a supply of envelopes with the company's name printed on them would be valued at their cost. This would not be the case if the company were going out of business. In that case, the envelopes would be difficult to sell because the company's name is on them. When a company is going out of business, the values of the assets usually suffer because they have to be sold under unfavourable circumstances. The values of such assets often cannot be determined until they are actually sold.

The Principle of Conservatism

The principle of conservatism provides that accounting for a business should be fair and reasonable. Accountants are required in their work to make evaluations and estimates, to deliver opinions, and to select procedures. They should do so in a way that neither overstates nor understates the affairs of the business or the results of operation.

The Objectivity Principle

The objectivity principle states that accounting will be recorded on the basis of objective evidence. Objective evidence means that different people looking at the evidence will arrive at the same values for the transaction. Simply put, this means that accounting entries will be based on fact and not on personal opinion or feelings.

The source document for a transaction is almost always the best objective evidence available. The source document shows the amount agreed to by the buyer and the seller, who are usually independent and unrelated to each other.

The Time Period Concept

The time period concept provides that accounting take place over specific time periods known as fiscal periods. These fiscal periods are of equal length, and are used when measuring the financial progress of a business.

The Revenue Recognition Convention

The revenue recognition convention provides that revenue be taken into the accounts (recognized) at the time the transaction is completed. Usually, this just means recording revenue when the bill for it is sent to the customer. If it is a cash transaction, the revenue is recorded when the sale is completed and the cash received.

It is not always quite so simple. Think of the building of a large project such as a dam. It takes a construction company a number of years to complete such a project. The company does not wait until the project is entirely completed before it sends its bill. Periodically, it bills for the amount of work completed and receives payments as the work progresses. Revenue is taken into the accounts on this periodic basis.

It is important to take revenue into the accounts properly. If this is not done, the earnings statements of the company will be incorrect and the readers of the financial statements misinformed.

The Matching Principle

The matching principle is an extension of the revenue recognition convention. The matching principle states that each expense item related to revenue earned must be recorded in the same accounting period as the revenue it helped to earn. If this is not done, the financial statements will not measure the results of operations fairly.

The Cost Principle

The cost principle states that the accounting for purchases must be at their cost price. This is the figure that appears on the source document for the transaction in almost all cases. There is no place for guesswork or wishful thinking when accounting for purchases.

The value recorded in the accounts for an asset is not changed later if the market value of the asset changes. It would take an entirely new transaction based on new objective evidence to change the original value of an asset.

There are times when the above type of objective evidence is not available. For example, a building could be received as a gift. In such a case, the transaction would be recorded at fair market value which must be determined by some independent means.

The Consistency Principle

The consistency principle requires accountants to apply the same methods and procedures from period to period. When they change a method from one period to another they must explain the change clearly on the financial statements. The readers of financial statements have the right to assume that consistency has been applied if there is no statement to the contrary.

The consistency principle prevents people from changing methods for the sole purpose of manipulating figures on the financial statements.

The Materiality Principle

The materiality principle requires accountants to use generally accepted accounting principles except when to do so would be expensive or difficult, and where it makes no real difference if the rules are ignored. If a rule is temporarily ignored, the net income of the company must not be significantly affected, nor should the reader's ability to judge the financial statements be impaired.

The Full Disclosure Principle

The full disclosure principle states that any and all information that affects the full understanding of a company's financial statements must be included with the financial statements. Some items may not affect the ledger accounts directly. These would be included in the form of accompanying notes. Examples of such items are: outstanding lawsuits, tax disputes, and company takeovers.

Glossary

A

Account   A specially ruled page used to record financial changes. There is one account for each different item affecting the financial position. All of the accounts together form the ledger.

Account balance   The value of an account showing the dollar amount and an indication as to whether it is a debit or a credit value.

Account form of balance sheet   A balance sheet which presents the information in a horizontal format, the assets being shown to the left and the liabilities and equity being shown to the right. *Contrast* Report form of balance sheet.

Account title   The name of the item for which an account is prepared, entered at the top of the account page.

Accountability   The obligation of management (or other group or person) to supply evidence, usually periodic, of its action or performance as required by custom, regulation, or agreement.

Accountant   A professional person who develops and maintains the accounting systems, interprets the data and prepares reports; supervises the work of accounting employees and participates in management decisions.

Accounting   The process of gathering and preparing of financial information about a business or other organization in a form that provides accurate and useful records and enables decisions to be made.

Accounting clerk   An employee who ensures that transactions are properly recorded and that supporting documents are present and correct. Carries out routine calculations and banking transactions. *Same as* Bookkeeper.

Accounting cycle   The total set of accounting procedures that must be carried out during each fiscal period.

Accounting entry   All the changes in the accounts caused by one business transaction, expressed in terms of debits and credits. For each accounting entry, the total of the debit amounts will equal the total of the credit amounts.

Accounting period   The period of time over which the earnings of a business are measured. *Same as* Fiscal period.

Accounts payable   The money that a business owes to its trade creditors. This money is a liability of the business.

Accounts payable ledger   A book or file containing all the accounts of ordinary creditors representing amounts owed to them by the business.

Accounts receivable   The money that is owed to a business by its customers. This money is considered an asset of the business.

Note: For Generally Accepted Accounting Principles (GAAPS), see Appendix.

844

Accounts receivable aging schedule A detailed breakdown of customers' accounts showing how long they have been unpaid.

Accounts receivable ledger A book or file containing all the accounts of debtors (customers) representing amounts owed by them to the business.

Accounts receivable turnover The number of days it takes a business to collect an account receivable. *Same as* Collection period.

Accrued expense An expense incurred during an accounting period for which payment is not due until a later accounting period. This results from the purchase of services which at the time of accounting have only been partly performed, are not yet billable, and have not been paid for.

Acid-test ratio The ratio current assets, excluding inventory, to current liabilities. *Same as* Quick ratio.

Adjusting entry An entry made before finalizing the books for the period to apportion amounts of revenue or expense to the proper accounting periods or operating divisions. For example, the apportioning of wages between accounting periods when the current period ends between two paydays.

Appropriation account An account to which some retained earnings are transferred to restrict their availability for dividends.

Asset Anything owned that has a dollar value. *Contrast* Liability.

Audit An examination of the accounting records and internal controls of a business in order to be able to express an opinion about the business's financial position and results of operation.

Auditing The process of conducting an audit. *See* Audit.

Audit strip In a cash register, a paper tape that provides a continuous record of all transactions that occur on a business day and can be accessed only by authorized persons. *Same as* Detailed audit tape.

B

Balance column account The most commonly used type of account, in which there are three money columns, one for the debit amounts, one for the credit amounts, and one for the amount of the balance. *Same as* Three-column account.

Balance sheet A statement showing the financial position (the assets, liabilities, and capital) of an individual, company, or other organization on a certain date.

Bank credit advice A business form by means of which a bank informs a depositor that an increase has been made in the bank account and the reason for the increase.

Bank debit advice A business form by means of which a bank informs a depositor that a decrease has been made in the bank account and the reason for the decrease.

Bank deposit An amount of money or its equivalent placed in a bank account.

Bank reconciliation A routine procedure to find out the reasons for a discrepancy between the balance on deposit as shown by the bank and the balance on deposit as show by the depositor.

Bank reconciliation statement A statement showing the differences between a bank account as reflected in the books of the bank and the same account as reflected in the books of the depositor.

Board of directors   The committee of persons elected by the shareholders of a corporation to supervise its affairs.

Book of original entry   Any journal; that is, the book that contains the first, or original, record of each transaction. *Same as* Journal.

Bookkeeper   An employee who ensures that transactions are properly recorded and that supporting documents are present and correct. Carries out routine calculations and banking transactions. *Same as* Accounting clerk.

Business transaction   A financial event that changes the values in certain accounts and therefore affects the financial position of the business.

C

Capital   The difference between the total assets and total liabilities of a business. *Same as* Net worth, Owner's equity.

Capital Stock account   The capital invested by shareholders when they purchased company shares.

Cash discount   A reduction that may be taken in the amount of a bill provided that the full amount is paid within the discount period shown on the bill.

Cash payments journal   A special columnar journal used to record all transactions that directly cause a decrease in the bank balance.

Cash receipts daily summary   A business paper, prepared daily, that lists the monies received by a business from customers on account and other sources.

Cash receipts journal   A special columnar journal in which are recorded the accounting entries for all transactions that directly cause an increase in the bank balance.

Cash refund   The return of money to the buyer by the seller in respect to deficient goods that were paid for and later returned.

Cash sales slip   A business form showing the details of a transaction in which goods or services are sold to a customer for cash.

Cash short or over   The amount of money by which the business's cash receipts for the day are more or less than what they should be.

Certified cheque   A cheque for which the bank takes the funds out of the payer's account in advance, and puts them aside to honour the cheque when it is presented by the payee.

Change fund   A small quantity of bills and coins, usually between fifty and one hundred dollars, placed in the drawer of a cash register at the beginning of the day for the purpose of making change for customers. *Same as* Float.

Chart of accounts   A list of the accounts of a business and their numbers, arranged according to their order in the ledger.

Charter   The document by which a corporation is created under the provisions of the Canada Business Corporations Act, or the corresponding act of a province. *Same as* Letters patent.

Cheque copy   A copy of a cheque, used as the source document for a payment made by cheque.

Classified balance sheet.   *See* Classified financial statement.

Classified financial statement   A financial statement in which data are grouped according to major categories.

Closing an account   To cause an account to have a nil balance by means of a journal entry.

C.O.D. (Cash on delivery)   A term of sale whereby goods must be paid for at the time they are delivered.

Collection period   The ratio of accounts receivable to charge sales for the year, multiplied by 365. It indicates the average number of days it takes the business to collect an account receivable. *Same as* Accounts receivable turnover.

Commission   An amount paid periodically to a salesperson or an agent calculated as a percentage of the amount of goods or services sold by that person.

Common shareholder   The holder of common stock. *See* Common Stock.

Common Stock   The class of capital stock representing the residual equity in the company's assets and earnings. *Contrast* Preferred stock.

Common-size financial statement   A financial statement that shows individual items as percentages of a selected figure, known as the base figure.

Comparative financial statement   A financial statement that presents the figures for successive years side by side, along with the amount of change.

Contra account   An account that must be considered along with a given asset account to show the true book value of the asset account. *Same as* Valuation account.

Contributed surplus   For a corporation, an equity item arising primarily from premiums or discounts on stock

transactions, gifts of plant or property from outsiders, and donations of stock or assets from shareholders.

Control account   A general ledger account, the balance of which represents the sum of the balances in the accounts contained in a subsidiary ledger.

Corporation   A legal entity as determined by statute, separate and distinct from its owners, with a capital divided into shares which, when issued, are held by shareholders. The liability of the shareholders is limited to the amount of the capital for which they have subscribed. *Same as* Limited company.

Correcting journal entry   An accounting entry to rectify the effect of an error.

Cost of goods sold   The total cost of goods sold during an accounting period.

Credit   To record an amount on the right-hand side of an account. *Contrast* Debit.

Credit invoice   A business form issued by a vendor to reverse a charge that has been made on a regular sales invoice. The reason for the reversal is explained in detail on the invoice. *Same as* Credit note.

Credit note   A business form issued by a vendor to reverse a charge that has been made on a regular sales invoice. The reason for the reversal is explained in detail on the note. *Same as* Credit invoice.

Creditor   Anyone who is owed money by the business. *Contrast* Debtor.

Cross balancing   The procedure whereby the total of all the debits in a journal is checked against the total of all the credits in the journal to make sure that the two totals agree.

Cross-referencing   Part of the posting sequence in which the journal page number for a given entry is recorded in the appropriate account, and the account number, in turn, is recorded on the journal page.

Cumulative preference share
A share in an incorporated company where, if the preferred dividend is not paid in any year, the unpaid dividend must be made up in following years before any dividends can be paid to the common shareholders. *Contrast* Non-cumulative preference share.

Current asset   Unrestricted cash, an asset that will be converted into cash within one year, or an asset that will be used up within one year.

Current bank account   A type of deposit account offered by the bank specifically to meet the needs of businesses.

Current liability   A short-term debt, payment of which is expected to occur within one year.

Current ratio   The ratio of current assets to current liabilities. *Same as* Working capital ratio.

Customer's statement of account
A record of a customer's account for a one-month period, showing purchases made during the period, payments received during the period, and the unpaid balance remaining. Statements of account are usually sent out each month by a business to its customers.

D

Daily interest savings account
A bank account that offers fairly high interest, calculated on a daily basis, on fluctuating savings. Cheques cannot be used with this account.

Debit   To record an amount on the left-hand side of an account. *Contrast* Credit.

Debt ratio   The ratio of the total liabilities of a business to the total assets. This measures the proportion of total assets acquired through borrowed money. The debt ratio is complementary to the equity ratio. *See* Equity ratio.

Debtor   Anyone who owes money to the business. *Contrast* Creditor.

Declining balance method of depreciation   A method of calculating the annual depreciation of an asset as a fixed percentage of the remaining value of the asset. Under this method, the asset's annual depreciation becomes progressively smaller. The percentages to be used are determined by government regulation. *Contrast* Straight-line method of depreciation.

Deficit   In a corporation, the financial condition that results when there is a debit balance in the Retained Earnings account.

Delivery expense   Transportation charges on outgoing merchandise. *Contrast* Freight-in.

Depreciation   The decrease in value of a fixed asset over time. For accounting purposes, this decrease is calculated according to a mathematical formula.

Detailed audit tape   In a cash register, a paper tape that provides a continuous record of all transactions that occur on a business day and can be accessed only by authorized persons. *Same as* Audit strip.

Discrepancy item   An item arising out of a transaction that has not been recorded equally in both the bank statement and the records of the depositor. *See* Bank reconciliation.

Dividend   An amount of earnings declared by the board of directors for distribution to the shareholders of a corporation in proportion to their holdings, having regard for the respective rights of various classes of stock.

Double entry system of accounting
The system of accounting in general use in which every transaction is recorded both as a debit in one or more accounts and as a credit in one or more accounts. Under this system, the total of the debit entries equals the total of the credit entries.

Doubtful account   An account receivable that may not be collectible.

Doubtful debt   *Same as* Doubtful account.

Drawings   A decrease in owner's equity resulting from a personal withdrawal of funds or other assets by the owner.

Dual purpose sales slip   A business form showing the details of a transaction in which goods or services are sold either for cash or on account.

Duty   Special charges imposed by the government of a country on certain goods imported from a foreign country.

E

Earnings per share   The net income (after income tax) of a company divided by the number of common shares outstanding. This figure measures the performance of a corporation and its executives.

Employee's earnings record   A form used to provide a cumulative record of all the payroll data during a calendar year for a particular employee. One is prepared for each employee.

Equity ratio   The ratio of the total equity to the total assets of a business.

This measures the proportion of total assets acquired by invested capital. The equity ratio is complementary to the debt ratio. *See* Debt ratio.

Expense   A decrease in equity resulting from the costs of the materials and services used to produce the revenue. *Contrast* Income, Revenue.

F

Financial position   The status of a business, as represented by the assets, liabilities, and owner's equity.

Fiscal period   The period of time over which earnings are measured. *Same as* Accounting period.

Five-journal system   An accounting system in which five journals are kept in process at the same time, each one recording transactions of a particular type.

Fixed asset   A long-term asset held for its usefulness in producing goods or services. *Same as* Plant and Equipment.

Float   A small quantity of bills and coins, usually between fifty and one hundred dollars placed in the drawer of a cash register at the beginning of the day for the purpose of making change for customers. *Same as* Change fund.

Forwarding   The process of continuing an account or journal on a new page by carrying forward all relevant information from the completed page.

Freight-in   Transportation charges on incoming merchandise. *Contrast* Delivery expense.

Fully participating preference shares
Shares in a corporation where the annual dividend paid to the common shareholders may not be higher than the ratio of the

Common Stock account to the Preferred Stock account.

Fundamental accounting equation
The equation that states that total assets minus total liabilities are equal to owner's equity. $A - L = OE$.

G

GAAP   *See* Generally accepted accounting principles.

General ledger   A book or file containing all the accounts of the business other than those in the subsidiary ledgers. The general ledger accounts represent the complete financial position of the business.

Generally accepted accounting principles   Guidelines established by professional accountants to be followed in the preparation of accounting records and financial statements.

Goodwill   An intangible asset of a business that has a value in excess of the sum of its net assets.

Gross pay   Earnings before deductions.

Gross profit   In a trading business, the excess of net sales over the cost of goods sold.

I

Imprest method   The method of handling petty cash in which the removal of monies is only recorded in the accounts at the time when the fund is replenished.

In balance   A state in which the total value of all the accounts (or columns in a journal) with debit balances is equal to the total value of all the accounts (or columns in a journal) with credit balances. *Contrast* Out of balance.

Income   An increase in equity resulting from the proceeds of the sale of goods or services. *Same as* Revenue. *Contrast* Expense.

Income statement   A financial statement that summarizes the items of revenue and expense, and shows the net income or net loss of a business, for a given fiscal period.

Income summary account   The temporary account to which the total revenues and the total expenses are transferred during the closing process. The balance of the account represents the net income or the net loss for the period and is transferred to the owner's capital account, or to the Retained Earnings account of a corporation as part of the closing process.

Income- or loss-sharing ratio   The ratio in which partners share net income or net loss, after first deducting for salaries and interest.

Insiders   The owners, managers, and executive group of a company who have access to company information not available to others. *Contrast* Outsiders.

Internal control   The plan of organization and all the coordinated methods used to protect assets, ensure accurate, reliable accounting data, encourage efficiency, and adhere to company policies.

Inventory turnover   For a trading business, the cost of goods sold figure divided by the average merchandise inventory. This represents the number of times the business has been able to sell its inventory in a year.

J

Journal   A specially ruled book in which accounting entries are recorded in the order in which they occur. A transaction is recorded in the journal before it is recorded in the ledger. *Same as* Book of original entry.

Journal entry   An accounting entry in the journal.

Journalizing   The process of recording entries in the journal.

L

Late deposit   A deposit that is made on the last day (usually) of the period covered by the bank statement but does not appear on the bank statement until the following period.

Ledger   A group or file of accounts that can be stored as pages in a book, as cards in a tray, as tape on a reel, or magnetically on disk. *See* Account.

Letters patent   The document by which a corporation is created under the provisions of the Canada Business Corporations Act, or the corresponding act of a province. *Same as* Charter.

Liability   A debt of an individual, business, or other organization. *Contrast* Asset.

Limited company   A legal entity as determined by statute, separate and distinct from its owners, with a capital divided into shares which, when issued, are held by shareholders. The liability of the shareholders is limited to the amount of the capital for which they have subscribed. *Same as* Corporation.

Limited liability   In a corporation, the shareholders are financially liable for actions of the corporation only up to the value agreed upon for their shares.

Liquidity   The ease with which an asset can be converted into cash.

Liquidity ratio   One of a number of ratios or numbers calculated by formula and used to help assess the ability of a company to pay its debts. *Same as* Solvency ratio.

Long-term liability   A liability which, in the ordinary course of business, will not be paid within one year.

M

Manufacturing business   A business that buys raw materials which it converts into new products and sells to earn a profit.

Merchandise inventory   The goods handled by a merchandising business. *Same as* Stock-in-trade.

Merchandising business   A business that buys goods to resell them at a profit. *Same as* Trading business.

Multi-columnar journal   A journal containing a number of columns in which items of a similar nature are grouped during the recording phase. Its purpose is to reduce the labour of posting.

N

Net income   The difference between total revenues and total expenses if the revenues are greater than the expenses. *Contrast* Net loss.

Net loss   The difference between total revenues and total expenses if the expenses are greater than the revenues. *Contrast* Net income.

Net pay   Earnings after deductions.

Net worth   The difference between the total assets and total liabilities of a business. *Same as* Capital, Owner's equity.

No par value share   A share of capital stock which has no nominal or face value.

Non-profit organization   A non-profit organization carries on activities to meet certain needs within society and not for profit. Examples are churches, community hockey leagues, or cancer societies.

NSF cheque   A cheque that was not cashed when presented to the issuer's bank because there were not sufficient funds in the issuer's bank account to cover the amount of the cheque.

O

Opening an account   The process of setting up a new account in the ledger.

Opening entry   The first accounting entry in the general journal, the entry that records the beginning financial position of a business, thereby opening the books of account.

Organization costs   The initial costs of incorporating a company.

Out of balance   A state in which the total value of all the accounts (or columns in a journal) with debit balances does not equal the total value of all the accounts (or columns in a journal) with credit balances. *Contrast* In balance.

Outsiders   A company's bankers and other creditors, prospective investors, shareholders, government agencies such as Revenue Canada, and others who do not have access to company information as do insiders. *Contrast* Insiders.

Outstanding cheque   A cheque that is issued and recorded, but not cashed, during the period covered by a bank statement, and therefore is not recorded on the bank statement. *See* Discrepancy item.

Owner's equity   The difference between the total assets and total liabilities of a business. *Same as* Capital, Net worth.

P

Par value share   The nominal or face value of a share.

Partnership   The relationship that exists between persons carrying on a business in common for shared profits. Does not apply to the members of a corporation.

Partnership agreement   A legal contract that sets forth the specific terms and conditions of a partnership.

Payment on account   Money paid to a creditor to reduce the balance owed to that creditor.

Payroll   The total process of calculating and preparing the employees' earnings.

Payroll journal   A columnar page on which are recorded the details for calculating individual net pays of employees as well as the total payroll figures for the period. *Same as* Payroll register.

Payroll register   A columnar page on which are recorded the details for calculating individual net pays of employees as well as the total payroll figures for the period. *Same as* Payroll journal.

Pencil footings   Tiny pencil-figure totals used in accounts and journals. *Same as* Pin totals.

Periodic inventory method   A method of accounting for merchandise inventory in which the record of items in stock is updated only at the end of an accounting period. *Contrast* Perpetual inventory method.

Perpetual inventory method   A method of accounting for merchandise inventory in which the record of items in stock is kept up to date on a daily basis. *Contrast* Periodic inventory method.

Personal chequing account   A bank account that pays no interest on the account balance, designed for those who write a lot of personal cheques.

Petty cash fund   A small quantity of cash, usually no more than $200, that is kept in the office for small expenditures.

Petty cash voucher   A form that is filled out when money is removed from the petty cash fund and no bill for the expenditure is available.

Physical inventory   The procedure by which the unsold goods of a merchandising business are counted and valued at the end of a fiscal period.

Pin totals   Tiny pencil-figure totals used in accounts and journals. *Same as* Pencil footings.

Plant and equipment   Long-term assets such as trucks, held for their usefulness in producing goods or services, and not normally for sale. *Same as* Fixed assets.

Point-of-sale terminal   A sophisticated electronic cash register that is connected to and is able to interact with a central computer.

Post-closing trial balance   The trial balance that is taken after the closing entries have been posted.

Post-dated cheque   A cheque that is dated for some time in the future and cannot be cashed until that date arrives.

Posting   The process of transferring the accounting entries from the journal to the ledger.

Preferred stock   A class of capital stock with special rights or restrictions compared with other classes of stock of the same company. The preference generally involves the distribution of divi-

dends at a stipulated rate. Such stock usually carries no voting rights to elect the company's directors. *Contrast* Common Stock.

Prepaid expense   An expense, other than for inventory, with benefits that extend into the future, paid for in advance.

Price-earnings ratio   The ratio of the current market price per share of stock to the earnings per share. This measures the confidence that outside investors have in the stock of a company.

Private corporation   A corporation that must raise funding privately and that cannot have more than fifty shareholders. *Contrast* Public corporation.

Profitability percentage   One of a number of percentages calculated by formula and used to help assess the company's ability to earn a profit.

Prospectus   An offer of shares published by a corporation giving financial and other information about the company.

Proving the cash   The process of counting the cash receipts at the end of the day and comparing the total of the book figure for total cash receipts for the day as determined by the company records.

Public accountant   An accountant who offers services professionally to the general public.

Public accounting   The profession of the public accountant who offers a variety of accounting services to the public for a fee.

Public corporation   A corporation that obtains its funds from the sale of bonds or shares to the general public. *Contrast* Private corporation.

Purchase invoice The name given to a supplier's sales invoice in the office of the purchaser. *See* Sales invoice.

Purchase on account A purchase that is not paid for at the time it is made; also called a purchase on credit.

Purchase order A business form initiated by the Purchasing Department authorizing the supplier to ship certain goods or to perform certain services as detailed on the form, and to send a bill for these goods or services.

Purchases journal A special columnar journal in which are recorded the accounting entries for all transactions involving the buying of goods or services on account.

Pure savings account A bank account which pays a high interest rate and allows no cheques to be written. Used mainly for savings.

Q

Quick ratio The ratio of current assets, excluding inventory, to current liabilities. *Same as* Acid-test ratio.

R

Rate of return on net sales The ratio of net earnings to net sales, expressed as a percentage, used comparatively to measure the net income performance of a company.

Rate of return on owner's equity The ratio of net earnings to average owner's equity, expressed as a percentage, used to evaluate the company's performance relative to other investment opportunities such as government bonds.

Real accounts An account the balance of which is not closed out at the end of the fiscal period but which is carried forward into the succeeding period.

Receipt on account Money received from a debtor to reduce the balance owed by that debtor.

Receiving report A business form initiated by the Receiving Department that contains detailed information about goods received from suppliers.

Registered pension plan A private pension plan, registered and approved by the government, for which contributions, up to a given maximum, are tax-free. *Same as* Registered retirement savings plan.

Registered retirement savings plan (R.R.S.P) A private pension plan, registered and approved by the government, for which contributions, up to a given maximum, may be deducted when calculating taxable income. *Same as* Registered pension plan.

Remittance advice The tear-off portion of a cheque, or a separate business form accompanying a cheque, which explains what the cheque is for.

Replenishing petty cash The procedure whereby the petty cash fund is renewed when it reaches a lower limit.

Report form of balance sheet A balance sheet which presents the information in a vertical format, the assets section being presented above the liabilities and equity section. *Contrast* Account form of balance sheet.

Restrictive endorsement One that places a condition on the cashing or depositing of a cheque.

Retail sales tax A percentage tax based on and added to the price of goods sold to a customer.

Retailer   A merchandising business that buys goods from wholesalers and manufacturers and sells them to the general public with a view to making a profit.

Retained Earnings account.   The capital that comes from company profits which have not yet been paid out to shareholders.

Revenue   An increase in equity resulting from the proceeds of the sale of goods or services. *Same as* Income. *Contrast* Expense.

Reversing entry   An entry made at the beginning of an accounting period to cancel an adjusting entry made at the end of the prior accounting period. Made as part of the process for recording revenues and expenses in their proper accounting period.

S

Salary   A fixed amount paid regularly to an employee for services, regardless of the number of hours worked. Salary is usually set at a certain amount per week, per month, or per year, and is paid weekly, half-monthly, or monthly.

Sale on account   A sale for which no money is received at the time it is made; also known as a sale for credit.

Sales invoice   A business form, prepared whenever goods or services are sold on account, showing a description of goods or services, the price, and other information. *See* Purchase invoice.

Sales journal   A special columnar journal in which are recorded the accounting entries for all sales of merchandise on account.

Service business   A business that sell a service, not a product.

Share certificate   A certificate given to each shareholder in a corporation, representing a number of shares that person owns.

Shareholder   The legal owner of shares of a corporation. *Same as* Stockholder.

Sole proprietorship   A business enterprise, the equity of which belongs entirely to one person.

Solvency ratio   One of a number of ratios or number calculated by formula and used to help access the company's ability to pay its debts. *Same as* Liquidity ratio.

Source document   A business paper, such as an invoice, that is the original record of a transaction and that provides the information needed when accounting for the transaction.

Statement of account   A detailed record of a customer's account, usually for a period of one month.

Statement of distribution of net income   A statement that shows how the net income of a business is divided among its partners.

Statement of partners' capital   A statement that shows the continuity of partners' Capital accounts for a fiscal period.

Stockholder   The legal owner of shares of a corporation. *Same as* Shareholder.

Stock-in-trade   The goods handled by a merchandising business. *Same as* Merchandise inventory.

Straight-line method of depreciation   A method of calculating the depreciation of an asset whereby the depreciation is apportioned equally to each year of the asset's life. *Contrast* Declining-balance method of depreciation.

Subsidiary ledger   A separate ledger that contains a number of accounts of a similar type, such as the accounts receivable ledger or the accounts payable ledger. The accounts in a sub-sidiary ledger make up the detailed information in respect to one particular control account in the general ledger.

Synoptic journal   A multi-columned journal with a number of selected special columns and two general columns. The special columns are used to record the more frequently occurring items; the two general columns are used to record the less frequently occurring items. Each of the special columns is reserved for a specific type of entry as indicated in the column heading. At posting time, the totals of the special columns and not the individual items contained in the columns are posted to the general ledger.

T

T4 slip   A formal document prepared by employers for all employees showing payroll data for the year, such as total gross pay and total income tax deducted, which is used to work out an individual's income tax return.

Taking off a trial balance   The process of comparing the total value of the debit accounts in a ledger with the total value of the credit accounts in a ledger. *See* Trial balance.

Taxable earnings   These equal the employee's pay after the premiums for Canada Pension Plan, unemployment insurance, and any registered pension plan have been deducted from the gross pay.

Temporary account   An account that accumulates data for only one fiscal period at a time. Revenue, expense, and drawings accounts are temporary. *Same as* Nominal account.

Terms of sale   The conditions agreed to at the time of sale, between the buyer and the seller, in respect to the length of time allowed for payment and whether a cash discount can be taken.

Three-column account   The most commonly used type of account, in which there are three money columns, one for the debit amounts, one for the credit amounts, and one for the amount of the balance. *Same as* Balance column account.

Timecard   A card that records the times that an employee starts and fin-ishes work each day. A timecard is usu-ally for a one- or two-week period.

Times interest earned ratio   The number arrived at by formula to show the company's ability to cover its inter-est expense out of net earnings.

Total personal exemption   An amount made up of several items, limited by regulation, the total of which may be deducted from earnings for income tax purposes.

Trading business   A business that buys goods in order to sell them at a higher price for profit. *Same as* Merchandising business.

Transaction   *See* Business transaction.

Transposition error   A mistake caused by the interchanging of digits when transferring figures from one place to another. The trial balance difference that results from such an error is always exactly divisible by 9.

Trend analysis   A document that presents financial data in percentages, for a number of periods, so that tendencies can be seen that are not evident when looking at the dollar figures alone.

Trial balance   A special listing of all the account balances in a ledger, the purpose of which is to see if the dollar value of the accounts with debit balances is equal to the dollar value of the accounts with credit balances. *See* Taking off a trial balance.

Two-column general journal   A simple journal with two money columns, one for the debit amounts and one for the credit amounts.

V

Valuation account   An account that must be considered along with a given asset account to show the true value of the asset account. *Same as* Contra account.

Voucher   A business document that establishes the validity of accounting records.

Voucher jacket   A file folder, containing all the information and documents belonging to a single purchase order.

Voucher system   A rigid set of procedures by which the documents supporting all expenditure transactions must be verified before any payments are authorized.

W

Wages   An amount paid periodically to an employee based on the number of hours worked or the quantity of goods produced. Wages are usually paid on a weekly or biweekly basis.

Wholesaler   A merchandising business that buys goods from manufacturers and other suppliers and sells them to retailers with a view to making a profit.

Work sheet   An informal business form prepared in pencil on columnar bookkeeping paper, used to organize and plan the information for the financial statements.

Working capital   The difference between the current assets and the current liabilities of a business.

Working capital ratio   A measure of a business's ability to pay its debts by the ratio of current assets to current liabilities. *Same as* Current ratio.

CREDITS

Cover Photo
Ken Davies/Masterfile

Chapter 4
Figure 4.1:a., b. Luckett Loose Leaf, Ltd.; c. IBM Canada Ltd.
Entrepreneur Profile Photo: Don Bain, Calgary

Chapter 7
Entrepreneur Profile Photo: Electraslide Corporation, Calgary

Chapter 10
Entrepreneur Profile Photo: Paul Martin, Saskatoon

Chapter 11
Entrepreneur Profile Photo: Pat Higinbotham/Studio 54, Vancouver

Chapter 12
Entrepreneur Profile Photo: College Pro Painters

Chapter 13
Various (Visa) photos, examples: The Bank of Nova Scotia
Figure 13.5 Photo: Moore Business Forms and Systems Division
Figure 13.7 Photo: NCR Corporation

Chapter 14
Figure 14.1 Photo: Simplex International Time Equipment Co. Ltd.
Figure 14.4: With the permission of Employment and Immigration Canada.
Figure14.7a, b, 14.27, 14.28, Table 14.1, 14.2, 14.3: Revenue Canada Taxation.
   Reproduced with permission of the Minister of Supply and Services Canada.

Chapter 15
Entrepreneur Profile Photo: Michael Creagan, Halifax

Chapter 16
Entrepreneur Profile Photo: George Syme

Chapter 17
Selection from *The Financial Times*, March 10, 1989

Chapter 18
Entrepreneur Profile Photo: George Syme

Index